P9-CQV-917

# Principles and Types of Public Speaking

## FIFTEENTH EDITION

**Raymie E. McKerrow**
*Ohio University*

**Bruce E. Gronbeck**
*The University of Iowa*

**Douglas Ehninger**

**Alan H. Monroe**

Boston ▪ New York ▪ San Francisco
Mexico City ▪ Montreal ▪ Toronto ▪ London ▪ Madrid ▪ Munich ▪ Paris
Hong Kong ▪ Singapore ▪ Tokyo ▪ Cape Town ▪ Sydney

*Vice President, Editor in Chief:* Karen Hanson
*Executive Editor:* Karon Bowers
*Editorial Assistant:* Jennifer Trebby
*Marketing Manager:* Mandee Eckersley
*Editorial–Production Service:* Susan Freese, Communicáto, Ltd.
*Composition and Prepress Buyer:* Linda Cox
*Manufacturing Buyer:* Megan Cochran
*Cover Administrator:* Linda Knowles
*Interior Designer:* Denise Hoffman, Glenview Studios
*Cover Designer:* Studio Nine
*Photo Researcher:* PoYee Oster, PhotoQuick Research
*Illustrations:* Precision Graphics
*Electronic Composition:* Denise Hoffman, Glenview Studios

For related titles and support materials, visit our online catalog at www.ablongman.com.

Copyright © 2003 Pearson Education, Inc.

All rights reserved. No part of the material protected by this copyright notice may be reproduced or utilized in any form or by any means, electronic or mechanical, including photocopying, recording, or by any information storage and retrieval system, without written permission from the copyright owner.

To obtain permission(s) to use material from this work, please submit a written request to Allyn and Bacon, Permissions Department, 75 Arlington Street, Boston, MA 02116 or fax your request to 617-848-7320.

Between the time Website information is gathered and then published, it is not unusual for some sites to have closed. Also, the transcription of URLs can result in unintended typographical errors. The publisher would appreciate notification where these errors occur so that they may be corrected in subsequent editions.

A previous edition was published under *Principles and Types of Speech Communication,* copyright © 2000 Addison Wesley Longman, Inc.

**Library of Congress Cataloging-in-Publication Data**

Principles and types of public speaking / Raymie E. McKerrow . . . [et al.].
     p. cm.
     Rev. ed. of: Principles and types of speech communication. 14th ed. 2000.
     Includes bibliographical references and index.
     ISBN 0–205–34402–X
     1. Public speaking.   2. Oral communication.   I. McKerrow, Ray E.
  II. Principles and types of speech communication.

PN4121 .P72 2003
808.5'1—dc21                                        2002023212

*Photo credits appear on page 438, which constitutes a continuation of the copyright page.*

Printed in the United States of America

10  9  8  7  6  5  4  3  2     RRD-VA   08  07  06  05  04  03

# Brief Contents

**PART ONE**    **Public Speaking and the Liberal Arts**    1

Chapter 1    The Academic Study of Public Speaking    3

Chapter 2    Getting Started: Basic Tips for Speech Preparation and Delivery    23

Chapter 3    Setting the Scene for Community in a Diverse Culture: Public Speaking and Critical Listening    51

Chapter 4    Public Speaking and Cultural Life    77

**PART TWO**    **Preparation**    101

Chapter 5    Analyzing the Audience and Occasion    103

Chapter 6    Developing Ideas: Finding and Using Supporting Materials    133

Chapter 7    Structuring the Speech: Language Devices, Internal Organization Patterns, and the Motivated Sequence    159

Chapter 8    Maintaining Audience Attention and Involvement    189

Chapter 9    Developing the Speech Outline    213

**PART THREE**    **Channels**    229

Chapter 10    Using Language to Communicate    231

Chapter 11    Using Visual Aids in Speeches    265

Chapter 12    Using Your Voice and Body to Communicate    287

**PART FOUR**    **Types**    307

Chapter 13    Speeches to Inform    309

Chapter 14    Speeches to Persuade and Actuate    343

Chapter 15    Argument and Critical Thinking    375

Chapter 16    Building Social Cohesion in a Diverse World: Speeches on Ceremonial and Corporate Occasions    399

# Contents

**A Note to Students and Teachers**    xvii

**PART ONE**    **Public Speaking and the Liberal Arts**    1

**Chapter 1**

**The Academic Study of Public Speaking**    3

**Studying Public Speaking in Higher Education**    4
The Need for Speech Training    4
Ways to Learn More about Public Speaking    6

**The Functions of Public Speaking in Society**    7
Orality in Social-Political Life    7
Public Speaking and Decision Making in a Multicultural Society    8
Achieving Personal and Collective Goals through Public Talk    10

**The Centrality of Ethics in Public Communication**    13
Ethos in the Western World    13
The Moral Bases of Public Decision Making    14
  ■ HOW TO *Enhance Your Credibility as a Speaker*    14

**Skills and Competencies Needed for Successful Speechmaking**    16
Integrity    16
Knowledge    16
Rhetorical Sensitivity    16
Oral Skills    17
Self-Confidence    17

**Public Speaking as a Liberal Art**    18
  ■ HOW TO *Manage Your Fear of Public Speaking*    18
Freeing Yourself    19
Making a Free Society Work    19

**Chapter Summary**    20

**Key Terms**    20

**Assessment Activities**    20

**References**    21

Chapter **2**

## Getting Started: Basic Tips for Speech Preparation and Delivery    23

**Selecting the Subject**     24

**Narrowing the Subject**     26

■ HOW TO *Narrow a Topic: An Illustration*     26

**Determining the Purposes**     27

General Purpose     27

Specific Purposes     30

Central Idea or Claim     31

Creating the Title     34

Strategic Considerations     35

**Analyzing the Audience and Occasion**     37

**Gathering the Speech Materials**     38

**Outlining the Speech**     39

**Practicing Aloud**     39

■ ETHICAL MOMENTS *Ethics and Public Speaking*     40

**Delivering Your Speech Confidently**     41

Selecting the Method of Presentation     41

Communicating Self-Confidence     43

**Learning to Evaluate Speeches**     43

**Assessing a Sample Speech:** *"Clearing the Air about Cigars," by Dena Craig*     46

**Chapter Summary**     49

**Key Terms**     49

**Assessment Activities**     49

**References**     50

Chapter **3**

## Setting the Scene for Community in a Diverse Culture: Public Speaking and Critical Listening    51

**Basic Elements of the Speechmaking Process: A Model Overview**     52

The Speaker     52

The Message     55

The Listener     56

Feedback     57

The Channels        58

The Situation        58

■ COMMUNICATION RESEARCH DATELINE  *Listening and Your Career:*
   *Working across the Generational Gap*        59

The Cultural Context        60

**Critical Listening: Theory and Practice**        62

Knowing Purposes: An Orientation to Listening Behaviors        63

Critical Listening for Comprehension and Judgment        65

**The Ethical Listener**        69

■ HOW TO  *Be an Active and Ethical Listener*        70

**Taking Good Notes**        72

**Special Needs for Critical Listening in the Classroom**        73

**Chapter Summary**        74

**Key Terms**        74

**Assessment Activities**        75

**References**        75

Chapter **4**

# Public Speaking and Cultural Life        77

**Understanding Cultural Processes**        78

Orality and Cultural Life        79

The Dimensions of Culture        82

The Challenge of Speaking in a Multicultural Society        85

**Strategies for Unifying Multicultural Audiences**        86

Recognizing Diversity        86

Negotiating Multicultural Values        88

Accepting Multiple Paths to Goals        90

■ COMMUNICATION RESEARCH DATELINE  *Rhetorical Framing*        91

Working through the Lifestyle Choices of Others        92

Maintaining Self-Identity in the Face of Difference        94

■ ETHICAL MOMENTS  *Adapting to Moral Codes*        94

**Chapter Summary**        97

**Key Terms**        98

**Assessment Activities**        98

**References**        98

## PART TWO   **Preparation**    101

## Chapter 5

# Analyzing the Audience and Occasion    103

**Analyzing Audiences Demographically**    104
     Analyzing Demographic Categories    104
     Using Demographic Information    105

**Analyzing Audiences Psychologically**    107
     Beliefs    107
     Attitudes    108
     Values    109
     Desires, Visions, and Fantasies    112
     Using a Psychological Profile    114

**Analyzing the Speech Occasion**    114

**Using Audience Analysis in Speech Preparation**    117
     ■ HOW TO *Analyze the Speech Occasion*    117
     Audience Targeting: Setting Realistic Goals    118
     Audience Segmentation: Selecting Dominant Ideas and Appeals    122
     Creating a Unifying Vision or Fantasy    125
     ■ ETHICAL MOMENTS *Analyzing Audience and Occasion in Moments of Controversy*    126

**Sample Audience Analysis**    127

**Chapter Summary**    130

**Key Terms**    131

**Assessment Activities**    131

**References**    131

## Chapter 6

# Developing Ideas: Finding and Using Supporting Materials    133

**What to Look For: Forms of Supporting Materials**    134
     Explanations    135
     Comparisons and Contrasts    135
     Examples and Narratives    137
     Statistics    139

Testimony    141

■ ETHICAL MOMENTS *The Numbers Game*    142

**Where to Look: Sources of Supporting Materials**    143

The Electronic World    143

The Print World    149

The Face-to-Face World    152

Surveys and Questionnaires    153

Recording Information in Usable Forms    154

**Using Source Materials Ethically**    154

**Chapter Summary**    157

**Key Terms**    157

**Assessment Activities**    157

**References**    158

Chapter **7**

## Structuring the Speech: Language Devices, Internal Organization Patterns, and the Motivated Sequence    159

**Micro-Structures: Using Language to Organize Ideas**    160

**Meso-Structures: Patterns of Internal Organization**    161

Chronological Patterns    162

Spatial Patterns    165

Causal Patterns    166

Topical Patterns    167

**Macro-Structure: The Five Basic Steps of the Motivated Sequence**    169

■ HOW TO *Choose from among Meso-Structures*    169

The Attention Step    171

The Need Step    172

The Satisfaction Step    173

The Visualization Step    175

The Action Step    177

**Using the Motivated Sequence to Frame a Speech**    178

Framing the Speech to Inform    178

Framing the Speech to Persuade    179

Framing the Speech to Actuate    180

Framing the Speech to Entertain    180

**Assessing a Sample Speech:** *"Drug Testing: Outcome, Death,"* *by Justin D. Neal*    181

**Integrating Meso-Structures into the Motivated Sequence**    185

**Chapter Summary**    186

**Key Terms**    187

**Assessment Activities**    187

**References**    188

Chapter **8**

# Maintaining Audience Attention and Involvement    189

**Capturing and Holding Attention in American Culture**    190

Activity    192

Reality    192

Proximity    193

Familiarity    193

Novelty    194

Suspense    194

Conflict    195

Humor    195

The Vital    195

Visualization    195

**Framing the Speech: Rhetorical Orientation**    196

■ HOW TO *Get Your Audience's Attention*    197

**Types of Speech Introductions**    199

Referring to the Subject or Occasion    199

Using a Personal Reference or Greeting    200

Asking a Question    201

Making a Startling Statement    201

Using a Quotation    202

Telling a Humorous Story    202

Using an Illustration    203

Building a Speech Forecast    203

**Types of Speech Conclusions**    204

Issuing a Challenge    204

Summarizing the Major Points or Ideas    205

Using a Quotation    206

Using an Illustration     206

Supplying an Additional Inducement to Belief or Action     206

Stating a Personal Intention     207

**Selecting Introductions and Conclusions**     207

Sample Outline for an Introduction and a Conclusion     209

■ HOW TO *Frame a Speech*     209

**Chapter Summary**     210

**Key Terms**     211

**Assessment Activities**     211

**References**     211

C h a p t e r  **9**

## Developing the Speech Outline     213

**Requirements of Good Outline Form**     214

■ COMMUNICATION RESEARCH DATELINE *Perceptual Grouping: The Organization of Subordinate Points*     217

**Developing the Speech: Stages in the Outlining Process**     218

Developing a Rough Outline     219

Developing a Technical Plot Outline     220

Developing a Speaking Outline     222

Using PowerPoint to Integrate Verbal and Visual Outlines     226

**Chapter Summary**     227

**Key Terms**     228

**Assessment Activities**     228

**References**     228

P A R T  T H R E E   **Channels**     229

C h a p t e r  **10**

## Using Language to Communicate     231

**Using Language Orally**     232

**Using Language Competently**     234

Effective Word Choice     234

Definitions     238

Imagery    239
Metaphors    242

**Using Language Ethically**    243
Ad Hominem Attack    244
Linguistic Erasure    244
Critiquing Domination    245

**Selecting an Appropriate Style**    247
Serious versus Humorous Atmosphere    247
■ ETHICAL MOMENTS *Doublespeak*    248
Speaker-, Audience-, or Content-Centered Emphasis    249
Propositional versus Narrative Style    250

**Selecting Language That Communicates Civility**    252
Gendered versus Gender-Neutral Language    252
■ HOW TO *Avoid Offensive Language*    253
The Problem of Uncivil and Hateful Speech    254
The Commitment to a Multicultural Vision of the Audience    255

**Assessing a Sample Speech:** *"Coloring Outside the Lines: The Limits of Civility,"
by Raymie E. McKerrow*    255

**Chapter Summary**    261
**Key Terms**    262
**Assessment Activities**    262
**References**    263

**Chapter 11**

**Using Visual Aids in Speeches**    265

**The Functions of Visual Aids**    266
**Types of Visual Aids**    267
Physical Objects    267
Representations of Objects and Relationships    268
■ ETHICAL MOMENTS *Can Pictures Lie?*    270
Representing Textual Materials    277
**Acquiring Visual Aids**    279
■ HOW TO *Make the Most of Color Selection for Slides and Other Visuals*    279

Making Your Own 280
Downloading Visual Aids from the Web 280
Getting Visual Aids from Research/Others 281

**Strategies for Selecting and Using Visual Aids** 281
Consider the Audience and Occasion 281
■ HOW TO *Select the Right Visual Aids* 282
Consider the Communicative Potential of Various Visual Aids 283
Evaluate Computer-Generated Visual Materials 283
■ HOW TO *Use Visual Aids Effectively* 284

**Chapter Summary** 285
**Key Terms** 285
**Assessment Activities** 285
**References** 286

## Chapter **12**

## Using Your Voice and Body to Communicate 287

**Orality and Human Communication** 287
Aggregative 288
Agonistic/Invitational 288
Ethically Appropriate 289

**Public Speaking as a Social Performance** 290
**Using Your Voice to Communicate** 291
Perceptions of the Speaking Voice 291
■ HOW TO *Determine Your Delivery Time* 292
Controlling the Emotional Quality 296
Practicing Vocal Control 296

**Using Your Body to Communicate** 297
Assessing Different Dimensions of Nonverbal Communication 297
■ HOW TO *Improve Your Voice* 297
Adapting Nonverbal Behavior to Your Presentations 302

**Chapter Summary** 304
**Key Terms** 305
**Assessment Activities** 305
**References** 305

PART FOUR    **Types**    307

Chapter **13**

**Speeches to Inform**    309

    Facts, Knowledge, and the Information Age    309

    Motivational Appeals: Engaging Listeners Where They Are    311

        Classifying Motives    311

        Motive Clusters    313

        Using Motivational Appeals in Speech Preparation    316

        ■ ETHICAL MOMENTS *Your Ethical Boundaries*    318

    Essential Features of Informative Speeches    319

        Clarity    320

        ■ HOW TO *Use Psychological Principles for Clarity*    321

        Associating New Ideas with Familiar Ones    322

        Relevant Visualizations    323

    Types of Informative Speeches    323

        Definitional Speeches    324

        Instructional and Demonstration Speeches    328

        Oral Briefings    331

        Explanatory Speeches    334

    Assessing a Sample Speech: *"The Geisha," by Joyce Chapman*    337

    Chapter Summary    340

    Key Terms    340

    Assessment Activities    341

    References    341

Chapter **14**

**Speeches to Persuade and to Actuate**    343

    Contemporary Approaches to Changing Minds and Behaviors    344

        VALS: Adapting Messages to Listeners' Psychological Orientations    346

        ■ HOW TO *Use VALS to Craft a Persuasive Message for a Diverse Audience*    348

        ■ COMMUNICATION RESEARCH DATELINE *Resistance to Counterpersuasion*    350

        PRIZM: Adapting Messages to Listeners' Behavioral Patterns    351

        Reference Groups: Adapting Messages to Listeners' Group Loyalties    353

        Credibility: Adapting Messages to Your Own Strengths    354

**Basic Types of Persuasive and Actuative Speeches**    356

Persuasion as Psychological Reorientation    356

Persuasion as Impetus to Action    359

**Structuring Persuasive and Actuative Speeches**    359

■ ETHICAL MOMENTS *Using Fear Appeals*    360

Using the Motivated Sequence for Psychological Reorientation    361

Using the Motivated Sequence for Behavioral Actuation    365

**Assessing Sample Speeches:** *"Speech for Impeachment," by Rep. J. C. Watts, and "Speech against Impeachment," by Rep. Richard Gephardt*    369

**Chapter Summary**    372

**Key Terms**    372

**Assessment Activities**    372

**References**    373

Chapter **15**

**Argument and Critical Thinking**    375

**Argument and Cultural Commitments**    377

Commitment to Change Your Mind    377

Commitment to Knowledge    377

Commitment to Worthy Subjects    377

Commitment to Rules    378

**Argument as Justifying Belief and Action**    378

Types of Claims    378

Evidence    381

■ ETHICAL MOMENTS *The Use of Evidence*    382

Forms of Reasoning (Inference)    384

Testing the Adequacy of Forms of Reasoning    386

Detecting Fallacies in Reasoning    386

■ HOW TO *Test Arguments*    388

**A Model for Organizing and Evaluating Arguments**    390

**Assessing a Sample Speech:** *"Mending the Body by Lending an Ear: The Healing Power of Listening," by Carol Koehler*    393

■ HOW TO *Develop Argumentative Speeches*    393

**Chapter Summary**    397

**Key Terms**    397

**Assessment Activities**    398

**References**    398

Chapter **16**

## Building Social Cohesion in a Diverse World: Speeches on Ceremonial and Corporate Occasions     399

Ceremony and Ritual in a Diverse Culture     400

Social Definitions of Diversity     400

Public Address as Community Building     401

Building Community on Corporate Occasions     403

Speeches of Tribute     405

Farewells     405

■ ETHICAL MOMENTS  *A Counterexample: Challenging
the Community's Values*     406

Dedications     407

Memorial Services     407

Style and Content in Speeches of Tribute     407

Speeches to Create Goodwill     408

■ HOW TO  *Organize Speeches of Tribute*     408

Style and Content in Goodwill Speeches     409

■ HOW TO  *Organize Goodwill Speeches*     410

After-Dinner Talks: Entertaining with a Purpose     411

Style and Content in Speeches to Entertain     412

■ HOW TO  *Organize Speeches to Entertain*     412

Keynote Speeches     413

Panel Discussions at Meetings     414

■ HOW TO  *Organize Speeches of Introduction*     414

Preparing for Panel Participation     415

Assessing a Sample Speech: *"In Pursuit of the Tiger:
Traditions and Transitions," by Susan Au Allen*     416

Chapter Summary     419

Key Terms     419

Assessment Activities     420

References     420

**Index**     421

# A Note to Students and Teachers

*Principles and Types of Public Speaking* has been a mainstay in the basic speech course—a celebrated leader in communication studies—for over half a century because it not only follows but also sets educational standards in this field. Longevity comes from demonstrating adaptability to varied conditions. This book always has looked both backward and forward: backward to the timeless principles of speech that are central to the Euro-American cultural experience since the ancient Greeks and forward to the latest research and the leading challenges of today and tomorrow. This fifteenth edition of the book follows in that tradition.

The overarching goal of this revision is to strengthen those features that have made *Principles and Types of Public Speaking* a preeminent book within the field: a commitment to cultural sensitivity, with concrete advice to students on how they can talk effectively in a culturally diverse society, and a commitment to the best research base of any basic book in the field. As such, the text retains core concepts that have been its trademark (e.g., Monroe's motivated sequence) and leads the field with respect to bringing the best research in both humanistic and social science traditions to bear on the principles and practices of public communication. At the same time, the language of the text continues to be accessible to the entering college undergraduate. Conceptually complex ideas are introduced in a way that makes them both understandable and applicable to the act of speaking in public settings. Furthermore, the text is written for students who are computer literate and who often rely more on Internet sources than paper library sources for their speech materials.

In sum, developing competent communicators who have a sophisticated understanding of public communication is the ultimate goal of *Principles and Types of Public Speaking*. Presenting a text that instructors will be proud to use as an exemplar of the best the field has to offer is the means of achieving that goal.

## Highlights of This Revision

Some have criticized current public speaking textbooks for "dumbing down" content to such an extent as to lose credibility. This edition strengthens the move in the opposite direction. With a commitment to clarity in the presentation of concepts as the underlying principle, we introduce materials that are at the cutting edge of scholarship within the discipline. We also illustrate their connection to the practice of communicating in public.

We have increased the focus on two central issues in public communication: speaking within a multicultural society and speaking ethically. In addition, this edition introduces research on such topics as performance theory and its role in oral presentations and devotes specific attention to assessing the credibility of information obtained via the World Wide Web. The issue of assessment leads directly into another pervasive feature of this revision—a commitment to illustrating critical-thinking skills and their use in preparing for and critiquing public discourse. Thus, this revision highlights four specific achievements that differentiate this text from others in the field:

1. *A pervasive connection to culture studies as it assists in approaching and analyzing public discourse in a culturally diverse society.* We have updated the chapter devoted to the issue of how to use cultural information in making specific choices in language, arguments, and the like. While other texts have focused, as does this text, on illustrations throughout the chapters, we have developed the connection between culture and public speaking as a means of introducing students to the importance of attending to cultural differences. We offer specific strategies for unifying diverse audiences without losing a sense of who you are as the speaker. Beyond that, we have expanded the use of diverse examples from people of color to further illustrate the issues of concern as well as to indicate the style of reasoning/speaking. For example, to our knowledge, we are the first text to make extensive use of contemporary Native American speakers as exemplars. The chapter on audience analysis (Chapter 5) and those on informative and persuasive speaking (Chapters 13 and 14) draw upon the strategies noted in the chapter on cultural life (Chapter 4). Recognizing that ideas and their acceptance are culture bound is a major thrust of this revision.

2. *Increased attention to the role of new technologies in communicating (from critically assessing web-based resources to using PowerPoint in presentations).* While the World Wide Web is a fantastic resource for students in terms of accessibility, it also is a highly problematic source of information with respect to accuracy and credibility. Websites are established to promote specific points of view, and students need to be aware of the potential for bias and inaccuracy in assessing web-based information. We focus on this issue in the information-gathering chapter (Chapter 6) and raise it again in the context of understanding audiences through the use of the World Wide Web. We

also illustrate the careful use of authoritative websites as part of our own research in this edition.

The use of PowerPoint is discussed in the chapter on visual communication (Chapter 11). Strategies are provided for creating a PowerPoint presentation that is more than a convenient outline of content; the goal is to enhance the presentation's ability to convey ideas, not simply to impress the audience with technical skill. In addition, a booklet is available separately from Allyn & Bacon that provides guidelines and tips on preparing visual aids using such programs as PowerPoint.

3. *A thorough introduction to the scholarship bearing on public communication, including but not limited to performance theory as it affects orality, culture studies, and persuasion theory.* This text has a long and well-established reputation for having a current research base. In this edition, as already noted, we update information derived from recent research in culture studies. We also add new information drawn from performance theory in relation to physical presence in speaking (the rhetoric of the body). Other additions include the following topics:

   - Recent advances in motivational psychology (This is the only text to introduce more recent research on motivation, such as that drawn from McClelland.)
   - Recent advances in marketing psychology (This is also the only textbook working from VALS and PRIZM, two of the leading paradigms in political-economic persuasion.)
   - The reinterpretation of oral communication (*orality*) in light of the emerging theories of media ecology
   - The concept of *collective memory*, or *collective desire*, as a resource in audience analysis and its role in ceremonial speaking
   - The role of fantasy theme analysis as it contributes to research on audiences
   - A renewed and updated emphasis on how public language functions (for instance, in the guise of debates on political correctness)
   - A revised treatment of the role of uncivil and hateful speech as well as advice on how to avoid offensive language

4. *A focus on both ceremonial and corporate occasions for public talk and how both contribute to the creation and maintenance of community.* That oral discourse functions to bind people has never been so clear as in times of crises, such as that which occurred in the United States while this edition was being written. Emphasizing those occasions in which public talk builds consensus, unity, and community in the midst of tragedy is an important contribution to students' understanding of the role of communication in a democratic society. Merging ceremonial and corporate occasions—including attention to speeches of tribute and goodwill along with keynote addresses and speeches to entertain—allows instructors and students to see the connections among these diverse occasions.

## Key Strengths of the Text

In addition to the focus on what is new, *Principles and Types of Public Speaking* has earned its reputation because of traditional strengths, and we have been sure to retain those characteristics in this edition. The following are the key ingredients of our continuing commitment to a textbook that offers a clear and useable blend of theory and performance skills:

1. *The connection between theory and practice.* Although known for its solid grounding in rhetorical and communication research, this book maintains its focus on the actual experience itself: creating and presenting an effective public speech. For example, in keeping with the increased emphasis on oral communication skills—skills needed both to prepare and deliver effective speeches—we have continued to include the "How to" boxes. Each of these boxes contains specific advice on how the concepts discussed in the text can be used in a specific illustration, thereby putting theory into practice. The continued inclusion of the "Communication Research Dateline" boxes also underscores the dual focus on providing grounded knowledge as well as practical advice to speakers.

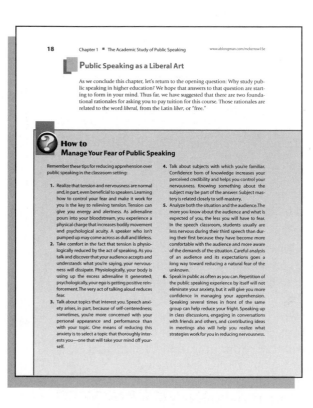

2. *A focus on both speechmaking in society and student presentations in class-rooms.* This book has an obligation to compel communication studies students to reflect seriously upon the electronic revolution and its implications for responsible dialogue between and among citizens. Throughout the text, we use examples and illustrations that focus attention on contemporary political, economic, religious, and social issues. We ask students to analyze these issues in a manner that will help them construct arguments and appeals that reflect their own beliefs and resonate with their audiences' beliefs, desires, and needs. Simultaneously, we recognize that students are seeking to survive and grow in their own environment—the college communication classroom. Thus, many of our examples, illustrations, and sample speeches are drawn from campus life as well as from student speakers. This book asks students not only to assess their skills where they are but also to look ahead to the experience of building community through communication after their college years.

3. *A continued commitment to critical thinking.* The chapter on argumentation (Chapter 15) focuses on the use of fallacies, both in terms of their illogical nature and in terms of their potential as rhetorically effective arguments. Critical thinking is not only about assessing arguments for logic and validity. It also implies paying close attention to the language choices made in speaking to a diverse audience and to the choices made in organizing a presentation. Throughout the text, we highlight the importance of thinking about the rhetorical choices that might be made in addressing specific audiences. The engagement of ideas and audiences is a matter of choice: It *does* matter what one says and how one says it in most circumstances. The "How to" boxes referred to earlier are one means of focusing attention on choices. Likewise, the illustrations drawn from current political and social discourse—how public discourse choices affect future rhetorical choices—also shed light on how public speaking influences public affairs.

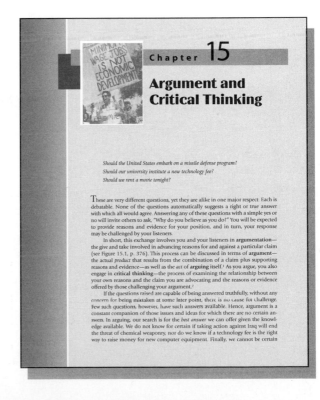

Chapter **15**

**Argument and Critical Thinking**

*Should the United States embark on a missile defense program?*
*Should our university institute a new technology fee?*
*Should we rent a movie tonight?*

These are very different questions, yet they are alike in one major respect: Each is debatable. None of the questions automatically suggests a right or true answer with which all would agree. Answering any of these questions with a simple yes or no will invite others to ask, "Why do you believe as you do?" You will be expected to provide reasons and evidence for your position, and in turn, your response may be challenged by your listeners.

In short, this exchange involves you and your listeners in **argumentation**—the give and take involved in advancing reasons for and against a particular claim (see Figure 15.1, p. 376). This process can be discussed in terms of **argument**—the actual *product* that results from the combination of a claim plus supporting reasons and evidence—as well as the *act* of **arguing** itself.[1] As you argue, you also engage in **critical thinking**—the process of examining the relationship between your own reasons and the claim you are advocating and the reasons or evidence offered by those challenging your argument.[2]

If the questions raised are capable of being answered truthfully, without any concern for being mistaken at some later point, there is no cause for challenge. Few such questions, however, have such answers available. Hence, argument is a constant companion of those issues and ideas for which there are no certain answers. In arguing, our search is for the *best answer* we can offer given the knowledge available. We do not know for certain if taking action against Iraq will end the threat of chemical weaponry, nor do we know if a technology fee is the right way to raise money for new computer equipment. Finally, we cannot be certain

4. *A continued commitment to the importance of ethics.* The "Ethical Moments" boxes were among the most positively received features of previous editions, and they have been maintained in this edition as well. New topics include plagiarism, sexism, the ethics of credibility and hyperemotionalism, ghostwriting, and statistical manipulations. Public speaking involves making moral decisions, both in terms of the choices that are made to tell the truth about what is known along with sharing that knowledge in ethically responsible ways.

5. *Streamlined coverage for today's public speaking classroom.* Without losing sight of what has made this text a valuable part of the communication field since its introduction in 1935, we have made several structural changes in this new edition:

   ■ The chapter "Getting Started" now follows an introductory chapter on the academic study of public speaking, so students can more quickly move to the practical matter of "What do I do next?" Instructors will find it easier to provide an overview of the basics as a precursor to the first speaking assignment.

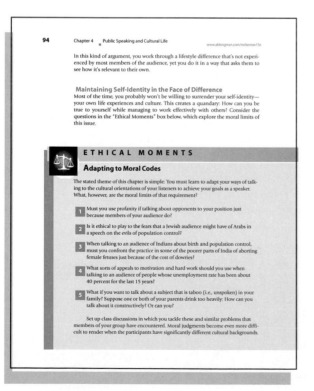

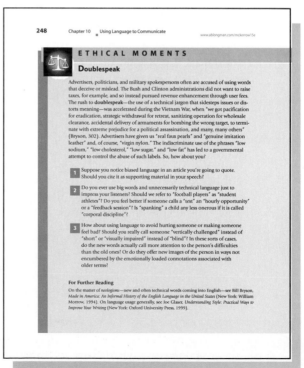

- The strategies for gaining and maintaining attention have been integrated with the specific advice on building introductions and conclusions (Chapter 8).

- The discussion of motivational appeals has been integrated into those chapters where their use is a priority—in the informative and persuasive speaking chapters (Chapters 13 and 14). This will allow instructors to highlight those appeals most likely to be effective as they focus attention on strategies for informing and persuading audiences.

- In addition, the chapter on special speaking occasions (Chapter 16) has been tightened to focus on how communication in ceremonial and business settings contributes to the creation and maintenance of community. This chapter covers speeches of tribute, farewell, dedication, and memorial as well as after-dinner talks, keynote speeches, and panel discussions at meetings.

6. *Continued pedagogical support.* Both teachers and students need to be well supported in the educational process. *Principles and Types of Public Speaking,* Fifteenth Edition, continues to be a leader in pedagogical support. Each chapter closes with a clear summary of content and a list of the key terms used in the chapter. These sections will help students in recalling concepts and building a vocabulary with which to discuss public communication events. Among the many ancillaries offered for instructors are a variety of videos, some of which cover topics such as speaker apprehension and audience analysis and others that contain sample student speeches. In addition, an Instructor's Manual provides teaching tips, bibliographies, chapter reviews, and additional tested exercises. For a full list of the supplements available with this edition, please see the list on pages xxiv–xxv or the catalog page for this book on the Allyn & Bacon website at www.ablongman.com/communication.

7. *A logical, teachable organization of topics.* As explained earlier, the basics of public speaking are introduced in Chapter 2; this allows instructors first to review the central issues in public speaking, as presented in Chapter 1, and then to introduce what will be discussed in more detail throughout the term. Additionally, some of the material on business and professional settings, which was presented in the last chapter of the previous edition, has been added to the chapter on ceremonial speaking (Chapter 16). This allows for a more coherent discussion of the role of communication in contemporary society.

Overall, we know that this edition of the most popular public speaking textbook of the twentieth century has merged traditional and innovative features to keep it at the forefront of communication studies in the twenty-first century. It is based on a speech skills tradition, which assures educators that course outcomes can be tested in concrete ways, yet it lives and breathes the liberal arts tradition, which makes the basic speech course but an introduction to the world of communication studies—to the scientific, theoretical, historical, and critical study of public communication and social life. What we seek through this revision is nothing less than the most refined, sophisticated, research-driven, application-oriented textbook available on the market. We are convinced that you will find *Principles and Types of Public Speaking* to be a solid yet malleable teaching and learning instrument.

## Supplementary Materials

The ancillary package for the fifteenth edition of *Principles and Types of Public Speaking* includes the following materials:

### Resources for Instructors

- *Instructor's Manual*
- *Test Bank*
- *Computerized Test Bank*
- PowerPoint Presentation Package for McKerrow (available only online: www.ablongman.com/ppt)
- Allyn & Bacon PowerPoint Presentation for Public Speaking (available only online: www.ablongman.com/ppt)
- Allyn & Bacon Public Speaking Transparency Package
- *ESL Guide for Public Speaking*
- *A Guide for New Public Speaking Teachers,* Second Edition
- *Great Ideas for Teaching Speech (GIFTS)*
- Allyn & Bacon Digital Media Archive for Communication, Version 2.0
- Allyn & Bacon Student Speeches Video Library (instructor's choice of one)
- Allyn & Bacon Public Speaking Video
- Allyn & Bacon Public Speaking Key Topics Video Library (some restrictions apply)
- Allyn & Bacon Communication Video Library (some restrictions apply)
- *ContentSelect* Research Database

### Resources for Students

- Companion Website with Online Practice Tests (www.ablongman.com/mckerrow15e)
- Allyn & Bacon Public Speaking Website (www.ablongman.com/pubspeak)
- *Preparing Visual Aids for Presentations,* Third Edition
- *Public Speaking in the Multicultural Environment,* Second Edition
- *Speech Preparation Workbook*

- Outlining Workbook
- iSearch: Speech Communication, including access to the ContentSelect research database
- Interactive Speechwriter Software, Version 1.1 (Windows)
- Speech Writer's Workshop CD-ROM, Version 2.0

## Acknowledgments

We owe a great debt to those instructors who took time to review the previous edition and to offer useful comments: Ferald Bryan, Northern Illinois University; Nanci Burk, Glendale Community College; Jean Perry, Glendale Community College; Jim Sayer, Wright State University; and David Walker, Middle Tennessee State University.

Gratitude is due, as well, to the University of Iowa's Obermann Center for Advanced Studies, especially its director Jay Semel and "operating magician" Lorna Olson; the facilities provided by the center helped the revision of this text proceed smoothly. Appreciation is offered, too, to Lotta Harviainen of the University of Jyväskylä, Finland, who helped with international connections during the process of revising this new edition.

Thanks also to Jakob and Ingrid Gronbeck, who continue to contribute their talents for library research and attempt to keep their father current. Finally, gratitude is owed to Gayle and Matthew McKerrow for their constant encouragement and continued support.

We also thank Allyn & Bacon for the resources and talents it invested in this project. This edition was executed under the careful watch of our Executive Editor, Karon Bowers, and the word-by-word manuscript preparation was handled by Kristinn Muller. Production was overseen by Production Administrator Donna Simons and carried out by Susan Freese of Communicáto, Ltd. We also appreciate the assistance of the permissions department in keeping us legal. We are pleased with the efforts of our Marketing Manager Mandee Eckersley. And finally, we thank the group of talented sales representatives who carry this book onto the campuses and ultimately to you.

You, of course, are the bottom line. We thank you for examining and using this book. In doing so, your own personal commitment to excellence as a public communicator will be enhanced and you will find new ways both to improve your own fortunes and to build a better community in a culturally diverse world. Your commitments are ours, as well, and we remain ever mindful of our obligation to enable you to succeed as an ethical communicator.

Raymie E. McKerrow

Bruce E. Gronbeck

# PART ONE

# Public Speaking and the Liberal Arts

What other power [than public speech] could have been strong enough either to gather scattered humanity into one place, or to lead it out of its brutish existence in the wilderness up to our present condition of civilization as [people] and as citizens, or, after the establishment of social communities, to give shape to laws, tribunals, and civic rights?

Cicero, *De oratore* I.33

# Chapter 1

# The Academic Study of Public Speaking

*"Why take a speech class? I've been speaking all of my life!"*

*"How in the world can you justify using expensive college and university resources on something as technique oriented as public speaking?"*

*"Sure, the business school needs to require speaking. Accountants need all of the help they can get! But why require it of the rest of us?"*

*"OK, maybe our international students profit from taking this class, but not somebody from Cleveland, Ohio!"*

*"If you want to take the easiest class at this school, sign up for public speaking!"*

*Teachers of public speaking have listened to these sorts of comments for all their years in the classroom. The course is too easy or too hard. It's too technique or theory oriented. It should be required, or it should be thrown out. Then, the time comes when the first speech must be delivered, and the comments change:*

*"What should I talk about?"*

*"How should I start my speech?"*

*"Why am I doing this? What do I want to achieve?"*

*"How should I stand? What should I do with my hands?"*

*"What if they can't understand my awkward English pronunciation?"*

*"What if someone asks a question I can't answer?"*

*"What if I forget what I want to say?"*

Such questions take you into specific concerns about the details of public speaking. But answering them involves more than giving advice—"Stand this way," "Hold your head that way," "Talk louder," "Check your fly." What is involved, ultimately, is understanding that while public speaking is a personal act, it's also a social act—one that involves other people who have their own roles and expectations. Because public speaking is a social act, you must think seriously about the culture within which you're speaking: its traditional rules for public talk, the usual ways of talking in specific situations (e.g., from a pulpit versus from a lockerroom bench), even relationships between males and females, the young and the old, and people from a range of racial, ethnic, and economic groups as they've developed in various regions of a country. Such rules, folkways, and relationships exist and can force you to think about more than your own sweaty palms and pounding chest. They also account for why public speaking is a mandated course in higher education.

In this chapter, we'll explore the study of public speaking in colleges and universities, the functions of public speaking in the social-political contexts of a multicultural society, why ethics, in fact, is always a central concern of the public speaker, and the most important skills and competencies you need to be a successful public speaker in a free society.

##  Studying Public Speaking in Higher Education

Before we plunge any farther into this book, think a bit more about why you need training in public speaking and how you can learn to do it better.

### The Need for Speech Training

As a student in a public speaking class, you're likely to feel a range of emotions: fear of what might happen to you in the middle of a speech, excitement at the prospect of learning how to better control yourself and your words in front of an audience, boredom when reading some of the chapters in this book, smugness when you find yourself saying "I already know [or do] that!" or even anger at being asked to do something you'd rather not do publicly.

While the prospect of speaking in public may seem scary, exciting, boring, or whatever other emotion you experience when you're about to talk, learning to channel your perfectly natural feelings in a positive direction to come across as poised, prepared, and even persuasive is one reason you're here. In addition, you're in this class because many people in higher education believe public speaking is something that well-educated, community-oriented people must be able to do well. Further, as the quotation from Cicero at the beginning of this unit indicates, the power of speech in building community is worthy of study. Preserving your own identity while creating a sense of community is a special challenge as the new century unfolds before us.

We can't deal with all of your feelings and all of the reasons that you should (or should not) be in this classroom. But as you start into a speech preparation process that Cicero said will make you *vir bonus, dicendi peritus,* "the good person, speaking well," we can discuss some of your more pressing feelings and reasons.

Actually, if you ask speech teachers why students need such training, you'll find no unanimity in their answers. Some will stress the **social imperative:**

Speech skills are necessary for all social beings, and speech training was mandated by the federal government as long ago as 1965 in the Primary and Secondary Education Act. Speech skills are necessary for any individual to participate in public events or, as pioneer rhetorical critics Lester Thonssen and A. Craig Baird noted some 50 years ago, "The fundamental purpose of oral discourse is social coordination or control."[1] The ability to control, to make function smoothly, various social events and confrontations also has been important to students of speech, as Kenneth Burke noted, because the public sphere is

> the Scramble, the Wrangle of the Market Place, the flurries and flare-ups of the Human Barnyard, the Give and Take, the wavering line of pressure and counter-pressure, the Logomachy, the onus of leadership, the Wars of Nerves, the War. . . . Rhetoric is concerned with the state of Babel after the Fall . . . [in] the lugubrious regions of malice and the lie.[2]

Speech skills must be sharpened through study and practice, because otherwise, you will not be able to participate with maximum effect in public events or, even worse, you might be victimized by unscrupulous others in the human barnyard.

This last point suggests another: You learn about the technicalities of public speaking not only to be a better maker of messages but also to be a more sophisticated receiver of public talk. There is a **consumer imperative** to speech education. Roderick P. Hart has written that a student of speech must engage in both *reflective complaining* and *reflective compliments*, that a student must become someone "who knows when and how to render an evaluation."[3] To understand how public communication works, you must have an understanding of basic processes and varied techniques, a vocabulary for talking about both, and some sense as to what kinds of standards can be used to make value judgments about speeches. A good course in public speaking will teach you as much about *listening* to as about *making* speeches.

Finally, behind any solid course in public speaking is an **intellectual imperative.** In fact, speech training is an important part of a liberal arts education. This has been so since Isocrates made it central to his training of the orator-statesmen of fourth-century B.C.E. Greece:

> For [the power to speak publicly] it is which has laid down laws concerning things just and unjust, and things honourable and base; and if it were not for these ordinances [i.e., of public speech] we should not be able to live with one another. It is by this also that we confuse the bad and extol the good. Through this we educate the ignorant and appraise the wise; for the power to speak well is taken as the surest index of a sound understanding, and discourse which is true and lawful and just is the outward image of a good and faithful soul.[4]

In this grand conception, the study of human speech is the study of the ethics, practical philosophy, and eloquent expression of the human spirit. The

*Sojourner Truth was an eloquent spokesperson for emancipation and women's rights.*

greatest examples of public speaking endure well past the time and place they were given: Pericles's Funeral Oration in 427 B.C.E. over the dead of the Peloponnesian War; William the Conqueror's exhortation to his troops before the Battle of Hastings in 1066; Jacques-Bénigne Bossuet's sermons before the bodies of French kings and queens in the seventeenth century; William Pitt the Elder's thunderous orations on British cruelties and stupidities in the American colonies; Abraham Lincoln's Gettysburg Address in 1863, soon after Sojourner Truth's identification of black women's problems with those of white women in "Ain't I a Woman?"; Mahatma Gandhi's message of nonviolent resistance in India, inspiring Martin Luther King, Jr.'s, "dream" speech at the Washington Monument in 1963; Barbara Jordan's explanation of what "We the people" means from her seat on the House Judiciary Committee as it was about to impeach President Richard Nixon.

You'll not likely be asked to comment eloquently on the human condition and ways of improving it generally, as did all of these individuals. But you must understand, clearly and unmistakably, that public speaking is about more than you and your problems. It's about you and your public relationships with others. You take courses in public speaking to improve your own self-confidence and sense of personal empowerment, of course, but also for social, self-protective, and intellectual reasons. That's why you need speech training.

## Ways to Learn More about Public Speaking

There are, naturally, many different ways to learn about public speaking. Your instructor probably won't have you pursue all of them, but some certainly will be part of his or her pedagogy. Consider the following:

1. *A speech classroom is a laboratory and, hence, an ideal place for trying new behaviors.* Try to develop new skills in your assigned speeches. Tell a story in the conclusion, use PowerPoint or access the World Wide Web to make visual aids, or deliver a speech from in front of rather than behind a lectern. The speech classroom is a comparatively safe environment for experimentation.

2. *Practice new speech techniques on friends, in a variety of settings, and in the speech classroom.* Practicing public speaking is every bit as important as practicing music instruments, soccer formations, or on-the-job interactions. You can't just read about speaking and then do it well. Speaking skills develop through the hit-and-miss process of practice: in the privacy of your own room, in front of friends willing to humor you, in other classes, and, of course, in your speech classroom. Get feedback whenever and wherever you can.

3. *Work on your speech consumer skills, as well.* In your lifetime, you'll be exposed to thousands upon thousands of public messages in the forms of speeches, classroom pitches, TV ads, and chatroom exchanges. Practicing listening—trying to accurately comprehend and fairly evaluate what others say publicly—will help you hone skills that are equally as important as speaking skills.

4. *Learn to criticize expertly the speeches of others.* You can use this book as a tool for analyzing speeches you find in print (e.g., with the *Speech Index*), hear in person, and access electronically.

Through activities both inside and outside your speech classroom—speaking and analyzing the speeches of others—you will develop and hone the skills that will make you a more productive and successful member of society.

## The Functions of Public Speaking in Society

It's time to get a bit more specific. What sorts of social, economic, political, and religious-moral functions do most societies—certainly Western societies—pursue through public talk? To answer this question, we first should consider why speech is so important to public life, even in the Electronic Age.

### Orality in Social-Political Life

You're literate, and so you can write a letter or even have a flyer printed and distributed from the street corner. You live in the Electronic Age, and so you can use a cell phone to call someone, hoping to sell him or her a product or an idea. Additionally, you can turn on your computer, enter a listserv or chatroom with folks who have the same interests you do, or even send a message to your congressional representative via his or her dot-gov address. And then, there are radio and TV call-in programs, minicams for making QuickTime movies, fax machines, and on and on. So, why in the world do presidents still give televised speeches, teachers still offer classroom lectures, business teams still do oral presentations, and lawyers duke it out with opening and closing courtroom speeches?

*There's something essentially, engagingly, and powerfully human about speaking publicly to others.* That's it, period. As far back as anyone can trace tribal relationships, human beings from parents to politicians have built their relationships through face-to-face talk. Speech flows directly out of your mouth and into the ears of others; your movements, vocal tones, bodily tensions, and facial displays are directly accessible to those who watch and listen. This sort of direct person-to-person contact in public simply cannot be wholly reproduced on paper, through electronically boosted sound waves, or via video or digital pictures.

The centrality of **orality**—of direct, in-person, spoken connections between people—to human relationships cannot be denied. Edward Hall argued almost 50 years ago that the "biological roots" of "all culture" can be found in speech, and more recently, Walter Ong urged us to remember that the "sounded word" is a tremendous source of "power and action."[6]

It is through sound that you act upon others—calling them ("Hey you!"), singling them out ("Come here, Danielle"), recognizing their group identities (the gladiators' "We who are about to die salute you!"). The ancients even practiced word magic, finding supernatural power in oral incantations, as you'll remember from Shakespeare's witches in *Macbeth:* "Double, double toil and trouble;/Fire burn, and caldron bubble." The power of naming was shown in the Bible in Genesis 2:20, where Adam named all of the animals in order to have dominion over them. And finally, speaking words calls up important events—their identities, motivations that should flow from them. "Remember the . . . [Titans, Alamo, Maine, etc.]!" is a speaker's demand to recall from memory an event that provides a reason for listeners to act together in particular ways.

## Public Speaking and Decision Making in a Multicultural Society

What is suggested by thinking about orality in the social world is this: Public speaking is a primary mechanism for bringing people together, for getting them to share perspectives and values, so that they can recognize who they are or can get something done.

That's easy to say, harder to do. The challenges of speaking publicly so as to affect people's self- and group perception or activities—in other words, to affect their decision making—center on three public activities:

1. *Self-presentation.* You must be able to present yourself convincingly as someone worthy of giving information and advice. Think of yourself not only in selfish ways but also as an instrument for changing others. (See the section on pp. 13–16, The Centrality of Ethics to Public Communication.)

2. *Packaging ideas and information.* From all of the things that you *could* say, you must select a relatively compact and relevant set of ideas, or a cluster of information, that will affect your listeners in the ways you want them affected. Suppose that you wish to convince your campus to quit selling school-labeled clothing that has been made in foreign sweatshops. You'll need one package of ideas and information to get fellow students behind your movement but another to convince the administration to join an academic cooperative that pressures manufacturers to offer reasonable pay to foreign laborers. You can't take the time to tell either group everything that could be said about Third World manufacturing practices nor, frankly, is everything relevant to your specific purpose: to keep sweatshop clothing out of your campus bookstore. Thoughtfulness and shrewdness are required as you select and arrange materials for your actual speeches.

3. *Selecting valuative frames.* Throughout the rest of this book, we'll have much to say about framing. Psychologists typically talk about **framing** as the mechanism by which our perceptions of the world are formed to fit with our existing values, knowledge, and experience.[7] The "facts" do not, cannot, speak for themselves. They become relevant and powerful by being situated inside human valuative frames—human-sensitive ways of understanding and evaluating the world.

Suppose, for example, you've discovered that 4 percent of the American population is unemployed. Is that a problem or not? From a legislative frame— the 1946 Full Employment Act —it's bad because anything over 3 percent unemployment requires federal programs to help put people to work. And personally, if you don't have a job but want one, it's likewise bad. Yet from a social perspective, where we assume that about 4 percent of the nonretired population has illnesses, disabilities, or living situations that make them unproductive or even dangerous workers, this level of unemployment is just about right. And from an economic perspective, if the figure were lower, it would make the process of finding labor when opening a new facility very difficult, requiring higher wages to lure workers from other jobs; from this view, a lower unemployment rate could be inflationary. Therefore, within the economic frame, 4 percent unemployment is ideal. And so the debate proceeds: The valuative or perceptual frame from which we view the facts makes them relevant to and judged within our individual human situations in different ways. Frameworks are the interpreters of the facts and, hence, central to public communication.

What we're suggesting is that, yes, when speaking in public, you must learn how to handle and present yourself in order to make your opinions worthwhile for your listeners. But you also face the even more difficult tasks of selecting and then packaging information and ideas and of interpreting that information in ways that make it relevant to collective decision making. That's yet another reason you're taking a course in public speaking.

*For Nelson Mandela, speech is a powerful means of maintaining cultural identity and fostering community.*

## Achieving Personal and Collective Goals through Public Talk

As you think about the personal and group-related reasons for learning to be a competent public speaker, several stand out.

First and foremost, to speak in public is to declare yourself to be a member of a community. By going public with your ideas, you demand that others accept you and your suggestions as worthy of consideration. Without Frederick Douglass, a former slave who urged the abolition of slavery, we would be less than we are today. In the language of his time, Douglass said, "Men may combine to prevent cruelty to animals, for they are dumb [mute] and cannot speak for themselves; but we are men and must speak for ourselves, or we shall not be spoken for at all."[8] Martin Luther King, Jr.'s, "dream" may not yet be fully realized, but the legacy of Douglass lives on as African Americans continue to speak on behalf of their cultural heritage. Similarly, the women attending the Seneca Falls, New York, convention for women's rights in 1848 argued they should be allowed to talk publicly. Originally, they had been assigned to watch the proceedings from the gallery, but they were determined to define their own rights. The words of Elizabeth Cady Stanton give eloquent testimony to the need to speak:

> I should feel exceedingly diffident to appear before you at this time . . . did I not feel that woman herself must do this work. . . . Man cannot speak for her, because he has been educated to believe that she differs from him so materially, that he cannot judge of her thoughts, feelings, and opinions by his own.[9]

Speaking in public, then, is a personal declaration of your beliefs and values and of your right to be a representative of your community. Not to speak is to surrender to silence. Silence can make you disappear, become invisible, a nonperson in the eyes of others. The Jews of Hitler's Germany were referred to as "silent animals" in *Mein Kampf*. African American slaves were thought of as the personal property of slave owners, and Native Americans were viewed as children and treated as such. Whole segments of populations have been treated as outcasts in their own lands and even "cleansed" in cases of ethnic genocide, as in the tragedies of Macedonia. When whole peoples are silenced, whether through force or intimidation, they are in danger of elimination. And that is why you, as an individual, sometimes must rise as a representative of a group to speak your (and their) mind.

Thus, a second reason for being a good public speaker—whether delivering a ritual performance or a specific address to right social wrongs—is to maintain or alter the communities to which we belong. In a culturally diverse land, maintaining community is a special right of those whose culture differs from that of others. With maintenance comes the obligation of respecting differences between cultures, even in the same physical community. In 1989, Henri Mann Morton, a member of the Cheyenne nation, addressed a multicultural conference and gave voice to the long-standing concern for preserving cultural diversity in these words:

> I am the granddaughter of those who welcomed many of our grandmothers and grandfathers—your grandparents—to this country. It is now our country.
>
> We were multi-tribal; heterogeneous as the indigenous people of America, and following Anglo contact exchanged the term "multi-tribal" for "multicultural," so we could embrace those who came to live with us. Prior to non-Indian contact, we as American Indians were culturally diverse. We were familiar with the concept of "cultural diversity," and recognized that those cultural differences made us strong. Cultural diversity made for strength—there was/is strength in cultural diversity. Cultural diversity makes our country strong. It has made us a great nation and we all have an opportunity to achieve the American dream.[10]

In a similar vein, on the opening night of the 1992 Democratic National Convention in New York City, the third keynote speech was given by the late Barbara Jordan, the former congresswoman from Texas who in 1976 was the first female African American to keynote a national political party convention. Dealing forthrightly with the issue of race relations in the United States, she implored her listeners to recognize and value difference in the midst of unity:

> We are one, we Americans, and we reject any intruder who seeks to divide us on the bases of race and color. We honor cultural identity. We always have, we always will. But separateness is not allowed. Separateness is not the American way. We must not allow ideas like political correctness to divide us and cause us to reverse hard-won achievements in human rights and civil rights. Xenophobia has no place in the Democratic party. We seek to unite people, not divide them.
>
> As we seek to unite people, we reject both white racism and black racism. This party, this party, this party will not tolerate bigotry under any guise. Our strength, our strength in this country is rooted in our diversity. Our history bears witness to that fact. *E pluribus unum*. "From many, one." It was a good idea when our country was founded, and it's a good idea today.[11]

That two speeches by female members of minority groups dealt with matters of cultural diversity, racial divisions, and social unity was no accident. We were then and continue to be rocked by a series of incidents that suggest the United States has not escaped the danger of splitting apart along lines of cultural difference. From the Rodney King incident to the lyrics of Eminem and death-metal groups such as Slayer to the slaughter of classmates because of differences in Littleton, Colorado, to gay, lesbian, bisexual and transgender bashing and even killing across the country, to the raping and pillaging of defenseless women and children—maintaining a sense of community while preserving diversity has been sorely tried. Someone (many someones) must stand up and have enough guts to condemn the verbal and physical violence spawned by social differences.

Third, even as you pursue the public expression of individual and collective identity in front of others, you also can pursue your own self-interest in learning how to be a more effective public speaker:

1. *Developing speaking skills will pay off, literally, on the job.* Companies want their new employees to have the skills to do basic research before making recommendations, to present ideas clearly and efficiently, to motivate their work teams once they get that first managerial position, to deal effectively with confused and underachieving team members, and to interact with the company's publics with grace and force. You should be working on these skills in this course. Your ability to speak to and with others is what is referenced in those job descriptions that say "Communication skills are required."

2. *These same skills, of course, will follow you out of the cubicle after work, as well.* Do you want to convince a group of friends at your local hangout to try a 100-mile charity bike ride this weekend? You'd better know how to persuade them. Did you volunteer to work a phone bank for the local crisis center's fund-raising? You'll do a much better job if you can turn that cold script you were given into warm, friendly speech tones. Do you want to teach the soccer group you're training on Saturday mornings to move the ball from backfielders to midfielders to the striker? You'll need to present instructions clearly, sequentially, yet excitingly to make 8-year-olds able to execute that drill.

3. *Finally, your whole attitude toward yourself will change if you're comfortable with some basic and a few more advanced public speaking skills.* Once you've had some success as a speaker, you'll gain confidence, and with confidence comes the willingness to take on more difficult speech tasks. No one ever loses all of his or her nervousness and the fear that something can go wrong when behind a lectern. For that matter, you'll not always be perfectly successful as a speaker. That's life. What's also life, however, is the sense of personal achievement—and, hence, self-confidence and self-liking—when you win a public battle over ideas or policies via public speaking. And because success tends to breed more success, you'll simply become better and better as you turn basic speech skills into more sophisticated ones.

The individual and collective goals of public speakers, therefore, can be wonderfully grandiose and profound even as they're intensely private and, in a way, selfish. But then, why would you expect otherwise? If speech has even half of the power that Cicero asserted it has, then you're working on skills that are essential to human life processes.

# The Centrality of Ethics in Public Communication

If speaking skills are so important to life's decisions and even to individual identity, what does that mean? How do they work? To approach answers to these questions, we need to explore the idea of *ethics* in public life, probably remaking a bit of your understanding of that term.

## Ethos in the Western World

We begin etymologically. The English word *ethics* is derived from the Greek word **ethos.** Actually, we still use the latter word, too, to mean something like "credibility" or "reputation." It had a larger meaning, however, in ancient Greece. "Motives and aims, no matter how pure or how grandiose," argued Hannah Arendt, "are never unique; like psychological qualities, they are typical, characteristic of different types of persons."[12] To Aristotle, a person who had ethos demonstrated while speaking that he or she shared characteristics with others in the community—that is, had good sense, goodwill, and good morals:[13]

1. *Good sense.* To demonstrate to others that the person is talking from a position of experience and knowledge, of information tempered by personal experience. To be talking knowledgably.
2. *Goodwill.* To communicate a sense of caring not only about oneself but, more importantly, about audience members—their needs, their status, and their future. To be talking caringly.
3. *Good morals.* To speak in the language of the beliefs and values of listeners, to share their visions, their fears, and their hopes. To be talking morally in the broad sense of that term.

Thus, for the Greeks, ethos was an orientation to life that individuals shared with their community. What made individuals people with ethos was their public demonstration of knowing and understanding what their community held as important—in other words, their shared commitments and living out those commitments in public talk. Ethos was a multifaceted idea, reflecting what people knew, cared about, and used as guidelines for living.

That such an understanding of ethos is relevant to us today can be seen in public opinions about President Bill Clinton in the 1990s. In surveys about his personal morals, he tended to score very low, usually with less than 25 percent of the respondents believing that he was personally moral. Yet when the same people were asked whether Clinton understood the country's needs and knew where to lead them, 60 percent or more supported him, and when asked what politician cared about them, more than two-thirds of the respondents believed that he did. President Clinton demonstrated that the Greek standards for ethos could sustain a politician in office even if his personal life was questionable.[14] The "How to" box below contains some guidelines for enhancing one's credibility as a speaker.

### The Moral Bases of Public Decision Making

We likewise must understand that the word *moral* comes from the Latin word *mores*, which refers to what most people believe to be important guidelines to shared values and activities. Stephen Carter calls *civility*—that is, the commitment to a civic life—"the sum of the many sacrifices we are called upon to make for the sake of living together. . . . We should make sacrifices for others not simply because doing so makes social life easier (although it does), but as a signal of respect for our fellow citizens, marking them as full equals, both before the law and before God."[15] Later, he notes that "all of us [must] learn anew the virtue of acting with love toward our neighbors."[16]

The idea of public morality or civility encompasses, therefore, both ethical commitments to community standards and also etiquette—that is, observation of

## How to
### Enhance Your Credibility as a Speaker

Research has verified that following these guidelines will help a speaker improve his or her credibility:

1. References to yourself and your experience (provided you're not boasting or excessive) tend to increase your perceived trustworthiness and competence. References to those who are acknowledged as authorities tend to increase your perceived trustworthiness and dynamism.

2. Using highly credible authorities to substantiate your claims will increase your perceived fairness.

3. Demonstrating that you and your audience share common beliefs, attitudes, and values will increase your overall credibility.

4. Well-organized speeches are more credible than poorly organized speeches.

5. The more sincere you are, the better your chance of changing your listeners' attitudes.

*Source:*  See Roderick P. Hart and Don M. Burks, "Rhetorical Sensitivity and Social Interaction," *Speech* [Communication] *Monographs* 47 (1980): 1–22.

acceptable ways of treating others. To be committed to the observation of community standards for thinking and activity does not mean that you simply think and do what everyone else does, nor does it mean that communities lack disagreement. In the 1830s, French writer and politician Alexis de Tocqueville toured the United States, marveling at a democracy in which Americans always were "at once ardent and relaxed, violent and enervated."[17] To act in accordance with community beliefs and values, however, is to work with **moral frames,** or shared values or ways of looking at and valuing the world.

To the public speaker, two implications of understanding community beliefs and values as moral frames for handling even disagreements or differences are especially important to public speakers:

1. *To be successful, you must find some moral frame you share with your listeners if you're going to convince them that you have their best interests at heart.* Donald Moon calls this the **skyhook principle.**[18] You will often speak to people whose backgrounds differ from yours, who hold values different from yours—even what have been called *incommensurate* or *absolutely opposed* values. How can you convince people whose values conflict with yours to do something? Moon's answer is to find a skyhook—a higher value, a higher appeal, that will transcend your differences. This is what Jesse Jackson did in 1988, for example, when trying to convince people of all ethnic backgrounds to work together in aid of the poor. He sought to demonstrate that, in spite of our ethnic, political ideological, economic, and geographical differences, Americans could survive and prosper only by overcoming those differences. To *survive* and *prosper*—stay alive, make progress—were moral or valuative frames, Jackson hoped, that were transcendent. "Keep hope alive!" he shouted. He hoped that the use of skyhooks would lift people's vision above their ethnic clashes, ideological differences, economic disparities, and geographical dispersion.[19]

2. *Finding a shared moral frame, however, still demands that you be true to what you believe.* Jackson sacrificed none of his own deeply seated beliefs and values when he called for "common ground" and "common sense" in his 1988 speech to the Democratic National Convention. His integrity was intact. You, too, should always look for moral frames you share with your listeners—not ones that only they accept but ones from which you both work. Then you'll both be true to yourself and interesting to your audience.

The moral bases for public speaking, therefore, are not merely ethical or religious tenets (although those can be a part of the moral bases for community). They're broader than that. They're all of the frames—social, psychological, legal, economic, scientific, philosophical, political, religious—that human beings in a community generally understand and even largely (though not necessarily universally) accept and live by. In communities as diverse, as multicultural, as those in the United States, the search for workable moral frames will be one of your most important tasks as a public speaker when your goal is to persuade people to change their minds or behaviors.

# Skills and Competencies Needed for Successful Speechmaking

Because public speaking is an interactive process through which people transact various kinds of business, you must acquire certain skills (psychomotor abilities) and competencies (mental abilities to identify, assess, and plan responses to communication problems) in order to be effective. From the beginning of your coursework, five basic qualities merit your attention: integrity, knowledge, rhetorical sensitivity, oral skills, and self-confidence.

## Integrity

Your reputation for reliability, truthfulness, and concern for others is your single most powerful means of exerting rhetorical influence. Integrity is especially important in this age of diversity, when various groups in a fragmented culture are wary of each other and of each other's purposes. Listeners who haven't had personal experience with a particular subject or with representatives of a particular social group must be convinced of your concern for them. If you are to succeed, you must earn their trust—demonstrate ethos—while speaking.

## Knowledge

No one wants to listen to an empty-headed windbag; a speaker must know what he or she is talking about. So, for example, even though you may have personal experience with motocross bike racing, do some extra reading, talk with other bikers and shop owners, and find out what aspects of the topic will interest potential listeners before giving a speech about it.

## Rhetorical Sensitivity

Sometimes, we talk publicly for purely expressive reasons—simply to give voice to ourselves. Usually, however, we speak for instrumental reasons—to pass on ideas or influence how others think or act. The most successful speakers are *other directed*, as we have been saying, or concerned with meeting their listeners' needs and solving their problems through public talk. These speakers are rhetorically sensitive to others.

**Rhetorical sensitivity** refers to speakers' attitudes toward the process of speech composition.[20] More particularly, rhetorical sensitivity is the degree to which speakers recognize that all people are different and complex and, hence, must be considered individually; adapt their messages and themselves to particular audiences; consciously seek and react to audience feedback; understand that, in some cases, silence is better than speaking; and work at finding the right set of arguments and linguistic expressions to make particular ideas clear and attractive to particular audiences.

What are your purposes? To what degree will they be understandable and acceptable to others? To what degree can you adapt your purposes to audience preferences while maintaining your own integrity and self-respect? These questions demand that you be sensitive to the needs of listeners and speaking situations as well as to your own need for self-respect. Being a rhetorically sensitive speaker attests to your competence as a communicator.

## Oral Skills

Fluency, poise, voice control, and coordinated body movements mark a skilled speaker. These skills don't come naturally; they develop through attention to the advice offered in this textbook and putting that advice into practice. As you practice inside and outside the classroom, aim to refine your skill as an animated, natural, and conversational speaker. Many competent public speakers seem to be merely conversing with their audiences. That should be your goal: to practice being yourself while engaging others in public conversation.

## Self-Confidence

As you think about speaking publicly, you're likely to feel some anxiety because you don't want to fail. This fear of failure or embarrassment may be even stronger than your desire to speak, leading to speech anxiety. Some people have deeply set phobias when thinking about their relationships to others; these people probably should be going through what are called *desensitization* programs or therapies. For most of us, however, anxieties arise in particular situations, such as speaking before others publicly. These anxieties can never be eliminated, but they can be controlled. It becomes important for listeners not to worry about you and your fears but rather to concentrate on what you're saying.

Gaining the kind of self-confidence that will allow you to break through that initial anxiety relatively quickly and move with enthusiasm into your discussions—in a word, to exhibit *self-confidence*—will come with preparation and practice. Prepare well enough to know what you're talking about, and practice speaking often enough to comprehend and even take delight in your own skills. The "How to" box on page 18 will give you some additional hints for gaining and maintaining self-confidence.

## Public Speaking as a Liberal Art

As we conclude this chapter, let's return to the opening question: Why study public speaking in higher education? We hope that answers to that question are starting to form in your mind. Thus far, we have suggested that there are two foundational rationales for asking you to pay tuition for this course. Those rationales are related to the word *liberal*, from the Latin *liber*, or "free."

# How to
# Manage Your Fear of Public Speaking

Remember these tips for reducing apprehension over public speaking in the classroom setting:

1. Realize that tension and nervousness are normal and, in part, even beneficial to speakers. Learning how to control your fear and make it work for you is the key to relieving tension. Tension can give you energy and alertness. As adrenaline pours into your bloodstream, you experience a physical charge that increases bodily movement and psychological acuity. A speaker who isn't pumped up may come across as dull and lifeless.

2. Take comfort in the fact that tension is physiologically reduced by the act of speaking. As you talk and discover that your audience accepts and understands what you're saying, your nervousness will dissipate. Physiologically, your body is using up the excess adrenaline it generated; psychologically, your ego is getting positive reinforcement. The very act of talking aloud reduces fear.

3. Talk about topics that interest you. Speech anxiety arises, in part, because of self-centeredness; sometimes, you're more concerned with your personal appearance and performance than with your topic. One means of reducing this anxiety is to select a topic that thoroughly interests you—one that will take your mind off yourself.

4. Talk about subjects with which you're familiar. Confidence born of knowledge increases your perceived credibility and helps you control your nervousness. Knowing something about the subject may be part of the answer: Subject mastery is related closely to self-mastery.

5. Analyze both the situation and the audience. The more you know about the audience and what is expected of you, the less you will have to fear. In the speech classroom, students usually are less nervous during their third speech than during their first because they have become more comfortable with the audience and more aware of the demands of the situation. Careful analysis of an audience and its expectations goes a long way toward reducing a natural fear of the unknown.

6. Speak in public as often as you can. Repetition of the public speaking experience by itself will not eliminate your anxiety, but it will give you more confidence in managing your apprehension. Speaking several times in front of the same group can help reduce your fright. Speaking up in class discussions, engaging in conversations with friends and others, and contributing ideas in meetings also will help you realize what strategies work for you in reducing nervousness.

*For Senator Ben Nighthorse Campbell of Colorado, the "Indian Way" places greater value on contributing to society than on acquiring material possessions.*

## Freeing Yourself

Taking a college- or university-level course in public speaking should be personally freeing for you. It should give you a self-confidence born of knowing you have the basic, and even some advanced, speaking skills that will allow you to talk publicly. In the process of speaking, of articulating and defending your opinions publicly, you also will come to better understand yourself: your commitments, those things that matter to you enough to make you disagree with others over them, your hopes for your own and others' development. Cicero was convinced that public eloquence not only made society possible but also made citizenship a reality. One could be a free citizen only by being able to talk publicly, freely with others.

## Making a Free Society Work

Cicero also wanted his readers to understand that a society works only when its members are free to speak. People who are silent—and worse, who are silenced—not only contribute nothing to the common good but even signal that society has oppressive corners where marginalized folks dwell. It's very easy for a society to forget about the rights and needs of its various segments—of women, the poor, the nonwhite, the illiterate, the deaf and blind and physically challenged communities. Only when all segments, no matter how different from the dominant group, have access to the public sphere and have the skills needed to say something publicly will that society, in fact, be free.

A liberal-pluralist society is not merely ideologically progressive. Rather, it is a place where all citizens have the right to speak and have been given, if necessary, training in how to speak their minds. You are getting that training in a collegiate or university setting. You should come away not only with some new skills but also with a larger vision about what public speaking can do in our personal, social, economic, political, and religious-moral lives. Good luck in gaining and spreading freedom in civil societies.

## ■ CHAPTER SUMMARY

Public speaking is comprised of a set of skills that are not acquired naturally. They must be learned, and colleges and universities can teach the social, consumer, and intellectual imperatives underlying them. We all need to learn to handle ourselves more effectively in front of others, and higher education is a good place to work in classroom laboratories, to practice talking seriously with friends, to learn how to defend yourself when listening to other speakers, and to gain training in systematic criticism.

Speech training is important because orality—face-to-face oral communication—is important to social life; in times of crises and need, people talk to each other directly. Decision making in politics, law, and most social relationships occurs through speaking, even in multicultural societies. Both per-

sonal and collective goals can be achieved through public talk.

This means that you must acquire not only speech skills but also the means by which you and others can come together valuatively; you must share an ethos with others. Moral framing—the personal, social, political, economic, philosophical, and religious-moral viewpoints from which one looks at and comprehends the world—becomes the means by which you and others can arrive at common ground and take shared action.

All speakers must possess some basic skills and competencies to succeed: integrity, knowledge, rhetorical sensitivity, oral skills, and self-confidence. Those who do can both free themselves and contribute to the running of a free society.

## ■ KEY TERMS

| | | |
|---|---|---|
| **consumer imperative**  (p. 5) | **intellectual imperative**  (p. 5) | **rhetorical sensitivity**  (p. 17) |
| **ethos**  (p. 13) | **moral frames**  (p. 15) | **skyhook principle**  (p. 15) |
| **framing**  (p. 9) | **orality**  (p. 8) | **social imperative**  (p. 4) |

## ■ ASSESSMENT ACTIVITIES

1. To learn how to assess both your own and other's speeches, watch a speech on videotape. Pause each time something strikes your attention. Jot down notes as you watch and listen. After viewing the speech several times, answer the following questions:

   a. Does the speech seek to define community, share information, take a position in a debate, or call for social change? State its main idea or argument.
   b. In what ways is the speaker taking into account the frames of his or her listeners?

c. Does the speaker appear to be rhetorically sensitive to the situation and the audience? Given the content, structure, and style of the speech, what image does the speaker appear to have of the audience?

d. What attitudes might the audience bring to this speech? Why would they want to listen to the speaker?

e. How would you rate the speaker's skills and competencies? Does the speaker seem knowledgeable, self-confident, and trustworthy? Does the speaker's use of verbal and nonverbal communication result in a message that is clear, forceful, and compelling? Why or why not?

f. List at least three ways the speaker could improve on this speech.

2. Explore a recent public event in which the ethics or credibility of a person was called into question. Prepare a three- to four-minute presentation in which you briefly summarize the ethical issue. Then, add your own views as to whether the person was fairly accused and, if so, what you think of the choice the person apparently made.

## ■ REFERENCES

1. Lester Thonssen and A. Craig Baird, *Speech Criticism: The Development of Standards for Rhetorical Appraisal* (New York: Ronald Press, 1948), 5.

2. Kenneth Burke, *The Grammar of Motives and the Rhetoric of Motives* (Cleveland: Meridian Books, 1962), 547.

3. Roderick P. Hart, *Modern Rhetorical Criticism*, 2nd ed. (Boston: Allyn and Bacon, 1997), 34.

4. Isocrates, *Isocrates II* [including *Antidosis*], translated by George Norlin (Cambridge, MA: Harvard University Press, 1927), 327.

5. Roberta Briggs Sutton, ed., *Speech Index: An Index to 259 Collections of World Famous Orations and Speeches for Various Occasions*, 4th ed., rev. & enl. (Metuchen, NJ: Scarecrow Press, 1966); and Charity Mitchell, *Speech Index: An Index to Collections of World Famous Orations and Speeches for Various Occasions*, 4th ed. suppl., 1966–1980 (Metuchen, NJ: Scarecrow Press, 1982). Also use search engines on your computer to find various collections of speeches on the Internet. One of the best is the Douglass Archive at Northwestern University.

6. Edward T. Hall, *The Silent Language* (New York: Fawcett World Library, 1966), 37; and Walter J. Ong, *Orality and Literacy: The Technologizing of the Word* (New York: Routledge, 1988), 31.

7. Shanto Iyengar is a well-known communication researcher who uses framing as his theoretical orientation. Among his recent research is a piece he wrote with Adam Simon on "New Coverage of the Gulf Crisis and Public Opinion: A Study of Agenda Setting, Priming, and Framing," in *Do the Media Govern? Politicians, Voters, and Reporters in America*, edited by Shanto Iyengar and Richard Reeves (Thousand Oaks, CA: Sage, 1997), esp. 250–251.

8. Frederick Douglass, "Speech at the National Convention of Colored Men (1883)," in *The American Reader: Words That Moved a Nation*, edited by Diane Ravitch (New York: HarperCollins, 1990), 172.

9. Elizabeth Cady Stanton, "Speech at the Seneca Falls Convention (1848)," in *Man Cannot Speak for Her*, vol. 2, *Key Texts of the Early Feminists*, edited by Karlyn Kohrs Campbell (New York: Praeger, 1989), 42.

10. Henri Mann Morton, "Strength through Cultural Diversity," in Jerry D. Blanche, *Native American Reader: Stories, Speeches, and Poems* (Juneau, AK: Denali Press, 1990), 196–197. Reprinted with permission of the publisher.

11. Barbara Jordan, keynote address to Democratic National Convention, July 13, 1992, New York City; telecast on C-SPAN television network; personal transcription.

12. Hannah Arendt, *The Human Condition: A Study of the Central Dilemmas Facing Modern Man* (New York: Doubleday Anchor Books, 1959), 184–185.

13. *Aristotle's Rhetoric and Poetics*, translated by Rhys Roberts (New York: Modern Library, 1954), Book 2, p. 91.

14. When you wish to follow trends in public opinion polls, a good place to go on the web is <http://www.PollingReport.com>, which assembles multiple polls, especially on political topics.

15. Stephen L. Carter, *Civility: Manners, Morals, and the Etiquette of Democracy* (New York: HarperPerennial, 1998), 11.

16. Carter, 18.

17. From de Tocqueville's *Democracy in America* (1840), vol. 2, bk. 2, ch. 13, as quoted in *The Faber Book of America*, edited by Christopher Ricks and William L. Vance (Boston: Faber and Faber, 1992), 270.

18. J. Donald Moon, *Constructing Community: Moral Pluralism and Tragic Conflicts* (Princeton, NJ: Princeton University Press, 1993), esp. 20–21.

19. See Jesse Jackson, "Common Ground and Common Sense," in *Diversity in Public Communication: A Reader*, edited by Christine Kelly, E. Anne Laffoon, and Raymie E. McKerrow (Dubuque, IA: Kendall/Hunt, 1994).

Chapter **2**

# Getting Started

## Basic Tips for Speech Preparation and Delivery

From reading the first chapter, you are aware of some reasons for studying public speaking, as well as its role in a diverse society. You also were introduced to some of the basic skills needed for success as a speaker. Since you will be asked to present speeches before you have actually read all of the chapters, or even most of them, this chapter presents an overview of speaking as a *practice:* planning what to say and how to say it. If you have already given speeches before groups, you have a sense of the preparation it takes and the kinds of things that can go wrong. This chapter serves to highlight the major tasks ahead of you in fulfilling class assignments.

Although this chapter will not cover all that you can learn about the intricacies and shortcuts of speech preparation and speechmaking, it will provide you with sufficient information to develop a **rhetorical frame of mind**. Doing so allows you to think your way strategically through the decisions you have to make as you prepare for any speech:

1. Selecting the subject
2. Narrowing the subject
3. Determining the purposes, including central ideas and claims
4. Analyzing the audience and occasion
5. Gathering the speech materials
6. Outlining the speech
7. Practicing aloud

Working through these steps in a systematic manner will keep you from wandering aimlessly through the library or waiting endlessly at your desk for inspiration. This chapter reviews each step to provide a basic foundation for planning your presentation (see also Figure 2.1, p. 24).

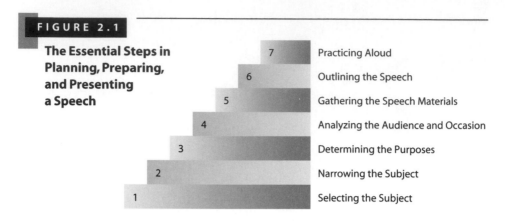

**FIGURE 2.1**

**The Essential Steps in Planning, Preparing, and Presenting a Speech**

7 — Practicing Aloud
6 — Outlining the Speech
5 — Gathering the Speech Materials
4 — Analyzing the Audience and Occasion
3 — Determining the Purposes
2 — Narrowing the Subject
1 — Selecting the Subject

There's no magical formula for getting ready to speak. However, if you pay close attention to these seven steps—either in the order presented here or in another that works for you—you'll be ahead of the game and ready for an audience. In addition to covering these steps, we will review how to decide on an appropriate method of presentation, how to project self-confidence, and how to evaluate your own and others' presentations. This last topic is a natural segue into the next chapter on the importance of becoming a critical listener.

## Selecting the Subject

One of the most difficult choices for many speakers, in classrooms and elsewhere, is choosing a subject. When you are confronted with a speech assignment, use these guidelines to help select a subject that is appropriate to the rhetorical situation:

**Select a subject about which you already know something and can find out more.** Begin with an inventory of what you already know. This will help focus your ideas and distinguish between strong and weak choices (i.e., less familiar topics are weaker choices). If you need to update statistical data or locate additional examples to flesh out your basic knowledge, consider whether the necessary information is readily accessible. Doing research will be easier if you know something about the subject because you will have some ideas regarding potential sources of information. Selecting a topic familiar to you also increases your self-confidence as you conduct research and prepare to speak.

**Select a subject that interests you and will interest your audience.** First, resist the temptation to speak on an issue that is more interesting to the audience than it is to you. This can be a disastrous choice, for gathering information will be unexciting and your presentation will reflect your lack of enthusiasm. Conversely, talking without regard to your audience may leave you with a subject that interests an audience of one—you. You need to balance your needs and interests with those of the audience. If you have a personal interest in an issue, your commitment will come across to the audience, and you will find it easier to gain and keep their attention. You'll also find researching the issue more interesting, and preparing the speech will become easier.

A topic may interest listeners for one or more of the following reasons:

■ *It concerns their health, happiness, or security.* For instance, you might talk to senior citizens about changes in Medicare regulations or to college students about job resources available on the World Wide Web.

■ *It offers a solution to a recognized problem.* You may suggest ways your group could raise funds in order to participate in a national competition or how college students might engage in volunteer activities within the community.

■ *It is surrounded by controversy or conflict of opinion.* You might speak on proposed restrictions on a university tradition, such as a Halloween street party, or on proposed strategies to restrict parking in the community.

■ *It provides information on a misunderstood or little understood issue.* You might speak to a local business group about the community service contributions of college students or to the class about the services provided by the campus writing and math centers.

**Select a topic appropriate to the occasion.** Often, the freedom to choose an appropriate subject may be virtually unlimited, such as an in-class speech assignment that does not limit the choice of a subject. Even in this situation, however, several factors may limit the degree of freedom that you have. Is the occasion the right setting for what you want to accomplish? A demonstration speech on body building might go over very well in your speech classroom, but bringing a dog to class to demonstrate training commands may not. Likewise, the speech on body building may not be appropriate at the dedication of a new senior citizens' center, but one describing the need for exercise at all ages and how to get the most out of the new center's exercise room would be fitting. In each instance, your choice would be affected as much by your personal interests as by the needs of the audience.

There will be times when your speech topic will be determined—at least in part—by the group to whom you will speak. Usually, you are invited to speak because you have specific expertise or knowledge to share with the group. As part of the invitation, you'll be asked to address a particular issue, policy, or question that relates to your work, community involvement, or special skills. In the classroom setting, the instructor may limit choices by requiring you to consider only certain issues or subject areas or may place certain topics (how to put a clarinet together or how to kill a chicken—these have been real topics in the past!) off limits.

In sum, whether the topic is a free choice or is assigned, it's best to approach it in a way that reflects interests shared by you and your audience. Further, it must be seen as appropriate to the speaking occasion.

## Narrowing the Subject

A general subject will be of little value until it is narrowed down to a manageable size. Narrowing a subject to a more precise speech topic involves three primary considerations:

**Narrow your subject so you can discuss it adequately in the time allotted for the speech.** If you are responding to an in-class speech assignment that will last 5 to 7 or 8 to 10 minutes, you cannot begin to do justice to a subject as large as the history of American football. Instead, you might review its earliest years or focus on the demise of the XFL. Fit the topic's breadth to the time you have to speak.

**Narrow your subject to meet the specific expectations of your audience.** Listeners expecting to hear an informative presentation on the new child-care center the university has opened may be upset if you request their financial support for new playground equipment for the center. The announced purpose of the meeting, the demands of the particular context, and the traditions of the group can influence an audience's expectations of what it is to hear. Violate audience expectations only when you feel it's absolutely essential, and be prepared for—and willing to accept—the consequences if you do.

## How to
## Narrow a Topic: An Illustration

**1.** Identify a broad subject you know and care about—for example, science fiction.

**2.** Identify subtopics within the broad subject area that also interest you. For example, subtopics of science fiction might include the following:
- The differences between science fiction and fantasy
- The nature of hard science in science fiction novels
- Major writers of science fiction: Heinlein, LeGuin, Asimov, McCaffrey

**3.** Ask five questions about each subtopic:
- Am I interested in this subtopic?
- Will the audience likely be interested in it?
- Is it appropriate to the occasion?
- Can I cover it in the time available?
- Will the audience comprehend it?

**4.** Narrow each subtopic until you can answer yes to all of these questions.

Time constraints might limit the first subtopic to *two or three* major differences between science fiction and fantasy and the third subtopic to *a single* major writer or a writer's *major series*. Since you really aren't that excited about the differences between fantasy and fiction, it would be difficult to seem enthusiastic when speaking about this topic, so it would be dropped. The audience's lack of background knowledge might cause you to discard the hard science topic if you have only 8 to 10 minutes to present your speech. Thus, the major writers of science fiction will be your best choice of topic.

**Gauge your subject to the comprehension level of the audience.** If, for example, you want to talk about laser technology or the existence of black holes to students in your speech class, focus on basic principles. If the audience is a group of senior physics majors, however, the nature and complexity of the material you present will necessarily change.

The process of narrowing may lead to a subject that is best for a particular occasion, or as the "How to" box on page 26 indicates, it may leave you with several possibilities. If this is the case, you need to decide which subject, given your time limit, will best fit your interests as well as those of the audience. Which topic can you make most interesting? Which will be most engaging for you and your audience?

## Determining the Purposes

Once you know what you want to talk about, the next task is to consider a series of *why* questions already implicit in much of what's been discussed: Why do you wish to discuss this subject? Why might an audience want to listen to you? Why is this topic appropriate to this occasion? These questions can be answered easily by considering the following four points in sequence:

1. Think about the *general purposes* that people have in mind when they speak in public.
2. Consider your own *specific purposes* for speaking.
3. Focus on the *central idea or claim* that expresses the principal message you wish to communicate.
4. Create a *title* for the presentation that captures your goals and tells the audience what your central idea or claim will focus on.

Following a review of each of these points, we also will examine strategic considerations relevant to selecting purposes.

### General Purpose

What do you want your listeners to do or to think once you've completed your speech? For example, are you trying to tell them something they do not know but should? Are you seeking to change how they feel about a social, economic, or political issue? Are you interested in having them do something as a result of your speech? Do you want them to laugh and learn at the same time?

Answering yes to any one of these questions will help focus your general purpose on the "end state" you wish to create in your audience. There are four **general purposes** for public speaking: to inform, to persuade, to actuate, and to entertain (see Figure 2.2, p. 28). Although these purposes are not mutually exclusive—you may be entertaining while persuading, for example—they are sufficiently discrete to treat them as individual purposes. We'll consider the types of speeches that accompany these general purposes later in the book, with a major emphasis on the processes of informing and persuading. In this section, we'll consider the major *goals* of informative, persuasive, actuative, and entertaining speeches.

**To Inform**     The general purpose of a **speech to inform** is to help listeners understand an idea, concept, or process or to widen their range of knowledge. This is the primary goal of elected officials when they seek to explain their actions to their constituents; of college professors when they teach chemistry, speech, philosophy, art, or any other subject; and of supervisors when they explain how to use new equipment to plant workers. Conveying new information changes the level or quality of knowledge your listeners possess. By providing examples, statistics, illustrations, and other material containing data and ideas, you seek to expand or to alter their concrete knowledge about an idea, policy, process, concept, or event. The message must be *comprehensive, accurate,* and *timely* in order to accomplish your informative goal. For example, an informative speech on the dangers of credit card debt must give an overview of the national scope of the problem, especially if the focus is on college students. Further, it must provide factual information about how debt builds, what interest rates are charged (and how they compare with other credit card interest rates), and what steps students can take to avoid being caught up in the debt cycle. This speech may well relate to audience experience; thus, you need to be sure you have accurate and complete information.

**To Persuade or to Actuate**     The purpose of a **speech to persuade** or **to actuate** is to influence listeners—whether to adopt a new point of view or to take a course of action. Because both types of speeches have similar goals, we'll consider them together. While it may be argued that all speeches are persuasive to some degree, there are many situations in which speakers have outright persuasion or action as their primary purpose.[1] For example, promoters and publicists try to make you believe in the superiority of certain products, persons, or institutions. Local citizens of a small town may protest plans to build a new Wal-Mart or other "Big Box" in their community. Politicians debate campaign issues and strive to convince voters that they will best represent their interests in the state legislature,

| FIGURE 2.2 | | |
|---|---|---|
| **The General Purposes of Speeches** | *To Inform* | Clear Understanding |
| | *To Persuade* | Acceptance of Ideas |
| | *To Actuate* | Action |
| | *To Entertain* | Enjoyment and Comprehension |

Congress, or the White House. For our purposes, speeches designed to influence beliefs and attitudes will be referred to as *persuasive speeches*, and those that go a step further in moving the audience to adopt a specific action—as in "Buy my product," "Join the protest," or "Vote for the preferred candidate"—will be referenced as *actuative speeches*. The distinguishing feature of an actuative speech is that instead of stopping with an appeal to listeners' beliefs and attitudes, you ask them to behave in a specified way.

To influence or alter your listeners' beliefs and actions, you need to present well-ordered arguments that are supported by facts, figures, examples, and expert opinions. You also need to do more than simply state the facts. To change people's minds and move them to action, you must be sensitive to both the rational and the motivational aspects of audience psychology, topics that will be discussed at length in later chapters. For the present, keep in mind the principle that facts alone—even if airtight, as far as the case for change is concerned—are often insufficient to change behavior.

Consider all of the information that connects cigarette, cigar, and pipe smoking to various forms of cancer as well as to the issue of secondary smoke effects. If facts alone were sufficient, wouldn't more people stop smoking? If you or a friend smokes, what about the current information is insufficient to warrant a change in behavior? What motivational appeal would lead a listener to take action in such an instance? Persuasion and actuation clearly involve far more complex tasks than simply telling people what you think.

**To Entertain**    To entertain, amuse, or provide other enjoyment for listeners is frequently the general purpose of an after-dinner speech, but talks of other kinds also may have enjoyment as their principal aim. A travel lecture, for example, contains information, but it may also entertain an audience by telling amusing tales of adventure or misadventure. Club meetings, class reunions, and similar gatherings of friends may provide the opportunity to "roast" one or more of the people present. In these situations, the effective use of humor is a key ingredient in being judged funny as opposed to tasteless by the audience.

A **speech to entertain** is *not* just a comic monologue. The humor is purposeful. Even the humor at a roast is intended to convey affection and genuine appreciation for the talents of the person being honored by friends and colleagues. Humor also can have a social role. Humorist Will Rogers used his radio talks and commentaries on political realities during the Depression to help create a sense of American unity and common effort. More recently, Whoopi Goldberg, Sinbad, and other comedians have used humor to call attention to social issues. In short, a speech to entertain is humorous yet serious.

As you have learned, to inform, to persuade, to actuate, and to entertain are the general purposes that guide your reason for speaking. Just as subjects are narrowed to subtopics, your general purpose needs to be narrowed to more specific purposes in order to focus your audience's attention on the content of your presentation.

## Specific Purposes

Given your topic, specifically what do you want the audience to know, value, or do? Within the context of a general purpose, a **specific purpose** focuses audience attention on the particular, *substantive* goal of your presentation. Once you determine your specific purpose, you can describe the exact response you want from your listeners—for example, "I want my audience to understand why interest in women's soccer has grown." In this instance, you want to inform your audience (general purpose), but more specifically, you want them to know the reasons behind the growth in the popularity of women's soccer (specific purpose).

You may have more than one specific purpose for a speech. Some may be clearly expressed; others may be held privately. For example, you will tell your listeners precisely what you want them to understand or do as a consequence of listening to your presentation. You also hope to make a good impression on the audience or receive a high grade for the presentation, but you are not likely to make these purposes explicit.

Specific purposes can be short term or long term. Suppose you are speaking to members of your class on the value of eating fat-free foods. A short-term purpose may be to get a decent grade; a long-term objective might be to induce them to change their eating habits.

Theoretically, you may have any number of public and private, short-term and long-term specific purposes when you speak. Practically, however, you will want to reduce your list of goals to a dominant one: *the response you wish to elicit from the audience.* Formulated as a clear, concise statement, this specific purpose delineates exactly what you want the audience to understand, enjoy, feel, believe, or do.

**An Illustration**    You've just decided on your topic for a speech that you'll give in one of your classes: the impact of MTV on recent presidential election campaigns. While your classmates may have seen some of the events, they probably do not have the whole picture with respect to MTV's participation. Hence, your general purposes will be to expand the audience's knowledge of MTV's role, and your specific purposes will include the following:

1. In terms of the subject, you want to provide background on MTV's actions in the 1988 campaign, contrast that with the 1992 and 1996 "Rock the Vote" campaigns, and finally discuss MTV's involvement in the 2000 campaign. You also want to highlight the specific events that took place, including interviews with the candidates. Finally, you want to cover MTV's actual impact in terms of voter participation by young adults.

2. In terms of yourself, a private goal may be the hope that if your classmates understand the role MTV plays, they also will see the value in greater participation in political campaigns and in voting. Undoubtedly, you want to convey to the class (and to the instructor) that you understand what it means

to plan and prepare an informative speech. You want to show the students and the instructor that you are knowledgeable and competent to speak on the issue.

The first specific purpose addresses a long-term goal of creating understanding and expanding knowledge, and your personal goal is private rather than public. Both of these specific goals can be summarized, however, in a statement of *the* dominant specific purpose: "to expand the audience's knowledge of MTV's role."

## Central Idea or Claim

For most speakers, this step flows directly from the preceding one. Can you state your message in a single sentence? If you are seeking to explain an idea or inform an audience about a process or event, that sentence is the **central idea.** It is a declarative statement that summarizes your speech: "This institution is taking specific steps to promote cultural diversity on campus." On the other hand, a **claim,** expresses the intent of your argument: "This institution should be taking specific steps to promote cultural diversity on campus." Thus, *central ideas* are characteristic of *informative speeches,* whereas *claims* form the core of *persuasive and actuative speeches.* Speeches to entertain also have a controlling thought—either as *a central idea aiming to convey information* or as *a claim making a moral point or moving the audience to action.* See Figure 2.3 (p. 32) for an overview of these types of speeches and the specific purposes they have.

Both central ideas and claims share the same function: They identify the primary thrust of your message. Precise phrasing of your central idea or claim is crucial because it focuses the audience's attention on *your* reasons for speaking rather than on *their* reasons for listening.

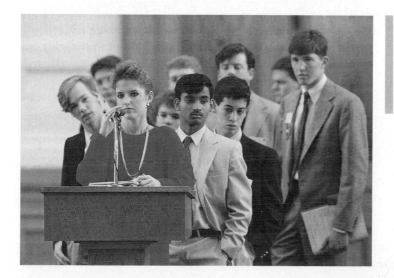

*Precise phrasing of your central idea or claim is important because your wording captures the essence of your subject matter and purposes and focuses audience attention on your reasons for speaking.*

FIGURE 2.3

**Central Ideas versus Claims**

| General Purpose | Inform | Persuade/Actuate | Entertain |
|---|---|---|---|
| Specific Purpose | Central Idea (preview main points) | Claim (preview main points) | Central Idea or Claim (preview main points) |

**Phrasing a Central Idea**     Assume that you're giving an informative speech on the relationship between business and social causes. Each of the following central ideas suggests a different emphasis for the speech:

> The Jerry Lewis Telethon for MDA illustrates how corporations can assist social causes.
>
> Ben Cohen, of Ben and Jerry's fame, illustrates how one can make money and donate to worthy causes.
>
> Ted Turner illustrates how a single individual can make a difference by donating to a cause.

A speech on central idea 1 would be developed differently than a speech on idea 2 or 3; each would utilize different kinds of material for support or illustration. The first speech would stress the history of the telethon and the amount of research funded over the years. The second would use the same theme but develop it through a close analysis of one specific company known for its commitment to social action. The third speech would change the focus to examine an individual's history of philanthropic giving.

**Phrasing a Claim**     Phrasing your claim can be an even more crucial preparatory step than casting the central idea because the wording colors the emotional tone of the message and its line of development. It will also suggest the relationship between you and your audience. Consider how each of the following claims will affect the audience's perception of your intensity:

> Allowing Wal-Mart to build in our community is *unwise.*
>
> Allowing Wal-Mart to build in our community is *a despicable act.*
>
> Allowing Wal-Mart to build in our community is *a moral outrage.*

As you move from claim 1 to 3, the feelings are phrased with greater intensity; each successive version expresses your attitude in more harsh and more graphic language.

In the next set of examples, note how you can vary the reasons for taking some course of action:

> Make use of the writing lab because it will help you in your English courses.
>
> Make use of the writing lab because you will get higher grades in all courses in which writing is expected.
>
> Make use of the writing lab because better writing will lead to a better job after graduation.

As these examples illustrate, your listeners may choose to act for a variety of reasons; phrase your claim in a way that captures the most compelling reason for *your particular audience*.

You can also vary the evaluative criteria for judging something:

> The old fine arts center is an *eyesore*.
>
> The old fine arts center is a *safety hazard*.
>
> While maintaining the old fine arts center would be *cheaper* than building a new one, we should still explore razing it and constructing a new one.

**Aesthetic Judgment**

**Personal safety judgment**

**Social value judgment**

Each of these claims condemns the same campus facility. The first version judges the art center's lack of beauty, the second considers its safety status, and the third implies that while maintaining it is a cheaper alternative, the community should value "the new" above economic cost. In each case, selecting particular criteria will control the main features of the speech's ultimate development: (1) to focus on aesthetics in relation to community development; (2) to emphasize the facts related to safety; and (3) to seek support for a social value, such as "New is better than old."

After you've decided the general and specific purposes of your speech and considered how to phrase the central idea or claim, you can start developing your speech outline. Doing so will focus your research efforts because the main points of your outline will indicate the type and quantity of information needed to accomplish your goals. More importantly, a succinctly phrased central idea or claim will enable you to preview the main points of your speech. As you flesh out the central idea or claim, it will be apparent that two or three main points will be necessary to cover the subject. For example, if you are going to talk about MTV, you could easily indicate to the audience how the speech will develop by leading into the main points in this manner:

> In explaining the role played by MTV in the recent election, I will focus on three key points: prior activities by MTV, specific events from the recent election, and the impact of MTV's role on participation among young viewers of voting age.

**Integrating General and Specific Purposes with Central Ideas and Claims**

The following examples illustrate how to integrate your general and specific purposes with your central idea or claim. By doing so, you will further focus your topic in preparing to create an outline.

INFORMATIVE SPEECH

**Subject:**  Business and social action

**General Purpose:**  To inform

**Specific Purpose:**  Includes dominant purpose, which is then recast as central idea

> The Jerry Lewis Telethon for MDA illustrates how corporations can assist social causes.
>
> Ben Cohen, of Ben and Jerry's fame, illustrates how one can make money and donate to worthy causes.
>
> Ted Turner illustrates how a single individual can make a difference in donating to a cause.

**Central Idea:**  Ben and Jerry's provides a prototype for businesses seeking to become socially responsible.

ACTUATIVE SPEECH

**Subject:**  Housing conditions of migrant farm workers

**General Purpose:**  To actuate

**Specific Purposes:**  Includes dominant purpose, which is then recast as claim

> To illustrate, with specific cases, the substandard housing provided for migrant laborers
>
> To force farmers hiring migrant laborers to provide adequate housing
>
> To be perceived favorably by the audience
>
> To overcome opposition from farmers to this proposal

**Claim:**  Farmers/owners who hire migrant laborers must provide adequate housing.

Central ideas and claims make different demands on the audience. Where a central idea explains and clarifies information, a claim gives the audience a reason to believe or act in a certain way. The speech to entertain encompasses both possibilities, since its goal may include either informing or persuading an audience.

## Creating the Title

To complete your initial thinking about purposes, you often will want to decide on **creating the title.** It may seem odd or even unnecessary to consider a title during the preliminary stages of speech preparation, but there are several concrete advantages to doing so. First, the title highlights the key concept or idea that the speech content will reflect. Second, as the experience of your authors attests, speakers are asked to announce titles ahead of time, so that planners can properly publicize their events. Just as a title helps the speaker focus on content, it also assists those who might attend in deciding whether the speaker's subject is of interest. The following guidelines will assist you in selecting and phrasing a title:

**A title should be relevant to you, the audience, and the occasion.** If you were to give a speech on business and political ethics, you might consider a title such as "The Eleventh Commandment," as did the speaker who claimed that the commandment "Thou shalt not steal" had been supplanted in some business and political circles by another: "Thou shalt not get caught."

**A title should be provocative.** One of the authors recently delivered a speech entitled "Coloring Outside the Lines: The Limits of Civility" at a professional conference.[2] Coloring outside the lines is something you learned *not* to do early in school, if not before; the notion of *civil society* does not normally connote "limits." Thus, the title created interest by appearing to break rules and suggest that civility might have limits.

**A title should be productive.** A title should convey to the audience the central idea or claim or, at the very least, give them a reason to attend to the message. A provocative title becomes unproductive, however, when it turns off a significant portion of the audience, hence lessening a speaker's chance of getting a fair hearing.

**The title should be brief.** Imagine the effect of announcing your title as "The Effects upon High-Track, Mean-Track, and Low-Track High School Juniors of Pretesting for Senior-Year Competency Testings." Besides not being terribly clear, this title is far too long and doesn't stimulate curiosity in your audience. A better choice might be "Tracking Juniors: A Means to Successful Testing as Seniors?" or "A Pretest in Time Saves Nine—or More." These latter two may lack some precision, but they are decidedly more provocative and productive than the first choice.

**When committing to a title for advance publicity, select a general phrase.** If you have to commit to a title well in advance, you want to preserve flexibility in how you develop the speech itself. The title "Ben and Jerry's: A Socially Responsible Company" is sufficiently precise to give the audience an idea of your general topic area while allowing you some freedom in exploring the subject as you plan the speech.

## Strategic Considerations

The preceding discussion has focused on the general and specific purposes in terms of the *desired response* you wish to obtain from your audience. What remains in this step of determining the purpose is to examine some of the reasons you may elect to (or have been asked to) inform, persuade, or entertain your audience. Some of the factors that will determine your actual decisions include an assessment of risks taken, the listeners' authority to act, their preexisting attitudes, the nature of the speech occasion, and the time available to speak.

**Taking Risks**    There are occasions when you will ask yourself how much you are willing to risk personally in front of others. For example, suppose you work for a firm that you're convinced is patently racist in its promotion policies. The company's record clearly suggests that it seldom promotes women of color to upper-level managerial positions. You are given a chance to talk about promotions at an open meeting of the firm. As a woman of color, how far do you go? What do you say? Your **private aim** may be to get your frustrations heard, regardless of the consequences. Your **ultimate aim** is to get some women of color—including yourself—into higher managerial positions. How you balance these purposes and the degree to which you put your own job at risk become real rather than theoretical issues.

**Listeners' Authority or Capacity to Act**    For a speaker to demand of students that they should "Abolish all required courses" is futile; any decision concerning course requirements is in the hands of the faculty. In this case, the listener's **authority to act** is nonexistent. As a speaker, limit your specific purposes and claims to behaviors that are clearly within the audience's authority or power.

**Listeners' Preexisting Attitudes**    If your listeners' **preexisting attitudes** are hostile to your message, you might, in a single speech, be able to convince them that there's merit in your side of the issue. You'll be hoping for too much, however, if you expect the audience to disavow their current beliefs and embrace yours or to take positive action based on your request.

**The Nature of the Speech Occasion**    Under most conditions, you automatically will seek to speak in a way that is in tune with what audiences expect. Violating audience expectations can have negative consequences. Hence, you should willingly go against the grain only when your principles dictate a need to say what needs saying, regardless of the audience's attitude. Be willing to accept the audience's anger, should you disappoint them. On most occasions, you'll find it easy and natural to adapt your specific purpose to the mood and spirit of the occasion.

**Time Limits**    The person assigning the speech, those inviting you to speak, or the occasion itself may dictate a **time limit** for how long you can speak. You will need to adjust what you hope to accomplish to fit the time constraints of the rhetorical situation. For example, you may be able to induce a hostile audience to postpone a decision without talking very long. If your goal is to change their feelings and convictions so they endorse your proposal, however, you'll need more than a few minutes. Similarly, if your subject is complex, a 15-minute speech may achieve listener comprehension but not convince the audience to act. Don't try to secure a response that an audience cannot give in the time available. Knowing more about the audience and occasion will assist you in making sound strategic choices.

## Analyzing the Audience and the Occasion

A good speech is one that reflects your interests while being seen as responsive to the interests, preferences, and values of the audience to whom it is presented. You must regularly ask yourself: How would I feel about this topic if I were in their place? How can I adapt this material to their interests and habits, especially at points where their experiences and understanding differ from mine?

To answer such questions, you need to analyze the people that compose your audience—their age range, gender, social-political-economic status, culture, background, prejudices, and fears. In a public speaking class, you can estimate these factors by listening to comments made during class discussions and by asking some class members what they think. In other circumstances, gathering this information is more difficult and requires you to become more creative in assessing the audience. Among the kinds of information you may wish to gather, consider the following:

**The audience's knowledge of and attitude toward you.** What does the audience already know about you, and what information would be useful in conveying your own expertise? Have they had a chance to form an opinion about you as a speaker?

**The audience's knowledge of and attitude toward the topic.** What they know and how they feel about the topic is critical; you may bore them if you simply duplicate their existing knowledge, and you may anger them if you ignore their own attitudes. Regardless of how it's done, **audience analysis** is a primary determinant of success. You also need to consider the setting and circumstances in which you're speaking.

**Are there specific rules or customs that you need to know and follow?** You need to be aware of anything that will affect the audience's reception of you or your message. Continually referring to an audience of African Americans or Asian Americans as "you people" distances you from them and, in so doing, may well anger them. What will the cultural mix likely be, and how will that affect what you want to say and how you express your ideas?

**How long will you have to speak? Will you precede or follow other speakers who could influence your reception?** If you overtalk your time limit, it may be the same as overstaying your welcome. When others will speak, knowing your place in the line-up will help you adapt to an audience who has heard too many speeches already.

**What impact will events before or after your speech have on topic selection, phrasing of your central idea or claim, or supporting materials?** As we will note later, timing is a critical variable. The decision of a Vermont senator to leave the Republican Party was far more critical at the outset of the Bush presidency than it would have been in the last months of the administration.

**Will the physical circumstances support your speaking style? If not, can you alter them?** Speaking to an audience in which some people are positioned behind pillars, as in a residence hall dining room, can make for anxious moments. You may have to move further from the lectern than normal, so parts of the audience can see you more easily, at least part of the time. Examining such issues in advance of speaking is the key. You want to be as forewarned and as comfortable as possible with the circumstances you face when it's your time to speak.

## Gathering the Speech Materials

Once you've analyzed the audience and context of the speech, you're ready to assemble ideas and information to support your central idea or claim. You need to do these things:

- Assess what information you think is needed in order to accomplish your objectives.
- Reflect on what you already know.
- Figure out what is relevant to your central idea or claim.
- Investigate where additional information can be found, if necessary.
- Obtain the additional information.

In almost every speech situation, you will need to gather additional information to develop, expand, or reinforce what you already know and believe. You may wish to talk to others, such as friends or local experts, to check out your perceptions. Critical listening is important here. You undoubtedly will want to gather other materials from newspapers, magazines, books, government documents, or radio and television programs. You'll soon learn about some traditionally solid sources: the "News of the Week in Review" section of the *New York Times;* articles in *Time, Newsweek, U.S. News and World Report;* journal articles surveyed in the *Readers' Guide to Periodical Literature* and more specialized indexes; and all of the annuals, yearbooks, almanacs, and so on that fill the reference area of your library. Surfing the web is a great means of obtaining information, but as we will note later, the accuracy and comprehensiveness of this information must be carefully scrutinized. Computerized index searches also will be helpful as you seek new information or supporting material for your ideas. We will review these and other resources in Chapter 6.

As we close this section, we also want to alert you to certain ethical issues that may arise in using the materials you locate. The "Ethical Moments" box on page 40 addresses this topic.

## Outlining the Speech

Once you've compiled your materials, you have to sort them. Developing a preliminary outline of your main ideas will help. An outline illustrates how your various materials relate to your central idea or claim, shows you where you have plenty of (or too little) material, and clarifies the structure of your speech. You'll probably jockey back and forth between your materials and your outline, looking for just the right fit between what you *know* and what you can *justify* publicly to a critical audience.

We will examine outlining in more detail later. For now, follow these rules:

- Arrange your main ideas in a clear and systematic order.
- Arrange the subpoints under each main idea in a manner that clearly illustrates their connection to the main point.
- Preserve the unity of your speech by making sure that each point, whether a main point or a subpoint, is directly related to your specific purpose and central idea or claim.

## Practicing Aloud

With your outline completed, you're ready for the most terrifying task of preparation: practicing your speech. This is not easy! You may feel like a fool talking alone in your room; the sound of your voice rings hollow and you find that some of the materials you wrote out come off as simplistic, clichéd, stiff, or silly. Rather than practice alone, enlist the aid of friends or students from your class to serve as listeners and critics. They may be brutal but better to be criticized in this situation than in the classroom following the speech. If you have an opportunity, have a friend videotape your practice session; play it back and, in viewing, keep in mind that you will be your own worst critic. This strategy also will help make you more comfortable in front of a camera; some instructors videotape speeches presented in class, and having prior experience makes it easier to handle the real thing. Practicing aloud is essential if you're to improve upon some of the decisions you've already made and work to refine your delivery skills.

## ETHICAL MOMENTS

### Ethics and Public Speaking

Occasionally, in this book, we'll include a box devoted to "Ethical Moments"—values-based decisions public speakers must make in preparing and delivering their talks. Some of these moments will fit you and your circumstances, and others will not. In either case, we hope that you'll take a moment to think about the problems presented and the solutions offered. Some of these problems might be discussed in class.

One of the primary ethical issues in public speaking concerns the use of source materials to support your central idea or claim. Consider the following:

**1**  When is it fair to borrow other people's ideas and words, and when is it not?

**2**  Suppose you recognize that a major portion of a speaker's informative speech came from a website that you have just investigated for your own speech on the same topic. The speaker does not cite the source. During the critique session, should you blow the whistle on the speaker?

**3**  Suppose an article says exactly what you want to say about the use of pesticides on garden vegetables. Then you find a more recent article claiming that new research contradicts the first article. Should you ignore the new evidence?

You will face ethical moments such as these regularly, both in your speech classroom and throughout your life. Taking a few moments to consider such situations, and even to articulate your position, can save you frustration and embarrassment later. Know what your moral stands are and why you take them—*before* you face ethical dilemmas on the platform.

Give practice a chance. It can, quite literally, save your communicative life. Talk through your outline in a confident, conversational (not a mumbling) tone that will help you get used to the sound. Listening to your own ideas is an excellent way to determine whether they make sense—if not to you, then will they to an audience? Repeatedly read through the outline until you've made changes that seem useful and until you can express each idea clearly and smoothly. Practice until the ideas flow easily, all the time talking in a conversational voice.

The steps we've covered so far—from selecting and narrowing a subject through practicing aloud—take you to the brink of public speaking with real audiences. Good work on preparation pays off in effective performance.

# Delivering Your Speech Confidently

For most beginners, delivering their first speech is very difficult. Many feel anxious and nervous: "I'm too nervous to stand up there." "What do I do with my hands?" "Will people think I'm a jerk?" Self-doubt, from actual fright to a more general lack of self-confidence, creeps into every speaker's mind; the trick is in learning to control it. In the remaining part of this chapter, we'll examine two strategies for self-control: selecting the right method of presentation and communicating self-confidence.

## Selecting the Method of Presentation

Which method should you use to present your speech? In addition to any restrictions imposed by an instructor, your choice should be based on several criteria: type of speaking occasion, the seriousness and purpose of your speech, audience analysis, and your own strengths and weaknesses as a speaker. Attention to these considerations will help you decide whether your method of presentation should be *impromptu, memorized, read from a manuscript*, or *extemporaneous*.

**The Impromptu Speech**    As the name suggests, the **impromptu speech** is delivered on the spur of the moment with little preparation. The speaker relies entirely on previous knowledge and skill. When an instructor in an organizational communication class calls on you for an explanation of an *organizational audit*, you don't have time to prepare more than a quick list of three or four words to remind you of points you want to make. Impromptu speeches are given in rhetorical emergencies—at public meetings, in classes, and at conventions. When using this method, try to focus on a single idea, carefully relating all significant details to it. This way, you'll avoid the rambling, incoherent remarks this method too often produces.

**The Memorized Speech**    The **memorized speech** is written out, word for word, and committed to memory. Although a few speakers are able to do this well, it presents problems for most of us. Instead of sounding conversational, a memorized speech often results in a stilted presentation. Speakers tend to pause too often while trying to remember the words or rush past ideas so as not to forget the words. In either case, meaning is at the expense of memory. This form is well suited to drama, as in the speeches in a Shakespearean play, and to intercollegiate competition in original oratory. But for general purposes, the memorized speech is not a recommended method of presentation.

**The Read Speech**    Like the memorized speech, the **read speech** is written out, but in this method, the speaker reads from a manuscript. If extremely careful wording is required—as in the president's annual message to Congress, in which a slip could undermine domestic or foreign policies—then the read speech is

*Appearing confident will help put your audience at ease as they listen to your ideas.*

appropriate. It also is useful in the presentations of scholarly papers, where exact, concise, often technical exposition is required. Reading a speech while retaining a conversational style is more difficult than it sounds. No matter how experienced you are, when you read your message, you'll inevitably sacrifice some of the freshness and spontaneity necessary for effective speechmaking. You'll also have trouble reacting to feedback and may be tempted to use more formal, written language. If you do use this method, talk through the speech over and over to ensure an effective oral style.

**The Extemporaneous Speech**     Representing a middle course between the memorized or read speech and the impromptu speech, the **extemporaneous speech** requires careful planning and a good outline. This chapter has been preparing you to present an extemporaneous speech. Working from your outline, practice the speech aloud, using different expressions for the ideas each time. Use the outline to fix the order of ideas in your mind, and try out various wordings to develop accuracy, conciseness, and flexibility of expression. Through such preparation, you'll be able to deliver the actual speech from a few notes.

If the extemporaneous method is used carelessly, the result will resemble a bad impromptu speech—inchoate and incoherent. When used well, however, the method will produce a speech that is nearly as polished as a memorized one but more relaxed, flexible, and spontaneous—hence, more like natural conversation than the other methods. The best lecturers at your college or university undoubtedly are extemporaneous speakers. Most of the advice in this textbook assumes the use of the extemporaneous method.

## Communicating Self-Confidence

The second matter you need to think about when speaking in front of a real audience is *yourself*. In Chapter 1, we discussed speech anxiety and some ways to overcome it. Now you need to consider how you can convey an air of dynamism and self-assuredness to your listeners. Many students ready to give their first speech ask: How should I deliver my speech? How can I communicate a sense of self-confidence to an audience? The following guidelines provide a start to answering these questions:

**Be yourself.** Act as if you were having an animated conversation with a friend. Avoid standing in an excessively rigid posture, but don't become so comfortable in front of the group that you sprawl all over the lectern. If there is a table, avoid the temptation to simply perch on it while talking. During the presentation, you want your listeners to focus on your ideas rather than your posture or lack of it.

**Look at your listeners.** Watch their faces for reactions. Without this feedback, you can't gauge the effectiveness of your speech or make adjustments as you speak. Also, people tend to mistrust anyone who doesn't look directly at them. They also may get the impression you don't care about them and aren't interested in their reactions. In speaking, "The eyes have it!"

**Communicate with your body as well as your voice.** Realize that as a speaker, you're being seen as well as heard. Bodily movements and changes in facial expression can help clarify and reinforce your ideas. Keep your hands at your sides so that when you feel an impulse to gesture, you can do so easily. If there is no lectern and you're working from an outline, use a hard backing to hold your papers firm. (This will make your nervousness less visible!) If you are using notecards, hold them up so you can see them clearly rather than hiding them. Your speech will flow more smoothly if your outline or notecards are easy to read from, as well. As you speak, don't become so relaxed you curl your papers or fold your cards. Let your body move as it responds to your feelings and message. If you hear a tremor in your voice or see one in your hand, remember that neither is as noticeable to listeners as it is to you. Overall, if you're being yourself, appropriate bodily responses will flow from the act of communicating.

## Learning to Evaluate Speeches

The classroom serves as a laboratory for studying and evaluating speech content and delivery. The evaluation form in Figure 2.4 (p. 44) is designed to help sharpen your critical-listening skills as well as your sensitivity to the fundamentals of the speechmaking process. A recent study of this and other evaluation forms has

| **FIGURE 2.4** | **Evaluation Form** |
|---|---|

Name _____     Date _____

Topic _____

Occasion _____     Speech length _____

### Introduction (15 points)

☐  Gained audience's attention.
☐  Established credibility and goodwill.
☐  Revealed nature of topic as central idea or claim.
☐  Prepared audience for rest of speech (forecasting).     **Points**  _____

### Body (40 points)

☐  Clearly identified main points.
☐  Developed each main point with appropriate materials.
☐  Developed topic appropriately for this occasion and audience.
☐  Arranged ideas logically.
☐  Used transitions effectively.
☐  Provided appropriate support (examples, expert opinion, statistics).
☐  Offered clear source citations.
☐  Related to and included audience.
☐  Made appropriate use of visual aids (if needed/used).     **Points**  _____

### Conclusion (15 points)

☐  Prepared audience for end.
☐  Reinforced central idea or claim in appropriate manner.     **Points**  _____

### Presentation and Delivery (20 points)

☐  Extemporaneous delivery.
☐  Enthusiasm for subject.
☐  Gestures/movements appropriate.
☐  Facial expressions appropriate.
☐  Eye contact appropriate.
☐  Pronunciation clear and accurate.
☐  Appropriate word choice for occasion and audience.
☐  Vocal variety.
☐  Fluent expression.     **Points**  _____

### Overall Evaluation (10 points)     **Points**  _____

**Total Points**  ____/100

*Source:*  Adapted with permission from Carlson and Smith-Howell, "Classroom Public Speaking Assessment: Reliability and Validity of Selected Evaluation Instruments," *Communication Education* 44 (April 1995): 87–97.

indicated that one can discriminate between good and not-as-good speeches through the use of such rating instruments.[3] You can use this form to evaluate speeches in classrooms, speaking events around your campus or community, and televised presentations on C-SPAN and other networks. Depending on the assignment, the audience, and the demands of the occasion, some checkpoints on the form will be more significant and applicable than others. For now, use the form as a general guide. Later, concentrate upon those parts that are relevant to specific assignments. In all likelihood, your instructor will use a comparable evaluation form. While it may use different terms or different weighting on items, it will nonetheless aim at the same goal: to evaluate your message and how effectively it reaches your audience.

What makes a good speech? While the answer to this question will vary among listeners, a positive response to each of the following questions will highlight some of the key issues involved:

- Does the speaker appear sincerely interested in the consequences of his or her speechmaking? That is, is the speaker willing to assume responsibility for what happens as a result of presenting ideas?

- Does the speaker take time at the beginning to indicate interest in and appreciation for divergent points of view? Does the speaker appear willing to consider opinions or perspectives other than those she or he is advancing?

- Is the information presented comprehensive and accurate, insofar as it is possible to obtain credible information on the topic being addressed?

- With respect to the central idea or claim advanced, is it supported with up-to-date and credible testimony, statistics, examples, and other supporting materials?

- Is the presentation understandable? That is, can you fathom what the speaker is talking about? Is the organization clear? Is the language appropriate? Is the delivery easy to listen to?

As you participate regularly in speech evaluations, even of early classroom assignments, use these broad questions, as well as others that seem appropriate, in providing direct feedback to your classmates. *Constructive* criticism is both positive and negative—but always personally supportive. Telling someone both what worked and what should be changed provides beginning speakers with much needed feedback. Being constructive also forces you, the listener, to formulate your thoughts and to acknowledge your own standards and expectations. In this way, both you and the speaker benefit.

As another strategy in this class, read the sample speeches in this book, such as the one that follows. Analyze them systematically to isolate the communication cues that facilitate listener comprehension and acceptance.

## Assessing a Sample Speech

The following speech by Dena Craig of Sante Fe Community College (New Mexico) is well adapted to a student audience and a persuasive speech assignment.[4] The initial paragraph introduces the issue, and the second paragraph indicates the major problem to be addressed and provides a clear preview of the main ideas and the order in which they will be discussed. Paragraphs 3 through 6 indicate the hazards associated with cigar smoking. Paragraphs 7 through 12 suggest why cigar smoking, though hazardous, has become popular. Paragraph 13 marks a transition from reviewing the problem to considering the solution in the next few paragraphs (14–17). The final paragraphs (18–19) provide a fitting ending to the speech with a specific plea for action.

---

### Clearing the Air about Cigars
#### Dena Craig, Santa Fe Community College

Denzel Washington, after finishing a hard day's work on an action film, unwinds with a premium Churchill cigar. Linda Evangelista walks down the runway modeling the latest fashions and holding a Cheroot cigar between her fingers. Jack Nicholson, after winning the Academy Award for best actor, celebrates with an expensive Macanudo cigar. Are they cool? Cigars may be smelly and expensive, but they are the hottest societal trend. Each year, according to the *Wall Street Journal*, February 8, 1998, Americans consume over 5.2 billion cigars annually. This represents a 53 percent increase in the last five years.    **1**

Alarmingly, despite potential carcinogenic effects, cigars carry no Surgeon General warning and users mistakenly believe that since they don't inhale, there is little danger. This is simply not true. Until recently, modern tobacco research has failed to illustrate the composition, use, and effects of cigars, focusing its attention instead on cigarettes. But the fact remains: Cigars are also toxic and addicting. Unlike cigarettes, cigars are completely unregulated. Today, we will look at first the dangers of cigar smoking; second, examine the reasons for the lack of control; and finally, suggest workable solutions to reduce the risk.    **2**

Since cigar smokers don't usually inhale, the dangers have always appeared negligible and, consequently, cigars have long had a benign quality. Many of us can remember a favorite uncle who always kept a stogie close at hand. And of course, many famous people smoke cigars: Winston Churchill, Groucho Marx, Bill Cosby, Bill Clinton, and Demi Moore. But recent research is clearing the air about cigars, and what it reveals shouldn't surprise us: Where there's smoke, there's fire!    **3**

Cigar smoking is dangerous to the smoker because the toxicity level determined during the slow curing process produces tars and nicotine which are readily absorbed into the mucous when placed in the mouth or absorbed into the skin when the moistened tip is held between the fingers. The problem is further complicated by the fact that the nicotine content varies from 0.77 to 21.2 percent, depending on how the cigar was made. Given the nature of cigars and their production, it is clear that there cannot be a one-size-fits-all method of researching its effects.    **4**

5     The American Health Foundation, July 1997, equates one large cigar to the toxicity of an entire pack of cigarettes. Cigar smokers might spend one full hour smoking a cigar but will spend several hours holding the unlit cigar, thus allowing more absorption of the toxic ingredients.

6     It cannot be denied that cigars produce poisons and that these poisons, in turn, lead to an array of health problems. *Newsweek,* July 21, 1997, indicates that cancers of the mouth, lung, larynx, pancreas, and esophagus are all associated with cigar smoking, and those risks are amplified if you drink alcohol while you puff. Furthermore, and perhaps more important to nonsmokers, the 23 poisons and 43 carcinogens released in cigar smoke make second-hand inhalation much more hazardous than second-hand cigarette smoke. James Repace, an advisor to the National Cancer Institute, states, "If you have to breathe secondhand smoke, cigar smoke is a lot worse than cigarette smoke." And we all are familiar with that lingering, musty odor that is cigar smoke; that's because we all have inhaled it, and at its current pace, cigars will soon replace cigarettes as the preferred weapon of smokers. Clearly, we are all affected. Cigars are poison to those who smoke and everyone else who breathes air polluted with cigar smoke.

7     Despite these risks, cigars have become the fashionable trend of the nineties. Upscale cigar stores, lounges, and magazines have become a booming business. The magazine *Cigar Aficionado,* now six years old, is highly successful. It commands advertising rates comparable to *People* and *Time,* and many famous people, such as Denzel Washington in February of 1998, have graced its cover. But somehow, all the cigar smoking has escaped the restrictions visited upon cigarette smoking. The *New York Times,* which wouldn't touch anything advocating cigarette smoking, happily runs full-page ads for *Cigar Aficionado.*

8     Cigar smoking has been made to look good, fun, and even sexy. Celebrity endorsers are having a drastic effect on the popularity of cigars. Basketball star Michael Jordan has been on the cover of *Sports Illustrated* with a cigar in his mouth. What kind of message is this sending to children? Arnold Schwarzenagger, whom we once saw standing on the White House lawn telling us to lead a healthy life, graced one of *Cigar Aficionado's* early covers.

9     Further, cigars are attracting a variety of people, including a growing number of women. According to *Fortune Magazine,* April 15, 1996, men often describe women cigar smokers as sexy. Tomina Edmark, author of *Cigar Chic—A Women's Perspective,* insists that every woman should smoke a cigar. She goes on to say that cigar smoking is good for relationships.

10     Too many teenagers are listening to this kind of advice. Because according to *Cancer Weekly Plus,* June 9, 1997, "More than a quarter of American teenagers have smoked a stogie in the past year." What makes this even worse is that two-thirds of the students who bought cigars said they were rarely or never asked their age.

11     Not only are sales unregulated, but the federal government has closed its eyes to the cigar industry in that it does not have regulations concerning content, additives, or processing. According to *Medical Update,* September 1997, the law does not require the package health warning on cigars that is found on cigarettes and other tobacco products, so users may not be aware of health risks. In addition, despite the fact that most cigars are imported, there are no regulations to monitor the quality of the product—for

*(continued)*

example, whether pesticides were used in growing tobacco—thus posing another risk to the smoker.

According to *Post Graduate Medicine,* September 1997, many cigar smokers believe that if they just chew on cigars instead of smoking them, that it reduces the cancer risk—but that just raises the risk of mouth cancer. Many cigar smokers believe that if they don't inhale the smoke, they are free from the dangers. This is simply not true. Because of the alkaline quality of cigars, the smoke does not need to be inhaled to get the nasty array of effects. It is these myths which cause society to misunderstand the dangers of cigars.    **12**

It is apparent that the cigar smoking fad is growing and is here to stay despite the risks involved. So what can be done to address this?    **13**

In April 1998, the Centers for Disease Control released a report confirming that the most recent research clearly demonstrates that cigars can be more harmful than cigarettes. It further indicates that the full extent of the risks is unknown due to the variables of importation, packaging, size, additives, and smoking patterns.    **14**

Therefore, on the national level, the first step must be additional research. Extensive research on the variation of product types and smoking patterns is needed to fully understand the dangers of cigars. According to the *Journal of the American Medical Association,* July 2, 1997, there are few long-term studies to indicate the extent of the harmful effects. Thus, it is necessary for the Centers for Disease Control to conduct an extensive study to quantify the exact harms. Secondly, money must be allocated to launch a national education program, similar to the antismoking campaign of cigarettes, to make the public fully aware of the harmful effects of cigars. Thirdly, the federal government must enact regulations that require warning labels on all brands—domestic and imported—and exact standards regarding the composition of cigars as well as any pesticides used in growing tobacco.    **15**

On the state level, stiff penalties, including both fines and imprisonment, must be implemented. Next, states must enforce laws which prohibit the sale of cigars to minors. And third, following the precedent of the Florida lawsuit against cigarette producers, advertising must be curtailed to prohibit cigar manufacturers from promoting their deadly products along interstates, in airports, and in newspapers.    **16**

Finally, on a personal level, first and most obvious, don't smoke cigars because they can kill you. If you're addicted to the high nicotine content, get help. Second, don't passively allow others to pollute your air with cigar smoke. Whether you're shy or just think you're being polite, stand up for yourself because their smoke can destroy your health. Finally, we must all act to bring to cigars the same stigma that hangs over cigarettes.    **17**

By implementing these responsible measures, we can extinguish its popularity and ensure that we begin tomorrow's day with a breath of fresh air.    **18**

Denzel Washington smoking a Churchill. Linda Evangelista, now pregnant, smoking a Cheroot. Jack Nicholson smoking a Macanudo. Arnold Schwarzenagger, Bill Cosby, Bill Clinton, Demi Moore, and Michael Jordan all smoking cigars and all well respected by children and adults …    **19**

Well, they are not cool. Hollywood may glamorize cigars, and cigar lounges may sell them, but the fact remains: Cigars may be a trend, but addiction never goes out of style.    **20**

# CHAPTER SUMMARY

In preparing a speech, the competent speaker will follow seven essential steps: selecting the subject; narrowing the subject; determining the purposes; analyzing the audience and occasion; gathering the speech materials; outlining the speech; and practicing aloud. In preparing an initial speech, the competent speaker will be able to select an appropriate method of presentation (impromptu, memorized, read, or extemporaneous), communicate self-confidence, and use the evaluative questions and form to check the adequacy of her or his and others' presentations.

# KEY TERMS

**audience analysis**  (p. 37)
**authority to act**  (p. 36)
**central idea**  (p. 31)
**claim**  (p. 31)
**creating the title**  (p. 34)
**extemporaneous speech**  (p. 42)
**general purposes**  (p. 27)

**impromptu speech**  (p. 41)
**memorized speech**  (p. 41)
**preexisting attitudes**  (p. 36)
**private aim**  (p. 36)
**read speech**  (p. 41)
**rhetorical frame of mind**  (p. 23)
**specific purpose**  (p. 30)

**speech to actuate**  (p. 28)
**speech to entertain**  (p. 29)
**speech to inform**  (p. 28)
**speech to persuade**  (p. 28)
**time limit**  (p. 36)
**ultimate aim**  (p. 36)

# ASSESSMENT ACTIVITIES

1. Listed below are two groups of three statements about a single topic: Group I about prisons and Group II about medical services. Read all three statements in each group, and then write what you believe to be the claim they make. Compare your phrasing of the claims with those of members of your class.

   **Group I**

   Many prison facilities are inadequate.

   Low rates of pay result in frequent job turnovers in prisons.

   Prison employees need on-the-job training.

   **Group II**

   There is a serious maldistribution of medical personnel and service.

   The present system of delivering medical service is in need of repair.

   Rural areas have a shortage of doctors.

2. Rewrite the following statements, making each a clear and concise central idea for a speech.
   a. Today, I would like to try to get you to see the way in which the body can communicate a whole lot of information.
   b. The topic for my speech has to do with the high amount of taxes people have to pay.
   c. A college education might be a really important thing for some people, so my talk is on a college education.

   Now rewrite statements (b) and (c) as claims. Be ready to present your versions in a class discussion.

3. Working in small groups, prepare an issues survey. Each group member will come to class prepared with five suitably narrowed subjects for an informative speech and five for a persuasive speech. (There may be some overlap.) Discuss your lists with your group, sorting out over-

lapping ideas in order to develop one list. (There may be more than five topics listed for informative and for persuasive speeches.) Have one person collate the list in readable form and bring copies for everyone to the next class. Using a simple three-point scale (1 = very interesting; 2 = interesting; 3 = very uninteresting), have class members respond to the subject lists of the various groups. The instructor and one or two students will collate responses and prepare a master copy for everyone in class. Select one informative or persuasive topic that scores among the lowest (i.e., most uninteresting) on this final list, and develop a speech about it that has arousing audience interest as a specific purpose.

4. Following the principles and guidelines presented in this chapter, prepare a three- to four-minute speech to inform. Narrow the subject carefully, so you can do justice to it in the allotted time. Concentrate on developing ways to gain and hold the audience's attention. Hand in an outline, along with a brief analysis of the audience and the occasion, when you present the speech. In your analysis, indicate why you think your approach to attention will work in this situation.

## ■ REFERENCES

1. It can be argued that all speeches are persuasive. *Any* change in a person's stock of knowledge, beliefs, attitudes, or behaviors represents the kind of adjustment in mental and emotional state that can be attributed to persuasion, as long as symbols were employed to induce the change. From a psychological perspective, it may be argued that it's impossible to separate *informative* and *persuasive* messages. We're taking a *rhetorical* perspective, in which the symbols used to evoke a certain kind of response, as well as the strategies employed in that process, provide an *orientation* that's overtly one of informing, persuading, actuating, or entertaining an audience. Hence, you'll find separate discussions of these later in this book. For a cogent discussion of persuasion, see Anthony R. Pratkanis and Elliot Aronson, *Age of Propaganda: The Everyday Use and Abuse of Persuasion*, rev. ed. (New York: H. H. Freeman, 2001) and Herbert W. Simons, Joanne Morreale, and Bruce Gronbeck, *Persuasion in Society* (Beverly Hills: Sage, 2001).

2. Raymie E. McKerrow, "Coloring Outside the Lines: The Limits of Civility," *Vital Speeches* 67 (15 February 2001): 278–281.

3. Robert E. Carlson and Deborah Smith-Howell, "Classroom Public Speaking Assessment: Reliability and Validity of Selected Evaluation Instruments," *Communication Education* 44 (April 1995): 87–97.

4. Dena Craig, "Clearing the Air about Cigars," *Winning Orations 1998*. Reprinted by permission of Larry Schnoor, Executive Secretary, Interstate Oratorical Association, Mankato, MN.

Chapter 3

# Setting the Scene for Community in a Diverse Culture

## Public Speaking and Critical Listening

*I arrived in Hong Kong ready to teach to a predominantly Chinese audience. Over the next four weeks, this veteran classroom lecturer was undone and remade. What I had been doing in the classroom on a university campus for several years bore little resemblance to the approach I learned to take, through trial and several errors, by the time I finished teaching. While several of the Chinese students spoke excellent English and wrote well in response to questions on exams, they were not familiar with most of the early examples I attempted to use in explaining concepts, nor were they familiar with my style of asking questions. Adapting my lectures to the audience and situation became easier as I began to draw on illustrations familiar to them. I also learned to speak slower and to avoid common idiomatic expressions that only someone raised in the United States might understand. In short, all of the elements of the process of public speaking were revamped or adapted to foster an environment more conducive to student learning.*

The experience just outlined is a real one. Speaking to a diverse audience in a U.S. college classroom is one thing; speaking to a predominantly non–native English speaking audience is quite another. This example brings home in clear terms what is at stake in the process of getting one's ideas heard. The Chinese students were polite and cordial at all times—even the one who responded with "I haven't a clue what you just said," smiling as he spoke. Not all audiences may be as forgiving, as the expectation that you will adapt to their level of knowledge and skill in listening may govern their responses. Whether in another country or in your own classroom, considering the differences that make a difference in how you speak will be critical to your success. As the example suggests, the information offered in this chapter cannot be taken for granted.

In the initial chapters, we set forth the rationale for the academic study of public speaking and outlined the basic tasks ahead of you. Before going into greater detail, this chapter provides a **model of the speechmaking process** and introduces a critical component that must be considered in all encounters, whether interpersonal or public: the process of critical listening.

## Basic Elements of the Speechmaking Process: A Model Overview

Speechmaking is comprised of a number of elements. A speaker, the primary communicator, gives a speech, which is a continuous, purposive oral message, to the listeners, who provide feedback to the speaker. Their exchange occurs through various channels in a particular communication situation and cultural context.

Before considering each of these elements individually, one way to conceptualize this process is to think in terms of your daily interactions with friends, significant others, instructors, and strangers. You bring to these interactions a specific *self-image*—how you want others to see you in a particular interaction, such as poised, self-confident, scared, responsible, or contrite. You also have an *image of the other* who is listening to you. You may see the person(s) as responsible, cooperative, or maybe highly critical of you and your ideas. Your listener likewise has a specific self-image to project in that particular setting and a particular image of you as the communicator. He or she may see you as petulant, irresponsible, or appropriately contrite.

In any case, the message that is communicated and heard by your listener(s) must touch on, in some way, all of these competing images. Specifically, it must accommodate them so as to bring closure to the communication event. If you are seen by your listener as irresponsible and petulant while you see yourself as responsible and justified in your complaint, and if your listener sees herself as open minded and flexible while you see her as judgmental and rigid, what chance is there for your message—however it is phrased—to be communicated effectively? In this particular scenario, communication success will be difficult to achieve. As our opening example suggests, communicating effectively is far more difficult in many situations than it may appear at first. Meeting the obligations imposed by the setting or the audience while holding true to your sense of self as a person may not always be easy. Reflect on the model presented in Figure 3.1 as you consider the more specific illustrations of the speechmaking process.

### The Speaker

A speaker must consider four key elements in every speech exchange or transaction: his or her purpose; knowledge of subject and communication skills; attitudes toward self, listeners, and subject; and degree of credibility.[1]

FIGURE 3.1

**A Model of the
Speechmaking Process**

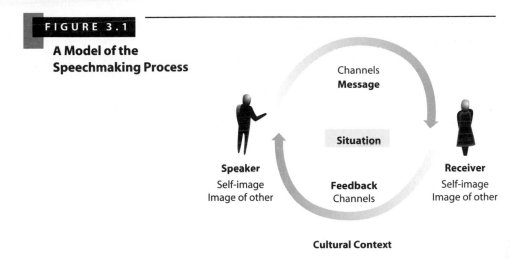

**The Speaker's Purpose**   Every speaker talks to achieve a goal. That goal can be as simple as a desire for social exchange ("Hi—you want to study together later?") or as complex as the desire to alter someone's ideas and actions ("We need to curb campus riots"). Your purpose or goal may be to entertain, call attention to a problem, refute an assertion, ward off a threat, or establish or maintain your status or power.

**The Speaker's Knowledge**   Your knowledge of the subject affects the character of your message and your effectiveness. If you have only surface knowledge of a topic, listeners feel cheated. They want you to say something important, new, relevant, and interesting. You also need to say it in a way that is understandable and enjoyable. In the chapters that follow, we address both areas, with an emphasis on communication goals, finding and assembling relevant information, organizing messages in coherent and powerful ways, illustrating them visually, and delivering them in a manner that convinces the audience you care about them.

**The Speaker's Attitudes**   Your attitudes toward yourself, your listeners, and your subject significantly affect what you say and how you say it. As suggested earlier, we all have mental pictures of ourselves—self-concepts or **self-images** of the kinds of individuals we are and of how others perceive us.

Your self-image—along with the self you wish to project in a specific situation—influences how you speak. Drawing on the opening example, suppose you're giving a speech in class about your experience communicating with international students. If you have little confidence in your abilities and haven't done any research beyond your own limited experience, you'll tend to speak hesitantly. Your voice will become weak, your body stiff, and you'll focus on the back wall rather than look directly at your audience. If you're convinced you know more than anyone else in class, however, you might move to the other extreme, becoming overbearing, disregarding listeners' needs or riding roughshod over their feelings. Doing research will improve your confidence in speaking in the first instance, and recognizing that your knowledge, while extensive, may not be complete will temper your expression in the second. Balancing research with sensitivity to your audience's own self-image will go a long way toward presenting ideas in keeping with a self-image you would like to project in that setting.

Part of your treatment of audiences comes from your power relations with them and the ways in which you perceive them—as instructors or fellow students, as supervisors or employees, as subordinates or equals. Giving a speech about cross-cultural communication in front of a teacher who is grading you involves an unequal power relationship; giving the same speech to a student research committee of which you're a member involves a relatively equal power relationship. As power relationships change, you adjust your speaking style accordingly.

Your comfort level in a specific setting also affects how you approach the speech. For example, a speech classroom will make you feel awkward at first, and that feeling will affect your speeches. As you grow more at home in this setting, however, your attitudes will improve—and so will your skills. Most people take a while to get used to speaking in church or synagogue or at a club or civic group meeting.

**The Speaker's Credibility**     Your listeners' estimation of your credibility will affect their reception of your message. Speaker **credibility** is the degree to which an audience judges a communicator as trustworthy, competent, sincere, attractive,

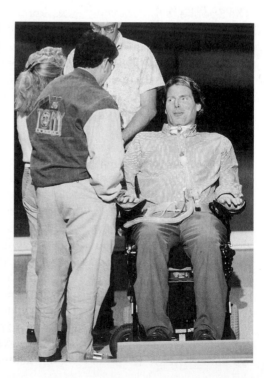

*Christopher Reeve has spoken eloquently on behalf of people with disabilities.*

and dynamic. The idea of credibility is rooted in the classical Greek concept of **ethos,** which, as you learned in Chapter 1, means "character." Research has demonstrated repeatedly that a speaker who can raise an audience's estimation of her or his trustworthiness, competency, sincerity, attractiveness, and dynamism will heighten the impact of any speech. In other words, you and your message are inseparable in people's minds. What Aristotle called the most important aspect of persuasion—your audience's perception of you—is the key to effectiveness.

## The Message

Your messages often are referred to as your ideas or information. In public speaking, three aspects of the message—content, structure, and style—are especially important.

**Content**    The speech's **content** is the message: the information you want to convey or the specific argument you want to advance. In deciding what to say, you will select some information or arguments and reject others, in part, because you will have more materials than you can use. These choices shape the information or argument for the audience. For example, the content of an informative speech on notebook computers is more than a recitation of brands, model numbers, and features ("The following criteria—price, performance, and use—provide a useful way to organize the variables involved in purchasing a notebook computer"). As a persuasive speech, the same points become arguments for a specific purchase ("Three factors—price, preference in disk operating systems, and use—should guide your decision on which notebook computer to purchase"). In each case, the central idea or claim changes the nature of the content and how it will be perceived and understood by the audience.

**Organization**    Any message you transmit is, of necessity, structured in some way, simply because you say some words first, others second, and so on. How clearly you phrase your central idea or claim will affect how you structure your message. As the previous examples suggest, the pattern imposes coherence on a subject that seems bewildering in its complexity. To keep the structure clear to the audience, *numbering* your points ("First I'll discuss, . . . Next I will . . . Finally, I'll . . .") or providing other *internal summaries* ("Having reviewed price, let's next consider performance") will help the audience keep track of where you are during the presentation.

**Style**    You are as you speak. Your words reflect more than your ideas. They also give the audience a sense of your personal values. Selecting and arranging words and revealing yourself to be a certain kind of person are matters of style. Style can be personal or impersonal, literal or ironic, plain or elevated, and even philosophical or poetic. Such labels refer to particular combinations of a speaker's vocabulary, syntax (sentence structure), and images. What we call *style,* therefore, really has little to do with the elegance (stylishness) of language. Rather, it refers to those aspects of language that convey impressions of you, details of the world, and emotional overtones.

## The Listener

Like speakers, listeners have purposes in mind; they are partners in speech transactions. The way they think about what is said is affected by their purposes, knowledge of and interest in the subject, level of listening skills, and attitudes toward self, speaker, and the ideas presented.

**The Listeners' Purposes**    Listeners always have one or more purposes when they come to a speech. No less than speakers, they're looking for something, be it information, confirmation of prior judgments about ideas or people, or simply entertainment. As we note in more detail in the second section of this chapter, speakers must take listeners' purposes into account or risk rejection.

**The Listeners' Knowledge and Interest Levels**    In speaking situations, listeners' knowledge of and interest in the subject will significantly affect how they respond to the message. One of your jobs is to figure out how much listeners know about your topic and whether they have any personal stake in it. Beyond assessing knowledge and interest, you also need to analyze cultural differences, if any, and how they will affect the audience's reception of your speech. For example, talking about time to a cultural group that does not place the same importance on being on time as your own requires an awareness of the difference. What shared experiences can you call on when talking with this audience?

**The Listeners' Command of Listening Skills**    As noted at the outset of this chapter, listeners vary in their abilities to process oral messages. Cultural differences may place greater responsibility on you as the speaker to ensure the ideas are clear; otherwise, the audience will tune out. Furthermore, even though college audiences have been listening to instructors for several years, they still want to know why they should listen to *you*. Motivating audiences to use the skills they have is as important as recognizing when they are not comprehending your message because of inadequate listening skills.

**The Listeners' Attitudes**    As the model in Figure 3.1 suggests, listeners' attitudes toward themselves, the speaker, and the subject affect how they interpret and respond to speeches. Listeners with low self-esteem, for example, tend to be swayed more easily than those with stronger self-images. Listeners who feel their opinions are confirmed by the speaker also are more easily influenced than those holding contrary ideas. Moreover, as a rule, people seek out speakers whose positions they already agree with and retain longer and more vividly those ideas of which they strongly approve.[2] **Audience analysis** is one of the keys to speaking success, because you need to know about people's attitudes before you can reach them.

## Feedback

You may think of public speaking as communication flowing in one direction—from speaker to listener. Information, feelings, and ideas, however, flow the other way, as well. **Feedback** is information that listeners return to you about the clarity and acceptability of your ideas (see Figure 3.2). Listeners may provide **immediate feedback** in the form of verbal or nonverbal responses during an interaction. Some immediate feedback is *direct*, such as when the audience asks questions, whereas some is *indirect*, such as when speakers look for frowns, smiles, nodding heads, and other nonverbal cues to audience reactions. Being able to read feedback for signs of comprehension and acceptability is important, as this skill allows you to make midcourse adjustments in the speech.

As noted earlier, however, in some cultures it is considered impolite to show disapproval through feedback. Instead, people smile cordially, as if all is well, when in reality they might not understand anything you say. Knowing in advance how different cultural values govern responsiveness will help you develop a sound perception of how effectively you have communicated your ideas. In some cases, you may not be certain until you have received additional concrete evidence through **delayed feedback**, which takes the form of oral, auditory, or visual signals received after the message has been transmitted. Examples include a voice vote on a matter a speaker has recommended, the sound of applause or boos, a written evaluation from an instructor, or discovering that the person listening was unable to follow your instructions even though he or she never said anything was amiss. (Again, it may be embarrassing to admit lack of understanding in some cultural interactions.)

**FIGURE 3.2**     **Types of Feedback**

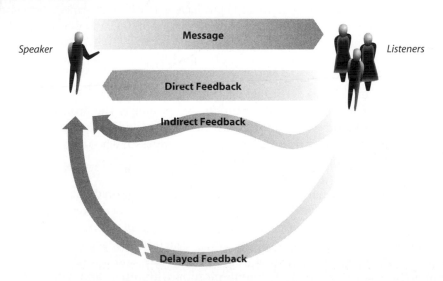

## The Channels

The public communication transaction occurs across multiple channels. The **verbal channel** carries words—society's agreed on symbols for ideas. The **visual channel** transmits the gestures, facial expressions, bodily movements, and postures of the speakers and listeners, and these tend to clarify, reinforce, or give an emotional tone to the words or to transmit necessary information about the audience's state of mind to the speaker. The visual channel sometimes is supplemented with the **pictorial channel** (visual aids such as diagrams, charts, graphs, sketches, and objects). The **aural channel**—also called the **paralinguistic channel**—carries the tone of voice and variations in pitch, loudness, and other vocal modulations; this channel carries cues to the emotional state of the speaker and the tone (ironic, playful, serious) of the speech.

Because these four channels are seen and heard simultaneously, the overall message really is a combination of several messages flowing through all of the pathways. Communication via multiple channels is what makes public speaking such a richly textured **transactional experience**. As a speaker, you must learn to shape and control the messages moving through all four channels.

## The Situation

What you say and how you say it are affected significantly by the situations in which you're speaking. For instance, you don't talk the same way at work as you do at a party. Your speech is affected by the physical setting and the social context in which it occurs.

**Physical Setting**    The physical setting influences listeners' expectations as well as their readiness to respond to your speech. People waiting at the convocation center for a graduation ceremony to begin have very different expectations from people attending a local politician's announcement of defeat at what might have been a victory party. Some settings have created formal conventions or rules for engaging in communication (a court of law), while others are far more informal (a social gathering at a local restaurant).

Even furniture and decor make a difference. Soft chairs and muted drapes put discussants at ease and promote productive exchange. The professor who has soft chairs and a lamp table in the corner of her or his office for interacting with students creates a different atmosphere than the professor who remains seated behind a large desk while leaving the student standing.

**Social Context**    Even more important to message reception than physical setting is the social context in which a speech is presented. A **social context** is a particular combination of people, purpose, and place interacting communicatively. In a social context, people are distinguished from each other by factors such as gender, age, occupation, power, degree of intimacy, ethnicity, and knowledge. Taken together, these factors shape your communication with others and conversely their communication with you. For example, you've learned not to talk in class while the instructor is talking. When you violate this communication rule, other students may be as displeased with your behavior as is the instructor. In other settings, you're expected to speak deferentially to your elders, your boss, a judge, or a high-status politician. The "Communications Research Dateline" box below looks at some of the work-related issues that stem from generational differences in communication. Moreover, certain purposes or goals are more or less appropriately communicated in different social contexts. A memorial service is not the context

## COMMUNICATION RESEARCH DATELINE

### Listening and Your Career:
### Working across the Generational Gap

If you've ever worked with or for supervisors who are your parents' age, you have already faced the differences that exist between the baby-boomer generation and your own. Listening to each other's needs becomes critical if both are to achieve their respective goals.

Finding common goals is one strategy recommended by Margaret Fitch-Hauser, managing partner for the Leadership Communication Group LLC and an associate professor at Auburn University. In a newsletter published monthly online by HighGain, Inc., Fitch-Hauser explains that "if you are talking to a younger person, it's very important to talk about why something is important, and what's in it for that individual. If you are talking to an older person, it would be important to talk about the good of the organization and the good of the group." It isn't the case that neither generation cares about what's important to the other; rather, focusing attention on what's of prime importance to each generation makes eminent sense if you wish to gain a hearing. Older workers tend to be willing to take the time necessary to examine data for relevance; younger workers are less patient generally, as they seek information that's relevant to their lives. It may be the case that older workers are more process oriented: How has the information been gathered, and is it valuable? Younger workers, on the other hand, may tend to be more results oriented: What is the information good for, and how can I use it?

As suggested in this chapter, the ethical listener is one who takes these differences into consideration. Andrew Wolvin, former president of the International Listening Association and a professor at the University of Maryland, suggests that "we need to recognize that people do have different needs, expectations, and styles and accept them. By listening conscientiously, we can stop the biases that plague good communication—particularly age and generational bias." In this way, the generational gap need not be a barrier to working as part of a team or to learning to adapt to the interests of people not in your own age group.

*Source: Sssh! Listen Up!* May 2001. Available online: <http://www.highgain.com/newsletter/back-issues/e-news-05-01/hg-enews-05-01.html>.

for attacking a political opponent, but a Meet the Candidates night is. Public offi-cials often are more easily influenced in their offices than in public forums, where they tend to be more defensive. Sensitive parents scold their children in private but never in front of their friends.

Societies are governed by customs, norms, and traditions that become the bases for **communication rules:** guides to communication behavior, specifying who talks to whom about what, in what style, and under what conditions. Some communication rules tell you what to do: "An audience will better remember what you have to say if you break your subject into three to five main points." Others tell you what to avoid: "Don't wander aimlessly across the stage while talking, because it will distract your audience." Such rules, of course, can be broken; some wander-ing speakers are listened to, probably because they have so many other virtues. Oc-casionally, rule breaking is inconsequential. Even so, it always involves a certain amount of risk, and sometimes it determines success or failure. The key is to deter-mine the level of risk acceptable to you and then act accordingly.

## The Cultural Context

Finally, elements of communication may have different meanings depending on the **culture:** the shared set of social understandings within which the communica-tion is taking place. Each society has its own rules for interpreting communication signals. Some societies frown on taking second helpings of food; in others, it's a supreme compliment to the host or hostess. Negotiating the price of a T-shirt is unheard of at a Sears store in Atlanta, yet it's a sign of active interest in an Istanbul bazaar or a Cleveland garage sale. Communication systems operate within the confines of cultural rules and the expectations of the members of any given society.

Cultural rules and expectations become important in two situations: during *intercultural contact* and during *cross-cultural presentations*. When talking to mem-bers of other societies on your home turf, you might offend them by violating some rule that they bring with them to your speech. A common violation during intercultural contact is being too familiar or informal with a new acquaintance. To call people by their first names in public, for example, is simply not acceptable in many countries.

Your problem may be even greater, of course, if you attempt to speak in pub-lic in another country. During such a cross-cultural presentation, you risk violat-ing not only personal standards of interaction but also the rules of the situation operating at that particular time and place. Americans soon learn they cannot joke publicly about royalty in Sweden in the same way they can about the presi-dent's family in the United States. If you are going to speak in another country, you will have to learn the communication rules governing how to introduce a per-son to an audience, to quote appropriate authorities, and to refer to yourself and audience members correctly. Rules for such communication situations tend to vary from country to country.

To tap into the cultural context for public speaking is to grapple with the most fundamental questions of diversity and sociality—how people in various countries interact with each other and transact public business. For example, dog meat is considered a delicacy in some parts of the world, while in the United States, eating dog meat would be considered almost criminal if not abhorrent. A speech that blames the Taiwanese, who do consider it a delicacy, for their "backward ways" would be inappropriate whether any Taiwanese were in the audience or not.[3] This is not to say that a speaker cannot be against such a choice; rather, she or he can argue against a cultural practice without at the same time devaluing the people for whom that practice is considered normal. Nor would it be true that all Taiwanese believe the same thing about a specific diet, any more than it would be to assume that because some Americans eat venison, all Americans approve of hunting deer. As we will note in more detail in the next chapter, cultural stereotypes have the distinct disadvantage of labeling all persons with the same characteristics. Speaking in a way that recognizes stereotypes for what they are—often misleading guides to individuals' beliefs and values—will go a long way toward maximizing success.

The cultural context for public speaking is the ultimate source of the communication rules you've been taught. Because speeches almost always represent transactions in which appropriateness is determined by cultural rules or expectations, you'll find throughout this book explicit pieces of advice—do's and don'ts. It's not really wrong, for example, to skip presenting a summary at the end of your speech, but most audiences expect one. If you omit it, the audience might question your **communication competence**: your ability to construct a speech in accordance with the audience's expectations. A male speaker who pulls a handkerchief out of his back pocket, blows his nose, and crumples it up and puts it back, all in the middle of his speech, may be considered rather odd in this country, but in Japan, the act would be seen as grotesque.[4] These sorts of expectations do not have to be followed in every case, because conditions, and even speaker talents, vary from situation to situation. You should follow the rules of communication most of the time, however, because you want listeners to evaluate your ideas, not your communication skills. A consistent theme of this book is the supreme importance of developing communication competence: the possession and execution of speech skills.

Speakers and listeners, messages and feedback, channels, context, and culture are the primary elements of the public speaking process. As you strive to refine your skills in managing all of them, consider the following points:

- *A change in one element usually produces changes in others.* During a speech on learning to use the campus computer system, for example, your attitude will affect your language and delivery, your listeners' attitudes toward you, and even the feedback that you receive from them.

■ *No single element controls the entire process.* You may think the speaker controls the entire process, but of course, she or he does not. Listeners can tune in or tune out, and cultural expectations often affect the listeners' perceptions of the speaker's talents.

Overall, public speaking is a transaction or exchange: You prepare a speech to give your listeners, and in turn, they give you their attention and reactions or feedback. From all of the things you could say, you select only a few and tailor them to the listeners' interests, wants, and desires, so they can absorb and accept your message. Just as you assert your right to speak, they assert their right to listen or not to listen. *Public speaking is a communication transaction, a face-to-face process of mutual give and take.*

The preceding model of the speechmaking process will be given greater attention later. For now, the main goal is to initiate some thought about what is important in the process and how you may gain more control over those elements that are open to change. In the next section, we examine one element of the model in greater detail: that of listening in an active and critically aware manner.

## Critical Listening: Theory and Practice

*George called his neighbor Frank, who ran a trucking business. "I want to ship three sows and seven sheep to market tomorrow," George said. "Fine, I'll be there at 6 A.M.," replied Frank. At 5:50 A.M., George looked out his kitchen window to see a fleet of semis. Frank climbed out of the front cab, came to the door, and said, "We're ready." "Ready?" said George. "Why all those trucks?" "Well," replied Frank, "I figured that if you had 3,007 sheep to ship, I'd need every truck I have."*

In your daily life, you spend more time listening than you do reading, writing, or speaking. Although you may assume you're a good listener from all that practice, you usually don't know about any problems you might have until you miss something important. The fact is, you've probably never had any training in listening, especially for situations such as class lectures, where you're expected to acquire technical or abstract materials aurally. Just ask Frank and George about the problems that can result from mishearing numbers!

**Hearing** is the first step in the listening process. Perhaps you recall your mother asking "Did you *hear* me?" To listen to a message, you first must hear it. Hearing loss of only 15 decibels, which can result from any number of physiological or neurological dysfunctions, is enough to create problems in learning. Moreover, hearing loss contributes to listening difficulties.[5]

**Listening**, on the other hand, is "the process of receiving, constructing meaning from, and responding to spoken and/or nonverbal messages."[6] Just how important is listening? One study of who gets promoted and who doesn't in corporations reports that "the common factor that differentiated the successful candidates for promotion was this: the executive was seen as a person who listens."[7]

In the remainder of this chapter, after more fully introducing the idea of listening, we focus on practical listening techniques you can use in almost any situation in which someone else is doing most of the talking. We finish by suggesting how you can put new listening skills to work in your classes.

## Knowing Purposes: An Orientation to Listening Behaviors

When it comes to listening, there are many ways to categorize appropriate and inappropriate behaviors (see Figure 3.3). The following approaches are not meant to be exhaustive but to orient you to the complexities involved in approaching audiences and in asking them to listen to what you have to say. Knowing their purposes, or styles, will assist you in gaining a hearing.

**The RRP Listening Styles**    This approach suggests that when you approach an audience, you should consider whether they need to know the *Reasons, Results, or Processes* (*RRP*) most relevant to your message. The **reasons-oriented listener** wants to know why your idea is a good one; he or she will approach your speech looking for the rationale behind your idea or proposal. The **results-oriented listener** wants to know the bottom line: What are you going to do? She or he will be impatient if you take too long getting to the bottom line. The **process-oriented listener** checks in when you begin to talk about how you went about making the decision, who will be affected by it, and how you will manage people's lives if they are unhappy with your choices. Stressing how your ideas will benefit the listener will help this person focus on your message.[8]

In adapting to these listening styles, look for immediate feedback from your audience. If they appear to be impatient as you go over the reasons for your proposal in painstaking detail, you may want to cut it short and move to the bottom line. Another strategy, especially if the audience contains people more focused on process, is to present the bottom line, develop the rationale in brief comments, and then illustrate the benefits and consequences at the close. In this manner, you cover the interests of all three listening styles without turning off any one listener.

---

**FIGURE 3.3**    **Styles of Listening**

*People may vary between and among these various approaches to listening. Knowing in advance what the person is listening for will assist you in developing your message.*

| RRP | VAT | SUR |
|---|---|---|
| Reasons | Visual | Self-Absorbed |
| Results | Auditory | Unfocused |
| Processes | Tactile | Rules-Driven |

**The VAT Listening Styles**    Another way to think about how listeners approach your presentation is to consider whether they are primarily *Visual, Auditory, or Tactile* (*VAT*) listeners. **Visual listeners** need something they can see; as the old saying from Missouri goes, "Show me." In this instance, visual aids become essential in drawing listeners into your presentation and getting them more involved in attending to your message. The kind of response you are looking for is "I can see what you mean." **Auditory listeners**, on the other hand, focus on what is said rather than on what is shown. The response they will give is "I hear what you are saying," where *hear* means they have processed your message. **Tactile listeners** want to become involved in some way; they want not only to see but also to get a hands-on exposure to your message. These are the listeners who will come forward if you are demonstrating how to do something and need volunteers from the audience. Their response is more on the order of "Now that I've worked with it, I understand what you mean."[9]

Using visual aids as part of your presentation, even going so far as to hand something out if you do not need volunteer assistance, is an excellent strategy in providing something for each. Chapter 11 ("Using Visual Aids in Speeches") provides advice for focusing on the needs of visual and tactile listeners.

**The SUR Listening Styles**    While the RRP and VAT styles generally are helpful in terms of active listening, other listening styles that people sometimes employ are not at all useful to you as a speaker, unless you can circumvent their influence. Listening with these styles can be called by many labels, but one study refers to them as *Self-absorbed, Unfocused, or Rules-driven* (*SUR*). **Self-absorbed listeners** are more interested in themselves and their view of the world than they are in you and your views. **Unfocused listeners** attend without regard to any plan or pattern, and without knowing what they are looking for, their attention soon wanders off, perhaps never to return. **Rules-driven listeners** are quite capable of listening, but their focus is so narrowly constructed around whether rules or guidelines are being adhered to or violated that once they find a violation, they tend to miss the big picture. These people will focus on all the reasons for *not* doing something, missing in the interim the arguments you present that might otherwise dissuade them.[10]

Dealing with such negative behaviors is difficult, unless you have the chance to interact one on one with such listeners. If they are part of a larger audience, however, and the opportunity is not present for a question-and-answer period or some other direct interaction, you may never know that they have been left on the sidelines. For those who may be self-absorbed, the best you can do is give them reasons to hear you out rather than focus on their own views. If you have knowledge of their specific views, however, then dealing with those ideas explicitly will at least gain their attention, if not their agreement. Unfocused listeners need structure; using PowerPoint to provide a handy outline may help keep their attention focused on one idea at a time. Giving them the pattern and then reinforcing it often during the speech may be the best way to keep them along for the ride. The rules-driven segment of your audience is harder to deal with, because you may not know for sure which rules, in their view, are being broken. Generally, if you are changing what they are accustomed to, you will, as with the "reasons" listeners, want to spell out why the change is important and, as with the "process" listeners, how the change will benefit them.

**Other Listening Styles**   As noted, these are not the only ways to characterize audiences in terms of their listening behaviors. A recent study of college student behaviors provides similar perspectives on the issue. In sum, the predominant reasons for ineffective or poor listening were daydreaming, being distracted by other events or the environment, thinking about other issues (often stimulated by something the speaker says), and simple lack of interest in what is being said.[11]

The first two styles (RRP and VAT) reflect positive if critical approaches to listening to you, whereas the last (SUR) reflects the downside of listening behavior. The same person may, at different times, work from any of these styles. You will not always know in advance, however, where the other person is coming from as a listener. Nor will the listener always be entirely focused on your message, even when being her or his most positive and critically aware self. Recognizing that your audience is not always going to be with you will help you remember to add internal summaries and other guideposts to make it easier for them to reposition themselves when they do return to active listening.

Sometimes, what you think is an example of poor or inattentive listening is not really that at all. A college professor used to listen to competitive debaters while playing solitaire. Once they were finished debating—and convinced that the judge had obviously not been paying the slightest attention (he never stopped and took notes)—they were amazed to find that his critique was sharp, incisive, and invariably on target in assessing the value of their respective arguments. While they might not have agreed with his decision, they had to respect that he had indeed been listening all the while. If you were speaking before an audience of Japanese businesspersons and some appeared to be sleeping, you should not automatically draw the conclusion that you were boring them. You may well be, but because Japanese people in general do not believe it appropriate to look you in the eye, they will probably look away or even cross their arms and appear to be asleep while listening.[12] Knowing why someone appears inattentive means more than just drawing natural inferences based on your own cultural experiences.

## Critical Listening for Comprehension and Judgment

Let's now switch positions from focusing on strategies you may use as a speaker in adapting to various audience listening styles to focusing on you as the person *listening*. Keep in mind that as a listener, you may fit into one or more of the preceding strategies at different times, and as a college student, you can identify with the

*Critical listening
is active listening.*

common problems most students express in terms of adequate listening behavior. As you probably know, you have to work hard to listen well. There's no alternative to brainwork if you're going to keep on task when receiving oral messages. The good news, though, is that you can train yourself to listen better. You can attack the problems of listening well in four ways: know your purposes when trying to listen, develop techniques that help you comprehend speeches, design questions that help you evaluate or assess speeches on criteria that matter to you, and sharpen your note-taking techniques.

**Why Are You Listening?**     This may sound foolish, but the first thing good listeners do is figure out why they're listening. As noted, this may be for specific reasons, for results, or for processing information. Knowing in advance which is most important to you will prepare you to focus on what is being said. That's not really as silly as it sounds, because you listen differently on specific occasions. On any given day, for example, you may listen intently to your instructors to learn new concepts and facts, listen to your favorite music to relax, and listen to a salesperson in a stereo shop to make sure she or he isn't skipping over some essential feature of the machine's performance or the dealer's guarantee. After reviewing listening research, Wolvin and Coakley identified five kinds of listening that reflect purposes you may have when communicating with others—appreciative, therapeutic, discriminative, comprehension, and critical:[13]

1. **Appreciative listening** focuses on something other than the primary message. Some listeners enjoy seeing a famous speaker; others appreciate the art of good public speaking. On these occasions, you listen primarily to entertain yourself.

2. **Therapeutic listening** provides emotional support for the speaker. Although it is more typical of interpersonal than of public communication, therapeutic listening does occur in public speaking situations, such as when a sports figure apologizes for unprofessional behavior, a religious convert describes a soul-saving experience, or a classmate reviews a personal problem and thanks friends for their help in solving it.

3. **Discriminative listening** requires listeners to draw conclusions from how a message is presented rather than directly from what is said. In discriminative listening, people seek to understand what the speaker really thinks, believes, or feels. You're engaging in discriminative listening when you draw conclusions about how angry your parents are with you based not on what they say but on how they say it. An important dimension of discriminative listening depends on your ability to draw relatively sophisticated inferences from messages.

4. **Listening for comprehension** occurs when you want to gain additional information or insight from the speaker. This probably is the form of listening with which you're most familiar. When you listen to radio or TV news, to a classroom speech on violence in high schools, or to a counselor explaining computerized registration procedures, you're listening to understand—to comprehend information, ideas, and processes.

5. **Critical listening** demands that you both interpret and evaluate the message, which makes it the most sophisticated and difficult kind of listening. It demands that you go beyond understanding the message to interpreting it, judging its strengths and weaknesses, and assigning it some value. You'll practice this sort of listening in class. A careful consumer also uses critical listening to evaluate sales pitches, campaign speeches, financial advice, and arguments offered by controversial talk-show guests. When you listen critically, you decide whether to accept or reject ideas and perhaps to act on someone's advice.

A common thread that runs through all of these strategies is that of **active listening:** listening with your whole body, not just your mind. You are demonstrating active listening when you face the person who is talking, adopt an open posture toward him or her, make direct eye contact, and reflect an attitude of comfort and relaxation. If your bodily posture is tense and your hands and feet are actively moving out of nervous energy, you may be active in one sense of the term but certainly not in the sense of creating a comfortable environment for the person speaking.

In addition to practicing active listening, you also can practice **reflective listening:** seizing the chance to talk to the person speaking, paraphrasing what you think you have heard to see if you have captured the person's meaning. Echoing the words of the other is especially helpful in meeting situations, where your purpose is to make sure you understand each other. Finally, in such settings, it is helpful to practice the 70–30 rule: Listen 70 percent of the time, and speak 30 percent of the time.[14] In this way, you will maximize your ability to actually comprehend and critique what is being said. It is much more difficult to accomplish these tasks if you are the one talking (or listening to yourself planning what you want to say, once you have the chance to speak)!

**Comprehending and Critiquing the Message**    Fully comprehending what's being said requires that you understand the three essential aspects of speech content: ideas, structure, and supporting materials. You must understand clearly what ideas you're being asked to accept, how they relate to each other, and what sorts of facts and opinions underlie them. A useful strategy to employ in gaining comprehension is to engage in what may be called **decentering,** which is the process of engaging others' ideas on their terms rather than your own. Your values and beliefs need to be decentered to place the other's rationale for speaking at the center of your analysis. As Johnson points out, "Decentering occurs during listening when the listener assumes the cognitive perspective of the speaker in order to understand the speaker's intended meaning."[15] The following questions may aid in cognitively assessing the speaker's meaning:

- Do I understand the ideas?
- What's the main thrust of the speech?
- Does the speaker's message correspond with other things I know to be true?
- Does the speaker provide supporting materials and acceptable explanations?
- Do these explanations support the speaker's conclusions?

Listening for any of these purposes may be your primary aim at a given time. You also may have other purposes during a specific occasion—perhaps listening to see if the speaker is angry or finding yourself impressed with the artful manner in which the speaker handles a controversial topic. However, this will not be the major reason for attending to what is said. Assuming that you are, for the most part, listening for comprehension and attempting to assess the value of the speaker's ideas or proposal, how do you employ decentering to make sure you can accomplish your objective? Asking three more questions will help you do so:

**What are the main ideas of the speech?**    Determine the central idea or claim, and look for the statements that help the speaker to develop it. These main ideas should be the foundation on which the speaker builds the speech. The next time you listen to a political commercial, listen for the main ideas: Are you encouraged to support a new candidate because of what she or he proposes to do? Or are you encouraged to vote because the incumbent has failed in some specific way to support goals the new candidate thinks should be supported? Does the commercial sell you on the candidate or negate the incumbent's value? Always know what ideas you're being sold.

**How are the main ideas arranged?** Once you've identified the main ideas, assess the relationships between them. If the speaker extols the accomplishments of the Clinton administration, for instance, but leaves out references to the sex scandals, is this an important or relevant omission? Does the account gloss over what otherwise might paint a different picture of that presidency? Let your experience in the world guide you here, but keep an open mind. In other words, identify what the structure of ideas is, and then probe the speaker's use of that form.

**What kinds of materials support the main ideas?** Consider the timeliness, quality, and content of the supporting materials. Are facts and opinions derived from sources too old to be relevant to today's problems? Is the speaker quoting the best experts? Ask yourself whether the materials clarify, amplify, and strengthen the main ideas of the speech. For example, if someone tells you to protest next year's 9 percent tuition increase, consider the following: If your school charges $15,000 tuition per year, which would increase costs $1,350, the protest may well be justified; if it charges $25 per credit hour, protesting an overall $70 to $75 increase (assuming 32 credits across a year, such an increase would raise the cost by about $72) may not be worth the effort and ill will. Examine the facts' ability to support the conclusion, and be sensitive to the types of supporting materials used: Are you getting facts and figures or only some vague endorsements from self-interested parties?

In other words, to comprehend the content, make sure you understand what ideas, relationships, and evidence you're being asked to accept.

## The Ethical Listener

Being an **ethical listener** is hard work. It means committing yourself to knowing why you are listening and to fairly assessing what you are hearing. It may mean postponing judgment until all of the evidence from this speech is in or until you've had a chance to check for yourself whether the ideas and information presented are worthy of belief or action. Above all, it means hearing the other person out before shutting down. Your opinion as to whether the speech is good/bad, just/unjust, fair/unfair, or true/false is critical in protecting yourself and others from inflated claims, dated information, and no-good cheats.

The "How to" box on the next page provides some general guidelines for how to be an active and ethical listener. In addition, an ethical listener is committed to asking most if not all of the following questions:

THE SITUATION

1. *How does the situation affect this speech and my understanding of it?* Is this the featured speaker or a warm-up act? Is the speaker expected to deal with particular themes or subjects? Am I in tune with this speech occasion?

Speeches in churches, at basketball games, and during business lunches are very different from each other, and you must adjust your judgment-making criteria accordingly.

2. *How does the physical environment affect speaking and listening?* Is it too hot or too cold? Is the room too big or too small? Are there other distractions? The physical environment can have an important effect on your listening, hence making active listening more difficult as well as more critical.

### THE SPEAKER

3. *What do I know about the speaker?* The reputation of this person will influence you whether you want it to or not. Are you being unduly deferential or hypercritical of the speaker just because of his or her reputation? Don't let such reactions get in the way of critical listening.

4. *How believable do I find the speaker?* Are there things about the person's actions, demeanor, and words that make you accepting or suspicious? Figure out why you're reacting positively or negatively, and then ask yourself whether it's reasonable for you to believe this person.

5. *Is the speaker adequately prepared?* Imprecise remarks, repetitions, backtracking, vague or missing numbers, and the lack of solid testimony are all signs of a poorly prepared speaker. For example, a talk about how audiences influence TV programming decisions should discuss, among other things, the networks' use of focus groups. If the speaker doesn't discuss this, you'll know that he or she hasn't gone very far into the topic. Similarly, if the speaker can't explain the difference between the Arbitron and Nielsen rating systems, you should question the reliability of other information in the speech.

## How to
## Be an Active and Ethical Listener

Use the **RRA technique** to improve your listening skills:

- *Review* what the speaker has said. Mentally summarize the key ideas presented thus far each time the speaker initiates a new topic.
- *Relate* the message to what you already know. As you bring more ideas to bear on what you're hearing, your ability to listen effectively will increase.

- *Anticipate* what the speaker might say next. Use your expectations to focus on the content of the message. If they are accurate, you know you're tuned in.

If you Review, Relate, and Anticipate, you will keep your attention centered on the message.

6. *What's the speaker's attitude toward the audience?* How is the audience being treated: cordially or condescendingly? Are they considered as individuals or as a general group? Does the speaker treat audience members as inferiors or as equals? Answering these questions will help you not only to understand your own experience but also to form some questions for the speaker after the speech.

THE MESSAGE

7. *How solid are the ideas being presented?* We've been hammering on this point throughout the chapter because it's crucial to assess the ideas presented in terms of your own knowledge and experience. Just one warning: You could be mistaken yourself, so don't automatically dismiss new ideas. That's how you stagnate intellectually. Do, however, listen all the more carefully when ideas seem strange. Also make sure that you understand them and that they're well supported.

8. *Are the ideas well structured?* Are important ideas missing? For example, anyone who talks about surfing the web and only refers to using Excite as a search engine is missing several other important means of finding information. In addition, if the speaker goes back and forth between search engines and Internet service providers without clearly demarcating the difference, you will have problems following the internal logic of the presentation. Structural relationships between ideas are what give them solidity and coherence as a package.

9. *Is sufficient evidence offered?* You can skip ahead to Chapter 15 and see some of the tests of evidence and reasoning that you should make when faced with crucial decisions based on a speech you're hearing. The world is filled with slipshod reasoning and flawed evidence. Bad reasoning and a refusal to test the available evidence are, after all, what led the U.S. high command to believe that Pearl Harbor was an absolutely safe port in 1941. The recent movie *Pearl Harbor* has brought that fact home to a new generation of listeners. Listen for evidence, and write down the key parts so you can mull them over, asking yourself if this information is good enough to use as a basis for changing your mind. Adopt a "show me" attitude.

You certainly won't ask all nine of these questions every time you hear a speech. Remember that your listening purposes vary considerably from occasion to occasion. You'll need all nine questions only when honing your critical-listening skills at times of significant decision making, such as determining which candidate to vote for, what lifestyle to follow, or which side to support over where to put an expensive municipal stadium. Tailor your listening practices to your purpose for attending a speech.

**Taking Good Notes**

What we said earlier bears repeating: You will have to practice your listening skills to improve them. You must train yourself, and one of the easiest ways to do that while in college is to work on notetaking. As you become a better notetaker, you'll also become a better listener. Here are some tips for improving your notetaking skills:

**Get organized.** Develop your own notetaking system, and then refine it. Some people like loose-leaf notebooks so that they can add, rearrange, or remove notes; others like the tidiness of spiral- or glue-bound notebooks. Whichever you choose, use separate notebooks for different courses and life experiences to avoid confusion—and learn to file. Also set aside a few minutes each day to review the syllabi for your classes, scan your readings, and review previous class sessions' notes. This will prepare you to ask questions while the lectures or readings are still fresh in your mind, and it will help you to keep oriented to the class. In turn, being oriented to what's going on helps you take notes on the most important materials.

**Leave 2- to 3-inch margins when taking notes.** When reviewing your notes later, that marginal area will provide space for making additional comments. A great way to review and study is to write critical comments about what you agree or disagree with, what you don't understand, what you think is significant, and what you've found to be confirmed or contradicted by another source. Providing such critical commentary is an important stage in merging the material in your notes with your own thoughts.

**Develop a notetaking scheme that works for you.** Consider the possibilities:

- *Outline form.* Making a conscious effort to outline a speech or lecture as you hear it will help you to isolate the important ideas, structure, and supporting evidence.
- *Abbreviations.* Some of the abbreviations you'll want to use are obvious: the ampersand (&) for *and* and *w/o* for *without.* Some abbreviations go with particular subject matters, as when business majors write *mgt* and *acctg* for *management* and *accounting,* respectively, and when biology majors use the *F* and *C* symbols for *male* and *female.* Other abbreviations will be your own. (Just make sure that you can remember the ones you invent!)
- *Multicolors.* You'll probably profit from color coding—for example, using black or blue ink for the main notes, red for questions or disagreements, and green for additional content.

By taking these actions, you're no longer a couch or a desk potato, a passive listener. You're an engaged, active listener who's demonstrating how public speaking should work as a two-way channel. The more you practice, the more effectively that channel will carry two-way traffic.

# Special Needs for Critical Listening in the Classroom

Your speech classroom is set up to teach you multiple listening skills that will be of great use for the rest of your life. You may not think these skills will be important, but others do. The American Management Association, for example, advertises a seminar called "Listen Up! A Strategic Approach to Better Listening" for sales professionals. This two-day seminar costs only $1,235 for nonmembers and $1,075 for members.[16] It is evident that the business world takes the issue of listening skills seriously.

Your classrooms are excellent settings for practicing new listening skills and for refining old ones. Use the Speech Evaluation Form (Figure 2.4, p. 44) as a checklist when listening to speeches. Doing so will sharpen your skills and force you to consider a full range of speechmaking dimensions. During this term, you also can improve your listening skills in the following ways:

1. Practice critiquing the speeches of other students. Practice outlining techniques. Take part in postspeech discussions, and ask questions of speakers. You can learn as much from listening well as you can from speaking yourself.

2. Listen critically to discussions, lectures, and student-teacher interactions in your other classes. You're surrounded with public communication that's worth analyzing. You can easily spot effective and ineffective speech techniques in all your classes.

3. Listen critically to speakers outside class. Attend public lectures, city council meetings, and political or religious rallies. You'll be amazed by the range of talent, techniques, and styles exhibited by the diversity of speakers and speeches around you.

4. Examine the supporting materials, arguments, and language used in newspapers and magazines. Refine your critical-listening skills by practicing critical reading. Together, critical listening and critical reading represent the skills of critical thinking that you need to survive in this world. **Critical thinking** is the process of consciously examining the content and logic of messages to determine their bases in the world of ideas and to assess their rationality. Critical thinking is the backbone of evaluation. It's what happens when you listen and when you read the messages of others with your brain fully engaged. Don't leave home without it!

5. Consider the role culture plays in the speaker's crafting of her or his ideas. Not everyone will speak as you do—not even people who agree with you. Taking cultural differences into account and, through decentering, taking the position of the other to assess the intended meaning will go a long way toward minimizing erroneous interpretations.

Overall, then, listening makes public speaking a reciprocal activity. Listeners seek to meet their diverse needs—ranging from personal enjoyment to critical decision making—through specialized listening skills designed for each listening purpose. When both speakers and listeners work at making the speech transaction succeed, public speaking reaches its full potential as a medium of human integration and social identity.

People may vary between and among these various approaches to listening. Knowing in advance what the person is listening for will assist you in developing your message.

## ■ CHAPTER SUMMARY

We began this chapter with an overview of the basic elements of the speechmaking process. The model stressed the importance of the images of self and others in the process of fashioning messages to communicate ideas clearly and effectively. The elements of that model—speaker, listener, message, feedback, situation, channel, and cultural context—were then discussed in more specific terms. Developing community within a culturally diverse world means that you must integrate the elements of the model in such a way as to enhance your effectiveness as a member of that community.

The second major section of this chapter focused on the role of listening. Developing an awareness of the manner in which people seek to learn from you makes it easier to adapt your message to gain their attention and, potentially, their support.

In addition to knowing how listeners approach the speech situation, being an ethical listener means understanding the role of comprehending and critiquing messages. In fact, having that knowledge will help you evaluate the adequacy of your own message. If you can satisfy your own understanding and critique, you've made progress toward meeting the expectations of others, as you often are your own worst critic. Given an understanding of the message, you are in a position to ethically assess what you hear. Taking good notes also will increase your listening ability and have a positive impact on your academic performance. Practicing and refining your listening skills in your speech class, as well as other classes, will help you to acquire improved tools for success in the worlds of college, business, politics, and social life.

## ■ KEY TERMS

active listening  (p. 67)

appreciative listening  (p. 66)

audience analysis  (p. 56)

auditory listeners  (p. 64)

aural channel  (p. 58)

communication
    competence  (p. 61)

communication rules  (p. 60)

content  (p. 55)

credibility  (p. 54)

critical listening  (p. 67)

critical thinking  (p. 73)

culture  (p. 60)

decentering  (p. 68)

delayed feedback  (p. 57)

discriminative
    listening  (p. 67)

ethical listener  (p. 69)

ethos  (p. 55)

feedback  (p. 57)

hearing  (p. 62)

immediate feedback  (p. 57)

listening  (p. 62)

listening for
    comprehension  (p. 67)

model of the speechmaking
    process  (p. 52)

paralinguistic channel  (p.58)
pictorial channel  (p.58)
process-oriented
  listener  (p.63)
reasons-oriented
  listener  (p.63)
reflective listening  (p.67)
results-oriented listener  (p.63)

RRA technique  (p.70)
RRP listening styles  (p.63)
rules-driven listeners  (p.64)
self-absorbed listeners  (p.64)
self-images  (p.53)
social context  (p.58)
SUR listening styles  (p.64)
tactile listeners  (p.64)

therapeutic listening  (p.67)
transactional experience  (p.58)
unfocused listeners  (p.64)
VAT listening styles  (p.64)
verbal channel  (p.58)
visual channel  (p.58)
visual listeners  (p.64)

## ASSESSMENT ACTIVITIES

1. To learn to assess your own and others' speeches, watch them on videotape. Pause each time something strikes your attention, and jot down notes as you watch and listen. After viewing a given speech several times, answer the following questions:

   a. Does the speech seek to define issues, share information, take a position in a debate, or call for social change? Does it have more than one of these general purposes? If so, which predominates? Why do you think so?

   b. How does the choice of channel influence the speaker's approach to this audience? Is this the most appropriate channel to use in conveying the speaker's message? Why or why not?

   c. Does the speaker appear to be rhetorically sensitive to the situation and the audience? Given the content, structure, and style of the speech, what image does the speaker appear to have of the audience? Does the speaker view listeners as passive consumers or as active, intelligent critics of the message?

   d. What attitudes might the audience bring to this speech? Why might they be listening to the speaker?

   e. How would you rate the speaker's skills and competencies? Does the speaker seem knowledgeable, self-assured, and trustworthy? Does the speaker's use of verbal and nonverbal communication result in a message that is clear, forceful, and compelling? Why or why not?

   f. List at least three ways the speaker could improve on this particular speech. Refer to the model discussed in this chapter as you formulate your answer.

2. Keep a listening log. For two days, record your oral communication interactions, noting to whom you were speaking, what your listening purposes were, and how effectively you listened given your purposes. Include talks with roommates, discussions in class meetings, coffee shop and lunchroom conversations, and chats that occur during evening activities. After completing the log, do a self-assessment: What are your strengths and weaknesses as a listener? What changes do you need to make to become a more consistently active and ethical listener?

## REFERENCES

1. Speechmaking is a transactional, rather than a one-way, mode of communication. Just as the speaker offers a message, so the listeners offer messages in the form of feedback. Speakers and audiences have mutual obligations to be forthright and honest in their appraisal and treatment of each other. Thus, they

play complementary roles during public speeches; hence, the word *transaction* clearly applies to this sort of communication exchange.

2. For a contemporary perspective, see James Price Dillard and Michael Pfau, eds., *The Persuasion Handbook: Developments in Theory and Practice* (Thousand Oaks, CA: Sage, 2002).

3. Kazuo Nishiyama, *Japan–U.S. Business Communication* (Dubuque, IA: Kendall-Hunt, 1995), 105.

4. Terri Morrison, Wayne A. Conaway, and George A. Borden, *Kiss, Bow, or Shake Hands: How to Do Business in Sixty Countries* (Holbrook, MA: Adams Media, 1994), 207.

5. Billie M. Thompson, "Listening Disabilities: The Plight of Many," *Perspectives on Listening*, edited by Andrew D. Wolvin and Carolyn Gwynn Coakley (Norwood, NJ: Ablex, 1993), 124–169. The information cited is on p. 138.

6. The quotation comes from the International Listening Association's webpage. Available online: <http://www.listen.org>.

7. Peter Meyer, "So You Want the President's Job . . ." *Business Horizons* 41 (1998): 2.

8. Rosemary V. Wood and Ruth T. Bennett, "Effective Communication via Listening Styles," *Business* 39 (1989): 45–48.

9. Jackie Taylor, "Learning Styles: A Practical Tool for Improved Communications," *Supervision* 59 (1998): 18–19.

10. Herbert Greenberg and Jay J. Avelino, "Can You Improve Someone's Listening Skills?" Available online: <http://www.aednet.org/ced/dec96/listen.htm>. Accessed June 10, 2001.

11. Mary Alice Griffin, Donnie McGahee, and John Slate, "Effective Listening Skills." Available online: <http://www.bvte.ecu.edu/ACBMEC/p1998/griffin.htm>. Accessed June 10, 2001.

12. Nishiyama, 112.

13. Andrew Wolvin and Carolyn Coakley, *Listening*, 5th ed. (Boston: McGraw-Hill, 1996).

14. Bill Prince and Patrick Milliken, "Tips on the Hiring Process: Effective Listening Skills." Available online: <http://www.geni-jobnet.com/hiringtips/home.htm>. Accessed June 10, 2001.

15. Jack Johnson, "Functions and Processes of Inner Speech in Listening," *Perspectives on Listening*, edited by Andrew D. Wolvin and Carolyn Gwynn Coakley (Norwood, NJ: Ablex, 1993), 170–181. The information cited is on pp. 178–179.

16. American Management Association. Available online: <http://www.tregistry.com/s0112271.htm>.

# Chapter 4

# Public Speaking and Cultural Life

*Monica was distraught. "I can't go out there!" As a delegate from the Speech Communication Student Association, she was about to speak at a gathering of the campus African American, Hispanic, and international students' associations on working together to make the city council reconsider a rezoning decision, one that would wipe out two blocks of student apartments and student-oriented stores. "Here I am, a white speech major born in Iowa, a state that's 94 percent white. And there they are, from Chicago and New York, even from foreign countries totally different from mine. They'll resent me. What do we have in common?" "That's the question you must answer," replied her best friend, Bill. "What do you have in common? You're all students here. You all live in or next to the neighborhood about to be destroyed. You all enjoy gathering at those stores and shops on Tripp Street. You have a lot in common!" "Well, I guess we do," said Monica, but . . ." "But nothing!" said Bill. "Quit emphasizing your differences. Sure, you have them, but think of what you share and how your differences will become a collective strength in front of the city council. You'll be part of a broad spectrum of students confronting city councilors who think of this only as a neighborhood with funny-smelling food. That's what you should talk about."*

Training in public speaking is, in part, a matter of learning about the cultural expectations of one's audience. Speakers must learn what those expectations are in order to be seen as socially competent and conceptually relevant to others. Speakers who want to affect audiences must learn to be exceptionally good at phrasing ideas and engaging the feelings of others within the communication traditions of their listeners' cultural traditions.

Learning about the cultural practices and expectations of one's listeners, however, is easier said than done. There is always, perhaps, a tension between one's self and society, between the individual and the collectivity, especially in the

United States, where almost all children have been taught to maximize their potentials and to be their own persons. On the one hand, you are you—a unique individual with your own life experiences and your own thoughts about the world. On the other hand, you always are marked by social categories. You are an individual, yes, but you also are reminded regularly that you're gay, of Polish descent, twenty-something, an Episcopalian, a junior in college who works as a salesclerk, or whatever the case may be. You are an individual, but part of your self-identity—and certainly a major part of others' perceptions of you—is socially and culturally determined.[1]

In a world where identities are both individually and collectively diverse, you must answer some difficult questions as you prepare to talk publicly:

- Can you respect individual differences and cultural diversity while attempting to get a group of people to think alike and work together?
- Can you recognize the diversity of your audience's experiences, even their ideological schisms, while you nonetheless attempt to enact a public image that is credible?
- Can you be true to yourself and your commitments while adapting to others?
- Can you successfully negotiate the differences between what audiences expect of you and what you expect of yourself?

These are not easy questions to answer, and you don't think of them every time you rise to say a few words. When you face an audience as different from you as Monica felt her audience was from her, however, you'll want to follow her friend Bill's advice and look for the **common ground**—the shared beliefs, attitudes, values, goals, and desires that turn a group of listeners into a people unified in thought and action.[2]

In this chapter, we discuss relationships between public speaking and cultural life by first examining the components of culture—especially oral culture—more specifically. Then, we review some strategies that you can use to unify and direct your listeners' thoughts and actions, even when they come from diverse cultural backgrounds.

## Understanding Cultural Processes

At its simplest, a **culture** is a social group's system of meanings. We can think of culture as the sorts of meanings that a given people attaches to persons, places, ideas, rituals, things, routines, and communication behaviors. You've been taught since you were an infant who is powerful or not (persons), how to act at home and in public buildings (places), what's true and false about the things you encounter in the world (ideas), how to greet family and strangers (routines), and the most effective and ineffective ways to get favors from your boss (communication behaviors). Your culture is thus comprised of pieces of social knowledge that represent how you've been taught to think and act successfully within the world of human beings.

All of this is true for everyone else, as well. We've all been taught about persons, places, rituals, ideas, and the rest. Unfortunately, the meanings that you've been given for those entities may not be the same meanings someone else has learned; after all, your experiences are different from those of others. This happens not only on an individual basis but on a group basis. In some important ways, men and women have been given different social educations. So have whites and Hispanics, people who are poor and rich, and those who hear and those who cannot.

All of our differences in psychological, social, political, economic, and behavioral—which is to say *cultural*—education can cause speakers some serious problems. But before you think about strategies for responding to key points of **cultural diversity** in your speeches, you should think more about how diversity affects your everyday life.

## Orality and Cultural Life

We talked briefly about *orality*, or oral culture, in Chapter 1. Now, let's think about that idea more concretely. Earlier, we noted that your relationships with others are built primarily via face-to-face talk. Direct, in person, spoken connections between people generate the essence of what it is to be human. Standing up in front of others—to recite a Christmas piece in a play, to declare your maturity in a Jewish community, to demonstrate you know how to read or spell in school, or to pledge allegiance to your sorority or fraternity family—is traditionally, in all societies, a way of manifesting and marking your membership in a community. Oral performance is simply the most fundamental method for bonding the individual to the group.

What makes face-to-face, oral communication so important to groups? Media theorist Walter Ong has identified a series of characteristics of the *sounded word*,[3] which include the following items, among others:

**Speech tends to be integrative.** In speech, you often draw together ideas or stereotypes held by the group, attaching them to people and events. Such aggregating or integrating of cultural beliefs and specific subject matters leads to oral formulae (not just "the student" but "the bright student," not just "the warrior" but "the brave warrior"). References in oral speech to "workable" or "practical" plans, "glorious" dawns and "star-lit" skies, and the like come off as clichés in written language but are used regularly in oral language because of their familiarity and shared use across groups. Speech thus integrates members of a society by identifying the personal characteristics that are valued by others and by recollecting reactions to the world that are shared across peoples. Speech, therefore, not only is about something, a *policy*, but it simultaneously reassembles a group, a *polity*.

**Speech tends to be redundant.** You often repeat yourself in public speaking, saying the same thing in more than one way. Notice that the last sentence could have ended at the comma, for the point was presumably clear as written. In speech, however, the second half likely would have been added, giving listeners a chance to catch the point again, in case it wasn't clear in its first phrasing. That's oral language: redundant or repetitious, with backlooping to help people keep up with the flow of the conversation.

**Speech tends to be traditionalist.** A group's traditional beliefs and values usually are reflected in public oral language. Sayings such as "It's six of one and half a dozen of another," "That's the way the ball bounces," "A bird in the hand is worth two in the bush," and "Better safe than sorry" capture traditional beliefs for many Westerners. That is, "There's no difference between two alternatives," "There are things you can't control in life," "You shouldn't risk what you already have for something that could go wrong," and "Take the sure alternative." Such sayings live in oral culture and so tend to appear in speeches. Not all such sayings are conservative; for instance, "Let your reach outstretch your grasp" urges you to take chances. Most of them are, however, probably because they have arisen out of situations in which the group or society is reining in individualism. "Strike while the iron's hot" also suggests that immediate action is valued over a wait-and-see attitude. So, in reality, traditionalist epithets or aphorisms can be either conservative or more radical in the West, for that's the way Western culture is: contradictory in its view of group safety and individual initiative. Oral communication draws on both kinds of sayings, which so often mark speechmaking.

**Speech tends to be concrete.** You might write "Relationships between blacks and whites in America are complex," but in a speech, you're more likely to be effective if you get specific:

> Two-thirds of our undergraduates of all ethnicities live within nine blocks of campus, side by side in the same student apartments. While blacks and whites in the state of Iowa tend to be separated, in Iowa City, the university draws them together, standing in the same lines at John's Grocery, drinking beer at the Sports Column and coffee at the Java House, listening to live music side by side on the Ped Mall. Sharing not only classrooms but life situations means that blacks and whites in Iowa City cannot ignore each other.

Here, the concrete references to particular places in the neighboring environment help listeners visualize ideas. This is important in oral communication, where the audience cannot reread something that wasn't grasped the first time.

**Speech is agonistically toned.**[4] This is Ong's phrase. It suggests that when people gather together to make decisions publicly by speech, things tend to get a little heated. It's as though public speaking has taken the place of ancient combat rituals. One can disengage when writing, building complex, philosophically structured bases for one's ideas. It's not so in speech. It's immediate. The disagreements usually occur between people who are present to each other and in front of the group that's making a decision. So, public speakers often become aggressive when a group's going to decide an issue. Speech is personal, flowing out of your mouth and body; you actually *perform* it. Writing can be circulated when you're not there and so is more distanced. Speech is immediate, personal—and therein lies its feistiness yet power.

**Speech is participatory.**  The audience, likewise, is personally involved. It's there, part of the environment; the speech is aimed at the folks who comprise the audience. They're often addressed directly, even personally. So, you might say:

> How many of you have plans to stop at the bloodmobile at the student
> union today? How many? How about you, Jill—are you going? Jake?
> Lisa? Maurice?

You cannot make people read something, but you have a very good chance of making them listen—of making them participate in public interaction.

**Speech is situational.**  It occurs in the here and now. You can read a newspaper in the bathroom or at the kitchen table; you might read a book a chapter at a time before you go to sleep. But speaking happens right here, right now. At its best, a public speech deals with issues that are visible in the immediate situation, in the actual lives of the listeners who are there. If listeners don't know that, you must convince them that such is the case:

> So, how many of you have stopped for a drink at a fountain in one of the
> university buildings today? How many times do you figure that you stop at
> a drinking fountain during a week? Three? Four? Twice a day? Even if you
> take a drink only three times a week, you have about a 1 in 20 chance of
> ingesting enough lead to make you sick. For, you see, . . .

Here, the speaker tries to make a water-quality speech relevant to the particular context within which listeners find themselves—as students living in a college campus environment.

So, oral culture tends to be dominated publicly by speech communication that is integrative, redundant, traditionalist, concrete, agonistically toned, participatory, and situational. All of these characteristics, really, suggest that the public speaker relies on group (cultural) resources when putting a speech together. This is not to say that knowledge of your topic, care in phrasing your own position on that topic, technical information, and awareness of how speeches usually are put together in a particular society are not important. Of course they are. It is to say, however, that the use of public, oral channels for communication within some group or society demands care in approaching the act of talking itself. Relationships between individuals and groups that are maintained in oral settings tend to require knowledge, as well, of oral language traditions of the kind we've been reviewing.

## The Dimensions of Culture

Public speaking, therefore, is a culture-bound activity or performance. If culture is a concept broad enough to include all of a society's meanings for ideas, things, and activities, then we need a systematic vocabulary to break it down into units for analysis and study. This vocabulary is a bit abstract, but it's easier to understand if you focus on three dimensions of culture: culture as lived, culture as thought, and culture as performed (see Figure 4.1).

**Culture as Lived: Demographic Categories of Social Organization**    One way to examine cultural life is via the social categories through which others define us. You've learned that others sometimes define you by gender (male, female, transsexual), racial or ethnic background (African American, Asian American), age (young, middle aged), sexual orientation (straight, gay, bisexual), nationality (Finn, Tibetan), educational background (high school dropout, college grad), reference group (Act Up! member, Disabled American Veteran), religion (Sufi, Presbyterian), disability (hearing impaired, visually challenged), socioeconomic status (under-class welfare recipient, upper-class taxpayer). Insofar as you think about yourself or others via such categories, these social markers become amazingly important in your relationships. In the story of Monica, for example, she thought about herself in terms of race, gender, and reference or organizational group. Such markers can become determinative of culture as lived.[5]

**FIGURE 4.1**    **The Dimensions of Culture**

*Culture is multifaceted and intermixed. Living, thinking, and performing culture is taken for granted within your own community of friends.*

*Culture as Lived:* **Social categories (gender, race) of identity**

*Culture as Thought:* **Ideas and values given to you by others**

*Culture as Performed:* **Ways you are taught to act publicly**

*Every culture includes subcultures and co-cultures that must be taken into account when communicating.*

Culture as lived—especially as you move out of your immediate neighborhood (i.e., away from the people who know you most intimately as an individual)—becomes increasingly focused on cultural differences. These differences have always been around, although the black, Hispanic, gay/lesbian, and women's empowerment movements of the 1960s and 1970s, the growing emphasis on cultural diversity in the 1980s, and passage of the Americans with Disabilities Act in 1991 have sensitized most of us to their roles. **Multiculturalism**—the recognition that a country such as the United States possesses not a unitary culture with several **subcultures** but rather **co-cultures** that interpenetrate yet are separate from one another—is a fact of life.[6] And you'd better be sensitive to cultural differences when you're speaking on topics that are subject to cultural variation.

**Culture as Thought: Ideology and Hegemony**     Not only have you been acculturated to act in particular ways through your experiences with others in everyday life, but you've also been conditioned to think in particular patterns, as well.[7] A system of thought that embodies social values and perceptual orientations to the world is called an **ideology.** Ideologies have a power in your life that is naturalized[8]—that is, thought of as "what everyone knows" or "how things are done around here." Ideologically grounded values and perceptions of the world are rooted in cognitions that always have been part of your environment, unquestioned and regularly reinforced by people important in your life—parents, siblings, friends, and authority figures in your community, church, and schools. A person in your locale who doesn't believe in love will be thought deviant, someone who prefers collard greens to lettuce will be regarded as a little strange, and someone who leaves his or her family (blood ties) to join a Hari Krishna community might even by chased down by deprogrammers.

Ideologies are powerful not only because familial, religious, social, and political institutions reinforce them but because of your own volition. You seldom question the fundamental tenets of living with like-minded others; you even reinforce them in your own talk to others. For example, you're liable to rein in a child running away from the lunch table without having first been excused by adults by saying, "That's not the way things are done around here, kid." In your own past, when a bigger and older bully pushed in front of you in the line for the drinking fountain, you likely thought that's simply the way the world is—that the bigger and older folks rule the roost. In these instances, you internalized a series of cultural rules and beliefs, integrating them into your perceptual and valuative equipment.

**Hegemony** is a word for relationships between more powerful and less powerful people that are maintained, either in part or in whole, through the complicity of the less powerful people. Hegemonic relationships often are signaled by phrases such as "That's the way we do things," "That's the way it goes," and "That's a fact of life." Relationships between social classes (rich and poor), racial groups (e.g., white and nonwhite), and even the sexes (male and female) often are maintained as much by complicitous acceptance of one's status as by direct force. The idea of hegemony accounts, in part, for why it's so difficult to change social relations quickly. Even when women or Hispanics or gays have been liberated from some dimension of their oppressions by others, not all of them join in the chorus of "Free at last! Free at last! Thank God Almighty, we're free at last!" There still are women who sneer at feminist thought, Mexican Americans who don't look forward to the revolution, and gays, lesbians, and bisexuals who haven't come out of the closet. Naturalized attitudes and social relations resist alteration. Culture as thought has a lock on many minds, thanks to the forces of ideology and hegemony.[9]

**Culture as Performed: Embodiment and Enactment**    The rules and thoughts governing life can be put into words, such as when you recite the Pledge of Allegiance, promise to tell the truth in court testimony, or decline to loan a friend money by saying "Neither a borrower nor a lender be." More usually, however, cultural rules and the social roles that we come to accept, or at least live out, are not only heard but also seen. **Embodiment** is the process whereby ideas, attitudes, values, and social character are given corporeal existence in communication acts.[10]

You come to understand what a *senator* is by watching your own senator's news conferences and reading his or her newsletters. A television show such as *Everyone Loves Raymond* exaggerates husband-wife and parent-child talk. The comedic acting out of gender and generational roles serves to critique the relationships between too many husbands and wives and too many parents and children. In addition, on *ER*, we see how the personal and professional aspects of people's lives actually are inseparable. The idea of police brutality was understood by one generation of Americans through watching the use of nightsticks and cattle prods on civil rights demonstrators in the 1960s and by another generation viewing the capture of Rodney King in the 1990s. You learn many, perhaps even most, of the cultural rules you know because particular people embody them in face-to-face or mass-mediated activities.

In turn, then, you work to enact them. **Enactment** is a communication process whereby a person behaves in a manner consistent with society's cultural rules. Lawyers go to school to learn to interview clients and present cases in court; in short, they learn to think and then act like lawyers are expected to in their country. Individual athletic achievements often are recounted with opening phrases such as "I couldn't have done this without my teammates, who . . ." Such modest behavior is consonant with rules for sports etiquette. In this course, you practice giving speeches with introductions, bodies, and conclusions on the assumption that such an arrangement for public talks is expected. Rules for speaking are grounded in audience expectations, which you try to enact so you'll be judged a competent speaker.[11]

Culture as performed, therefore, takes us to the heart of this book—how it is that members of a society communicate with each other. The forms of public talk (introductions, bodies, conclusions), the substance of public talk (accepted ways of reasoning), the relationships between speaker and audience (grounded in lived experiences), and even the outcomes of public speeches (who will listen to whom) are affected by your skills in performing those speeches in culturally sensible and accepted ways.

*Performance* should not be thought of here as a theatrical term, as acting out a script in such a way as to become someone else. In communication studies, the idea of performance is tied to life roles and cultural rules, not to artistic license.[12] Theatrical performance is judged by aesthetic standards. Speech performance is judged by community and pragmatic standards, by whether people accept you, by what you have to say, and by how you say it. You learn these standards by seeing others embody them, and then you enact them yourself in hopes of affecting the beliefs, attitudes, values, and behaviors of others. To quote historian Doris Kearns Goodwin, that enactment personalizes ideas "so that you can hear the music of the speaker's delivery—the pitch of the voice, the inflection, the cadence, the changing rhythm, the alliteration, the pulse, the sense of movement—and most of all, the passion that stirred the heart of an audience and left an indelible mark."[13]

## The Challenge of Speaking in a Multicultural Society

Earlier, we raised this question: Can you respect individual difference and cultural diversity while attempting to get a group of people to think alike and work together? Yes, we think that you can. You can embody in your public oral presentations some generally accepted cultural standards for public interpersonal relationships. What those standards are and how you can embody them are the next topics of discussion.

# Strategies for Unifying Multicultural Audiences

One of any speaker's primary jobs is to acknowledge relevant cultural experiences and expectations affecting listeners' reception of a message, even while calling for unified thought and action. *Relevance* is an important concept here. If you're giving a speech on how to fillet fish, for example, your audience's racial background probably is irrelevant, but if you're talking about federal programs for low-income housing, race likely becomes a relevant issue. If you're discussing police profiling, race is central. So, how can you recognize sociocultural differences and diversity while seeking to get people to work together? Consider the following strategies, which the best speakers have used regularly over the last few years (see also Figure 4.2).

## Recognizing Diversity

If cultural differences between and among audience members are likely to come to people's minds when you're speaking, you should probably recognize them. Even in their differences, after all, members of a group must learn to think and act together. A famous example of this challenge in recent years was the Million Man March on Washington, DC, organized by Minister Louis Farrakhan of the Black Muslin Nation in the fall of 1995. In fact, nearly 1 million people came, including many non-Muslims. Minister Farrakhan had to recognize his listeners' diverse backgrounds so that all, not just Black Muslims, would respond to his message. First, he read from a speech given by a white slaveholder in 1712 who advocated using fear, distrust, and envy to fracture the slave community. Then, he noted:

**FIGURE 4.2**    **Strategic Choices for Unifying Audiences**

*These strategies are not mutually exclusive or necessarily as ordered here. Paying attention to each, however, will assist you in developing messages that are adapted to the cultural context.*

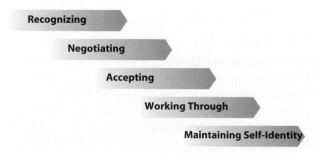

*Jesse Jackson epitomizes the role of the public speaker in acknowledging diverse communities, whether people in Chicago or in the hills of Appalachia.*

And so, as a consequence, we as a people now have been fractured, divided and destroyed, filled with fear, distrust and envy. Therefore, because of fear, envy and distrust of one another, many of us as leaders, teachers, educators, pastors, and persons are still under the control mechanism of our former slave masters and their children.

And now, in spite of all that division, in spite of all that divisiveness, we responded to a call and look at what is present here today. We have here those brothers with means and those who have no means. Those who are light and those who are dark. Those who are educated, those who are uneducated. Those who are businesspeople, those who don't know anything about business. Those who are young, those who are old. Those who are scientific, those who know nothing of science. Those who are religious and those who are irreligious. Those who are Christian, those who are Muslim, those who are Baptist, those who are Methodist, those who are Episcopalian, those of traditional African religion. We've got them all here today.[14]

Minister Farrakhan's reputation as a black militant almost demanded that he include a message of reconciliation between and among the various branches of African American culture. If the Million Man March was to succeed, he had to argue that African Americans, regardless of cultural diversity, had to commit themselves to common goals: "Black man, you don't have to bash white people. All we gotta do is go back home and turn our communities into productive places. All we gotta do is go back home and make our communities a decent and safe place to live."[15] In this case, the speaker recognized diversity but stated his goals in terms of the actions of individuals, not groups. Thus, diversity didn't turn into the kind of divisiveness advocated by the ancient slaveholder of 1712.

Inventorying the diversity of cultures in your audience is a technique that you can quickly learn to use. For example, in a speech on why students in your school's study-abroad program should consider going to school in Malta, you might say:

> Malta has earned its reputation as "The Crossroads of the Mediterranean," and for that reason, it can provide a wonderful social and educational experience for all of you. Those of you who want to learn in English will find classes taught in your native tongue; those with ears for foreign languages will discover a score of them spoken in apartment complexes and restaurants. Churchgoers can find Catholic, Protestant, and Islamic houses of worship. White Eurocentric people and Black Afrocentric people work and play together on Malta. You can take sidetrips to nearby sites reflecting a variety of cultural experiences: You can eat scampi in Italy, cous cous in Morocco, goulash in Croatia, tapas in Spain, or lamb in Sicily. Your palate, and your mind, will be opened to a dozen cultures on Malta, allowing all of you to find a niche for comfortable living in a foreign land.

Even if your topic doesn't seem inherently multicultural, you'll want to be sensitive to diversity all of the time. For example, if you plan to mention dating in a speech on teenage urban lifestyles, think about whether you can assume everyone in your audience practices only heterosexual relationships. When talking about the hypergrowth of city government, don't unnecessarily apply gender to the employees by calling the managers "he" and the secretaries "she."

## Negotiating Multicultural Values

Because audiences often form into groups based on the diverse characteristics of the individuals comprising them, it's likely that different segments see the world in different ways—use some of the same words as others but to mean quite different things. This is because people's **value orientations**—their habitual ways of thinking about positive and negative grounds for human thought and action—tend to become materialized in highly idiosyncratic ways. Consider, for example, how the phrase *family values* was talked about in the 1990s. Everyone supports family values, but a variety of valuative orientations—we can call them *liberal, middling*, and *conservative* ideologies—underlie different people's use of this phrase (see Table 4.1).

These, of course, are simplified versions of people's political positions, but when most people argue about a government policy toward family values, they deal in such simplifications. That *family values* can mean such different things to different people shouldn't be surprising because the issue is a strongly divisive one in American society today. The differences are so great that you can't ignore them when talking about this topic, either. Rather, you're better advised to recognize the differences and define the phrase *family values* carefully, so that your listeners know exactly what you're talking about. Even then, you may well want to negotiate among the varied definitions. You might have to say, "All right, then, on what do we agree? How far can we go together in helping parents raise their children?" It was precisely this kind of thinking that got liberals, conservatives, and middle-of-the-roaders together in 1993 to form a coalition in Congress. That coalition passed the Family and Medical Leave Act in the name of both fostering traditional families (by requiring businesses to pay a parent while staying at home with an infant) and recognizing a child's needs (by guaranteeing him or her parental support in the earliest stages of social life). The middle-of-the-roaders saw this act as a perfect example of family-business-government cooperation and so were equally supportive.

The tricky part of negotiating across valuative differences is to make sure that negotiation doesn't lead to erasure. Differences need not—and usually should not—be ignored or hidden. The best negotiators recognize differences but also assert that they should not stand in the way of cooperation. So, when

---

**TABLE 4.1**   The Diversity of *Family Values*

| IDEOLOGY | BELIEF |
| --- | --- |
| Conservative | American society is in moral decline and must return to older family values. We've become a permissive society characterized by divorce, illegitimacy, juvenile crime, and spoiled children. We must bolster the traditional, two-parent, heterosexual family as the best environment for children and eliminate government (including school) interference with the family's operations. |
| Liberal | American parents should receive more aid in raising their children. Everyone, not just parents, has a stake in making sure that children are cared for, supported, and raised to be good citizens. Because financial resources are so varied in the United States and so many families are troubled, government at the local, state, and national levels must help parents with child care, health care, paid parental leave when children are infants, and other forms of financial assistance. It is better to help all forms of families—single and dual parent, traditional and nontraditional—with their children now than to deal with juveniles in prisons later. |
| Middle-of-the-Road | Raising children should primarily be a matter of parental responsibility but with government safety nets in place. Parents must be made more responsible for the growth and actions of their children yet should have help available in the form of family-planning agencies, subsidized adoption and abortion services, and sex education in the schools. If parents neglect or abuse their children, the state should rescue the children, but overall, parents should be made to take responsibility for their children's care, feeding, and nurturing. |

Elizabeth Bird, director of the Human Rights Campaign and herself a lesbian, asked the antigay Christian Coalition to open a dialogue on family values and lifestyles, she recognized differences but sought a shared commitment to treat those differences respectfully:

> We are, all of us and those we represent, human beings. As Americans, you will have your political candidates; we will have ours. But we could, both of us, ask that our candidates speak the truth to establish their right to leadership, rather than abuse the truth in the interest of one evening's headline. We may work for different outcomes in the elections, but we can engage in an ethic of basic respect and decency.[16]

## Accepting Multiple Paths to Goals

A still more difficult challenge often is to convince people that there are many ways to reach a shared goal. Thus, for example, some colleges and universities allow students to meet a foreign language requirement in varied ways, such as a demonstration of skills (oral or written test), life experiences (having grown up in a household that speaks another language), or in-class instruction (taking enough classes to become proficient). Likewise, smoking-cessation programs often allow smokers to try different approaches to quitting, such as hypnosis, psychotherapy, the patch or nicotine gum, group therapy, and "cold turkey" regimes.

Suppose you're in a situation, however, in which people tend to say, as some parents do to their children, "There's only one way to do this: the right way!" In such a situation, how can a speaker create a sense of tolerance and acceptance of multiple paths leading to a common goal? Metaphors and allegories (see Chapter 10) are useful ways for letting people see the utility of allowing multiple paths to shared goals. In his speech at the Atlanta Exposition in 1894, black social activist Booker T. Washington used the metaphor of the hand, whereby individual ethnic groups (the fingers) were depicted as attached to and a part of the same social system (the hand). In urging the U.S. Forest Service to hire a more culturally diverse workforce, Native American Henri Mann Morton used the metaphors of a former chieftain to argue that multiple paths can lead to the same goal:

> Finally, I would like to leave you with the words of one of our Cheyenne philosophers, High Chief, who said:
>
> In this land there are many horses—red, white, black, and yellow. Yet, it is all one horse.
> There are also birds of every color, red, white, black, and yellow. Yet, it is all one bird. So it is with living things.
> In this land where once there were only Indians, there are difference races, red, white, black, and yellow. Yet, it is all one people.
> It is good and right.

## Rhetorical Framing

For the last 20 years, cognitive psychologists have done research on **framing**, which involves the use of a variety of conceptual borders that can be put on factually equivalent messages. The idea that human beings come to perceive, comprehend, and ultimately evaluate aspects of the world through cognitive frames is an essentially rhetorical notion. It demands that speakers be highly sensitive to how they tell their audiences how to go about looking at the world. According to recent communication research, speakers have several options:

*Metaphorical frames.* Simons argues that much political discussion depends on metaphors used as frames for policies. Benoit, for example, compared the use of bridge metaphors employed by Bill Clinton and Bob Dole in their 1996 acceptance speeches. Clinton was able to make his "bridge to the twenty-first century" metaphor a powerful tool for conceptualizing his agenda, but Dole did not take enough time to develop it well enough to do him any good.

*Narrative frames.* The work done through the 1990s by Stanford communication researcher Shanto Iyengar has focused on story forms in the news. A recent study is that done by Jay Rosen of NYU and Princeton Survey Research Associates of story forms on the front pages of the *New York Times, Washington Post,* and *Los Angeles Times* and four regional papers (*Atlanta Constitution, Idaho Statesman, Rocky Mountain News,* and *Minneapolis Star-Tribune*) during January–February 1999. It found that only 16 percent of the stories were "straight news accounts" of the who-what-when-why-how variety. Most (30 percent) were combative stories of conflict, winners, and losers; 12 percent were explanatory stories about larger trends or historical contexts; 8 percent dealt with public or political policy; and the rest of the stories were written in various minor narrative forms. In a study of the last two weeks of Campaign 2000, Alsina, Davies, and Gronbeck found that over 60 percent of the stories in the *New York Times* and *Washington Post* dealt with candidate personalities and activities, not the issues or policy stands they were taking.

*Valuative frames.* Issues can be framed by values—looking at them ethically, economically, socially, aesthetically, and the like. Gronbeck found that local news broadcasts tended to emphasize dominant community values when reporting the news. Detweiler, Bedell, Salovey, Pronin, and Rothman discovered that arguments featuring positive values ("gain-frames") were more persuasive than those featuring negative values ("loss-frames").

A good way, then, to think about your tasks as a public communicator is to start by thinking about the sorts of rhetorical frames that will most likely be attractive and understandable to your listeners.

*Sources:* Cristina Alsina, Philip E. Davies, and Bruce E. Gronbeck, "Preference Poll Stories in the Last 2 Weeks of Campaign 2000," *American Behavioral Scientist* 44 (2001): 2288–2305; Jerusha B. Detweiler, Brian T. Bedell, Peter Salovey, Emily Pronin, and Alexander J. Rothman, "Message Framing and Sunscreen Use: Gain-Framed Messages Motivate Beach-Goers," *Health Psychology* 18 (1999): 189–196; Bruce E. Gronbeck, "Tradition and Technology in Local Newscasts: The Social Psychology of Form," *Sociological Quarterly* 38 (1997): 361–374; Shanto Iyengar, *Is Anyone Responsible? How Television Frames Political Issues* (Chicago: University of Chicago Press, 1991); Shanto Iyengar and Richard Reeves, eds., *Do the Media Govern? Politicians, Voters, and Reporters in America* (Thousand Oaks, CA: Sage, 1997); Jay Rosen and Princeton Survey Research Associates, "Framing the News: The Triggers, Frames, and Messages in Newspaper Coverage," available online: <www.journalism.org/framing.html>; and Herbert W. Simons with Joanne Morreale and Bruce Gronbeck, *Persuasion in Society* (Thousand Oaks, CA: Sage 2001).

> High Chief was a wise man. He knew that cultural uniquenesses have a strength of their own. At the same time he recognized our common humanity.
>
> You, too, know this, as indicated by your powerful theme of "Strength through Cultural Diversity."[17]

The metaphor of colors is also useful. For instance, Jesse Jackson's political group of the 1980s was called the Rainbow Coalition. The concept of colors suggests how differences can be focused into a whole, just as the color spectrum is blended together to make light. Historical examples also are useful, such as pointing to the success of multinational forces in times of war (the Allies of World War II or the Kosovo campaign), interpersonal and group efforts in times of disaster (people-to-people medical programs in Honduras), and the overcoming of differences in times of celebration (the building of the multiracial South African Olympic team in 1996).

Teaching people to accept multiple paths or cooperative arrangements to shared goals is a technique you must learn to use almost daily in your speaking if you're going to successfully get past those matters that divide listeners into distrustful groups. Understanding the concept of rhetorical framing, as discussed in the "Communication Research Dateline" box on page 91, may help you do so.

## Working through the Lifestyle Choices of Others

An old saying recommends that "When in Rome, do as the Romans do." Often, you do. You might eat with chopsticks and a flat-bottomed spoon when in a Thai restaurant, kiss Romanians on both cheeks when greeting them, or take a siesta after lunch in Mexico. Urging people to accommodate to the lifestyles of other cultures is something you'll need to do on occasion, particularly if that's the only way to get them to come together and that's important to you.

A classic Western story of accommodation, of surrender to another's lifestyle, comes from the Book of Ruth in the Bible. Ruth, a Moabite, had been married to Mahlon, an Israelite from Judah. Mahlon and his brother died, so their mother, Naomi, decided to return from Moab to Judah. Ruth pleaded with Naomi to take her to Judah. Naomi kept thinking of reasons for Ruth not to move to what, for her, would be a foreign land. Ruth finally gave a short speech:

> Entreat me not to leave you or to return from following you; for where you go I will go, and where you lodge I will lodge; your people shall be my people, and your God, my God; where you die I will die, and there will I be buried. May the Lord so do to me and more also if even death parts me from you.[18]

The Book of Ruth records: "And when Naomi saw that she was determined to go with her, she said no more."[19] Furthermore, Ruth's actions led her future husband, Boaz, to notice her accommodation:

> All that you have done for your mother-in-law since the death of your husband has been fully told me, and how you left your father and mother and your native land and came to a people that you did not know before. The Lord recompense you for what you have done, and a full reward be given you by the lord, the God of Israel, under whose wings you have come to take refuge![20]

Here, we see an extraordinary effort at persuasion built around a full surrender to the lifestyle of others. In offering to engage in a series of acts reflective of another's lifestyle—living with Naomi, dwelling among her people, worshipping her deity, and being buried with her—Ruth was able to enter into a complete and apparently mutually satisfying relationship with Naomi and all of Israel. Indeed, as a result of these promises, Ruth became the great-grandmother of the most famous of Israel's kings, David. Obviously, such a strategy of accommodation can have great personal consequences; one's own lifestyle may well be sacrificed. That very sense of personal sacrifice, perhaps, is why it's such a powerful approach to the transcendence of difference. If you're willing to give up part of your own identity, then you are demanding to be taken with the utmost of seriousness.

Hence, in urging your classmates to pressure Congress to pass a more aggressive policy on protecting gay rights in governmentally funded charity programs, you might say:

> Now, for many, perhaps even most, people in this class, the issue of gay rights in government-subsidized faith-based charities seems irrelevant. You're not gay, right? And you don't plan on working for the Salvation Army, do you? You say, why worry? Well, there are plenty of reasons to worry. If charitable organizations can dictate the sexual lifestyles of their employees with the endorsement of the federal government, then such government tolerance for exceptions to antidiscrimination laws in the states can expand. If faith-based charities drive out gay employees with Washington's blessing, then they're weakening civil rights in this country as well as closing employment doors to about 10 percent of our population. If Washington allowed exceptions of antidiscrimination laws in areas of welfare, why not do it as well for companies that bid on federal construction contracts or serve as vendors to the American military? And if your sexual orientation can be dictated, how about dress codes, mandatory overtime, and work week? Even those of you who are straight, therefore, have to deal with important social and legal questions flowing from the Salvation Army's request for exceptions to government policy.

In this kind of argument, you work through a lifestyle difference that's not experienced by most members of the audience, yet you do it in a way that asks them to see how it's relevant to their own.

## Maintaining Self-Identity in the Face of Difference

Most of the time, you probably won't be willing to surrender your self-identity—your own life experiences and culture. This creates a quandary: How can you be true to yourself while managing to work effectively with others? Consider the questions in the "Ethical Moments" box below, which explore the moral limits of this issue.

# ETHICAL MOMENTS

## Adapting to Moral Codes

The stated theme of this chapter is simple: You must learn to adapt your ways of talking to the cultural orientations of your listeners to achieve your goals as a speaker. What, however, are the moral limits of that requirement?

**1** Must you use profanity if talking about opponents to your position just because members of your audience do?

**2** Is it ethical to play to the fears that a Jewish audience might have of Arabs in a speech on the evils of population control?

**3** When talking to an audience of Indians about birth and population control, must you confront the practice in some of the poorer parts of India of aborting female fetuses just because of the cost of dowries?

**4** What sorts of appeals to motivation and hard work should you use when talking to an audience of people whose unemployment rate has been about 40 percent for the last 15 years?

**5** What if you want to talk about a subject that is taboo (i.e., unspoken) in your family? Suppose one or both of your parents drink too heavily: How can you talk about it constructively? Or can you?

Set up class discussions in which you tackle these and similar problems that members of your group have encountered. Moral judgments become even more difficult to render when the participants have significantly different cultural backgrounds.

One technique for maintaining self-identity is to recognize your similarities with others even while maintaining your own identity. This is what President Lyndon Johnson did in 1965 when he urged Congress to pass civil rights legislation:

> There is no Negro problem. There is no Southern problem. There is no Northern problem. There is only an American problem. And we are met here tonight as Americans—not as Democrats or Republicans—we are met here as Americans to solve that problem.[21]

Johnson was searching for a transcendent identity with which, he hoped, everyone in his audience could associate.

Identity also can become complicated when speakers see themselves as having multiple identities that seem to conflict. Speaking to the 1996 Republican National Convention, Mary Fisher had a potential identity problem. She had AIDS and was speaking as an AIDS advocate, yet she was speaking to an audience in which the more conservative members, especially, wanted little to do with AIDS patients or with federal programs to help them. Fisher phrased the potential identity problem early in the speech:

> I mean to live, and to die, as a Republican. But I also live, and will die, in the AIDS community—a community hungry for the evidence of [political] leadership and desperate for hope.[22]

To make use of that distinction and to overcome it, Fisher chose to strip away the conservative political culture of her listeners to demand their action:

> The question is not political. It's a human question, sharpened by suffering and death, and it demands a moral response.[23]

Thus, she could argue, by the end of her speech, that political action should be undertaken not for ideological reasons but for social and cultural ones. Hugging a 12-year-old African American girl named Heidia, who was born with AIDS, Fisher concluded her speech as follows:

> The day may come when AIDS will have its way with me, when I can no longer lift my sons to see the future or bend down to kiss away the pain. At that moment Max and Zack will become the community's children more than my own, and we will be judged not through the eyes of politics but through the eyes of children. I may lose my own battle with AIDS, but if you would embrace moral courage tonight and embrace my children when I'm gone, then you and Heidia and I would together have won a greater battle, because we would have achieved integrity.[24]

To find ways of affirming your own self, your own ethos, while also recognizing and complementing your listeners' sense of self is a search that you'll continue throughout your lifetime when you speak publicly. Finding ways of achieving unity in the midst of social diversity is a central challenge to all who would inform and persuade others. You'll often find yourself saying such things as expressed in these three examples:

> Now, I'm not a farmer myself—I teach school right here at this college. But I live in the country and see everywhere the struggles of the subsistence farmer. I know something about the hours you put in trying to survive on marginal land. I know you're anxious about how you'll educate your kids when you need a new tractor, so you can rent more land. I know how you struggle to feed your family between your trips to market your cattle. You're facing the struggles of every low-income occupation in this country.
>
> • • •
>
> I'm not from the East Coast and seldom visit, yet I can understand that the stereotyping that makes us laugh at such sitcoms as *Everybody Loves Raymond* and *The King of Queens* is unsettling. Sure, comedy should help make us aware of our stereotypes by calling attention to them, but can that backfire? Might the behavior of Raymond's dominating parents or delivery-man Douglas in his never-ending schemes to shortcut hard work just reinforce our stereotypes about New Yorkers—especially lower-/middle-class New Yorkers?
>
> • • •
>
> OK, so college athletes not only get a free ride through school, but many also gain enough notoriety to gain a leg up on job hunting when they're done. But have you ever stopped to think about what they pay in time, stress, and physical problems for that glory? I never did until last fall, when I became the roommate of a football player.

One final point: Just as you'll often maintain your own identity in the face of the identities of others, so, too, will you want to urge others to act from a conviction that is rooted in their own cultural identities. Karl Marx began his treatise on the proletarian revolution with the call "Workers of the world, unite!" This first sentence signaled his argument that workers, as a class, had to take control of their own destinies because the upper (bourgeois) classes certainly weren't serving their interests. The phrases "Sisterhood is powerful" and "Black power" likewise were rallying cries in the 1960s for groups to recognize their own abilities to influence their social, economic, and political relationships with others. So, occasionally you will affirm not only your own but also others' identities as the bases of thought and action.

This is not to say that you'll always accept the lifestyle choices of others. There will be times you'll find it important to confront the socially dangerous or personally destructive behaviors of, for example, a drug addict or an alcoholic. The lifestyle choices that others have made may not appeal to you, and you may find it impossible to accept appeals for cultural consistency. Sometimes, appeals to male bonding or sisterhood, to your whiteness or brownness, to your youth or status as an elderly person will get nowhere. Some questions will transcend cultural practices in your mind, and you'll be forced to assault them, which is what happens when most Americans are confronted by white supremacists. Even then, however, it's vitally important to understand all you can about culture as lived, thought, and performed so you can select confrontational strategies with a chance of actually moving listeners to change their life patterns.

Throughout much of this book, we'll return to questions of cultural life, multiculturalism, and the search for social unity. We do not approach what are essentially the cross-cultural dimensions of social life for political reasons. Although multiculturalism assuredly has strong political dimensions, our focus is cultural, not political. If you don't understand that speakers must adapt to their listeners' cultural moorings, you'll have great difficulty speaking to any but your own close circle. Social life—and, hence, public communication—is rooted in cultural practices.[25] Thus, it becomes your job to understand and to adapt your public speaking strategies to those practices.

## ■ CHAPTER SUMMARY

Culture is a social group's system of meanings. One's culture is largely determined, referenced, maintained, and altered by public talk. Culture-sensitive public speech is integrative, redundant, traditionalist, concrete, agonistically toned, participatory, and situational. Thinking about culture as lived puts an emphasis on demographic or social categories for classifying people into groups. Cultural diversity represents differences in systems of meaning that are possessed by different groups in a society. Multiculturalism is a recognition that a country possesses not a unitary culture with several subcultures but a series of co-cultures that interpenetrate yet are separate from one another.

Culture also is a way of thinking. An ideology is a system of thought that embodies social values and perceptual orientations to the world. Hegemony is a concept that defines relationships between more powerful and less powerful people; those relationships are maintained, in part, by the complicity of the less powerful people.

Culture also is performed; you can see culture only when it is embodied. Embodiment is the process whereby ideas, attitudes, values, and social character are given corporeal existence in communication. Once you learn culturally significant behavior, you enact that culture when you speak. Enactment is a communication process whereby a person behaves in a manner consonant with a society's cultural rules.

The central cultural challenge that public speakers face is to respect individual difference and cultural diversity while attempting to get a group of people to think alike and act together. At least five primary strategies for communicating unity through diversity are available to public speakers: recognizing diversity while calling for unity, negotiating among diverse values, accepting multiple paths to shared goals, working through the lifestyle choices of others, and maintaining self-identity in the face of cultural difference.

## ■ KEY TERMS

agonistically toned  (p.80)

co-cultures  (p.83)

common ground  (p.78)

concrete  (p.80)

cultural diversity  (p.79)

culture  (p.78)

culture as lived  (p.82)

culture as performed  (p.84)

culture as thought  (p.83)

embodiment  (p.84)

enactment  (p.85)

framing  (p.91)

hegemony  (p.84)

ideology  (p.83)

integrative  (p.79)

multiculturalism  (p.83)

participatory  (p.81)

redundant  (p.80)

situational  (p.81)

subcultures  (p.83)

traditionalist  (p.80)

value orientations  (p.88)

## ■ ASSESSMENT ACTIVITIES

1. Do a demographic profile of your speech class-room. Have everyone anonymously record his or her sex, age, economic status, religious background, place of birth or home state, and ethnic/racial background. Your instructor will tabulate the results and then distribute them to everyone. Write down the central idea or claim for your next speech, and ask yourself how the cultural backgrounds of your listeners, as seen in the demographic profile, should affect how you handle this idea or claim. Turn it in for your instructor's comments.

2. Take one of the following topics, and by yourself or in class discussion, identify three or more valuative positions that might be held by ideologically liberal, conservative, and middle-of-the-road people. Then, suggest at least two shared goals you think might be acceptable to most people in all three groups. Work with one of the following topics:

   a. Undocumented (illegal) aliens
   b. Legalization of same-sex marriages
   c. Federal subsidies to faith-based charities
   d. Tuition as the basic method for financing higher education
   e. Construction of new nuclear power plants

## ■ REFERENCES

1. To explore the role of social categories of human beings is to begin dealing with the "consequences of differences and divergences, boundaries and borders," in the words of Angie McRobbie, *Postmodernism and Popular Culture* (New York: Routledge, 1994, 6). Differences and divergences should not be thought of as tools for shattering societies, as so often happens when scholars begin thinking about "the postmodern," but rather as phenomena that enrich your life experiences and provide you with interesting challenges when you're trying to adapt to other people's worlds in positive ways.

2. What is here called *common ground* is termed *radical categories* by cognitive scientist George Lakoff in *Moral Politics: What Conservatives Know That Liberals Don't* (Chicago: University of Chicago Press, 1996, 8). A radical category is a variation on some central model. So, in one of his examples, the category *mother* can have different radicals or variations in interpretation: "(1) The birth model: the mother is one who gives birth. (2) The genetic model: the mother is the female from whom you get half of your genetic traits. (3) The nurturance model: your mother is the person who raises and nurtures you. And (4) the

marriage model: your mother is the wife of your father." Radical categories thus represent different ways of looking at a particular phenomenon or idea. As such, the term will be useful to us when we talk about rhetorical framing later in this chapter.

3. Walter J. Ong, *Orality and Literacy: The Technologizing of the Word* (New York: Routledge, 1982), 31. The phrase *sounded word* is used in the first heading of Chapter 3 of Ong's book, "Some Psychodynamics of Orality" (pp. 31–77), which considers a wide range of characteristics of orality. We'll examine only some of those characteristics here.

4. Ong, p. 43.

5. You can gain an interesting and well-illustrated understanding of how different people's lived experiences are represented by reading the middle chapters of Stuart Hall's *Representation: Cultural Representations and Signifying Practices* (Thousand Oaks, CA: 1997), especially Chapters 3–5. Classic essays on speaking and lived culture include Gerry Philipsen, "Speaking 'Like a Man' in Teamsterville: Cultural Patterns of Role Enactment in an Urban Neighborhood," *Quarterly Journal of Speech* 61 (1975): 13–22; his "Places for Speaking in Teamsterville," *Quarterly Journal of Speech* 62 (1976): 16–25; and Phyllis M. Japp, "Gender and Work in the 1980s: Television's Working Women as Displaced Persons," *Women's Studies in Communication* 14 (1991): 49–74. To see someone complaining about being judged by her ethnic background rather than her individual personality, see Jordan Lite, "Please Ask Me Who, Not 'What,' I Am," *Newsweek*, 16 July 2001, p. 9.

6. For a discussion of co-cultures, see the introduction and essays in Alberto González, Marsha Houston, and Victoria Chen, eds., *Our Voices: Essays on Cultural Ethnicity and Communication*, 2nd ed. (Los Angeles: Roxbury Press, 1996). How these issues play out publicly is explored in Clint C. Wilson II and Félix Gutiérrez, *Race, Multiculturalism, and the Media*, 2nd ed. (Thousand Oaks, CA: Sage, 1995).

7. For discussions of relationships between thought/speech and culture, see Donald Carbaugh, "'Soul' and 'Self': Soviet and American Cultures in Conversation," *Quarterly Journal of Speech* 77 (1991): 123–151; Jay Fernback, "The Individual and the Collective: Virtual Ideology and the Realization of Collective Principles," in *Virtual Culture: Identity and Communication in Cybersociety*, edited by Steven G. Jones (Thousand Oaks, CA: Sage, 1997), 36–54; and Kristine Fitch, *Speaking Relationally: Culture, Communica-*

*tion, and Interpersonal Relations* (New York: Guilford Press, 1998), especially Chapter 6, "'A Set of Bonds to Others': Elaborating an Ideology of Connectedness," 146–179.

8. For more on the naturalization of myths and ideologies in our lives, see the classic work by French cultural theorist Roland Barthes, *Mythologies*, translated by A. Lavers (London: Paladin, 1973), especially the last chapter, "Myth Today."

9. The power of hegemonic relationships can be seen in Brenda Cooper's "The Relevancy of Gender Identity in Spectators' Interpretations of *Thelma & Louise*," *Critical Studies in Mass Communication* 16 (1999): 20–41.

10. Embodiment involves the symbolic marking of the body in communicatively significant ways. For interesting work on embodiment, see Elaine Scarry, "The Merging of Bodies and Artifacts in the Social Contract," in *Culture on the Brink: Ideologies of Technology*, edited by Gretchen Bender and Timothy Drucker (Seattle: Bay Press, 1994), 85–97; Dan Brouwer, "The Precarious Visibility Politics of Self-Stigmatization: The Case of HIV/AIDS Tattoos," *Text and Performance Quarterly* 18 (1998): 114–136; and, on the marketing of women's bodies commercially, Jean Kilbourne, *Deadly Persuasion: Why Women and Girls Must Fight the Addictive Power of Advertising* (New York: Free Press, 1999).

11. For studies of enactment, see Y. Griefat and Tamar Katriel, "Life Demands Musayara: Communication and Culture Among Arabs in Israel," *Language, Communication, and Culture*, edited by Stella Ting-Toomey and Filipe Korzenny (Thousand Oaks, CA: Sage, 1989), 121–137; Cheryl R. Jorgensen-Earp and Lori A. Lanzilotti, "Public Memory and Private Grief: The Construction of Shrines at the Sites of Public Tragedy," *Quarterly Journal of Speech* 84 (1998): 150–170; and, for the strong of stomach, Kirk W. Fuoss, "Lynching Performances, Theatres of Violence," *Text and Performance Quarterly* 19 (1999): 1–37.

12. Communication/rhetorical studies' principal theorist of performance and performativity is Judith Butler. See, for instance, her *Bodies That Matter: On The Discursive Limits of "Sex"* (New York: Routledge, 1993).

13. Doris Kearns Goodwin, "Foreword," in *In Our Own Words: Extraordinary Speeches of the American Century*, edited by Robert Torricelli and Andrew Carroll (New York: Kodanska International, 1999), xxiii.

14. From "Transcript from Minister Louis Farrakhan's remarks at the Million Man March," 17 October 1995, p. 4, available at CNN's website: <http://cnn.com/US/9510/megamarch/10-16/transcript/index.html>.

15. Transcript, p. 15.

16. Reprinted in Torricelli and Carroll, p. 419, from a speech given at the Hilton Hotel in Washington, DC, September 1995.

17. Henri Mann Morton, "Strength through Cultural Diversity," in Jerry D. Blanche, *Native American Reader: Stories, Speeches, and Poems* (Juneau, AK: Denali Press, 1990). Reprinted with permission of the publisher.

18. Ruth 1:16–17, *Holy Bible,* Revised Standard Version.

19. Ruth 1:18.

20. Ruth 2:11–12.

21. President Lyndon Baines Johnson, "We Shall Overcome," delivered to a joint session of Congress, 15 March 1965, reprinted in Theodore Windt, ed., *Presidential Rhetoric (1961 to the Present)* (Dubuque, IA: Kenndall/Hunt, 1994), 67.

22. Mary Fisher, address to the Republican National Convention, 12 August 1996, transcript done from the C-SPAN broadcast of the address. Printed with the express permission of the Republican National Committee and Mary Fisher.

23. Fisher.

24. Fisher.

25. See Chapter 8 on social criticism in Malcolm O. Sillars and Bruce E. Gronbeck, *Communication Criticism: Rhetoric, Social Codes, Cultural Studies* (Prospect Heights, IL: Waveland Press, 2001).

# PART TWO

# Preparation

Let no one however demand from me a rigid code of rules such as most authors of textbooks have laid down.... If the whole of rhetoric can be thus embodied in one compact code, it would be an easy task of little compass: but most rules are liable to be altered by the nature of the case, circumstances of time and place, and by hard necessity itself. Consequently, the all-important gift for an orator is a wise adaptability since he [sic] is called upon to meet the most varied emergencies.

**Quintilian,**
*Institutio Oratoria*, I.xlii.1–2

# Chapter 5

# Analyzing the Audience and Occasion

The Roman rhetorician Quintilian was correct in observing that "the all-important gift for an orator is a wise adaptability." Adapting your ideas to the audience and the occasion is an essential task in achieving success as a public speaker. Speaking is purposeful—you speak to have a positive effect on the information the audience knows and understands, impact the cognitive and emotional state of your listeners, or affect their behavior. You also speak in a context already influenced by prior rhetoric or others. The words that have been said before may constrain or enhance your ability to address an audience. *Where* the words have been said also impacts what you can say—ceremonial settings, courthouses, classrooms imply standards of decorum and respect that you must consider in speaking. In the words of Donald C. Bryant: Since ancient Greece, the essence of public rhetoric has been that of "adjusting ideas to people and people to ideas."[1] Without engaging a particular audience at a particular time and place, you're just talking, not speaking.

A primary theme will be stressed throughout this chapter: The goal of *audience analysis* is to discover those *demographic* and *psychological* characteristics of your audience that are relevant to your speech. Understanding these characteristics allows you to adapt your ideas to those that will have the most potential impact on the acceptance of your message. You also need to be sensitive to the demands the *occasion*—a time and place set aside for particular events and activities—places on your choice of themes and language. Speakers must learn what people expect and be as responsive as possible to their expectations. To prepare you for the dual task of adapting to audiences and occasions, we first discuss the demographic and psychological features of listeners. We then take apart the rules governing speech occasions and indicate some of the specific moves you should be making while constructing your speeches to maximize your chances for rhetorical success.

**103**

# Analyzing Audiences Demographically

A **demographic analysis** is a study of the social and physical traits people hold in common. People often group themselves by such traits. For example, your gender has affected the way you have played since you were a child, the young and the old often bring very different ways of thinking to bear on topics under discussion, and your level of education can affect what jobs you can apply for. Phrases such as "All professional women agree that . . . ," "White America is . . . ," and "The better-educated voter will . . ." signal that some group trait is particularly important to a subject under discussion. Such claims may well be exaggerated. "All professional women" is not really a monolithic body of people who do in fact agree, yet this group may characterize enough people to warrant referencing in relation to a specific claim or central idea.

Many of these analyses are available publicly (e.g., public opinion polls distinguishing between men's and women's attitudes toward a set of presidential candidates), and many others can be located through research (e.g., government studies of the comparative costs of health care by age). Because you can directly observe many demographic characteristics of an audience just by looking at them, it's a good idea to begin an audience analysis with demographic factors. For most audiences, you can identify certain traits, at least generally: age, gender, sexual orientation, education, some group memberships, and cultural and ethnic background.

## Analyzing Demographic Categories

The competent speaker asks questions about the demographic characteristics of audiences to see which, if any, are relevant to the speech she or he is delivering. Consider the following categories:

- *Age:* Will the expected listeners primarily be young, middle aged, or elderly, or will the group more likely be of mixed ages? Is there a special relationship between age groups, such as parent/child or teacher/student? Is your speech likely to be more familiar and interesting to one age group than to another?

- *Gender:* Will the listeners primarily be male or female, or will the group be split? Is this a topic likely to divide the audience along gender lines?

- *Sexual orientation:* Is this a topic that addresses issues of sexual orientation or one that, if not phrased carefully, will make you appear insensitive to such issues?

- *Education and experience:* How much will the listeners already know about the subject? Will their educational or experiential backgrounds allow them to grasp easily the essential ideas you want to convey?

- *Group membership:* Will the listeners belong to groups that represent specific experiences, attitudes, or identifiable values? Think how varied your answer to this question would be if you were talking to the Young Republicans, a Rotary International chapter in downtown Chicago, a League of Women Voters political platform meeting, or a social hour sponsored by the Society of Black Journalists.

- *Cultural and ethnic background:* Will the listeners predominantly belong to specific cultural or ethnic groups? Are those group identifications likely to be raised by your speech? A speech arguing that English should be designated the only language spoken in elementary schools will make cultural/ethnic background relevant because some school districts use Spanish as a primary language. A speech on where to find wildflowers for a fall bouquet, however, will not.

## Using Demographic Information

The importance of demographic analysis for you as a speaker doesn't lie in simply answering these questions. Rather, the key is to decide if any of these demographic factors will affect your listeners' ability or willingness to understand and accept what you want to say. That is, does a particular group affiliation, age, or gender have any relevance in the situation you face? Does it influence the rhetorical choices you make in selecting a subject and developing a central idea or claim? Just as critical, you also do not want to fall into the trap of overgeneralizing regarding any one of these demographic *markers*. Just because someone is from a particular cultural group, is female, or at a certain educational level does not mean that he or she will form a unified body who thinks alike on particular issues. These markers serve as starting points for asking yourself questions about the nature of the audience's experience, information possessed, and attitudes held.

If you're addressing a group of students, faculty, administrators, and community members gathered to consider building a new student center on campus, for example, you should consider all of these questions. You would be safe in assuming that some would be opposed to the very idea, some would be mildly curious, some would be interested but undecided, and some would be strongly in favor. Some of the students would have as their major concern who is paying (and most likely, student fees will be the chief source of funding to repay bonds). Community members will wonder what they can gain from the presence of yet another new building on the campus. Their tax base won't be affected, but they will wonder if new space for university/community events will be planned into the new structure. Some faculty members and university administrators in the audience will wonder why this is the priority for funding instead of a new science building or a new performing arts center. Campus groups, from the student senate to the rugby club, will wonder if space has been provided for their activities and interests. Students of color in the audience will wonder if their needs have been met. Some students will be older and have less interest in the kinds of activities provided for by a student center —their concerns will be focused on the cost projection and payoff plan.

Overall, these are some of the demographic characteristics of the audience that would be invited to and interested in a new campus facility. With these demographic characteristics in mind, you might adapt your speech to your listeners by using the following strategies:

■ Avoid technical jargon. Your audience will not be interested in a highly technical presentation on bond structures, interest, and how payments will be amortized over time.

■ Give examples of the variety of groups that will be housed in and be able to use the new facility. Cast the net widely in covering all of the various interests represented by a diverse audience.

■ Recognize that some in the audience will oppose the structure for various reasons, and attempt, in your presentation, to indicate that you are aware of and respect their concerns. While you may not be able to address all of the concerns in detail, recognizing their existence will help foster a positive atmosphere for an open discussion of differences of opinion.

Demographic analysis can help you select and phrase your key ideas, and it sensitizes you to crucial factors that may influence your choice of themes, examples, and other supporting material. If your analysis is cursory or incomplete, you decrease your chances of being understood and of reaching agreement. Even when you're aware of the demographic characteristics, however, you still may create problems with your choice of language. A white person addressing a group of African Americans, for example, who refers to them as "you people" and "your people" demonstrates a lack of sensitivity and judgment—as it marks them as different and perpetuates a superiority over them as a distinct cultural group. Appropriate use of demographic information can help you avoid such problems and convey a sensitive and caring attitude toward your listeners.

Not all groups will be as easy to analyze as the group considering a new student center on campus. Because you are in a college setting, these groupings, and the interests they represent, would come naturally to you. In this instance, the more active you are in campus affairs, the more easily you will arrive at a list of potential audience members and their respective attitudes and values in relation to your subject. The same will be true for other audience analyses you will undertake. If you have never been around retired people or been to an assisted-living center, preparing to address such an audience can be a scary prospect. In this instance, a lack of familiarity can be alleviated by doing research on older Americans—what is the average age of those in assisted living, what percentage are women, and so on. You also can gain a sense of the demographics by visiting a center prior to the speaking engagement and observing a typical lunch or dinner hour when all are gathered. In addition, you can ask friends and relatives about their experiences with such centers. The manner in which you obtain your information will vary with the particular situation, but using your own knowledge and doing research will be the key strategies in fleshing out the demographic picture.

# Analyzing Audiences Psychologically

Dividing audience members into **psychological profiles** on the basis of their beliefs, attitudes, and values also helps you adapt to their needs and interests. This is especially important if you intend to influence your listeners' thinking on issues. You need to know what ideas they already accept before you try altering their thoughts and actions. Sometimes careful demographic analysis will create such groupings naturally and provide clues about what your audience members think. For example, at a gathering of farmers who still farm quarter-sections (160 acres) or less, you can assume that most will strongly oppose so-called macroswine production facilities, where 2,000 or more hogs are raised at a single location. This demographic group likely will be worried about the smell, the fouling of the air when liquid manure is sprayed over fields to dispose of it, the possibility of polluting the local watershed, and the arrival of other signs of corporate farming. You can be pretty sure that they'll have great interest in legislation controlling the size of swine production facilities and the positions of gubernatorial candidates on such issues. When you have a more diversified audience, however, you might need to work on psychological profiling without much help from demographics. You'll have to explore beliefs, attitudes, values, and desires or fantasies in other ways.

## Beliefs

The first task of psychological profiling is to understand an audience's beliefs. **Beliefs** are convictions about what is true or false. They arise from firsthand experience, public opinion, supporting evidence, authorities, and even blind faith. For example, you might believe that anatomy is a difficult course based on your own experience. At the same time, you may believe that calculus is important because it's required for the premed sequence, which you want to pursue as a concentration. So, although each belief is held for different reasons, both are considered true.

Beliefs come in many different forms:

1. Beliefs that can be demonstrated and held confidently are called **facts.** Generally, facts are supported by strong external evidence. When you say "Research has proven that smokers can clear almost all damaging materials out of their bodies by not smoking for 10 years," you're very sure of that belief. You hold facts with certainty because you have hard evidence to support them (in this case, many scientific studies)

2. **Opinions** are personal beliefs that may not be supported by strong external evidence. You may think that all cats are nasty animals, either because cats have scratched you in the past or because you're allergic to them. However, your experience is limited. Many people like cats, even if you don't. An opinion is a personal belief supported with less compelling external evidence than a fact. Sometimes many people hold the same opinion—that President Bush "stole the election" from Al Gore or that the use of tanning booths is

safer than direct exposure to sunlight—though they may not have a lot of strong, independent verification of the truth of those opinions. No matter how many hold it, it's still an opinion, not a fact.

3. Beliefs will vary in the intensity with which they are held. **Fixed beliefs** are those that are highly resistant to change; they have been reinforced through-out a lifetime, making them central to one's thinking. Many beliefs—such as "Things happen for a reason," "If you work hard, you'll succeed," and "Rich people have cheated to get where they are"—are fixed beliefs. The problem with these types of stereotyped beliefs is that rich people may pay the taxes they owe and sometimes hard work does not payoff as expected. **Stereo-types** ignore individual differences and exceptions to rules. Fixed beliefs often can be too rigid.

4. **Variable beliefs** are less well anchored in your mind and experiences. You might enter college thinking that you want to be a computer programmer; however, after an instructor praises your abilities in a speech class, you may consider becoming a political campaign consultant. Then, you take a mar-keting class and find you're good at planning advertising campaigns. This sort of self-discovery continues as you take additional classes. Your beliefs about your talents change with your personal experiences. The same is true, of course, for members of your audience. One of your jobs in assessing be-liefs is figuring out which of the listeners' beliefs relevant to your speech are variable. That is, which of their beliefs can you change to get them to agree with your central idea or claim?

Fact or opinion, fixed or variable, beliefs are those parts of people's psycho-logical profiles that you should assess first because they'll determine what kinds of supporting materials you'll want to use in clarifying a central idea or in defend-ing a claim. See Figure 5.1 for an overview of the types of beliefs.

## Attitudes

The second task of psychological profiling is to identify audience attitudes. **Atti-tudes** are tendencies to respond positively or negatively to people, objects, and ideas. Attitudes are emotionally weighted, as well. They express individual prefer-ences and feelings, such as "I like my public speaking class," "Classical music is better than rap music," and "Cincinnati is a beautiful city."

As a speaker, you should consider the dominant attitudes of your listeners. Audiences may have attitudes toward you, your speech subject, and your purpose. Ideally, your listeners may think you know a lot about your topic, and they may be interested in learning more. If they do not like you as a person, you will have more difficulty getting beyond that opinion in convincing them to change their ideas or actions. For example, if a speaker says that you can earn extra money in your spare time by working at a telemarketing company, you might have a com-plex set of attitudinal reactions: You feel good about earning extra money, but you

| FIGURE 5.1 | **The Varieties of Beliefs** |

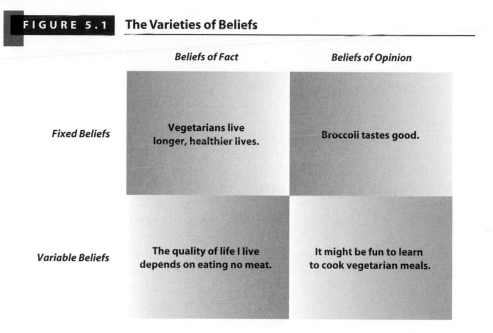

|                  | *Beliefs of Fact*                                 | *Beliefs of Opinion*                              |
|------------------|---------------------------------------------------|---------------------------------------------------|
| *Fixed Beliefs*  | **Vegetarians live longer, healthier lives.**     | **Broccoli tastes good.**                         |
| *Variable Beliefs* | **The quality of life I live depends on eating no meat.** | **It might be fun to learn to cook vegetarian meals.** |

don't know enough about telemarketing to have an opinion on the topic. You also didn't especially care for the speaker when you talked with that person in the cafeteria last week, which affects how you feel about the proposal. Relationships among your attitudes toward the speech topic, purpose, and speaker can be complex, and how you trace those relationships in your own mind will influence your final decision about telephoning strangers. Attitudes express your and other people's orientations toward the world—and even the factual conditions existing in the world. They're the keys to human reactions and, hence, to a willingness to accept or reject ideas.

## Values

The third component of psychological profiling is understanding audience values. **Values** are relatively enduring conceptions of ultimate goods and evils in human relationships and of the best and worse ways of pursuing those goods and evils. According to Milton Rokeach, such a definition recognizes that human beings have both **terminal values** and **instrumental values**—values toward which they aspire as well as values about the best ways of living out those aspirations.[2] As an example, you and a friend might agree that obtaining increased financial reward is a *terminal value* worth pursuing in your first job yet disagree about how to best go after it. You might hold "efficiency" as an *instrumental value* and, hence, look for ways to gain salary and raises quickly and with the least effort. Your friend might hold "stability" as a parallel *instrumental value* and, hence, want to make more money only within a conservative company that offers good benefits.

Both of you can cite popular wisdom guiding your action—you, "A stitch in time saves nine," and your friend, "Haste makes waste"—so it's not as though one of you is legitimated by society and the other is not. Rather, you hold conflicting instrumental values while pursuing the same terminal value.

Because values are the overarching concepts that we use to organize our beliefs and attitudes, they become central to rhetorical decision making. As noted by Elliott Jaques, CEOs must do audience analysis, with a focus on values, if they're to be successful in impacting corporate culture: "If the CEO can establish overarching corporate values and philosophies, which are nested within basic societal values, and which meet people's own generic values, he or she can get the whole organization working effectively in the same broad direction. . . . It is our values that move us, bind us together, push us apart, and generally make the world go round."[3] As is suggested, values are more foundational than beliefs and attitudes because they represent the broad conceptual categories that help attitudes and beliefs cohere. For example, a person may hold a value, such as "Life is sacred." That value can be expressed in multiple attitudes, including "Abortion is wrong" and "Hunting is immoral." That value also may be expressed in beliefs such as "The death penalty is wrong" and "Hunting animals in the wild causes them cruel suffering." Once learned, the intent is that these would underlie a person's particular attitudes and beliefs.

Notice in the following quotation how billionaire entrepreneur George Soros works from common economic values to argue for "the decisive role that international financial capital plays in the fortunes of individual countries":

> The system is very favorable to financial capital, which is free to go where it is best rewarded. This has led to the rapid growth of global financial markets. The result is a giant circulatory system, sucking capital into the financial markets and institutions at the center and then pumping it out to the periphery either directly, as credits and portfolio investments, or indirectly through multinational corporations. . . . Until the Thai crisis in 1997.[4]

Notice that Soros argues that "financial capital" is valued by its ability to travel easily around the world. He makes factual assertions about the rapidity of capital growth, using an analogy of the circulatory system in making his statements clear to listeners. Then, he begins an example to show that his valuing of financial capital over other economic factors can explain the operation of the real world—Thailand in 1997.

Because values exist in broad mixtures for most of us, as for Soros, they're often thought about collectively as **value orientations** or **ideologies.** Value orientations are aggregations of values shared by large numbers of people (see Figure 5.2). One goal of education is to impart core community values to youth. For example, the Michigan Education Portal for Interactive Content has created a set of *democratic core values* to be used in teaching elementary schoolchildren the basic values of democracy. They present the following seven as core values to be used in teaching: equality; personal property; right to petition the government; freedom

**FIGURE 5.2**    **Belief, Attitude, and Value Clusters**

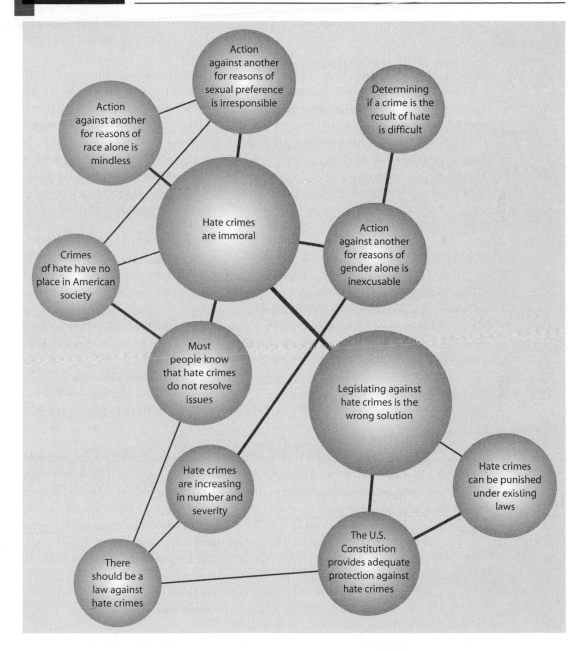

of assembly; majority rule; minority rights; and common good and pursuit of happiness.[5] Once learned, these become the value orientations within which attitudes and beliefs are formed. Together, they function as the ideological system governing how a person looks at democracy. Each of these also serves as what

Kenneth Burke calls *terministic screens*—sieves that let some ideas through while filtering out others.[6] Being able to refer to value orientations held by audience members is a great advantage for speakers.

## Desires, Visions, and Fantasies

Closely related to value orientations are **desires** and **fantasies.** We live in an era when desire, pleasure, and fantasy are understood less as escape mechanisms—a lecture often given by parents to their children—and more as vehicles for cultural identity and even political statements. At least since Dick Hebdige offered his now classic study of *style,* we have realized that items of art, literature, music, dress, and expressed attitudes are both identity markers—showing the world who we are— and political statements. The fans of reggae who wear dreadlocks as a style and re- live Bob Marley's music as a political statement are exploring desire, pleasure, and fantasy as means of self-definition and political persuasion.[7]

Ernest Bormann calls group fantasies **rhetorical visions,** or "the unified putting-together of the various scripts which give the participants a broader view of things."[8] That putting-together may occur around a master analogy, such as Franklin Roosevelt's New Deal or John F. Kennedy's New Frontier. Even more po- tent, perhaps, is the narrative center of such visions: the story of the New Israel that the Puritans used to envision the society they were building in seventeenth-century America; the story of the proletarian revolution and upheaval of the social world that lay at the base of Marxism; and the vision of a new society created in love, cre- ative suffering, and soul force that Martin Luther King, Jr., regularly described for his audiences. When all of an audience's existence is captured in such depictions, Bormann calls them *life-style rhetorical visions.*[9] These function as the grounding value set on which people receive your ideas and claims on their attention.

Expressions of collective desire commonly are found in the conclusions of speeches, when speakers hope to leave listeners in a state of agreement and a frame of mind to work to achieve that which has been agreed on. It was just such a hope for common desire that Abraham Lincoln tried to articulate at the end of his first inaugural address:

> We are not enemies, but friends. We must not be enemies. Though passion may have strained it must not break our bonds of affection. The mystic chords of memory, stretching from every battlefield and patriot grave to every living heart and hearthstone all over this broad land, will yet swell the chorus of the Union, when again touched, as surely they will be, by the better angels of our nature.[10]

Rhetorical visions of society and of listeners' lives within that society also are regularly built by powerful speakers to renew or redirect an audience's politi- cal energies, to justify traditional courses of action, and to articulate new motiva- tions for moving down new paths. They become the lenses through which group members are asked to view the world and to act within it. For example, notice the use of a rhetorical vision in the following quotation from Henri Mann Morton, a Native American woman addressing the Colville and Okanogan National Forest Conference on cultural diversity:

> I share your . . . vision of a racially, culturally, gender-based, and humanistically representative workforce in which attitudes of respect, acceptance, and understanding are all pervasive.
>
> The vision I see is dedicated to a love of life, to a love of people, and love of the environment, particularly the land—the earth, she who is our grandmother, who must be revered and protected; she upon whom we walk and live; she who supports our feet and gives us life; she who nurtures us, her children. We all share this bond and as culturally diverse people we can draw strength from our rich cultural diversity.
>
> I would like to share with you this Cheyenne philosophical belief: "A nation is not conquered until the hearts of its women are on the ground. Then it is done, no matter how brave its warriors nor how strong its weapons."
>
> This shows the acceptance of, and respect for, the power of women. As equal partners of men, who too, have their own power, we then can see why the most powerful of all pairs in the universe are men and women working together.[11]

Notice how Morton intertwines a general vision of cultural diversity with a specific depiction, through quotation, of the male/female union. The source of social life is seen in a feminine image of the grandmother and then is elaborated in the Cheyenne aphorism. This allows Morton's rhetorical vision to have breadth yet a unitary focus—on Grandmother Earth as the center of her dream.

Rhetorical desires, visions, and fantasies are the outgrowths of our complex of beliefs, attitudes, and values; they are the manifestation of what we believe about ourselves and others. They are as cognitively grounded and as well reasoned as the core concepts that form them. To understand them is to understand your audience. But gaining that information may be difficult, as people do not attend with such concepts stamped on their foreheads in sound-bite style. You will have to interrogate potential members of your audience, asking them what they see as the overarching terminal values underlying the topic you are speaking about, as well as the instrumental values that they might endorse in getting to that point. Further, you will be able to hear in their responses a more abstract sense of what their own desires, visions, and fantasies are in relation to the issues you wish to address. Recall the earlier example of speaking at an assisted-living center. To learn more about the psychological makeup of your audience, visit beforehand and engage residents in informal discussion. Asking how they are faring, what their hopes are, is a way of eliciting information that will give you a better sense of who they are and what they value. This is not about being *politically correct*. It *is* about respecting the dignity and values of the audience members and illustrating that respect by doing the homework necessary to prevent the insensitive handling of a topic.

## Using a Psychological Profile

After you've developed a profile of your audience's beliefs, attitudes, values, and rhetorical visions, how can you use this information? Three ways are obvious:

1. *Understanding your audience's beliefs, attitudes, values, desires, and visions will help you frame your ideas.* For example, if an audience generally believes that childhood is crucial to human development, you might persuade them to volunteer for a day-care cooperative. If they espouse family values, your job should be even easier. If you have no indication that they're particularly interested in child development, however, you'll have to establish the crucial nature of youth and its development before you can ask for volunteers.

2. *Understanding your audience's beliefs, attitudes, values, desires, and fantasies will help you select your supporting materials.* Statistics generally work well with highly educated audiences but less well with those having little education. People who are attitudinally and valuatively involved with a topic are much more likely to scrutinize the evidence you use than people who are not.[12] Churchgoers, for example, are likely to understand and appreciate a rhetorical vision in which divine intervention in human life is described. Atheists, to use Burke's expression, would employ a terministic screen that interprets such references very differently: same words, different meanings. In both cases, the groups' involvement in or considered rejection of an idea or value affects how seriously they will consider your evidence.

3. *Understanding your audience's beliefs, attitudes, values, desires, and rhetorical visions allows you to set realistic expectations as you plan your speech.* Not all audiences are equally amenable to change. You must always look for signs of resistance—deeply anchored beliefs and values, deep feelings of distrust or fear—when designing a speech. It's not likely that you'll convert a Christian to Islam or a Muslim to Judaism in one shot. In a group of college sophomores, however, several people are likely to be looking for a new major and are probably anxious about the process, in which case a speech on the usefulness and value of majoring in technology studies might prove most provocative.

# Analyzing the Speech Occasion

Sometimes, analyzing the speech occasion is simple: You know you're attending a National Communication Association Speech Club meeting, you've been there often, and you know what's expected from you when asked to present a 5- to 10-minute report on public relations internship possibilities in local medical organizations. At other times, the occasions are complex, with rules and traditions governing what can be said, who can talk, how and when people can talk, and in what manner you must treat other people. While you may not have thought much about it, an occasion can control how you behave when talking to others.

As we've suggested, an **occasion** is a set of activities that occurs in a time and place set aside expressly to fulfill the collective goals of people who have been taught the special meanings of those activities. Let us unpack this definition:

- *In a time and place . . .* Regular occasions, such as religious services, usually occur at special times (Fridays, Saturdays, Sundays) and in special places (mosques, synagogues, churches). Special events, such as political conventions, happen at specific times in halls designed to accommodate the people present and decorated to capture the value orientation and rhetorical vision of the party. These times and places take on special meanings of their own. Sunday morning in the United States is such a special time that many activities are scheduled around church services. The places where justice is handed down—courtrooms—are specially designed to emphasize permanence (made of marble), spaciousness (high ceilings in oversized rooms), elevation (the bench is raised above all other chairs, so the judge looks down on everyone else), and impartiality (a black robe hides the individual features of the judge). As such, courtrooms have come to be known as quiet, decorous places where respect is shown to all parties.

- *Fulfilling collective goals . . .* Most important, perhaps, people design occasions to meet the particular needs of particular groups, such as worship (church), justice (courts), passage to adulthood (bar mitzvahs, confirmations, debutante balls, commencement ceremonies), remembrance of basic values and heroes (monument dedications, holidays such as Memorial Day), and recognition of leadership and power (inaugurals, coronations). These are all activities in which individuals tend to participate as part of a group; a one-person ceremony or dedication doesn't mean much.

*Speakers must determine what they can expect to accomplish with a particular audience in the time they have available.*

■ *Special meanings . . .* You don't enter the world knowing how to pray, cheer, dedicate, mourn with others, or inaugurate. These are social activities that you must learn, through either instruction or imitation.[13] Knowing and understanding what is expected of you and others are signs of belonging to a particular group. Outsiders do not possess this knowledge; insiders do. You understand this best when you or others have violated the unwritten code of conduct for a specific occasion.

The purpose, complexity, and even formality of occasions vary widely. A presentation to your public relations club may be an informal yet an important occasion. Funerals and political conventions are much more formal. No matter what their formality, however, all occasions are governed by *rules* (do's and don'ts), *roles* (duties or functions that different people perform), and *judgments of competency* (assessments about how well people play their parts). Occasions normally involve rather precise expectations of what will happen, to whom it will happen, who will participate, and how they will take part.[14]

A speech occasion is thus every bit as demanding as any other social or political event. Like any other occasion, a speech occasion is characterized by rules, expected roles, and judgments of competency—in other words, by audience expectations. Those expectations take two forms. **General audience expectations** are those associated with any public speaker working in a particular society. In the United States, this includes such rules as "Speakers shouldn't mumble"; "The larger the room, the larger your gestures should be"; "Trusted speakers look audience members right in the eyes"; and "An excessive number or random gestures detracts from your message." Not all of these rules hold in every society; they're the products of U.S. society.

The second form, **specific audience expectations,** arise from habitual speaking practices in particular settings. Politicians on the campaign trail are expected to be enthusiastic, celebrate their own virtues, and attack their opponents. In some churches, preachers are expected to be even more excited and to deliver speeches filled with divine energy. Insurance salespeople are trained to ask questions of their listeners in the middle of their presentations ("How does this sound to you?" "Are these problems you face?" "Doesn't this make sense, given how young your children are?"). In some situations, you're expected to be an informer (orientation meeting), in others a comic (an after-dinner speech honoring a close friend), and in others, a persuader (a real estate office).

You do have choices in responding to an occasion's expectations. Obviously, you can either ignore the tradition associated with an event or simply say everything the audience wants to hear on that occasion. Being true to your own principles is the best guide; in keeping with your personal ethics, you want to say what you think needs to be said, irrespective of the constraints in the situation. As you take this stance, you also need to be prepared for the consequences that you may face from an audience that reacts negatively to your spurning tradition. Saying what needs saying in a way that both meets the expectations as much as one can yet does not compromise principle is the key. You must find a way to express yourself so that you are seen as a person whose personal ethics are consistent with the audience's own ethical standards.

Audience expectations, in other words, should be seen as opportunities to find ways into people's minds, not as barriers that stop communication. For that to happen, you must learn to read occasions—to interpret their effects on your speaking. The "How to" box below provides a useful summary of how to analyze the speech occasion.

## Using Audience Analysis in Speech Preparation

Neither demographic analysis nor psychological profiling is an end in itself. Nor will merely thinking about the speech occasion produce foolproof speech preparation strategies. Rather, you need to perform these twin analyses to discover what

# How to
## Analyze the Speech Occasion

- ***What is the nature and purpose of the occasion?*** Make sure the subject and purpose of your speech relate to the purpose of the meeting. If your speech is part of a series or will follow other speeches, find out the other speakers' approaches and decide how you will distinguish yours. If you are facing a **captive audience** (a group that is forced to attend), make an extra effort to show the significance of your subject to them.

- ***What are the prevailing rules or customs?*** Find out what customs are accepted in the speech situation: Is there a fixed program into which your speech must fit? Will listeners expect a formal speaking manner? An expression of respect for a tradition or concept? Also find out whether there are more specific rules. For example, the audience at the Friars Club in New York expects the speaker to mercilessly "roast" (verbally abuse) the object of the speech—but in a good-natured way.

- ***What are the physical conditions?*** Will you speak outdoors or indoors? Will the audience sit or stand? How large will the room be? Will you need to bring your own audiovisual equipment? If the conditions will negatively affect your presentation, consider moving your audience closer together or helping them change locations to avoid excessive heat or moisture. If outside noise interferes, speak more loudly and distinctly than you normally would.

- ***What events precede and follow your speech?*** If you will speak right after a meal or at the end of a long program, acknowledge your listeners' reduced interest and potential drowsiness. Give them time to stretch and otherwise get comfortable. If you are the warm-up speaker, be careful to follow the customs and rules of the occasion. Consider the character of any other items on the program to get a sense of how the group functions, perhaps even getting clues about its basic values.

- ***Have you figured out ways to target specific appeals to each significant segment of the audience?***

- ***Can you create a rhetorical vision that will encompass both your purpose and your listeners' understandings of the world?***

might affect the reception of you and your message. You're searching for relevant factors that can affect the audience's attitudes toward you, your subject, and your purpose. In turn, these factors should guide your rhetorical choices regarding subject matter, themes covered, language used, and the appropriateness of visual aids in the speech setting.

## Audience Targeting: Setting Realistic Goals

Begin with your purpose in speaking: Are you attempting to inform or persuade your audience, move them to action, or entertain them while imparting a moral lesson? Once this is determined, you are ready to set up the audience as a target of your address and relate what the analysis tells you to the general purpose of your speech. Five considerations are relevant in **audience targeting:** your specific purpose, the audience's areas of interest, their capacity to act, their willingness to act, and the degree of change you can expect. While what appears to be reasonable or realistic may fall short of your actual goal, working within these parameters will make it far easier for you to obtain audience support for your ideas. Moving too far beyond what is realistic will, in general, increase the risk that your listeners won't follow you—even if they're sympathetic to the thrust of your remarks.

**Your Specific Purpose**   Suppose that you have a part-time job at your college's career services office. You're familiar with its general goals and programs, and you have sufficient personal interest to speak about them to other campus groups. What you have discovered about different audiences should help you determine appropriate, specific purposes for each. If you were to talk to a group of incoming first-year students at new-student orientation, for example, you would know these things beforehand:

- They probably know little or nothing about the functions of a career services office. (They have few, if any, fixed beliefs about the office.)
- They probably are predisposed to look favorably on the office once they know how it functions (given their own career aspirations).
- They probably are, at their current stage of life and educational level, more concerned with practical issues such as selecting their courses, seeing an advisor, registering, and learning about basic degree requirements (whether a foreign language is required for English majors, whether a calculus course is required for business majors). While they want to be well positioned to make the most of their junior or senior year, learning specifics about what they can do "if and when" is not a high priority at this time. Hence, they may require external motivation (provided by your arguments and illustrations) to develop interest in the subject.
- They are likely to see you as an authoritative speaker, especially if you're introduced (or you introduce yourself) as a student employee in career services, and they likely are willing to listen to what you have to say.

*Effective persuasion depends on the speaker's analysis of both demographic and psychological profiles of the audience.*

Given these audience considerations, you probably should keep your presentation fairly general. Explain the principal functions of the career services office, and review the programs that the office sponsors (career fairs, résumé writing assistance, etc.). Stress how becoming familiar with the office and its programs can give new students an early start on a possible career or introduce them to new career possibilities. You might phrase your specific purpose as follows:

> To brief incoming first-year students on the range of service offered by the career services office

That orientation would include a basic description of each service and a general appeal for students to use these services early in order to position themselves for job hunting when they are seniors.

Were you instead to talk about this subject to a group of college seniors, you would address the audience differently. You also would know these things beforehand:

- They are more likely to be aware of the general goals and programs of the career services office, but they may be misinformed—or even uninformed—about details.
- They generally have positive feelings about the advantages of career services, but some may be unsure of whether it offers the opportunities for interviews in their specific majors.
- They may view your qualifications with somewhat more skepticism because you're one of their peers. At the same time, if you have worked in the office since you were a sophomore, your credibility regarding "do's" and "don'ts" will be fairly high.

Given these factors, you should be much more specific in some areas. You should describe the specific interactions you've had with employers who have been on campus, your own recent experience attending a career fair, and the specific strategies that students need to go through in arranging to be on a company's interview list. First-person stories will help convince the audience that a wide variety of students can profit from becoming involved with the activities at the career services office. In addition to fleshing out particulars about the "what" of career services, you'll need to spend time on the "how": How should students who are interested become involved? How should they pursue employers on their own? If they know an employer, how can she or he get involved?

You might phrase your dominant specific purpose in this way:

To inform juniors about the benefits gained by becoming involved in Eastern University's career services program

Your subordinate purposes might include "To demonstrate the ease with which students can become involved in the program" and "To illustrate that almost every student may be served."

**Areas of Audience Interest**    You can use both demographic analysis and psychological profiling to help you decide what ideas will interest your listeners. This is critical in narrowing your topic choice and in choosing specific ideas to develop. Suppose that you know something about communicating with people from diverse cultures. An audience of new management trainees for an international firm would probably be very interested in hearing how communication may differ as one moves from a Japanese to a Latin American market. An audience of midlevel managers for the same company could want to know more, if only to assess for themselves whether a new training program should be put online. An audience of vice-presidents and regional managers would want to know how insensitivity to communication across cultures might affect employee morale as well as company productivity and profits.

Sometimes, however, you will want to create a new set of interests in an audience. For example, you might want to inform a group of college students about southwestern cooking. Some audience members already may have more than a passing interest in the culinary arts, while others may be relatively uninformed and uninterested. For those already interested, you can draw connections between traditional midwestern, meat-and-potatoes flavors and those of southwestern cuisine. For those not already interested, you should work from the backgrounds in southwestern food they already have. You could show how southwestern cuisine is built around some flavors they already know from fast-food Mexican restaurants and how easy it is for them to broaden their taste by learning how to order different courses. For this speech, you might phrase your central idea as "Knowing more about southwestern cooking will open up whole new, exciting, food-preparation and eating experiences." Phrasing the central idea in this way ties the subject to both segments of your audience.

**The Audience's Capacity to Act**    As noted in the section on narrowing speech subjects, you should limit your request to an action that lies within your listeners' range of authority. Don't ask them to accomplish the impossible. To demand that a group of college students take direct action to stop the netting of tuna is unrealistic, for example, especially if you're in the corn belt of the United States. However, you can ask them to boycott tuna and other products associated with tuna harvesting that are not marked as "dolphin safe." You also can urge them to write their local congressional representatives to implore their support for more stringent fishing regulations and put them in touch with larger organizations already lobbying on this problem.

Sometimes an audience analysis reveals that different segments of your audience have varying capacities to undertake actions. If so, you'll want to address those segments separately in the action step of your speech. For example, in addressing an open meeting of the city council on why the city should sponsor a major fund-raising bicycle race, you'll want to target different subgroups with different calls to action:

**Council members:** Pass a special appropriation to the recreation services budget that funds a part-time race director and publicity chair.

**Potential race sponsors:** Support the race by contributing money, food, and prizes for the various race categories.

**Riders:** Use your contacts at other races to bring out of towners to this event.

By using this method, each call for action is suited to the range of authority and talents possessed by each subgroup of listeners.

**The Audience's Willingness to Act**    An audience may have the authority to act but not the will. You'll need to assess the degree to which listeners are willing to put themselves on the line for your ideas or proposals. For example, a speech urging students to support creation of same-sex bathrooms on campus has a better chance of success when given at a fraternity or sorority meeting about service projects than it does in your speech classroom. People attending the meeting are committed to the idea of public service—or they wouldn't have come to listen. On the other hand, people in your classroom are strongly aware that you're practicing public address. Hence, they're usually more distanced from you, more attuned to the quality of your appeals and style of speaking, and less caught up in the spirit of advice following. They are difficult listeners to reach because they hear so many appeals from fellow students during the term.

Your assessment of an audience's will or desire may influence the wording of your claim. Addressing a fraternity, sorority, or a panhellenic council comprising both groups, you might phrase a claim in this fashion:

Running a campaign to create same-sex bathrooms is the best service project our organization can undertake this semester.

In your speech classroom, you might phrase this same claim differently:

> You should support the creation of same-sex bathrooms as a matter of personal commitment.

The first version acknowledges both the purpose of the meeting (identifying a service project) and the willingness of the listeners to act on some project. The second version plays down or ignores the occasion (a classroom speech) because that occasion doesn't encourage listeners to take your advice. Instead, the wording personalizes the subject, allowing the speaker to tug on at least a few heartstrings.

**Degree of Change**    Finally, as suggested earlier, you must be realistic in targeting the degree of change you can reasonably hope to obtain. In an informative context, there is a natural limit on how much information you can present about the topic due to the time limits and the complexity of the subject. For instance, it would take more than a 5-minute speech to do justice to the controversy surrounding the death penalty in the United States. Demographic factors such as age, work location, and educational development will influence how much change you can effect. In addition, deciding whether the information is new or already known will influence how much material you can cover in a single speech.

In other words, audience analysis should help you determine how to phrase your specific purpose, central ideas, and claims for maximum effectiveness. The understanding you gain about your audience in this manner also gives you a more realistic expectation of the degree of change in behavior, beliefs, attitudes, values, and commitments to action that is possible.

## Audience Segmentation: Selecting Dominant Ideas and Appeals

The preceding discussion of demographic analysis and psychological profiling of relevant beliefs, attitudes, values, and desires or fantasies focused on targeting your audience as a group. Keep in mind, however, that no matter how people are crowded together, arranged in rows, or reached electronically, they're still individuals. Although influenced by culture and society, each person holds unique beliefs, attitudes, values, and aspirations. You also function as a unique individual when approaching the audience as a speaker.

Ideally, approaching each listener one on one would be most effective. Sometimes you can, but such communication is time consuming and inefficient in matters of broad public concern. Imagine the current president of the United States taking time to talk to each one of us individually. If you assume 160 million adults and 5 minutes per person, it would take 300 million minutes—or more than 570 years of nonstop talking! Rather than take that approach, it's no wonder that political leaders have resorted to broadcasting their messages simultaneously to millions of television viewers. Through adroit stage management and attention to a conversational style, they can simulate the atmosphere of a personal conversation. In so doing, they can begin to think of listeners as individuals hearing the message in the privacy of their own homes.

Political leaders and televangelists, as well, have adopted a technique long familiar to advertisers: audience segmentation. **Audience segmentation** is a matter of dividing a mass audience into subgroups—or *target populations*—that hold common attitudes, beliefs, values, and demographic characteristics. The earlier illustration of addressing city council members, sponsors, and riders in terms of their different capacities to act is an instance of such segmentation. A typical college-student audience might be segmented by academic standing (freshmen through seniors), academic majors (art through zoology), or extracurricular activities (officer training programs, varsity sports, recreational clubs, political groups). It is up to you to decide which segments make the most sense for your speeches.

**Accurately Identifying Subgroups/Segments**    The process of identifying subgroups must be accurate and relevant to the speech purpose and occasion. This will not only allow you to better phrase your appeals, but it will also help you avoid irritating your listeners unnecessarily. A speaker who begins with "Now you girls are going to have to realize that we guys are more interested in your bodies than your minds" probably would alienate three subgroups in the audience. The female members probably would be irritated at being called "girls" and identified as mere bodies. The male members who, in fact, are attracted to females who are literate, smart, and capable of clever conversation also would be offended by having been excluded. Gay and lesbian members might see, once again, the heterosexual parts of the world getting all of the attention. The appeal would be better phrased as "Because we're all interested in establishing satisfying interpersonal relationships, . . ." This appeal aims at the proper audience segments—all people interested in various kinds of relationships—and allows audience members to fill in the individual relationships about which they're worried.

**Selecting Relevant Psychological Statements**    Audience segmentation also should help you identify statements of belief, attitudes, values, and desire to include in your speech. If you can accurately identify the relevant subgroups, you can include psychological appeals for each in your speech, thereby greatly increasing the personal appeal and potential effectiveness of your message.

Recall the earlier example of a proposed new student center on campus. If you were defending the claim that "The new student center will, in the long run, greatly improve the overall atmposphere on this campus," you'd want to suggest factual and valuative benefits for various segments of the audience:

> **Student groups:**  How many of you here have been denied office space in the present building? Of the 45 groups on campus, there has been space for only 25. The new building is designed for current groups and will allow for some growth, as well.

**Appeals to access and opportunity**

**Appeals to access and to prestige; also note recognition of alternative priorities—doesn't diminish those but suggests reason to accept proposal**

**Appeals to access and to prestige; also note recognition of alternative priorities—doesn't diminish those but suggests reason to accept proposal**

**Appeals to thrift and convenience**

**Faculty and administrators:**  How many times have you been frustrated when the current student center has been unable to accommodate your meeting? While there remain pressing priorities for additional space for academic programs—we won't deny that need exists—this facility will also enhance recruitment efforts in bringing the best and brightest students to our campus.

**Nontraditional students:**  We realize that many of you are on limited budgets, are working your way through school, and are very concerned about the cost of this new facility. It's impact on you will be smaller than you think—repaying the bond issue through a student fee of $90 per academic year is $10 per month or 33 cents per day. Considered in those terms, we believe this is a reasonable investment for the return. You will have far more space to study, many more eating options in the new food court, and the new commuter lockers will be a convenient place to store your books while on campus.

Although this segmentation has not used every conceivable value term, the procedure should be clear. Think through the possible reasons people might accept your claim because of values they hold, and use a value-sensitive vocabulary to phrase your actual appeals for acceptance. Thus, audience analyses—in combination with audience segmentation—are valuable tools for selecting your main lines of appeal and argument.

**Choosing among Valuative Appeals**   Finally, as you might guess, audience segmentation will help you select a **valuative vocabulary** for your speeches. Even informative speeches must contain appeals to audience interests. You can use a valuative vocabulary to motivate different segments of the audience to listen to and accept your information. For a class speech on banning the use of cell phones by motorists, you might begin this way:

**Efficiency value**

**Safety value**

**Safety value**

**Satisfaction/ freedom/pragmatic values**

> Cell phones, while not as popular in the United States as in Hong Kong or other places, are fast becoming a quick and easy way to stay in touch. Having your own cell phone means you can get a call anywhere at any time (even while in class, if you left it on). When you are traveling, it provides a quick way to contact authorities in an emergency. But there is a movement across the country to limit their use: The claim is made that using a cell phone while driving increases the risk of an accident. My purpose today is not to argue for or against this claim but to review for you the evidence and arguments that are being made. In this way, you can decide whether this is a good idea or if it imposes a limit on our personal freedom.

With that statement, you give your audience different reasons for listening and have a good chance of appealing to every listener, even those who do not yet use cell phones.

Appealing to every listener can be especially challenging when your topic is a controversial one. The "Ethical Moments" box on the next page looks at how to analyze the audience and occasion in this situation.

## Creating a Unifying Vision or Fantasy

Ultimately, an audience must act together. Therefore, although you can individualize appeals to particular segments, ideally, you should find a vision—a big picture—that brings all the segments back into a whole. One of two approaches is traditionally used.

When addressing the 1988 Democratic National Convention, Jesse Jackson used the *additive method*, reassembling the segments but allowing each subaudience to keep its own identity. After describing how his grandmother in Greenville, South Carolina, sewed together old, mismatched pieces of cloth to make blankets, he admonished his audience to do likewise:

> Now, Democrats, we must build such a quilt. Farmers, you seek fair prices and you are right, but you cannot stand alone. Your patch is not big enough. Workers, you fight for fair wages. You are right. But your patch, labor, is not big enough. Women, you seek comparable worth and pay equity. You are right. But your patch is not big enough. Women, mothers, you seek Head Start and day care and prenatal care on the front side of life, you're right, but your patch is not big enough.
>
> Students, you seek scholarships. You are right. But your patch is not big enough. Blacks and Hispanics, when we fight for civil rights, we are right, but our patch is not big enough. . . . Conservatives and progressives, when you fight for what you believe, right-wing, left-wing, hawk, dove—you are right, from your point of view, but your point of view is not enough.
>
> But don't despair. Be as wise as grandmama. Pool the patches and the pieces together, bound by a common thread. When we form a great quilt of unity and common ground, we'll have the power to bring about health care and housing and jobs and education and hope to our nation. We the people can win.[15]

Jackson thus added the segments of his audience together, sewing their patches into a large, Democratic quilt. Using the additive method, he enabled each segment to retain its identity in the rhetorical vision. Although spoken in 1988, his quilt metaphor has entered the national lexicon as a key rhetorical term in recognizing difference while seeking unity. Words do matter, and their choice may well have an impact beyond the immediate occasion.

The *integrative method* for constructing a vision works in the opposite direction: stripping the individual segments of their identities, attempting to make everyone feel like everyone else. When using such a technique, the speaker hopes to make the audience members feel as one. This was the tactic used by Minister Louis Farrakhan at the Million Man March to Washington, DC, in the fall of 1995.

# ETHICAL MOMENTS

## Analyzing Audience and Occasion in Moments of Controversy

In every speaking situation, the ethical considerations—honesty, openness, integrity, and the like—come into play. These are everyday considerations in being an ethically responsible speaker. But what happens when the ethics of the situation or topic are heightened by the seriousness of the issue, the existence of strongly held religious and/or political positions, and the need to take a stand that will, inevitably, cause even some of your close friends to disagree with you?

Consider the following controversy that is causing concern in several communities: When a pregnant women is killed by a drunk driver and the fetus does not survive, should the driver be charged with causing one death or two? Does the unborn fetus have victim rights? In specific terms:

"Should a fetus be granted legal status separate and distinct from its mother?"*

Imagine if you were talking to your own classmates about this issue. Some will agree if you say yes. Some will agree if you say no. Regardless of the position you take, the audience's values will be targeted in specific fashion. What is the right thing to do?

Speaking in a way that openly acknowledges the differences in opinion and judgment that exist is the best strategy. Taking a position consistent with your own beliefs and values, you will need to express your arguments in terms that will not cause opponents to believe you are insensitive to their values. The notion that "Reasonable people can disagree reasonably" is the key value you wish to hang your position on in this setting. Pointing out that, ultimately, this will be a case fought in courts of law does not mean that citizens should not be informed or should not advocate their understanding of what should be done in such controversies.

Adding your voice to those arguing both sides of the issue is a means of advancing understanding and appreciation of the intensity with which views are held by those in the community, including you and members of your audience.

*Stephanie Simon, "One Killing—or Two?" *Columbus Dispatch,* 17 June 2001, p. C1.

He built his final appeal around a pledge, asking the audience to forget about their former activities and become new men, committed to each other and their society. The pledge was long. Here is the opening:

> Now, brothers, I want you to take this pledge. When I say I, I want you to say I, and then say your name. I know that there's so many names, but I want you to shout your name out so that the ancestors can hear it. Take this pledge with me. Say with me please, I, say your name, pledge that from

this day forward I will strive to love my brother as I love myself. I, say your name, from this day forward will strive to improve myself spiritually, morally, mentally, socially, politically, and economically for the benefit of myself, my family, and my people. I, say your name, pledge that I will strive to build businesses, build houses, build hospitals, build factories, and then to enter international trade for the good of myself, my family, and my people. I, say your name, pledge that from this day forward I will never raise my hand with a knife or a gun to beat, cut, or shoot any member of my family or any human being, except in self-defense.[16]

When a vision is well crafted, it surrounds an audience, helping it feel like an integrated group. When listeners are caught up in the same vision, they can be forged into a working unit.

# Sample Audience Analysis

In this chapter, we have surveyed various factors that you will consider as you analyze your audience and occasion. If you work systematically, these choices will become clearer. Suppose you belong to a citizens action group—Citizens for Safe Driving—that advocates a ban on using hand-held cell phones while driving. Favoring the use of hands-free phones in cars, you decide to talk at a public hearing in your county being held by the state Senate Transportation Safety Committee. You might prepare the following comprehensive analysis of your audience as you prepare your speech.

---

### *Promoting Safer Driving through Responsible Phone Use*

I. General description of speech
   A. *General purpose:* To persuade
   B. *Specific purpose:* To persuade the Senate Transportation Safety Committee to support a bill banning the use of hand-held phones in vehicles

II. General description of audience: At this public hearing are several representatives of your citizens action committee; representatives of the Cellular Telecommunications and Internet Association who will speak against the proposal; managers of local cellular phone companies; students from the local campus who use cell phones on a regular basis while driving back and forth from home; local citizens who are both for and against the proposal; representatives of local and regional newspaper, radio, and television operations; and about three dozen people who have come out of curiosity and general interest in the issue.

III. Audience analysis
   A. Demographic analysis
      1. *Age:* Most individuals attending the meeting are between 18 and 65. The age range means that I'm facing mostly experienced adults, who can vote and

---

*(continued)*

pressure their legislators if I can get through to them. My own age (19) will be a factor, as some may see me as too young to be in such a responsible position as an advocate. On the other hand, I am among those who typically use phones while driving.

2. *Gender:* The audience is a mixed group, with slightly more men than women. With this issue, gender differences are not a relevant factor in appealing to state legislators.

3. *Education:* This is a well-educated community, and among members of this audience are people who are aware of the current drive in many states to enact a similar ban such as in New York and who are aware of accidental deaths that have been linked to phone use while driving. I can assume some level of knowledge, so I don't have to detail particular aspects of the problem, though I'll want enough details to get major stories in the press.

4. *Group membership:* All listeners are politically active or they would not have taken time out to attend this hearing; those eligible are registered voters. I can assume that most are ready to act (or to oppose action).

5. *Cultural and ethnic background:* Ethnic background is mixed though primarily European. It is not a major factor here. Culturally, people attending have a sense that this is a safety issue that cuts across social and ethnic lines. In this community, the audience generally envision themselves as heartland people, with courtesy, common sense, civic pride, and neighborliness values that are spoken of often. There are some "town-gown" conflicts on occasion. This issue is one that cuts across the others—it is not a case of students/professors against the "townies."

B. Psychological profile

1. *Factual beliefs:* Not everyone in the audience uses a cell phone, but they have seen others use them while driving. They are, for the most part, aware of recent news articles, such as the one chronicling New York's approval of a ban on hand-held devices. They have some facts but are not all well informed. Their present beliefs should be capable of being altered.

2. *Opinions:* As noted, given their observations of phone use while driving, some will have strong opinions on the dangers they perceive and will be in favor of the action you propose. Others will be less certain that the problem can be easily remedied by a ban. I must address both groups, as their opinions conflict.

3. *Attitudes:* As noted above, some listeners may consider me too young, hence naive and idealistic in seeking change. Their attitude is premised in part on distrust of government in acting in the people's interest. I must demonstrate that I know what I'm talking about, and I must not convey a similar attitude of distrust in addressing legislators. I have to be forceful in making my points without seeming insensitive to their willingness to listen and act with reason.

4. *Values:* Listeners are committed to the democratic process and take pride in community political involvement at the state and national levels. They see themselves as common people—"the heart of America"—fulfilling the American dream. They value common sense and compromise, protecting the individual while celebrating community.

With this prespeech audience analysis completed, the next steps in preparing the speech are clearer. The audience analysis points to the kinds of supporting materials needed. For instance, for the Senate committee members, you need facts on the size of problem in the state and the nation. Also useful would be information about other states (e.g., New York) and other countries (e.g., Switzerland and Italy) that have acted to ban the use of hand-held phones in vehicles. For the press, spectacular, specific instances are attractive pieces of evidence. To blunt your opponents' counterarguments, know why New York has acted and why other states are considering such actions. To locate this information, do the following:

1. Use the library's computerized database to investigate cell phone bans.

2. Obtain a copy of the 1997 *New England Journal of Medicine* (*NEJM*) study that suggests cell phone use quadruples the risk of an accident.

3. Access electronic versions of the *New York Times* and other major newspapers that have articles on the issue. (Note that some search sites that stockpile articles are required to delete these after a two- to three-week period— just because the search engine references an article's existence, it may no longer be available on the web.)

4. If possible, contact the public policy director for Verizon Wireless, and ask if she or he or a representative from Verizon could attend the session—as the company supports national legislation making such a ban uniform across all states.

5. Interview students and business leaders who use cell phones while driving.

6. Get a copy of an American Automobile Association (AAA) study that contradicts the evidence provided in the 1997 *NEJM* article—know the differences between the two studies, as your opponents will cite the AAA study as proof there is no reason for a ban.

7. Although not directly related to the present issue, know enough about other bans on cell phone use to speak knowledgeably should the issues arise (e.g., students being suspended from their high schools for having cell phones in the school building).

While this list may seem extensive, it is likely to yield useful information because it is a specific rather than a general search for facts on cell phone use. Then, with the demographic and psychological profile of the audience completed and your research compiled, you can adapt your ideas and appeals to your audience. You might include the following main ideas in your speech:

1. Stress the openness and fairness with which the legislators have addressed problems facing the state. Make it clear that you understand these decisions are not necessarily easy because the freedom of individuals to buy and use cell phones as they wish is as important as the duty of the state to assist in protecting citizens from actions which may endanger their lives. Point out

that safety is the prime issue here; it is not a question of impinging on personal freedom, as citizens can still use hands-free phones in their vehicles. Rather, it is a question of preventing needless accidents through responsible driving.

2. Make it clear that this is not an economic issue. You are not talking about who can and cannot afford to install hands-free phones. You are instead focusing on the dangers inherent in hand-held usage. Aim these issues particularly at the senators and the family people in the audience.

3. Use the evidence that has been collected on accidents related to cell phone use to demonstrate, specifically, that such use is dangerous.

4. Cite evidence from recent national studies that show 70 percent to 90 percent of those polled favor some kind of ban on drivers using hand-held phones.

5. Recognize that this is a national problem. If the nation as a whole does not act, it will remain critical for state legislatures to take the lead in protecting their own states and communities from undue harm. Given that you are in a university community, stress the need for continued study. All of this points not to the dismantling of rights but to a carefully thought-out rationale for reducing the dangers from hand-held phone use while driving.[17]

## ■ CHAPTER SUMMARY

Public speaking is audience centered and occasion centered. The primary goal of audience analysis is to discover the aspects of listeners' demographic and psychological backgrounds that are relevant to your speech purposes:

- *Demographic analysis:* the age, gender, education, group membership, and cultural as well as ethnic background of the audience
- *Psychological analysis:* the beliefs, attitudes, values, desires, visions, and fantasies of the audience

Once you can profile your listeners, you can adapt your speech purposes and ideas to them.

Analysis of the occasion complements analysis of the audience. An occasion is a set of activities that occurs in a time and place set aside for the express purpose of fulfilling collective goals for and by people who have been taught the special meanings of those activities. You should attempt to analyze your speech occasion's rules for speaking, habitual roles played by both speaker and audience, and the standards of competency that will be applied to your speech.

The analysis of both audience and occasion will help you with audience targeting: deciding on realistic specific purposes, areas of audience interest, the audience's capacity and willingness to act, and the degree of change you can expect. Your analysis also will aid you in audience segmentation: creating basic appeals that accurately identify subgroups, applying psychological statements that are relevant to their lives, and using appropriate valuative appeals. The ability to adapt your speech to the needs of a particular audience and occasion is the mark of a competent public speaker.

# ■ KEY TERMS

attitudes  (p. 108)
audience segmentation  (p. 123)
audience targeting  (p. 118)
beliefs  (p. 107)
captive audience  (p. 117)
demographic analysis  (p. 104)
desires  (p. 112)
facts  (p. 107)
fantasies  (p. 112)

fixed beliefs  (p. 108)
general audience
    expectations  (p. 116)
ideologies  (p. 110)
instrumental values  (p. 109)
occasion  (p. 115)
opinions  (p. 107)
psychological profiles  (p. 107)
rhetorical vision  (p. 112)

specific audience
    expectations  (p. 116)
stereotypes  (p. 108)
terminal values  (p. 109)
valuative vocabulary  (p. 124)
value orientations  (p. 110)
values  (p. 109)
variable beliefs  (p. 108)

# ■ ASSESSMENT ACTIVITIES

1. Using the Sample Audience Analysis outline on pages 127–128 as a checklist, respond to each item for your next speech and turn it in two class periods before you're due to speak. Your instructor will examine and comment on it before you speak to be sure that you've maximized your chances of success.

2. Study the occasion of presenting a speech in your classroom. Working either in groups or alone (depending on your instructor's instructions), answer the following questions. Then, after you've answered the questions, write down three things you will do to adapt to the occasion.
   a. What are the prevailing rules and customs you must follow in this classroom?
   b. What physical conditions affect the way you speak?

   c. How do speech days work? (What will precede and follow your speech? Are there any special challenges presented in the ways speech days are run in this class?)

3. Secure a copy of Minister Louis Farrakhan's 1995 speech, either from the Information Arcade at the University of Iowa Libraries or from CNN U.S. News (cnn.org). (Both are on the Internet.) After reading the speech, do the following:
   a. Identify any beliefs, attitudes, values, and visions that you think are hostile to those of the white viewers of that day.
   b. Note how, if at all, Minister Farrakhan narrows the gaps between his beliefs, attitudes, and values and those of his white audience.
   c. Name or label the tactics he uses, and discuss briefly in what kinds of situations you can use them.

# ■ REFERENCES

1. Donald C. Bryant, *Rhetorical Dimensions of Criticism* (Baton Rouge: Louisiana State University Press, 1973), 19.
2. For more discussion, see Lawrence E. Harrison, ed., *Culture Matters: How Values Shape Human Progress* (New York: Basic Books, 2000); Milton M. Rokeach, *Beliefs, Attitudes, and Values: A Theory of Organization and Change* (San Francisco: Jossey-Bass, 1968); Milton Rokeach, *Understanding Human Values* (New York: Free Press, 1979). Cf. the discussion of polarized policy warfare because of contraposed, extreme values in Deborah Tannen, *The Argument Culture: Moving from Debate to Dialogue* (New York: Random House, 1998), especially Chapter 2.

3. Available online: <http://www.leader-values.com/leader%20values/Lead8.htm>. Accessed June 16, 2001.

4. George Soros, "The Crisis of Global Capitalism," excerpted in *Newsweek*, 7 December 1998, p. 78.

5. Available online: <http://www.michiganepic.org/coredemocratic.html>. Accessed June 16, 2001.

6. See Kenneth Burke's ideas on terministic screens in his *Language as Symbolic Action: Essays on Life, Literature, and Method* (Berkeley: University of California Press, 1966).

7. Dick Hebdige, *Subculture: The Meaning of Style (New Accents)* (London: Routledge, 1981). This is a large topic: Exploring the social force and politics of desire, pleasure, and fantasy takes you into many worlds, such as the music of Madonna (especially during the late 1980s and early 1990s); advertising; political statements such as Martin Luther King, Jr.'s, "I Have a Dream" speech of 1963; dressing-for-success or for expressions of self-identity; and the like. For applications, see overviews in Stuart Hall, ed., *Representation: Cultural Representations and Signifying Practices* (Thousand Oaks, CA: Sage, 1997). On the "aesthetization" or "fashioning" (p. 5) of social identities and political attitudes, consult Paul du Gay, ed., *Production of Culture/Cultures of Production* (Thousand Oaks, CA: Sage, 1997). For summaries of current advertising theory and analysis, see Katherine Toland Frith, ed., *Undressing the Ad: Reading Culture in Advertising*, 2nd ed. (New York: Peter Lang, 1998); and for discussions of the politics of pleasure and other feeling-states, see Kathleen Hall Jamieson, *Everything You Think You Know About Politics . . . and Why You're Wrong* (New York: Basic Books, 2000) and Roderick P. Hart, *Seducing America: How Television Charms the Modern Voter*, rev. ed. (Thousand Oaks, CA: Sage, 1999).

8. The idea of rhetorical vision was introduced in Earnest G. Bormann, "Fantasy and Rhetorical Vision: The Rhetorical Criticism of Social Reality," *Quarterly Journal of Speech* 58 (1972): 396–407. All of his ideas, as well as his analysis of the history of rhetorical visions in political speechmaking, are found in his book *The Force of Fantasy: Restoring the American Dream* (Carbondale, IL: Southern Illinois University Press, 1985); this quotation is from p. 8.

9. Bormann, *The Force of Fantasy*, 8. See also Bruce E. Gronbeck, "Rhetorical Visions from the Margins, 1963–1988," *Retoriska Frågor: Texter on tal och talare från Quintilianus till Clinton tillägnade Kurt Johannesson*, edited by Christer Åsberg (Stockholm: Nordstedts Förlag, 1995), 267–281.

10. Abraham Lincoln, "First Inaugural Address [4 March 1961]," *The American Reader: Words That Moved a Nation*, edited by Diane Ravitch (New York: HarperCollins, 1990), 143.

11. Henri Mann Morton, in Jerry D. Blanche, *Native American Reader: Stories, Speeches, and Poems* (Juneau, AK: Denali Press, 1990). Reprinted with permission of the publisher.

12. For further information, see Robert H. Gass and John S. Seiter, *Persuasion, Social Influence and Compliance Gaining* (Boston: Allyn and Bacon, 1998).

13. Edward Hall argues that you learn about culture and social expectations in three ways: formally (when someone tells you what to do), informally (when you imitate what others are doing), and when you are older, technically (when you learn why members of a society do certain things and not others through explanations). See Hall, *The Silent Language* (Greenwich, CT: Fawcett, 1959), Chapter 4, "The Major Triad," 63–91.

14. For an analysis of the rhetorical roots of occasion, see John T. Kirby, "Occasion," in *Encyclopedia of Rhetoric*, edited by Thomas O. Sloane, 529–532. (New York: Oxford University Press, 2001).

15. Excerpt from "Common Ground and Common Sense," by Rev. Jesse Jackson, from *Vital Speeches of the Day*, Vol. 54, August 15, 1988, p. 651. Copyright © 1988 by Jesse Jackson. Reprinted by permission of the author.

16. Louis Farrakhan, "Transcript from Minister Louis Farrakhan's Remarks at the Million Man March, October 17, 1995." Available online: <www.arcade.uiowa.edu>. Used with permission.

17. Material taken from "States Consider Motorist Cell Phone Bans," *Athens Messenger*, 12 June 2001, p. 1; "Cell Phones in Cars—More Accidents on Highways." Available online: <http://www.voiceoftheinjured.com/a-aa-cell-phones-accidents-injuries.html>. Accessed June 23, 2001.

# Chapter 6

# Developing Ideas
## Finding and Using Supporting Materials

*A student wanted to do a speech on President George W. Bush. She accessed the World Wide Web, pulled up the Google search engine, typed in "President Bush," and in 30 seconds, got about 750,000 hits. Stunned, she decided to check on Bush's opponent in the election, Al Gore. In about the same time, that search returned only 670,000 hits. Thinking she had better narrow the search field a bit, she typed in "Presidential Debates." Things were looking better, as that yielded only 41,200 hits. She noticed a reference to C-Span in one of the hits and decided to give that a try: "C-Span+Presidential Debates." This returned 13 hits—suffi cient to remodel the speech on Bush to a speech on C-Span's coverage of the debates. While a "C-Span" search alone turned in over 200,000 hits, "C-Span+ History" turned in only 50, and one of those (www.cspan.org/about/milestones/) provided a linear history of major achievements since its inception in 1979. Now she had a historical overview she could use to frame a more current discussion of C-Span's role in the debates. With a bit more work, she was able to access other sites, and within a half hour, she had all of the information she needed without leaving her desk.*

This student's experience reflects a search process that, in just the last few years, has become a common approach to managing the acquisition of information. She was overwhelmed by the number of hits at a general level, and only when she narrowed the search was she able to decide what was useful and what was irrelevant to her specific need. Whether speaking to inform, to persuade, or even just to entertain, you'll want to convey ideas that have substance and are worthwhile. To do so, you need materials that are concrete, reasonably connected to claims you are making, and sufficient to convince an audience that you do know what you are talking about. The search tools of today—such as the World Wide Web, where you can access libraries and home pages from around the globe, electronic card catalogs, CD-ROM search technologies for major newspapers and special in-dexes—will deluge you with enough information not just for a six-minute speech of explanation but for dozens of such speeches.

In this chapter, we explore the kinds of supporting materials speeches de-mand. A good speech burns supporting materials like jet fuel, and this chapter dis-cusses the various kinds of energy that fuel speeches. We then tackle the questions of where to find those fuels and how to burn them. We discuss electronic, print, face-to-face, and mailed forms of supporting materials, and we look at some strate-gies for putting them together to achieve maximum power and effectiveness.

Thinking through the kinds of materials you need before you actually hit the library or an "http" command on your computer is a habit you must cultivate. Searching for supporting materials purposively is the key to success—and to sanity.

## What to Look For:
## Forms of Supporting Materials

Competent speakers regularly use five types of supporting materials: explana-tions, comparisons and contrasts, examples and narratives, statistics, and testi-mony (see Figure 6.1).

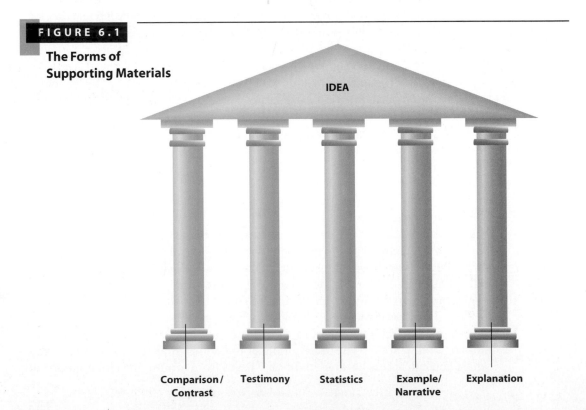

**FIGURE 6.1**

**The Forms of Supporting Materials**

IDEA

Comparison/Contrast    Testimony    Statistics    Example/Narrative    Explanation

## Explanations

An **explanation** is a description or expository passage that makes a term, concept, process, or proposal clear or acceptable. Explanations tell "what," "how," or "why," and they show relationships between a whole and its parts. They also may make it easier to understand concepts that are difficult to grasp. As with other forms of support, explanations must be presented clearly and attached explicitly to the central ideas of your speech to be useful.

An explanation tells an audience what something is by offering defining and clarifying details. Elie Wiesel, a Holocaust survivor and 1986 recipient of the Nobel Peace Prize, spoke on the perils of indifference at a White House symposium:

> Indifference, after all, is more dangerous than anger and hatred. Anger can at times be creative. One writes a great poem, a great symphony, has done something special for the sake of humanity because one is angry at the injustice that one witnesses. But indifference is never creative. Even hatred at times may elicit a response. You fight it. You denounce it. You disarm it. Indifference elicits no response. Indifference is not a response.
>
> Indifference is not a beginning, it is an end. And, therefore, indifference is always the friend of the enemy, for it benefits the aggressor—never his victim, whose pain is magnified when he or she feels forgotten. The political prisoner in his cell, the hungry children, the homeless refugees—not to respond to their plight, not to relieve their solitude by offering them a spark of hope is to exile them from human memory. And in denying their humanity we betray our own.
>
> Indifference, then, is not only a sin, it is a punishment. And this is one of the most important lessons of this outgoing century's wide-ranging experiments in good and evil.[1]

Notice that the explanation begins with a comparison with a more familiar concept in demarcating what indifference means. Explanations are helpful in setting up an understanding of a concept or practice—what something means or how something is done. An explanation should not be too long, as the audience may lose the larger point in the myriad details. Nor should it be expected to carry the weight of an argument, as it seldom provides sufficient justification for belief or action.

## Comparisons and Contrasts

Comparisons and contrasts are useful verbal devices for clarifying ideas—to make them distinctive and focused. Pointing out similarities and differences helps listeners comprehend your ideas and opinions.

**Comparisons**   A **comparison** is an analogy that connects something already known or believed with ideas a speaker wishes to have understood or accepted. Comparisons, therefore, stress similarities. Andrew B. Wilson, a speechwriter, spoke to the Peterson Conference of Banking Communicators and introduced a comparison between skiing and public speaking:

> I was sitting on a sofa in front of a roaring fire, leafing through a recent issue of *Skiing* magazine, when I came across an article entitled, "To Air (that's air—a . . . i . . . r) Is Human," by Kristen Ulmer. Ms. Ulmer specializes in what is known as "extreme skiing." In other words, she is a kind of an Evel Knievel on skis.
>
> This may not be everyone's cup of tea, but what Ms. Ulmer has to say about ski jumping is strikingly apropos to public speaking—particularly public speaking at a time of crisis.
>
> Let's begin with her observation that "There is a narrow line between total control and overwhelming terror." If you really want to go airborne—in skiing or in public speaking—everything depends upon a positive and purposeful attitude. You must "ache for the impact!" because, as Ms. Ulmer says, "Once in the air, he who hesitates is lunch."[2]

In this fashion, Wilson offers a clear comparison between what is felt by an extreme skier and a public speaker and what both must do to succeed.

**Contrasts**     A **contrast** helps to clarify a complex situation or process by focusing on differences. A speaker explaining arena football would want to contrast it with the more familiar rules governing interscholastic football. To clarify the severity of the 1996 drought, the news networks contrasted the average rainfall for a normal summer with the rainfall that year. Contrasts not only can clarify unfamiliar or complex problems but also can strengthen the arguments you wish to advance. In her acceptance speech for the Green Party's Nomination for vice president during the 2000 election, Winona LaDuke highlighted the treatment given Native Americans in contrast to that offered to business corporations:

> How is it that when the people of the White Earth reservation ask the federal government for the return of the Tamarac National Wildlife Refuge or to manage the Tamarac National Wildlife Refuge—lands taken illegally from our people—we are refused or put off? Yet these same lands are basically given to Potlatch and Champion. Why is it that the state and other officials refer to last year's wind shear on my reservation that took down over 200,000 acres of trees as a natural disaster? Yet Potlatch expands present mills and they will be cutting a square mile of Minnesota's northwoods daily—the equivalent of an eight foot pile of logs piled across both the north and south bound lanes of 35W from Minneapolis to Duluth—and that is referred to as economic growth.[3]

Helping an audience reason along with you by visualizing differences is an excellent strategy for getting them to understand and accept your ideas.

**Using Comparisons and Contrasts**   Whenever using a comparison or contrast, make sure that one of the items is familiar to listeners. Comparing arena football and interscholastic football will make no sense to listeners from Ireland, for example, who probably don't know anything about either one. You'd have to compare and contrast arena football and European soccer to clarify the arena game for them. You also can use comparison and contrast together by focusing first on the similarities between football and soccer and then on the differences.

## Examples and Narratives

A detailed **example** of an idea you wish to support is either an **illustration** or a **narrative.** If the example describes a concept, condition, or circumstance, it's called an *illustration;* if it's in story form, it's called a *narrative.* An illustration or narrative is always, however, a big "for instance"—something concrete that makes an abstract or general idea easier to comprehend. If the illustration is undeveloped or set up as a string of quick examples, it's called a **specific instance.**

Some illustrations and narratives are hypothetical (made up); others are factual—recitations of actual events or references to persons, places, and things. If you were giving a speech on why students should move out of dormitories and into apartments, you might narrate a typical evening in a dorm: loud music, a constant flow of pizza delivery people through the hall, a traveling party, a false fire alarm, nonstop card games, illegal alcohol, and an engagement shower. Although not all of these may occur on the same night, asking listeners to imagine what life would be like if they did would help you convey the intensity of your antidormitory feelings through a made-up narrative.

For many audiences, fact-based illustrations and narratives are more potent. Courtney Love offered the following account of what happens to a recording artist who receives what appears to be a huge advance for a new recording in her presentation at the Digital Hollywood Online Entertainment Conference:

> I want to start with a story about rock bands and record companies, and do some recording-contract math:
>
> This story is about a bidding-war band that gets a huge deal with a 20 percent royalty rate and a million-dollar advance. (No bidding-war band ever got a 20 percent royalty, but whatever.) This is my "funny" math based on some reality and I just want to qualify it by saying I'm positive it's better math than what Edgar Bronfman Jr. [the president and CEO of Seagram, which owns Polygram] would provide.
>
> What happens to that million dollars?
>
> They spend half a million to record their album. That leaves the band with $500,000. They pay $100,000 to their manager for 20 percent commission. They pay $25,000 each to their lawyer and business manager.
>
> That leaves $350,000 for the four band members to split. After $170,000 in taxes, there's $180,000 left. That comes out to $45,000 per person.
>
> That's $45,000 to live on for a year until the record gets released.[4]

Through a clear narrative, Courtney Love exposes what she calls "piracy" throughout her presentation: that record companies are getting rich at the expense of performers. Specific instances are undeveloped illustrations or examples; usually, they are grouped into a list, so they pile one upon the other to drive the speaker's point home.

The Roman orator Cicero was the first advocate of "filling the mind" with examples. He called the technique *accumulatio*, or "accumulation," in Book III of his treatise on rhetoric, *De Oratore*. An example from the *Rhetorica ad Herennium* (author unknown) is instructive:

> He [the defendant] is the betrayer of his own self-respect, and the way-layer of the self-respect of others; covetous, intemperate, irascible, arrogant; disloyal to his parents, ungrateful to his friends, troublesome to his kin; insulting to his betters, disdainful of his equals and mates, cruel to his inferiors; in short, he is intolerable to everyone.[5]

The power of an example comes from cumulative effect rather than from vivid detail. Sometimes, you can use a single specific instance if all you need is a quick example:

> You're all familiar with the windows in this classroom, but you might not have noticed their actual construction. I want to talk about windows like the ones around you—these double-glazed, low-emissivity, gas-filled windows—and how the use of such seemingly expensive windows contributes to reduced energy consumption on campus and in your life.

More often, though, speakers pile on instances either to clarify their point or to prove it. That's what Erin Gallagher did in an original oration written for forensics competition. Speaking on the issue of donated tissue, she shared these observations:

> Too often skin is sold to companies to *improve* lives, while hospitals search in vain for that same skin to *save* someone's life. The April 17, 2000, *Orange County Register* tells the story of Seton Hall University student Dana Christmas, who suffered burns on 60 percent of her body in the dormitory fire there last January. Even though the country's largest tissue bank, the Musculosketal Transplant Foundation, was just 20 minutes south of Dana's hospital, it couldn't provide the needed skin. That's because 100 percent of its skin was committed to a firm that markets a product for plastic surgery. And the June 10, 2000, *Sarasota Herald-Tribune* reports that the Grossman Burn Center in Anaheim, California, faced a similar problem last fall. After calling 15 different skin banks but still failing to find enough skin, doctors were forced to leave a patient's wounds open, leading to his death. In fact, the website of the American Red Cross, copyright 2001, reports that "only $1/6$ of the skin needed for burn patients is currently available."[6]

With these accumulated instances, Gallagher was able to illustrate the severity of the problem before going on to explain the reasons that skin tissue is regularly unavailable where it is most needed.

## Statistics

**Statistics** are numbers that show relationships between or among phenomena—relationships that can emphasize size or magnitude, describe subclasses or parts (segments), or establish trends. By reducing large masses of information into generalized categories, statistics can clarify situations, substantiate potentially disputable central ideas, and make complex aspects of the world clear to listeners.

We often use statistics to describe a situation or to sketch its significance in terms of its **size** or **scope.** When one statistical description of the size of a problem is piled upon others, the effect on listeners can be especially strong. So, a speech reviewing President Bill Clinton's relationship with the public during the 1998 impeachment process could cite three, four, even five polls that all showed him with the support of 55 to 65 percent of the public as the House Judiciary Committee and the full House worked on articles of impeachment.

Not all references to the size or scope of a problem, of course, need such an accumulation of instances. Simple, hard-hitting information sometimes works even better. For example, as Courtney Love demonstrated in drawing out her narrative on record company payments:

> That leaves $350,000 for the four band members to split. After $170,000 in taxes, there's $180,000 left. That comes out to $45,000 per person. That's $45,000 to live on for a year until the record gets released.

Her point that an original million-dollar advance reduces to a little money is clearly made.

*A speaker can use statistics to describe a situation or to sketch its scope or magnitude. By reducing large masses of information into general categories, statistics can clarify and substantiate a claim.*

Statistics also are used to isolate the parts of a problem or to show aspects of a problem caused by separate factors; parts or aspects can be treated as statistical **segments.** In discussing the wisdom of renovating the University of Iowa's student union, for example, a speaker might point to a survey indicating that 54 percent of the student body said it would pay $60 per student for the renovation; 21 percent, $45; 6 percent, $30; and 20 percent, nothing.[7] You then could say:

> In other words, four out of five students are willing to help finance the renovation out of their own funds.

Statistics also often are used to point out **trends**—indicators that tell us where we were, where we are now, and where we may be heading. The comparison of statistical representations across time allows you to say that a particular phenomenon is increasing or decreasing. Another student used the following table from a website to illustrate the growth of the Internet as a source for merchandise:[8]

**Internet commerce: Companies that allow consumers to purchase merchandise via the web fall into this category**

| Quarter 1 2000 | Growth over Q1 1999 | Quarter 2 2000 | Growth over Q2 1999 |
|---|---|---|---|
| $1,020,416 | 12.6% | $1,033,159 | 8.2% |

In making use of this kind of visual information, the speaker also needs to make sure the audience understands what the basis for reporting is—just copying the table, as done above, from the website is not sufficient. Corroborating this data with other information that tells a similar story goes a long way toward enhancing the believability of what has been extracted from a single web source.

The different ways in which size or scope, segments, and trends might be used in support of an issue are illustrated in Table 6.1.

---

**TABLE 6.1**   **Types of Statistics**

In a speech to inform, a speaker might use three types of statistics to describe students at Central University. What other forms of supporting material could complement these numbers?

| SIZE/SCOPE | SEGMENTS | TRENDS |
|---|---|---|
| "Three-fourths of all Central University students come from the state." | "Sixty percent of all Central University students major in business; 25 percent are humanities majors; the remaining 15 percent are in fine arts." | "Since 1975, enrollment at Central University has increased by 20 percent every five years." |

**Using Statistics**    When you use statistics in the ways just described, you can help your listeners by making the numbers more user friendly. Follow these guidelines:

1. *Translate difficult-to-comprehend numbers into more immediately understandable terms.* In a speech on the mounting problem of solid waste, Carl Hall illustrated the immensity of 130 million tons of garbage by explaining that trucks loaded with this amount would extend from coast to coast three abreast.[9]

2. *Don't be afraid to round off complicated numbers.* "Nearly 300,000" is easier for listeners to comprehend than "296,454." Likewise, "Just over 33 percent" or, better yet, "about a third," is preferable to "33.5 percent."

3. *Use visual aids to clarify complicated statistical trends or summaries whenever possible.* Hand out a photocopied sheet of numbers, draw a graph on the chalkboard, or prepare a pie chart on an overhead transparency. Such aids allow you to concentrate your words on explaining the significance of the numbers rather than on making sure the audience understands and remembers them.

4. *Use statistics fairly.* It's easy to mislead with statistics—even if you don't exactly lie. Arguing that professional women's salaries increased 8.3 percent last year may sound impressive to listeners until they ask what the actual salaries are in real dollars. The listeners may then realize that the increase is based on a lower salary, on average, than men earn for the same work. Provide a fair context for your data.[10]

This final point is examined further in the "Ethical Moments" box on page 142, which looks at the ethical issues involved in using statistics.

## Testimony

When you cite the opinions or conclusions of others, you're using **testimony**. Testimony sometimes merely adds weight, clarity, or impressiveness to an idea, as when you quote Mahatma Gandhi or a clever turn of a phrase by Rosie O'Donnell. All testimony should meet the twin tests of *pertinence* and *audience acceptability*. When used to strengthen a statement rather than merely to amplify or illustrate an idea, testimony also should satisfy four more specific criteria:

1. *The person quoted should be qualified, by training and experience, to speak on the topic being discussed.* Athletes are more credible talking about sports equipment or exercise programs than endorsing breakfast food or local furniture stores.

2. *Whenever possible, the authority's statement should be based on firsthand knowledge.* An Iowa farmer is not an authority on a Mississippi drought unless she or he has personally observed the conditions.

3. *The judgment expressed should not be unduly influenced by personal interest.* Asking a political opponent to comment on the current president's performance will likely yield a self-interested answer.

# ETHICAL MOMENTS

## The Numbers Game

The rise of science in the twentieth century was accompanied by the rise of numerical data—and its public exhibition. By now, you've been told by one poll that the public favors a liberalization of abortion laws by 2 to 1 but by another poll that the public favors tightening abortion laws by an equal percentage. You know that 4 out of 5 dentists surveyed recommend a particular brand of toothpaste. You've heard that a brand of cigarettes has the lowest level of tar and nicotine—from more than one manufacturer. As both listener and speaker, you have to make some ethical calls when encountering such data:

1. Contradictory polls, such as those on abortion, usually result when questions are asked in slanted ways. "Do parents have to right to know when their under-aged teen seeks a dangerous abortion?" tends to encourage a positive answer, whereas "Should women have the right to control their own bodies without external interference from others?" also encourages a positive answer—but one in favor of a very different public policy than the first. Questions can be loaded in favor of opposing public policies. You're wise to report the actual questions when quoting poll results.

2. Who were those "4 out of 5 dentists surveyed"? Is it ethical to cite statistics without reviewing how they were gathered and calculated?

3. If your favorite brand of cigarettes is one of five brands that all have the same low tar and nicotine content, then technically, of course, yours has the lowest—and so do the other four brands. Is it ethical, however, to claim your brand is "the lowest," or must you say that it is "one of the lowest"?

It's easy to fiddle with numbers: to round up or down, to compare only parts rather than wholes, and to ignore key details that would properly contextualize information for listeners. If you play fast and loose with numbers, however, you might get caught. Learn to play the numbers game honestly so as to protect your reputation.

4. *Listeners should perceive the person quoted as being an actual authority.* An archbishop may be accepted as an authority by a Roman Catholic audience but perhaps not by a Protestant or Hindu audience.

When citing testimony, don't use big names simply because they're well known. The best testimony comes from experts whose qualifications your listeners recognize. Finally, always acknowledge the source of an idea or particular phrasing. As we will elaborate further later, avoid plagiarism as if it were the plague itself. Claiming someone else's ideas, information, or phraseology as being your own is stealing. Give your source credit for the material, and give yourself credit for having taken the time to do the research. (See the section "Using Source Materials Ethically," pp. 154–157.)

# Where to Look: Sources of Supporting Materials

So, you may know what kinds of materials you want for your speech—some solid numbers, a nice list of specific instances, a well-developed illustration or story, testimony from credible people, and some clarifying comparisons and contrasts. Now, where do you find such materials? You'll find them exactly where you find all ideas in this world: in electronic networks and storage technologies, in print, in interaction with others, and in information-gathering instruments that you construct yourself. Use the checklist presented in Figure 6.2 (p. 144) to evaluate and plan your supporting materials.

## The Electronic World

You've seen the ads: AT&T promising you access to information from everywhere, the newest Pentium chip bringing you sounds and images from every imaginable society, and your own college or university linking you with other institutions of learning and ideas throughout the world. Working your way through government, commercial, and educational networks takes a few skills, though probably not as many as the novice might think. At most schools and through an increasing number of inexpensive commercial services, you now can surf the Internet, upload information from CD-ROMs in libraries, and search your own library electronically with relative ease.

**The Electronic Card Catalog**    Most college and university libraries have a computerized search system for their holdings and also for journals and magazines in general. If you have access to such a system, it should be your first stop. For example, the University of Iowa uses the Oasis system, which is popular among larger research libraries. It allows you to search the university's card catalog, that of a consortium of libraries, the *Humanities and Social Science Indexes,* and several versions of *Psychological Abstracts.*

Suppose you want to do a speech on health communication, with a specific focus on research done on hospices. Using a communication database for your search (www.cios.org), you access communication journals. Typing in "Hospice" generates only one article from 1992 that may be relevant to your interests. Deciding to broaden the search, you type in "Health" and generate 85 resources from a variety of communication journals. Your quick review has taken you from too little to too much. To check other resources, you click back to the library's "Book Search" page, type in "Health Communication," and generate (at Ohio University) a list of 550 books—way more than you can sort through. Using "Hospice" as the key term, you come up with 159; narrowing that to "Hospice+Communication," you find

| FIGURE 6.2 | Checklist for Supporting Materials |
|---|---|

You should evaluate your supporting materials when you plan your speeches. Answer the questions on this checklist as you plan your supporting materials.

**General Considerations**

☐  1.  Have I included sufficient supporting materials?
☐  2.  Are my supporting materials distributed throughout my speech?
☐  3.  Do I provide extra support for confusing or controversial ideas?
☐  4.  Are my supporting materials interesting and clear?
☐  5.  Do I adequately credit the sources of my supporting materials?

**Explanations**

☐  1.  Are my explanations short and direct?
☐  2.  Do I provide other forms of support in addition to explanations?

**Comparisons and Contrasts**

☐  1.  Is at least one of the items in a comparison or contrast familiar to my listeners?
☐  2.  Is the basis of the comparison clear?
☐  3.  Is the contrast distinct enough?

**Examples and Narratives**

☐  1.  Is the illustration or narrative clearly related to the idea it's intended to support?
☐  2.  Is the illustration or narrative typical?
☐  3.  Is the illustration or narrative vivid and adequately detailed?
☐  4.  Have I provided enough specific instances?
☐  5.  Can listeners easily recognize or understand the instances I mention?

**Statistics**

☐  1.  Are my statistics easy to understand?
☐  2.  Have I rounded off complicated numbers?
☐  3.  Am I using statistics fairly?
☐  4.  Should I use visual materials to clarify complicated numbers?
☐  5.  Have I adequately interpreted the statistics I've cited for my listeners?

**Testimony**

☐  1.  Is the authority qualified to speak on the topic being discussed?
☐  2.  Is the authority's statement based on firsthand knowledge?
☐  3.  Is the authority's opinion subject to personal influence or bias?
☐  4.  Do my listeners know the authority's qualifications?
☐  5.  Will my listeners accept this person as an authority?

one book. This gives you a solid start. You may yet need more material, but at least you can begin with these resources—each one will list other resources in the bibliography that will make connections between communication and hospices.

Learning to narrow through precise specification of topic or subcategorization will make your searches less frustrating. Many systems offer **Boolean searching,** where you use words such as "AND," "OR," and "NOT" to control the subject matter. So, "Medieval OR Architecture" gets you all references with either word, "Medieval AND Architecture" pulls up references with both words, and "Medieval AND Architecture NOT England" highlights medieval architecture everywhere except England. Knowing authors, titles, and the like will help you even more. Take time to look at the pamphlet or online "Help" menu, and make sure you use your local electronic card catalog with maximum efficiency.

One last point: Find out what databases you can access through your library system. ERIC (Educational Resources Information Center) will help you locate scholarly papers in the humanities, MEDLINE will get you into psychosocial and physiological studies of disease and associated medical problems, and LEXIS-NEXIS will give you access to a staggering number of public and commercial information sources. As mentioned earlier, CIOS will give you access to communication research. You will need to check to see whether your library/department is a member of this research service.

**CD-ROM Searches**   We're living through an explosion in the use of the CD-ROM—a technological device that uses the compact disk (CD) to store computer data. CDs hold much more information than floppy disks; hence, they are used to store and to retrieve data from multiple volumes' worth of materials. Check to see what your local libraries have, perhaps the *New York Times Index*, the *Oxford English Dictionary* on CD-ROM, the *Modern Language Association Indexes*, or the *Table of Contents to Communication Journals* (which includes all articles published in National Communication Association journals since 1990). As more and more databases become available on CD-ROM, you'll be able to link electronically with the actual articles you want.

**The World Wide Web**   The **Information Superhighway** was the great metaphor of the 1980s and early 1990s—a system allowing everyone to access information electronically from around the globe. Today, you can use a variety of search tools to access unlimited information sources, yielding truckloads of data. You also can link pages of data, and, with a mere click of a mouse or tap of an "Enter" key, access the **World Wide Web.** The highway is transportation; the web is a way of reading many assembled sources at once. The web is an access protocol that allows you to enter the maze of computerized language, pictures, and sounds from any point in that maze—and then to move from site to site simply by clicking on a word or a symbol. Knowing a little vocabulary will help you work through the Web:

> *URL, Uniform Resource Locator:* The address of some site. Addresses include .com = commercial company; .edu = an educational institution; .net = a company that connects you to the Internet; .gov = a governmental site; .org = a

nonprofit organization; .mil = a military group; .us = someone in the United States who doesn't fit into another category; and specific codes for other countries (e.g., .uk for the United Kingdom, .se for Sweden, .fi for Finland, etc.).

*http, HyperText Transport Protocol*: A command to your computer to take you to some site.

*WWW, World Wide Web:* The network of servers (computers online) that provides hypertext searches on the web.

*HTML, HyperText Markup Language:* Used to create the main or homepage of a website.

*Hypertext*: Highlighted words that, when clicked, transport you to other texts (if you're on the web).

*FTP, File Transfer Protocol:* Allows you to retrieve file and directory information.

*Usenet:* Interactive accounts that link you to newsgroups or interactive discussions.

*Archie, Gopher, Veronica, WAIS (Wide Area Information Servers):* Multiple tools for accessing information sites in useful ways.

*FAQs, Frequently Asked Questions:* Check this page when you're unsure about something.

**Speech Research on the Web**     By now, you probably cannot tune into a sports broadcast, a news hour, or even a prime-time television show without being told you can use a "www" command to get to its homepage, such as ESPNET's sports scores for the day, CNN International's informational background on big stories, *USA Today* online, National Public Radio's discussion group, or propaganda from the Republican and Democratic parties. You soon discover you can go to Mississippi State University for the Internet Movie Database, to SCREENsite for links between the Library of Congress and directories on film and television resources, to the Harvard-MIT-Tufts consortium on negotiation and conflict resolution, to the University of Maryland's site full of resources and simulations for high school students, and to state and federal government sources through ".gov" locations.

Taking time to discover how to draw on such information will make your time for speech preparation not only well spent but even fun. Here is a sample of useful sites for speech research:

| SUBJECT | SITE |
| --- | --- |
| Facts | http://www.refdesk.com |
| | http://www.factsonfile.com |
| Genealogy | http://www.genealogy.org/~ngs |
| Health (disease control) | http://www.cdc.gov/cdc/htm |
| Electronic newspapers | http://www.enews.com |
| *USA Today* | http://www.usatoday.com |
| City networks | http://www.city.net |

| Maps | http://www.mapquest.com |
|------|--------------------------|
| Links to people | http://www.bigfoot.com |
| | http://www.altavista.com |
| Sports | http://www.wwcd.com/hp/sports.html |
| White House | http://www.whitehouse.gov |
| U.S. House of Representatives | http://www.house.gov |
| U.S. Senate | http://www.senate.gov |

When opening websites around the world, you'll discover utterly amazing places, such as where the Aryan (white power) women hang out, the homepages of individuals paying homage to Marilyn Monroe or Nostradamus, full texts of song lyrics, places to watch election returns from many countries, sites with sound bites and video clips, and even sites where you can shop for John Deere tractors or find parts for your 1948 9N Ford tractor. Because almost anyone can put up a website, however, you must learn to evaluate websites both for quality of information and for importance of opinion. Figure 6.3 (p. 148) presents a checklist for doing so, as outlined by Esther Grassian of the UCLA College Library.

Elaine Cubbins, at the University of Arizona, raises similar questions in a webpage dedicated to those seeking information on Native American peoples through the web. While focused on a specific group, several of the criteria are applicable to all web searches:[11]

### EVALUATION GUIDELINES FOR WEBSITES

#### General Website Guidelines

- Is the site so sophisticated that to access it requires computer software and hardware that are state of the art?
- Is the site well organized and easy to move around in? Does it take a long time for the site to load onto your computer?
- Is the site kept up to date, with current links, new material added from time to time, and a creation or revision date?
- Is the purpose of the site clear? Does the stated purpose match the actual content?
- What links are included to other sites? How well do these links meet criteria for quality websites?

#### Authority Guidelines

- Who is the web builder for the site? Is an e-mail address included?
- Does the site's URL give you any information as to the authority and validity of the site?

Taken together, these two sets of queries provide a fairly comprehensive review of the kinds of things you should look for or know about, the website you are using for information. An old saying still has merit in this new electronic world: *"Don't believe everything you read (or see on the web!)."*

| FIGURE 6.3 | **Checklist for Evaluating Websites** |

Use these questions to help determine whether a website is credible and contains useful information.

**Content and Evaluation**

☐ 1. How complete and accurate are the information and the links provided by this source?

☐ 2. How good is this site vis-à-vis other sites or print sources? (A librarian can help answer this question.)

☐ 3. What are the dates on the site and its materials?

☐ 4. How comprehensive is the site? Is the site builder interested only in certain aspects of a topic (e.g., the Arab side of the Arab-Israeli conflict)? Does she or he attempt to cover everything available—and if so, how? Are evaluations of links to other sources provided?

**Source and Dates**

☐ 1. Who produced the site? Why? What authority or knowledge does the site builder have? Is there a sponsoring organization with a vested interest in what results from people using the site?

☐ 2. Is there evident bias in the materials you find?

☐ 3. When was the site mounted, and when was it last revised? How up to date is it?

☐ 4. Is it easy to contact the site builder with questions?

**Structure**

☐ 1. Does the site follow good graphics principles? Is the use of art purposive or decorative?

☐ 2. Do the icons clearly represent what is intended?

☐ 3. Does the text follow basic tenets of good grammar, spelling, and composition?

☐ 4. Can the text be used by both line-mode (text-only) and multimedia (words/sound/pictures) users?

☐ 5. Are links provided to web subject trees in directories—lists of web sources arranged by subject?

☐ 6. How usable is the site? Can you get through it in a reasonable time?

**Other**

☐ 1. Is appropriate interactivity available?

☐ 2. Can you transfer secure information to and from the site?

☐ 3. Are links to search engines provided?

*Source:* Used with permission of Esther Grassian, Electronic Services Coordinator, UCLA College Library. Excerpted from "Thinking Critically about World Wide Web Resources." Available online: <http://www.library.ucla.edu/libraries/college/instruct/web/critical.htm>. 1997.

**Search Help**    Grassian's last point above also is ours: You need to be able to use search engines to help you through the maze of material available electronically. A **search engine** is an online database that allows you to explore broad subjects and find specific information by being directed to a source. Search engines are like the bibliographies in a library's reference area, and some—the "super" engines—are like the bibliographies of bibliographies. They come with different virtues, as well.

A "one-stop-shopping place" for search engines on the web is http://www.searchenginewatch.com/. This site will enable you to review the various sites and their strengths in engaging in your own research. Large databases include Google, Yahoo!, AltaVista, HotBot, Northern Light, Excite, InfoSeek, and Lycos. Advanced search features on InfoSeek and AltaVista allow you to easily search within your results or refine your questions. Annotated directories that tell you how to get into searches as you search include AlphaSearch and the University of Iowa Gateway (both guides to especially academic searches), the Britannica Internet Guide, Look-Smart, Snap!, and The Mining Co. Business directories include Livelink Pinstripe, Dow Jones Business Directory, SearchZ, and Northern Light Industry Search. See Table 6.2 (p. 150) for advice on which search engines to use for which approaches to information finding and retrieving.

## The Print World

Books and newspapers have not died! They still exist—check your campus library. Not all information gathering needs to, or even should, be done by browsing the web. Not all information accessible there is as up to date as that available through magazines, newspapers, and other print-based resources. For this and other reasons, most teachers and experts will tell you to watch out when you use information from the web and to do additional research in the print world. There simply are more controls on print than electronic sources, generally speaking. The trick for using traditional print competently is to look for the different kinds and qualities of information in different places.

**Newspapers**    Newspapers obviously are useful sources of information about events of current interest. Moreover, their feature stories and accounts of unusual happenings provide a storehouse of interesting illustrations and examples. You must be careful, of course, not to accept everything in a newspaper as true because the haste with which news must be gathered sometimes makes complete accuracy difficult. Your school or city library undoubtedly has copies of one or two highly reliable papers—such as the *New York Times,* the *Observer,* the *Wall Street Journal,* or the *Christian Science Monitor*—as well as of the leading newspapers in your state or region. If your library has the *New York Times Index,* you can locate that paper's accounts of people and events from 1913 to the present. Another useful and well-indexed source of information on current happenings is *Facts on File* (also on the web: http://www.factsonfile.com/), which has been issued weekly since 1940. (Some newspapers also can be accessed and searched on the web or on CD-ROMs from your library.)

**TABLE 6.2**     **Internet Search Engines**

Note that some sites require *http://* without *www* in front of a specific site name.

| KIND OF INFORMATION NEEDED | SEARCH RESOURCE(S) |
| --- | --- |
| A search strategy; new sites | www.NoodleQuest.com;  www.mamma.com/ http:www.metacrawler.com/;  http://scout.cs.wisc.edu/archives http://www.searchenginewatch.com/links/ |
| Fast search for good hits | www.Google.com;  www.vivismo.com;  www.ixquick.com www.alltheWeb.com |
| Narrowing a broad academic speech topic | www.encarta.msn.com;  www.altavista.com;  www.Infomine.com www.northernlight.com;  http:www.Encarta.msn.com/reference/ |
| Popular or general topic | www.yahoo.com;  www.go.com |
| Refining key words | www.HotBot.com;  www.surfwax.com;  www.excite.com |
| Topic already searched by others | www.askjeeves.com;  www.directhit.com |
| Generating links prepared by subject experts) | http://home.about.com;  www.clearinghouse.net; http://bubl.ac.uk (European focus) |
| Phrase or word | www.infoseek.com;  www.altavista.com |
| Specific name/person | www.infoseek.com;  www.altavista.com;  www.hotbot.com |
| Biographic information | www.s9.com/biography;  www.biography.com;  www.amillionlives.com |
| U.S. government data | www.firstgov.gov |
| Late-breaking news | www.moreover.com;  www.dailynews.yahoo.com www.northernlight.com |
| Magazine or newspaper articles online | http://fullcoverage.yahoo.com;  http//arj.newslink.org www.totalnews.com;  http://www.pbs.org/newshour/newshour-index |
| Hot topics with accurate information | http://library.sau.edu/bestinfo/Hot/hotindex.htm www.multnomah.lib.or.us/lib/homework/sochc.html |
| Ideas from other countries | http://Websearch.about.com/internet/Websearch |
| Statistical data | http://nilesonline.com/data/;  http://odwin.ucsd.edu/idata/ |
| Almanac-type information | www.infoplease.com;  www.odci.gov/cia/publications/factbook/ |
| Primary sources | www.digitallibrary.net; http://www.perseus.tufts.edu/ (Classical Greece) http://lcWeb2.loc.gov:8081/ammem/ndlpedu/resource/history/ (History) |
| Multimedia/pictures/visuals | http://www.ncrtec.org/picture.htm;  http://www.findsounds.com/ http://www.thinker.org/fam/thinker.html; http://multimedia.lycos.com/ http://lcweb2.loc.gov/ammem/collections/ |
| Scientific information | www.altavista.com |
| Quotations | http://www.quotationspage.com;  http://www.aphids.com/quotes/ http://www.quoteland.com/;  http://www.bemorecreative.com/ |
| Usenet news | www.dogpile.com;  www.webtaxi.com |
| Expert opinions/editorials | http://www.opinion-pages.org/;  www.askanexpert.com;  www.listz.com |
| Free/inexpensive software | http://www.data-wizard.de/SoftCrawler |
| Automatically rerun a search | http://informant.Dartmouth.edu |

*Source:*  Adapted from Debbie Abilock, Curriculum Coordinator, Nueva School. Full listing available online: <http://nuevaschool.org/~debbie/library/research/adviceengine.html>. Accessed July 2, 2001.

**Magazines**   The average university library subscribes to hundreds of magazines and journals. Some, such as *Time, Newsweek,* and *U.S. News & World Report,* summarize weekly events. The *Atlantic* and *Harper's* are monthly publications that cover a wide range of subjects, both of passing and of lasting importance. *The Nation, Vital Speeches of the Day, Fortune, Washington Monthly,* and *The New Republic,* among others, publish commentary on current political, social, and economic questions. More specialized magazines include *Popular Science, Scientific American, Sports Illustrated, Field and Stream, Better Homes and Gardens, Wired, National Geographic,* and *The Smithsonian.*

This list is, of course, just the beginning. Hundreds of periodicals are available that cover thousands of subjects. To find specific kinds of information, use the *Readers' Guide to Periodical Literature,* which indexes most of the magazines you'll want to consult in preparing a speech. If you'd like more sophisticated material, consult the *Social Sciences Index* and the *Humanities Index,* which now are computerized in most libraries. Similar indexes are available for publications in technical fields and from professional societies; a reference librarian can show you how to use them.

**Yearbooks and Encyclopedias**   The most reliable source of comprehensive data is the *Statistical Abstracts of the United States,* an annual publication covering subjects ranging from weather records and birth rates to steel production and election results. Information on Academy Award winners, world records in various areas, and the "bests" and "worsts" of almost anything can be found in the *World Almanac,* the *People's Almanac,* the *Guinness Book of World Records,* the *Book of Lists,* and *Information Please.* Encyclopedias such as the *Encyclopedia Britannica* and *Encyclopedia Americana* attempt to cover the entire field of human knowledge and are valuable chiefly as initial references or for background reading. Refer to them for important scientific, geographical, literary, and historical facts; for bibliographies of authoritative books on a subject; and for ideas you don't need to develop completely in your speech.

**Documents and Reports**   Various government agencies—state, national, and international—as well as many independent organizations publish reports on special subjects. The most frequently consulted government publications are the hearings and recommendations of congressional committees in the publications from the U.S. Department of Health and Human Services and the Department of Commerce. Reports on issues related to agriculture, business, government, engineering, and scientific experimentation also are published by many state universities. Endowed groups—such as the Carnegie, Rockefeller, and Ford Foundations— and special interest groups—such as the Foreign Policy Association, Brookings Institution, League of Women Voters, Common Cause, and the U.S. Chamber of Commerce—also publish reports and pamphlets. Though by no means a complete list, *The Vertical File Index* serves as a guide to some of these materials. Also search "Newsletters" with LEXIS-NEXIS.

**Books**    As suggested earlier, book publishing continues of both fiction and non-fiction materials. Edited collections of recent research, expert opinion, historical treatments, and the like abound—but it does take some work to determine which books are the most helpful. If your "Health" search locates 550 books in the university library, you will need to be more precise in using the electronic card catalog to access what is most useful to you. Most subjects suitable for a speech have been written about in books. Generally, you'll find authoritative books in your school library and more popularized treatments in your public library. You now can access your and other libraries' card catalogs electronically. This often makes your search more efficient and productive.

**Biographical Dictionaries**    The *Dictionary of National Biography, Dictionary of American Biography, Who's Who, Who's Who in America, Current Biography,* and more specialized works, organized according to field, all contain biographical sketches. These works are especially useful in locating facts about famous people and in documenting the qualifications of authorities whose testimony you may quote.

## The Face-to-Face World

As you become a more proficient oral communicator during this course, you should not forget that you can use the skills you're gaining in speech preparation and analysis to help you acquire information, as well. You can prepare and conduct interviews with people who can supply you with facts, opinions, background information, and leads to other sources.

**Conducting Informational Interviews**    The goal of an **informational interview** is to obtain answers to specific questions. In conducting the interview, you hope to elicit answers that can be woven into your speech. These answers also can increase your general understanding of a topic so that you avoid misinforming your audience or drawing incorrect inferences from information obtained through other sources. The interviewee may be a content expert or someone who has had personal experience with the issues you'll discuss. If you are addressing the topic of work at absolute zero, who better to help you than a physicist? If you are explaining the construction of farm ponds, you might contact a local civil engineer.

You should observe the following general guidelines when planning an informational interview:

- *Decide on your specific purpose.*  What precise information do you hope to obtain during the interview? One caution: If you are interviewing controversial figures, don't attack them. Even if you disagree with the answers being given, you're not someone from *Law and Order,* seeking to win a jury's vote by grilling the witness. This does not mean that your purpose cannot encompass tough questions or those that seek further clarification of answers that don't seem right. You can raise such questions without provoking an argument.

- *Structure the interview in advance.*  The beginning of an interview clarifies the purpose and sets limits on what will be covered. You also can use this time to establish rapport with the person being interviewed. The middle of the interview comprises the substantive portion: Information being sought is provided. Structure your questions in advance, so you have a rough idea of what to ask and when. Finally, the list will be useful as you summarize your understanding of the major points; this will help you avoid misinterpreting the meaning given to specific points by the person interviewed.

- *Remember that interviewing is an interactive process.* There is a definite pattern of turn-taking in interviewing that allows both parties to concentrate on one issue at a time and also assists in making the interview work for the benefit of both. This interactive pattern requires that both parties be careful listeners because one person's comment will affect the next comment of the other. Should you forge ahead or ask intervening questions to clarify or elaborate on a previous response? Constantly ask yourself that question.

**Communicative Skills for Successful Interviewers**     By now, it should be clear that adept interviewers must have certain communicative skills:

- *A good interviewer is a good listener.*  Unless you take care to understand what someone is saying and interpret the significance of those comments, you may misunderstand that person. You can achieve clarification only if you are a good listener. (See Chapter 3 on listening for comprehension.)
- *A good interviewer is open.*  Many of us are extremely wary of interviewers. We are cynical enough to believe they have hidden agendas—unstated motives or purposes—that they are trying to pursue. Too often, interviewers have said they only want a little information when actually they were selling magazine subscriptions or religious ideals. Frankness and openness should govern all aspects of your interview.
- *A good interviewer builds a sense of mutual respect and trust.*  Feelings of trust and respect are created by revealing your own motivation, getting the person to talk, and expressing sympathy and understanding. Sometimes, of course, your assumptions of integrity and goodwill can be wrong, but to start with suspicion and distrust is to condemn the relationship without giving it a fair chance.

## Surveys and Questionnaires

You can collect information informally by asking a number of your friends what they think about an issue or by developing a more formal survey or questionnaire that you may hand out or, if time permits, mail out to potential respondents. If, for example, you wanted to give a speech on a proposed halfway house for people with disabilities, you might survey residents in the vicinity. You could send a questionnaire to people chosen randomly from the phone book or to all residents within a three-block radius from the proposed site. If you're seeking information on a new college advising program, you could go door to door and talk to several of the residents or pass out surveys in the dorm dining hall. With the results, you then may construct your own statistical summaries for presentation as part of your speech.

When developing a questionnaire, keep the following guidelines in mind:

- Be sure the form explains the exact purpose of the questionnaire and the procedures to follow in responding to the questions.
- Keep the form short and focused on the specific points for which you wish to have responses.
- For ease of summarizing, use closed questions (e.g., ask for "yes/no" responses where appropriate, use categories such as "strongly agree/agree/disagree/strongly disagree" if you want ranges of opinion).
- Phrase questions in clear, neutral language. Do not use loaded terms (e.g., "Do you wish to see mentally unbalanced, unpredictable people living next door to your children?").
- Pilot-test the form with a few people to see if the instructions are clear and to determine if any need to be rephrased.
- If mailing the questionnaire, include a stamped, self-addressed envelope to encourage returns.

## Recording Information in Usable Forms

When you find the information you've been looking for, either photocopy it or take notes. Whether you use 4- × 6-inch notecards or a notebook, it is helpful to have an accurate, legible record of the materials you wish to consider for your speech. An incomplete source citation makes it difficult to find that information again if you need to recheck it; hurried scribbles are hard to decipher later, as well.

Many people find that notecards are easier to use than a notebook because they can be shuffled by topic area or type of support. If you use a notebook, however, try recording each item on half a page. Most of your information will not fill a page, so this will save paper. Cutting the sheets in half will make it easier to sort your data or to adopt a classification scheme and relate information to particular themes or subpoints of your speech.

## Using Source Materials Ethically

Now that we've discussed locating and generating materials for your speeches, we come to a major ethical issue—**plagiarism**, "the unacknowledged inclusion of someone else's words, ideas, or data as one's own."[12] One of the saddest things an instructor must do is cite a student for plagiarism because in speech classes, students do occasionally take material from a source they've read and present it as their own. And with the increased use of the web as a resource, it has become far easier to download information and paste it into a speech text or outline without citing the source.

*The world of supporting materials that is now at your fingertips is still subject to the requirements of proper citation.*

One of the major clues in written texts is the change in style that occurs—you and the source do not write in the same way. The same may occur in the context of a public speech. Even if listeners have not read the material being used, it soon becomes apparent that something is wrong: The wording differs from how the person usually talks, the style is more typical of written than spoken English, or the speech is a patchwork of eloquent and awkward phrasing. In addition, the organizational pattern of the speech may lack a well-formulated introduction or conclusion or not be one normally used by speakers. Often, too, the person who plagiarizes an article reads it aloud badly—another sign that something is wrong. In writing a paper, a student interspersed quoted material (appropriately referenced) with what appeared to be his own writing. In double-checking the source (the class textbook), it was clear that the student also borrowed phrases and sentences verbatim on the same pages from which the quoted material was taken. This was not particularly smart.

Plagiarism is not, however, simply undocumented, verbatim quotation. It also includes undocumented paraphrases of others' ideas and undocumented uses of others' main ideas. For example, if you paraphrase a movie review from *Newsweek* without acknowledging that staff critic David Ansen had those insights or use economic predictions without giving credit to *BusinessWeek*, you are guilty of plagiarism. Suppose you ran across the following idea while reading Neil Postman's *Amusing Ourselves to Death: Public Discourse in the Age of Show Business:*

> The television commercial is not at all about the character of products to be consumed. It is about the character of the consumers of products. Images of movie stars and famous athletes, of serene lakes and macho fishing trips, of elegant dinners and romantic interludes, of happy families packing their station wagons for a picnic in the country—these tell nothing about the products being sold. But they tell everything about the fears, fancies and dreams of those who might buy them. What the advertiser needs to know is

> not what is right about the product but what is wrong about the buyer. And so, the balance of business expenditures shifts from product research to market research. The television commercial has oriented business away from making products of value and toward making consumers feel valuable, which means that the business of business has now become pseudotherapy. The consumer is a patient assured by psycho-dramas.[13]

Imagine that you wanted to make this point in a speech on the changing role of electronic advertising. Of course, you want to avoid plagiarism. Here are some ways you could use these ideas ethically:

1. *Verbatim quotation of a passage.* After introducing the author and title, simply read the passage aloud word for word:

> Neil Postman, in his 1985 book *Amusing Ourselves to Death: Public Discourse in the Age of Show Business*, said this about the nature of television advertisements.

2. *Paraphrasing of the main ideas.* Summarize the author's ideas in your own words:

> We've all grown up with television advertising, and most of the time we endure it without giving it much thought. In his book *Amusing Ourselves to Death: Public Discourse in the Age of Show Business*, Neil Postman makes the point that instead of selling us on the virtues of a product, advertisers sell us our own fears and dreams. Advertisements are more about us than about the products being sold.

3. *Partial quotation of phrases.* Quote a brief passage, and then summarize the rest of the author's ideas in your own words:

> Postman suggests that the shift from product research to market research indicates a shift in emphasis away from the product being sold and to the consumer. He says that business now focuses on making the consumer feel better through "pseudo-therapy. The consumer is a patient assured by psycho-dramas."

Be sure to pause, however, and say "quote" to indicate when you are quoting the author's words.

Plagiarism is easy to avoid if you take reasonable care. Moreover, by citing such authorities as Postman, who are well educated and experienced, you add their credibility to your own. Avoid plagiarism to keep from being expelled from your class—or even from your school. Avoid it for positive reasons, as well: to improve your ethos by associating your thinking with that of experts. Ultimately, the warnings and possible punishments are to no avail: You have to decide whether to cheat yourself. For that is, in fact, what you are doing: You are not cheating the class so much as devaluing your own self, as integrity and self-worth are measured in the absence of such shortcuts. Your teacher, and we, as authors, can point out the problems, but the choice to cheat or not to cheat is yours to make. Can you get caught? Maybe yes, maybe no. If you don't get caught, will it matter in the long run? We believe it will, irrespective of the risks you take to get by without doing the real work. If you cheat on a speech, what else will you cheat on? How quickly does getting away with cheating become a pattern of behavior? The safest route is to take extra care in noting on an outline, in the presentation itself, and on printed visual aids, where your information comes from.

Finding and using supporting materials expertly gives your speeches power and drive. As we noted at the beginning of this chapter, supporting materials are the fuel—have plenty along for the journey!

## ■ CHAPTER SUMMARY

Competent speakers use five primary forms of supporting materials to clarify, amplify, and strengthen their presentations:

- Explanations, which answer the questions "what," "how," or "why"
- Comparisons and contrasts, which explain the similarities and differences between ideas and processes familiar and unfamiliar to listeners
- Examples and narratives, which provide detailed illustrations, undeveloped specific instances, or stories
- Statistics, which show the numerical relationships between or among phenomena

- Testimony, which cites the opinions or conclusions of qualified experts

These materials can be assembled from the electronic world (electronic card catalogs, CD-ROM indexes, World Wide Web searches), the print world (newspapers, magazines, yearbooks and reports, books, biographical dictionaries), the face-to-face world (informational interviews), and the so-called snail-mail world (letters of inquiry, questionnaires). Record information from any source both fully and accurately, either on notecards or notebook pages. Avoid plagiarism.

## ■ KEY TERMS

**Boolean searching**  (p. 145)
**CD-ROM**  (p. 145)
**comparison**  (p. 135)
**contrast**  (p. 136)
**example**  (p. 137)
**explanation**  (p. 135)
**illustration**  (p. 137)

**Information Superhighway**  (p. 145)
**informational interview**  (p. 152)
**narrative**  (p. 137)
**plagiarism**  (p. 154)
**search engines**  (p. 149)

**segments**  (p. 140)
**size/scope**  (p. 139)
**specific instance**  (p. 137)
**statistics**  (p. 139)
**testimony**  (p. 141)
**trends**  (p. 140)
**World Wide Web**  (p. 145)

## ■ ASSESSMENT ACTIVITIES

1. Read one of the speeches in this textbook, and identify the forms of supporting materials. Down the lefthand side of the page, record the idea or assertion being made. Across from it, on the righthand side, indicate the type(s) of supporting materials used to clarify, amplify, or

strengthen it. Then, assess the speaker's use of supporting materials: Were good choices made (or not)? In other words, was the material adequate to clarify, amplify, and strengthen ideas? What could have been done better? How?

2. Work in groups of two to four students, trying to make sure at least one member of the group has access to the Internet (though all of this information can be found in a good library). Work in pairs, with each pair assigned four items to find—one student working in print resources and the other electronically, if possible. (If that's not possible, students should work together in the print resources.) When the pairs turn in their reports, they should include careful citations of where they found these items of information:

   a. A weekly or daily summary of current national news

   b. A daily summary of stock market action

   c. The text of George W. Bush's inaugural address

   d. The text of a business leader's (any) speech in the prior six months

   e. A mission statement for the National Rifle Association

   f. At least three different meanings for the word *wit* and dates when those meanings came into use

   g. The current status of California legislation on educational reform

   h. A description of a recent traffic accident, locally or nationally reported

   i. A list of CDs by Mariah Carey

   j. A brief sketch of the Big Ten's basketball schedules

## ■ REFERENCES

1. Elie Wiesel, at a White House symposium, speaks on the perils of indifference, Washington, DC, April 12, 1999. Available online: <http://www.pbs.org/greatspeeches/timeline/index.html#1990>. Accessed June 23, 2001.

2. Andrew Wilson, speech excerpt. Available online: <www.executive-speaker.com/spch003.htm>. Accessed June 23, 2001

3. Winona LaDuke, speech excerpt. Available online: <http://gos.sbc.edu/l/laduke/html>. Accessed June 23, 2001.

4. Courtney Love, speech excerpt. Available online: <http://gos.sbc.edu/l/love2.html>. Accessed June 23, 2001.

5. *Ad Herennium*, 4.40.52. Downloaded from Silva Rhetoricae website. Available online: <http://humanities.byu.edu/rhetoric/Figures/ACCUMULATIO.HTM>. Accessed June 23, 2001.

6. Erin Gallagher, Persuasive Speaking, "Saving America's Skin Donation System," presented at the National Forensics Association's Championship Tournament, April 2001, Western Kentucky University, Bowling Green, KY, and the American Forensics Association's National Individual Events Tournament, April 2001, George Mason University, Fairfax, VA.

7. "Union Needs Make-Over, Students Say," *The Daily Iowan*, 16 December 1998, p. 1.

8. Information drawn from Center for Research in Electronic Commerce, Graduate School of Business, University of Texas at Austin, © 2001. Available online: <http://www.cnn.co.uk/interactive/career/0101/computersci2/internet.html>. Accessed June 23, 2001.

9. Carl Hall, "A Heap of Trouble," *Winning Orations*, 1977.

10. Go to <http://literacy.kent.edu/Midwest/Math/refsites.html> to pursue many works on how to use statistics. Such a study area is called the study of *numeracy*.

11. Material extracted from larger discussion on the University of Arizona website. Available online:<http://www.u.Arizona.edu/~ecubbins/webcrit.html>. Accessed June 23,2001.

12. Louisiana State University, "Academic Honesty and Dishonesty," adapted from *LSU's Code of Student Conduct*, 1981.

13. Neil Postman, *Amusing Ourselves to Death: Public Discourse in the Age of Show Business* (New York: Viking Penguin, 1985), 128.

# Chapter 7

# Structuring the Speech

## Language Devices, Internal Organization Patterns, and the Motivated Sequence

*Jake had just taken part in the wedding of his sister. He was amazed at what went into planning it, so he decided to talk about that for his second speech. He opened with a hilarious story about the groom dancing and throwing his bride into the punch bowl and then discussed what the wedding cost his parents, the odd little guy who did the flowers, the way the caterer tried to rip them off with extra appetizers, the flower girl who fell flat on her face coming down the aisle, and the combo that had trouble playing together most of the night. As Jake looked around, he saw a significant number of puzzled looks. After the speech, he asked his audience, "Didn't you think that was funny?" "Well, I guess so," replied Jacqui, "but I didn't understand: What was your point? Why should I have listened to you just laugh at your own stories about people I don't know?"*

Jake's experience is not unusual. When you speak without considering the audience, the audience notices. Jake had assumed that because students go to lots of weddings and maybe are thinking about getting married themselves, they would automatically find his descriptions funny and worthwhile. He had given no thought to the audience's interests or needs. Hence, he didn't even bother to think about ways to interest them in his topic. He also hadn't bothered to structure his speech to keep the flow of events clear in the audience's mind. If he forgot to mention something, he just circled back and filled in the missing information: "When I talked about the caterer, I forgot to tell you that she also . . . ," or "Oh, you also need to make sure that you listen to a band before you hire it," or, "Lastly, but before I get to that, you should also realize that most of these folks need to be prepaid."

Having personal familiarity with a topic is not the same as spending time to make sure the audience can follow the development of ideas, as Jake discovered. Audiences dislike rambling, unconnected, incoherent patterns that draw more attention to the speaker than to the ideas being discussed. Structuring ideas provides direction for the audience; it lets them follow the development of your message so that by the time you conclude, they know the central idea or claim, understand how it was explained or supported, and see its relevance to them personally.

In this chapter, we explore organizational patterns that will assist you in arranging your materials in the most effective manner. We'll ask you to think of organizational patterns at three levels of structure: **micro-structure,** the most basic level, which includes relationships built between ideas by the use of structuring words; **meso-structure,** or middle-level organization, which is made up of packaging techniques that bundle ideas together in recognizable patterns; and **macro-structure,** or a way of organizing a whole speech, which includes introductory and concluding sections attached to the center of the speech. The *motivated sequence* is a well-known, general purpose approach to macro-structure that approximates how audiences think as they respond to your message—the questions they ask themselves as you move through each phase of your presentation.

## Micro-Structures: Using Language to Organize Ideas

People actively seek organization in their environment, imposing it if they cannot find it naturally. Watch young children. They learn early that one set of furniture goes in the bedroom, another in the kitchen, and a third in the living room. By elementary school, they can determine what is foreground in a picture and what is background or supporting detail. Such processes of differentiation lend coherence to their perceptions of objects and events. They also can complete or fill in missing elements in sequences or patterns of words or drawings. For example, if someone says "One, two, three, four," you almost automatically continue with "Five, six, seven, eight." If a cartoonist draws a few pen lines of a well-known person, you probably can identify the individual.[1] Generally speaking, the principles of **differentiation** and **closure** are central to our understanding of verbal organization or order.

The key idea underlying verbal organization is this: People use language to structure and, thereby, make sense of their world. Think of some language strategies you use to organize parts of your life:

- *Numerical order:*  "In the first place . . ." Such language establishes sequence.
- *Temporal order:*  "Before I . . ."; "After you do . . ." This language establishes when things might be done.
- *Physical space:*  "In the middle"; "To the west, east, and, south." Establishing spatial relationships allows you to see physical order through language.

- *Topics or types:* "Executive, legislative, and judicial branches of government"; "Animal, vegetable, and mineral"; "Past, present, and future." Dividing a subject into manageable and memorable topics helps clarify relationships.

- *Narrative order:* "Once upon a time"; "I heard a story the other day"; "I awoke with a start that morning." Turning a series of events into a story—with a beginning, middle, end, and even a moral or message—is a way of making disorganized experiences coherent and giving them a point or application.

- *Logical inference:* "Because of this . . . , therefore . . ."; "As evidence for this assertion"; "I believe that because." These phrases show connections between ideas, thereby indicating what follows from what.

- *Hierarchies:* "Higher, lower"; "Inside, outside"; "Under-class, middle-class, upper-class"; "Important, unimportant"; "Main points, secondary points." We often build hierarchies out of social or intellectual judgments to help us understand or argue for what is more or less central to our lives.

These are just some of the language devices used in organizing or ordering life experiences. These phrases show relationships among ideas, events, and objects, and as we convey our perceptions to others, these phrases become indispensable aids in making ideas clear.

# Meso-Structures: Patterns of Internal Organization

Now it is time to think about how to package the substantive center of your speech—the body of the speech, its **main points.** You should meet five key criteria for communicating ideas to an audience as you think about speech organization:

1. *The organization of main points must be easy for the audience to grasp and remember.* Listeners find it easier to track your ideas if they see relationships among the main points. If the structure is clear, they even anticipate your next point through the pattern.

2. *The pattern must allow full, balanced coverage of the material it organizes.* When making three arguments in support of a claim, you usually want to spend roughly the same amount of time on each, because the first point might be important for some listeners while the second and third points may appeal to others. Audiences usually can sense proportion, and they may well wonder why you spend far more (or less) time on one point than another.

3. *The pattern should be appropriate to the occasion.* As noted, on some occasions, you're expected to observe group traditions. Political fund-raising speeches, for example, almost always are built around a problem-solution format—with a call for contributions as the action step. Audiences on this and other occasions expect certain topics and even certain organizational patterns.

4.  *The pattern should be adapted to the audience's needs and level of knowledge.*
    Patterns of internal organization depend on audience awareness of an issue
    or problem. If listeners are not well informed, a historical chronology that
    contextualizes the issue may be necessary for them to understand the evo-
    lution of events. If they are knowledgeable, a cause-effect pattern that com-
    pacts such an analysis in the need step—but then develops a more compli-
    cated satisfaction step—probably will work better. Start where the audience
    is, and take them where you want to go. (We will come back to these steps
    later in this chapter.)

5.  *The speech must move forward steadily toward a complete and satisfying end.*
    Keeping listeners with you is easier if they have a clear idea of where you're
    heading during the speech. Repeated backtracking to pick up lost points
    confuses and aggravates them, as Jake found out. Using clear transitions be-
    tween main points—"Now that we've seen why we must change, what are
    we going to do?"—will assist audiences in tracking your ideas.

These are the primary criteria that should guide development of the body of materials going into your speeches. The four most useful patterns for structuring the
bodies of speeches are *chronological, spatial, causal,* and *topical.*

## Chronological Patterns

The defining characteristic of a **chronological pattern** is the temporal structuring
of happenings or events. Chronology can be used in a temporal sequence to orient listeners who know little about a topic, or it may be used to unfold a story or
narrative.

*A subject often suggests the most
effective organizational pattern. A
chronological pattern, for instance,
is well suited to explaining a process
or a sequence of events.*

**Temporal Sequence**    To use a **temporal sequence,** you begin at some period or date and move forward (or backward) systematically to provide background information. So, for a speech on why the United States has devoted so much more time and money to manned rather than unmanned space flights, you'd do well to use a temporal sequence, examining the unmanned rocket flights of the 1950s and 1960s, the Kennedy-era commitment to manned flights to the moon, the Nixon-era commitments to a manned space station and shuttle technology, and the deep-space probes that have continued until our own time. Such a selection and sequencing of events—both of which are strategic moves made by a speaker who uses a temporal sequence—allows you to use the past to explain the present.

**Narrative Sequence**    If you want to do more than explain or provide background for some problem, however, a narrative (story) allows you to draw conclusions about a series of events. For example, Aesop's fables are narratives with morals about human motivations and actions. Lawyers, too, tell stories in arguing for their defendants' guilt or innocence. In a **narrative sequence,** therefore, stories are the source of supporting material for some claim or moral-of-the-story.[2] Notice the following speech outline, which tells two stories—a specific one about Election Night 2000 and a more general one about television networks and news organizations' collusion in the 1990s—to argue for reform of election-night information processes.

USING NARRATIVE SEQUENCE:
*How the Networks Blew Election Night 2000*

I. Everyone knows by now that the national television networks blew Election Night 2000, but how did it happen and what can be done to prevent it from happening again?

II. The details of November 7–8, 2000, ran as follows:
   A. At 7:40 P.M. (Eastern Time), the computerized analysis of voter exit polls in Florida showed Gore with a lead big enough to call the state for Gore. By 7:55 P.M., that call became labeled "Win Gore," and the networks announced that win.
   B. At 10:13 P.M., the computer operators changed their call to a no-call, saying they would need to examine data from absentee ballots before actually declaring a winner.
   C. At 2:05 A.M. the morning of November 8, with 96 percent of the vote counted, Bush led by more than 29,000 votes, so the computer service called "Win Bush," with every network calling him the winner of the presidency within five minutes.
   D. In a little over an hour, Bush's lead was down to 600 votes, and an hour after that, down to 224 votes—a 0.0004 percent difference! Florida again was declared "No call."

III. The fact that all networks made the same calls within minutes or even
    seconds of each other is another story—the story of election data pools.
    A. This, the larger story, begins in 1966, when the news organizations
        formed the News Election Service (NES).
        1. The NES was organized to phone selected precincts around the
            country for their actual vote counts.
        2. This was innocent enough and got factual information to the public
            efficiently.
    B. Then, in 1990, the organizations formed a second project, the Voter
        Research and Surveys (VRS) team.
        1. The VRS pooled exit polls—interviewers asked people leaving polls
            for whom they voted.
        2. Now, there was only one set of exit polls used by all networks to call
            winners and losers early in each of the states.
    C. In 1993, the NES and the VRS were combined into a single organiza-
        tion—the Voter News Service, or VNS, a label you see spread across the
        TV screen every election night.
        1. Here was the best of polling science!
        2. Actual votes could be compared with exit-poll data to check on
            accuracy.
        3. The use of a single organization to gather and compare exit-poll data
            probably resulted in an illegal activity—industrial collusion, subject
            to antitrust laws.
    D. Therefore, just so that the networks and other news organizations could
        save themselves $5 million to $10 million apiece, a presumably illegal
        cartel was built and did what probably would not have happened if each
        major network and newspaper information source had done its own
        interviews: That cartel miscalled not only one state's election but that of
        the entire country.

IV. The moral of both the specific story of Election 2000 and of vote counting
    on election night generally is this: Dismantle the Voter News Service.
    A. Restore competition between the networks and the news services, which
        will provide them motivation to get the stories right and save us from
        Big Brother–type public information.
    B. Allow the public to compare multiple polling results so as to give it a
        bigger role in election results.
    C. Having different media corporations design various ways for measuring
        election results will actually help produce accuracy and restore public
        confidence in the people who provide them with their election-night
        news.[3]

It is the narrative form's dramatically structured story, together with the possibility of adding a moral-of-the-story—which directs human action that in turn
reinforces the results of "happy" stories and prevents "unhappy" stories from
being lived through again—that makes the chronological pattern so powerful.

## Spatial Patterns

Generally, a **spatial pattern** arranges ideas or **subpoints** in terms of their physical proximity or relationship to each other. A specialized form, the **geographical pattern,** organizes materials according to well-known regions or areas. So, the evening weather forecast reviews today's high-pressure dome over your area, then the low-pressure area lying to the west, and the arctic cool-air mass that seems to be coming in behind that low-pressure area from Canada. The notion of geography, however, need not be applied only to land masses. You can use it to talk about physical spaces, such as the different services available on the four floors of a university library. In an age when travel is highly popular and comparatively inexpensive, you might well find yourself giving a speech using a geographical pattern, as in the following speech.

USING SPATIAL PATTERNING: *Volcanoes of the World*

I. During the summer of 2001, Italy's Mount Etna spewed lava and provided spectacular fireworks of shooting flames and rocks.
   A. It may seem odd that such an old, famous volcano should be acting up again.
   B. It's not, however, unusual for volcanoes to periodically make comebacks.

II. If you wanted to tour volcanoes around the world that have been recently active, you could start right here in the United States and then move around the world.
   A. Start at Mt. Saint Helens in the state of Washington (1991 eruption).
   B. Journey to the Aleutian Islands off the Alaska coast to Mt. Akutan (1990 eruption).
   C. Cross the Pacific to Japan to Mt. Asama (1991 eruption).
   D. Drop down to Sumatra to find Mt. Kerinci (1987 eruption).
   E. Head west to Zaire in Africa to Mt. Nyamuragira (1988 eruption).
   F. Then go north to Europe to see Italy's Etna (1990 and 2001 eruptions) and Iceland's Hekla (1991 eruption) before returning home.

III. Even if the whole trip's expensive, a visit to any of these active volcanoes could be the trip of a lifetime.
   A. You'll learn firsthand how Earth itself is composed.
   B. You'll experience a sense of power, endurance, and the never-ending remanufacturing that makes this planet a special home.[4]

Giving your audience a sense of physical relationship through spatial ordering also works with single arguments or ideas. A speech on the effects of nuclear fallout could organize damage assessments from "ground zero" (the point of impact) through areas 1 mile away to regions 10, 50, and 100 miles out.

The great utility of spatial patterns is their visual component. Helping audiences see ideas is a virtue for someone using the oral medium of communication.

## Causal Patterns

As the name implies, a **causal pattern** of organization moves either from a description of present conditions to an analysis of the causes that seem to have produced them or from an analysis of present causes to a consideration of future effects (see Figure 7.1). Because ideas are developed in direct relationship with each other, a sense of coherence is communicated to listeners. When using a cause-effect pattern, you might first point to the increasing number of closed courses (i.e., too few places) in your college each semester and then show the result—it takes students longer to graduate. Or using an effect-cause pattern, you could argue that everyone knows how long it takes students to graduate and then argue that closed classes are the cause (at least in part).

USING CAUSE-EFFECT AND EFFECT-CAUSE PATTERNS:
Two Sample Outlines

*Option 1: Requiring Community Service for High School Graduation*

**Claim:** Requiring that high school students engage in community service as a condition of graduation (cause) leads to an erosion of the very volunteer spirit it is designed to promote (effect).

I.  Several students have forced the issue by appealing to the courts.
    A.  Students in Bethlehem, Pennsylvania, who already were active refused to report their activities to school authorities.
        1.  They lost in court.
        2.  The school denied their diplomas.
    B.  Students in Chapel Hill, North Carolina, filed suit.
        1.  As one student, already an Eagle Scout, suggested, requiring what should be a volunteer activity leaves "no heart" for the activity.
        2.  The case has not been completed.

II.  Community service is important, but it will become a part of people's social consciousness only when they are properly motivated to undertake it.

---

**FIGURE 7.1**   **Developing a Causal Pattern**

*Note how one specific cause is identified as the force behind specific effects. What kind of support would be necessary to illustrate the connection between the cause and each effect?*

**Purpose:** To argue that deforestation of the Amazon Region must stop.

| *Causes* | *Effects* |
|---|---|
| **Deforestation** | **Imbalance in the bioregion**<br>**Air pollution**<br>**Destructive runoff** |

*Option 2: Requiring Community Service*

**Claim:** Community service (cause) offered within formal educational settings provides students with an enriched understanding of others and a strong sense of self-achievement (effects).

I. Students are enriched through their exposure to community service.
   A. In Hebbville, Maryland, an elementary teacher regularly incorporates students' visits to nursing homes.
      1. Students get to practice their reading in the presence of an eager audience.
      2. In the process, they gain a greater understanding of and empathy for the elderly.
   B. Young veterans of the Hebbville program are quiet testimony to its success.
      1. One fourth-grader who came back to help the younger class prepare for their experience played a garbled tape and then pointed out that this is how many elderly might hear the students if they are almost deaf.
      2. As another fourth-grader noted, it is fun to make people happy.

II. The trick here is make community service a part of schoolchildren's education from a young age, long before it is discussed as an obligation, so that it is naturalized.
   A. It then becomes part of the social studies curriculum—an application of one's learning.
   B. It also builds within students a strong sense of what they can accomplish, even as kids, in local and concrete ways, improving their self-images.[5]

Both outlines share a common characteristic: Each starts with the aspect of the situation better known to audience members and then develops more fully the lesser-known facets of the problem. As a guiding principle, use a cause-effect sequence when listeners are generally well acquainted with the cause, but use an effect-cause sequence when the effect is better known. Note also that each option illustrates a different view of the same issue. Such activities are rarely one sided. You must be ready for different sets of cases.

## Topical Patterns

Some speeches on familiar topics are best organized in terms of standardized subject-matter divisions. Financial reports customarily are divided into assets and liabilities; discussions of government into legislative, executive, and judicial matters; and comparisons of telescopes into celestial and terrestrial models. In these instances, the topic suggests its own pattern of development. **Topical patterns** are useful in speeches that enumerate aspects of persons, places, things, or processes.

Your coverage of these aspects may be a **complete enumeration** of a subject, as in an analysis of the "who-what-when-where-how-why" scheme that encompasses any story you wish to report on, or a **partial enumeration,** as you might use in a speech on stress in students' lives.

USING A TOPICAL PATTERN: *Stress in College Students' Lives*

I. I'll bet you complain about stress in your life all of the time around here.
   A. How will your instructor like that paper you wrote hurriedly last night?
   B. Will he—or will she—ask me out for tomorrow night?
   C. Where did that last five pounds come from, and why is it located right around my belt line?

II. Students typically experience three kinds of stress inducers.
   A. Physical stress inducers tend to result from shifts in your lifestyle once you enter college.
      1. You eat more even as you sit around more, losing muscle mass and gaining fat.
      2. You sleep less, giving your body less time to relax and making you more susceptible to disease.
   B. Emotional stress inducers then complicate your physical changes.
      1. Fear of failure in the classroom is experienced by almost everyone.
      2. Many face speech anxiety when having to talk in class.
      3. Your inability, sometimes, to comprehend theoretical or other kinds of abstract materials puts pressure on your feeling-states.
   C. The social side of college life always creates stress—concerns over making the team or the rush, dating, partying, having fewer financial resources, or maintaining relationships with the family you left at home.

III. Even if you can't solve all of your problems overnight, you can start right now, at least, to reduce the stress that accompanies them.
   A. Force yourself to exercise several times a week, relaxing yourself mentally and toning your body.
   B. Learn physiological relaxation techniques you can use even while sitting at a desk—stretching, flexing, and muscle-tensing exercises.
   C. Attend one of the weekly introductions to meditation available to you at the student memorial union every Wednesday night, where you'll learn mental techniques for controlling your bodily processes and orientation.

Topical patterns are among the most popular and easiest to use in organizing a speech. Given the usual practice of a partial, rather than complete, enumeration of topics, you may need to justify your limitations by indicating why you're not talking about other facets. If someone asks, "Why didn't you talk about biofeedback as a means of reducing stress?" you could answer, "I focused on the three most common approaches to stress reduction where people don't need special equipment or much in the way of technical training to get started." All that's required is that the audience members understand why some items were included and others were not. That understanding can come either from your logical development of the topic or from an explicit statement about its scope.

As you might notice if you look back at the sample outlines, meso-structuring is a matter of finding generally understood ways of organizing the heart of a speech—its main points. (See the "How to" box below for some advice on choosing the best meso-structure for your speech.) We have added some introductory claims to drive home the point that you always must search for ways to get inside a listener's head and heart, but primarily, we've featured small outlines of the bodies of speeches. Now it is time to move to the whole talk: macro-structure, including beginnings, middles, and endings.

## Macro-Structure: The Five Basic Steps of the Motivated Sequence

**Monroe's motivated sequence** was constructed out of a method for improving sales in the 1920s. The first author of this book, Alan Monroe, turned sales techniques into a broadly useful approach to persuasion, combining some principles from traditional motivational psychology with traditional principles of speech organization.[6] The steps of the motivated sequence conform to a listener's desire for need satisfaction, rational decision making, and order. As a holistic way of organizing speeches, it reflects thought processes that listeners often follow when receiving new information or solving problems. When you find yourself listening to

## How to
### Choose from among Meso-Structures

- *Does your subject matter guide you toward a particular pattern?* For example, to explain basic principles of professional flower gardening, a spatial pattern would be a natural choice.
- *Does your specific purpose suggest which pattern is most serviceable?* For example, to explain changing definitions of rape and the social effects of these definitions, a chronological pattern for the main points and cause-effect units for the subpoints would be logical choices.
- *Do the needs or expectations of your audience call for a specific topical pattern?* For example,

an audience listening to a speech urging the rerouting of three creeks to make room for a new highway might expect you to address particular points: positive impacts of the highway, environmental impact of the rerouting, and costs of the project.

- *Does the occasion call for a specific topical pattern?* For example, every presidential inaugural address must mention the historicity of the occasion, the binding up of wounds after an ugly political campaign, domestic problems, foreign policy problems, and a call for citizens to help.

a classroom speech, you probably experience a predictable series of reactions: "Why should I listen?" "OK, what do you mean?" "Why is that true?" "How does this affect me?" "So, what do you want from me as a result of this speech?" These and other questions are typical responses by audience members as they listen to an informative or persuasive presentation.

The motivated sequence provides a template of sorts, arranged in five basic steps, for this natural progression of audience queries (see Figure 7.2). As a starting place, you must get people to *attend* to a problem or feel strongly enough to want to hear more about the deficiency you want them to help correct. Then, you

## FIGURE 7.2  The Motivated Sequence

| Steps | | Audience Response |
|---|---|---|
| **1. Attention** Using attention factors from Chapter 8: gain attention. |  | I want to listen. |
| **2. Need** Using supporting materials and motive appeals as needed, demonstrating why listening is important, articulating central idea/claim. |  | I understand the importance of the central idea or claim and see why I should continue to attend to the message. |
| **3. Satisfaction** As above, pull together information that fleshes out central idea, offers support for resolution of the claim. |  | I understand the central idea now that it has been explained; I see how the reasons support the resolution of the claim. |
| **4. Visualization** Illustrate how the central idea affects their lives— what you want them to know when you finish. Illustrate why claim resolves problem identified. |  | I see how the central idea relates to me, why the information is useful to know; I see how the claim is resolved; I see what the future would be with this claim supported. |
| **5. Action** Illustrate importance of their commitment to accept your claim, act on your request. |  | I can see why I should retain this information; I accept the central idea or claim. |

can address more specific needs or desires in relation to an individual's personal sense of *need*. Once these have been established, you can attempt to *satisfy* the audience by showing what can be done to solve the problem or alleviate its impact on their lives. Simply describing a course of action may be insufficient to move an audience to act, so move to *visualizing* what the situation would be like if the action were carried out or, conversely, what it would be like if the action were not taken. With these motivational tasks completed, you can appeal to the audience members to *act*—to put into practice the proposed solution to the problem. Two key moves make the motivated sequence a powerful macro-structure:

- Use this pattern as a template for thinking about what questions the audience likely will ask.
- Construct motivational appeals that engage individuals even as you reasonably lead them from personal needs to ways that they can satisfy them.

Now that we've briefly introduced the motivated sequence, we examine more closely the individual steps. In particular, we note their internal structuring, the methods for developing them, and the kinds of materials that can be used effectively in each.

## The Attention Step

As a speaker, your first task is to gain attention. In planning the **attention step,** you need to read ahead and examine the nine factors of attention discussed in Chapter 8: activity, reality, proximity, familiarity, novelty, suspense, conflict, humor, and the vital. In general, you always need to begin your speech with something more innovative than "Today I'd like to . . ." or "My speech today is on . . ."

Your manner of delivery also affects the attentiveness of your audience. The vigor and variety of your gestures and bodily movements and the flexibility and animation of your voice are important determinants of audience enthusiasm and interest. Your credibility—or *ethos*—as it is judged by your listeners also assists you in securing their attention. The color and impressiveness of your language and style also affect the audience's willingness to attend to your message. Just take a look on a Sunday morning at the beginning of an evangelical preacher's message. You'll probably not start your speeches with the same flamboyant delivery and barrage of colorful language, but you will see an expert gaining listeners' attention.

Fundamentally, however, you capture and hold your listeners' attention through the types of ideas you present. Your ideas must resonate with your listeners' social interests and personal needs before they will feel compelled to listen. Gaining attention is an initial step in bringing your ideas to an audience, but remember that keeping their attention also is vitally important. Use the same attention devices (see Chapter 8) as you develop the remaining steps of the motivated sequence. In particular, these devices can be used to heighten attention during the need and visualization steps.

## The Need Step

Assuming the audience is attending to you and your message, you must set forth reasons for their concern about the issue you're discussing. That's the goal of the **need step.** Why is the information or viewpoint vital to their interests? Why should they think the problem is urgent? How can you create **intrinsic motivation,** or self-motivation, in listeners? Extrinsic motivation—hopes to win a lottery, fears of bullying personalities or conspiracies, and the like—may or may not move listeners to act. But intrinsic motivation, that which comes from their own experiences and self-understandings, certainly will.[7] To provide answers, the need step can be set up effectively using four parts:

1. *Statement:* Offer a clear statement of the need. State the central idea or claim, and phrase it in more than one way to make the point clear.

   > Among people of color, there is a growing need for social and political activism on the part of young adults—activism that makes a difference.[8]

2. *Illustration:* Present one or more illustrations or specific instances to give listeners an initial idea of the problem's seriousness and scope—its importance or significance.

   > Mary Kay Penn, 32, is president of the Institute of African American Folk Culture in Harlem; she recently raised $50,000 for the institute and convinced a Hispanic organization to donate a photo-processing lab.

   > The New Progressive Party in Wisconsin, largely African American and Latino, has elected 22 officials from its ranks.

   > The Black Student Leadership Network, a college-based arm of the Children's Defense Fund, aided more than 2,000 children this past summer; its southern region coordinator is only 23.

3. *Ramification:* Using the types of supporting materials discussed in Chapter 6, clarify your statement of need and justify the concern you're expressing. Add more examples, statistics, testimony from experts, and other forms of support to drive your analysis forward.

   > Nationally, there are four reasons why such activism must continue: First, proposed cuts in student aid may affect as many as 1.5 million students; people of color will be among those affected. Second, historically black colleges and universities, such as Howard University, which depends on federal subsidies for 55 percent of its budget, will be adversely affected by reductions in federal aid to education. Third, court-ordered changes in voting districts may adversely affect communities of color, thereby changing, literally, the complexion of Congress. Fourth, the transition to block grants to states, with state

caps on spending for programs like Aid to Families with Dependent Children, will mean lessened flexibility in meeting needs. To the extent people of color are recipients, they, along with others, will find it more difficult to receive needed assistance.

4. *Pointing:* Impress upon your listeners the issue's seriousness, scope, and significance to them. Tie it to their health, happiness, security, or other interests.

> Given the national deficit, it is clear that some cuts, especially in the social areas just noted, will be coming. What can you do? Lamont Harris, 27-year-old founder of a center devoted to giving people survival skills, Reality Plus One, says this in response: "It's gonna make people fight back. Maybe this time we won't stop short like we did in the seventies." Are you ready to fight back—to organize on your own and provide services where shortages and the absence of assistance will occur?

In the need step, you have two primary goals: to make your subject clear and to relate your subject to the concerns and interests of your audience. Although you may not need to use all four tactics every time you discuss some need, you at least should try fitting your material to this framework to see what it produces.

## The Satisfaction Step

The purpose of the **satisfaction step** is to help your listeners understand the information you're presenting or to show them how they can handle the needs you've raised in them. The structure of this step varies, depending on whether your purpose is primarily informative, entertaining, or persuasive.

**In a Speech to Inform**   Giving your listeners a clear understanding of a topic is the key to meeting this step. Consider a speech on the need for social and political activism. If cast as an informative speech, it does not include a well-developed plan for how to respond to such activism, as would a speech to persuade or actuate, but you certainly would want your listeners to know that activism is alive and well in communities of color. Follow this plan:

1. *Initial summary:* Briefly state the main ideas you'll cover.

> Responding to the challenge will not be easy; it will take personal commitment and hard work. But as the following examples suggest, it can be done.

2. *Detailed information:* Discuss the facts and explanations pertaining to each of the main ideas. For our speech on activism among people of color, give further examples of the social service work being done and the political organizing taking place in communities of color.

3. *Final summary:* Restate the main ideas you've presented together with any important conclusions you want to leave with your listeners. If your purpose in this speech is informative rather than persuasive, this step would fall short of actually asking them to act on their own.

> In this speech, I've given you a number of examples of social service and political activity currently being carried out by young people of color. We need to be concerned about the effects of funding cuts on our lives and those of people in need. We can learn from the examples set by our sisters and brothers.

**In a Speech to Persuade or Actuate**     In these types of speeches, the satisfaction step is developed as a major subdivision of the speech. The following elements can be included:

1. *Statement:* Briefly state the attitude, belief, or action you wish the audience to adopt.
2. *Explanation:* Make sure your statement is understood by the audience. Diagrams or charts may be useful in explaining a complex proposal or plan.
3. *Theoretical demonstration:* Show how this belief or action logically meets the problem illustrated in the need step.
4. *Workability:* If appropriate, present examples showing that this solution has worked effectively in the past or that this belief has been supported by

*In the satisfaction step of a speech to actuate, the speaker can explain the new action, belief, or attitude that will remedy the problem.*

experience. Use facts, figures, and expert testimony to support your claim about the workability of your proposal or idea.

5. *Meeting objections:* Forestall opposition by answering any possible objections that might be raised.

These elements may not be needed in every speech to persuade or actuate, and they may not always appear in this order. For instance, if workability is key to the success of your proposal and the audience already is well informed, you can shorten the preceding steps and spend most of your time persuading the audience your idea can work. Conversely, if workability is not the central issue but an explanation of how your solution solves the problem is in order, you may spend more time on this facet. In any case, the elements—in sequence—offer a useful framework for presenting a solution to a problem. Briefly state what you propose to do, explain it clearly, show how it remedies the problem, demonstrate its workability, and answer any objections.

**In a Speech to Entertain**    When your purpose is to entertain—to present a useful thought or sentiment in a lighthearted, humorous manner—the satisfaction step can constitute the major part of your speech. Your goal is to satisfy the audience that the speech is, in fact, entertaining and has conveyed an idea or sentiment worth their time and attention. When developing the satisfaction step in a speech to entertain, follow these guidelines:

1. *Initial statement of theme:* Briefly indicate the sentiment or idea you will discuss.

2. *Humorous elaboration:* Develop the theme with particular attention to hypothetical and factual illustrations and specific instances that convey a lighthearted yet meaningful message to the audience.

3. *Final summary:* Restate your main theme by connecting your illustrations to the point you wish to make.

## The Visualization Step

The **visualization step** most commonly is included in speeches to persuade and actuate. The function of this step is to intensify the audience's desire or willingness to act—to motivate listeners to believe, feel, or act in a certain way. The primary strategy is to project listeners into the future and illustrate vividly the results of accepting or denying the proposed belief or of acting or failing to act as the speaker directs. The step may be developed in one of three ways:

1. The **positive method of visualization** describes the favorable conditions that will prevail if the audience accepts your beliefs or proposal. Use specific examples and illustrations to give audience members a clear sense of what they can look forward to by their agreement.

2.  The **negative method of visualization** describes the adverse conditions that will prevail in the future if the audience does not adopt your ideas or proposal. Graphically describe the danger or unpleasantness that will result from their denial or inaction.

3.  The **contrast method of visualization** combines both positive and negative perspectives on the future. Forecast the negative possibilities first, and then introduce the positive attributes that can be expected if the audience embraces your ideas or acts upon your proposal. By means of such contrast, the bad and good effects—the disadvantages and advantages—are more striking than if they were presented in isolation from one another.

Whichever method you use, realize that the visualization step must always stand the test of reality: The conditions you picture must appear believable and probable. In addition, you must make every effort to put your listeners into the picture. Use vivid imagery to create mental images that allow the audience members to see, hear, feel, taste, or smell the advantages or disadvantages you describe. The more real you make the projected situation, the greater your chances of getting a significant, positive response from your audience.

Suppose you were helping your listeners get ready for Campaign 2004 by comparing and contrasting issues that have dominated male and female campaigns and affected their comparative success on election night. You might move into visualization in this way:

**Summary**

> So, as the University of Maryland's Center for American Politics and Citizenship's Campaign Assessment and Candidate Outreach Project has demonstrated, most women's political campaigns stress education, social issues, social welfare, and local issues more than men's campaigns. And men's political campaigns generally stress economic, governmental reform and some specialized issues related to specific occupations. So, what should you expect to be hearing from female and male candidates in this state in 2003 and 2004?

**Positive method, contrast method**

> Suppose you have a female Democrat running for the state legislature out of your district. She'll likely talk about state support for smaller elementary school class size, pay for teachers, spousal abuse legislation, the need for retraining programs as part of the welfare system, and county control of hog manure settling ponds. Her Republican male opponent likely will hammer on completely different issues: property tax reduction bills, the need to streamline the state agribusiness bureaus, reduction of the size of county-level educational agencies, and regulatory relief for small business owners.

**Negative method**

> So where does this leave the voter? When females stress the issues upon which females have won major offices in the past and when males do the

same, the voter is left with a most difficult decision. The poor voter has no bases for doing solid comparisons between the candidates. So what does the Republican think about job retraining? What does the Democrat think about small business regulations in this state? The voters in your district will hem and haw, and local polls will show that 35 to 40 percent of them still are undecided two weeks before the election. The candidates will panic and start calling each other every name in the book because issue-stands, obviously, haven't forced voting decisions. And in the end, everyone—the winner, the loser, and the public—will feel worse about politics than they did that spring.

I'm not suggesting that men and women shouldn't be running against each other—of course they should. Rather, I'm saying that if political issues continue to be organized by gender, we'll not get anywhere in making the political process a place where both men and women can work together in governing our cities, counties, states, and country.[9]

**Summary of the visualization step**

## The Action Step

The only speech that always requires an **action step** is one that seeks specific action on the part of the audience. With other speech purposes, such as to inform, persuade, or entertain, you seek in this step to answer the question: So, what do you want me to do with this information or as a result of being entertained? Urging further study of the topic, illustrating a moral point through humor, or seeking to strengthen a belief or attitude in meeting a persuasive purpose are ways the action step is used naturally to answer this question.

The action step should be relatively brief. Two adages apply: "Stand up, speak up, shut up" and "Tell 'em what you're going to tell 'em, tell 'em, and then tell 'em what you told 'em." In the case of the social activism speech discussed earlier, an action step might be phrased as follows:

> In this speech, I've claimed that young sisters and brothers need to act on behalf of our own communities. I've presented four reasons why we must continue: Cuts in student aid, education aid, changes in Congress, and reductions in social service support will adversely affect communities of color. We can either bury our heads in the sand and hope this crisis will pass, that it won't hurt too much, that our brothers and sisters will not suffer too much, or we can take matters into our own hands and act.
>
> Whether your own interests lead you into social service or political organizing, Tammy Johnson, a member of the New Progressive Party, says it best: "There are those of us who have been doing community work for a while, and we decided that we could establish ourselves through our closeness to the community. If you really want to do the democracy thing, you have to do it block by block."

# Using the Motivated Sequence to Frame a Speech

As an overall pattern of development, the most obvious use of the motivated sequence is in persuasive or actuative situations, but it also can be easily adapted to other situations. The following illustrations will make it much easier for you to use this overall pattern. (See Chapters 13 and 14 for more detailed information and examples on using the motivated sequence.)

## Framing the Speech to Inform

Generally, informative speeches concentrate on the first three steps of the motivated sequence. Of course, you need to elicit the listeners' initial attention and then sustain it throughout the rest of the speech. You also must motivate them to listen, approaching the need step in this way: Why should anyone want to know the information you're about to present? Then, to satisfy this need, you actually supply the material on the subject of your speech. Sometimes an action step is added in response to the "So what?" question: What should your listeners do with this information?

You don't emphasize the action step in an informative speech, but it can provide a nice conclusion. All five steps of the motivated sequence are applied in the following overview of the steps in an informative speech.

*Stopping the Energy War*

**Specific Purpose:** To inform students about the federal energy war

**Attention Step**

I. Did the 2001–2002 controversy over oil drilling in the Arctic National Wildlife Refuge confuse and frustrate you?

**Need Step**

I. It should have, for that battle between environmentalists and energy advocates was waged because the American public is ambivalent about this issue.

II. We want to protect the environment, yet we won't give up on gas-guzzling SUVs, still more electrical appliances, and high-consumption air conditioning.

III. We want to protect the environment, yet we won't buy high-fuel-efficiency cars, high-efficiency appliances, and air-circulating rather than air-cooling machines.

**Satisfaction Step**

I. The public will have to accept energy consumption taxes or environmental risks for Washington to quit waging this war.

**Visualization Step**

I. Think about a campaign where politicians take clearly proenvironment or clearly proenergy stands, allowing the public to vote for one or the other.

**Action Step**

I. Start thinking now about how you can influence the election and the governing processes to stop the energy war soon.[10]

## Framing the Speech to Persuade

The speech to persuade (or *to actuate,* as you will later see in Chapter 14) utilizes all of the steps in the motivated sequence. After gaining the attention of listeners, you will need to pay particular attention to the need and satisfaction stages as well as to the action step at the close of the speech. If your focus is on a problem with a proposed solution, what is the nature and scope of the problem and why has it not yet been resolved? How does the solution work to satisfy the needs you have outlined? In the visualizing step, involving the audience in seeing how the solution works will assist in preparing them for the final step. The action you propose to solve the problem needs to be reinforced through a strong closing statement: What do you, precisely, want the audience to do as a consequence of your message?

> *Snoring Is No Laughing Matter*
>
> **Specific Purpose:** To convince listeners that snoring should be considered a medical problem worth exploring before it's fatal

I. Did your mom or dad snore loud enough to wake you?    **Attention Step**

II. Was snoring a laughing matter to you?

I. For 1 out of 10 snorers, it may not be, and for their families, it may need treatment even if not fatal.    **Need Step**

    A. Some snorers suffer from sleep apnea—short moments of oxygen deprivation and carbon monoxide buildup that can affect the heart, brain, and other vital organs.

    B. These persons stop breathing for short periods of time and can experience hypertension, headaches, marital problems, and possibly fatal consequences, especially if one's heart is diseased.

    C. Others with less severe cases are tired and irritable, the subject of family complaints, and probably even depressed.

II. The causes of snoring are multiple, making it difficult to relieve.

    A. Physiological problems can include a deviated septum (usually, a broken nose), sinus problems, thickened tissues inside the nose, an elongated uvula (the little thing hanging down in the back of your throat), a softened palate, and a thickened tongue.

    B. Snoring can be affected by smoking, which irritates yet dries membranes, and by alcohol consumption, which numbs some of the neurological controls of your nose and throat.

    C. Even your mental health might be related to snoring by affecting how long and how well you sleep.

I. Snoring, therefore, is no laughing matter, but there are steps you can take to improve your sleep and control your snoring.    **Satisfaction Step**

    A. You can assess the possibility of sleep apnea through a number of methods—monitor your own sleep pattern with a tape recorder, have a sleep partner do it, or have a professional sleep study.

> B. Treatments vary widely—everything from changing your sleeping position and taking a sleeping aid to sleeping masks and surgery.

**Visualization Step**

> I. Just think how your life can change if you correct a snoring problem.
>    A. Visualize more comfortable sleep, if corrected.
>    B. Visualize difficult relationships with others, if not corrected.

**Action Step**

> I. So, talk to a friend today about your snoring, bring it up at your next physical exam, and take the first small steps toward controlling it today—it's no laughing matter anymore.[11]

## Framing the Speech to Actuate

All five steps of the motivated sequence are used in a speech to actuate. The audience is asked to go beyond a change in belief or awareness of new information and to actually behave in new ways. The following overview illustrates how the steps lead naturally to an action step.

> *The Lifeblood of Your Community*
>
> **Specific Purpose:**  Urging classmates to join a blood donors group being formed on campus

**Attention Step**

> I. If you had needed an emergency transfusion for a rare blood type in Choteau County on December 23, 1998, you might not have received it.

**Need Step**

> I. Blood drives seldom collect sufficient quantities of blood to meet emergency needs in rural areas such as this one—a major multicar accident on Interstate 80 tonight would severely strain Choteau County's supply once more.

**Satisfaction Step**

> I. A blood donors association guarantees a predictable, steady supply of needed blood to the medical community.

**Visualization Step**

> I. Without a steady supply of blood, our community will face needless deaths; with it, any emergency you face can be met with prompt treatment.

**Action Step**

> I. You can help by filling out the blood donors cards I am handing out and joining me this afternoon at the county bloodmobile, which will be parked in front of the student union.

## Framing the Speech to Entertain

The speech to entertain may exist for humor in its own right, but more often, it uses humor to make a serious point. When you expect the audience only to sit back and enjoy the presentation (e.g., at a comic revue), the attention step is the only one required. When you want both to entertain your audience and make a serious point, however, additional steps are needed. In the following outline, all steps of the motivated sequence are appropriate to the moral that the speaker draws from the discussion of optimism versus pessimism and the concluding appeal for acting as an optimist.

*A Case for Optimism*

**Specific Purpose:**  To contrast optimistic and pessimistic people humorously

I. Perhaps you've heard the expression "The optimist sees the doughnut; the pessimist, the hole."    **Attention Step**

I. To the pessimist, the optimist is a fool: The person who looks at an oyster and expects to find pearls is engaging in wishful thinking.    **Need Step**

II. To the optimist, the pessimist is sour on life: The person who looks at an oyster and expects to get ptomaine poisoning is missing out on the richer possibilities life can offer.

I. The pessimist responds to every event with an expectation of the worst that could happen.    **Satisfaction Step**

II. The optimist, on the other hand, looks for the bright side.
   A. The day after a robbery, a friend asked a store owner about the loss. After acknowledging that he had indeed suffered a loss, the store owner quipped, "But I was lucky; I marked everything down 20 percent the day before—had I not done that, I would have lost even more."
   B. The optimist is one who cleans her glasses before she eats grapefruit.

I. When you look on the bright side, you find things to be happy about.    **Visualization Step**

I. Be an optimist: Keep your eye on the doughnut and not on the hole.[12]    **Action Step**

Before going on to more specific organizational patterns, look at the following sample speech, which exemplifies use of the motivated sequence. Read it by focusing on how the structure of the speech leads the audience toward a specific conclusion.

## Assessing a Sample Speech

As you read the following speech, prepared by Justin D. Neal of Berry College, Georgia, note that the attention step (paragraphs 1–2) creates initial curiosity, an orientation to the topic, and then a shift from animal testing to human testing in a shocking (but not overstated) manner.[13] In paragraph 3, Justin forecasts the speech's structure and then develops the need with examples and authoritative testimony across paragraphs 4 through 9. In a series of three paragraphs (10–12), he satisfies the need as presented and then moves in paragraph 13 to visualizing an activist solution by pointing to other instances where student pressure helped bring about reform. Such visualization, then, makes the call for action even by students in the final paragraph seem a powerful move.

### *Drug Testing: Outcome, Death*
**Justin D. Neal**

**Attention Step**

In the high-tech, high-stakes world of drug testing, one assistant has proven irreplaceable: the research rodent. Lab rats and guinea pigs have provided valuable insight into human health. Consider the case of 6587-0069. This guinea pig was given the experimental drug Trovan designed to combat meningitis. Over the next three days its condition deteriorated, its strength evaporated, and one eye froze in place. And while another, proven treatment was available, the Pfizer records report what happened next: Action taken, "Dose unchanged." Outcome, "Death." **1**

Another regrettable rodent death in the name of human medical advancement? Not exactly. You see 6587-0069 was not a literal guinea pig. She was a 10-year-old girl from Kano, Nigeria, whose name never made the corporate record books. She and 10 other children were victims of the search by U.S. pharmaceutical firms for the next miracle drug. As one citizen stated in the *African News Service* of January 10, 2001, "We were just their guinea pigs." And while this may sound like a horror story from the Tuskogee Syphilis experiment or from Nazi Germany, it is happening now all around the world, and our drug companies and tax dollars are supporting it. **2**

Drug testing in developing nations is exchanging human rights for corporate wrongs. Today, we are going to look at the appalling treatment of these human guinea pigs, then examine why the experiments occur, and finally, outline some steps we can take to help unlock the cages and end the abuse of human test subjects around the world. **3**

**Need Step**

In recent years, more and more industries have gone global, and due to lax regulations and lower costs, the pharmaceutical industry has followed suit. The resulting studies and trials have caused tragic consequences in the developing world. But while defining the problem is difficult, the *Washington Post* provides a glimpse into the nightmare of drug testing in developing nations. The paper sent 12 reporters to five continents to cover the issue over 11 months. Their findings were reported in a series that ran from December 17–22, 2000. **4**

A world tour of the pharmaceutical fiasco includes a stop in: **5**

- Kano, Nigeria, where patient 6587-0069 was one of 11 deaths in a study of 200 children. Other patients suffered from blindness, deafness, lameness, seizures and paralysis.
- Over to South America in Sao Paulo, Argentina, where over 80 forged consent forms were uncovered in a study of experimental heart medication that left 13 out of 137 patients dead.

- And then to Bangkok, Thailand, where 101 pregnant HIV-positive women were studied to determine how HIV is transmitted from mother to embryo. To preserve the purity of the study, the already proven drugs were withheld and according to the *International Herald Tribune* of December 22, 2000, 22 babies were born with HIV.
- And according to the same article, under similar circumstances, another Bangkok study resulted in 37 babies born HIV positive.

6    More time would allow us to consider:

- The Argentinean study where life threatening renal complications were unreported in a study of 966 HIV patients
- Or Mexico where authorities were persuaded to allow a drug to be tested on humans which had already produced dangerous complications in dogs

7      And these are just a few of the ones that we know about. I would like to provide comprehensive statistics, but we don't have any, because as the *Washington Post* of December 18, 2000, points out, the FDA aggressively protects the drug companies and the results of the overseas tests are kept secret. One thing we know is that the number of drug trials in developing countries is accelerating at reckless speeds. In its June 12, 2000, report, the Department of Health and Human Services states that in 1992, there were 988 registered drug researchers abroad. By 1998, that number had jumped to 5,380.

8      Pharmaceutical companies are perpetuating a legacy of detestable action. With the opportunities for abuse multiplying exponentially, it is vital we learn why human beings are being turned into guinea pigs. As in all business, the causes of the problem are economic: demand, supply, and lack of efficient government oversight. In industry, it all comes down to the dollars. As researcher Dianna Rogers said in the *Toronto Star* of December 42, 2000, "Their bottom line is profit, and I think that's why drug companies seem insensitive to the needs of the Third World." To get FDA approval so a drug can be sold in the United States, the firms need clinical results. As the *Ann Arbor News* of February 11, 2001, reports, every day a major drug is delayed in getting to market costs $1.3 million in unrealized sales. Large numbers of test subjects are needed to stay on schedule, and the problem is that as need grows, the available pool of test patients in the developed world is shrinking.

9      And that is where the supply side enters the equation. With millions of diseases people without health care in the developing nations, it is easy to find subjects. The *Health Letter,* a publication of Public Citizen, from September 2000, quotes one advertisement from a human experimentation firm that promises the company can "even help you tap the vast drug naïve patient populations of China, Korea and other emerging markets." As was reported on *National Public Radio* of December 21, 2000, "Some countries ... who are really short on money for health care, are trying to finance large parts of their health-care systems by doing clinical trials for American companies." And why do patients get involved?

*(continued)*

As one Hungarian woman quoted in the *International Herald* tribune from December 20, 2000, states, "I believe they can cure me sooner. I am honored to be chosen for an American experiment."

A final reason that clinical trials are abusing these human guinea pigs is the lack of government regulation. Before the FDA approves a drug, it reviews the data collected in the testing process. But as the *New England Journal of Medicine* from June 22, 2000, points out, instead of being scrutinized by regulatory agencies, research is protected. And ironically, as the *New York Times* of April 23, 2000, reports, our tax dollars are actually subsidizing many of these studies.     **10**

**Satisfaction Step**

The guinea pigs are available, and the drug companies are eager to exploit them. If we choose to be apathetic on this issue, then the abuse will continue. To end these injustices in the developing world, there must be solutions on three levels: international, national, and personal. The world has already declared its position on this issue in the Declaration of Helsinki of the World Health Organization. The declaration spells out the fact that, "In research on man, the interest of science and society should never take precedence over consideration related to the well-being of the subject." We need to give that declaration teeth through the United Nations. The world, through the World Health Organization, must speak with one voice on this issue. If any issue deserves attention from a global authority, it is this one. Beyond this, our nation does not have to bear the reproach of the world if we'll act unilaterally to curb these immoral practices.     **11**

First, we have to end confidentiality of drug trial results. The FDA's protection of the pharmaceutical industry must stop. This will certainly ruffle feathers on Wall Street, but when profits are being valued more highly than people, we have to draw the line. Second, it's time to discontinue federal funding of drug research overseas if it would not be allowed in the United States. And according to the *Washington Post* of January 24, 2001, the Department of Health and Human Services has started the ball rolling, stating that it is going to start monitoring publicly funded research abroad to make sure it's not exploitive.     **12**

But we need to step it up a level. We need to make it illegal to conduct privately funded research abroad if it would not be allowed in the Unites States. And while this may seem extreme, if American children were being abused in these trials, we would not hesitate to employ such policies. And right now, we have a great opportunity to set the standard. According to *WebMD,* an online medical news service, from February 23, 2001, a U.S. pharmaceutical company is asking the FDA to approve a study that will allow 325 infants in South America with a life-threatening disease to receive a placebo in a study that will cause many of those infants to die while effective treatments remain unused.     **13**

**Visualization Step**

An all-out campaign is needed to bring Congressional attention to these issues. And the *Washington Post* article just cited points out that we already have two friends on this issue: Congressman Sherrod Brown and Senator Edward Kennedy. Constituent action may seem old fashioned, but it can be effective when used with persistence and vigor. But we all know the sluggish pace of legislative change, so we also need to pursue more dynamic and time efficient methods. In recent years, college students have led the movement for human     **14** rights in standing up against injustice in cases from Slobodam Milosevic in Serbia to Nike and Pepsi in the Far East. Students and educators can offer a voice to the world's guinea pigs. Every person in this room has the ability to write a letter to their local campus paper concerning this issue, and every person in this room can lobby for change and reform. We did it with Nike, and we can do it again.

15     Today, we've seen the tragedy of human guinea pigs, we've learned the reasons that the labs stay open, and we've discovered how to unlock the cages and end the abuse. Around the globe, U.S. pharmaceutical companies are engaging in unthinkable, deplorable practices. The faces in our comfortable living rooms are no more valuable than 6578-0069. And while we don't know her name, we do know her fate—and the plight of hundreds like her. Let us consider our own involvement now. Let's not follow Pfizer's example. Action taken: Dose unchanged. Outcome: Death.

**Action Step**

## Integrating Meso-Structures into the Motivated Sequence

Finally, you must consider the relationship between the motivated sequence and the chronological, spatial, causal, and topical patterns, or meso-structures, we reviewed earlier. They are easily fit into the overall, macro-structure of the complete speech:

1. *Attention step—Introduction to speech:* As introductory devices, you might use chronological or spatial methods in beginning a hypothetical story. Overall, organize the introduction to satisfy the functions discussed in Chapter 8.

2. *Need step—Body of speech:* Use chronological, spatial, causal, or topical patterns to relate the main points to one another. You may even use one pattern for main points and another to organize subpoints—as long as it's clear when you, say, use a topical pattern but organize each subpoint chronologically. You'll notice that's what we did in the speech outline earlier in the chapter on how the networks blew their coverage of Election 2000.

3. *Satisfaction step—Body of speech:* Use any of the patterns to organize this step. Whatever pattern is used should be tied to needs, however, because the relationship between the need step and the satisfaction step is key to the body of your speech.

4. *Visualization step—Body or conclusion of speech:* You can highlight the positive or negative benefits, or you can contrast these to illustrate why your proposal is worth considering. A chronological pattern running from past to future or a geographical pattern illustrating effects in different regions also might be employed in creating a visual picture for the audience.

5. *Action step—Conclusion of speech:*  A specific pattern is not needed. A conclusion can call for specific actions or review the main ideas to give listeners a sense of what they could do with the information, ideas, and proposals you've presented.

In conclusion, organizing a speech is a big job because it demands your attention to the overall pattern (macro-structure), the internal packages of ideas (meso-structure), and the language that sets out relationships between individual ideas (micro-structure). When you see all of these structuring patterns in one place, they can overwhelm you. Well, they shouldn't, because you've actually used most of them all of your life. The language of relationships is likely a part of your everyday vocabulary. You probably use narrative, causal, and other patterns in your conversations with friends and associates. When pushed, you probably even demand attention, build need cases, offer solutions, use visual language, and request action from others.

So far as speech structures are concerned, you should now be thinking about these matters consciously, strategically. If Jake had done that in his speech about his sister's wedding, he would have articulated relationships between incidents at the micro-level, packaged his narrative so as to spread out the funny bits and the good advice for planning, and laid out the whole thing with a motivating introduction and a summarizing conclusion. The best structure takes the listeners on a clear, understandable, and engaging journey with the speaker.

## ■ CHAPTER SUMMARY

The human need to find or create order in the world is the basis for the need to organize public presentations. At the micro-level of organization, listeners need speakers to provide emphasis via distinctions between foreground and background differentiation and via a sense of completeness that provides closure to messages. At the meso-level of structure, you must build a conceptually clear pattern, let the pattern be sensitive to your topic, purpose, and the expectations of the audience and occasion. Five criteria should guide you toward some pattern:

1. The organization of the main points must be easy for the audience to grasp and remember.
2. The pattern should allow full, balanced coverage.

3. The pattern should be appropriate to the occasion.
4. The pattern should be adapted to the audience's needs and level of knowledge.
5. The speech must move steadily forward.

The four types of internal, or meso-structural, organizational patterns include chronological (temporal, narrative), spatial (as well as geographical), causal (effect-cause, cause-effect), and topical (complete and partial enumeration). Different patterns can be combined, especially by ordering main points in one pattern and subpoints in another.

At the macro-level, Monroe's motivated sequence was introduced in the early 1920s as a means of combining problem- and motivated-centered structures for ideas. It provides an orderly approach to problem solving within a motivational framework. Its five steps—attention, need, satisfaction, visualization, and action—can be used to structure any speech, informative, entertaining, persuasive, or actuative.

## KEY TERMS

action step (p. 177)
attention step (p. 171)
causal pattern (p. 166)
chronological pattern (p. 162)
closure (p. 160)
complete enumeration (p. 168)
contrast method of visualization (p. 176)
differentiation (p. 160)
geographical patterns (p. 165)
intrinsic motivation (p. 172)

macro-structure (p. 160)
main points (p. 161)
meso-structure (p. 160)
micro-structure (p. 160)
Monroe's motivated sequence (p. 169)
narrative sequence (p. 163)
need step (p. 172)
negative method of visualization (p. 176)

partial enumeration (p. 168)
positive method of visualization (p. 175)
satisfaction step (p. 173)
spatial pattern (p. 165)
subpoints (p. 165)
temporal sequence (p. 163)
topical patterns (p. 167)
visualization step (p. 175)

## ASSESSMENT ACTIVITIES

1. Choose a social controversy as a topic for a speech, and specify two audiences for it: one opposing the issue and the other supporting it (e.g., a speech on the need for additional daycare facilities presented to a liberal audience and a conservative audience). Using the motivated sequence as a pattern, specify how you would develop each step so it is appropriate to each audience. Write a concluding paragraph that explains the differences between the two speeches as adapted to the two audiences. Think about such topics as the following:
   a. Partial-birth abortions
   b. Off-shore drilling
   c. Demanding that collegiate clothing sold on campus be made in unionized shops only
   d. Bringing in outside companies to run your college's bookstore, laundry, meal services, or concession services

2. Prepare a 5- to 7-minute speech on a subject of your choice for presentation in class. Before

you present the speech, critically appraise the meso-structure that you have used, and write a brief paper defending your approach in organizing the main points and subpoints. Immediately after you have presented the speech—and taken into account class feedback—write a brief addendum on the experience of presenting your speech. Did it work the way you anticipated? Would you change your approach in any specific area of the speech? Hand in the analysis to your instructor.

3. Working in small groups in class, suggest how the main points can be organized in each of the following topics (assuming the end product is to be a short in-class speech):
   a. Why many small businesses fail
   b. Developments in laser technology
   c. Doing a web search for your next speech
   d. Eat wisely and live long
   e. Problems of the part-time student

## ■ REFERENCES

1. The concept of closure is central to Gestalt psychology. The term *gestalt* (meaning "wholeness") refers to psychological studies of these kinds of cognitive processes. For reviews, see John R. Anderson, *Cognitive Psychology and Its Implications* (New York: W. H. Freeman, 1980); and Philip G. Zimbardo, *Psychology and Life*, 13th ed. (New York: Addison-Wesley/Longman, 1992), 266–268.

2. Walter R. Fisher argues that narrative persuasion is the most powerful kind of speaking because it so easily carries an audience along in the drama of the story. See his *Human Communication as Narration: Toward a Philosophy of Reason, Value, and Action* (Charleston: University of South Carolina Press, 1987). In *The Politics of Misinformation* (New York: Cambridge University Press, 2001), Murray Edelman explains the power of particular stories about particular people in this way: "We are often unable to see the whole picture and so make decisions that are based on a small part of the relevant total" (p. 2).

3. The material for this outline is from two stories in *Brill's Content* (February 2001): Steven Brill, "Fixing Election Night" (pp. 26–30); and Seth Mnookin, "It Happened One Night" (pp. 94–98, 150–153).

4. The data for this outline are from *The World Almanac and Book of Facts 1992* (New York: World Almanac, 1991), 529–530, as well as various news reports from the late 1990s and 2001.

5. The information for this outline is from Suzanne Goldsmith, "The Community Is Their Textbook," *The American Prospect* (Summer 1995): 51–57.

6. The preface to the first edition of Monroe's book, *Principles of Public Speaking* (Chicago: Scott, Foresman, 1936), narrates his thinking and sources as he put the motivated sequence together.

7. On intrinsic and extrinsic motivation, see Jeff Kerssen-Griep, "Teaching Communication Activities: Activities Relevant to Student Motivation: Classroom Facework and Instructional Communication Competence," *Communication Education* 50 (2001): 256–273.

8. Information for these speech segments is from Raoul Dennis, "Retroracism," *Young Brothers and Sisters* (September 1995): 80–86.

9. Information on men's and women's campaign tendencies is used with permission from Kevin McNeill and Cheryl Klock, "Connecticut Upset: How a Longshot Challenger Bucked Tough Attacks and Top-of-the-Ticket Trends to Defeat a 20-Year Incumbent," *Campaigns & Elections*, May 2001, pp. 38–43.

10. The idea for this outline is from Robert J. Samuelson, "The Energy War within Us," *Newsweek*, 28 May 2001, pp. 28–29.

11. This information is from Steve Kaplan, "Snoring," *World and I*, 2 (July 1987): 298–303; and from *Nasal Surgery* (San Bruno, CA: The StayWell Co., 2000).

12. Based, in part, on information from *Friendly Speeches* (Cleveland: National Reference Library, n.d.).

13. Justin D. Neal, "Untitled [Drug Testing: Outcome, Death]," *Winning Orations 2001*. Reprinted by permission of Larry Schnoor, Executive Secretary, Interstate Oratorical Association, Mankato, MN.

# Chapter 8

# Maintaining Audience Attention and Involvement

*The moment arrives—it is your turn to walk to the front of the classroom and begin your speech. You know the subject well. You've done the research, including finding statistical support for the main point, as well as a nice quotation from William Shakespeare to use as a summary of the third point. You've even practiced each argument carefully so that you can be clear and forceful. On your way to the podium, a question strikes you: How are you going to start? When you practiced, you just started with "Today, I'm going to talk about . . ." In focusing on the substantive points, you forgot to think about ways to gain audience attention in the introduction of your speech so that your listeners will, in fact, decide to listen. You also forgot about how your information would maintain their attention throughout the speech and how you would structure a conclusion that reminds listeners of what you said and why they should believe or act on your words. Without time to think of a different beginning, your introduction—"Today, I'm going to talk about . . ."—sounds lame and unoriginal. "Next time," you promise yourself as you begin, "I'll do it better next time."*

Audiences need more than your information and arguments to stay with you. As suggested, you don't just start; you *introduce* a speech. You also don't just quit; you *conclude* a speech. How you accomplish these tasks will make a major difference in whether the audience will listen attentively to your ideas. This chapter provides the information you need to "do it better next time."

The initial topic, strategies for gaining and maintaining **audience attention,** serves as the basis for a discussion of orienting listeners through an astute introduction and closing the presentation with a conclusion that gives the audience a clear sense of what you want them to remember or what actions you want them to take. The overarching concept that we introduce is that of *rhetorical orientation:* the art of framing your presentation in a way that lets the audience know what is expected from them as listeners. Leaving an audience with a clear understanding of what you want them to know, believe, or do also takes more than a "Well, that's it" type of ending. The strategies that we review, coupled with those for introducing a speech, will give you the advantage you need to keep the audience tuned into your message. Finally, we show you how introductions and conclusions can be easily integrated into a speech built around the motivated sequence (discussed in Chapter 7). Introductions fulfill the attention step, and conclusions are tied either to the visualization or the action step. We also concentrate on making beginnings and endings fit around speeches organized in other ways because it is in those other cases that genuine rhetorical orientation is occurring.

##  Capturing and Holding Attention in American Culture

The strategies discussed here are specifically attuned to how American audiences may react to presentations. We are an active, busy people, with little time to "stop and smell the roses." In fact, "Time is money" is a favorite saying, and the more time you ask of your listeners, the more money they may well feel they are losing.

*Conveying belief in your ideas and sincere interest when speaking helps to maintain audience attention throughout your presentation.*

Thus, making your presentation worth their time is critical. Essentially, your listeners need reasons for wanting to listen. Even when you have their attention, it tends to ebb and flow. So, you must constantly watch for lapses. James Albert Winans, a twentieth-century pioneer in public speaking instruction, expressed the problem succinctly: Attention determines response. If the audience does not attend, they cannot respond as you wish. By gaining their attention—and striving to maintain it throughout the presentation—you have a better chance they will still be there with you at the conclusion of your presentation.

What is **attention?** For our purposes, it can be thought of as a focus on one element in a given environment, with other elements fading from conscious perception as a result.[1] To give attention, then, is to perceive "in relation to a goal [either] internally or externally motivated."[2] What does this mean? If you want your audience to listen to you, they have to be motivated to attend to your words. And what motivates them? They need a reason to listen. A forensics student provides an illustration in a speech on a topic likely not to be of direct interest to her audience—bioacoustic technology. Why would anyone care to listen to this topic? You cannot just start this kind of speech; you need to provide a link between the topic and the personal lives of those listening:

> Poets tell us that "the eyes are windows to our souls," and romantics imagine that gazing into their depths will reveal secrets hidden within. However, some of the more scientifically inclined among us have recently proposed another portal to access our inner workings—the human voice. The November–December 2000 *Nexus Magazine* explains recent research has revealed that variations in the tone and frequency of our voices can indicate changes in the health and functioning of our bodies. Sound too good to be true? Amazingly, this technique is real, and for the thousands of patients who have already benefited from the emerging field of bioacoustics, the idea of diagnostic vocal analysis is truly music to their ears.[3]

With this beginning, Erin Gallagher, an undergraduate at Ohio University, offers a clear reason for listening: The sound of our voice may tell us something about how healthy we are. In this fashion, Gallagher taps into an interest that many in her audience will share—their personal health. She also taps into a second interest: a natural curiosity about how new technology aids in the diagnosis of our health. Obviously, some in the audience will remain unmotivated by this—you may not reach all members equally well. Nevertheless, as the example suggests, a topic that at first blush is not of interest can be made interesting to listeners.

Words alone may not be sufficient. Had Gallagher presented this in a dry and deadpan manner, the audience would likely wonder if even she were interested; a lively and varied delivery helps provide motivation for listening. Likewise, your reputation as a trustworthy and honest person (positive ethos) can command respect—and attention. Lively and picturesque language shows audiences word pictures and makes it easier for them to stay with you.

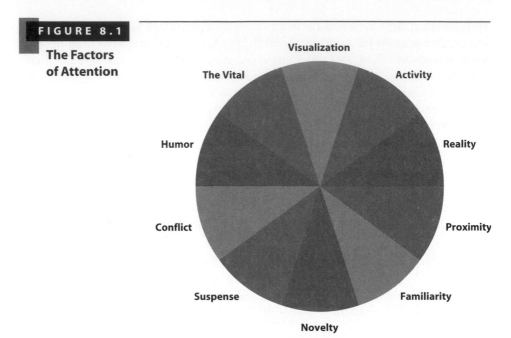

**FIGURE 8.1**

**The Factors of Attention**

If you were to rework the example from Gallagher's speech, what would be necessary in motivating you to listen? What else might the speaker have done to interest you in a topic such as bioacoustics? Alternately, think of a recent lecture you've listened to. What strategies did the lecturer use that made you stay tuned? What strategies should she or he have used? Consider the following **attention gaining/maintaining strategies** (see also Figure 8.1). Which of these might the lecturer have used to better involve you in the presentation?

## Activity

Suppose you have two TV sets, side by side. One shows Ricky Martin performing motionless behind a microphone, and the other carries one of his music videos—a fully choreographed production number. Which one will you look at? Nothing is so boring as talk that seems to stand still, providing far too much detail on a minor point. Instructions and demonstrations, in particular, demand orderly, systematic progress. Nothing is worse than a lecturer who stands still, locked in place, delivering ideas in a monotone. You need to create **activity**—a sense of movement in the presentation that shows the audience you are alive.

## Reality

The earliest words you learned were names for tangible objects—"Mama," "milk," "dog." While the ability to abstract or generalize is one mark of human intelligence, we all have an interest in **concrete reality**—the here-and-now of sense data. American audiences are attuned to the real. Human-interest stories spark attention and gain audience involvement in the ideas being presented. Being abstruse and abstract may work in a written essay, but live audiences need a touch of realness to latch onto as they listen.

## Proximity

Consider the following:

> Do you realize how much fast food is consumed on this campus? Within four blocks of this classroom are nine restaurants, including a McDonald's, a Wendy's, and a Pizza Hut. Two are local submarine houses. Even the student union runs a fast-food bar. A key question we face is this: What are our lunch habits doing to our nutrition—to our body and mind?

Such an example, whether used as an introduction or later in the speech, brings the topic close to home, thus providing **proximity.** A topic that is far away from the daily concerns of the audience needs to be brought home. The United States' stance on the Kyoto treaty on global warming is such a topic: You need to illustrate how or in what sense the issue affects the audience where they sit.

## Familiarity

Especially in the face of new or strange ideas, references to the familiar create and sustain attention. One way to use **familiarity** to your advantage is to employ analogies: Noting, for example, that the London postal or zip codes are arranged like directions on a compass (the initial letters indicate directions and the next set of numbers represent degrees or positions) uses something familiar to explain something unfamiliar. Another positive use of familiarity is to begin a speech with references to proverbs or well-known slogans, such as "A stitch in time saves nine" or "Just do it."

Adrienne Mayo, an undergraduate at Morgan State College, used the familiar image of the school bully to introduce her audience to a new bully in town—the corporate bully—in this way:

> Some of us may remember all the memories of the elementary school playground. Everything from the games to the different groups of people there were. Let's see: There were the athletes, and the tomboys, the bookworms and the bullies. But the bullies usually got a lot of the attention. Whether we were the victims or just sympathetic observers, we hoped these antics would soon end. . . . However, according to the National Resources Committee, September 1999, over 4.3 million people are bullied in the workplace annually.[4]

Within American culture, audiences are responsive to what they already know. When such a reference is used in a unique or appropriate way, it brings the audience into the presentation and incites them to listen further.

## Novelty

As the old adage has it, "When a dog bites a man, it's an accident; when a man bites a dog, it's news." Citing the unusual aims at a "Wow, that's different" reaction from the audience. Justin D. Neal, an undergraduate at Berry College, worked from the normal to the unusual in his introduction of unprosecuted criminal cases:

> A crime is committed. It happens all the time, right? This is not exactly going to catch our attention. A crime is committed. This time we're lucky: We know who did it, and the police produce a warrant. A crime is committed, and another, and another, and another and 70 more. A total of 75. Seventy-five crimes, 75 warrants for one man.[5]

In using novel materials, be careful not to inject elements that are so different or unusual as to be unfamiliar. **Novelty** gains its strength from an initial familiarity with the allusion; using the familiar in new and unique ways gives it added punch.

## Suspense

Much of the interest in mystery and detective stories arises from the uncertainty about their outcome. When giving a speech, you also can create **suspense** by structuring stories so they build to a surprising climax. Stephanie Aduloju, an undergraduate student at Creighton University, used this strategy in introducing a speech on sex education for the elderly:

> I bumped into my friend, George, the other day. Now he's a babe magnet if I've ever seen one. I mean, he gets lucky even more than, well, me. And he had, what now—15 sex partners in the last year? Get this, though: George never uses a condom. Doesn't think he has to. You probably wouldn't be surprised if I said George was a strapping, young, 21-year-old alpha male who just didn't care. But what if, instead, I said that George was 71?[6]

As another example, you might begin a speech on mental retardation with the scenario of a developmentally disabled child; then, after describing the causes of and care for people who are developmentally disabled, you reveal that you've been talking about your brother. If your speech runs long, however, you need other strategies to keep the audience's attention—they will not follow you to the surprising end if they tire of listening in the meantime.

## Conflict

Controversy compels attention. Just consider the ratings of prime-time TV soap operas that emphasize extremely strong interpersonal **conflict** in their plots. Over 30 years ago, Malcolm X gave voice to the frustration of African Americans in that generation with these now-classic words:

> If you never see me another time in your life, if I die in the morning, I'll die saying one thing: the ballot or the bullet, the ballot or the bullet.[7]

The contrast was vivid, and the implication of conflict was equally vivid.

## Humor

Listeners usually pay attention to a speech when they're enjoying themselves, and **humor** provides a chance for listeners to participate more actively in the transaction by sharing their laughter. When using humor to capture or hold attention, follow three guidelines:

1. *Be relevant:* Beware of wandering from the point. Don't tell a joke just for the sake of telling a joke. If the humor doesn't reinforce an important idea, leave it out.

2. *Be appropriate:* You don't want to tell a knee-slapper during a funeral, for example. You should avoid off-color stories, as well, because they will offend most—if not all—audience members.

3. *Be quick:* A long, drawn-out story loses its value as listeners struggle to figure out where you are going—and what the story has to do with the point you've been making. A short, concise, humorous anecdote, however, can be very helpful in reducing audience tension while making your point.

## The Vital

People nearly always pay attention to matters that affect their own well-being. When you hear "Students who take an internship while in college find jobs after graduation three times as fast as those who don't," you're likely to pay attention. Appealing to **the vital**, therefore, is a matter of personalizing your speech, of making it unavoidably relevant not just to the group but also to specific individuals in your audience.

## Visualization

As we will note in more detail in Chapter 12, word choice will also assist in gaining and maintaining attention. You can create word pictures in your audience's mind, drawing them into the scene that you describe, and thereby gain or keep

*The forceful delivery and use of language by Dr. Martin Luther King, Jr., worked together to capture and hold the attention of his audiences.*

their attention focused on your ideas. Martin Luther King, Jr., was an astute student of **visualization** in creating such word pictures, especially in his "I Have a Dream" speech. Winston Churchill was another wordsmith whose use of language gave courage to a nation in a perilous hour. This particular strategy is one that can be used in combination with others; in fact, most of the strategies we've discussed are capable of being used alone or in combination.

Although these 10 generic strategies do not exhaust the ways in which you can obtain and hold attention, they do provide an easy-to-use repertoire of ways to enliven your presentation. See the "How to" box on the next page for an overview of these strategies. Keep them in mind not only for introducing and concluding your speech but also for maintaining attention throughout. Focusing only on openings and closings, while critically important, is not sufficient in itself to maintain audience attention as you develop your central idea or claim with evidence and illustrations. As the next section illustrates, however, by considering the overall strategy of orienting your listeners, you can adapt these attention strategies at the start and continue using them all the way to the conclusion of your speech.

## Framing the Speech: Rhetorical Orientation

As noted earlier, **rhetorical orientation** is the process of effectively positioning listeners in relation to the substance of your speech—to the central idea or claim you are advancing, the arguments you are making, and the supporting materials you've assembled. The new homeowner is likely to say to an admiring visitor, "Here. Stand here so you can see the effect we were going for when we designed this house for this lot." Likewise, the effective introduction says, "Look at my central idea in this way. If you do, you'll see that it's interesting and relevant to your life." The successful conclusion says, "Look at the speech in this way. If you do, you'll see that the ideas I've talked about are important, significant for you and your life, and compelling."

A competently built **introduction** accomplishes three goals:

1. *The well-framed introduction orients the listeners' attention.* It gets them to focus on the subject matter at hand, and it piques their interest. The strategies for gaining and maintaining attention discussed earlier are relevant here, but you must find ideas that will convince an audience your speech is important to their lives.

2. *The well-framed introduction orients the listeners to the speaker's qualifications.* The audience must believe that you know what you're talking about (good sense), that you're a straight shooter (good morals), and that you have their best interests in mind (goodwill). These are the three grounds—good sense, good morals, and goodwill—that Aristotle identified as being central to a speaker's **ethos,** or credibility.

## How to
## Get Your Audience's Attention

- *Activity:* Keep it moving! Ideas that "move" tend to attract attention; like ideas, the speech should march or press forward.
- *Reality:* Keep refocusing on the here-and-now. Refer to specific events, persons, and places. Audiences can hang abstract ideas on specific details.
- *Proximity:* Bring the topic close to home. A direct reference to something nearby in time and space often orients an audience who may be wondering what you're talking about.
- *Familiarity:* Show how the unfamiliar is like the familiar. People generally are more comfortable when you refer to familiar ideas.
- *Novelty:* Introduce novelty. New and unusual developments attract wide notice. Just be careful that your audience can relate what you're saying to things they know about.

- *Suspense:* Add suspense. Create uncertainty by pointing to puzzling relationships or unpredictable forces. Use suspense in the stories you use to illustrate your ideas, building up to a surprising climax.
- *Conflict:* Note conflicts and controversies. Controversy compels attention. Like suspense, controversy suggests uncertainty, and like activity, controversy is dynamic.
- *Humor:* Share humor. Listeners pay attention when they're enjoying themselves. Humor allows listeners to participate actively, diffuses tension, and revives a tired audience.
- *The Vital:* Personalize your speech. People pay attention to matters affecting their health, reputation, property, or employment. Make your speech unavoidably relevant.
- *Visualization:* Create vivid images with words. If people can picture what is said as they listen, they will be more attentive.

3. *The well-framed introduction orients listeners to the speech's ideas and their development.* An audience must come to understand what you're talking about, why you're talking about it, and how you'll develop those ideas. At least in part, this aspect of rhetorical orientation usually takes the form of a good **forecast** or **preview**. Evelyn Breznik, an undergraduate at Eastern Michigan University, set up her discussion of unsolved rape cases and then previewed her presentation as follows:

> You do not need me to tell you that rape is serious and that none of us are immune to it. But what you might not realize is that we have the evidence to solve over 180,000 rape cases, and we are not doing it. Because rape knows few boundaries, it becomes imperative that we make every effort to put rapists behind bars. Therefore, we must first address the problems associated with allowing evidence in 180,000 rape cases to go unanalyzed. Then, we must ask ourselves why this is happening. And finally, we will examine solutions to the devastatingly real problem.[8]

In a speech introduction, therefore, rhetorical orientation situates listeners to best see the potential of the speech: "why" they should listen, "to whom" they're listening, and "how" they should go about following the speech. You also need to adopt a similar rhetorical orientation strategy in ending the speech, because a good **conclusion** has focus, flair, and a sense of finality:

- *Focus:* Even average speakers remind listeners what they've been talking about—the focus of the speech—and why listeners should be interested—the focus of their attention.

- *Flair:* Better speakers also show a bit of their rhetorical talents during conclusions by wording ideas in compelling ways, finding just the right quotation or final appeal that captures the tone of the speech—thus reengaging the listeners' needs and interests—and by pacing their oral delivery to capture the sense of an ending.

- *Finality:* All speakers must be able to create a sense of **The End**, the feeling that the speech, in fact, is over, which is to say that nothing else needs to be said at this time on this topic by this speaker. You want to end speeches in such a way that listeners say "Amen!"—which means "Yes, it shall be so." Seeking that sort of affirmation of you and your ideas should become the dominant purpose in your conclusions.

The three F's—*focus, flair,* and *finality*—represent the dimensions of your conclusion's objective—orienting listeners to your ideas, your talents, and areas of expertise—and to The End of their listening experience.

Use the attention strategies to frame your presentation, to seek and maintain attention throughout, and finally to orient your listeners to what has been said that is worthy of belief and/or action. What follows is practical advice on accomplishing this objective—creating introductions and conclusions that entice an audience to listen to what you have to say.

# Types of Speech Introductions

Although you will use attention strategies throughout your speech, you have some special requirements in this regard during those first few seconds. Your listeners are making judgments about you and the speech in that first half-minute:

| | |
|---|---|
| Interesting or boring? | Relevant or irrelevant? |
| Profound or dumb? | Forceful or limp? |
| Prepared or just running at the mouth? | Clear or muddy? |
| Confident or unsure? | Worthy or unworthy? |

With all these questions to answer, listeners will actually give you their attention readily—but only for a few seconds. Once most of the questions are answered, they're ready to *tune in, tune out,* or *graze.* The *grazers* constantly shift their focus from you to a person sitting a row ahead to a sound outside to this evening's activities and back to you, their minds working like remote control devices, zipping from channel to channel. It's your job to make sure they tune in—and stay long enough to want to come back. You need to draw them into your world. As noted, you need to tie your speech to the listeners' needs and interests to hold their attention, to convince them you know what you're doing, and to help them comprehend your main ideas and their development. The following techniques aim at one or all of these functions.

## Referring to the Subject or Occasion

If your audience already has a vital interest in your subject, you need only state that subject before presenting your first main point. The speed and directness of this approach signals your eagerness to address your topic. International award–winning journalist Christiane Amanpour used a direct style in beginning her remarks at the 2000 Murrow Awards Ceremony:

> When I was thinking about, you know, what I'd say when I came here it occurred to me that it's exactly 17 years to this very day that I walked into CNN, and I wonder whether my bosses remember that day. They probably actually think that it's seventeen hundred years, because I've aged them, I've beaten up on them for all these years and tonight will be no different.[9]

Although such forthrightness may strike exactly the right note on some occasions, you should not begin all speeches this way (and the "you know" may be troublesome if you keep using it throughout the speech!). To a skeptical audience, a direct beginning may sound immodest or tactless; to an apathetic audience, it may sound dull or uninteresting. When listeners are receptive and friendly, however, an immediate reference to the subject often produces a clear, engaging opening.

Instead of referring to your subject, you may sometimes want to refer to the occasion that has brought you and your audience together. Then 82 years old, social activist Mary Harris, a.k.a. "Mother" Jones, spoke to militant coal miners at Charleston, West Virginia, on August 15, 1912:

> This, my friends, marks, in my estimation, the most remarkable move ever made in the State of West Virginia. It is a day that will mark history in the long ages to come. What is it? It is an uprising of the oppressed against the master class.
>
> From this day on, my friends, Virginia—West Virginia—shall march in the front of the Nation's States. To me, I think, the proper thing to do is to read the purpose of our meeting here today—why these men have laid down their tools, why these men have come to the statehouse.[10]

In this manner, Mother Jones acknowledged the critical nature of the occasion and why it was important to consider the reasons for gathering on this day.

## Using a Personal Reference or Greeting

At times, a warm, personal greeting from a speaker or the remembrance of a previous visit or scene also serves as an excellent starting point. Personal references are especially useful when a speaker is well known to the audience or has just been introduced to the audience. For example, one of the authors used this strategy in acknowledging the person who had just introduced him to the audience:

> Thank you, Jim, for that fine introduction. You are to be commended for the theme of this convention and for the excellent work you have done in fulfilling its promise; I can only hope to do further justice to engaging the discipline in the comments to come.[11]

If a personal reference is sincere and appropriate, it will establish goodwill as well as gain attention. Avoid extravagant, emotional statements, however, because listeners are quick to sense a lack of genuineness. At the other extreme, avoid apologizing. Don't say, "I don't know why I was picked to talk when others could have done it so much better" or "Unaccustomed as I am to public speaking . . ." Apologetic beginnings suggest that your audience need not waste time listening. Be cordial, sincere, and modest, but establish your authority and maintain control of the situation.

## Asking a Question

Another way to open a speech is to ask a question—or series of questions—to spark thinking about your subject. For example, Kari Hammer of the University of South Dakota opened a speech about the plight of American high schools as follows:

> High school is a world of pep rallies, pop quizzes, gossip, and sports events. If you're lucky enough to find a date, you might even get to go to the prom. However, have you ever stopped to ponder the real benefits of high school?[12]

Such a question introduces a topic gently and, without actually expecting a quick answer from the audience, both introduces the topic and engages the interest of her listeners. That they have, for the most part, just recently graduated from high school also helps pique their interest.

## Making a Startling Statement

On certain occasions, you may choose to open a speech with the shock technique—making a startling statement of fact or opinion. This approach is especially useful when listeners are distracted, apathetic, or smug. It rivets their attention on your topic. For example, Stephanie Wolfe of Berry College used this single line as the opening of her speech on heart arrhythmia:

> It was determined to be drowning.

"What was?" and "Drowning, how?" were perhaps the initial questions in the audience's mind. She went on to explain:

> There really wasn't another explanation. Michael London was a strong swimmer for an 11-year-old. It seemed so odd that one moment he was swimming around in just a few feet of water; the next he was unconscious, floating at the top of the pool. Michael's parents were destroyed, even more so when they discovered that there was an explanation for Michael's death, and it wasn't drowning. It was a congenital heart arrhythmia.[13]

> Shocking an audience takes adept timing—you want to cause them to raise the questions just suggested but also want to move forward to answer them in a forthright manner. You also must be careful not to give offense by using a shocking phrase or statement that gets their attention but disgusts them to the point that they cease to listen.

## Using a Quotation

A quotation may be an excellent means of introducing a speech because it can prod listeners to think about something important and often captures an appropriate emotional tone. Amy Brin, of Ball State University, opened a speech on Vietnam-era war veterans by referencing a cult figure, Timothy Leary:

> Former Harvard professor and famed drug user Timothy Leary asserted, "If you can remember the 1960s, then you probably weren't there."

She then went on to suggest that some do, in fact, remember the sixties with more reason than most:

> In 1968, Tom Jefferson graduated from high school. Like many other young men at that time, just one year later, he found himself fighting in the jungles of Southeast Asia. However, when he returned home, he found a whole new war—this time with the same government he had served.[14]

The opening has an element of humor and a not-so-veiled allusion to the drug use during that era. It also turns on itself in suggesting, without being explicit, that for some, Leary was dead wrong, thereby piquing the interest of the audience and inviting listeners to consider what life was like for returning veterans.

## Telling a Humorous Story

You can begin a speech by telling a funny story or relating a humorous experience. When doing so, however, recall the three earlier cautions in making sure that humor works for you rather than against you: be relevant, be appropriate, and be quick. Earnest Deavenport, chair and CEO of Eastman Chemical Company, observed all three of these rules when addressing the American branch of the Société de Chimie Industrielle:

> I want to begin with a story about a tightrope walker who announced that he was going to walk across Niagara Falls. Well, nobody believed that was possible, and the crowd that had gathered tried to talk him out of it. But to everyone's amazement, he made it safely across and everybody cheered. Then he asked, "Who believes I can do it blindfolded?" And everyone cried, "Don't do it, you'll fall!" But again, he made it safely across.
>
> Then he said, "Who believes I can ride a bicycle across?" And they all said, "Don't do it, you'll fall!" But he got on his bicycle and made it safely across.
>
> Then he said, "Who believes I can push a full wheelbarrow across?" Well, by that time, the crowd had seen enough to make real believers of them, and they all shouted, "We do! We do!" At that he said, "OK . . . Who wants to be the first to get in?"

Well, that's how many investors feel about companies who have adopted the philosophy that balancing the interests of all stakeholders is the true route to maximum value.

They are skeptical at first, then believers after they see some solid results, but are very reluctant to get in that wheelbarrow.[15]

After telling that story and tying it to his topic, Deavenport was ready to develop a picture of Eastman Chemical Company's approach to balancing the interests of various groups who watch developments in the industrial world of chemicals.

## Using an Illustration

A real-life incident, a passage from a novel or short story, or a hypothetical illustration also can get a speech off to a good start. As with a humorous story, however, an illustration should be interesting to the audience as well as relevant to your central idea. Travis Kirchhefer of Sheridan College used this technique to introduce a speech on the dangers of sleep deprivation:

A short time ago in White Plains, New York, a propane truck slammed into an overpass and exploded. The explosion hurled the tanker into a nearby neighborhood. Erupting into a massive fireball, the truck leveled several homes and injured 23 people. Was the driver drunk? No, but he might as well have been. The man, chronically sleep deprived, had fallen asleep at the wheel. This story illustrates how one person with insufficient sleep endangers the lives of those around him.[16]

The existence of a problem with sleep deprivation is clear from this introduction. This is a common way of introducing a persuasive or argumentative speech, as the story serves to highlight the serious issue the speaker wishes to address. In addition, it offers compelling evidence of the problem and invites the audience, implicitly, to begin thinking about why it exists and what can be done about it.

## Building a Speech Forecast

As suggested several times, highly competent speakers always are careful to forecast the development of their speeches. The simplest forecast merely enumerates the sections of a speech, as Travis did in the speech on sleep deprivation cited above:

To assess this dangerous situation, we first need to sound the alarm about the harms we face; second, open our eyes to how this dangerous situation has developed; and finally, wake up to some solutions we must take to end this nightmare.[17]

This approach is simple without being simplistic: In clear terms, it previews the inner logic that will guide the speech's development.

# Types of Speech Conclusions

The best conclusion mirrors a good introduction by returning to the viewpoint articulated early in the speech, recapturing the tone with which it started, and reaffirming the speaker's goals for—and control over—the speech. A good speech often feels like a circle. An audience understands that it has entered a universe of thought and action at some point, taken a trip around that universe, and then returned to the place where it entered, now much wiser and more knowledgeable than when it came in (see Figure 8.2). Creating a sense of having taken an interesting and worthwhile journey through important ideas requires careful attention to various types of speech conclusions.

## Issuing a Challenge

You may conclude your speech by focusing directly upon the audience, hoping that you can inspire your listeners to get up and act in constructive ways. Such a conclusion attempts to involve listeners directly—intimately—with your speech. Jennifer Sweeney, University of Arizona, closed her presentation on racial profiling with this challenge:

> Today we have explored the crime of racial profiling and its causes. The main solution is simple; it relies on us. This community, this forensics community, has the potential to create change. Look at the number of people who can become aware today and start making a difference tomorrow.

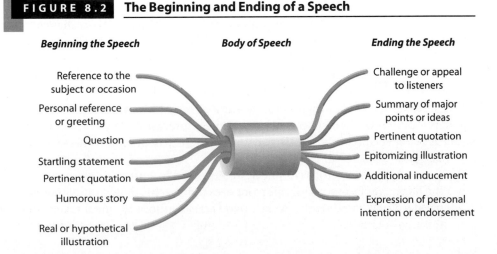

**FIGURE 8.2**     **The Beginning and Ending of a Speech**

*Beginning the Speech*

Reference to the subject or occasion
Personal reference or greeting
Question
Startling statement
Pertinent quotation
Humorous story
Real or hypothetical illustration

*Body of Speech*

*Ending the Speech*

Challenge or appeal to listeners
Summary of major points or ideas
Pertinent quotation
Epitomizing illustration
Additional inducement
Expression of personal intention or endorsement

Make racial profiling unacceptable. In this case, the solution really is in our hands. Lead by example. Let changing our minds lead to changing our actions. Teach your children; hold a rally; tell a friend; vote. How we choose to create change is up to the individual. That a change is necessary—well, that should be understood.[18]

Rather than review each of the main points in the speech, Sweeney chose instead to focus on the main theme and the action that audience members could take in making a difference.

## Summarizing the Major Points or Ideas

In an informative speech, a summary allows the audience to pull together the main strands of information and evaluate the significance of the speech. In a persuasive speech, a summary gives you a final opportunity to present—briefly—the major points of your argument. For example, in the informative speech on bioacoustics quoted earlier, Erin Gallagher ended with a review of the main themes:

Today, we've explored the emerging field of bioacoustics, examined the ability of the technique of vocal analysis to detect and prescribe for physical afflictions, and considered the ramifications of this technology. It's certainly not news that humans use their voices to communicate. Yet perhaps in the not so distant future, our voices will routinely convey necessary health information about our bodies, and that help may be just a phone call away.[19]

Stephanie Wolfe ended her persuasive speech on testing for congenital heart arrhythmia's at birth with a precise recapitulation of the main themes:

So today we've seen the traumatic effects of congenital heart arrhythmias and how they can be prevented with neonatal EKGs, we've seen why we don't perform regular EKG screening on newborns, and finally we looked at some ways to help make neonatal EKGs common practice in hospitals. You can tell a champion by looking at their heart. It seems so simple—all it requires is a 10-second EKG at birth. Newborns can't speak for themselves. It takes people with care and compassion to speak for them. It takes a person with the heart of a champion to champion the cause of the heart.[20]

In each case, summarizing the main ideas of the speech gives the speaker another opportunity to reinforce the message. Information can be reiterated in the summary of an informative speech, or the major arguments or actions can be strengthened in the summary of a persuasive speech.

## Using a Quotation

You can cite the words of others to capture the spirit of your ideas in the conclusion of your speech. In fact, quotations often are used to end speeches. Poetry may distill the essence of your message in uplifting language, and quoted prose—if the author is credible—may gather additional support for your central idea.

## Using an Illustration

Illustrations engage your listeners emotionally, and a concluding illustration can set the tone and direction of your final words. Your illustration should be both inclusive and conclusive—inclusive of the main focus or thrust of your speech and conclusive in tone and impact. Sometimes, a single illustration can even tie together a whole speech. For example, Amy Brin (cited earlier) refers back to her opening illustration in closing her speech on the plight of Vietnam veterans:

> After indicting the Department of Veterans Affairs, exploring the roots of their abuse, and finally establishing a means to bring about some meaningful change, we now understand the importance of protecting our veterans. Tom Jefferson went to Vietnam because it was his duty. He returned home to be abandoned by the very system of care created to protect him and abandoned by those that he fought to keep free. We, as Americans, are justified in the shame we feel. It is now our duty to protect those who did their part for us.[21]

## Supplying an Additional Inducement to Belief or Action

Sometimes, you may conclude a speech by quickly reviewing the principal ideas presented in the body and then supplying one or more additional reasons for endorsing the belief or taking the proposed action. In his speech, Michael Twitchell spoke at length about the devastating effects of depression. After proposing numerous reasons for people to get involved in the battle, Twitchell offered in his conclusion an additional inducement:

> Why should you really care? Why is it important? The depressed person may be someone you know—it could be you. If you know what is happening, you can always help. I wish I had known what depression was in March of 1978. You see, when I said David Twitchell could be my father, I was making a statement of fact. David is my father. I am his son. My family wasn't saved; perhaps now yours can be.[22]

## Stating a Personal Intention

Stating your own intention to adopt the action or attitude you recommend in your speech is particularly effective when your prestige with the audience is high or you have presented a concrete proposal requiring immediate action. By professing your intention to take immediate action, you and your ideas gain credibility. In the following example, a speaker sets himself up as a model for the actions he wants his listeners to take:

> Today I have illustrated how important healthy blood is to human survival and how blood banks work to ensure the possibility and availability of blood for each of us. It is not a coincidence that I speak on this vital topic on the same day that the local Red Cross Bloodmobile is visiting campus. I want to urge each of you to ensure your future and mine by stopping at the student center today or tomorrow to make your donation. The few minutes that it takes may add up to a lifetime for a person in need. To illustrate how firmly I believe in this opportunity to help, I'm going to the student center to give my donation as soon as this class is over. I invite any of you who feel this strongly to join me.

## Selecting Introductions and Conclusions

So far, we've talked about the functions of introductions and conclusions, about fitting them together to provide a solid rhetorical orientation to your speech, and about a variety of strategies to begin and end speeches. At this point, you should be able to build a generally serviceable opening and closing for a speech. Suppose you want to stretch yourself a bit farther, however, to move beyond the skills of the average speaker and into the world of highly competent speechmakers, of the kind we've been quoting throughout this chapter. What then? How do you become a superior opener and closer?

The answer—as always in this textbook—is that you must learn to assess yourself, your listeners, the subject matter, and the requirements of the occasion. The answers to four questions should help you construct high-quality introductions and conclusions.

**What are your own experiences and abilities?** The best source of powerful illustrations is your own life. Stories of your own experiences usually come across as natural and involving, especially if your own reactions to those experiences are like those your listeners would feel in the same situation. Anecdotes that you've found elsewhere, however, must be practiced and, at the very least, put into your own words to make them a part of you. Your abilities as a speaker also may constrain your choices. If you don't tell funny stories in a natural, relaxed manner, attempting a humorous anecdote may not be wise. On the other hand, if you're known as a clown and want to be taken seriously for a change, you need to set forth your qualifications explicitly and, when concluding, create a serious mood for the consideration of your views. Humor may not be your best vehicle under these circumstances.

**What is the mood and commitment of the audience?** If you're speaking on a subject already announced and known to be controversial, gaining attention through a startling statement or a humorous anecdote may be highly inappropriate. If the audience is indifferent or has already heard several presentations on the same subject, a direct reference to the subject may be perceived as dull and unoriginal. A rhetorical question that forces them to think for a moment or a startling statement that creates curiosity, however, may be appropriate because both will induce listeners to participate directly rather than listen passively.

**What does the audience know about you and your commitment to the subject?** If you're already known as an expert in an area, stating your qualifications would be repetitious and may even convey conceit. If your personal experience and depth of feeling generally are unknown, however, you'll want to reveal these through personal reference or, as Michael Twitchell did, through an additional inducement at the close of your address. Either approach establishes both your knowledge and your personal involvement in the subject. Allow time to pass before you attempt to bring deeply felt experiences—especially those involving loss of life—before an audience. If you appear emotionally shaken or teary eyed, the tension level will increase as the audience shares your personal discomfort, and the effectiveness of your personal revelation will correspondingly decrease. Finally, using a challenge or statement of personal intent also is an effective means of demonstrating your commitment to the subject.

**What constraints are imposed by the situation or setting?** A somber occasion (a funeral or dedication of a war memorial) is hardly the place for a hilarious story. On the other hand, some serious occasions (commencements) can be enlivened by humor. The student speaker who ended his high school address by waving a beer bottle and proclaiming "This Bud's for you" quickly discovered that his attempt at humor was well received only by part of his audience. The faculty and parents did not react as pleasantly as his peers. Not everything goes—even when you see nothing wrong with the story or allusion. A reference to the occasion or personal greeting, however, may be an appropriate reminder to the audience that you, as well as they, appreciate the significance of the occasion. Pertinent quotations and epitomizing illustrations, whether at the beginning or the end, also may convey a sense of the event's meaning for everyone present.

This discussion of appropriate introductions and conclusions is not intended to be exhaustive. Rather, it illustrates the general approach to thinking through possible audience reactions as you select various means of introducing and concluding your speech. The "How to" box below provides a quick overview of points to consider in creating an introduction and conclusion that frame your speech. A thought-through speech will be perceived as being well prepared by your listeners—whether they ultimately agree with you or not.

## Sample Outline for an Introduction and a Conclusion

An introduction and conclusion for a classroom speech on doing research using the World Wide Web might take the following form. Notice that the presentation begins with an illustration that will engage the listeners, as they've been there before. The presentation then outlines, in brief, the development of the speech. In concluding, the short summary of key points serves to pull the ideas together as a final reminder and then circles back to the opening illustration to provide a fitting closure.

### INTRODUCTION

I. It is 11 P.M., almost time to shut down for the night, when your eye catches a textbook leaning precariously on a stack of other texts—and then it hits you a paper is due at 11 A.M. tomorrow, and no, you didn't do the research you promised you'd do, much less start the paper.

    A. What next? A few excuses run through your tired brain as you try to think of ways to dodge the inevitable late night—and finally you turn to the computer and begin to settle in. But first, where do you find materials at this time of the night?

## How to
## Frame a Speech

### In Your Introduction:

- Focus on gaining your audience's attention, especially if they aren't likely to be interested in your topic.
- Establish your expertise, particularly if the audience isn't aware of your qualifications.
- Satisfy any special demands of the occasion; if you depart from custom, justify your reasons for doing so.
- Work to create goodwill when the audience isn't sympathetic to you or your ideas.

### In Your Conclusion:

- Signal the audience that the speech is about to end by refocusing them on the message.
- Answer the question "So what?" for your listeners.
- Influence the audience with your own enthusiasm and interest to help keep them involved in the message.

B. As many of you have already guessed, the prime resource for that late-night crisis is none other than the World Wide Web—an all-night delicatessen of information, if only you know where to look for the right stuff.

II. Knowing how and where to look for resources is the trick—and in this presentation, I will review the reasons the web is an excellent resource, talk about specific search phases, and then provide some useful tips to assist in finding the right materials.

CONCLUSION

I. The search phases we have discussed—using metasearch engines, using the most powerful of the crawlers, and using sources with hyperlinks—make it possible to find the kind of materials needed in less time.

II. The tips—using quote marks, using words such as NOT and truncating words—also make the process more streamlined and enhance your chances of finding the material you need.

III. It is now midnight, and a brief half hour of searching the web has provided the key materials needed for your research paper. In fact, you found more materials than you could use! The paper is now well underway, and it looks, with any luck, like you'll still get some sleep.

## ■ CHAPTER SUMMARY

Recall Winans's advice in noting that "Attention determines response." The 10 strategies for gaining and maintaining attention—activity, concreteness, proximity, familiarity, novelty, suspense, conflict, humor, the vital, and visualization—provide ways to motivate your listeners to attend to your ideas. More specifically, introductions and conclusions provide a rhetorical orientation to your speeches, thus framing them in ways audiences can understand and appreciate.

A well-framed introduction orients an audience's attention, shows them your qualifications, and directs them to your ideas and their development. A well-framed conclusion provides focus, flair, and a sense of finality for your talk. Useful ways of beginning a speech include referring to the subject or occasion, using a personal reference or greeting, asking a question, making a startling statement, using a quotation, telling a humorous story, using an illustration, and building a speech forecast. A speech can be concluded by issuing a challenge, summarizing the major points or ideas, using a quotation, using an illustration, supplying an additional inducement to belief or action, and stating a personal intention.

Your decision regarding which strategies you use, whether singly or in combination, should depend on you and your experiences, the mood and commitments of the audience, the audience's knowledge of you and your commitments, and any constraints imposed by the situation or setting. The most competent speakers carefully think through strategies for moving into and out of their speeches because of the importance of rhetorical orientation in making them successful behind the lectern.

## ■ KEY TERMS

activity  (p. 192)

attention  (p. 191)

attention gaining/maintaining
   strategies  (p. 192)

audience attention  (p. 189)

conclusion  (p. 198)

concrete reality  (p. 192)

conflict  (p. 195)

ethos  (p. 197)

familiarity  (p. 193)

forecast  (p. 198)

humor  (p. 195)

introduction  (p. 197)

novelty  (p. 194)

preview  (p. 198)

proximity  (p. 193)

rhetorical orientation  (p. 196)

suspense  (p. 194)

The End  (p. 198)

the vital  (p. 195)

visualization  (p. 196)

## ■ ASSESSMENT ACTIVITIES

1. Following the principles and guidelines presented in this chapter, prepare a 3- to 4-minute speech to inform. Narrow the subject carefully, so you can do justice to it in the allotted time, and concentrate on developing ways to gain and hold the audience's attention. Hand in an outline, along with a brief analysis of the audience and the occasion, when you present the speech. In your analysis, indicate why you think your approach to attention will work in this situation.

2. You've been asked to speak on a controversial issue. Assume that the settings for three versions of the speech will include three different occasions: a classroom at your school, where audience members are mixed in their support or rejection of the issue; a favorable ("pro") audience, highly sympathetic to you and your position; and an unfavorable ("con") audience, hostile to you and your position. Write three introductions, one for each setting. Include a brief paragraph explaining your rhetorical orientations to those three audiences, and then turn in the introductions and rationales to your instructor.

3. Devise a 1-minute introduction and conclusion for your next informative speech. Deliver them to a small group in class, in round-robin fashion, so that everyone gets a turn with the group. Have each member of the group rate your introduction in terms of attention value, perception of your qualifications, and forecast of your speech's development and your conclusion in terms of focus, flair, and sense of finality. Collect the ratings from everyone, and use their feedback to refine your opening and closing.

## ■ REFERENCES

1. Psychologist Philip G. Zimbardo has likened attention to "a spotlight that illuminates certain portions of our surroundings. When we focus our attention on something and thus become conscious of it, we can begin to process it cognitively—converting sensory information into perceptions and memories or developing ideas through analysis, judgment, reasoning, and imagination. When the spotlight shifts to something else, conscious processing of the earlier material ceases and processing of the new content begins." From *Psychology and Life*, 12th ed. (Glenview, IL: Scott, Foresman, 1988), 225.

2. Gibson E. and N. Rader, "Attention: Perceiver as Performer," in *Attention and Cognitive Development*, edited by Gordon A. Hale and Michael Lewis (New York: Plenum 1979), 1–22. Cited in Russell A.

Barkley, "Critical Issues in Research on Attention," in *Attention, Memory, and Executive Function,* edited by G. Reid Lyon and Norman A. Krasgegor (Baltimore, MD: Brookes, 1996).

3. Erin Gallagher, Informative Speaking, "BioAcoustic Technology," presented at the National Forensics Association's Championship Tournament, April 2001, Western Kentucky University, Bowling Green, KY, and the American Forensics Association's National Individual Events Tournament, April 2001, George Mason University, Fairfax, VA.

4. Adrienne Mayo, "Corporate Bullying," *Winning Orations 2000.* Reprinted by permission of Larry Schnoor, Executive Secretary, Interstate Oratorical Association, Mankato, MN.

5. Justin D. Neal, "Leaving Justice Unserved," *Winning Orations 2000.* Reprinted by permission of Larry Schnoor, Executive Secretary, Interstate Oratorical Association, Mankato, MN.

6. Stephanie Aduloju, "It's Never too Late: Sexual Education for the Elderly," *Winning Orations 2001.* Reprinted by permission of Larry Schnoor, Executive Secretary, Interstate Oratorical Association, Mankato, MN.

7. Malcolm X, "The Ballot or the Bullet," in *Diversity in Public Communication: A Reader,* edited by Christine Kelly, E. Anne Laffoon, and Raymie E. McKerrow (Dubuque, IA: Kendall-Hunt, 1994), 138.

8. Evelyn Breznik, "Our Nation's Shame: The Injustice of Idle Rape Kits," *Winning Orations 2000.* Reprinted by permission of Larry Schnoor, Executive Secretary, Interstate Oratorical Association, Mankato, MN.

9. Christiane Amanpour, remarks at the 2000 Murrow Awards Ceremony, Sept. 13, 2000. Available online: <http://gos.sbc.edu/a/amanpour/html>. Accessed June 9, 2001.

10. Mother Jones's speech excerpt. Available online: <http://www.pbs.org/greatspeeches/timeline/index.html#1990>. Accessed June 9, 2001.

11. Raymie E. McKerrow, "Coloring Outside the Lines: The Limits of Civility," *Vital Speeches of the Day* 67 (15 February 2001): 278.

12. Kari Hammer, "The Plight of America's High Schools," *Winning Orations 2000.* Reprinted by permission of Larry Schnoor, Executive Secretary, Interstate Oratorical Association, Mankato, MN.

13. Stephanie Wolfe, "Champions of the Heart," *Winning Orations 2001.* Reprinted by permission of Larry Schnoor, Executive Secretary, Interstate Oratorical Association, Mankato, MN.

14. Amy E. Brin, "Forgotten Heroes and Broken Promises: Reforming Our Department of Veterans Affairs Hospitals," *Winning Orations 2000.* Reprinted by permission of Larry Schnoor, Executive Secretary, Interstate Oratorical Association, Mankato, MN.

15. Earnest W. Deavenport, "Walking the High Wire: Balancing Stakeholder Interests," *Vital Speeches of the Day* 62 (1 November 1995): 49.

16. Travis Kirchhefer, "The Deprived," *Winning Orations 2000.* Reprinted by permission of Larry Schnoor, Executive Secretary, Interstate Oratorical Association, Mankato, MN.

17. Kirchhefer.

18. Jennifer Sweeney, "Racial Profiling," *Winning Orations 2000.* Reprinted by permission of Larry Schnoor, Executive Secretary, Interstate Oratorical Association, Mankato, MN.

19. Gallagher.

20. Wolfe.

21. Brin.

22. Michael Twitchell, "The Flood Gates of the Mind," *Winning Orations 1991.* Reprinted by permission of Larry Schnoor, Executive Secretary, Interstate Oratorical Association, Mankato MN.

Chapter **9**

# Developing the
# Speech Outline

$W$hy outline a speech? Recall the opening story about Jake in the preceding chapter: Had he taken the time to outline his speech, he likely would have reminded himself to think about audience interest, and he certainly would have put ideas and stories about a particular event all in the same place, making it easier for listeners to follow him. An outline keeps you on track, allows you to concentrate on what needs to be said, and reminds you of points you otherwise may forget to mention. In addition, you can make side notes to remind yourself when to show a slide or to pause, so audience members can focus on a graph you have presented or absorb an important point you have made.

Although your past experiences with outlining may not have been the most pleasant (remember outlining in eighth or ninth grade?), the fact is that outlining is an important tool for the speaker. In addition to providing guidance, an outline helps you evaluate the coherence of your ideas: You can discover what ideas you've overemphasized to the exclusion of others, see more clearly what should be added, and tell at a glance that you've buried your most important point. And while public speaking is an oral event, a few well-crafted notes can help you manage the actual presentational process. Thus, while the outline is written for the speaking situation, it serves as an evaluative and a mnemonic tool, as well.

Speech outlines come in many forms, depending on the purpose for which they've been constructed. In this chapter, we review the elements of good outline form—in case you've forgotten those earlier lessons from eighth or ninth grade! Then, we get into the heart of the matter: the process of moving from your initial ideas to an outline you can use in presenting a speech.

# Requirements of Good Outline Form

There are many useful outline forms, each appropriate for a certain use. The following four requirements are applicable to all outlines, regardless of their purpose or form. To help point out the difference between a sloppy outline and a logical one, we alternate between "Wrong" and "Right" illustrations. This should make application of the rules easier to understand.

**Each item in the outline should contain one main idea.** When two or more ideas are included in a main point, an audience has more difficulty tracking the development of the point.

WRONG

I. When you buy pork chops or bacon at the supermarket, you probably don't think about the problems that hog manure settling ponds can cause those living nearby them because the manure can leech into nearby water sources and can smell just terrible on a hot day, especially when liquid manure is sprayed as fertilizer on other fields, but of course the larger the farming operation, the more clout it has with government, and so of course the lives of those who live around it don't get any help.

This is a mess. It is hard to discern what the main point of the speech is from this sentence. It appears the speaker is angry about the presence of large hog farms (perhaps the speaker has personal experience?), but the series of examples and the unsupported allegation about big business makes this too large a claim to swallow whole.

RIGHT

I. Large or macro-hog farms need to be regulated by county and state governments.
   A. Manure settling ponds need to meet strict county standards that will prevent them from leeching into underground water sources.
   B. The state must set air quality standards to control odor and timetables for when liquefied manure can be sprayed on fields as fertilizer.
   C. Both county and state governments should outline procedures that allow for citizen input on size and location of macro-hog farms.

In this case, the claim is clearly focused on regulations. The initial point sets forth the position that the speaker wants to establish and then dictates the evidence requirements. To support it, the speaker would need statistics on the amount of manure produced by, say, a 2000-hog farming operation and on the nature and extent of water pollution and noxious odors that would be produced by typical operations in the area.

**Less important ideas in the outline should be subordinate to more important ideas.** You already know this is true; the trick is to actually carry it out so that listeners will understand the rational structure of your arguments.

**WRONG**

I. The cost of medical care has skyrocketed.
  A. Operating room fees can run to tens of thousands of dollars.
    1. Hospital charges are high.
    2. A private room can cost $1,500 a day.
  B. X-rays and laboratory tests involve extra charges.
  C. Complicated operations may cost over $100,000.
    1. Doctors' charges constantly go up.
      a. Office calls usually cost between $30 and $90.
      b. Surgical costs have increased.
    2. Drugs are expensive.
    3. Most antibiotics cost from $2 to $3 per dose.
  D. The cost of nonprescription drugs also has mounted.

This outline is sloppily arranged. Listeners would feel bombarded by numbers and general references to hospitals and doctors—and probably would not be able to sort it all out. To help listeners grasp the main ideas, notice what happens when the material is sorted by cost in a basic outline identifying reasons and support:

**RIGHT**

I. The cost of medical care has skyrocketed.
  A. Hospital charges are high.                                    **Reason**
    1. A private room may cost as much as $1,500 a day.            **Support**
    2. Operating room fees may be tens of thousands of dollars.
    3. X-rays and laboratory tests involve extra.
  B. Doctors' charges constantly go up.                           **Reason**
    1. Complicated operations may cost more than $100,000.        **Support**
    2. Office calls usually cost between $30 and $90.
  C. Drugs are expensive.                                         **Reason**
    1. Most antibiotics cost from $2 to $3 per dose.              **Support**
    2. The cost of nonprescription drugs also has mounted.

This outline highlights the three main topics and subordinates the examples, which are the supporting materials, to the three main arguments. The key word here is *fit*: What example fits within or under what topic? Reasons (A, B, C) fit within or under claims, and supporting materials (1, 2, 3) fit within or under reasons.

**A consistent set of symbols should be used.**  The levels of indentation should be designated by the same set of symbols. The most common set looks like this:

I.  Main idea
   A.  Major subpoint or topic
      1.  Aspect of the subpoint or topic
         a.  Perhaps a statistic or quotation
            (1) Perhaps bolstering support

You can use other sets of symbols (A, 1, a if you only need three levels). However, the primary concern is to be consistent so that the rational structure of your thoughts emerges clearly, both for evaluative and for guidance purposes.

**The logical relation of items in an outline should be shown by proper indentation.**  Why? Doing so makes it easier to see what is subordinate to what. As noted earlier, reasons and supporting materials should not be placed on the same level. By indenting and using a consistent format for the levels used in outlining, the process of evaluating your claim or central idea becomes much easier. In addition, indentation helps you see precisely where you are when you're looking down at your notes. You will be able to follow your own speech while talking, when you're liable to be a little nervous or forgetful.

WRONG

I.  Picking edible wild mushrooms is no job for the uninformed.
   A.  Many wild species are highly toxic.
      1.  The angel cap contains a toxin for which there is no known antidote.
      2.  Hallucinogenic mushrooms produce a short-lived high, which is followed by convulsions, paralysis, and possibly death.
   B.  Myths abound regarding ways to choose safe mushrooms.
      1.  Mushrooms easily peeled still can be poisonous.
      2.  Mushrooms eaten by animals are not necessarily safe.
      3.  Mushrooms that do not darken a silver coin in a pan of hot water can be toxic.
      4.  Join a mushroom club to learn from others and keep a journal, with drawings, of mushrooms you have found.

RIGHT

I.  Picking edible wild mushrooms is no job for the uninformed.
   A.  Many wild species are highly toxic.
      1.  The angel cap contains a toxin for which there is no known antidote.
      2.  Hallucinogenic mushrooms produce a short-lived high, which is followed by convulsions, paralysis, and possibly death.
   B.  Myths abound regarding ways to choose safe mushrooms.
      1.  Mushrooms easily peeled still can be poisonous.
      2.  Mushrooms eaten by animals are not necessarily safe.

      3. Mushrooms that do not darken a silver coin in a pan of hot
         water can be toxic.
   C. Protect yourself before you get into trouble.
      1. Join a mushroom club to learn from others.
      2. Keep a journal, with drawings, of mushrooms you have found.[1]

Before moving on, consider the information in the "Communication Research
Dateline" box below, which looks at the thought process involved in organizing

## COMMUNICATION RESEARCH DATELINE

### Perceptual Grouping: The Organization of Subordinate Points

What basic principles do we use to organize information into meaningful patterns? Gestalt psychologists, who believe that organization is basic to all mental activity and reflects the way the human brain functions, provide some useful clues. As suggested in this chapter, psychologists argue that we learn by adding new bits of information to old constructs. Although the information that we encounter changes, the constructs remain constant. We use several relatively common constructs to group new bits of information:

1. *Proximity:* We group stimuli that are close together.
2. *Continuity:* We tend to simplify and to find similarities among things rather than differences.
3. *Contiguity:* We connect events that occur close together in time and space.
4. *Closure:* We complete figures by filling in the gaps or adding missing connections.
5. *Similarity:* We group items of similar shape, size, and color.

You can use these constructs to enhance the audience's understanding of your ideas.

Your speech outline can be cast in a pattern of thinking that is familiar to your audience. Consider the constructs for organizing subordinate points shown in Table 9.1 (p. 218).

These constructs also may assist you as you evaluate your outline, especially as you develop the technical plot outline. Are your most important ideas near, or *proximate*, to each other? Do they advance a chain of thinking in a coherent manner, thus implying *continuity?* Are they linked, or *contiguous?* Are they sufficiently comprehensive to permit accurate *closure?* Are they *similar* enough to suggest they belong together as main points?

### For Further Reading

Beck, Jacob, ed. *Organization and Representation in Perception* (Hillsdale, NJ: Erlbaum, 1982).

Palmer, Stephen E. "Gestalt Psychology Redux," in *Speaking Minds*, edited by Peter Baumgartner and Sabine Payr (Princeton, NJ: Princeton University Press, 1995), 157–176.

Rock, Irvin, ed. *The Legacy of Solomon Asch: Essays in Cognition and Social Psychology* (Hillsdale, NJ: Erlbaum, 1990).

Smith, Barry, ed. *Foundations of Gestalt Theory* (Munich: Philosophia Verlag, 1988).

www.gestalt.org

www.enabling.org/ia/gerhards/links.html

| TABLE 9.1 | Strategies for Organizing Speech Information | | |
| --- | --- | --- | --- |
| **ORGANIZING STRATEGY** | **MAIN CONSTRUCT** | **EXPLANATION** | **EXAMPLE** |
| Parts of a whole | Proximity | Help your audience perceive how the new information is all part of a whole. | "The grip, shaft, and head are the main parts of a golf club." |
| Lists of functions | Continuity | Show your audience the connections between pieces of new information. | "The mission of a police department consists of meeting its responsibilities of traffic control, crime detection, and safety education." |
| Series of causes or results | Contiguity | Show your listeners the precise relationship between pieces of new information. | "The causes of high orange juice prices may be drought, frost, or blight in citrus-producing states." |
| Items of logical proof | Closure | Connect separate items of information along a coordinated line of reasoning. | "We need a new high school because our present building (a) is too small, (b) lacks modern laboratory and shop facilities, and (c) is inaccessible to students who are disabled." |
| Illustrative examples | Similarity | Help your audience accept your main point by grouping specific cases or examples. | Cite the outcome of experiments to prove that adding fluoride to your community's water supply will help prevent tooth decay. |

information into useful patterns. As described in the box, we use several common constructs to group new information. Table 9.1 also provides some strategies for organizing information in your speeches, offering examples as well as explanations.

## Developing the Speech: Stages in the Outlining Process

You should develop your outline of a speech through a series of stages. At each stage, your outline will become increasingly complex and complete as the ideas evolve and you move closer to the final form of your speech. We will examine each of the major stages, beginning with the rough outline, and then consider in sequence the technical plot outline and the speaking outline.

## Developing a Rough Outline

Suppose your instructor has assigned an informative speech and allowed you to choose the subject. You decide to talk about World Wide Web (WWW) search strategies, which might be helpful to classmates looking for speech materials. In the 6 to 8 minutes you have to speak, you obviously cannot cover such a broad topic adequately. After considering your audience (see Chapter 5) and your time limit, you decide to focus your presentation on the steps to take—and avoid—in finding useful information.

As you think about narrowing your topic further, you jot down some possible ideas. How much history do they need? Probably none. Should you show both productive and unproductive searches? Sure! How many search engines can you deal with in the time available? Only the most popular. Should you do simple or advanced searches? Start with simple ones. You continue to expand and then narrow your list until your final ideas include the following:

1. General information about Internet and WWW searches to set the scene
2. Search phases: Moving through various search engines
3. Search strategies that are useful
4. Search strategies that are not as useful

Your next step is to consider the best pattern of organization for these topics. Because searching is itself a sequential process, a **chronological pattern** will allow you to discuss the initial steps in preparing to search and then move forward in time to more sophisticated searching. Because you are not posing this as a problem, patterns such as **cause-effect** and **effect-cause** will not be as easy to work into the structure of this speech. After examining the alternatives, you finally settle on a **topical pattern,** which allows you to present four topics that are related to the search process:

1. Setting the context in terms of the WWW as a research resource
2. Elaborating on search phases: Moving from metasearch engines to more specific ones
3. Discussing search strategies that further focus the search
4. Discussing search strategies that are not as useful

These four topics form the basis for your **rough outline,** which identifies your topic, provides a reasonable number of subtopics, and shows a method for organizing and developing your speech:

I. General discussion of the WWW
   A. As a research resource
   B. Key terms to be used

   II. Search phases
      A. Metasearch engines and what they can do
      B. More specific search engines: If you are looking for *x,* use search engine *y*

  III. Search strategies and tips that will focus the research
      A. Using quotation marks
      B. Using NOT or –
      C. Using AND or +

  IV. Search strategies that will not be as useful

Notice that you've arranged the main points topically and used a general-to-specific ordering under main point II, which also suggests a sequential process for searching. Under main point II, you also have organized the subpoints topically.

*A word of warning:* As you refine your outline, make sure that the speech does not turn into a "string of beads" that fails to differentiate between one topic and the next.

## Developing a Technical Plot Outline

After completing your rough outline and learning more about your topic through background reading, you're now ready to assemble a **technical plot outline,** which is a diagnostic tool used to determine whether a speech is structurally sound. Use your technical plot outline to discover possible gaps and weaknesses in your speech.

Begin this process by laying your current outline beside a blank sheet of paper. On the blank sheet, write down opposite each outline point the corresponding supporting materials, types of motivational appeals, factors of attention, and other devices. For example, indicate on the blank sheet wherever you use statistics. You also might include a brief statement of the function of the statistics. Then, examine the list of supporting materials, motivational appeals, factors of attention, and so on. Consider these questions:

- Is there adequate supporting material for each point in the speech?
- Is the supporting material sufficiently varied?
- Do you use motivational appeals at key points in the speech?
- Do you attempt to engage your listeners' attention throughout the speech?

Answering these questions with your technical plot outline can help you determine whether your speech is structurally sound, whether there is adequate supporting material, whether you've overused any forms of support, and whether you have effectively adapted your appeals to the audience and content.

What follows typifies the kind of outline you will initially construct, as it mixes full sentences with phrases as needed to clearly indicate your thoughts.[2] In most cases, however, you will use a more precisely phrased speaking outline—provided that will fulfill your instructor's goals regarding how detailed to make your outline. (Note that the introduction and conclusion of this outline are assumed. This is the *content* portion of the presentation.)

## Sample Technical Plot Outline

### *Search Strategies for Successful Research on the WWW*

I. Conducting research on the WWW is an excellent tool in locating speech materials.

    A. The web is an amazing library resource.

        1. Both Google and AltaVista, the great San Francisco Bay–area megasearch engines, can tap into more than 1 billion webpages as of August 2001.

        2. AltaVista estimates there are more than 2 billion webpages as of 2001.

        3. AltaVista does 50 million searches a day in 30 languages of full-text databases, and Google likely does more.

        4. The Babel Fish translation program pioneered by AltaVista moves across languages from around the world.

        5. The "I'm Feeling Lucky" feature of Google takes you to the single-most important site for a search to let you have an in-depth look at it.

        6. Yet no web search engines, including the two giants, access all the pages available—you need to use several.

    B. The WWW is a convenient resource.

        1. If you have an Internet connection, you can log on any time, day or night.

        2. Information never sleeps.

        3. The search engines even rank resources, helping you with quality of information.

    C. Before you start, you should know some key terms.

        1. *HTTP:* Hypertext Transfer Protocol

        2. *URL:* Uniform Resource Locator

        3. *Hyperlinks:* Links by words or symbols to more texts

        4. *Boolean:* The algebraic system for relating search terms to each other in specific ways

II. Search phases

    A. Phase one: Use metasearch engines.

        1. Inference find: www.inference.com/infind

        2. MetaFind: www.metafind.com

        3. MetaCrawler: www.metacrawler.com

        4. Dogpile: www.dogpile.com

**Annotations (right column):**

- **First main topic**
- **First subtopic**
- **Statistics**
- **Second subtopic**
- **Motivational appeal**
- **Transition topic**
- **Definitions [use blackboard, tripod, or PowerPoint slides for terms]**
- **Second main topic**
- **Specific instances [list on board or use slides to make it easy for audience to see and copy the terms]**

*(continued)*

| | |
|---|---|
| **Specific instances [illustrate as above]** | B. Phase two: Use those with the most power to locate specific information.<br>  1. Infoseek: www.infoseek.com<br>  2. AltaVista: www.altavista.com<br>  3. Northern Light: www.northernlight.com<br>  4. Hotbot: www.hotbot.com<br>  5. For other search engines: www.home.co.il/search.html |
| **Third subpoint** | C. Phase three: Use "webliographics" resources—focus on sites with hyperlinks to your subject area.<br>  1. Yahoo!: www.yahoo.com<br>  2. Argus Clearinghouse: www.clearinghouse.edu<br>  3. Google: www.google.com |
| **Third main topic** | III. Search tips: Experiment with the search engine you are using in trying these features, because not all engines accept the same codes. |
| **Explanation** | A. Place more than one word in quotation marks. |
| **Specific instances** | 1. "Web search engines"<br>  2. "Presidential Commission on Debates" |
| **Explanation**<br>**Specific instances** | B. Use either NOT or – to eliminate hits on a specific word.<br>  1. "Rhetoric NOT speeches"<br>  2. "Politics NOT American" |
| | C. AND or + also will assist in focusing the search.<br>  1. "Rhetoric AND public spheres AND criticism"<br>  2. "Geological AND rock AND formations" |
| | D. OR produces hits on both terms used in a search.<br>  1. "Arguing OR conflict"<br>  2. "Legal OR forensic" |
| | E. Truncate words to find as many variations as possible.<br>  1. "Femini"—retrieves *feminist, feminism, feminine* on AltaVista<br>  2. "Polit"—retrieves *polit* as an English abbreviation, a Russian noun, and a stem for a variety of words for politics in different languages (*politik, politicas, politique*) when using AltaVista |
| **Final main point** | IV. Search strategies to avoid. |
| **Explanation** | A. Typing in a general subject term and seeing what pops up |
| **Explanation** | B. Using "Subject Directories" within the search engine menu |

## Developing a Speaking Outline

As you probably realize, the technical plot outline is not intended for actual speaking use. It gives you a chance to see what is needed or how to make sure the audience understands the information, but it is not the kind of outline you actually would use in giving a speech on WWW search strategies.

Remember what we said about the oral style and interactive moments while speaking (especially in Chapter 1)? The speaker/audience relationship in public speaking is a fluid one, with the listeners taking part in the event. Their reactions

*By sketching out the structure of your speech in advance of presentation, you can determine whether the major sections fit together smoothly.*

are integral to successful communication. This means that the speaker must be able, at least somewhat, to go with the flow, speeding up when the listeners are bored or when she or he is talking about something they already know and slowing down and becoming more redundant when they look puzzled.

To allow yourself this flexibility, you need to do two things. First, compress the technical plot outline into a **speaking outline,** using the same indentation and symbol structure. The major difference between the two types of outlines is that each item in a speaking outline is referred to in shorthand—using phrases and single key words. Second, be ready to drop any materials you don't need to include and to insert additional examples. Developed with these two injunctions in mind, the previous technical plot outline looks like this:

## Sample Speaking Outline

### Search Strategies for Successful Research on the WWW

I.  Conducting research on the WWW
   A.  The WWW as a library resource
      1.  AltaVista and Google est. 2 billion webpages
      2.  A-V gets 50 million hits/day in 30 languages
      3.  A-V's Babel Fish—multilingual materials
      4.  G's I'm Feeling Lucky selects one—in-depth examination
   B.  Convenience of the WWW
      1.  Modem/Internet connection
      2.  Information never sleeps
      3.  Best engines rank resources

*(continued)*

C. Key terms [SHOW POSTERS!]
   1. HTTP: Hypertext Transfer Protocol
   2. URL: Uniform Resource Locator
   3. Hyperlinks: links to relevant resources
   4. Boolean: algebraic system of relationships

II. Search phases
   A. Phase one: Use metasearch engines
      1. Inference find
      2. MetaFind
      3. MetaCrawler
      4. Dogpile
   B. Phase two: Specific engines
      1. Infoseek
      2. AltaVista
      3. Northern Light
      4. Hotbot
      5. Search Engine Listing
   C. Phase three: "webliographics" resources
      1. Yahoo!
      2. Argus Clearinghouse

III. Search tips
   A. Quotation marks
   B. NOT or –
   C. AND or +
   D. OR
   E. Truncate words—*femini, polit*
   F. [Extra examples as needed: *geolog, sociopat*]

IV. Search strategies to avoid
   A. General subject terms
   B. Subject directories

What you use in writing out your speaking outline depends on your personal preference. Some people like to work with small pieces of paper, and others prefer notecards (see Figure 9.1). Whatever your choice, however, your speaking outline should serve several functions while you're addressing your audience:

1. It should provide you with reminders of the direction of your speech—main points, subordinate ideas, and so on.

2. It should record technical or detailed material, such as statistics and quotations.

**FIGURE 9.1**  **Sample Speaking Outline on Notecards**

*Notecards for a speech on web search strategies.*

**I. Conducting research on the World Wide Web**

A. The web as a library resource
   1. AltaVista — 2 billion web pages as of fall 2001
   2. None access fully
B. Convenience of the web
   1. Modem/Internet connection
   2. Information never sleeps
C. Key terms [SHOW POSTER]
   1. HTTP: hypertext transfer protocol
   2. URL: uniform resource locater
   3. Hyperlinks: links to relevant resources

**II. Search phases**

A. Phase One: Use meta-search engines
   1. Inference Find
   2. MetaFind
   3. MetaCrawler
   4. Dogpile
B. Phase Two: Specific engines
   1. Infoseek        4. Hotbot
   2. AltaVista       5. Google
   3. Northern Light
C. Phase Three: "webliographics" resources
   1. Yahoo!
   2. Argus Clearinghouse

**III. Search tips**

A. Quotation marks
B. "NOT" or "–"
C. "AND" or "+"
D. "OR"
E. Truncate words

**IV. Search strategies to avoid**

A. General subject terms
B. Subject directories

3. It should be easy to read so it does not detract from the delivery of your speech. Each notecard or piece of paper should contain only one main idea.

4. It should give you directions on presentation (such as extra examples included on the outline) and delivery (such as when to show a poster or a PowerPoint slide).

A properly prepared speaking outline has these four main characteristics:

1. Most points are noted with only a key word or phrase—a word or two should be enough to trigger your memory, especially if you've practiced the speech adequately.

2. Ideas that must be stated precisely are written down fully—for example, "Information never sleeps."

3. Directions for delivery—for example, "SHOW POSTER"—are included.

4. Emphasis is indicated in a number of ways—capital letters, underlining, indentation, dashes, and highlighting with colored markers. Find methods of emphasis that will easily catch your eye, show the relationship of ideas, and jog your memory during delivery.

## Using PowerPoint to Integrate Verbal and Visual Outlines

As noted in the previous chapter, **PowerPoint** is a highly useful tool in making sure both you and your audience know where you are as you present your ideas. The speech on WWW search strategies lends itself especially well to the use of PowerPoint, as the listing of websites needs to be clear for the audience: Simply hearing the names and addresses will not be a sufficient means of conveying useful information to the audience.

The primary advantage in using PowerPoint is that you can make notes about each slide you show. When you go into the "View" menu and select "Notes Page," you get a smaller version of the slide and a space to add notes below. You can print out this file and use it to stay on track with the information presented (see Figure 9.2). Because PowerPoint also allows you to bring each subpoint to the screen as you refer to it, you also can manage the information given so that the audience will focus on each point as it is discussed. In this way, you integrate what you are saying to the audience, as they see the evidence for themselves on the projection screen.

One last idea here: This particular speech on WWW research would be even more interesting if you had available **Elmo** or another presentational projection technology that attaches to a computer that, in turn, has WWW access. Then you could move out onto the Internet, go to Hotbot or InfoSeek, and do an actual search, illustrating the use of Boolean manipulations of terms and projecting the results on a screen.

**FIGURE 9.2**

**PowerPoint Slides/Notes**

**Listening Styles**

- RESULTS–bottom line, action or task oriented
- REASONS–logic/analysis oriented; test rationale for request/action
- PROCESS–affiliation oriented; look at the "big picture"

Listening Styles

RRP–Results, Reasons, Process
Results: Focuses on "What is to be done?"
Reasons: Focuses on "Why should this be done?"
Process: Focuses on "How has this recommendation been reached?"

In summary, when you spent that late Thursday night worrying about outlining exercises in preparation for the Friday ninth-grade test on form, you gave outlining a bad rap. To be sure, the technical plot outline still can give you the willies. But both the rough outline, which gets you started, and the speaking outline, which is your greatest help in remembering what you want to say while you're saying it, can carry you to success when speaking in public. The outline combines form and content in ways calculated to increase your oral clarity and power. Use it.

## CHAPTER SUMMARY

Arranging and outlining need not be tedious tasks. If you have understood the fundamentals presented in this chapter, you now realize that an outline is both a diagnostic tool and a guide to delivering ideas. You also are aware of the elements of a good outline:

- Each item should contain only one idea.
- Less important ideas should be subordinate to more important ones.
- Logical relationships should be shown by using proper indentation.
- A consistent set of symbols should be used.

You also should be able to work through the logical progression involved in developing ideas, from the construction of a rough outline, followed by the addition of a technical plot, and then the drafting of a final speaking outline. Should you desire and should your instructor approve, you might take some shortcuts in the actual process by eliminating the technical plot outline. You also could write out those comments that you want to make sure you say in a specific way and leave other materials as key words and phrases. Whether or not you risk using an abbreviated method, you should be aware of the evaluative role that outlining can play in the speaking process.

## ■ KEY TERMS

**cause-effect** (p. 219)          **Elmo** (p. 226)          **speaking outline** (p. 223)
**chronological pattern** (p. 219)   **PowerPoint** (p. 226)   **technical plot outline** (p. 220)
**effect-cause** (p. 219)          **rough outline** (p. 219)   **topical pattern** (p. 219)

## ■ ASSESSMENT ACTIVITIES

1. Revise each of the following using the guidelines for correct outline form:
   a. The nuclear freeze concept is a good idea because it will allow us to stop nuclear proliferation and will help make us feel more secure.
   b. I. We should wear seatbelts to protect our lives.
      II. Studies indicate seatbelts protect children from serious injury.
      III. Studies indicate seatbelts reduce risk of head injury.

2. For a speech assigned by the instructor, develop a rough outline and a technical plot outline in accordance with the samples provided in this chapter. Hand in both outlines in time to obtain feedback before presenting your speech.

3. Working in small groups, select a controversial topic for potential presentation in class. Brainstorm possible arguments that could be offered on the "pro" and the "con" sides. Using these as a basis, develop a rough outline of the main points to be presented on both sides. Here are some possible topics:
   a. Whaling in the Pacific Ocean
   b. Stem cell research and biological engineering
   c. The value of the World Trade Organization
   d. School voucher systems
   e. National Endowment for the Arts public programming grants

## ■ REFERENCES

1. The information used in creating these outlines is from Vincent Marteka, "Words of Praise—and Caution—About Fungus Among Us," *Smithsonian*, May 1980, pp. 96–104; and *The Audubon Society Field Guide to North American Mushrooms* (New York: Knopf, 1992), esp. Introduction.

2. The information used in creating this outline is from several sources: John A. Courtright and Elizabeth M. Perse, *Communicating Online: A Guide to the Internet* (Mountain View, CA: Mayfield, 1998); <www. AltaVista.com>; <www.google.com>; <www.lib. berkeley.edu/guides/interent/findinfo.html>; <freelance.co.nz/webpages.htm>; and Barry Nance, "Managing Tons of Data," available online: <www. computerworld.com>, accessed April 23, 2001.

# PART THREE
# Channels

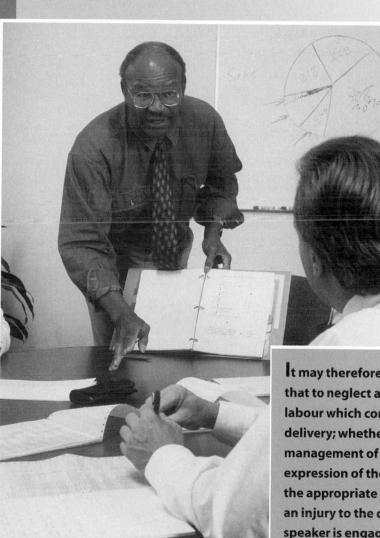

It may therefore be fairly concluded, that to neglect all or any part of the labour which constitutes correct delivery; whether it be the due management of the voice, the expression of the countenance, or the appropriate gesture, is so far an injury to the cause in which the speaker is engaged, and so far deprives his composition of its just effect.

Gilbert Austin, *Chironomia: Or a Treatise on Rhetorical Delivery* (1806)

# Chapter 10

# Using Language to Communicate

*When Neil Armstrong set foot on the moon in 1969, millions of Americans heard him say, "That's one small step for man, one giant leap for mankind." It seemed an appropriate thing to say: a two-phrase speech that captured in a simple, eloquent way the realization that another "ball of rock" in the universe had been traversed by an earthling. Yet as people thought about Armstrong's words, at least some noticed that they formed a tautology; the distinction between "step for man" and "leap for mankind" was not clear at all. After Armstrong heard the rebroadcast, he was quick to say that a key word—the word a—had been lost in transmission. The words he had actually intoned were, "That's one small step for a man, one giant leap for mankind." Then, the two phrases actually asserted two different actions—those of an individual and those of the people for whom that individual acted. Within another year or so, however, the astronaut faced still another question: Why did he talk only about the male half of the population? While the astronauts (at that point) were all male, the NASA team included both males and females, and all of humankind—not just mankind—took that leap into the future in late July of 1969. Neil Armstrong had no answer to that question and probably decided to quit explaining his speech while he was still a hero.*

As Armstrong discovered, language functions on multiple levels of meaning. Language is a referential, relational, and symbolic medium of communication. As a **referential** tool, language refers to aspects of the world: *dog, bagel, man*. Through its **relational** powers, language suggests associations or relationships between people: *Give me a bagel* not only points to bagels but indicates that one person has the power or authority to command another, as well. Armstrong's little speech also asserted that he was not only an individual—a *man*—but also a representative of all others—*(hu)mankind*—and thus, related to his audience in a particular way. As noted in the opening illustration, Armstrong's selection of the words *man* and *mankind* were taken to be signs of a gendered focus—perhaps **symbolic** of the male's penchant for seeing his half of the species as being the achievers and the lords of society. So, it's not enough to know words and what they mean abstractly when preparing speeches. You also must understand how language in use reflects human relationships and shared senses of reality—your culture and your thinking. In other words, not only do words *mean,* but the act of using some words rather than others can be crucial to successful (or unsuccessful) communication. Both language and language use are symbolic processes.

In the next three chapters, we turn our attention to the processes involved in **encoding**—creating ideas and images through words and actions—and **decoding**—interpreting those words to understand the ideas or images being transmitted. The **codes** you use—the channels through which ideas are communicated to listeners—include verbal language, visual aids, bodily and vocal behaviors, and even movements, postures, and sounds. In this chapter, we focus on **word choice:** using language strategically to convey the meaning you wish to impart. Your use may be very precise—"Please pass the salt"—or relatively ambiguous—"The full implementation of the actions contemplated has not yet been effected." Which words you use, when you use them, and where you use them as you talk with others publicly will have a major impact on the achievement of your goals.

## Using Language Orally

Before we tackle the questions of choosing words and styles for effective speeches, we should stop and think about *speech* as a particular kind of language use. Long before written language developed, speech—**orality**—was the principal mode of communicating thought. Written language is only about 3,000 years old (give or take a century or two). Orality reaches back into the unknowable preliterate ages. Even with the coming of written language to the ancient world, orality maintained its ascendancy in the language world for centuries. Scribes recorded speech, and speech still created ideas and guided human action. The power of oral rhetoric was at its greatest in ancient Greece precisely at the time—the fifth and fourth centuries B.C.E.—when Greek was being stabilized as a written language.

Why is all this important to you even now, centuries after orality held sway? Quite simply, because speech, or **oral style,** is not the same as written prose. Speech practices differ significantly from writing practices because of the kinds of social and business transactions people conduct through talk. We reviewed some of the reasons for the importance of orality in Chapter 1. Here, we will take the discussion further. What determines how language should be used in face-to-face oral communication? The following characteristics typify this sort of communication:

**Speech is strongly social.** In other words, when speaking, individuals have the potential to bond with each other into concrete relationships. Speech is especially relational in its force because there is *copresence*—people who are directly apprehending each other and, thus, constructing or embodying relationships. Sometimes, the relationship preexists, as when an employee talks with a boss. At other times, the relationship is built on the spot, as when two strangers start talking to each other on the bus.

**Speech is ephemeral.**   Your words disappear into nothingness as soon as they are uttered. Some of the sound waves strike the tympannus (eardrum) of anyone within range, but the rest dissipate completely. You can reread a paragraph, but you cannot hear oral words again (unless you ask for a repetition, and then it is never the exact duplicate). Speakers seldom repeat everything, so they must find other ways to help listeners remember, especially when the speakers are stringing together several ideas or arguments. This is why it's so important for oral language to be concrete or specific and why, as we will see, connectives, metaphors, images, and so on are essential to public speaking.

**The best speech is enthymematic.**   When talking to others, you assume that they can fill in the missing elements in your presentation. If they are comfortable with your language use, the ideas you project connect to things they already know; you do not have to spell everything out, and you don't have to give the full background on every point you want to make. In speaking **enthymematically** about sending American troops to a foreign "hot spot," for example, you may argue that "We should because doing so is consistent with our status as a world leader." This argument makes sense only if the audience already connects "sending troops" to "world leadership" and believes that, in this instance, such action is justified. Building speeches enthymematically—on audiences' preexisting beliefs, attitudes, values, and interests—is a key to success (as we've been noting all through this book).

**Speech is less formal.**   Even in more formal settings, public speech will be less formal than a written essay. When someone has *written* out a speech, it probably begins something like this:

> I am most pleased that you could come this morning. I would like to use this opportunity to discuss with you a subject of inestimable importance to us all—the impact of inflationary spirals on students enrolled in institutions of higher education.

Translated into an oral style, this speech might begin like this:

> Thanks for coming. I'd like to talk today about a problem facing all of us—the rising cost of going to college.

Notice how much more natural (to the ear) the second version sounds. The first is wordy, filled with prepositional phrases, complex words, and formal sentences. The second addresses the audience directly and contains shorter sentences and a simpler vocabulary that make it easier to hear and to understand.

Oral style has other characteristics, as well, when used by the most competent speakers, and in examining these, we will focus first on different strategies for making word choices competently and ethically. Second, we will examine the appropriateness of oral style. Finally, we will examine your social responsibilities in using language publicly to strengthen rather than destroy the social fabric of your community and country.

# Using Language Competently

Because you are speaking in front of others, the language you employ is **public speech**—the language used by people when conversing with others in public spaces. You have used **private speech** when talking with a tight group of friends or your siblings, but those private words and phrases will not mean the same things at all when you're talking to people from outside your social group or family. Therefore, you must be especially sensitive to what audiences in general will judge as being *good* or *competent* language use as well as *ethical* public speech. Think how often you use "you know" or "like" in conversing with friends and how conscientious you are in limiting those same phrases when presenting ideas to the class as a whole. **Competent language use** in speeches involves selecting words that make your public talk clear, powerful, and credible. You should choose words that make your speech comprehensible and capable of affecting your listeners' beliefs, attitudes, values, and behaviors.

## Effective Word Choice

Clear and effective word choice depends upon five features: accuracy, simplicity, coherence, language intensity, and appropriateness.

**Accuracy**     Pick words that help listeners understand precisely what you're talking about. If you tell a hardware store clerk "I broke the doohickey on my hootenanny, and I need a thingamajig to fix it," you'd better have the hootenanny in your hand, or the clerk won't understand you. Thus, when you speak, one goal is **accuracy.** You should leave no doubt about your meaning.

Words are symbols that represent concepts or objects, but your listener may attach a meaning to your words that's quite different from the one you intend. This misinterpretation becomes more likely as your words become more abstract. *Democracy*, for example, doesn't mean the same thing to a citizen in the suburbs as it does to a citizen in the ghetto. It also will elicit different meanings from Americans who belong to the Republican Party than it will from those who belong to the Green Party.

**Simplicity**     "Speak," said President Abraham Lincoln, "so that the most lowly can understand you, and the rest will have no difficulty." Because electronic media reach audiences more varied than Lincoln could have imagined, you have

*Abraham Lincoln said, "Speak so that the most lowly can understand you, and the rest will have no difficulty."*

even more reason to follow his advice today. Say "learn" rather than "ascertain," "try" rather than "endeavor," "use" rather than "utilize," and "help" rather than "facilitate." Do not use a longer or less familiar word when a simple one is just as clear. Evangelist Billy Sunday illustrated the effectiveness of familiar words in this example:

> If a man were to take a piece of meat and smell it and look disgusted, and his little boy were to say, "What's the matter with it, Pop?" and he were to say, "It is undergoing a process of decomposition in the formation of new chemical compounds," the boy would be all in. But if the father were to say, "It's rotten," then the boy would understand and hold his nose. "Rotten" is a good Anglo-Saxon word, and you do not have to go to the dictionary to find out what it means.[1]

**Simplicity** doesn't mean *simplistic*. Never talk down to your audience. Just remember that short, direct words convey precise, concrete meanings.

**Coherence**    People listening to you speak don't have the luxury of reviewing the points you have made, as they do with a written essay. Nor are they able to perceive punctuation marks that might help them distinguish one idea from another as you speak. To be understood, oral communication requires **coherence,** or the logical connection of ideas. To achieve coherence, you must use **signposts,** or words or phrases such as "first," "next," and "as a result," that help listeners follow the movement of your ideas. Signposts such as "The history of this invention begins in . . ." also provide clues to the overall message structure. **Internal transitions** also help to focus the listener on what is said and prepare them for what is coming next:

> Thus far, we have discussed three reasons why smoking in restaurants should be limited. Next, I want to focus on what happens if we don't take action quickly.

Other examples of such **connectives** are also useful in moving audiences with you as you speak:

In the first place . . . My second point is . . .

In addition to . . . notice that . . .

Now look at it from a different angle . . .

You must keep these three things in mind to understand the importance of the fourth . . .

What was the result?

Turning now to . . .

**Summaries,** like signposts and transitions, provide clues to the overall speech structure. **Preliminary** and **final summaries** are especially helpful in outlining the major topics of the speech. A preliminary summary (also called a *forecast* or *preview*) precedes the development of the body of the speech, usually forming part of the introduction. A final summary follows the body of the speech, usually forming part of the conclusion. Consider the following examples:

| PRELIMINARY SUMMARIES | FINAL SUMMARIES |
|---|---|
| Today, I am going to talk about three aspects of . . . | I have talked about three aspects of . . . |
| There are four major points to be covered in . . . | These four major points— [restate them]—are . . . |
| The history of the issue can be divided into two periods . . . | The two periods just covered— [restate them]—represent . . . |

You can improve the coherence of your speeches by indicating the precise relationships among ideas, including *parallel/hierarchical, similar/different,* and *coordinate/subordinate* relationships. Here are some examples:

**Parallel:**  Not only . . . but also. . .        **Hierarchical:**  More important than these . . .

**Different:**  In contrast . . .        **Similar:**  Similar to this is . . .

**Coordinated:**  One must consider X, Y, and Z . . .        **Subordinated:**  On the next level is . . .

All of these strategies—signposts, transitions, summaries—are useful in illustrating the coherence of your message and thereby keeping your audience focused on the ideas you present.

**Intensity**  You can communicate your feelings about ideas and objects through word choices, and you can communicate your attitude toward your subject by choosing words that show how you feel. For example, consider these attitudinally weighted terms:

| HIGHLY POSITIVE | RELATIVELY NEUTRAL | HIGHLY NEGATIVE |
|---|---|---|
| Savior | G.I. | Enemy |
| Patriot | Soldier | Baby-killer |
| Freedom fighter | Combatant | Alien devil |

These nine terms are organized by their **intensity,** ranging from the highly positive "Savior" to the highly negative "Alien devil."

How intense should your language be? In research that has stood the test of time, communication scholar John Waite Bowers suggested a useful rule of thumb: Let your language be, roughly, one step more intense than the position or attitude held by your audience.[2] For example, if your audience already is committed to your negative position on tax reform, then you can choose intensely negative words, such as "regressive" and "stifling." If your audience is uncommitted, you should opt for comparatively neutral words, such as "burdensome." And if your audience is in favor of tax changes, you can use still less negative words, such as "unfair" and "unevenly applied." Figure 10.1 shows how positive, neutral, and negative language can be combined effectively to produce different levels of intensity.

**FIGURE 10.1**  **Language Intensity Chart**

| | | Subject | Verb | Object |
|---|---|---|---|---|
| **+** | *Positive* | A Doctor of Philosophy at an institution of higher learning | discussed | dialectical perspectives on life and living. |
| **+ −** | *Neutral* | The philosophy professor at State U | outlined | Karl Marx's economic and social theories. |
| **−** | *Negative* | An effete intellectual snob at the local haven for druggies | harangued our children with | political drivel. |

**Appropriateness**     Use language that's **appropriate** to the speech topic and situation. Solemn occasions call for restrained, dignified language. Joyful occasions call for informal, lively language. The language you use at a party would not work for a formal speech and vice versa. Suit your language to the tone of the occasion, and watch your use of slang with audiences from different generations.

## Definitions

Audience members need to understand the fundamental concepts of your speech. You cannot expect them to understand your ideas if your language is unfamiliar. As a speaker, you have several options when providing definitions of unfamiliar or difficult concepts. You're probably most familiar with a **dictionary definition**, which categorizes an object or concept and specifies its characteristics: "An orange is a *fruit* [i.e., category] that is *round, orange* in color, and a member of the *citrus family* [i.e., characteristics]." Dictionary definitions sometimes help you learn unfamiliar words, but they do not help an audience much.

Occasionally, a word has so many meanings that you need to choose one. In this case, use a **stipulative definition** to orient your listeners to your subject matter. A stipulative definition designates the way a word will be used in a certain context. You might say, "By *rich*, I mean . . . "or something like the following:

> By *mass media*, scholars traditionally have referred to such public communication media as newspapers, magazines, films, radio broadcasting, and telecasting. I want to expand that concept to include the Internet. While it's not *mass* in the sense of being only a one-to-many medium, it's being used that way by marketers selling you books, cars, computer programs, and even pets and personal services. So, by a *mass medium*, I'll mean any communication technology capable of permitting a source to reach large numbers of people it has no personal contact with.

You can further clarify a term or concept by telling your audience how you are *not* going to use it—by using a **negative definition.** Courtney Love further clarified her use of *piracy* in this manner:

> What is piracy? Piracy is the act of stealing an artist's work without any intention of paying for it. I'm not talking about Napster-type software. I'm talking about major label recording companies.[3]

Using a negative definition along with a stipulative definition, as did Love, allows you to specify how a word is going to be used during the presentation.

Sometimes, you may reinforce an idea by telling your listeners where a word came from, and one way to do this is by using an **etymological definition.** You might talk about the fact that the words *communication, community,* and *communion* all have the same Latin roots—*com* ("with") and *munis* ("public work")—suggesting that all three words involve working together for the public good. You then could argue that communicators have a shared obligation to communicate publicly to commune (i.e., share) with others the work of society (i.e., the community).

If the concept is unfamiliar or highly technical, using a reference to a place or object that the audience is already familiar with, as an *exemplar*, is helpful:

> The building we're in today, the administrative center, is a perfect example of what I want to talk about—Bauhaus art and architecture. This style of architecture represented a redefinition of aesthetics that has affected many buildings, paintings, and plays with which many of you are familiar.

Whereas an **exemplar definition** connects a key concept to specific thing, a **contextual definition** tells listeners how a word is used in a specific context or how the context accounts for its meaning. For example, Ben Johnson, a student at the University of Nevada, Reno, focused on a medical condition called *deep vein thrombosis* by referencing its more common name: *economy class syndrome,* or *ECS:*

> ECS was first coined in 1988 to describe airline passengers who developed blood clots after long flights.[4]

Still another means of making technical or abstract notions easier to understand is the **analogical definition,** which compares a process or event that is unknown with ones that are known. For example, Valerie Waldock, a student at Minnesota State University, Moorhead, began her speech with a description of the U.S. interstate highway system and then compared that to the "digital divide":

> Built on the principle of free access, the U.S. interstate highway system was established for opportunities to flourish from coast to coast, making the "American Dream" within reach of all Americans. Recently, a new national highway infrastructure was developed, but it steered from the principle of free access. Those able to pay the price of admission were able to go places they had never gone before, but rather than easy on-ramps, the new highway was only accessible to affluent neighborhoods and the toll for entrance was steep. This class-based system is our nation's Information Superhighway, dividing rather than uniting our country.[5]

Overall, select a definitional strategy that makes sense for your subject matter, listeners, and purposes.

## Imagery

A third kind of competent language use involves linguistic word pictures—**imagery.** People grasp their world through the senses of sight, smell, hearing, taste, and touch. To intensify listeners' experiences, you can appeal to these senses.

Imagery consists of sets of sensory pictures evoked in the imagination through language. The language of imagery is divided into seven types, each related to the particular sensation it seeks to evoke: visual (sight), auditory (hearing), gustatory (taste), olfactory (smell), tactile (touch), kinesthetic (muscle strain), and organic (internal sensations) (see Figure 10.2).

**Visual Imagery**    As we noted in the discussion of attention, *visualizing* is a means of enhancing audience interest in what is being said. Using language to stimulate recognition of size, shape, color, and movement helps create an active picture in the audience's mind and recount events in vivid visual language. Telling a story in visual terms entices people—it awakens their imaginations in ways that dull language cannot. Stephanie Aduloju, a student at Creighton University, used such a narrative to involve listeners in her discussion of how race is depicted on television:

**FIGURE 10.2**    **Types of Imagery**

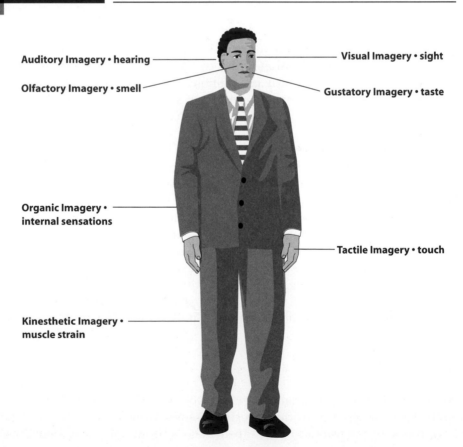

Every Tuesday, my posse comes over to chill at my crib. They throw up their kicks and flip on the TV. They change the channel to *The PJ's*. You know, I love that show. My life is JUST like that. It's so realistic. I mean, every night I go home to my ghetto and eat fried chicken and collard greens. Well, maybe I don't, but you'd think so given the way African Americans are portrayed on TV.[6]

Note as well the use of *vernacular* language—"posse," "chill," "crib," and "kicks" are terms that have specific meanings in this context. You need to be careful in using such idiomatic expressions, as some in your audience will not understand the references.

**Auditory Imagery**    To create auditory imagery, use words that help your listeners hear what you're describing. Auditory imagery can project an audience into a scene. For example, during a fictional conversation in his movie *Hannibal*, Thomas Harris allows the reader to hear the voice of a character through language choice:

> Margot, her voice rough and low, tough-mouthed as a livery pony
> and resentful of the bit.[7]

**Gustatory Imagery**    Gustatory imagery depicts sensations of taste. Sometimes you may even be able to help your audience taste what you're describing. Mention its saltiness, sweetness, sourness, or spiciness, and remember that foods have texture as well as taste. If demonstrating how to prepare homemade honey mustard, describe the bite on your tongue of the powdered mustard overlaid with the sweetness of the honey yet also with the savor of the salt. Detailed descriptions allow your listeners to participate in the experience through their imaginations.

**Olfactory Imagery**    Olfactory imagery describes sensations of smell. Smell is a powerful sense because it normally triggers a flood of associated images. You can stimulate this process by describing or comparing one odor with more familiar ones:

> Theft in the college dorm is on the rise, but why anyone would steal
> my roommate's shoes from outside our door is beyond me. Ever picked
> up moldy socks from the bottom of the hamper, put there wet from a
> torrential rain and left for days? Ever had to wash the smell of skunk off
> your body? These are pleasant odors compared to my roommate's tennis
> shoes, and it is the reason they were left outside our room, in the hallway.
> They must have been really needed by someone.

**Tactile Imagery**    Tactile imagery is based on the sensations that come to us through physical contact with external objects. Let your audience feel how rough or smooth, dry or wet, or slimy or sticky modeling clay is (texture and shape). Let them sense the pressure of physical force on their bodies, the weight of a heavy laundry bag, the pinch of jogging shoes, or the blast of a high wind on their faces (pressure). Sensations of heat or cold are aroused by thermal imagery. General Douglas MacArthur's great speech to the cadets of West Point on "Duty, Honor, and Country" used vivid examples of tactile imagery as he described soldiers of the past:

> Bending under soggy pack on many a weary march, from dripping dusk to drizzly dawn, slogging ankle deep through mire of shell-pocked roads; to form grimly for the attack, blue-lipped, covered with sludge and mud, chilled by the wind and rain, driving home to their objective, and for many, to the judgment seat of God."[8]

**Kinesthetic Imagery**   Kinesthetic imagery describes the sensations associated with muscle strain and neuromuscular movement. Let your listeners experience for themselves the agonies and joys of running a marathon—the muscle cramps, the constricted chest, the struggle for air—and the magical serenity of getting a second wind and gliding fluidly toward the finish line.

**Organic Imagery**   Hunger, dizziness, nausea—these are organic images. There are times when an experience is not complete without the description of inner feelings. The sensation of dizziness as a mountain climber struggles through the rarefied mountain air to reach the summit is one example. Another is how the bottom drops out of your stomach when the rollercoaster rattles down the steep decline. Because such imagery is powerful, you shouldn't offend your audience by overdoing it. If you call attention to sheer technique—to description for its own sake—your imagery will lose its power, and overdone organic imagery becomes gruesome, disgusting, or grotesque when you get too far into the description of blood and guts or cramps and nausea.

**Combining Types of Imagery**   The seven types of imagery—visual, auditory, gustatory, olfactory, tactile, kinesthetic, and organic—directly involve the listeners' sensory equipment in your speech. Sensations become avenues into their minds. Not every image will work with everyone, however, so use a variety throughout your speech to engage various segments of your listeners. To be effective, such illustrations must be plausible and keep the listeners' attention focused on the subject matter—not on the technique being used. Artistry that calls attention to itself risks losing the point it is intended to project.

## Metaphors

Images created by appealing to the senses often are metaphors. A **metaphor** transfers the meaning of one person, place, thing, or process to something else. "They were lions in battle" transfers the characteristics we associate with *lions*—authority, power, commanding presence—to the group doing battle. As rhetorical scholar Michael Osborn notes, good metaphors should "result in an intuitive flash of recognition that surprises or fascinates the hearer."[9] If the hearer is not jolted, informed, or given a clear orientation to whatever's being discussed, the metaphor probably is dead (as in "the legs of the table," where *legs* is a dead metaphor) or just plain ineffective.

Once-fresh metaphors also can turn into **clichés**—metaphors so far gone they can have almost a reverse effect. Clichés can diminish your ideas rather than enhance or clarify them—unless they're used humorously, as in the advertisement for the book *The Dictionary of Clichés:* "Not to beat around the bush, or hedge the bet, this is a must-read for every Tom, Dick, and Harry under the sun!"[10]

Good metaphors can create new understanding and uplift an audience. Such metaphors even can be drawn from everyday experiences, which give them wide audience appeal. For example, relying on our common experiences of lightness and darkness, Martin Luther King, Jr., intoned a solemn message that was driven by metaphor:

> With this faith in the future, with this determined struggle, we will be able to emerge from the bleak and desolate midnight of man's inhumanity to man, into the bright and glittering daybreak of freedom and justice.[11]

This light/dark metaphor allowed King to suggest contrasts between inhumanity and freedom as well as the inevitability of social progress (as "daybreak" inevitably follows "midnight"). The metaphor communicated King's beliefs about justice and injustice, and it urged others to act, now that daylight had come.

Competent language use, as this section has illustrated, takes care and attention. Words don't just magically appear on your tongue when you wish for them. Having misspoken in the past on occasion, all of us know that the ill-timed or ill-chosen word has costs. Words are not neutral pipelines for thoughts flowing from one person to another. Words reflect the world outside the mind and also help shape and create perceptions of people, events, and social contexts—referentially, relationally, and symbolically. The effective use of language enables you to move others to believe, think, and act.

## Using Language Ethically

*Competent* public language use makes your ideas both clear and powerful. *Ethical* public language use makes them culturally acceptable and respectful of others' thinking. Some of the issues we discuss later (under the heading "Selecting Language that Communicates Civility," pp. 252–255) also have ethical dimensions. But here, we want to deal with three common uses of language that possess clear ethical dimensions: linguistic attacks upon others (ad hominem attacks), the refusal to mention groups of people who should be referenced (linguistic erasure), and conspiratorial attacks on people and institutions (critiquing domination).

*Getting your point across depends on making appropriate language choices. What kinds of choices might be involved in this scene?*

## Ad Hominem Attack

The phrase *ad hominem* is Latin for "to the person" or, more usually, "to personal circumstances."[12] An **ad hominem attack** is an argument made against another person rather than against the ideas that she or he espouses. Saying "You certainly can't support him for Congress; he's been married and divorced twice" presents an ad hominem argument. Irrespective of what you think of the person's judgment or morals in marriage and divorce, is it relevant to his decision making in office? Ad hominem attacks often are based on stereotypes of groups or collectivities. Thus, some think that African Americans cannot really be Republicans because they should favor a liberal agenda and a welfare state, that real men suppress their softer emotions and cannot be expected to be warm and caring, and that all Catholics oppose state-sponsored abortions. It's the "Everyone knows that . . ." aspect to ad hominem attacks that makes them so powerful with some audiences.

Is an ad hominem attack ever fair? Usually not. In fact, they may well represent the most common kind of unethical attack on others that you'll run into—or be tempted to use—as a speaker. Sometimes, of course, the personal circumstances of a counterarguer are relevant. In presidential campaigns, for example, it's impossible to have positions on all the issues, so most of us rely on some assessment of the candidates' character—evidence of their good sense, goodwill, good morals, vision, and caring for the electorate—to help us decide for whom to vote.[13] Generally speaking, however, always examine the ad hominem attack very, very closely to make sure it's just not a diversionary or ungrounded, stereotyped reaction to an opponent.

## Linguistic Erasure

A concept that is difficult to explain but nonetheless important to public talk is **linguistic erasure,** or *not* labeling or talking about a person or group of people that demands to be mentioned. This language phenomenon is called the *third* *persona* by rhetorical theorist Philip Wander.[14] If a picture of the speaker constructed in words is the *first* persona and the picture of the audience built into the speech is the *second*, then people who are important to a speech but not actually mentioned in it comprise the *third* persona—and are erased.

Suppose you are giving a speech on the quincentenniary celebration in the United States of the arrival of Christopher Columbus. Suppose you also are talking about the heroism and faith that drove Columbus and his crew to venture into uncharted lands and found colonies for other Europeans in the New World. In this speech, you will probably construct an image of yourself as someone interested in history—and good at it—by using multiple sources and good speechmaking techniques. That's the picture of the first persona built into the speech. The picture of the noble Italians and Spaniards who initiated the Age of Discovery at the end of the fifteenth century will be the second persona—a vision of European adventurers who made life on this continent possible for others. And the third persona? If you do not mention the coastal Native Americans awaiting the Pilgrims; the Cubans, blacks, and Central American Indians whom Hernán Cortéz enslaved in the early sixteenth century; or the Florida Indians ravaged by European diseases when Sir Francis Drake tried to conquer Saint Augustine in the 1580s, then the native peoples of the American territories are the third personae.[15] They are not mentioned in your heroic tale yet obviously were extremely important players in that story: "What about the locals, the natives?" some in your audience will ask.

Linguistic erasure is a matter of eliminating someone's presence in a story or argument by simply not mentioning them. "The Final Solution" could be talked about in Hitler's Germany without actually saying the word "Jews": The metaphor of the *solution* made it unnecessary for believers in National Socialism to mention them. Speeches about nuclear families often ignore the needs of single-parent and nonheterosexual families. Talk about being prochoice and granting women control over their own bodies and destinies often avoids references to dead fetuses (which is frequently the talk of prolife advocates).

Now, of course, there are times when you actually choose to concentrate on just part of a story. If you decide, for example, to talk only about the European explorers in the Age of Discovery because you're interested primarily in the effect of exploration upon Europe, then tell that to your audience. In that way, the listeners know there is a Native American side of the story but that it is not relevant to your speech. Thus, you'll not be questioned ethically for your lack of discussion regarding their fate.

## Critiquing Domination

Another ethical question you face when selecting language has to do with a decision on whether to talk about *conspiracies.* That may seem like an odd decision until you think about all the conspiratorial talk that floats through American media: talk that the CIA supplied drugs to the African American community to keep it from rising up, references by Hillary Clinton in early 1998 to a vast right-wing conspiracy trying to drive her husband out of politics, discussions in the Middle East of a Euro-American conspiracy to keep the area destabilized to make the U.S. presence there necessary or to keep an eye on their oil, and arguments that the white community controls the standardized tests that measure intelligence, thus keeping itself in a superior position.

The point is not whether any of these are true. Conspiratorial talk about dominant groups holding down others, controlling institutions, or enslaving different segments of society does not depend upon facts. After all, if the facts could be ascertained—for instance, if someone could prove that the Trilateral Commission runs the world economy for its own purposes—then something could be done about the problem. In the 1950s, Senator Joseph McCarthy claimed he had a list of 208 Communists in the U.S. State Department. He never showed the whole list to anyone else, however, because then each person could have had a security check. No, conspiracies—and, indeed, domination of one group by another in general—depend upon fear and anger, upon shadows and not substance. **Critiquing domination,** thus, is the linguistic strategy of charging that some situation has been brought about by a widespread—usually societywide—operation wherein a group or social segment suppresses the rights, chances to succeed, and even identities of other groups.[16] So, when arguing that television helps establish the power of white—and especially male—Americans to dominate U.S. policy toward other countries, Kent Ono built this argument:

> One of the most obvious ways television has contributed to neocolonialist relations is by aiding the U.S. government in demonizing people of color worldwide, such as Saddam Hussein, Moammar Kadafi, Manuel Noriega, the Ayatollah Khomeini, and Fidel Castro. Whenever the U.S. government and military want to justify a military intervention to reestablish their domination over economically, technologically, and militarily less powerful peoples, they manufacture a demonic view of someone, almost always a swarthy male, as a psychopathic, uncontrollable, irrational, and fascistic leader.[17]

The point here, again, is not whether these charges are true—they may well be. Rather, the point is that the entire rationale for economic, political, and military policy has been reduced to a conspiracy of the white world to control the world of color. The actual rationales for U.S. foreign policy have been flattened to a single dimension—the will to dominate—which Ono believes must be critiqued.

Should U.S. foreign policy be reduced to a single rationale? Is it ethical to use such language as "demonizing," "establish their domination," and "manufacture a demonic view"? Such language, of course, is an ad hominem attack, but if it's true, the character attack fits the situation. If Ono is right, the image that is constructed of the "other" is one that creates fear, not respect, suspicion, not trust, before the other is even known. Is it ethical to call attention to the way our language creates images of those we do not know when that image is negative? Think carefully, as did Ono, about your purposes and options before launching into conspiratorial arguments about domination.

Ad hominem attack, linguistic erasure, and critiquing domination are but three of the common ways in which language choices (or nonchoices, in the case of erasure) engage important ethical questions. We discuss other ethical decisions speakers must make in the following sections of this chapter. In addition, the "Ethical Moments" box on the following page looks at the deceptive use of language through *doublespeak*.

## Selecting an Appropriate Style

Now, we can think more systematically about how not just words but also oral style generally should guide how you talk with other people and how you present yourself orally. The combination of stylistic decisions you need to make generally is called **tone**, which is the predominant effect or character of a speech. It is an elusive quality of speech, but we can identify four dimensions of tone that you should consider: serious versus humorous atmosphere; speaker-, audience-, or content-centered emphasis; and propositional versus narrative style.

### Serious versus Humorous Atmosphere

You cultivate the **atmosphere** of the speaking occasion largely through your speaking style. During a graduation speech or an awards banquet address, you want to encourage the personal reflection of your listeners, but during a fraternity gathering or holiday celebration, you want to create a social, interactive atmosphere.

Sometimes, the atmosphere of the occasion dictates what speaking style should be used. You don't expect a light, humorous speaking style during a funeral. Even so, sometimes a minister, priest, or rabbi will tell a funny story about the deceased. The overall tone of a funeral eulogy, however, should be somber. In contrast, a speech after a football victory, election win, or successful drive to change collegiate graduation requirements seldom is solemn. Victory speeches are times for celebration and unity. Humorous speeches can have serious goals, as well. Even speeches designed to entertain have worthy purposes. These speeches can be given in grave earnestness. The political satirist who throws humorous but barbed comments at pompous, silly, or corrupt politicians aims to amuse the audience as well as urge political reform.

The speaking atmosphere is the mindset or mental attitude that you attempt to create in your audience. A serious speaker urging future professors to remember

# ETHICAL MOMENTS

## Doublespeak

Advertisers, politicians, and military spokespersons often are accused of using words that deceive or mislead. The Bush and Clinton administrations did not want to raise taxes, for example, and so instead pursued revenue enhancement through user fees. The rush to **doublespeak**—the use of a technical jargon that sidesteps issues or distorts meaning—was accelerated during the Vietnam War, when "we got pacification for eradication, strategic withdrawal for retreat, sanitizing operation for wholesale clearance, accidental delivery of armaments for bombing the wrong target, to terminate with extreme prejudice for a political assassination, and many, many others" (Bryson, 302). Advertisers have given us "real faux pearls" and "genuine imitation leather" and, of course, "virgin nylon." The indiscriminate use of the phrases "low sodium," "low cholesterol," "low sugar," and "low fat" has led to a governmental attempt to control the abuse of such labels. So, how about you?

**1** Suppose you notice biased language in an article you're going to quote. Should you cite it as supporting material in your speech?

**2** Do you ever use big words and unnecessarily technical language just to impress your listeners? Should we refer to "football players" as "student athletes"? Do you feel better if someone calls a "test" an "hourly opportunity" or a "feedback session"? Is "spanking" a child any less onerous if it is called "corporal discipline"?

**3** How about using language to avoid hurting someone or making someone feel bad? Should you really call someone "vertically challenged" instead of "short" or "visually impaired" instead of "blind"? In these sorts of cases, do the new words actually call more attention to the person's difficulties than the old ones? Or do they offer new images of the person in ways not encumbered by the emotionally loaded connotations associated with older terms?

### For Further Reading

On the matter of *neologisms*—new and often technical words coming into English—see Bill Bryson, *Made in America: An Informal History of the English Language in the United States* (New York: William Morrow, 1994). On language usage generally, see Joe Glaser, *Understanding Style: Practical Ways to Improve Your Writing* (New York: Oxford University Press, 1999).

the most important things in life might say, "Rank your values, and live by them." That same idea expressed by actor Alan Alda sounds more humorous:

> We live in a time that seems to be split about its values. In fact it seems to be schizophrenic. For instance, if you pick up a magazine like *Psychology Today*, you're liable to see an article like "White Collar Crime: It's More Widespread Than You Think." Then in the back of the magazine they'll print an advertisement that says, "We'll write your doctoral thesis for 25 bucks." You see how values are eroding? I mean, a doctoral thesis ought to go for at least a C-note.[18]

Which atmosphere is preferable? The answer depends on the speaking situation, your speech purpose, and your listeners' expectations.

## Speaker-, Audience-, or Content-Centered Emphasis

Because you use speeches to conduct different kinds of personal, social, and professional business, you can emphasize various aspects of the communication process in your message. Sometimes, you stress your thoughts or your opinions—your position as a knowledgeable or sensitive person. On such occasions, much of the speech is constructed in the first person: "I." At other times, however, the focus is on the audience or things you and the audience can accomplish together. In those circumstances, you're likely to address the audience in the second person ("you") or in the first-person plural ("we"). Then, there are times when the subject matter itself is the center of attention, such as in a class lecture, in which case references to "I" and "you" or "we" all but disappear.

Sometimes, the emphasis of the whole speech is **speaker-, audience-,** or **content-centered,** but the emphasis more often shifts from one section to another. This clearly happened in a speech given by Allen H. Neuharth, Chair of the Freedom Foundation, when he accepted the DeWitt Carter Reddick Award for Outstanding Achievement in Communication given him by the College of Communication of the University of Texas at Austin. In this speech, Neuharth employed all three emphases:

SPEAKER-CENTERED: "I"

> In 1952, just two years out of the University of South Dakota, a classmate and I started a weekly statewide sports tabloid newspaper called *SoDak Sports.* We begged, borrowed and stole all the money we could—about $50,000. Two years later, we had lost it all, our venture went belly-up and we were bloodied and bowed. I ran away from home, went to Miami, found a job as a reporter for $95 a week.

### AUDIENCE-CENTERED: "YOU/WE"

We must overcome our reluctance to criticize ourselves or our co-workers or competitors. Most in the media are unbelievably thin-skinned. We spend most of our lifetime criticizing or analyzing everyone else—politicians, business people, academicians. But we seldom turn that spotlight on ourselves. Our egos are enormous.

### CONTENT-CENTERED: "THEY/IT"

The media, thanks to instant satellite communication, is the glue that is bringing this globe together. Without the satellite—and instant global communication—there would have been no Tiananmen Square sit-in in Beijing. No breakdown of the Berlin Wall. No marches in Poland, Romania, and Czechoslovakia. And the hardliners would not have flunked Revolution 101 in the old Soviet Union last August.[19]

In mixing speaker-, audience-, and content-centered emphases, Neuharth was able to achieve multiple purposes: He established a personal bond with his audience (relational communication), gave them some messages to act on (referential communication), and added to his expert credibility by talking clearly about the world of the journalists (symbolic communication). You, too, should decide whether to emphasize yourself (personal revelations), your audience (directives to your listeners), or the subject matter (ideas and arguments about the external world) in various combinations during your talks.

## Propositional versus Narrative Style

Finally, speaking styles can be largely propositional or narrative. A **propositional style** emphasizes a series of claims, with supporting evidence for each, that culminate in a general proposition. In this style, the claims suggest what action should be taken or what policy should be adopted or rejected. A **narrative style**, however, couches claims and evidence in a more informal, often personal story that epitomizes the general claim being advanced. While both styles make claims on an audience's attention, belief, and action, they present their arguments in radically different ways. In the following illustrations of propositional and narrative approaches, assume that you—the speaker—want to persuade your classmates to consult with their academic advisors on a regular basis:

### PROPOSITIONAL STYLE

I. You should see your advisor regularly because he or she can check on your graduation requirements.
   A. Advisors have been trained to understand this school's requirements.
   B. Advisors also probably helped write the departmental requirements for your major, so they know them, too.

II. You should see your advisor regularly because that person usually can tell you something about the careers in your field.

    A. Most faculty members at this school regularly attend professional meetings and know what schools and companies are hiring in your field.

    B. Most faculty members have been here a long time and, thus, have seen what kinds of academic backgrounds get their advisees good jobs after graduation.

III. You should see your advisor regularly to check out your own hopes and fears with someone.

    A. Good advisors help you decide whether you want to continue with a major.

    B. If you decide to change majors, they often will help you find someone in another department who can work with you.

NARRATIVE STYLE

  I. I thought I could handle my own advising around this school, and that attitude got me into trouble.

    A. I could read, and I thought I knew what I wanted to take.

    B. I decided to steer my own course, and here's what happened.

 II. At first, I was happy, taking any course I wanted to.

    A. I skipped the regular laboratory sciences (i.e., chemistry, biology, physics) and took a course called Science and Society instead.

    B. I didn't take statistics to meet my math requirement but instead slipped into remedial algebra

    C. I piled up the hours in physical education so I could have a nice grade-point average to show my parents.

III. When I was about half done with my program, however, I realized two things.

    A. I hadn't met about half of the general education requirements for graduation.

    B. I wanted to go into nursing.

IV. Therefore, I had to go back to freshman- and sophomore-level courses, even though I technically was a junior.

    A. I was back taking the basic science and math courses.

    B. I was still trying to complete the social science and humanities requirements.

  V. In all, I'm now in my fifth year of college—with at least one more to go.

    A. My classmates who used advisors have graduated.

    B. I suggest you follow their example, rather than mine, if you want to save time and money.

Either style can be effective, depending upon the audience's expectations and the speaker's resourcefulness in generating an effective argument.[20] The propositional form provides a concise, logical series of "should" statements to direct audience action. The narrative form puts your talent as a storyteller to the test. These examples suggest the use of either style as the structure for the body of an entire speech, but speeches may combine both. As mentioned, Neuharth used a narrative style in discussing his own life experience and then moved on to a propositional form in relaying his views regarding the kinds of reforms in which journalists must engage.

Building an oral style appropriate to you, your audience, the occasion, and the subject matter takes serious thought on your part. Think through the degree of seriousness, the appropriate emphasis, and the use of propositional or narrative form, because shaping these carefully is the mark of a sophisticated and talented speaker.

# Selecting Language That Communicates Civility

Ultimately, public speaking is a collective activity. It is the way that a society transacts its important business in face-to-face and, in some cases, in televisual ways. If we think of public speaking as the *conversation of the culture,* as a society having dialogues about important and even difficult matters, then we are faced with important questions regarding the degree to which a speaker has an obligation to help maintain the social system and move people forward collectively.

Especially during the 1990s, American society witnessed a good deal of concern about violations of civility—and about what some see as a hyperconcern for the treatment of others in the language we use. Here, we consider these under two topics, each related to communicating inclusivity and sincere respect for everyone who may hear our words: gendered language and uncivil and hateful speech.

## Gendered versus Gender-Neutral Language

Words themselves are not intrinsically good or bad, but as noted at the beginning of this chapter, they communicate your values and attitudes to your listeners and can suggest relationships between you and your audience. **Gender-linked words**—particularly nouns and pronouns—require special attention as they directly or indirectly identify males and females, such as *policeman, washerwoman, waiter,* and *waitress.* Pronouns such as *he* and *she* and adjectives such as *his* and *her* also obviously are gender-linked words. **Gender-neutral words** do not directly or indirectly denote males and females—*chairperson, police officer,* and *firefighter.*

As rhetorical critic Kenneth Burke suggested, naming is not a neutral act.[21] Rather, the name we select and use toward someone conveys an attitude and deflects from consideration other names or labels that might apply. This is especially the case in using gendered language, as it reflects a specific character of the person so named and narrows the range of possible images that may be associated with that person. Calling a person a "skunk" may be funny in some situation, but think of the image it conjures and the images it simultaneously eliminates—can a skunk be cuddly or warm? Is this the right language to use in any situation?

Inclusivity requires that we pay special attention to avoiding inaccurately excluding members of one sex. Some uses of gendered pronouns inaccurately reflect social-occupational conditions in the world: "A nurse sees her patients 8 hours a day, but a doctor sees his for only 10 minutes." Many women are doctors, and many men are nurses. Most audience members are aware of this and may be displeased if they feel you're stereotyping roles in a particular profession.

In addition, you will want to avoid stereotyping psychological and social characteristics in gendered terms: "Real men never cry." "A woman's place is in the home." "The Marines are looking for a few good men." "Sugar 'n spice 'n everything nice—that's what little girls are made of." Falling back on these stereotypes gets speakers into trouble with audiences—both male and female. Audiences are insulted to hear such misinformed assertions. In addition, these stereotypes conceal the potential in individuals whose talents are not limited by their gender.

A speaker who habitually uses sexist language is guilty of ignoring important speaking conventions that have developed over the last several decades. Ultimately, the search for gender-neutral expressions is an affirmation of mutual respect and a recognition of equal worth and the essential dignity of individuals. Gender differences are important in many aspects of life, but when they dominate public talk, they're ideologically oppressive. Be gender neutral in public talk to remove barriers to effective communication.[22] Follow the guidelines provided in the "How to" box below.

# How to
# Avoid Offensive Language

### Avoiding Sexist Phrases

- Speak in the plural. Say "Bankers are often . . . They face . . ." This tactic often is sufficient to make your language gender neutral.
- Switch to "he or she" when you must use a singular subject. Say "A student majoring in business is required to sign up for an internship. He or she can . . ." This strategy works well as long as you don't overdo it. If you find yourself cluttering sentences with "he or she," switch to the plural.
- Remove gender inflections. It's painless to say "firefighter" instead of "fireman," "chair" or "chairperson" instead of "chairman," and "tailor" instead of "seamstress."
- Use gender-specific pronouns for gender-specific processes, people, and activities. It is acceptable to talk about a mother as "her" or a current or former president of the United States as "him." Men do not naturally bear children, after all, and a woman has not yet been elected to the presidency.

### Avoiding Giving Offense in Other Ways

- When speaking to an audience that is primarily from other cultures or ethnic groups, use "we" rather than "you people" or "your kind." Such phrases as the latter serve to create separation between you and the audience, rather than bring you closer together.
- Be sensitive to changes in names for various groups. "Retarded" conveys negative connotations: use "developmentally challenged" instead. Use names for ethnic groups that are accepted by the ethnic community.
- Avoid off-color and ethnic jokes. Period.
- When there are international students or people from other countries in your audience, recognize that your colloquial expressions may not be understood. Would a student from India or Korea understand Stephanie Aduloju's opening line, quoted earlier: "Every Tuesday, my posse comes over to chill at my crib"? How would you reword this so as to make the meaning clear?

## The Problem of Uncivil and Hateful Speech

More general than the issue of gendered language is choosing names that demonstrate respect for and appropriately include others. While *PC*, or **political correctness,** as a term of derision appears to be waning, the principle of respect for others remains a central concern in a civil society.[23] Why is it correct to say "people of color" but not "colored people" in the United States? Isn't a phrase such as "environmentally challenged" an awkward way of referring to "people with disabilities"? There are simple answers to these questions: "Colored" focuses on a single attribute of the person named, whereas "people of . . ." focuses on who they are, and color is secondary to that distinction. In the case of "challenged" versus "disabled," the latter term carries with it negative associations that the new term avoids—images of people incapable of contributing to society due to their disabled status.

Using civil language means treating others with dignity. But this is not as simple a claim to enforce as it might seem. Should you avoid or boycott a speaker who is said to demean feminists? Should you avoid hearing a feminist who is thought by some to sound radical or people who are too aggressively straight or gay in the language they use? To be sure, uncivil, racist, and hateful speech should be confronted, but to react in knee-jerk fashion to someone who talks about a "disabled man" rather than a "person who is physically challenged" without examining what actually is being said may prove counterproductive. At the same time, to people who are physically challenged, the failure to appreciate their condition through learning and using appropriate language can be as important to them as the use of sexist or racist language is to a female or a person of color. As noted earlier, your language reveals you—your attitude toward the other—and clearly communicates your level of respect for his or her situation, as well as your willingness to employ language that does not carry the emotional baggage associated with rejected names or terms.

**Hate speech,** the most virulent form of uncivil discourse, is public talk that attacks or denigrates a group or class of people. It is similar to an ad hominem attack except that it is aimed at a whole segment of society. Talking about women as "girls" or "chickies" is seen by some as being degrading, but other terms put them down as a group. Ethnic slurs always have been a part of the American experience, especially since the heavy immigration of the late nineteenth century. Colloquial, negative terms have been invented for the Irish, the Italians, the Puerto Ricans, the Mexicans, the African Americans, and others.

Hate speech is only possible, of course, because the First Amendment to the U.S. Constitution guarantees freedom of speech. It is what is called *protected speech*—you are permitted to call people names publicly. The United States has guarantees on freedom of expression, but the exclusive emphasis on such individual freedom may jeopardize collective responsibilities. The U.S. Constitution recognizes individual rights. However, it is constructed in the name of "We, the people," as its opening line names us. Public name-calling of whole segments of society can destroy the "We."

This is not to say that you should never attack someone's thinking, motives, evidence, or timing. There even are times when you should question the intentions of others publicly, but that can and should be done with rhetorical tools other than hate speech. Some rights are better left unexercised in the name of the collective good.[24]

## The Commitment to a Multicultural Vision of the Audience

In a sense, people who assert their right to call others whatever they want and judge others' motives simply on the basis of their language use need to move to another ground: the relationships between language and both the language user and the world outside the user. As we've suggested throughout this chapter and this book, how you use language publicly reflects both your view of the world and your understanding of your relationship with listeners. When you say "Gimme that pork chop," you've not only referred to an object in the environment but you have also communicated your attitude toward the others around you.

Public, oral language is both referential and relational, as we noted at the beginning of this chapter. Thus, whenever you speak publicly, you both talk about something and suggest (however indirectly or tacitly) your attitudes toward others—the people you're talking about and the people you're talking to.

This is why a **multicultural vision** is essential to socially constructive public speaking. You almost always will be talking to a multicultural audience—men and women, young and old, rich and poor, disabled and not, and people with varied ethnic backgrounds. To ignore one or another cultural segment is to ignore potential believers in your position. Further, to use language that seemingly demeans or rejects portions of your audience is to potentially injure your credibility or ethos. This is not to say you'll never be angry with one group of people or you'll always believe in everything another group advocates. Of course not. Strong differences in opinion and action can exist between men and women, young and old, white and brown.

Multicultural vision does not mean that everyone melts into one lumpen society. When Americans say their civic slogan is "Out of many, one," they do not mean "Out of many, all the same." We are all part of what's called a *body politic*, a social-political group. Not all parts of your body are the same, however, just as not all parts of a civic body are the same. We are legitimate parts—and should be accorded respect when we speak about them. The oral, public use of language can work for good or ill, for collective action or divisiveness. Each time you use language publicly, you're participating in a destructive or a constructive social act.[25]

## Assessing a Sample Speech

Raymie E. McKerrow, one of the authors, presented the following speech on November 11, 2000, as his Presidential Address at the National Communication Association (NCA) convention in Seattle, Washington.[26] The presentation is especially fitting as a sample for this chapter, as it deals directly with the issues just discussed, especially the question of civility. The imagery, especially the personal narrative used with reference to life experience as a Montana farm boy, helps to convey both sincerity and commitment to the audience.

## Coloring Outside the Lines: The Limits of Civility
**Raymie E. McKerrow**

Thank you, Jim, for that very fine introduction. You are to be commended for the theme of this convention and for the excellent work you have done in fulfilling its promise; I can only hope to do further justice to engaging the discipline in the comments to come. **1**

Over the past three years, it has been my privilege to work with the national office staff as an officer of this association. Just this morning, we presented the national office staff with a Presidential Citation in honor of their dedication and commitment to the association. That we are here in Seattle, and in our new home in the District, given the unplanned events of the past several weeks, is a testament to their steadfastness in the face of adversity. My service has been made possible by their assistance, as well as the work of the administrative committee and members of the legislative council. In addition, I want to express a special thank-you to my colleagues at Ohio University; the support I have received has made it possible to take the time necessary to attend to NCA affairs. I also owe a great deal more than I can repay to members of my family, Gayle—my best friend for the last 35 years, my son Matthew, and Alina; the constancy of their love has sustained me. My close friends—and I will not attempt to cite names, as I will surely miss one—also have suffered through my doubts and, as friends will, told me what I didn't want to hear. That I am here at this moment is a testament to the patience, love, and support of my colleagues, family, and friends. **2**

The time has come, then, to consider the topic I have chosen. If we are truly to be an engaged discipline, it means we must come to grips with what it means to valorize civil discourse. The central question for this address is this: Are there limits on what civility brings to the solution of human problems? I ask this question in the spirit of the 1999 NCA convention theme, "Coloring Outside the Lines." That theme struck a fairly responsive chord within our academic community. Only one or two found it necessary to suggest that the theme was demeaning, while I had only intended it to be demanding. If Coloring Outside the Lines is to engage the free play of our imaginations, where might we transgress prohibitions, cross borders, or otherwise challenge and redraw boundaries, all the while remaining engaged with others in a common pursuit? For lines appear to be ever present in our social and political lives, whether as academics or as citizens of the world. The understanding we give to the expression "They've crossed the line" would give clear evidence to the salience of lines in our everyday interactions. Playing with the dimension of color in relation to lines also is implied in this theme, as several programs at the Chicago convention took to heart and played out in imaginative and provocative ways. Drawing connections between and among disparate groupings, reconceptualizing conventional strategies, and rethinking what is most important in our academic pursuits took center stage in a way that I could not have planned alone. **3**

4        That was then; this is now. What might I say that would continue the conversation, that would move the project forward in ways that reconfigure the very nature of our interactions? In the context, then, of Coloring Outside the Lines, I will highlight two arenas in which we might challenge ourselves with respect to the lives we now lead: our lives in an academic and social community and our lives as political beings in the larger world.

5        While the lines I will draw here are highly artificial, let us focus for a moment on our lives as members of an academic and social community. In recruiting students and faculty to our campuses, and specifically to our discipline, we have a common desire to foster cultural diversity. If we can accept the aphorism that civility begins at home and that, for the time being, the campus is our home, what might we say of our behavior on campus, especially in fostering diversity? If there are to be persons of color within our discipline, they must exist first as students—as undergraduates who find within the discipline a receptive place to continue advanced studies and, ultimately, as an inviting and personally rewarding place to work as professors. While readily affirming the goal, many of us already within the academy are relatively clueless as to what life is truly like for persons of color who have entered the discipline. An example from an international student's experience in our academic community may help clarify the distance we have yet to travel:

6        I cannot understand many expressions, I cannot follow jokes, and I cannot actively engage in exciting discussions. I have many experiences that I watch myself smiling and nodding and pretending that I am understanding what the other person is saying, even though I could not follow the conversation.

7        The feeling of "being comfortable"—and those of us in communication may justly pride ourselves as a discipline on creating or striving to create such a feeling among our students—is not an issue solely with respect to our international students. We have other students of color who may not have the same barriers to cross as our international students but for whom other barriers, equally invisible to many of us in our daily habits, also exist. In too many places, college students have been pulled over, not on suspicion of a DUI or DWI but for the simple act of DWB, or "Driving While Black." Racial profiling, as Jesse Jackson, Al Sharpton, and others have so eloquently reminded us, does not need to be an official policy to be *in place* within a local community. That we have not yet found a reason to coin the parallel acronym, DWW, or "Driving While White," should suggest something about the lines that yet exist in our campus communities. In our lives as teachers and scholars, it also should underline the importance of our critique of language's power in perpetuating the dominance of whiteness. No wonder many African Americans, at campuses across the country, express a multivalenced attitude toward their educational experience: They don't want to leave a campus where they have friends, but they also can't say they are truly comfortable or feel welcome in that same community. And the experience and attitude is not in any way restricted to African Americans or others of color. The members of NCA's gay, lesbian, bisexual, and transgendered division would equally note the problem of "being comfortable" in our academic communities. While we attack racism and sexism in our scholarship, we do not necessarily recognize its everydayness in our own immediate community. The campus is our community—whether mine or yours. And yet, we often remain silent when

*(continued)*

we should speak—all of us, irrespective of color, have an obligation to color outside the lines as it were through our own spoken challenge. And it is the case that those of us who speak from the privilege of whiteness must share a greater sense of moral duty when faced with the kind of idiocy reflected in the following example: When asked, in reference to the racial profiling noted earlier, "Why not hire some of those students of color who are interested in law enforcement? They understand the community, and would serve as role models for others" the reply has been "Well, they'd have to pass the civil service exam." Keep in mind that one needs only a high school diploma if one is white, but if one is a person of color (and, in a special case I'm aware of, also an athlete) …what do or can you say? Is this a time for incivility?

8    Before addressing that question, it is important to recognize that the issue of civil discourse may NOT be the most critical problem facing our society. I don't mean to downplay it at the outset, but I do want to suggest that, at times, I wonder whether simple STUPIDITY is not more prevalent and more in need of redress than is the issue of CIVILITY. Consider these recent real-life events:

9    A day-care administrator, apparently captured by the aphorism that duct tape can do anything, decided to put it to the test. The administrator wrapped a baby in duct tape and stuck the baby to the wall to see if the tape would hold the child in place. It worked. That the administrator and others found this funny might lead us in the direction not of civility training but of the need to educate the presumably educated.[27]

10    From a perspective that might be humorous if not such a sad commentary, consider three instances of what might be accounted for as stupidity, rather than as acts of incivility:

11    A young inmate broke out of jail, only to be recaptured when he stopped a police officer and asked for directions to a known drug-dealing area. A person using stolen ATM cards, while hiding his face from the surveillance camera, kept his company's hat on, with the logo clearly depicted. Police simply took the photo to the company and within minutes had identified a suspect. An alleged robber, prior to entering a shop, inadvertently stood in front of the surveillance camera practicing how he would disguise himself.[28]

12    My next illustration arguably reveals either an acculturated blindness or simple stupidity moreso than an uncivil action. The organizers responsible for selecting finalists for the creation of the Sojourner Truth statue received 49 entries, about equally divided between male and female artists; the initial five finalists were …and you know what is coming …all male.[29] What are the chances that at least one female applicant might have been worthy of selection as a finalist?

13    One may tire of the social requirement to remain civil in the face of this and similar actions. Whether or not we should be civil gives rise to a central question: Is there ever a reason for the expression of an uncivil rhetoric? In responding, I want to shift our focus toward our lives as citizens of the larger world. While the line between our campus and society is more artificial than real, my goal in this discussion is to recognize that privileging civil discourse as a solution to human problems carries with it the promise of what might be called the *tyranny of civility*. Civil behavior may be more than politeness,

but in its execution, it may also serve to mask very real differences in power relations. In a word, civility may perpetuate *servitude*.

14      Rest assured that I will not be dismissing civility in what remains to be argued, for "Who can be against civility?"[30] Nevertheless, we should not uncritically accept the positive rhetoric about how we should all "Just get along." You may recall the plaintive cry "Why can't we all just get along?" from a few years ago; one could answer this in various ways:

15      First: We can't get along; we are, after all, a product of our own limits as humans, limits presumably so powerful and ever present as to preclude getting along with others.

16      *Second:* We could but we won't get along; it is not because we are limited by our own natures but because we don't wish to put these natures under any sort of control.

17      These two answers affirm our destiny as closed to the possibility of living in harmony with one another. I would suggest that neither response is entirely accurate—though to be sure, there are people in our society who would fit either of these characterizations. There is a third alternative that is closer to the mark: **We should not get along—at least not all of the time**. Getting along may be well and good in most circumstances. (To go along is to get along, as the saying suggests.)

18      Unfortunately, the presence of getting along, and the civility it projects, may be simply illusory. As a Montana farm boy, I got along with the Native Americans living in railroad cars up on Hill 57 just outside of Great Falls. They kept, for the most part, to their world, and I kept to mine; and when we did cross, it was with a civil silence that protected each from the other. I am not, now, proud of the civil indifference my actions projected in those days. But what I hope to have taken from that experience is the recognition that merely getting along is woefully inadequate as a response to social issues.

19      I am equally sure that the well-intentioned white women in the South who acted to prevent lynchings "got along" with the black women they interacted with.[31] But do I think that getting along in this instance meant that civility alone produced positive results for the emergence of an equal status between two groups? I'd be willing to bet that nothing changed in the primary relationships between white and black. That the black women were recognized for their color was affirmed; that they were accepted as equals was not. To have done so would have torn the fabric of an otherwise well woven tapestry of prejudice and have placed white women in direct opposition to the prevailing attitudes. To alter the social landscape in such a fashion was not the intent of these white women. Rather, they walked the tightrope of an objection to a scurrilous practice while maintaining the cultural truths about difference to which they were so well accustomed. In being civil citizens, they adopted a common perception of what it means to be civil, in which civility bespeaks "a willingness to conduct oneself according to the socially approved rules even when one would like to do otherwise."[32] Isn't that enough? Before answering in the affirmative, consider this example: "Mississippi slave owners of the nineteenth century were renowned for exhibiting impeccable manners, conversational decorum and knowledge of the social graces, namely, the requisite components of social civility." Then, as in the case of the Southern women protesting against lynching, life went on "because everyone knew his or her place and recognized the often severe penalty for stepping out of it."[33] In this context, who controls the rules determines what occurs.

*(continued)*

This approach to civil behavior is ever so clearly expressed in the following ration-ale, advanced as a means of justifying repression in the perpetuation of a civil society:[34] **20**

Democratic discourse, then, posits the following qualities as axiomatic: activism, autonomy, rationality, reasonableness, calm, control, realism, and sanity. The nature of the countercode, the discourse that justifies the restriction of civil society, is al-ready clearly implied. If actors are passive and dependent, irrational and hysterical, excitable, passionate, unrealistic, or mad, they cannot be allowed the freedom that democracy allows. On the contrary, these persons deserve to be repressed, not only for the sake of civil society, but for their own sake as well. **21**

What is present in this description is a recognition of the centrality of discourse in constructing the symbolic codes. What is equally absent is any recognition of who is defining what it means to be either calm or excitable, active or passive, rational or irra-tional. Such a sense of civil society is meaningless in that it merely serves to perpetuate the dominance of those already in positions of power. It is one thing to play nice with the cultural other; it is quite another to accept that person as an equal—an inescapable condition of being civil in the first place. **22**

Civility is not, as Stephen Carter would have us believe, a sacrifice we make.[35] For if seen as sacrificial, as playing nice, in all cases, the act of civility is constantly tainted with the potential of inauthenticity. If you must sacrifice your better nature to be civil to me, I may then wonder what you really think and whether your civil face is, in fact, sincere and trustworthy. If we must both sacrifice, it also suggests a Hobbesian view of who we really are: Humans whose natural condition requires the overlay of a sacrificial act of pretense that we express ourselves in a manner other than what we would most desire. Nor is it "morally better to be civil than to be uncivil."[36] Admittedly, that seems like a rea-sonable assertion on its face, but who is determining what counts as civil? Keep in mind that within the councils of civility that have occurred in the past few years, those invited to the table have been the "civil ones"—mostly white, mostly male, and always in a posi-tion to decry, denigrate, and demean the actions of those not invited to the table.[37] Is it always better to be civil to these self-appointed arbiters of what will count as good be-havior? To raise these questions is to consider where the lines are that define the con-tours of a civil society and what it might mean to transgress those lines in advancing one's cause. **23**

What is the solution? One that might be proposed is the call to transcendence—if we can just get beyond our differences, we can eliminate the problems. But transcen-dence alone does not provide all the answers, for it makes invisible those differences that may well matter in the outcome. Reality recedes from view in a transcendent world, wherein differences that do change the way we interact are no longer of import. Bringing the Other to my table, within my white world, also is the wrong path—for it is still my table, set with my patterns of interaction and control. Claiming a commitment to tolerance that "allows" difference its space to play also is the wrong path—for the language of "to allow" perpetuates the cultural dominance of the person doing the "allowing."[38] Nothing changes if we simply allow the Other to come over. Going to the world of the Other likewise is the wrong path, as the same holds true, if only in reverse. Compromising our identity, or seeking to compromise the identity of the Other, is also **24** the wrong communicative path. Being civil in a manner that erases our collective soul may yield agreement but may also impoverish us as a people.

25    To challenge civility, to Color Outside the Lines of accepted social practice, is to affirm the presence of difference—difference that matters to the social reconstruction of relationships created in and through communication. A civility that masks or covers over the presence of deep disagreement retards social progress rather than, as it would otherwise seem, advancing it. A civility that smothers discontent destroys. If we reinvoke the phrase Coloring Outside the Lines as a response to civil discourse that masks or hinders the expression of difference, it would mean taking our everyday taken-for-granted practices and turning them inside out, upside down—interrogating them before altering or readopting them.

26    How, then, might we conclude this sojourn? From choices we make in our academic community, we can construct a more comfortable community for all, and from choices we make in our larger role as citizens, we can determine the limits of civility and utilize those opportunities to recognize when incivility may be a positive force for change.

27    As already implied, all challenges are not equally right, all choices are not destined to be correct. There is an implicit balance between the impetus to conserve that which we know and the desire to live that which is new. Put in these terms, it might be pictured as follows: To conserve is to protect and to defend those rights accorded a people—not to strip away or deny those self-same rights. To call conservatives to task, then, is simply to remind them of the originating duty. It is a state of being in the world to defend and protect that which is accorded humanity by virtue of its nature as human

28    To liberate, on the other hand, is to set free, to loosen the lines or boundaries which set a person within a place, fixing one's options to always already delineated contours. To call liberals to task, then, is simply to remind them of the duty to see beyond the lines, beyond the present place. It is a state not of being in but of acting out of the world, not toward any one predetermined place but to act toward the future in a manner that preserves the ability to move beyond the lines that define one's place at any moment in time. In this regard, then, the conservative is the defender of human and civil rights, and the liberal is the promoter of the new and as yet untried, which a people might come to enjoy in an as-yet-undefined future. Once accorded, these new rights become the province of the conservative as defender or conservator of the present. We need both forces—those holding us fast within the lines and those impelling us forward across the lines—in active tension. Enacting a civil, or at times uncivil, discourse, in this scenario, is not simply an option to consider but a fundamental necessity of being actively human.

# ■ CHAPTER SUMMARY

Language is a referential, relational, and symbolic medium of communication, which means that speakers must be sensitive to how they encode their messages for the listeners who decode them. Central to effective speaking is the challenge of capturing an oral style, because public speaking is social, ephemeral, enthymematic, and less formal. One key to an oral style of language use is the need to use language competently through effective word choice: accurate, simple, coherent, properly intense, and appropriate language choices. Other aspects of competent language use include attention to definitions (dictionary, negative, etymological, exemplar, contextual, and analogical), imagery (visual, auditory, gustatory, olfactory, tactile, kinesthetic, and organic), and metaphors.

Oral language use also must be ethical, and speakers should think about their use of ad hominem attack, linguistic erasure, and critiquing domination (i.e., conspiratorial appeals). In selecting language that creates an oral style appropriate to you, the occasion, the subject matter, and the audience, you must make good decisions regarding a serious versus humorous atmosphere; a speaker-, audience-, or content-centered emphasis; and a propositional versus narrative style. You also should think about the larger picture—how your speech contributes to a civil society through recognizing the difference between gendered and gender neutral language, avoiding uncivil and hateful speech, and crafting multicultural visions of audiences.

Language choices—and the resulting ways that the oral style of a speaker is created—comprise the speaker's most crucial channel of communication.

## ■ KEY TERMS

accuracy  (p. 234)

ad hominem attack  (p. 244)

analogical definition  (p. 239)

appropriateness  (p. 238)

atmosphere  (p. 247)

audience-centered emphasis
   (p. 249)

clichés  (p. 243)

codes  (p. 232)

coherence  (p. 235)

competent language use
   (p. 234)

connectives  (p. 236)

content-centered emphasis
   (p. 249)

contextual definition  (p. 239)

critiquing domination  (p. 246)

decoding  (p. 232)

dictionary definition  (p. 238)

doublespeak  (p. 248)

encoding  (p. 232)

enthymematic  (p. 233)

etymological definition  (p. 238)

exemplar definition  (p. 239)

final summaries  (p. 236)

gender-linked words  (p. 252)

gender-neutral words  (p. 252)

hate speech  (p. 254)

imagery  (p. 239)

intensity  (p. 237)

internal transitions  (p. 235)

linguistic erasure  (p. 244)

metaphor  (p. 242)

multicultural vision  (p. 255)

narrative style  (p. 250)

negative definition  (p. 238)

oral style  (p. 232)

orality  (p. 232)

political correctness  (p. 254)

preliminary summaries  (p. 236)

private speech  (p. 234)

propositional style  (p. 250)

public speech  (p. 234)

referential  (p. 231)

relational  (p. 231)

signposts  (p. 235)

simplicity  (p. 235)

speaker-centered emphasis
   (p. 249)

stipulative definition  (p. 238)

summaries  (p. 236)

symbolic  (p. 231)

tone  (p. 247)

word choice  (p. 232)

## ■ ASSESSMENT ACTIVITIES

1. Choose one of the items listed, and describe it using seven types of imagery to create a portrait you could use in a speech. Highlight each of the images that you use, and label it for your instructor.
   a. Eating freshly picked berries on the shores of Lake Michigan

   b. A complicated machine of some kind
   c. One of the creatures from *Shrek* (or any other popular movie)
   d. The oldest (or newest) building on campus

2. Read the sample speech at the end of this chapter, and identify what methods the speaker uses to make the language effective. Were the essen-

tials of effective word choice observed? Did the speaker create what seems to you an appropriate style, as defined in this chapter? Were the rhetorical strategies of definition, imagery, and metaphor used well? Grade the speaker's competence (e.g., minimal, average, superior) as an oral stylist, and justify your grade.

## ■ REFERENCES

1. Quoted in John R. Pelsma, *Essentials of Speech* (New York: Crowell, Collier, and Macmillan, 1934), 193.
2. John Waite Bowers, "Language and Argument," in *Perspectives on Argumentation*, edited by G. R. Miller and T. R. Nilsen (Glenview, IL: Scott, Foresman, 1966), 168–172.
3. Courtney Love, "Address at Digital Hollywood Online Entertainment Conference," New York City, May 16, 2000. Available online: <http://gos.sbc.edu/l/love2.html>. Accessed June 16, 2001.
4. Ben Johnson, "Flying the Friendly Skies: How Safe Are You?" *Winning Orations 2001*. Reprinted by permission from Larry Schnoor, Executive Director, Interstate Oratorical Association.
5. Valerie Waldock, "Bridging the Digital Divide," *Winning Orations 2001*. Reprinted by permission from Larry Schnoor, Executive Director, Interstate Oratorical Association.
6. Stephanie Aduloju, "Whitewashed," *Winning Orations 2000*. Reprinted by permission from Larry Schnoor, Executive Director, Interstate Oratorical Association.
7. Thomas Harris, *Hannibal* (New York: Random House, 1999), 269.
8. Douglas MacArthur, "Duty, Honor, and Country," in *The Dolphin Book of Speeches*, edited by George W. Hibbit (Garden City, NY: Doubleday, 1965).
9. Michael Osborn, *Orientations to Rhetorical Style* (Chicago: Science Research Associates, 1976), 10.
10. Quoted on the cover of James Rogers, *The Dictionary of Clichés* (New York: Ballantine Books, 1985). On clichés, see Joe Glaser, *Understanding Style: Practical Ways to Improve Your Writing* (New York: Oxford University Press, 1999), ch. 5.
11. From Martin Luther King, Jr., "Love, Law and Civil Disobedience" (Martin Luther King, Jr., 1963). Reprinted by arrangement with The Heirs to the Estate of Martin Luther King, Jr., c/o Writers House, Inc. as agent for the proprietor. Copyright 1963 by Martin Luther King, Jr., copyright renewed 1991 by Coretta Scott King.
12. Technically, the phrase *ad personam* means "to the person" in an individual sense, whereas *ad hominem* is an attack on the life circumstances of someone. So, if one argues, "You're a liar and a cheat and, hence, cannot be trusted to be telling the truth on this question," that's an ad personam argument, but if one argues, "You must be pro-life on the abortion question because you're a Catholic," that's an ad hominem argument. Ad hominem arguments often are class or group based rather than individual based. Keep in mind, however, that this distinction is a technical one; people commonly use *ad personam* and *ad hominem* interchangeably.
13. For arguments about the centrality of character arguments to (especially American) politics, see Bruce E. Gronbeck, "Character, Celebrity, and Sexual Innuendo in the Mass-Mediated Presidency," in *Media Scandals: Morality and Desire in the Popular Culture Marketplace*, edited by James Lull and Stephen Hinerman (London: Polity Press, 1997), 122–142. For a discussion of ad hominem and other fallacies in political debate, see Jerry L. Miller and Raymie E. McKerrow, "Political Argument and Emotion: An Analysis of 2000 Presidential Campaign Discourse," in *Contemporary Argument and Debate* 22 (2001): 43–58.
14. Philip Wander, "The Third Persona: An Ideological Turn in Rhetorical Theory," *Communication Studies* 35 (1984): 197–216.
15. For details and beautiful illustrations, see Herman J. Viola and Carolyn Margolis, eds., *Seeds of Change: A Quincentennial Celebration* (Washington, DC: Smithsonian Institution Press, 1991).
16. For the originary discussion of the critique of domination (and the critique of freedom), see Michel Foucault, *Power/Knowledge: Selected Interviews and Other Writings*, edited by Colin Gordon; translated by Colin Gordon, Leo Marshall, John Mepham, and Kate Soper (New York: Pantheon Books, 1980). It is turned into a theory of *critical rhetoric* in Raymie E. McKerrow, "Critical Rhetoric: Theory and Praxis," *Communication Monographs* 59 (1989): 91–111.
17. Kent Ono, "Power Rangers: An Ideological Critique of Neocolonialism," in *Critical Approaches to Television*, edited by Leah E. Vande Berg, Lawrence A. Wenner, and Bruce E. Gronbeck (Boston: Houghton Mifflin, 1998), 274.

18. Alan Alda, "A Reel Doctor's Advice to Some Real Doctors," in *The Art of Public Speaking*, edited by Stephen E. Lucas (New York: Random House, 1983), 364.

19. Allen H. Neurath, "Acceptance Address," *DeWitt Carter Reddick Award: Address by the 1992 Recipient* [pamphlet] (Austin: University of Texas at Austin, 1992). Used with permission of the author.

20. See Bruce E. Gronbeck, "Characterological Argument in Bush's and Clinton's Convention Films," *Argument and the Postmodern Challenge: Proceedings of the Eighth SCA/AFA Conference on Argumentation*, edited by Raymie E. McKerrow (Annandale, VA: National Communication Association, 1993), 392–397.

21. Kenneth Burke, *The Philosophy of Literary Form* (Baton Rouge: Louisiana State University Press, 1941), 5–7.

22. For reviews of these and other issues relative to gendered communication, see P. J. Kalbfleisch and M. J. Cody, eds., *Gender, Power, and Communication in Human Relationships* (Hillsdale, NJ: Erlbaum, 1995); and Sarah Benor, ed., *Gendered Practices in Language* (Chicago: University of Chicago Press, 2001).

23. To examine the debate over political correctness, see such works as Richard Feldstein, *Political Correctness: A Response from the Cultural Left* (Minneapolis: University of Minnesota Press, 1997); Cary Nelson, *Manifesto of a Tenured Radical* (New York: New York University Press, 1997); and Alan Charles Kors and Harvey A. Silvergate, *The Shadow University: The Betrayal of Liberty on America's Campus* (New York: Free Press, 1998). For an attack on the excesses of political correctness, see Tammy Bruce, *The New Thought Police: Inside the Left's Assault on Free Speech and Free Minds* (Roseville, CA: Prima Publishing, 2002).

24. Your library probably has a shelf of works on hate speech. Here are some recent works worth your time: James Weinstein, *Hate Speech, Pornography, and the Radical Attack on Free Speech Doctrine* (Boulder, CO: Westview Press, 1999); Robin Tolmach Lakoff, *The Language of War* (Berkeley: University of California Press, 2000); Judith P. Butler, *Excitable Speech: A Politics of the Performative* (New York: Routledge, 1997); Richard Abel, *Speaking Respect, Respecting Speech* (Chicago: University of Chicago Press, 1998); and Martin P. Golding, *Free Speech on Campus* (Lanham, MD: Rowman & Littlefield, 2000).

25. The idea of multiculturalism has been vigorously debated in American society. For some of the positions taken, see Thomas S. Popkewitz, ed., *Educational Knowledge: Changing Relationships between the State,* *Civil Society, and the Educational Community* (Albany, NY: SUNY Press, 2000); Susan Stanford Friedman, *Mappings: Feminism and the Cultural Geographies of Encounter* (Princeton, NJ: Princeton University Press, 1998); Mark P. Orbe, *Constructing Co-Cultural Theory: An Explication of Culture, Power, and Communication* (Thousand Oaks, CA: Sage, 1998). 1997); and John J. Miller, *The Unmaking of America: How Multiculturalism Has Undermined the Assimilation Ethic* (New York: Free Press, 1998).

26. Earlier versions of this address were presented at the 2000 Southern States Communication Association Convention, New Orleans; at the University of Maryland; and at the 2000 Arizona Communication Association Convention in Phoenix.

27. *Athens News*, 15 May 2000, p. 22.

28. *Athens News*, 1 May 2000, p. 22; 4 May 2000, p. 26

29. "Artist Selection for Sojourner Truth Statute in Dispute," *Columbus Dispatch*, 20 February 2000, p. 9A.

30. Gören Ahrne, "Civil Society and Uncivil Organizations," in *Real Civil Societies: Dilemmas of Institutionalization*, edited by Jeffrey C. Alexander (Thousand Oaks, CA: Sage, 1998), 85 (see pp. 85–95).

31. Kimberly A. Powell, "The Association of Southern Women for the Prevention of Lynching: Strategies of a Movement in the Comic Frame," *Communication Quarterly*, 43 (1995): 86–99.

32. Randall Kennedy, "The Case against 'Civility,'" *The American Prospect* (November–December 1998): 84 (see pp. 84–90).

33. Constance Hilliard, as quoted in Sam Smith, "Building a Civil Society: Let Them Eat Discourse," *Progressive Review*. Available online: <http://emporium. turnpike.net/P/PreRev/civsoc.htm>. Accessed October 8, 2000.

34. Jeffrey C. Alexander, "Citizen and Enemy as Symbolic Classification: On the Polarizing Discourse of Civil Society," *Cultivating Symbolic Boundaries Differences and the Making of Inequality*, edited by Michèle Lamont and Marcel Fournier (Chicago: University of Chicago Press, 1993), 292 (see pp. 289–308).

35. Stephen L. Carter, *Civility: Manners, Morals, and the Etiquette of Democracy* (New York: Harper, 1998).

36. Carter.

37. Benjamin DeMott, "Seduced by Civility: Political Manners and the Crisis of Democratic Values," *The Nation*, 9 December 1996, pp. 11–19.

38. I am indebted to Jennifer Willis-Rivera for this suggestion (personal communication, December 1999).

# Chapter 11

# Using Visual Aids in Speeches

*Sue had everything ready to show slides as part of her speech—she had spent a long time working in PowerPoint to make sure points slid in as she desired, the graphics she'd added were appropriate, and even the materials downloaded from the web fit her needs. She also had practiced timing the speech, so she knew how long to show each slide before moving on. The classroom had a pull-down screen, so she didn't need to bring one. The windows had shades, so she could darken the room to enhance the visual effect. She had reserved a laptop from the department as well as the LCD projector. The day of the speech, she brought the equipment in (and she remembered to bring an extension cord, in case it was needed), set it up, and began her speech. As she hit the first slide, she realized something was wrong—all her codes for bringing subpoints up on the slide one at a time had disappeared. Instead, the whole slide came up at once, which lessened the visual effect she had planned. After her speech, she discovered that the version of PowerPoint she had used and the one on the department's computer were not identical. The difference in versions was sufficient to affect her slide presentation.*

Sue's experience is like that of other speakers: Even with attention to preparation, one missed detail may ruin the use of visuals or lessen their impact. We fully expect that you will repeat Sue's experience—perhaps not with different versions of software but in some other way. From a practical perspective, using visuals requires a great deal more thought and attention to detail than might at first meet the eye.

Given that, you might wonder: Why use visuals at all? One answer is to consider the general impact of visuals in contemporary society. We live in a time that has been called **ocularcentric**[1] (i.e., *ocular* = "eye"; *centric* = "centered")—one in which sight threatens to be the dominant sense. Television, film, transparencies,

VCRs and videotape, videodiscs, CD-ROMs and related digital technologies, over-head and opaque projectors, billboards, poster art, banners trailing from air-planes, sidewalk tables with samples from a store's "Today only" sale—our world is filled with visual communications. No time or place before ours has been so vi-sually oriented. Entire companies—from famous media studios to small-town graphics shops in basements—exist because of our willingness to pay for pieces of visual rhetoric that entice the eye and affect the mind.

The public speaker, of course, always has been in the visual communication business. A speaker's physical presence before an audience is a powerful visual statement. Body language, facial expression, eye contact, and gestures—all these combine to make the visual channel of public speaking a carrier of significant messages. The use of **visual aids** makes the world of sight an essential part of oral communication transactions, as well. From the objects a second-grader brings to school for "show and tell" to the flipcharts sales trainers use, speakers multiply and deepen their communication messages when they use visual channels well.

Research on visual media, learning, and attitude change has revealed help-ful information about the impact of visual aids on audiences.[2] Much advice, how-ever, still flows directly from veteran speakers to those who are new at public pre-sentations. In this chapter, we mix advice from both sources to maximize your potential in creating effective, value-added visual materials. First, we deal with the general functions of visual aids, and then, we examine various types and look at some advice on how to use them to greatest effect.

## The Functions of Visual Aids

Visual materials provide added value to your presentation. There are several reasons for including some form of visual aid in speaking. One source lists the following:

- To enhance understanding of the topic
- To add authenticity
- To add variety
- To help your speech have lasting impact
- To enhance speaker ethos[3]

These are fairly self-explanatory rationales for taking the time and effort to locate and/or design effective visual supports for your presentation. Based on your own experience in listening to classroom lecturers, you know that watching something (at times, anything!) helps you focus on the ideas being communicated to you by the instructor. If you were to stand at a lectern for an hour, not moving from the single spot, and only talked to your audience, how long would they really listen?

Which lectures, and lecturers, do you recall more vividly after time passes—those who stood their ground (literally) or those who moved about, from the chalkboard to the TV monitor, to the laptop or overhead projector or Elmo (a document camera) to *show* rather than simply *tell?* By adding visuals, you truly enhance the power and forcefulness of your presentation. Visual materials satisfy the "show-me" attitude prevalent in a vision-oriented, or ocularcentric, age and provide a crucial means of meeting listener expectations.[4]

## Types of Visual Aids

To give you the broadest possible look at visual aids, we divide them into two large classes: **physical objects** and **representations of objects and relationships.** Then, we examine more particular types and give you some tips on how to use them in your talks.

### Physical Objects

The objects that you bring to a presentation, including your own body, can be categorized under two headings: **animate** (living) **objects** and **inanimate** (nonliving) **objects.**

**Animate Objects**    Live animals and plants can, under some circumstances, be used to enhance your speeches. If your speech explores the care and feeding of gerbils, you can reinforce your ideas by bringing to the speech one or two gerbils in a properly equipped cage. Likewise, describing the differences between two varieties of plants may be easier if you demonstrate the differences with real plants. You might be stretching your luck, however, by bringing a real horse into the classroom to show how one is saddled or an untrained puppy to show how one is paper trained. You also will want to be careful with other animals—spiders, snakes—as some in your audience will be made uncomfortable. Your purpose is to focus audience attention on your speech, not to distract the audience with the object. A registered Persian cat may seem to be a perfect visual aid for a speech about what judges look for in cat shows—until a person in the first row has an allergic reaction to your pet. You may think your python is cute and harmless, but some may be truly frightened. In a classroom setting, you will have an opportunity in advance to ask if anyone would be upset or worried about using a specific animal in a demonstration. In other settings, asking those who may attend or who would have a sense of what the occasion is like will assist in making a well-informed decision.

You also can use your own body as a visual aid: Demonstrating warm-up exercises, ballet steps, or tennis strokes adds concreteness and vitality to such presentations. Such demonstrations, however, need to be seen to be appreciated (and this goes for any visual you use). In using your body to demonstrate a yoga position, use a sturdy tabletop rather than the floor. Slow the tempo of a tennis stroke, so the audience can see any intricate action and subtle movements. Exaggerate an action, so it can be seen by those in the back of the room. One advantage of properly controlled visual action is that you can direct the audience's attention to your demonstration. Discretion and common sense about what's possible and in good taste will help make animate visuals work for you rather than against you.

**Inanimate Objects**    Demonstrations often are enhanced by showing the actual object under discussion: A speech about stringing a tennis racket is enhanced by a demonstration of the process with an actual racket. A speech about the best way to repair rust holes in an automobile fender is clarified by samples of the work in various stages. (Bring in pieces, not the whole fender!) Demonstrations of cooking or house remodeling are enlivened with samples prepared before the presentation because the presenter usually does not have time to complete the actual work during the presentation. Take a tip from TV cooking shows—they work with several copies of a dish to illustrate different stages. You can do the same if your purpose is to illustrate a sequence of events in remodeling or making something.

Whether an object is animate or inanimate, you want to keep the audience's attention focused on the message of your speech. Thus, when you are through with your gerbils in the cage, move the cage out of direct sight if possible to avoid having the audience watch the gerbils rather than listen to you. Endeavor to control the audience's focus on what you want them to hear and understand, and use visuals in a manner that maximizes their attention on you.

## Representations of Objects and Relationships

When you cannot use actual objects or your own physical movements to clarify your message, you can resort to using representations—or images—that help convey an understanding of what you are discussing. These representations may be relatively concrete—such as photographs, slides, transparencies, and film or videotape segments—or more abstract—such as drawings, graphs, charts, and models. They may involve a simple chalkboard or a flipchart or even equipment such as overhead transparencies, slide projectors, VCRs with television monitors, or computer-generated and controlled slides. There are advantages and disadvantages to each, however (see Figure 11.1).

**Photographs**    With photographs, you can illustrate flood damage to ravaged homes or depict the beauty of a wooded area threatened by a new shopping mall. One problem with photographs, however, is that audiences may not be able to see details from a distance. You can compensate by enlarging photos, so people

FIGURE 11.1

### Rollerblade Visuals

*Representations convey information in various ways. For instance, a photograph of an inline skate (right) gives the audience a realistic but complicated view of the object, whereas an abstract representation, such as a diagram (bottom right), strips away unnecessary details to illustrate the parts of the object more clearly. An action shot (bottom left) provides a feeling of a three-dimensional object.*

*Source:* Diagram is reprinted by permission of Rollerblade, Inc. Copyright © Rollerblade, Inc. Photos also used courtesy of Rollerblade, Inc.

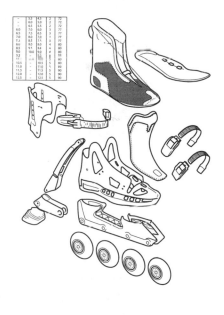

can see them more easily. Avoid passing small photos through the audience, however, because such activity is noisy and disruptive. The purpose of a visual aid is to draw the attention from all members of the audience simultaneously.

Another potential problem with photographs is that they can be altered. See the "Ethical Moments" box on the next page for some examples.

# ETHICAL MOMENTS

## Can Pictures Lie?

Can a picture lie? Isn't each one worth a thousand words because seeing is believing, because showing is better than telling? Not really, especially in the ocularcentric age. Consider these examples of photo faking:

**1**  Hopes for finding U.S. soldiers missing in action (MIAs) in Vietnam often depended upon photos taken by the North Vietnamese that seemed to show American soldiers standing with signs having current dates on them. Those pictures were faked.

**2**  Thanks to sophisticated scanning and graphics technology, you now can easily add to or subtract from a photo and print the altered version so cleanly that the forgery is almost impossible to detect.

**3**  During the 1992 presidential campaign, political action committees (PACs) ran ads that showed Bill Clinton holding hands in victory on the Democratic convention stage with Ted Kennedy. What the PAC had done was put a picture of Kennedy's head on Al Gore's body.

Pictures can be altered to say things that aren't true. They may also create impressions that will intensify the words being spoken or focus on the wrong message. For example, the 1992 PAC ad seemed to be saying, "Bill Clinton is much more liberal than you think."

The visual channel can be very helpful to both speaker and audience when used in morally defensible ways. It can destroy the truth, however, when it is not.

**Slides**  Slides allow you to depict color, shape, texture, and relationships. If you are giving an informative speech on Salvador Dali, you will want to have two or three slides that illustrate his work. If you're giving a speech on horror writer Stephen King, using a picture of the famous author or of the iron gates at the front of his home in Bangor, Maine, would be a logical way to focus attention on your topic.

Using slides requires familiarity with projection equipment. Recall Sue's experience—attention to small, seemingly inconsequential details will make a major difference in how smoothly the presentation goes. For example, if you're using a slide projector instead of an LCD projector and PowerPoint—that is, you have actual slides to illustrate with—what happens if the bulb goes out in the middle of your presentation? Did you bring a spare, and do you know how to change the bulb? Will you need an extension cord? Do you know how to remove a jammed slide? If you are using a laptop you have borrowed from another person or an office, are you familiar with how the cables are attached between the laptop and projector? If the room has a ceiling-mounted LCD projector, with a remote control unit, which button works what on the remote? If you operate on the assumption that whatever can go wrong will, you will be prepared for most problematic circumstances.

**Transparencies**    If you do not have access to a slide projector or to PowerPoint and an LCD projector and screen, you can still dress up the visual portion of your presentation using **transparencies** and an overhead projector. Most copy machines will allow you to reproduce directly from a print version of a document (and in color, if the machine has that capability), and many printers will allow you to print transparencies directly from your file (and in color, if your printer has color capability). Transparencies allow for more information on the printed page than slides.

You also can download information from the World Wide Web, put it directly into your file, and then print the graphic or other visual as part of your transparency. You are not limited to just words in using an overhead projector. Because you cannot click new items to appear on the slide, as you can in Power-Point, you'll need to cover part of the transparency to focus audience attention on the feature you wish to discuss. As you move to the next item, you also need to uncover that item. This is perhaps more cumbersome and inefficient than using PowerPoint, but it can work just as well in terms of directing audience attention to the points you want to make. Transparencies of graphs also work well using an overhead projector—and may be easier to build, depending on your skill at creating slides. You also can cover the entire transparency or simply turn the machine off when you have finished with the key visuals and then turn it on again later if you need to return to specific transparencies. You even can mark the transparency quickly with respect to emphasizing a specific term or statistic or direct audience attention to one element in a table or drawing.

**Document Cameras**    Some classrooms and other meeting room facilities will have a **document camera** (sometimes called an *Elmo*) that you can use. In this instance, your original print document can be brought in (e.g., a magazine advertisement) and placed on the camera. The image then is transferred to the screen via an LCD projector. If you have more than one ad to illustrate, you simply need to remove one and place the other on the camera bed. You also can zoom in to focus attention on specific elements of the ad, or you can use a felt-tip marker to circle specific objects or attributes you want to highlight. As with any use of visuals, however, you'll want to do this fairly quickly, so as not to consume valuable time.

**Visuals**    If the room you are using is wired to the Internet, you can use a laptop and LCD projector to connect to the web and put specific pages up for the audience to see. You will need to be certain of the web address and proficient in typing it in correctly, in order not to waste time trying to locate a site. You also should double-check the site's availability as close to the speaking time as possible. Some sites, especially newspaper reports, are not available after a specific period of time. (This is a good reason for noting in an outline when a site has been accessed. It indicates at the very least that you were there—and so was it—once.) This resource is especially useful for an image that you want to show briefly and then remove. During a class discussion of hate speech, for example, a "hate site" can be shown and then removed from visual sight. Removal is in keeping with a central principle across all such visuals: Keeping them in the audience's line of vision beyond your direct use will distract the audience from other points you want to make.

**Videotapes and Films**    These types of visual aids also can be useful in illustrating your points. Two or three videotaped political ads can help illustrate methods for packaging a candidate. Again, familiarity with the operation of a VCR and its TV monitor or of a film projector will ensure a smooth presentation. Too often, speakers assume the equipment will be provided—and a skilled technician will be available—only to find that no one knows how to run the machine properly. Such delays increase your nervousness and detract from your presentation. Slide and film projectors will require time to set up. You also may need to wheel in a monitor/VCR cart, hook it in, and get it running. Some classrooms are cable ready, hence allowing you to show a live excerpt, should the timing work out.

**Models**    You can use **models**—reduced or enlarged scale replicas of real objects—to convey plans or illustrate problems. Architects construct models of new projects to show clients. Developers of shopping malls, condominiums, and business offices use models when persuading zoning boards to grant needed rights-of-way or variances. You can use models of genes to accompany your explanation of gene splicing. As with other inanimate physical objects, models need to be manageable and visible to the audience. If a model comes apart so that different pieces can be examined, practice removing and replacing these parts beforehand.

**Drawings**    Whether drawn in advance or as you speak, it will be useful, in some instances, to construct rough line drawings or provide the audience with more formally drawn pictures to represent ideas. How finished these are will depend on the formality of the situation. Drawings on flipcharts may be sufficient to explain cell division to a small group, but when presenting the same information to a large audience, more refined visual support materials are needed. The care with which you prepare these visuals will convey to your audience an attitude of indifference or concern.

*Chalkboard drawings are quick sketches that illustrate your ideas.*

Drawings on **whiteboards** and **chalkboards** also are useful in conveying an understanding of a step-by-step process. By drawing each stage as you discuss it, you can control the audience's attention to your major points. Coaches often use this approach when showing players how to execute a particular play or defend against an opponent's play. Take care, however, not to rely on the board so much that you spend most of your speech with your back to your audience. Make sure the audience can see what you are drawing. Standing in front of the drawing, with your back to the audience while talking, does little to communicate your ideas. Stand to the side and draw away from your body, stopping to turn back to the audience at intervals, so they are kept in contact with you and the development of your ideas. Since you will use colored markers on a whiteboard or flipchart, you can more easily use different colors to distinguish what you are illustrating.

Regardless of the medium used to create your drawings—a flipchart, whiteboard, chalkboard, or document camera (i.e., take a blank sheet, place it on the camera bed, and draw)—keep the following points in mind: First, make your drawings large enough so that the audience can see them. Second, if you continue talking to the audience as you draw, be brief. Your audience's attention will wander if you talk to the board or the light source or with your head down (concentrating on drawing on the document camera's bed) for more than 30 seconds. Third, as noted, consider the visual field while you draw—where should you stand to avoid blocking the audience's view of your visuals? Fourth, when you're through talking about the illustration, erase it, cover it, or turn off the projector.

**Graphs**    A graph shows the relationships among the various parts of a whole or variables across time. There are several types of graphs:

1. **Bar graphs** show the relationships between two or more sets of figures (see Figure 11.2). If you were illustrating the difference between lawyers' and doctors' incomes or between male lawyers' and female lawyers' incomes, you would probably use a bar graph.

2. **Line graphs** show relationships between two or more variables, usually over time (see Figure 11.3). If you were tying to explain a complex economic correlation between supply and demand, you would use a line graph.

3. **Pie graphs** show percentages by dividing a circle into the segments that are being represented (see Figure 11.4). A charitable organization could use a pie graph to show how much of its income goes to administration, research, and fund-raising campaigns. Town governments use pie graphs to show citizens what proportions of their tax dollars go to municipal services, administration, education, recreation, and law enforcement.

4. **Pictographs** represent size and number with symbols (see Figure 11.5, p. 276). A representation of U.S. and Russian exports of grain might use a miniature drawing of a wheat shock or ear of corn to represent 100,000 bushels. This representation would allow a viewer to see at a glance the disparity between the exports of these two countries.

---

**FIGURE 11.2**    **Bar Graphs**

_Bar graphs visually illustrate relationships. Be wary, however, in constructing them, as changing the spacing and sizes of the bars can affect the visual message. This graph illustrates the projected growth of PC units between 2000 and 2005._

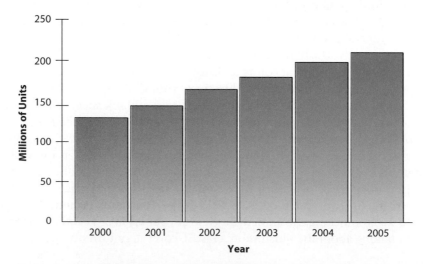

_Source:_  Data from "By the Numbers," _Infoworld,_ 2 April 2001, p. 18.

---

**FIGURE 11.3**    Line Graphs

Line graphs can reveal relationships, but they also can be deceptive. These two graphs show the same data, but the use of different spacing makes the increase in hotel room prices seem much steeper in the right-hand version than in the left. Always look at the scales and their units when trying to interpret line graphs.

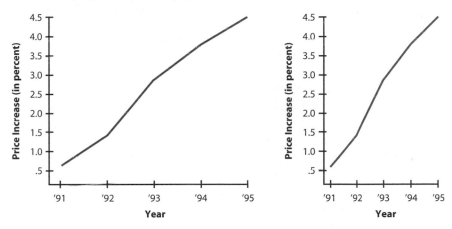

Source: Adapted from Smith Travel Research, as reported in USA Today, 27 October 1995, p. B1.

---

**FIGURE 11.4**

**Pie Graphs**

A pie graph shows percentages of a whole; this graph shows the percentages of different language populations who are online.

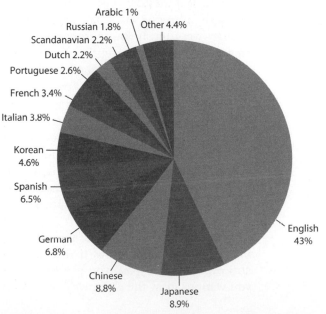

**Online Language Populations
Total: 529 Million People
(December 2001)**

Arabic 1%
Russian 1.8%    Other 4.4%
Scandanavian 2.2%
Dutch 2.2%
Portuguese 2.6%
French 3.4%
Italian 3.8%
Korean — 4.6%
Spanish — 6.5%
German 6.8%
Chinese 8.8%
Japanese 8.9%
English 43%

Source: Information available online: <http://www.euromktg.com/globstats/>.

**FIGURE 11.5**   **Pictographs**

*The speaker can use artistic skill to depict the relative sizes of the largest tech companies by using a dollar bill to create a pictograph showing annual revenues.*

| Rank | Company | 2000 revenue (in $10 billion increments) |
|------|---------|------------------------------------------|
| 1. | IBM | [$][$][$][$][$][$][$][$][$] |
| 2. | HP | [$][$][$][$][$] |
| 3. | Compaq | [$][$][$][$] |
| 4. | Motorola | [$][$][$][$] |
| 5. | Intel | [$][$][$] |
| 6. | Dell | [$][$][$] |
| 7. | Cisco Systems | [$][$] |
| 8. | Microsoft | [$][$] |
| 9. | Sun | [$][$] |
| 10. | Oracle | [$] |

*Source:* Data from "By the Numbers," *Infoworld,* 2 April 2001, p. 18.

Your choice of a bar, line, pie, or pictorial graph will depend on the subject and the nature of the relationship you wish to convey. A pie graph, for example, cannot easily illustrate discrepancies between two groups, nor can it show effects of change over time. If your purpose is to illustrate trends, line graphs will show increases and decreases over time, whereas bar graphs will work better to illustrate comparisons between different variables. Pie charts are excellent if your purpose is to illustrate the proportions "owned" by different variables.[5]

Regardless of the type of graph you choose, you must be very careful not to distort your information when preparing it. A bar graph can create a misleading impression of the difference between two items if one bar is short and wide but the other is long and narrow. A line graph can portray very different effects of change if the units of measurement are not the same for each time period. You can avoid misrepresenting information by using consistent measurements and generating your graphs on a computer.

**Charts and Tables**   **Charts** and **tables** condense large blocks of information into single representations. If you want to discuss what products are imported and exported by Japan, you can break down imports and exports in a table. If you want to show the channels of communication or lines of authority in a large company, your presentation will be much easier to follow if your listeners have an organizational chart for reference.

There are two special types of charts: A **flipchart** unveils ideas one at a time on separate sheets, and a **flowchart** shows the chronological stages of a process on a single sheet. Both flipcharts and flowcharts may include drawings or photos. If you present successive ideas one at a time with a flipchart, you'll focus audience attention on specific parts of your speech. If you present successive ideas all at once with a complete chart, however, the audience may stray from your order of explanation to read the entire chart. You can use a flowchart to indicate what actions might be taken across time—for example, the sequential stages of a fund-raising campaign.

If the information is not too complex or lengthy, tables and charts may be used to indicate changes over time and to rank or list items and their costs, frequency of use, or relative importance. Tables and charts should be designed so they can be seen and convey data simply and clearly. Too much information will force the audience to concentrate more on the visual support than on the oral explanation. For example, a dense chart showing all the major and minor offices of a company may overwhelm listeners as they try to follow your explanation. Thus, if the organization is too complex, you may want to develop a series of charts, with each one focusing on a smaller unit of information.

## Representing Textual Materials

You are not limited to these representational forms of displaying information. You also can use any of the mentioned equipment to convey textual materials, such as an outline of your talk, a list of the key items to be covered, or a quotation from an authoritative source. All these can be displayed on a chalkboard or through slides, overhead transparencies, and so on. Corporate trainers, for example, often use slides created through a computer program such as PowerPoint and displayed electronically from a ceiling-mounted or table-top projector to outline the presentation and convey key information (see Figure 11.6, p. 278). If you are giving a seminar on how to navigate the World Wide Web, you might use visuals that duplicate what is seen on a computer screen. Saying "Click the mouse here" is much easier if your audience can see where the cursor is on the screen at the front of the seminar room.

There are three things to consider when working primarily with text materials. First, keep enough *white space* on the page or slide so the audience does not get lost among the verbiage. Second, make sure the type size is large enough for the audience to see. Even though you can magnify type to some extent by adjusting the distance between projector and screen, some may yet remain too small to read. Third, for slides in a presentation program like PowerPoint, the background color needs to contrast with the text color. What you see on your computer screen as you develop your slide may be easy to read, but consider the effect when you

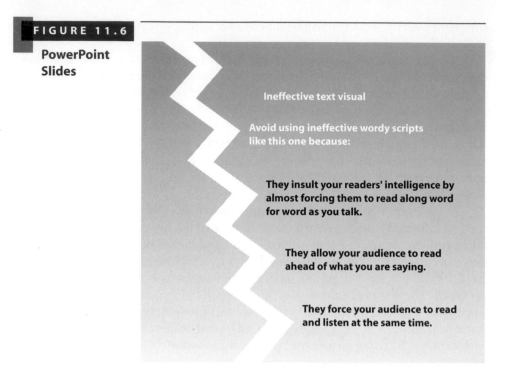

**FIGURE 11.6**

**PowerPoint Slides**

put it on a larger screen. Will the text be readable, or will the background color and text color blend to make the words hard to see? For further practical advice on the use of color in visuals, see the "How to" box on the next page.

**Using Handouts**    Information also can be put on handouts and referred to while you are speaking. Charts, graphs, outlines, rough drawings—all of these can be photocopied and given to each audience member. Giving one to each member is better than passing around only a few copies, which will distract each listener as she or he gets involved in reading and passing things to one another. Often, giving each member a copy is the strategy of choice, such as if you want each person to have the material in her or his possession at the close of your talk.

The primary difficulty you have to work against with handouts is the audience's tendency to read ahead of where you are. If you have more than one handout, you can control this by sequencing when they are given out—and by having someone handle the actual distribution while you talk. You also can control the audience's access to information, at least to some extent, by using an overhead transparency. Use a separate sheet to uncover the items as you go. This won't stop all members from reading ahead, but it will focus attention on where you are at any given moment. You also can wait until the conclusion of your speech and then distribute materials that you want the audience to take away with them.

Lecturers have used the slide "View" function of Power Point, for instance, to copy the slides they will present. They also could use the "Outline" function in the "View" menu to list the key content of each slide. In passing this information out in advance, the assumption is that more will be said about each slide or major point. Otherwise, the audience could simply collect the outline and leave without waiting for the listener to start, much less finish.

## Acquiring Visual Aids

Where do you get your visual aids? Making your own, searching the web for specific examples that you can use, and acquiring them from others are three logical resources.

### How to
### Make the Most of Color Selection
### for Slides and Other Visuals

When using color, consider these three qualities:

1. **Background:** Black causes problems; dark blue works best; but red and blue appear to "jump" when used together.
2. **Mood:** Warm colors (oranges, reds) are more vibrant and exciting. Cool colors (greens and blues) are more sedate and calming. Choose colors to communicate the mood you want the audience to be in as they consider the information contained in the visual. If you want to sell an idea to your audience, choose colors that excite. If you are discussing downsizing or an upsetting topic, use colors that calm.
3. **Contrast:** What looks good on your computer may not be so pleasing on the large screen. Black on yellow is easy to read. Purple letters on blue background is not. White on light yellow also is hard to read. Red type against a green background also is harder to distinguish (and some audience members may have difficulty distinguishing red from green due to color blindness).

Also make sure you know your audience. A conservative audience may be turned off by a yellow background; a blue background is more conservative. Finally, remember three tips:

1. **Be consistent:** Use the same color theme throughout your presentation.
2. **Be judicious:** Do not use more than three or four colors.
3. **Be smart:** Use bright colors to highlight important data.

**For Further Reading**

Hoffman, B. (1995). "Exploring Color," in *Encyclopedia of Educational Technology.* Available online: <http://edWeb.sdsu.edu//EET/Color/Color.html>. Accessed April 18, 1997.

*Technology for Teachers.* Available online: <http://199.78.128.9/tft/pedagogy/present/color.htm>. Accessed April 18, 1997.

*Sources:* Adapted from Dan Cavanaugh, *Preparing Visual Aids for Presentations*, 2nd ed. (Boston: Allyn and Bacon, 2000); and "Color Selection," available online: <http://Webbase.emporia.edu/slim/]]li812/project/812971/t2color.htm>. Accessed July 28, 2001.

## Making Your Own

If you are making your own posterboard to bring to class, you'll need to make sure the classroom is set up to display the board. Not all classrooms have cork strips above the chalkboard or whiteboard that can be used to tack up a poster. So, rather than attempt to hold the poster while trying to refer to items on it, consider enlisting the assistance of a classmate who can hold and then put it away when you are finished. As already noted, too much information on a poster, including small letters or numbers, will make it difficult for the audience. It may take more than one poster to get all of the information across so people sitting 15 feet away can see your drawing and read your text.

## Downloading Visual Aids from the Web

Searching the web for a suitable image or outline of the key issues you wish to discuss—and downloading that information into a slide or a file that can be printed as a transparency—has become much easier. **Website visuals,** in particular, are easy to capture and move into slides. If you are using an IBM-compatible PC with a mouse, move the cursor over the image, click on the right side, and select from the menu the "Save As" option. You will be directed next to a dialog box that asks you to select a place to file the image. You can rename it and save in any one of your file directories for easy access.[6] You then can select the file and open it in a website and onto your slide. For example, the website for the Library of Congress includes a link to the "American Memory" online collections of a variety of text and graphics. Starting from <http://memory.loc.gov>, you can enter the collections and search on a topic and format. This photo of Eleanor Roosevelt was clicked on and saved as a JPEG file; then, with a text onscreen, the file can be clicked to open onto the page.

Once there, left-clicking with the mouse moves you to "Edit" mode, and with the left button down, you can move the slide, positioning it on the page where you want it. You can move it over printed text, and when done, the text will rearrange itself around the image. As another strategy, right-click on the picture and click "Copy"; then move to your text, click "Edit" and then "Paste," and *voila*—the picture you see on the right is imbedded in your slide/text.

*Eleanor Roosevelt*

The same process will work within your slide: You can alter the size of the image and position it where you wish to have it. If your presentation will be broadcast to other sites, you'll need to place the image so that room remains for a technician to put a small picture of you speaking in one corner of the slide. Otherwise, the audience at a different site will only see the slide, or your "corner box" will cut off part of the text/image that you are attempting to illustrate.

### Getting Visual Aids from Research/Others

You also can rely on your research skills as well as ask friends for assistance in locating appropriate images. (See the advice on gathering information in Chapter 6.) If you wish to illustrate a specific interpersonal interaction, such as the importance of appearing credible and believable in conflict situations, think in terms of recent movies you have seen. A 30-second video excerpt from a well-known movie, for example, may be the best way to illustrate what you're talking about regarding the role of credibility in negotiating conflict. When using equipment, try and get to the classroom early enough to give the equipment (in this case, a VCR) a trial run, and make certain the tape is at the right spot to introduce the idea.

## Strategies for Selecting and Using Visual Aids

With these brief suggestions for acquiring visuals in mind, you also need to consider some of the more important ways to maximize their utility. To decide which visual aids will work best for you, take into account these three factors:

1. The characteristics of the audience and occasion
2. The communicative potential of various visuals
3. The potential of computer-generated visual materials to help with your communication tasks

### Consider the Audience and Occasion

Before you select specific visual aids, common sense will tell you to think about your listeners: Do you need to bring a map of the United States to an audience of college students when discussing the westward movement of the U.S. population? If you're going to discuss a football team's offensive and defensive formations, should you diagram them for your audience? Can you expect an audience to understand the administrative structure of the university without providing an organizational chart?

How readily an audience can comprehend *aurally* (by ear) what you have to say is another, more difficult question to answer. It may be quite difficult, for example, to decide what your classmates know about the organization of groups such as the National Red Cross or what Rotary Club members know about the administrative structure of your college. Probably the best thing to do is speak with several of your listeners ahead of time. This and other forms of audience research can help you decide how to use the visual channel.

As part of your preparation process, take into account the speaking occasion. Certain occasions demand specific types of visual support materials. The corporate executive who presents a report on projected future profits to a board of directors without providing a printed handout or diagram probably will put his or her credibility in jeopardy. The military adviser who calls for governmental expenditures on new weapons without presenting pictures or drawings of the proposed systems and printed technical data on their performance is not likely to be a convincing advocate. An athletic coach without a whiteboard at half-time on which to diagram plays probably will confuse some of the players.

In short, if you speak in situations where speakers traditionally use certain visual aids, meet those expectations in your own work. If an occasion does not appear to require certain visual supports, analyze the occasion and your topic further to determine different visual possibilities. The guidelines in the "How to" box below can help you make that analysis. Use your imagination. Be innovative. Don't overlook opportunities to make your speech more meaningful, exciting, and interesting for your listeners.

## How to
## Select the Right Visual Aids

Consider the following when choosing which type of visual aids to use in a particular presentation:

1. ***The purpose of the presentation.*** If specific points are to be highlighted, transparencies or word slides might be appropriate. If the procedure is of utmost importance, a model or physical demonstration might be needed. Travel presentations often use slides or video.

2. ***The nature of the audience.*** What the audience knows about the subject will determine the most appropriate types of visual aids. For a presentation on diseases of vegetables to a group of homeowners with limited knowledge about gardening, it would be appropriate to have real plant specimens and slides. For commercial vegetable farmers with good knowledge of such diseases, however, perhaps you would need only slides to illustrate your point.

3. ***The physical setting.*** The shape, size, lighting, and equipment available in the particular speaking environment are major considerations. Will the seating arrangement allow everyone to see the visual aids being used? If total darkness is required, is it possible? Are there enough electrical outlets for the equipment? Is an overhead projector available? A slide projector? The physical setting should be explored well before the presentation date. Time allowed for the presentation also is critical. If a short timeframe is allowed, then fewer visual aids—and ones that require little explanation—should be used.

4. ***The presenter's skill in using visual aids.*** Only use visual aids with which you feel comfortable. Don't try using a slide projector for the first time during an important presentation without practice. Any visual aid should fit naturally into the presentation. It should not draw excessive attention to itself or be the main focus of the presentation.

*Source:*  Adapted from information available online: <http://hammock.ifas.ufl.edu/txt/fairs/11513>. Accessed July 28, 2001.

## Consider the Communicative Potential of Various Visual Aids

Remember that each type of visual aid is best at communicating a particular kind of information. Each type also must blend with your spoken presentation as well as with your audience. In general, pictorial and photographic visuals can make an audience *feel* the way you do. For example, you can use slides, movies, sketches, and photographs of your travels in Thailand to accompany a speech on social conditions in equatorial Asia. Direct representations can be filled with feeling and show an audience what you experienced in another place or situation. Visuals containing descriptive and written materials, however, will be especially useful in helping an audience *think* the way you do. Models, diagrams, charts, and graphs about the population and economy of Thailand or the increase in AIDS cases in that country could help you persuade your listeners to conclude that the United States should increase its aid to this nation.

See the "How to" box on page 284 for some tips on using different types of visual aids effectively.

## Evaluate Computer-Generated Visual Materials

When considering visual aids, you can tap into the expanding world of computer graphics. You may not be able to produce results similar to those on the latest televised football game, but you still can use readily available **computer-generated visual materials.** Here are some suggestions:

**Use computer graphics to create an atmosphere.** It's easy to make computer banners with block lettering and pictures, so hang a banner in the front of the room to set a mood or establish a theme. For example, one student urging her classmates to get involved in a United Way fund-raising drive created a banner with this campaign slogan: "Thanks to you, it works, for all of us." Initially, the banner captured attention. During her speech, the banner reinforced the theme.

**Enlarge small computer-generated diagrams.** Most computer diagrams are too small to be seen easily by an audience. You can use a photo-duplicating machine, however, to enlarge an image (sometimes to 140 to 200 percent of the original size) and make a more visible diagram. Depending on the facilities available, you may be able to transfer your visual image to a large screen through use of a projector wired to your computer. This also will enlarge the diagram so that it can be seen.

**Consider enhancing the computer-generated image in other ways.** Use markers to color in a pie chart or darken the lines of a line graph. Use press-on letters to make headings for your graphs. Convert computer-generated images into slide transparencies for projection during your speech. Mixing media in such ways can give your presentations a professional look. If you have access to the right technology, you also can create three-dimensional images of buildings, machines, and the human body.

**Know the limitations of computer technology.**  Remember that you're the lead actor and that your visuals are props. Choose visuals that fit your purpose, physical setting, and audience. Computers are most effective when processing numerical data and converting them into bar, line, and pie graphs.

# How to
# Use Visual Aids Effectively

Here are some tips and reminders to assist you in preparing and using visual aids in your presentation:

1. **Good visuals reinforce the spoken message.** They do not convey the entire message.
2. **Have a presentation plan.** Begin with an introduction, and end with a summary or set of conclusions. Identify several major points you want to cover. Supporting points reinforce the main points but can be sacrificed if you're running out of time.
3. **Words and graphics on visual aids should be kept simple.**
   - Complex ideas belong in a handout or paper.
   - Tables generally are not effective. Schematic drawings often are too detailed, but you can modify and simplify a drawing to illustrate only the point you are making, leaving out unnecessary details.
   - Organizational charts cannot be read. Simplify the chart to show only the segments you are discussing.
   - Equations, by themselves, are not effective visual aids. You can make an equation more visually appealing, however, by adding pictorial elements.

4. **If you are using text only:**
   - To show a trend, use a line graph.
   - To show relationships, use a pie chart.
   - To compare quantities, use a bar graph.
   - To illustrate criteria/variables, use a table or chart.
5. **Design visuals to maximize their effectiveness.**
   - Use bullet points, and limit the number of words.
   - When preparing flipcharts in advance or writing on a blackborad or whiteboard during the presentation, write larger than normal: Titles should be 3 inches high; subtitles, 2 inches; and other text, 1½ inches.
   - When using computer-generated slides, the title font should be at least 24-point; subtitles, 18-point; and other text, 14-point.
   - Use bullets and dashed lines to delineate subtopics, but avoid having too many subtopics.
   - Use a ragged-right (i.e., unjustified) margin.
   - Bold text is preferable to underlined text.
   - Avoid overcrowding.
6. **Use—but don't abuse—available technology to produce visuals.**
7. **Use your "spill" check (spell), and then proofread. Inaccuracy will reduce your credibility.**
8. **TEXT IN ALL CAPITALS IS HARD TO READ.**

*Sources:*  Adapted from information available online: <http://omar.llnl.gov/EFCOG/tips.html>; Anne Miller, "Visual Aid Virtuosity," available online: <http://www.presentersuniversity.com/courses>, accessed July 28, 2001; and Dan Cavanaugh, *Preparing Visual Aids for Presentations*, 2nd ed. (Boston: Allyn and Bacon, 2000).

# ■ CHAPTER SUMMARY

We asked a question in the introduction to this chapter: Why use visuals at all? At this point, the reasons should be abundantly clear. We live in an ocularcentric age. Visuals offer several assists, including enhancing understanding and heightening the persuasive impact of a speech. We cannot, in a single chapter, make you proficient at all the possibilities available, but you should be able to consider your topic and occasion and make informed judgments about whether to use visuals—and about which forms would be most appropriate in your situation. You also should be able to categorize potential visual aids as physical objects and concrete or abstract representations.

You should know a bit more about using animate (i.e., living) and inanimate (i.e., nonliving) objects and about using representations such as pictures, slides, transparencies, document cameras, videotapes, whiteboard or chalkboard drawings, graphs, charts, tables, handouts, and computer-generated materials. Just as important, you should be able to select which visual aids—and in what forms—to use in particular speeches after considering the following: the audience and occasion; the communicative potential of various visual aids; the best use of computer-generated materials; and how to coordinate verbal and visual channels for maximum effect.

# ■ KEY TERMS

animate objects   (p. 267)
bar graphs   (p. 274)
chalkboards   (p. 273)
charts   (p. 276)
computer-generated visual
    materials   (p. 283)
document camera   (p. 271)
flipcharts   (p. 277)

flowcharts   (p. 277)
inanimate objects   (p. 267)
line graphs   (p. 274)
models   (p. 272)
ocularcentric   (p. 265)
physical objects   (p. 267)
pictographs   (p. 274)
pie graphs   (p. 274)

representations of objects and
    relationships   (p. 267)
tables   (p. 276)
transparencies   (p. 271)
visual aids   (p. 266)
Website visuals   (p. 280)
whiteboards   (p. 273)

# ■ ASSESSMENT ACTIVITIES

1.  Think of several courses you have taken in high school or college. How did the instructors use visual aids in presenting the subject matters of these courses? Were such materials effectively used? Was there a relationship between the subject matter and the type of visual aid used? Give special consideration to proper and improper uses of the chalkboard by instructors. When was using the chalkboard helpful, and when did it detract from the topic? Are there special problems with using visuals when audience members are taking notes while listening? Prepare a brief, written analysis that answers these and other questions that occur to you, including several illustrations from the classes, in answering this general question: What, in your view, constitutes appropriate and inappropriate uses of visual materials?

2. Visual aids capture appropriate moods, clarify potentially complex subjects, and sometimes even carry the thrust of a persuasive message. Examine magazine advertisements and "how-to" articles in periodicals, look at store windows and special displays in museums and libraries, and observe slide-projection lectures in some of your other classes. Then, using the types of the visual materials considered in this chapter, do the following:

   a. Classify those that you have encountered.
   b. Assess the purposes these materials serve—clarification, persuasion, attention focusing, mood setting, and others.
   c. Evaluate the effectiveness of each of the materials you have examined.
   d. Finally, prepare a report, paper, or journal entry on the results of your experiences and observations.

3. Using a web source such as www.presentations.com, research and evaluate the advice given online for the effective preparation of visuals. Prepare a short speech explaining your findings to the class. Use your own judgment as to the value-added nature of the tips offered, and be a critical reviewer of what is suggested.

## ■ REFERENCES

1. Martin Jay, "The Rise of Hermeneutics and the Crisis of Ocularcentrism," in *The Rhetoric of Interpretation and the Interpretation of Rhetoric*, edited by Paul Hernadi (Durham, NC: Duke University Press, 1989), 55–74.

2. Consult these sources: Theo Van Leeuwen and Carey Jewitt, eds., *The Handbook of Visual Analysis* (Thousand Oaks, CA: Sage, 2001); Paul Martin Lester, *Visual Communication: Images with Messages*, 2nd ed. (Belmont, CA: Wadsworth, 2000); and Gillian Rose, *Visual Methodologies: An Introduction to the Interpretation of Visual Materials* (Thousand Oaks, CA: Sage, 2001).

3. "Virtual Presentation Assistant—Using Visual Aids." Available online: <http://www.ukans.edu/cwis/units/coms2/vpa/vpa.7.htm>. Accessed July 28, 2001.

4. For more practical tips on using various kinds of visual materials, see the following: Dan Cavanaugh, *Preparing Visual Aids for Presentations*, 2nd ed. (Boston: Allyn and Bacon, 2000); Gene Zelazny, *Say It with Charts: The Executive's Guide to Visual Communication* (New York: McGraw-Hill, 2001); and Sherron Bienvenu, *The Presentation Skills Workshop: Helping People Create and Deliver Great Presentations.* (New York: American Management Association, 2000).

5. This is adapted from information available online: <http://www.cs.engr.uky.edu/~lewis/visuals/notes3.html>. Accessed July 28, 2001.

6. See John A. Courtright and Elizabeth Perse, *Communicating Online: A Guide to the Internet* (Mountain View, CA: Mayfield, 1998).

# Chapter 12

# Using Your Voice and Body to Communicate

*Have you ever worried that your voice just wasn't up to the job of speaking in front of others? Would it help to know that you aren't alone in that worry? The great Greek orator Demosthenes initially had such a weak and indistinct voice that he reputedly practiced speaking by shouting into the coastal winds of the Aegean Sea and loading his mouth with pebbles to practice articulating around them. Abraham Lincoln suffered from severe stage fright. Eleanor Roosevelt appeared awkward and clumsy, speaking with a high-pitched, hoarse voice; only after years of practice could she command an audience with her delivery. John Kennedy's strong, regional dialect and his repetitive, wood-chopping gestures were parodied throughout the 1960 presidential campaign and became the objects of intense speech-training sessions. Robert Dole had such trouble with speech dynamism that in the 1996 presidential campaign, his staff resorted to making campaign ads of quick cuts from line to line to make him appear more animated. During the 2000 campaign, neither Al Gore nor George Bush won praise for the use of their voices.*

In this chapter, we will consider ways to work with your own voice qualities to enhance confidence and improve performance. We will begin with a reminder of orality's role in American culture, followed by a more precise discussion of the role of public speaking as a social performance. Then we will focus on practical ways to improve your use of both voice and body in communicating ideas.

## Orality and Human Communication

That people of the stature of Greek orators, U.S. presidents, internationally famous humanitarians, and candidates for high office all took the time to improve their speech delivery skills should not be surprising. These cultural heroes realized that public service comes from thinking great thoughts, yes, but also from forging strong interpersonal bonds that allow those great thoughts to become shared values and actions. Even in the age of electronic interconnectivity, it is still person-to-person contact that forms the basis of social formations. We share ideas, values, and courses of action, most fundamentally, through speaking with others.

The question remains, however: What are the basic characteristics of **oral delivery**—the use of voice and body to communicate with others in your presence—that enhance the importance and power of public speaking? Communication theorist and critic Walter Ong has devoted his life to answering that question in broad terms, trying to understand the ways in which oral (preliterate) cultures worked.[1] Drawing from Ong's work, there are three important characteristics that, taken together, illustrate the power of the voice. For our purposes, we'll discuss them under these headings: aggregative, agonistic/invitational, and ethically appropriate.

## Aggregative

The best human speech gathers together ideas—commonly shared notions—and relates the subject matter to them. Maxims, folk sayings, and even clichés often are *accumulated* or *aggregated* in speeches. Even though you probably were not around when President John Kennedy gave his inaugural address, you undoubtedly are familiar with the refrain "Ask not what your country can do for you . . ." (The ease with which you finish this memorable phrase is proof of its staying power as a political cliché.) The rhetorical potency of this phrase comes from its symbolism of a people willing to act on behalf of and for their country. An almost perfect political slogan, it taps into what is known as *American optimism* or *exceptionalism:* the idea that the United States believes it can always grow and overcome any problem because it is a flexible democracy with problem-solving skills provided by people assembled from all other countries.[2] The best speeches are **aggregative** in that they draw together pieces of wisdom and tie them to the subject matter. If you gather together only clichés, of course, your speech will be empty. The maxims and pieces of wisdom are there to bond your ideas and yourself to other members of the community, not to take the place of new ideas.

## Agonistic/Invitational

There is an ineluctable tension within human speech between the forces of a combative style and those fostering a cooperative, caring spirit. On the one hand, speakers know they are struggling with ideas and with listeners, looking to speak ideas in forceful and commanding ways and to engage listeners not only intellectually but also emotionally. Although not as strong politically as he was in 1996, during the 2000 campaign, Pat Buchanan kept up his fierce attack, pushing his more conservative antigovernment views. At the other end of the scale was Crystal Cathedral preacher Robert Schuller, a smooth, witty, and accommodating speaker. He, too, pleaded with audiences and reached out with sympathy, love, and the power of positive thinking to burrow into their psyches. Both Buchanan and Schuller understood that **agonism**—struggle with others—is something that makes speeches work and that represents a form of public talk that gets things done.

At the other extreme is a form of **invitational rhetoric** that "constitutes an invitation to the audience to enter the rhetor's world and to see it as the rhetor does. In presenting a particular perspective, the invitational rhetor does not judge or denigrate others' perspectives but is open to and tries to appreciate and validate those perspectives, even if they differ dramatically from the rhetor's own."[3] This style also strives for the same end—to get things done—but it seeks to do so by creating an atmosphere that is conducive to the speaker and audience coming to an understanding together, arriving at a vision of the future that is mutually held and acted upon. Seeking cooperation ("Your ideas may be as valued and viable as mine, but I invite you to consider my rationale") rather than confrontation ("It's my way or the highway") as a resource may be more useful in rhetorical settings.

## Ethically Appropriate

The most **ethically appropriate** speech always is grounded in the concreteness of the here-and-now, in the specific situation. Philosophical essays and poetry can try to be timeless, but speeches should always be timely, made for now. The Greek idea of *kairos*—"appropriateness for time and place"—was a concept important to classical rhetoricians.[4] That sense of timely specificity develops because speakers usually are called upon or expected to speak when something is in need of repair or celebration and that something itself is concrete (e.g., you need help understanding a city council resolution, feel anger and sorrow at a friend's death, want someone to express the joy you feel when winning a game).

Concreteness is important because of the sheer physicalness of person-to-person speech: Words seem to flow on material sound waves from the speaker's mouth to the listeners' ears, the bodies of the speaker and listeners are present, and touch occurs when handshakes follow a talk. The very ideas discussed seem to flow from the total human body—the mouth, yes, but also the arms and legs, head and torso, the clothing and jewelry that adorn that body, and the technologies that amplify sound and vision. The material situatedness of public speech gives it a sense of command and presence that simply is not possible with written language, radio or television broadcasts, or Internet chatrooms.

This discussion of the power of the voice may come across as too theoretical and idealistic for your tastes. Nevertheless, theory frames practice; it gives you the reasons for acting as you wish to enhance your chance of success. While you've been talking all of your life and probably have gotten along all right, at the same time, you've also formed a clear sense of what works and what doesn't. The same is true here: When you grab onto a lectern to address a waiting audience, hoping to achieve your general and specific purposes, you must stop to think how best to aggregate ideas, tone them powerfully, and situate yourself and your thoughts concretely enough among today's concerns to meet the audience's expectations and needs. If you do all of that well, you'll have the satisfaction of knowing you've spoken in as competent and socially successful a way as you can. That competence is furthered by an understanding of orality as a social performance.

# Public Speaking as a Social Performance

Just as you perform culture (see Chapter 4), you also perform as a public speaker. Your every action and expression is a performance of self. Whether you speak in an agonistic, combative style or in an invitational, cooperative style, what you say and how you say it intertwine to form the audience's impression of who you are as a person. Your physical body speaks, as well: "Bodies speak, without necessarily talking, because they come coded with and as signs. They speak social codes."[5] Consider the constraints placed on street performers—without the trappings of the theater, they must communicate through their physical presence that they have the competence to recreate, on the street, the images and events that would normally be "staged" in a theatre.[6] The lectern functions as your "theatre" with respect to granting a sense of authority for the presentation. When you have an opportunity to perform without the benefit of a lectern, your body is more fully present to the audience, and like the street performer, much more is demanded of it in establishing your legitimacy as a speaker.

There is a clear, gendered aspect to what might be called a *rhetoric of the body*—the manner in which the body expresses itself is socially conditioned by the roles that men and women play in the public sphere. As one scholar has noted, "For men at least, the higher the role in society, the less importance the body has."[7] What this means is that for men, looks become less important than ideas or status as one climbs the social ladder. For women, appearance remains a critical component of their success. Performing the body depends, in part, on the social expectations created by a society prone to differentiate on the basis of gender.

Conceiving of the body as performer is not simply a Western view of the role of discourse in society. The account of a leader of the Merina peoples of Madagascar is instructive: "The speaker began very slowly, hesitantly, and very quietly, head down, and only gradually would he appear to gain more confidence, although at no time did any excess of expression creep into his manner of delivery."[8] In the Akan society of Ghana, the norms for performance in formal situations "include the non-exclusive use of the left hand in gesticulating, baring of the shoulders, removal of footwear while addressing the chief or his proxy, and finally avoiding proxemic confrontation with the chief."[9]

In every society, adherence to the cultural norms for performing the body become part of the necessary tasks; in moving into such different cultural norms, you must be aware of what expectations are placed on your performance of self. Integrating the bodily presence with the manner of delivery is essential if you're to be considered a legitimate resource for the audience's decisions and actions. What you are seeking is **synchronicity**—a sense of oneness between your physical performance and the specific audience's expectations of that performance. In this way, you advance on a common ground with the audience. Promoting the legitimacy of your ideas will be much easier if the audience is not distracted or turned off by the manner in which your voice or body performs. Delivering your classroom speech while seated on a table or desk in the front of the room, dangling your legs (and because of nervous energy, keeping them in constant motion), probably is not the best means of expressing ideas. The audience expects a much more formal address. If, however, you are demonstrating how to do something, moving from the podium and engaging the audience's attention in a relaxed and casual manner will put them at ease. They will sense that you are comfortable with the artifacts or objects you use in the demonstration and that they have nothing to worry about as you move forward in the speech.

How you use your voice, in addition to your body, also becomes a part of your overall performance. The next section focuses on practical advice in using the voice, and the final section of this chapter focuses on similar advice for using the body as a communicative medium.

# Using Your Voice to Communicate

The human voice is the physical instrument that shapes the meanings of words and ideas. Since preliterate times, when all cultures were oral, the voice has been the primary connector between people, creating a sense of identification and community. You must learn to control your vocal sound stream to make it central to your communication habits.

You communicate your enthusiasm to your listeners through your voice. By learning about the characteristics of vocal quality, you can make your ideas more interesting. Listen to a stock market reporter rattle off the daily industrial averages. Every word might be intelligible, but the reporter's vocal expression may be so repetitive and monotonous that the ideas seem unexciting. Then, listen to Gary Thorne doing play-by-play coverage of a baseball or hockey game or to Billy Packer covering a basketball game. The excitement of their broadcasts depends largely on their use of voice.

American society prizes one essential vocal quality above all others: a sense of **conversationality**.[10] The conversational speaker creates the sense of a two-way, interpersonal relationship—even from behind a lectern. The best hosts of afternoon talk shows and evening newscasts speak as if they're engaging each listener in a personal conversation. Program hosts who have developed a conversational quality—Katie Couric, Matt Lauer, and Oprah Winfrey, for example—have recognized that they are talking with, not at, an audience.

## Perceptions of the Speaking Voice

The perception that successful speakers want to create for their audiences is that their voice, as they use it to shape their ideas and emotionally color their messages, is sincere. A flexible speaking voice has intelligibility and variety.

**Intelligibility**   This quality refers to the ease with which a listener can understand what you're saying, and it depends upon loudness, rate, enunciation, and pronunciation. Most of the time, inadequate articulation, a rapid speaking rate, and a soft volume are acceptable, both because you know the people you are talking with and because you are probably only 3 to 5 feet from them. In public speaking, however, you may be addressing people you do not know and often from 25 feet or more away. When speaking in public, you have to work on improving your **intelligibilty.** Try the following techniques:

**Adjust your volume.**  Probably the most important single factor in intelligibility is how loudly you speak. **Volume** is related to the distance between you and your listeners and also to the amount of noise that is present. You must realize that your own voice sounds louder to you than it does to your listeners. Obviously, you need to project your voice by increasing your volume if you're speaking in an auditorium filled with several hundred people. You shouldn't forget, however, that a corresponding reduction in volume also is required when your listeners are only a few feet away. The amount of surrounding noise with which you must compete also has an effect on your volume, as illustrated in Figure 12.1.

**Control your rate.**  Rate is the number of words spoken per minute. In animated conversation, you may jabber along at 200 to 250 words per minute. This rate is typical of people raised in the American North, Midwest, and West. As words tumble out of your mouth in informal conversation, they're usually intelligible because they don't have to travel far. In large auditoriums or outdoors, however, rapid delivery can impede intelligibility. Echoes sometimes distort or destroy sounds in rooms. Ventilation fans interfere with sound. In the outdoors, words seem to vanish into the open air. When addressing larger audiences, cut your rate by one-third or more. Obviously, you don't go around timing your speaking rate, but you can remind yourself of potential rate problems as you prepare to speak. In fact, knowing your speaking rate is a critical part of determining the delivery time of a given speech (see the "How to" box below). Get feedback from your instructors and classmates regarding your speaking rate.

# How to
## Determine Your Delivery Time

The best speaking rate is between 120 (slow) and 170 (medium) words per minute. If you take the time to write out your speech, use the "Word Count" feature of your software to determine the number of words you have written. (In Microsoft Word, click "Tools" and then "Word Count"; in WordPerfect, click "File" and then "Properties" and then "Information.") Simply divide the number of words by the rate at which you wish to speak (or divide by the amount of time available, and you'll get the rate).

For example, if you decide to use Victoria Woodhall's 18,612-word oration and plan to speak at 120 words per minute, it will take you a little over 2½ hours. If you only have 30 minutes, you probably won't make it, as 620 words per minute will be a bit fast.

*Sources:* Tina Santi Flaherty, "Gender Communication: Mute Issue?" *Working Women/Executive Female,* April 2000, p. 15; and "How to Figure the Delivery-Time of a Speech," available online: <http://gos.sbc.edu/find.html>, accessed June 23, 2001.

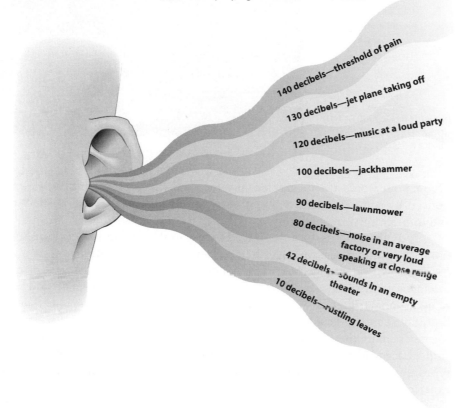

| FIGURE 12.1 | Loudness Levels |
|---|---|

*As you can see, noise varies considerably. How could you adjust your volume if you were speaking in a small room with little noise distraction? What if you were competing with a lawnmower outside the building or a baby crying in the back of the room?*

140 decibels—threshold of pain

130 decibels—jet plane taking off

120 decibels—music at a loud party

100 decibels—jackhammer

90 decibels—lawnmower

80 decibels—noise in an average factory or very loud speaking at close range

42 decibels—sounds in an empty theater

10 decibels—rustling leaves

**Enunciate clearly.  Enunciation** refers to the crispness and precision with which you form words. Good enunciation is the clear, distinct utterance of syllables and words. Most of us are "lip lazy" in normal conversation, however. We slur sounds, drop syllables, and skip over the beginnings and endings of words. This laziness may not inhibit communication between friends, but it can seriously undermine a speaker's intelligibility.

When speaking publicly, force yourself to say "going" instead of "go-in," "just" instead of "jist," and "government" instead of "guvment." You will need to open your mouth wider and force your lips and tongue to form the consonants firmly. If you're having trouble enunciating clearly, ask your instructor for some exercises to improve your performance. (See the "How to" box on page 297 for more information.)

**Meet standards of pronunciation.** To be intelligible, you must form sounds carefully and meet audience expectations regarding acceptable **pronunciation.**

*Projecting your voice may require an amplifier, as is the case here.*

Even if your words are not garbled, any peculiarity of pronunciation is sure to be noticed by some listeners, and your different pronunciation may distract them and undermine your credibility as a speaker.

A **dialect** is language use—including vocabulary, grammar, and pronunciation—unique to a particular group or region. Your pronunciation and grammatical or syntactical arrangement of words determine your dialect. You may have a foreign accent, a white southern or black northern dialect, a New England twang, or a Hispanic trill. A clash of dialects can result in confusion and frustration for both speaker and listener. Audiences can make negative judgments about the speaker's credibility—education, reliability, responsibility, and capacity for leadership—based solely on dialect.[11] Paralinguists call these judgments **vocal stereotypes.**[12] Wary of vocal stereotypes, many news anchors have adopted a midwestern American dialect, a manner of speaking that is widely accepted across the country. Many speakers also become *bilingual,* using their own dialects when facing local audiences but switching to midwestern American when addressing more varied audiences. When you speak, you'll have to decide whether you should use the grammar, vocabulary, and vocal patterns of middle America. The language of your audience is the primary factor to consider.

**Variety**     As you move from conversations with friends to the enlarged context of public speaking, you may discover that listeners accuse you of monotony in your pitch or rate. When speaking in a large public setting, you should compensate for the greater distance that sound needs to travel by varying certain characteristics of your voice. **Variety** is produced by changes in rate, pitch, stress, and pauses:

**Vary your rate.**     Earlier, we discussed normal rates of speech. Alter your speaking rate to match your ideas. Slow down to emphasize your own thoughtfulness, and quicken the pace when your ideas are emotionally charged. Observe how Larry King varies his speaking rate from caller to caller or how an evangelist changes pace regularly. A varied rate keeps an audience's attention riveted to the speech.

**Change your pitch.**  **Pitch** is the frequency of sound waves in a particular sound. Three aspects of pitch—level, range, and variation—are relevant to effective vocal communication. Your **optimum pitch level**—whether habitually soprano, alto, tenor, baritone, or bass in range—is adequate for most of your everyday communication needs. The key to successful control of pitch depends on understanding the importance of **pitch variation.** As a general rule, use higher pitches to communicate excitement and lower pitches to create a sense of control or solemnity. Adjust the pitch to fit the emotion being expressed.

**Vary the stress.**  A third aspect of vocal behavior is **stress,** which is how sounds, syllables, and words are accented. Without vocal stress, you would sound like a computer. Vocal stress is achieved through **vocal emphasis**—the way that you accent or attack words. You create emphasis principally through increased volume, changes in pitch, and variations in rate. Emphasis also can affect the meaning of a sentence. Notice how the meaning of "Now is the time for action" varies with these changes in word emphasis:

| | |
|---|---|
| NOW is the time for action. | **Action needs to take place now, not later.** |
| Now is the TIME for action. | **This is an appropriate time for action.** |
| Now is the time for ACTION. | **We need to act, period.** |

A lack of vocal stress not only gives the impression that you are bored, but it also causes misunderstanding of your meaning. Changes in rate can be used to add emphasis, as well. For example, relatively simple changes can emphasize where you are in an outline: "My s-e-c-o-n-d point is . . ." Several changes in rate also can indicate the relationship among ideas: "We are a country faced with . . . [moderate rate] financial deficits, racial tensions, an energy crunch, a crisis of morality, environmental depletion, government waste . . . [fast rate], and - a - stif - ling - na - tion - al - debt [slow rate]." The ideas pick up speed through the accelerating list of problems but then come to an emphatic halt with the speaker's main concern: the national debt. Such variations in rate emphasize for an audience what is—and what is not—especially important to the speech.

**Use helpful pauses.**  **Pauses** are the intervals of silence between or within words, phrases, and sentences. When placed immediately before a key idea or the climax of a story, a pause can create suspense: "And the winner is [pause]!" When placed after a major point, it can add emphasis: "And who on this campus earns more than the president of the university? The football coach [pause]." Inserted at the proper moment, a dramatic pause can express feelings more forcefully than words. Clearly, silence can be a highly effective communicative tool if used intelligently and sparingly—and if not embarrassingly prolonged.

Sometimes, speakers fill silences in their discourse with sounds: "um," "ah," "er," "well-ah," "you-know," and other meaningless fillers. Undoubtedly, you've heard a speaker say, "Today, ah, er, I would like, you know, to speak to you, um, about a pressing, well-uh, like, a pressing problem facing this, uh, campus." Such vocal intrusions convey feelings of hesitancy and lack of confidence. Make a concerted effort to remove these intrusions from your speech. In addition, avoid too many pauses and those that seem artificial because they can make you appear manipulative or overrehearsed. On the other hand, do not be afraid of silences. Pauses allow you to stress important ideas, such as the punchline in a story or argument. Pauses also intensify the involvement of listeners in emotional situations, such as when Barbara Walters or Dan Rather pauses for reflection during an interview.

## Controlling the Emotional Quality

A listener's judgment of a speaker's personality and emotional commitment often centers on that speaker's **vocal quality**—the fullness or thinness of the tones and whether the sound is harsh, husky, mellow, nasal, breathy, or resonant. Depending on your vocal quality, an audience may judge you as being angry, happy, confident, fearful, sincere, or sad.

Fundamental to a listener's reaction to vocal quality are **emotional characterizers,** which are cues about a speaker's emotional state. These include laughing, crying, whispering, inhaling, and exhaling.[13] Emotional characterizers combine with your words to communicate subtle shades of meaning. Consider a few of the many ways you can say "whatever." You might say it as if it were a matter of no importance, as if you were wishing the person speaking would finish, or with a vocal emphasis that indicated you, too, were reaching the end of your patience. As you say the word to express these different meanings, you might laugh or inhale sharply, altering your emotional characterizers. Such changes are important cues to the audience regarding how to understand what you're saying.

The vocal qualities you can control become prime determiners of your vocal style: Intelligibility is a base characteristic, for without it you have no chance whatsoever of reaching anyone with your message. Emotional characterizers add the human dimensions, providing invaluable cues as to how your message should not only be understood but also responded to—how the audience is to feel about your subject matter. These sorts of **paralinguistic** or vocal connections knit the speaker and the audience together.

## Practicing Vocal Control

Do not assume that you'll be able to master in a day all the vocal skills we've described. To attain them, you have to train your mind, convincing yourself to express certain kinds of feelings publicly before you can, for example, fully modulate multiple vocal qualities. You also have to work on your vocal instrument—to practice aloud. The "How to" box on the next page contains a variety of exercises you can do to work on your voice. Practice may not make perfect, but it certainly won't hurt. Speak in front of as many different kinds of audiences as you can, working in intelligibility, variety, and stress. This will help you engrain constructive changes in your speaking style and into everyday conversation. Then, you should be ready to seek the sense of conversationality so highly valued in U.S. society in the enlarged context of public speaking itself.

# Using Your Body to Communicate

Just as your voice communicates and shapes ideas through the oral-aural channel, so your physical behavior before an audience helps control listeners' understandings of and reactions to what you're saying. The visual channel is so important that even our word *idea* is derived from the Greek word "to see."[14] Both the oral and visual channels can be used to create a common understanding of your ideas and how you want others to feel about them. Questions of physical behavior usually are talked about as *nonverbal communication*.

## Assessing Different Dimensions of Nonverbal Communication

Some use the phrase **nonverbal communication** to refer to all nonlinguistic aspects of interpersonal interaction, but here, we focus on physical behavior in communication settings. In recent years, research has reemphasized the important role of physical behavior in effective oral communication.[15] Basically, three generalizations about nonverbal communication should guide your speechmaking:

## How to Improve Your Voice

The Instructor's Manual that accompanies this textbook has several exercises for voice improvement. Your instructor can get it from Allyn and Bacon. If you or others are concerned about how you use your voice, those exercises can be most useful. Here's a sample of what you can do:

- **Breath control.** Say the entire alphabet, using only one breath. As you practice, try saying it more and more slowly so as to improve your control of exhalation.
- **Pitch control.** Sing "low, low, low, low," dropping one note of the musical scale each time you sing the word, until you reach the lowest tone you can produce. Then, sing your way back up the scale. Now, sing "high, high, high, high," going up the scale to the highest note you can reach. Sing your way back down. Go up and down, trying to sense the notes you're most comfortable with— your so-called *optimum pitch*. Give most of your speeches around your optimum pitch.

- **Articulatory control.** Pronounce each of the following word groups, making sure that each word in the group can be distinguished from the others. Have someone check your accuracy:

    jest, gist, just
    thin, think, thing
    roost, roosts, ghost, ghosts
    began, begun, begin
    wish, which, witch
    affect, effect
    twin, twain, twine

Or, try the following tongue twisters:

    The sixth sheik's sixth sheep's sick.

    Three gray geese in the green grass grazing; gray were the geese and green was the grazing.

    Barry, the baby bunny's born by the blue box bearing rubber baby buggy bumpers.

1. *Speakers reveal and reflect their emotional states through their nonverbal behaviors.* Your listeners read your feelings toward yourself, your topic, and your audience from your facial expressions. Consider the contrast between a speaker who walks briskly to the front of the room, head held high, and one who shuffles, head bowed and arms limp. Communications scholar Dale G. Leathers summarized a good deal of research on nonverbal communication processes: "Feelings and emotions are more accurately exchanged by nonverbal than verbal means. . . . The nonverbal portion of communication conveys meanings and intentions that are relatively free from deception, distortion, and confusion."[16]

2. *The speaker's nonverbal cues enrich or elaborate the message that comes through words.* A solemn face reinforces the dignity of a wedding. The words "We must do either this or that" can be illustrated with appropriate arm-and-hand gestures. Taking a few steps to one side tells an audience you're moving from one argument to another, and a smile enhances your comment on how happy you are to be there. The degree of formality expressed through nonverbal channels also depends on the cultural context. In some cultures (Denmark, Italy), the expectation is for greater informality in public settings; in others (France, Germany), being highly formal is the requisite behavior.[17]

3. *Nonverbal messages form a reciprocal interaction between speaker and listener.* Listeners frown, smile, shift nervously in their seats, and engage in many types of nonverbal behavior. The physical presence of listeners and the natural tendency of human beings to mirror each other when close together mean that nonverbal behavior is a mechanism of social bonding. For this chapter, though, we concentrate on the speaker's control of physical behavior in four areas: proxemics, movement and stance, facial expressions, and gestures.

*A person's body also can be a communicative vehicle. Artists depend as much on the rhythm of their bodies as on their voices to communicate personality and emotional flavoring in a message.*

**Proxemics**    The use of space by human beings is called **proxemics**. Two components of proxemics are especially relevant to public speakers:

1. *Physical arrangement:* The layout of the room in which you're speaking, including the presence or absence of a lectern, the seating plan, the locations of whiteboards and similar aids, and any physical barriers between you and your audience

2. *Distance:* The extent or degree of separation between you and your audience

Both of these components bear on the message you communicate publicly. Typical speaking situations involve a speaker facing a seated audience. Objects in the physical space—the lectern, a table, several flags—tend to set the speaker apart from the listeners. This setting apart is both physical and psychological. Literally as well as figuratively, objects can stand in the way of open communication. To create a more informal atmosphere, reduce the physical barriers in the setting: You might stand beside or in front of the lectern instead of behind it. In very informal settings, you might even sit on the front edge of a table while talking. So, what influences your use of physical space?

3. *The formality of the occasion:* The more solemn or formal the occasion, the more barriers will be used. On a highly formal occasion, the speaker may even use an elevated platform or stage.

4. *The nature of the material:* Extensive quoted material or statistical evidence may require you to use a lectern; the use of visual aids often demands equipment such as an easel, laptop computer, VCR, or overhead projector.

5. *Your personal preference:* You may feel more at ease speaking from behind rather than in front of the lectern.

The distance component of proxemics adds a second set of considerations. In most situations, you'll be talking at what anthropologist Edward T. Hall has termed a *public distance*—12 feet or more from your listeners"[18] (see Figure 12.2, p. 300). To communicate with people at that distance, you obviously cannot rely on your normal speaking voice or subtle changes in posture or movement. Instead, you must compensate for the distance by using larger gestures, broader shifts of your body, and increased vocal energy. In contrast, you should lower your vocal volume and restrict the breadth of your gestures when addressing only a few individuals at a closer distance.

**Movement and Posture**    The ways you move and stand provide a second set of bodily cues for your audience. **Movement** includes physical shifts from place to place, and **posture** refers to the relative relaxation or rigidity and vertical position of the body. Movement and posture can communicate ideas about you to an audience. The speaker who stands stiffly and erectly may, without uttering a word, be saying, "This is a formal occasion" or "I'm tense, even afraid, of this audience." The speaker who leans forward, physically reaching out to the audience, often is

**FIGURE 12.2**    **Classification of Interhuman Distance**

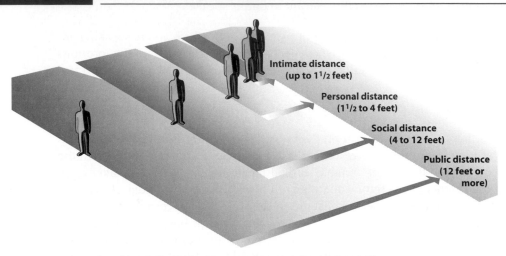

*Source:*  Based on Edward T. Hall, *The Hidden Dimension* (New York: Doubleday, 1969).

saying, "I'm interested in you. I want you to understand and accept my ideas." The speaker who sits casually on the front edge of a table and assumes a relaxed posture may suggest informality and readiness to engage in a dialogue with listeners. Note, however, that sitting on a table, crossing your legs, and showing the soles of your shoes to the audience, while normal in most U.S. settings, is viewed as anything but in some other cultures, where such actions are perceived as impolite— or even insulting.

Movement and postural adjustments regulate communication. As a public speaker, you can, for instance, move from one end of a table to the other to indicate a change in topic. You also can accomplish the same purpose by changing your posture. At other times, you can move toward your audience when making an especially important point. In each case, you're using your body to reinforce transitions in your subject or to emphasize a matter of special concern.

Keep in mind that your posture and movement can work against you, as well. Aimless and continuous pacing is distracting. Nervous bouncing and swaying makes listeners seasick. An excessively erect stance increases tension in listeners. Your movements should be purposeful and meant to enhance the meanings of your words. Use your stance and movement to help your communicative effort and produce the impressions of self-assurance and control that you want to exhibit.

**Facial Expressions**    When you speak, your facial expressions function in several ways. First, they communicate much about you and your feelings. Researchers Paul Ekman, Wallace V. Friesen, and Phoebe Ellsworth call these **affect displays**— facial signals of emotion that an audience perceives when scanning your face to see how you feel about yourself and about them.[19]

Second, facial changes provide listeners with cues that help them interpret the contents of your message. Are you being ironic or satirical? Are you sure of your conclusion? Is this a harsh or a pleasant message? Researchers tell us that a high percentage of the information conveyed in a typical message is communicated nonverbally, and psychologist Albert Mehrabian has devised a formula to account for the emotional impact of the different components of a speaker's message. Words, he says, contribute 7 percent; vocal elements, 38 percent; and facial expressions, 55 percent.[20]

Third, the display elements of your face—your eyes, especially—establish a visual bond between you and your listeners. American culture values eye contact. The speaker who looks people squarely in the eye is likely to be perceived as earnest, sincere, forthright, and self-assured. In other words, regular eye contact with listeners helps establish a speaker's credibility. Speakers who look at the floor, read from notes, or deliver speeches to the back wall sever the visual bond with their audiences and lose credibility. Conversely, some cultures place a higher value on indirect eye contact, wherein the speaker avoids making direct contact with the audience. You need to consider the people you will be talking to and ascertain their degree of comfort with direct eye contact. You cannot assume that just because you like it and understand its meaning, the audience likewise will accommodate your behavior.

Of course, you cannot control your face completely, which may be why listeners search speakers' faces so carefully for clues to their feelings. You can, however, make sure that your facial messages do not belie your verbal ones: When you're uttering angry words, your face should be communicating anger; when you're pleading with your listeners, your eyes should be engaging them intently. In short, let your face mirror your feelings. That's one of the reasons it's there!

**Gestures**   To help support and illustrate your ideas, make **gestures**—purposeful movements of the head, shoulders, arms, hands, and other areas of the body. Fidgeting with your clothing and notecards, clicking a pen, or playing with your hair are *not* purposeful gestures. They distract from the ideas you're communicating. The effective public speaker commonly uses three kinds of gestures:

1. **Conventional gestures** are physical movements with specific meanings assigned by custom or convention. These gestures condense ideas: They are shorthand expressions or symbols of things or ideas that would require many words to describe fully. A speaker can use the raised-hand "stop" gesture to interrupt listeners who are drawing premature conclusions or the "V for victory" sign when congratulating them for a job well done.

2. **Descriptive gestures** are physical movements that describe the idea to be communicated. Speakers often depict the size, shape, or location of an object by movements of their hands and arms—they draw pictures for listeners. You might indicate the size of a box by drawing it in the air with a finger or raise an arm to indicate someone's height.

3. **Indicators** are movements of the hands, arms, and other parts of the body that express feelings. Speakers throw up their arms when disgusted, pound the lectern when angry, shrug their shoulders when puzzled, and point a

threatening finger when issuing a warning. Such gestures communicate emotions to listeners and encourage similar responses in them. Facial expressions and other body cues usually reinforce such gestures.[21]

You can improve your gesturing through practice. As you practice, you'll obtain better results by keeping in mind four factors that influence the effectiveness of gestures:

1. *Relaxation is the key.* If your muscles are tense, your movements will be stiff and your gestures awkward. You should make a conscious effort to relax your muscles before you start to speak. You might warm up by taking a few steps, shrugging your shoulders, flexing your muscles, and breathing deeply.

2. *Useful gestures have vigor and definiteness.* Useful gestures are natural and animated. They reflect your emotional state and help you to physiologically describe ideas in ways that others would. Exaggerated arm movements, repetitive chopping, and random twitches of your hands call attention to your body itself, not to the ideas being formed with its aid. The best gestures reflect important mental and emotional states.

3. *Proper timing is crucial to effective gestures.* The stroke of a gesture (the shake of a fist or movement of a finger) should fall on or slightly before the point the gesture is emphasizing. Just try making a gesture after the word or phrase it was intended to reinforce has been spoken. If you do that repeatedly, you may create a comedic effect. If that is your purpose, go for it; otherwise, time it. Timing gestures effectively demands that you be in a state of readiness, usually with arms by your sides and often with your hands resting on the lectern or held in a relaxed fashion in front of your bellybutton, so they're ready to move into action. Practice making gestures until they're habitual, and then use them when you want to visualize your ideas and feelings.

4. *Appropriateness is a serious matter when facing diverse cultural groups.* Pointing at an audience or using the "A-OK" gesture may work well with most Caucasian audience members, but for non-Caucasians, these gestures are seen as insulting.[22] A quick review of information at the "webofculture" site will provide useful information on what is considered appropriate across different cultures.[23] Knowing in advance what will insult your audience or reveal your insensitivity to their cultural norms allows you to concentrate on those gestures that are appropriate to the context.

## Adapting Nonverbal Behavior to Your Presentations

You'll never completely control your physical behavior, but you can gain skill in orchestrating your gestures and other movements. You can make some conscious decisions about how to use your body together with the other channels of communication to communicate effectively. Here are some suggestions:

**Plan a proxemic relationship with your audience that reflects your own needs and attitudes toward your subject and your listeners.** If you're comfortable behind a lectern, use it; however, remember that it's a potential barrier between you and your listeners. If you want your whole body to be visible to the audience and you feel the need to have your notes at eye level, stand beside the lectern and arrange your notecards on it. If you want to relax your body, sit behind a table or desk, but compensate for the resulting loss of action by increasing your volume. If you feel relaxed and want to be open to your audience, stand in front of a table or desk. Consider your listeners' needs, as well. The farther you are from them, the more important it is for them to have a clear view of you, the harder you must work to project your words, and the broader your physical movements must be. The speaker who crouches behind a lectern in an auditorium of 300 people soon loses contact. Think of large lecture classes you've attended or outdoor political rallies you've witnessed. Recall the delivery patterns that worked effectively in such situations, and put them to work for you.

**Adapt the physical setting to your communicative needs.** If you're going to use visual aids—such as a whiteboard, flipchart, or working model—remove the tables, chairs, and other objects that might obstruct your audience's view. Increase intimacy by arranging chairs in a small circle, or stress formality by using a lectern.

**Adapt the size of your gestures and amount of your movement to the size of the audience.** Remember what Hall noted about public distance in communication, and realize that subtle changes of facial expression and small hand movements cannot be seen clearly in large rooms or auditoriums. Although many auditoriums have a raised platform and a slanted floor to enhance visibility, you should adjust to the distance between yourself and your audience by making your movements and gestures larger.

**Continuously scan your audience from side to side and front to back, looking specific individuals in the eye.** Your head should not be in constant motion, however; *continuously* does not imply rhythmic, nonstop bobbing. "Bobbleheads" may be popular collectibles right now, but you don't want to be perceived as one. Rather, take all your listeners into your field of vision periodically, and establish firm visual bonds with individuals occasionally. Such bonds enhance your credibility and keep your auditors' attention riveted on you. Some speakers identify three audience members—one to the left, one in the middle, and one to the right—and make sure they regularly move from one to another of them. For those who do not have trouble moving from side to side, another technique is to do the same thing from front to back, especially if the audience is not too big. Making sure that you're achieving even momentary eye contact with specific listeners in different parts of the audience creates the sense of visual bonding that you want.

**Use your body to communicate your feelings about what you're saying.** When you're angry, don't be afraid to gesture vigorously. When you're expressing tenderness, let that message come across your relaxed face. In other words, when you communicate publicly, use the same emotional indicators as you do when you talk to individuals on a one-to-one basis.

**Use your body to regulate the pace of your presentation and to control transitions.** Shift your weight as your speech moves from one idea to another. Move more when you're speaking more rapidly, and move less and gesture accordingly when you're slowing down to emphasize particular ideas.

**Use your full repertoire of gestures while talking publicly.** You probably do this in everyday conversation without even thinking about it, so recreate that behavior when addressing an audience. Physical readiness is the key. Let your hands rest comfortably at your sides, relaxed but ready. Then, as you unfold the ideas of your speech, use descriptive gestures to indicate sizes, shapes, and relationships, making sure the movements are large enough to be seen in the back row. Use conventional gestures to give visual dimension to your spoken ideas. Keep in mind there is no right number of gestures to use, but as you practice, think of the kinds of bodily and gestural actions that will complement your message and purpose.

Using your voice and body as the actual instruments of communication—as the vehicles that inject mere ideas with the presence and emotions of an actual human being—will significantly enhance your chances for gaining audience support for those ideas. With practice, the vocal adjustments and the physical movements that we've reviewed here will become second nature to you. You may not move with the grace of a ballerina, but you can still have impact on your audience through vocal and physical changes.

You live in a society that prizes great sound and great pictures—digitized audio and video experiences. Keep telling yourself that even more powerful than digitized reproduction is the compelling presence of a living, breathing human being. That's *you* behind the lectern. Unleash your vocal-visual potential for energized public talk.

## ■ CHAPTER SUMMARY

Speakers must learn to maximize the advantage of their face-to-face presence in oral communication, in part, by understanding that oral communication processes are at their best when talk is aggregative, agonistic/invitational, and ethically appropriate—that is, when it is completely adapted to the particular time and place in which it is occurring. Your body is a site of performance—it performs the self as you speak. Seeking synchronicity with your audience, wherein the message the body communicates is one that meets the expectations of the audience, will assist in legitimizing your performance as a speaker. Regarding practical advice on controlling your voice, remember that a flexible speaking voice

has intelligibility, variety, and understandable stress patterns. Volume, rate, enunciation, and pronunciation affect intelligibility, as do dialects. Changes in rate, pitch, stress, and pause patterns create variety in your presentations. Emotional characterizers communicate subtle shades of meaning to listeners.

Regarding nonverbal (i.e., physical or bodily) communication, three generalizations are significant: Speakers reveal and reflect their emotional states through their nonverbal behaviors; nonverbal cues enrich or elaborate the speaker's message; and nonverbal messages form bonds between the speaker and listener. Speakers knowledgeable about proxemics can use space to create physical and psychological distance or intimacy. A speaker's movement and posture can regulate thought and feeling states. Facial displays communicate feelings, provide important cues to meaning, establish a visual bond with listeners, and enforce speaker credibility. If relaxed, definite, and well-timed, gestures enhance listener response to ideas. Speakers commonly use conventional gestures, descriptive gestures, and indicators. Practice is the name of the game—practice making your voice and body effective instruments of oral communication in a society that prizes good sound and good pictures.

## KEY TERMS

affect displays (p.300)
aggregative (p.288)
agonism (p.288)
conventional gestures (p.301)
conversationality (p.291)
descriptive gestures (p.301)
dialect (p.294)
emotional characterizers (p.296)
enunciation (p.293)
ethically appropriate (p.289)
gestures (p.301)

indicators (p.301)
intelligibility (p.292)
invitational rhetoric (p.289)
*kairos* (p.289)
movement (p.299)
nonverbal communication (p.297)
optimum pitch level (p.295)
oral delivery (p.288)
paralinguistics (p.296)
pauses (p.295)
pitch (p.295)

pitch variation (p.295)
posture (p.299)
pronunciation (p.293)
proxemics (p.299)
rate (p.292)
stress (p.295)
synchronicity (p.290)
variety (p.294)
vocal emphasis (p.295)
vocal quality (p.296)
vocal stereotypes (p.294)
volume (p.292)

## ASSESSMENT ACTIVITIES

1. Divide the class into teams and play charades. (For rules, see David Jauner, "Charades as a Teaching Device," *Communication Education* 20 [1971]: 302.) A game of charades not only will loosen you up psychologically, but it will also help sensitize everyone to the variety of small but perceptible cues you read when interpreting messages. Talk about those cues at the end of the game.

2. Select a poem, and read it aloud. As you read, change your volume, rate, pitch, and emphasis and use pauses. Practice reading the poem in several ways to heighten different emotions and emphasize alternative interpretations. Record three or four readings, and play them back for evaluation. Write a paragraph on each reading—describing the sound of your voice and emotional texture—and turn them in along with the tape.

## REFERENCES

1. See, especially, Chapter 3 on the psychodynamics of sound in Walter J. Ong, *Orality and Literacy: The Technologizing of the Word* (London: Methuen, 1982).

2. Harold M. Zullow, "American Exceptionalism and the Quadrennial Peak in Optimism," in *Presidential Campaigns and American Self Images*, edited by Arthur H. Miller and Bruce E. Gronbeck (Boulder, CO: Westview Press, 1994), 214–230.

3. Sonja K. Foss and Cindy L. Griffin, "Beyond Persuasion: A Proposal for an Invitational Rhetoric," *Communication Monographs* 62 (1995): 2–18.

4. For a discussion of *kairos*, see Jane Sutton, "Kairos," in *Encyclopedia of Rhetoric*, edited by Thomas Sloane (Oxford: Oxford University Press, 2001), 413–417.

5. Elizabeth Grosz, "Bodies and Knowledge: Feminism and the Crisis of Reason," in *Feminist Epistemologies*,

edited by Linda Alcoff and Elizabeth Potter (New York: Routledge, 1993), 199. For an analysis of bodies and rhetoric, see Raymie E. McKerrow, "Corporeality and Cultural Rhetoric: A Site for Rhetoric's Future," *Southern Communication Journal* 63 (1998): 315–328.

6. David Graver, "The Actor's Bodies," *Text and Performance Quarterly* 17 (1997): 221–235.

7. Catherine Fouquet, "The Unavoidable Detour: Must a History of Women Begin with the History of Their Bodies?" in *Writing Women's History*, translated by Felicia Pheasant, edited by Michelle Perrot (Oxford: Blackwell, 1992), 55.

8. Maurice Bloch, "Introduction," in *Political Language and Oratory in Traditional Society*, edited by Maurice Bloch (New York: Academic Press, 1975), 7.

9. Kwesi Yankah, "Oratory in Akan Society," *Discourse and Society* 2 (1991): 58.

10. Thomas Frentz, "Rhetorical Conversation, Time, and Moral Action," *Quarterly Journal of Speech* 71 (1985): 1–18.

11. Mark Knapp, *Essentials of Nonverbal Communication* (New York: Holt, Rinehart and Winston, 1980).

12. Klaus R. Scherer, H. London, and Garret Wolf, "The Voice of Competence: Paralinguistic Cues and Audience Evaluation," *Journal of Research in Personality* 7 (1973): 31–44; Jitendra Thakerer and Howard Giles, "They Are—So They Spoke: Noncontent Speech Stereotypes," *Language and Communication* 1 (1981): 255–261; and Peter A. Andersen, Myron W. Lustig, and Janis F. Andersen, "Regional Patterns of Communication in the United States: A Theoretical Perspective," *Communication Monographs* 54 (1987): 128–144.

13. Bruce L. Brown, William J. Strong, and Alvin C. Rencher, "Perceptions of Personality from Speech: Effects of Manipulations of Acoustical Parameters," *Journal of the Acoustical Society of America* 54 (1973): 29–35.

14. Chris Jenks, "The Centrality of the Eye in Western Culture,"in *Visual Culture*, edited by Chris Jenks (New York: Routledge, 1995), 1.

15. For a review of research, see Judee K. Burgoon, David B. Buller, and W. Gill Woodall, *Nonverbal Communication: The Unspoken Dialogue*. 2nd ed. (New York: McGraw-Hill, 1996). For more recent research in nonverbal communication, see one or more of the following: Peter A. Andersen, Laura K. Guerrero, David B. Buller, and Peter F. Jorgensen, "An Empirical Comparison of Three Theories of Nonverbal Immediacy Exchange," *Human Communication Research* 24 (1998): 501–535; April Trees and Valerie Manusov, "Managing Face Concerns in Criticism: Integrating Nonverbal Behaviors as a Dimension of Politeness in Female Friendship Dyads," *Human Communication Research* 24 (1998): 564–583; Edward Woods, "Communication Abilities as Predictors of Verbal and Nonverbal Performance in Persuasive Interaction," *Communication Reports* 11 (1998): 167–178; and David Lapakko, "Three Cheers for Language: A Closer Examination of a Widely Cited Study of Nonverbal Communication," *Communication Education* 46 (1997): 63–67.

16. Dale G. Leathers, *Successful Nonverbal Communication: Principles and Applications*, 3rd ed. (Boston: Allyn and Bacon, 1997).

17. For a succinct review of how one might act, see Elizabeth Urech, *Speaking Globally: Effective Presentations across International and Cultural Boundaries* (Dover, NH: Kegan Page, 1998). Also see online: <www.webofculture.com>.

18. Edward T. Hall, *The Hidden Dimension* (New York: Doubleday, 1969). The important matter here is not the exact distance, of course, but the idea that speakers must vary multiple aspects of their physical and vocal behaviors as distances between them and their audiences grow.

19. Paul Ekman, Wallace V. Friesen, and Phoebe Ellsworth, *Emotion in the Human Face*, 2nd ed. (Cambridge, England: Cambridge University Press, 1982).

20. Cited in Robert Rivlin and Karen Gravelle, *Deciphering the Senses: The Expanding World of Human Perception* (New York: Simon and Schuster, 1984), 98. Of course, such numbers are only formulaic estimates and are important only as rough proportions of each other. Even if Mehrabian is off by a considerable margin, his basic point—that voice and face are the primary vehicles for emotionally bonding speakers and their audiences—is indisputable.

21. For a more complete system of classifying gestures, see Paul Ekman and Wallace V. Friesen, "Hand Movements," *Journal of Communication* 22 (1972): 360.

22. For a succinct review of gestures that are perceived as obscene, see Elizabeth Urech, *Speaking Globally: Effective Presentations across International and Cultural Boundaries* (Dover, NH: Kegan Page, 1998).

23. The "webofculture" site: http://www.webofculture.com/worldsmart/gestures.htm>.

# PART FOUR

# Types

All the ends of speaking are reducible to four; every speech being intended to enlighten the understanding, to please the imagination, to move the passion, or to influence the will. Any one discourse admits only one of these ends as the principal.

George Campbell,
*The Philosophy of Rhetoric* (1776)

# Chapter 13

# Speeches to Inform

*A student, Ben, came in one day to ask his instructor how he could make an informative speech about endangered languages relevant to his listeners. He indicated he'd checked resources on the web and had not found what he was looking for. "Well, Ben, electronic resources are fine for some things, but they are not the 'be all and end all' of research. Take a look at* Cultural Survival Quarterly, *as a recent issue focused on exactly that topic. In addition, check the media services department in the library, and ask if they have access to documentaries on native cultures," advised his instructor. Ben took the advice to heart in conducting additional research, finding that, indeed, the* Quarterly *was useful and that the library did have additional resources he could use.*

As we've tried to suggest, limiting your research to the web, as easy a resource as that is to connect with for many, does not necessarily provide all of the information you might find useful. Finding relevant information that attracts the attention of your audience is what informative speaking is all about.

In this chapter, we first talk about information and the processes whereby *facts* become usable human *knowledge.* Conveying knowledge, however, without motivating your audience to listen to what you have to say is an exercise in futility. Hence, as we begin the focus first on informative and then on persuasive, argumentative, and ceremonial speeches, it is well to take some time to examine the basic motives that you might tap in gaining and maintaining audience interest. Then, we discuss the essential features of informative speeches, after which we can examine four types of speeches and ways of building them to maximize your chances for success.

## Facts, Knowledge, and the Information Age

American society seems to worship facts. A staggering amount of information is available to us, particularly because of technologies such as electronic media, photostatic printing, miniaturized circuitry, fax machines, and digitized data storage and retrieval systems. Jumping onto America Online or your school's access to the World Wide Web puts you on an Information Superhighway with more—and bigger—lanes than the Santa Monica Freeway. The entire Indiana University library is available online, as are major collections of data from around the world. Today, Detective Joe Friday from the old *Dragnet* television series would never dare say "Just the facts, Ma'am," for he'd immediately drown in data.

Furthermore, as Joe Friday knew, mere facts are not enough. Until he put those facts into a coherent order that turned them into the elements of a scenario—a story of a crime—he had nothing but isolated factoids. Only after that information was patterned and hooked in cause-effect chains, and only after those chains were contextualized into the lives of particular people, did the facts produce the story of the crime. Joe Friday not only had to gather the facts but also humanize them—that is, use them to probe motivations, plausible human activities, and matters of opportunity and access to the means of crime. Without structuring, clarifying, and interpreting facts, the information at hand is all but useless.

Information must be turned by competent speakers into knowledge. Think of **facts** as statements about the world upon which two or more people agree. "The Gronbecks' house is 44 feet long" is a fact, which could be verified by some folks taking a tape measure to it. **Information** is a collection of facts associated with some topic. Consider the information shown in Table 13.1, which is derived from the 2,567 sites Shopsearch lists for those wishing to order items via the Internet.

The challenge is to turn this collection of information into human **knowledge**—information given human significance—through your own interpretation. For example, approximately 70 percent and 80 percent of the stores in Table 13.1 report orders via traditional means: mail and phone, respectively. A little less than two-thirds of the sites report orders coming via fax or e-mail. What does this mean? The Internet is growing as a source for orders via e-mail, but the many orders using more traditional means suggest people still are accustomed to older—and perhaps slower—ways of doing things. On the other hand, the growth of

**TABLE 13.1**     **Ordering Methods on the Internet**

| ORDER METHOD | NUMBER OF STORES | PERCENT |
|---|---|---|
| E-mail | 1,514 | 58.97 |
| E-mail (PGP) | 9 | 0.35 |
| Fax | 1,532 | 59.68 |
| Form (secure) | 1,079 | 42.03 |
| Form (unsecure) | 630 | 24.52 |
| Mail | 1,740 | 67.78 |
| Phone | 2,010 | 78.30 |

*Source:* Information available online: <http://www.shopsearch.com/stats/htm>, accessed August 25, 2001.

e-mail and fax orders also suggests that e-commerce is a growing phenomenon. Your *interpretation* connects the *facts* with human activity, thereby transforming mere facts into useful *knowledge* of buying habits.

This is what informative speaking is about: turning facts into information and then information into knowledge. To make the most of your interpretation of facts and their presentation to audiences, you also need to think in terms of the motives people have for listening to your ideas.

# Motivational Appeals: Engaging Listeners Where They Are

For our purposes, human behavior will be divided into two categories: activity that results from biological needs, drives, and stimuli and activity that results from social motives, desires, and deliberate intent.[1] External stimuli such as a stuffy room also can affect your physiological state, and attending classes between noon and 1 P.M. affects students' concentration because they're thinking about food. Satisfying a **biological need,** then, is a matter of giving in to or meeting a physiological urge. **Social motives,** however, are individual goals, desires, and behaviors that result from acting in accordance with your understanding of what others expect or value. Appeals can tap both biological and social motives. "What's a baseball game without a hot dog?" has the potential to appeal to hunger (you rushed to get to the game and haven't eaten yet) and to tradition (eating a hot dog just goes with the game). As this example attests, most biological and social motives are relatively enduring and intimately linked to the cultural environment of your own community. A word to the wise: Never underestimate the power of speech in tapping human desires and, thus, in altering beliefs, attitudes, and values.

## Classifying Motives

To enable you to tap into those desires, we first introduce two classification systems that can help you group or cluster individual motives. Then, we define *motivational appeal* and illustrate ways of expressing individual motives within speeches.

**Maslow's Hierarchy of Needs**    A now-classic approach to the study of motives was proposed by Abraham Maslow. **Maslow's hierarchy of needs** has had a major impact on consumer-oriented studies of marketing and sales and on the field of communication studies. According to Maslow, the following categories of needs and desires drive people to think, act, and respond (see also Figure 13.1, p. 312):

- *Physiological:* The needs for food, drink, air, sleep, and sex—the basic bodily tissue requirements

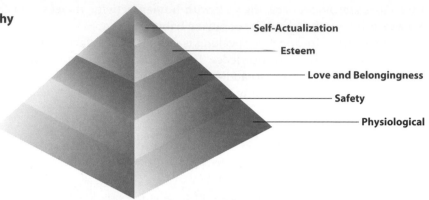

**FIGURE 13.1**

**Maslow's Hierarchy of Needs**

Self-Actualization

Esteem

Love and Belongingness

Safety

Physiological

■ *Safety:* The needs for security, stability, protection from harm and injury, structure, orderliness, predictability, and freedom from fear and chaos

■ *Love and belongingness:* The needs for devotion and warm affection from lovers, spouses, children, parents, and close friends; for feeling a part of social groups; and for acceptance and approval

■ *Esteem:* The needs for self-esteem based on achievement, mastery, competence, confidence, freedom, and independence and for recognition by others expressed in reputation, prestige, recognition, and status

■ *Self-actualization:* The needs for self-fulfillment, for realizing individual potential and actualizing capabilities, and for being true to the essential self and satisfying an aesthetic sensibility[2]

These needs and desires interrelate biological and social motives. In Maslow's theory, lower-level needs usually must be satisfied, either in whole or in part, before higher-order desires become operative. Maslow labels this interrelationship the **hierarchy of prepotency,** which is best exemplified by considering the plight of people who are homeless: They have little time and energy to worry much about esteem or self-actualization, so appeals to such needs would fall on deaf ears in the soup kitchens of U.S. cities. To Maslow, needs or motivational appeals must be aimed at that level in the hierarchy where individuals' lives are centered. For the homeless, which needs are most salient at any given moment? Food and shelter would appear to be more significant needs than self-actualization. Using Maslow's strategy focuses your message on the most critical level of the hierarchy—where your audience will receive the greatest impact of the appeal being made.

**McClelland's Motive Types**     Generally, there are three primary motives under which more specific drives can be subsumed: affiliation, achievement, and power or social influence. **Affiliation motives** focus on the desire to belong to a group, to be well liked and accepted. **Achievement motives** relate both to the intrinsic and extrinsic desires for success, adventure, creativity, and personal enjoyment. **Power motives** involve activities in which influence over others is the primary objective.[3] These broad clusters are critical in considering your overall purpose in speaking. For example, consider the distinction between affiliation and power: Will you appeal to your listeners' sense of belongingness or their sense of dominance? It's important, as well, to think of the relationships between power and achievement motives: Do you approach audience members with a focus on their desires to control others or their hopes for personal development and self-satisfaction? **McClelland's motive types,** also discussed in motivational literature under the heading **three needs theory,** help you target your exploration of the specific appeal that might be most useful in addressing your audience. These motive clusters also fit well with Maslow's hierarchical approach, as Table 13.2 illustrates.

## Motive Clusters

Thus far, we've treated motives as general concepts. Translating any of these into specific appeals is the focus of this section. We now are ready to move from Maslow's hierarchy and McClelland's motive types to employing specific appeals in speeches. By understanding the general thrust of each **motive cluster** and its specific appeals, you'll be in a good position to choose from among the appeals we've identified when preparing your speeches and to come up with others we don't deal with. In selecting specific appeals, be guided by one principle: Motivational appeals work only when they are relevant to audience members and have features that listeners can visualize or relate to beliefs or values on which they want to act. Because the motive terms virtually are self-explanatory, the following list identifies a motive term and a phrase that would be typical in its use. As you read, see how many more phrases you can create that express the motive term. For ease of reference, we employ *affiliation, achievement,* and *power* as the key clusters or groupings under which the motive terms fall.

**The Affiliation Cluster**　　Affiliation motives are dominated by a desire for acceptance or approval. They're focused more on the social or interpersonal bonds attributed to people than on personal success or power over others.[4]

**TABLE 13.2**　　**Comparing Maslow and McClelland**

| MOTIVE APPEAL | MASLOW | McCLELLAND |
| --- | --- | --- |
| Prestige | Esteem | Achievement |
| Loyalty | Belongingness | Affiliation |
| Authority | Self-actualization | Power |

**Companionship:**  Birds of a feather flock together.

**Conformity:**  To get along, you need to go along.

**Deference/dependence:**  Nine out of ten doctors recommend . . .

**Sympathy/generosity:**  For only one dollar a day, you could be the parent this child has never known.

**Loyalty:**  For the past 10 years, those who have worked for the company the longest, who have lived through the bad times as well as the good times, have been the foundation on which our success is based; as new employees, I hope you will follow their example; if you do, we will surely prosper well into the future.

**Tradition:**  It is through our sacred rituals and ceremonies that we are known as a people.

**Reverence/worship:**  As God gives us the light to see the right, so will we act.

**The Achievement Cluster**     Achievement motives are focused on individual urges, desires, and goals—concerns for self and for excellence, prestige, and success. The fourth and fifth levels of Maslow's hierarchy generally fit here. Once your basic physiological and social needs are satisfied, you become centered on personal accomplishment. These motivational appeals are aimed at individual members of the audience.

**Acquisition/saving:**  Earn good money now in our new Checking-Plus accounts!

**Success/display:**  Successful executives carry the Connerton electronic organizer.

**Pride:**  Lose weight through our diet plan, and feel great about your body.

**Prestige:**  Harley Davidson—The Legend Rolls On.

**Adventure/change:**  Come to Marlboro Country!

**Perseverance:**  If at first you don't succeed, try, try again.

**Creativity:**  Dare to be different: Design your own major!

**Curiosity:**  Curiosity killed the cat; satisfaction brought him back.

**Personal enjoyment:**  Let the good times roll!

**The Power Cluster**     All appeals in the power cluster focus on influence or control over others or the environment. All motives in this group feature appeals to one's place in the social hierarchy—a dominant place. People with power motives seek to manipulate or control others, but not all uses of power are negative. With power comes social responsibility—the demand that power be used in socially approved ways to benefit the group, community, and society. Appeals to power also depend heavily on appeals to affiliation because power is most constructively used when people see it as being in their best interest to grant power to another. Appeals to power are not equivalent to forcing people to do things. Ethically, you'll need to reconcile appeals to power with those to the affiliation needs of your audience to maximize your chance of success.

**Aggression:** We must fight for our rights—if we are to be heard, we dare not allow others to silence us.

**Authority/dominance:** Under our organization's by-laws, we have the right to pursue issues in the manner we have undertaken.

**Defense:** Only a mean-spirited and vindictive person would draw conclusions prior to having heard all of the available information; we need to give the accused the chance to clear her name.

**Fear:** Friends don't let friends drive drunk.

**Autonomy/independence:** Just do it.

In specific terms, a **motivational appeal** is an attempt to code or translate a biological or social motive into language. Consider using the social motive *prestige:* "If you're elected president of this organization, people will look up to you" is an attempt to work an appeal to prestige into the language of a speech. You have two choices when attempting to encode motives into the language of speech: the **visualization process** (verbal depiction),[5] in which you project a scene or setting in which people are enjoying the advantages of accepting your ideas, and the **attribution process** (verbal association), in which you claim that someone is acting on the basis of specific motives.

Suppose you want your classmates to join in a demonstration against a proposed tuition hike when the board of regents is in town next month. Most students would, of course, like to see the school hold the line on tuition, but many will be reluctant to protest publicly. Your best bet to engage them might well be to visualize various motives:

Just think of what we can accomplish. If we all `Affiliation` gather in front of the administration building, we can show the regents that this is a serious matter. We can show the regents that we're as much a part of the decision-making process as they are `Authority` and that our voice `Independence` deserves to be heard as much as theirs. When we present our petition to the president of the board, even after he's tried to ignore us, `Perseverance` he'll see that we're serious and will have to admit we have a right to be heard `Success/display` . There's no need to be afraid `Fear` when you're among friends `Companionship` in a cause that's right `Pride` . On that day, we'll demonstrate our solidarity `Loyalty` and force the board `Aggression` to listen to our side of the story!

You also can relate motivational concepts directly to other concepts through what is technically called *a process of attribution*. Instead of seeking to visualize the appeal in the audience's mind, you assert an association between an object and a specific motive appeal. You do this everyday when claiming someone acted on the basis of specific motive, such as honesty or conformity. In addition, through *redefinition* and *relabeling*, you can change the audience's attributes that they associate with a specific event or person:

> While the political candidate for governor has been labeled in the press as uncaring and unconcerned about our situation, I can tell you from firsthand experience that she is indeed committed to our cause.

This process of attribution attempts to shift from a negative motive attributed to a person to one that is positive.

This discussion of individual motivational appeals is not designed to present the human psyche as if it were orderly and consistent. Rather, we're trying to give you a basic understanding of human motivation and various kinds of appeals you can use to enhance your rhetorical effectiveness. Even in all their confusing aspects, humans usually act in a motivated way. Hence, we turn next to questions concerning the use of these appeals in speech development.

## Using Motivational Appeals in Speech Preparation

The material we've discussed thus far raises an extremely important question: How do you decide which motivational appeals to use in your speech? Precise choices depend on the specific group of listeners you face, the occasion, and even your own preferences and motives for speaking. Even so, three general factors should guide your thinking about motivational appeals: the type of speech you are to give, the demographic characteristics of your audience, and your personal predilections.

Throughout the discussion of motivational appeals, we've suggested that thinking about the type of speech you're delivering will help you select appeals. For example, appeals to individuality often appear in persuasive and actuative speeches, the goals of which are to free people from previous modes of thinking.

MOTIVATIONAL APPEALS: DEVELOPING AN INTEGRATED SET

**General purpose:**  To persuade/actuate

**Specific purpose:**  To have classmates pursue a flexible Bachelor of General Studies (BGS) degree

**Claim:**  For many students, the BGS is the best available college degree.

**Appeal to creativity**

Without a major and with few requirements, the BGS allows you to build a program suited to your individual desires.

Break away from the crowd, and do something unique in structuring your life here.

Appeal to adventure

Explore subjects as deeply as you wish.

Appeal to curiosity

Get a feeling of achievement from designing and completing your own program.

Appeal to success

In contrast, speeches also can tap into collective motives—tradition, companionship, defense, deference, conformity, and loyalty. Exploring the demographic characteristics of your audience members—their age, educational level, and so on—also helps you sort through possible motivational appeals. As noted, for example, people who have little need to be concerned about survival and safety will more likely respond to appeals to creativity, independence, personal enjoyment, and generosity. As Maslow's hierarchy of prepotency suggests, a speech on urban renewal presented to inner-city tenement dwellers should feature discussions of food, shelter, and safety rather than achievement and self-actualization. Appeals to ethnic traditions and a sense of belonging work well with homogeneous audiences gathered to celebrate such occasions as Hispanic Heritage Week (*Cinco de Mayo*) and Norwegian Independence Day (*Syttende Mai*). Consider, too, McClelland's analysis of motive types, particularly the relationship between affiliation and power motives.

*Advertisers adapt motivational appeals to target audiences. This advertisement appears in a magazine aimed at a professional female audience. How might it be revised for a magazine with an audience of homemakers?*

# ETHICAL MOMENTS

## Your Ethical Boundaries

What appeals would you refuse to make? What are your ethical limits? Consider the following examples:

**1** Afraid that your listeners will not take your concerns about inadequate protections against theft seriously, you embellish statistical data obtained from campus security. Some incidents happened, but you make them appear more frequent and more serious than the statistics suggest.

> **Honesty in relation to appropriateness of authority appeal**

**2** Would you show third-graders pictures of mouth sores and completely decayed teeth as a way of getting them to brush and floss better?

> **Appropriateness of fear appeal**

**3** Would you bring pictures of fetuses to class to show the audience what happens to the unborn during an abortion?

> **Appropriateness of fear appeal**

**4** Would you tell your classmates they can earn up to $5,000 a month selling encyclopedias, even though commissions average only $300 dollars a month?

> **Honesty/openness in relation to success appeal**

Your reputation, credibility, or ethos is created largely by what you say and what others think about what you say. Know the limits of your audience, and more importantly, know your *own* limits. In that way, you won't be surprised when listeners question the motivational appeals you have employed. In the process, anything you do to promote the common good and the basic humanity of others will earn you many points in life.

ILLUSTRATING THE INTEGRATION OF MOTIVATIONAL APPEALS

**General purpose:** To persuade/actuate

**Specific purpose:** To convince the nonprofessional employees at your school that they need a labor union

*On joining the union for reasons of affiliation:*

**Conformity**    All your friends are joining.

**Dependence**    The union has leaders with the strength to stand up for your rights.

**Sympathy**    Unions understand the way you live and what you need better than university professors do.

*On joining the union for reasons of power:*

If you don't fight for your rights, who will?

**Aggression**

With the union, you can take charge of your workplace and run it properly.

**Dominance**

Without a union, you can be dismissed from your job at any time and for any reason.

**Fear**

**General purpose:**  To persuade/actuate

**Specific purpose:**  To convince listeners to take a summer trip to Europe

The tour is being offered for a low price of $2,000 for three weeks.

**Acquisition and savings**

There'll be a minimum of supervision and regimentation.

**Independence**

You'll be traveling with friends and fellow students.

**Companionship**

These two examples give you a clear sense of how to integrate affiliation and power and add achievement to the mix in planning a speech. Never will it be the case, of course, that the audience is all achievement oriented, affiliation oriented, or power oriented; life is not that simple. Assessing tendencies, however, will help you select the appeals you want to feature.

In addition, always look to your personal predilections—your own beliefs, attitudes, and values—when framing motivational appeals. Ask yourself questions like these: Am I willing to ask people to act out of fear, or am I committed instead to higher motives such as sympathy and generosity? Do I actually believe in the importance of loyalty and reverence as they relate to this situation? See the "Ethical Moments" box on the preceding page for some scenarios that will help test your ethical boundaries.

In short, use the appeals that you think are important—and that you can defend to yourself and others. Appeals mean little without a context for their activation, and informing audiences is one such context.

# Essential Features of Informative Speeches

Your goal as an informative speaker is to make it easy for your listeners to acquire and retain new information. In addition to using motivational appeals, three other tactics will help ensure your listeners understand and remember what you say: (1) the clearer your message, the better they will follow your ideas; (2) associating new ideas with familiar ones will also assist in their understanding, and

(3) visualizing ideas through words in a manner that is relevant to their experience will aid in their ability to recall your message. Ultimately, your goal is to communicate in a manner that is directly relevant to the lives of your listeners.

## Clarity

Informative speeches achieve maximum clarity when listeners can follow and understand what you're saying. Clarity is largely the result of two factors: effective organization and word choice.

**Effective Organization**    Effective organization is a matter of grouping or clustering your ideas clearly and connecting then into a coherent whole. This can be accomplished in three specific ways:

**Limit your points.**  Confine your speech to three or four principal ideas, grouping whatever facts and ideas you wish to consider under these main headings. Even if you know a tremendous amount about your subject matter, remember that you cannot make everyone an expert with a single speech.

**Use transitions to show relationships among ideas.** Word your transitions carefully. Make sure to indicate the relationship of the upcoming point to the rest of your ideas. Consider these example, which use transitions to allow listeners to follow you from point to point:

> Second, you must prepare the chair for caning by cleaning out the groove and cane holes.
> The Stamp Act Crisis was followed by an even more important event—the Townshend Duties.
> To test these hypotheses, we set up the following experiment.

**Keep your speech moving forward.**  Rather than jump back and forth between ideas, charging ahead and then backtracking, develop a positive, forward direction. Move from basic ideas to more complex ones, from background data to current research, or from historical incidents to current events.

You can also use your listeners' natural perceptions to help cluster information. The next "How to" box discusses principles of perception and cognition that are useful in organizing ideas.

**Word Choice**    The second factor in achieving clarity is being understood. You can develop understanding through careful selection of your words. For a fuller discussion on use of language, see Chapter 10; for now, think about the following ways to achieve clarity:

**Keep your vocabulary precise and accurate—not too technical.** For instance, to tell someone how to finish off a basement room, you might say:

> Next, take one of these long sticks, cut it off in this funny-looking gizmo with a saw in it, and try to make the corners match.

An accurate vocabulary, however, will help your listeners remember what supplies and tools to get when they approach the same project:

> This is a ceiling molding; it goes around the room between the wall and the ceiling to cover the seams between the paneling and the ceiling tiles. You make the corners of the molding match by using a mitre box, which has grooves that allow you to cut 45-degree angles. Here's how you do it.

# How to
# Use Psychological Principles for Clarity

Many speakers find clustering items of information is often useful because it makes ideas much easier for listeners to grasp and retain. For more than a century, psychologists have been interested in discovering why things appear the way they do to us. Four principles of perception and cognition are still current in the literature:

1. *Proximity* suggests that elements close together seem to organize into units of perception; you see a pair made up of a ball and a block, not sets of blocks and sets of balls.
2. *Similarity* suggests that like objects usually are grouped together; you see three columns rather than three rows of items.
3. *Closure* is the tendency to complete suggested shapes; you see the figure of a tiger even though the lines are not joined.
4. *Symmetry* suggests that balanced objects are more pleasing to perceive than unbalanced ones.

These four principles suggest ways to cluster ideas in your speeches:

1. Put your most important ideas close together, so they can play off each other.
2. Construct your main points in similar ways grammatically to make the structure stand out.
3. Offer enough typical examples to allow for closure.
4. Balance your treatments of the main ideas to give a sense of symmetry—for example, use parallel sentences.

Following these principles can help you organize your speeches to take advantage of your listeners' natural perceptions.

**For Further Reading**

Anderson, John R. *Cognitive Psychology and Its Implications*, 5th ed. (New York: W.H. Freeman, 2000).

Rock, Irvin. *Perception*, reprint ed. (New York: W. H. Freeman, 1995).

Spence, Robert. *Information Visualization* (Boston: Addison-Wesley, 2000).

**Simplify when possible.**  If your speech on the operation of a two-cycle internal combustion engine sounds like it came from the documentation for computer software, then it's too technical. An audience bogged down in unnecessary detail and complex vocabulary can become confused and bored, so include only as much technical vocabulary as needed.

**Use reiteration to clarify complex ideas.**  Rephrasing helps solidify ideas for those who did not get them the first time. You might say, for example:

> Unlike a terrestrial telescope, a celestial telescope is used for looking at moons, planets, and stars; that is, its mirrors and lens are ground and arranged in such a way that it focuses on objects thousands of miles—not hundreds of feet—away from the observer.

In this case, the idea is rephrased; the words are not simply repeated.

## Associating New Ideas with Familiar Ones

Audiences grasp new facts and ideas more readily when they can associate them with what they already know. In a speech to inform, try to connect the new with the old (see Figure 13.2). To do this, you need to know enough about your audience to choose relevant experiences, images, analogies, and metaphors.

Sometimes, the associations you should make are obvious. A college dean talking to an audience of manufacturers on the problems of higher education presented her ideas under the headings of raw material, casting, machining, polishing, and assembling. She translated her central ideas into an analogy that her audience, given their vocation, would understand. If you cannot think of any

---

**FIGURE 13.2**

**Association of New Ideas with Familiar Ones**

**Snail Shell
(Single Unit)**

**House
(Single Unit)**

**Honeycomb
(Multiunit)**

**Condominum
(Multiunit)**

obvious associations, you may have to rely on common experiences and images. For instance, you might explain the operation of the pupil in a human eye by comparing it to the operation of a camera lens aperture, or you could explain a cryogenic storage tank by comparing it to a thermos bottle.

## Relevant Visualizations

Perhaps the bottom line in presenting information to others is the matter of *relevance:* Unless you make the information relevant to the needs, interests, anxieties, areas of known ignorance, or material conditions of people in your audience, they'll ignore you. You cannot be clear unless you know what they already know, and you cannot associate new ideas with familiar ones if you don't know what's familiar to them. Clustering ideas works only if the scheme you choose piques their interests, and motivational appeals are nothing without knowledge regarding the motivational triggers of others. You have to know what sets them off.

In seeking to make information relevant to audiences, you're going to have to create word pictures, such as these drawn by Jesse Jackson:

> The very issues that seem racial in content when viewed from the lens of a place like Chicago turn out not to be racial at all when viewed from the lens of Appalachia.
>
> If I were to give the same speech in Harlem as I'm giving you tonight, America would miss the point.
>
> That's why Robert F. Kennedy held a white baby from Appalachia in his arms when he was trying to rouse the conscience of a nation. That's why LBJ came to Athens when he launched his war on poverty.[6]

Jackson uses specific illustrations that are strong in affiliative appeals to connect his ideas to his listeners. *Verbal depiction,* or **visualization**, is a classic yet contemporary strategy for making information and viewpoints relevant to listeners' lives.[7]

# Types of Informative Speeches

Now that we've looked at some of the essential features of competently executed informative speeches, let's examine some of the types of informative speeches you'll be asked to make during your lifetime. There are many different types of speech forms into which information is placed, and the choice of which form to use depends upon the situation and level of knowledge possessed by listeners. Four of those forms—definitional speeches, instructional and demonstration speeches, oral briefings, and explanatory speeches—occur so frequently, however, that they merit our attention. They represent four different yet common ways in which people package or integrate information to meet the needs of others.

*Informative speeches take many forms. A definitional speech presents concepts or processes so as to make them relevant to listeners. An instructional speech explains a complex process verbally, and a demonstration speech adds a nonverbal illustration of such a process. A speaker giving an oral briefing assembles, arranges, and interprets information in response to a group's request. In an explanatory speech, a speaker clarifies the connections among concepts, processes, or events.*

## Definitional Speeches

> Dad, what's a *latchkey kid?*

> Professor Delroy, what are the differences among copper wire phone connections, ISDN phone connections, and coaxial cable connections so far as modem operations are concerned?

> Now, John, I know this is a dumb question, but what's a *dual-agency realtor,* and what's in it for me?

You've been asking questions like this all of your life. In many cases, a dictionary definition just does not help. A **definitional speech** seeks to present a concept or process in a way that makes it relevant to listeners. Once Sarina knows what a latchkey kid is, she'll understand what she's been called and will want to know whether that's good or bad. Once you know about different modem-computer connections, you'll be able to assess how much it's worth to you to pay for faster data transmission. Once you understand that John's able to serve both you and a seller better if he's a dual-agency realtor, you'll know how to approach an offer you want to bid on a house. As these examples suggest, definitional speeches demand that you present ideas clearly and coherently. This means that the ways in which you structure them are very important.

**Attention**     Because definitional speeches treat either unfamiliar or familiar concepts in a new light, their introductions must create curiosity about the issues to be discussed. Creating curiosity is a special challenge in speeches on unfamiliar concepts. We're all tempted to say, "Well, if I've made it this far in life without knowing anything about black holes or carcinogens or trap blocking, why should I bother with learning more about these ideas now?" You need to make people wonder about the unknown. Use new information to attract attention and arouse curiosity.

**Need**    Definitional speeches also must be attentive to the needs or wants of the audience. In other words, their introductions should include explicit statements that indicate how the information can affect the listeners, such as the following:

> Understanding the dynamics of trap blocking will help you better appreciate line play in football and thereby increase your enjoyment of the game every Saturday afternoon in our stadium.

**Satisfaction**    Most definitional speeches use a topical pattern in satisfying the need to listen that has been created. In many cases, these speeches describe various aspects of an object or idea. It seems natural, for example, to use a topical pattern for a speech on computer programming careers, organizing the satisfaction portion of the speech around topics such as the duties of a computer programmer, the skills needed by a computer programmer, and the training needed to become a computer programmer.

There are occasions, however, when other patterns may serve your specific purpose even better than a topical pattern. You might use an effect-cause pattern, for example, when preparing an informative speech on the laws of supply and demand. You also could enumerate a series of effects with which people are already familiar—changing prices at the gas pump—and then discuss the laws of supply and demand that account for such changes.

**Visualization**    Once you have satisfied the need to know, you will want to add this step if you have not yet illustrated how this information impacts the audience—what difference it makes in knowing the information. Although visualization is primarily useful in persuasive/actuative speeches, conveying to your audience in explicit fashion why the information is useful to them may be desirable.

**Action**    In drawing the speech to a close, as suggested in Chapter 7, focus on what you want the audience to carry away with them—the central point that is essential to remember as you conclude. Generally, the action step in a definitional speech has two characteristics: a summary of the main points and a stress on the ways in which people can apply the ideas presented. For example, a speaker discussing diabetes could conclude by offering listeners the titles of books containing more information, the phone number of the American Diabetes Association, the address of a local clinic, or the meeting time and place of a diabetics support group.

**Sample Outline**    A speech defining diabetes could be outlined in a topical pattern as in the following sample outline.[8] Notice several features of this speech:

- The speaker attempts early in the speech to engage listeners' curiosity and review listeners' personal needs to draw the audience into the topic. The use of a personal example is particularly good for this kind of speech.
- The speaker offers statistics on diabetes early so that the audience knows the disease is widespread and serious.

■ Three topics are previewed and then developed in the body of the speech to engage three aspects of listeners' thinking.

■ After offering a summary of the central idea, the speaker returns to the personal example, adding closure to the speech.

## Sample Outline for a Definitional Speech
### *What Is Diabetes?*

**ATTENTION**

A motivation for listening is provided.

I. I never knew my grandmother. She was a talented artist. She raised six kids without all the modern conveniences, like microwave ovens and electric clothes dryers, and my dad still talks about the time she foiled a would-be burglar by locking him in a broom closet until the police came. My grandmother had diabetes. It finally took her life. Now my sister has it. So do 13 million other Americans.

**NEED**

Supporting testimony shows the severity of the disease.

I. Diabetes threatens millions of lives, and it's one of nature's stealthiest diseases.

II. It's important to understand this disease because more than likely, you or someone you know will eventually have to deal with it.

Listeners are warned that ignorance makes the problem worse.

   A. Diabetes is the third-leading cause of death behind heart disease and cancer, according to the American Diabetes Association.

   B. More than one-third of those suffering from the disease don't even know they have it. That simple knowledge could make the difference between a happy, productive life and an early death.

The scope of the problem is expanded.

   C. Furthermore, diabetes is implicated in many other medical problems: It contributes to coronary heart disease; it accounts for 40 percent of all amputations and most new cases of blindness.

The three main ideas of the speech are previewed.

   D. In the next few minutes, let's look at three things you should know about "the silent killer," diabetes—what it is, how it affects people, and how it can be controlled.

**SATISFACTION**

The first main point is stated.

I. What is diabetes?

Diabetes is defined in medical terms.

   A. Diabetes is a chronic disease of the endocrine system that affects your body's ability to deliver glucose to its cells.

The symptoms of diabetes are explained.

   B. The symptoms of diabetes, according to Dr. Charles Kilo, are weight loss despite eating and drinking, constant hunger and thirst, frequent urination, and fatigue.

The second main point is provided.

II. How does diabetes affect people?

Type I diabetes is operationally defined.

   A. Type I diabetes occurs when your body cannot produce insulin, a substance that delivers glucose to your cells.

1. Only 5 to 10 percent of all diabetics have Type I.
2. This type, also known as *juvenile diabetes,* usually shows up during the first 20 years of life.
3. Type I diabetes can be passed on genetically but also is thought to be triggered by environmental agents, such as viruses.
4. Type I diabetics must take insulin injections to treat the disease.

B. Type II diabetes occurs when your body produces insulin but fails to use it effectively.
1. Of all diabetics, 90 to 95 percent have Type II.
2. This type usually shows up after a person turns 40.
3. It often affects people who are overweight; more women are affected than men.
4. Insulin injections sometimes are used to treat the disease.

**VISUALIZATION**

I. How is diabetes controlled?
A. Type I diabetes cannot be cured, but it can be controlled.
1. Patients must take insulin injections, usually several times a day.
2. Patients need to monitor their blood sugar levels by pricking a finger and testing a drop of blood.
3. According to *Science News,* several new treatments are available:
   a. One new device uses near-infrared beams to determine blood sugar level.
   b. Insulin can be taken through the nose or in pill form.
   c. Pancreatic transplants have been performed with limited success.
B. Type II diabetes can be controlled through lifestyle modifications.
1. Usually, these diabetics are required to lose weight by exercising, according to Dr. JoAnn Manson.
2. Changes in diet also are required.
3. Some people take oral hypoglycemic medications that stimulate the release of insulin and foster insulin activity.
4. If these modifications fail, Type II diabetics must take insulin injections.

**ACTION**

I. Diabetes is a serious disease in which the body no longer can produce or use insulin effectively.

II. The two types of diabetes occur at different stages in life and require different measures for control of the disease.

III. My grandmother lived with her diabetes for years but eventually lost her life to it. My sister has the advantages of new treatments and future research in her fight with diabetes.

IV. As we age, many of us will be among the 600,000 new cases of diabetes each year. Through awareness, we can cope effectively with this silent killer.

---

**Supporting statistics show the scope of this type.**

**Type II diabetes is operationally defined. Notice how this section of the speech parallels the preceding section in development.**

**The third main point is provided.**

**The treatments for Type I are explained.**

**The treatments for Type II are explained.**

**The three main ideas are reiterated.**

**The speech reaches closure by referring to the introductory personal example.**

**Listeners are warned that diabetes could affect them.**

talking—demonstrating your material while explaining aloud what you're doing. Decide where you'll stand when showing a slide, so the audience can see both you and the image. Practice talking about your aerobic exercise positions while you're actually doing them. Work a dough press in practice sessions as you tell your mythical audience how to form professional-looking cookies. If you do not, you'll inevitably get into trouble before your real audience. For other tips on using visual aids, see Chapter 11.

**Action** In instructional and demonstration speeches, this stage usually has three parts:

1. ***Summary.*** Most audiences need this review, which reminds them to question any procedures or ideas they don't understand.
2. ***Encouragement.*** People trying new processes or procedures usually get in trouble the first few times and need reassurance that this is predictable and can be overcome.
3. ***Offer to help.*** What sounded so simple in your talk may be much more complicated in execution. If possible, make yourself available for assistance or point to other sources of further information and assistance:

    As you fill out your registration form, just raise your hand if you're unsure of anything, and I'll be happy to help you.

    Here's the address of the governor's office.

    Such statements not only offer help, but they also assure your listeners they won't be labeled as dimwitted if they ask for it.

**Sample Outline** Thinking through requirements of instructional and demonstration speeches might result in a speaking outline like the following one on how to make Shanghai wontons.[9]

## Sample Outline for a Demonstration Speech

### *How to Make Shanghai Wontons*

**ATTENTION**

**Listeners' interest is aroused by using questions.**

I. Have you ever eaten small Chinese dumplings, or *wontons?*

II. Have you ever made wontons? Well, you can learn, as I did from my Shanghainese mother. The steps are very simple and easy to follow, as I will illustrate.

    1. Only 5 to 10 percent of all diabetics have Type I.

    2. This type, also known as *juvenile diabetes,* usually shows up during the first 20 years of life.

    3. Type I diabetes can be passed on genetically but also is thought to be triggered by environmental agents, such as viruses.

    4. Type I diabetics must take insulin injections to treat the disease.

  B. Type II diabetes occurs when your body produces insulin but fails to use it effectively.

    1. Of all diabetics, 90 to 95 percent have Type II.

    2. This type usually shows up after a person turns 40.

    3. It often affects people who are overweight; more women are affected than men.

    4. Insulin injections sometimes are used to treat the disease.

> Supporting statistics show the scope of this type.
>
> Type II diabetes is operationally defined. Notice how this section of the speech parallels the preceding section in development.

## VISUALIZATION

I. How is diabetes controlled?

  A. Type I diabetes cannot be cured, but it can be controlled.

    1. Patients must take insulin injections, usually several times a day.

    2. Patients need to monitor their blood sugar levels by pricking a finger and testing a drop of blood.

    3. According to *Science News,* several new treatments are available:

      a. One new device uses near-infrared beams to determine blood sugar level.

      b. Insulin can be taken through the nose or in pill form.

      c. Pancreatic transplants have been performed with limited success.

  B. Type II diabetes can be controlled through lifestyle modifications.

    1. Usually, these diabetics are required to lose weight by exercising, according to Dr. JoAnn Manson.

    2. Changes in diet also are required.

    3. Some people take oral hypoglycemic medications that stimulate the release of insulin and foster insulin activity.

    4. If these modifications fail, Type II diabetics must take insulin injections.

> The third main point is provided.
>
> The treatments for Type I are explained.
>
> The treatments for Type II are explained.

## ACTION

I. Diabetes is a serious disease in which the body no longer can produce or use insulin effectively.

II. The two types of diabetes occur at different stages in life and require different measures for control of the disease.

III. My grandmother lived with her diabetes for years but eventually lost her life to it. My sister has the advantages of new treatments and future research in her fight with diabetes.

IV. As we age, many of us will be among the 600,000 new cases of diabetes each year. Through awareness, we can cope effectively with this silent killer.

> The three main ideas are reiterated.
>
> The speech reaches closure by referring to the introductory personal example.
>
> Listeners are warned that diabetes could affect them.

## Instructional and Demonstration Speeches

> This is not your real life; if it were, you would have been given better instructions.

This statement testifies to the importance of instructions in daily life. You're bombarded by instructions in the classroom, at work, and when purchasing or assembling a new product. Sometimes, the instructions are complicated enough that you have to be shown: how a food processor works, what you need to do in a lab to isolate oxygen, how to install a water filtration system on your cold-water pipes. An **instructional speech** offers a verbal explanation of a complex process, but a **demonstration speech** goes further by providing a visual dimension, illustrating the actual product or process for the audience. To help with clarity and concreteness, both types of speeches can use visual aids—pictures, graphs, charts, overheads, and the rest.

**Attention/Need**    In some speaking situations, such as presentations in speech communication classrooms, listener attendance may not be voluntary. On these occasions, you'll have to pay attention to motivational matters. If your audience has invited you to speak or is attending your talk voluntarily, however, you can assume listener interest. When giving instructions or offering a demonstration, you'll usually need to spend only a little time generating curiosity and motivating people to listen. After all, if you're instructing listeners in a new office procedure or giving a workshop on how to build an ice boat, they already have the prerequisite interest and motivation—otherwise, they wouldn't have come. When your audience is already motivated to listen, you can concentrate your attention/need stages on two other tasks:

1. *Preview your speech.*  If you're going to take your listeners through the steps involved in making a good tombstone rubbing, give them an overall picture of the process before you start detailing each operation.

2. *Encourage listeners to follow along.*  Even though some of the steps may be difficult, urge everyone to listen. A process such as tombstone rubbing, for example, looks easier than it is. Many people are tempted to quit listening and give up somewhere along the way. If, however, you forewarn them and promise special help with the difficult techniques, they'll be more likely to bear with you.

**Satisfaction/Visualization**    As we suggested earlier, most speeches of demonstration and instruction follow a natural chronological or spatial pattern in satisfying the audience's attention and need to listen. In addition, since they often include visual aids, they implicitly convey reasons for why an audience member might find the information useful. Consequently, you'll usually have little trouble organizing the satisfaction-visualization stages of a speech of demonstration or instruction. Your problems are more likely to be technical and may include the following:

- *The problem of rate.* If the glue on a project needs to set before you can go on to the next step, what do you do? You cannot just stand there and wait for it to dry. Instead, you could have a second object that's already dried and ready for the next step. You also need to preplan some material for filling the time—perhaps additional background or a brief discussion of what problems can arise at this stage. Preplan your remarks carefully for those junctures so you can maintain your audience's attention.

- *The problem of scale.* How can you show various embroidery stitches to an audience of 25? When dealing with minute operations, you often must increase the scale of operation. In this example, you could use a large piece of posterboard or even a 3- by 4-foot piece of cloth stretched over a wooden frame. By using an oversized needle, yarn instead of thread, and stitches measured in inches instead of millimeters, you could easily make your techniques visible to all audience members. At the other extreme, in a speech on how to make a homemade solar heat collector, you should work with a scaled-down model.

- *The coordination of verbal and visual methods.* Both instructions and demonstrations usually demand that speakers *show* while they *tell*. To keep yourself from becoming flustered or confused, be sure to practice doing while

*Practice coordinating the verbal and visual elements before giving a demonstration or instructional speech.*

talking—demonstrating your material while explaining aloud what you're doing. Decide where you'll stand when showing a slide, so the audience can see both you and the image. Practice talking about your aerobic exercise positions while you're actually doing them. Work a dough press in practice sessions as you tell your mythical audience how to form professional-looking cookies. If you do not, you'll inevitably get into trouble before your real audience. For other tips on using visual aids, see Chapter 11.

**Action**   In instructional and demonstration speeches, this stage usually has three parts:

1. *Summary.* Most audiences need this review, which reminds them to question any procedures or ideas they don't understand.
2. *Encouragement.* People trying new processes or procedures usually get in trouble the first few times and need reassurance that this is predictable and can be overcome.
3. *Offer to help.* What sounded so simple in your talk may be much more complicated in execution. If possible, make yourself available for assistance or point to other sources of further information and assistance:

> As you fill out your registration form, just raise your hand if you're unsure of anything, and I'll be happy to help you.
>
> Here's the address of the governor's office.

Such statements not only offer help, but they also assure your listeners they won't be labeled as dimwitted if they ask for it.

**Sample Outline**   Thinking through requirements of instructional and demonstration speeches might result in a speaking outline like the following one on how to make Shanghai wontons.[9]

---

### Sample Outline for a Demonstration Speech
#### *How to Make Shanghai Wontons*

**ATTENTION**

I. Have you ever eaten small Chinese dumplings, or *wontons*?

II. Have you ever made wontons? Well, you can learn, as I did from my Shanghainese mother. The steps are very simple and easy to follow, as I will illustrate.

*Listeners' interest is aroused by using questions.*

**NEED**

I. Making wontons is easy, and presenting them to friends at a meal will cause them to envy you.

**SATISFACTION/VISUALIZATION**

I. First, you must have the proper materials.
   A. Utensils: chopsticks, dish, cup
   B. Ingredients of wonton filling
      [Use transparency to list ingredients]
   C. Ready-made wonton wrappers

II. Demonstration: folding wonton wrappers
   A. This is a step-by-step procedure that is easy to watch and to do for yourself.
      [Hold up empty wrapper to show steps; then put filling in a new wrapper and repeat same steps]
   B. With a volunteer from class, I will now show you how easy it is to do, as I have done in wrapping a wonton.
   C. Serving wontons
      1. Wontons can be served in chicken soup.
         [Show picture of soup with dumplings]
      2. Wontons can be deep-fried and served with a hot pepper sauce.
         [Show picture of deep-fried wontons]

**ACTION**

I. With the proper utensils, the right ingredients, and ready-made wrappers, you, too, can enjoy this tasty food from my home.

II. Even if you don't make them yourself, you know what they are and can try them the next time you go out to a Chinese restaurant.

*A chronological pattern is used to reference what is needed first.*

*The steps are shown to the audience.*

*Using a volunteer helps support the idea that this is an easy process.*

*The "So what?" question is answered in this section.*

*The conclusion summarizes the main points.*

## Oral Briefings

An **oral briefing** is a speech that assembles, arranges, and interprets information gathered in response to a request from a particular group. A briefing may be *general,* as in an overview of the general education requirements being discussed by a university committee, or *technical,* as in a class report on the award-winning concrete boat that was created by a university engineering team. A briefing is either *factual,* as in reviewing the specification for the concrete boat race and how the winning boat compared, or *advisory,* as in going beyond the factual information to provide specific recommendations for how such a boat might be built by a new team.

An oral briefing also demands that you consider your role as an expert—as the source of predigested information for a group of people who, in turn, will act on what you have to say. That role carries the obligation to prepare with special care and the necessity to present ideas with clarity and balance. The following guidelines will help ensure your concentration on the tasks at hand:

- *The information you present must be researched with great care.* The audience will expect you to have concrete data on which the generalizations are based, especially if those generalizations are controversial or seem extraordinary.

- *When making recommendations, rather than merely reporting information, be sure to include a complete rationale for your advice.* Suppose, for example, that as a wheelchair-bound person, you have been called on to brief your student government on the status of access for people with disabilities on your campus and to recommend how the assembly can help make the campus more accessible. First, you can use your own experience in listing the problems. Second, you need to gather additional information about the current status of access, especially in relation to the requirements specified in the 1991 Americans with Disabilities Act. The information gleaned from these sources will begin to build the rationale for the speech because you want audiences to be clear about the current status of handicapped access on campus.

- *Make full use of visual aids when briefing audiences.* If your speech is short and to the point yet contains information that may be complex and new to the audience, use visual aids.

- *Stay within the boundaries of the charge you are given.* Whether your briefing assignment is general or technical, factual or advisory, you are the primary source of information at that moment. Thus, being sensitive to the audience's expectations and needs is essential: Were you asked to present information only, or were you charged with offering recommendations? Does the audience assume that you'll emphasize information from the past, current trends, or future prospects? Are cost implications expected in assessing a proposal?

Oral briefings require more attention to structural considerations than other informational speeches. The following provides an overview of each phase of the speech.

**Attention**    The audience is more interested in content than in being motivated to listen—they know why you are speaking. A brief reminder or recapping of the charge given sets the context. Describing the procedures used assures the audience you did your job, and forecasting the ideas or issues to be covered in the presentation prepares the audience to listen.

**Need**    What you want the listeners to do, believe, or know as a result of the information needs to be highlighted early in the presentation. In essence, orient listeners through a review of the past (their expectations and your preparation), the present (your goal in this presentation), and the future (their responsibilities following the presentation).

**Satisfaction**    Adhere to this structural principle: Use the pattern best suited to the topic and audience expectations. For example, a chronological pattern will best answer the topic and expectations in a speech on the history of a group's existence or a specific problem. A cause-effect pattern would best answer an expectation for awareness of why a problem or a group exists.

**Visualization**    In closing, make very clear what you want the audience to do with your information. What are their responsibilities following the briefing? If not already clear, be explicit in stressing what needs to happen next.

**Action**    Direct reference to the introductory comments is a common tactic in concluding, as is thanking those who participated and made a difference in the outcome. In giving a revised charge to a group, the action step may focus on reminding them that it is now their duty to carry out the revised charge to the best of their ability. You also may offer a motion to accept a report if the circumstances call for this parliamentary step. Inviting audience questions is another move that can be made at the close of the presentation. In essence, conclusions of oral briefings should be quick, firm, efficient, and specific regarding what you want the audience to know.

**Sample Outline**    The sample outline that follows shows how these points can be applied in an oral briefing that presents the findings of a report.

## Sample Outline for an Oral Briefing
### *Report from the Athletic Advisory Committee*

**ATTENTION/NEED**

I.  Our committee was asked to evaluate the current charge to the advisory committee and suggest changes to the president.      **The reporter's charge is reviewed.**
    A.  First, you need to know that the committee is composed of faculty, staff, and students.
    B.  Second, you need to know that our committee is advisory to the president—we do not make policy, but we do recommend actions to make the lives of student-athletes better.      **The orientation has been completed.**

(continued)

**The deliberative process is summarized.**

**SATISFACTION**

I. We conducted an orderly and systematic review.
   A. First, we examined the relevance of each specific task in the current charge.
   B. Then, we interviewed two key committee members—the athletic director and the senior women's athletic official—to assess their views of the current charge.
   C. Next, we evaluated recent actions undertaken by the group to get a better sense of what we have been considering and its relation to the charge.
   D. With this as a baseline, we then brainstormed additional new activities with which the group could become more involved.

**The recommended course of action is justified.**

II. We also went outside the committee for further information.
   A. We interviewed the president to get the opinions of central administration.
   B. We interviewed officers in the faculty senate.
   C. We interviewed student government officers.

III. Using this information as a basis, we then drew up a list of duties for discussion.
   A. We ranked each item as to its relative importance.
   B. We indicated our commitment to each item.
   C. Reviewing the results of A and B, we ascertained which items received unanimous, solid support from the committee.
   D. The final list was approved.

IV. The final revised document was presented to the president for approval.

## Explanatory Speeches

An **explanatory speech** has much in common with a definitional speech; both share the function of clarifying a concept, process, or event. Normally, though, an explanatory speech is less concerned with the word or vocabulary involved than with connecting one concept to a series of others. For example, a speech of *definition* on political corruption would concentrate on that term, telling what sorts of acts committed by politicians are included by it. An *explanatory* speech on corruption, however, such as on the scandal surrounding the awarding of Olympic sites, would go further into the subject and indicate the social-political conditions likely to produce corruption or the methods for eliminating it. The clarification involved in an explanatory speech is considerably broader and more complex than that of a definitional speech.

The key to most explanatory speeches is how the speaker constructs a viewpoint or rationale. Suppose, for example, that you want to explain what is happening to undocumented workers in the United States. You would want your audience to be aware of the marches in New York, California, Oregon, Illinois, and Washington, DC, and about meetings and rallies in other states. You would also want to explain the purposes behind legislation for these workers, including the actions that designated undocumented workers as "illegals." This will be a difficult topic to work with, as your purpose is to provide information and not necessarily suggest what you think about the situation—is it fair or unjust? As you move toward one of these attitudes, you move toward persuading or moving your audience to precise action.[10] To ensure against misunderstanding, you need to preface your satisfaction step with a precise statement of your purpose:

> Let me tell you the story of undocumented workers. My intent is not to provide a position on this issue but to make you aware of the current situation. As news reports occur about undocumented workers on labor sites in your community, you will have a better understanding of the issues involved.

Such a statement recognizes that you're not trying to offer every possible explanation and tells your listeners what to listen for. Identifying a viewpoint helps you—and your listeners—keep the story straight.

Unlike definitional speeches, explanatory speeches can be complex and difficult to organize. We now discuss this aspect.

**Attention**    For this type of speech, motivational appeals are far more important in getting audiences interested in your topic. The need to connect your topic to audience members' everyday lives is paramount. In addition, forecasting the main points will help orient the audience to your topic's development.

**Need**    When dealing with complex materials, indicate a willingness to elaborate or note that you'll go into more detail as needed later in the presentation. Note the specific viewpoint you are taking toward the information and why it is imperative that the audience understands not only the information but your purpose in providing it.

**Satisfaction/Visualization**    Causal or topical patterns fit most explanatory speeches. Explaining why something exists or operates as it does calls for either cause-effect or its reverse. Topical patterns allow you to order items without worrying which comes first or second.

**Action**    In this type of speech, most conclusions develop additional implications or calls for particular actions. Knowing what causes a disease, for example, may lead the audience to wonder how to avoid the cause or treat the effects.

**Sample Outline**    Suppose your major is sociology, and you decide to discuss the movement to protect undocumented workers, or so-called illegal aliens. Consider the following outline to see how some of this advice about explanatory speeches can be put to work.[11]

# Sample Outline for an Explanatory Speech
## *The Movement to Protect Undocumented Workers*

**ATTENTION**

**Raise your listeners' curiosity.**

I. Listen to the story of Carmen: She is 17 years old and works 11-hour days for less than $2.70 an hour. She washes dishes, cleans bathrooms, mops floors, and makes homemade tortillas. She works in Mexico, right? Wrong! She works in the United States.

**Tie new knowledge to the purpose for listening.**

II. Carmen's story epitomizes the reason there is an immigrant rights movement in the United States.

**NEED**

**State your purpose; clarify your intent.**

I. My purpose in this presentation is not to take a stand, though some of the facts and examples may suggest that, but rather to make you aware of this new movement. As you read about so-called illegals working in our community or elsewhere, you will have a better understanding of the issues.

**SATISFACTION**

**Interpret the facts to make knowledge claims.**

I. The history of immigrant status provides a context for examining this new movement.
   A. The criminalization of moving across borders without papers or documents proving you were a citizen took place in 1929.
   B. At that time, the government established language that labeled undocumented workers as "illegals," subject to immediate deportation.
   C. In 1986, as part of the Immigration Reform and Control Act, it became illegal to work without papers.

II. Gaining admission thus requires documentation; its absence fosters long waiting lists for those without specific technical skills and money.
   A. Migrants from some areas may wait as long as 15 years for papers.
   B. Women of color are particularly affected by the current policies.

III. An underground economy has been created, with undocumented or illegal workers continuing to work for U.S. firms.
   A. The average wage for such a worker in a New York City restaurant is $200 for a 72-hour work week, or $2.77 per hour, well under minimum wage.
   B. Sweatshop workers face even more difficulty, as they may work for weeks without being paid.

**Enlarge the interpretations to make them relevant to today's issues.**

IV. Activism is taking place across the country.
   A. In Texas, an Immigration Law Enforcement Monitoring Project works on behalf of those without papers.
   B. In Chicago, local activists were successful in presenting a petition to request amnesty for undocumented workers.
   C. Marches have occurred in major cities in New York, California, Illinois, and Washington, DC.

V. The issues are complex and not easily resolved.
   A. Amnesty is not a simple fix for the problem.
      1. María Jiménez notes:"Amnesty from what? We die in the desert, we die in the workplace, and we sacrifice our lives for our families' survival— why should they 'forgive' us? I prefer to describe our struggles as a fight for the rights of residency and mobility and for demilitarization of borders."
      2. Legislation legitimating current undocumented workers may adversely affect the number of new immigrants who can be approved, thereby exacerbating the waiting-list problem.
      3. Other underrepresented groups may see in this action a threat to their own livelihood.

**VISUALIZATION**

I. You have heard stories about undocumented workers on construction projects in our community. It is a real issue and one that is not likely to be resolved easily.

II. It is a problem that is larger than the immigrants themselves, as Maricela García points out:"At every step of our organizing work, we need to main-stream the issue of immigrants as a broader issue affecting others in society."

**ACTION**

I. The question of legalizing undocumented workers, then, will continue. Whatever position you take, you hopefully will be better informed as a consequence of this presentation.

II. In closing, I can do no better than continue with the words of Maricela García: "The discussion of immigration has been placed outside of the struggles of other people. But we need to bring it back into the struggle for social justice so we see ourselves as players with other movements—African American, gay and lesbian, environmental, and others—whose progressive agenda should include immigration."

*Finish the satisfaction step with an undisputable knowledge claim.*

*Connect your purpose to the audience's interests through visualization.*

*Closing with a quotation helps make the case real and vivid for listeners.*

## Assessing a Sample Speech

The following speech, "The Geisha," was delivered by Joyce Chapman when she was a first-year student at Loop College in Chicago.[12] It illustrates most of the virtues of a competent informative speech: It provides enough detail and explanation to be clear to a Western audience; it works from images of Geishas familiar to at least some audience members, adding new ideas and correcting old ones within the frames of reference listeners might have; its topical organization pattern is simple and easy to follow; and it gives the audience reasons for listening.

## The Geisha
### Joyce Chapman

A personal reference establishes an immediate tie between Chapman and her topic.

Chapman works hard to bring her listeners—with their stereotyped views of Geishas—into the speech through comments many might have made and references to familiar films.

The central idea is stated clearly.

A transition moves the listeners easily from the introduction to the body of the speech via a forecast.

The first section of the body is devoted to an orienting history, which cleverly wipes away most of the negative stereotypes of the Geisha.

A nice transition moves Chapman to her second point on the rigors of

As you may have already noticed from my facial features, I have Oriental blood in me and, as such, I am greatly interested in my Japanese heritage. One aspect of my heritage that fascinates me the most is the beautiful and adoring Geisha.

I recently asked some of my friends what they thought a Geisha was, and the comments I received were quite astonishing. For example, one friend said, "She is a woman who walks around in a hut." A second friend was certain that a Geisha was "A woman who massages men for money and it involves her in other physical activities." Finally, I received this response: "She gives baths to men and walks on their backs." Well, needless to say, I was rather surprised and offended by their comments. I soon discovered that the majority of my friends perceived the Geisha with similar attitudes. One of them argued, "It's not my fault, because that is the way I've seen them on TV." In many ways my friend was correct. His misconception of the Geisha was not his fault, for she is often portrayed by American film producers and directors as: a prostitute, as in the movie, *The Barbarian and the Geisha;* a streetwalker, as seen in the TV series, *Kung Fu;* or as a showgirl with a gimmick, as performed in the play "Flower Drum Song."

A Geisha is neither a prostitute, streetwalker, or showgirl with a gimmick. She is a lovely Japanese woman who is a professional entertainer and hostess. She is cultivated with exquisite manners, truly a bird of a very different plumage.

I would like to provide you with some insight into the Geisha, and, in the process perhaps, correct any misconception you may have. I will do this by discussing her history, training, and development.

The Geisha has been in existence since 600 A.D., during the archaic time of the Yakamoto period. At that time the Japanese ruling class was very powerful and economically rich. The impoverished majority, however, had to struggle to survive. Starving fathers and their families had to sell their young daughters to the teahouses in order to get a few yen. The families hoped that the girls would have a better life in the teahouse than they would have had in their own miserable homes.

During ancient times only high society could utilize the Geisha's talents because she was regarded as a status symbol, exclusively for the elite. As the Geisha became more popular, the common people developed their own imitations. These imitations were often crude and base, lacking sophistication and taste. When American GIs came home from World War II, they related descriptive accounts of their wild escapades with the Japanese Geisha. In essence, the GIs were only soliciting with common prostitutes. These bizarre stories helped create the wrong image of the Geisha.

Today, it is extremely difficult to become a Geisha. A Japanese woman couldn't wake up one morning and decide, "I think I'll become a Geisha today." It's not that simple. It takes 16 years to qualify.

8      At the age of six a young girl would enter the Geisha training school and become a Jo-chu, which means house keeper. The Jo-chu does not have any specific type of clothing, hairstyle, or make-up. Her duties basically consist of keeping the teahouse immaculately clean (for cleanliness is like a religion to the Japanese). She would also be responsible for making certain that the more advanced women would have everything available at their fingertips. It is not until the girl is 16 and enters the Maiko stage that she concentrates less on domestic duties and channels more of her energies on creative and artistic endeavors.

9      The Maiko girl, for example, is taught the classical Japanese dance, Kabuki. At first, the dance consists of tiny, timid steps to the left, to the right, backward and forward. As the years progress, she is taught the more difficult steps requiring syncopated movements to a fan.

10     The Maiko is also introduced to the highly regarded art of floral arrangement. The Japanese take full advantage of the simplicity and gracefulness that can be achieved with a few flowers in a vase, or with a single flowering twig. There are three main styles: Seika, Moribana, and Nagerie. It takes at least three years to master this beautiful art.

11     During the same three years, the Maiko is taught the ceremonious art of serving tea. The roots of these rituals go back to the thirteenth century, when Zen Buddhist monks in China drank tea during their devotions. These rituals were raised to a fine art by the Japanese tea masters, who set the standards for patterns of behavior throughout Japanese society. The tea ceremony is so intricate that it often takes four hours to perform and requires the use of over 17 different utensils. The tea ceremony is far more than the social occasion it appears to be. To the Japanese, it serves as an island of serenity where one can refresh the senses and nourish the soul.

12     One of the most important arts taught to the Geisha is that of conversation. She must master an elegant circuitous vocabulary flavored in Karyuki, the world of flowers and willows, of which she will be a part. Consequently, she must be capable of stimulating her client's mind as well as his esthetic pleasures.

13     Having completed her 16 years of thorough training, at the age of 22, she becomes a full-fledged Geisha. She can now serve her clients with duty, loyalty, and most important, a sense of dignity.

14     The Geisha would be dressed in the ceremonial kimono, made of brocade and silk thread. It would be fastened with an obi, which is a sash around the waist and hung down the back. The length of the obi would indicate the girl's degree of development. For instance, in the Maiko stage the obi is longer and is shortened when she becomes a Geisha. Unlike the Maiko, who wears a gay, bright, and cheerful kimono, the Geisha is dressed in more subdued colors. Her make-up is the traditional white base, which gives her the look of white porcelain. The hair is shortened and adorned with beautiful, delicate ornaments.

15     As a full-fledged Geisha, she would probably acquire a rich patron who would assume her sizable debt to the Okiya, or training residence. This patron

**Geisha training. She discusses the training in language technical enough to make listeners feel they're learning interesting information but not so detailed as to be suffocating.**

**The third point of the speech—how a Geisha develops her skills in actual work—is clearly introduced and then developed with specific instances and explanations.**

*(continued)*

| | |
|---|---|
| The conclusion is short and quick. Little more is needed in a speech that has offered clear explanations, though some speakers might want to refer back to the initial overview of negative stereotypes to remind the listeners how wrong such views are. | would help pay for her wardrobe, for each kimono can cost up to $12,000. The patron would generally provide her with financial security.<br><br>The Geisha serves as a combination entertainer and companion. She may dance, sing, recite poetry, play musical instruments, or draw pictures for her guest. She might converse with them or listen sympathetically to their troubles. Amorous advances, however, are against the rules.    **16**<br><br>So, as you can see the Geisha is a far cry from the back-rubbing, street-walking, slick entertainer that was described by my friends. She is a beautiful, cultivated, sensitive, and refined woman.    **17** |

## ■ CHAPTER SUMMARY

Overall, informative speeches provide more interesting and greater challenges than most people realize. Facts and information are not particularly useful to listeners until they're turned into knowledge—assembled and structured in ways that help human beings find those facts and that information relevant to their lives.

Audiences are not always automatically interested in every topic; hence, you need to appeal to their personal motives for listening. Motives can be thought of as springs—needs or desires tightly coiled and waiting for the right appeal or verbal depiction to set them off. Worked by a skillful speaker, these motives can convert the individuals comprising an audience into a cohesive group, ready to think and act in ways consistent with a specific purpose. These motives, phrased in language appealing to biological needs or social motives, include three categories: affiliation motives, which reflect the desire for acceptance and approval by others; achievement motives, or individual urges, desires, and goals; and power motives, desires to influence or control others or the environment. The competent speaker will be able to draw on these motives, singly or in combination, to meet the speech purpose in an ethically sound manner. In doing so, the speaker will avoid the obvious, select appeals appropriately for the subject and occasion, and organize them effectively.

In preparing informative speeches, you must be sensitive to certain matters: clarity through effective organization and word choice; ways to associate new ideas with old ones so the audience can more easily understand the new ones; and relevant visualization, to show listeners how information is relevant to them. The four kinds of informative speeches discussed in this chapter—definitional speeches, instructional and demonstration speeches, oral briefings, and explanatory speeches—occur often enough in your life to demand your attention. Evaluate the organizational strategies available to you in structuring these presentations, so they meet the needs of the situation and your listeners.

## ■ KEY TERMS

achievement motives  (p. 313)
affiliation motives  (p. 312)
attribution process  (p. 315)
biological need  (p. 311)

definitional speech  (p. 324)
demonstration speech  (p. 328)
explanatory speech  (p. 334)
fact  (p. 310)

hierarchy of prepotency
  (p. 312)
information  (p. 310)
instructional speech  (p. 328)

knowledge (p.310)

Maslow's hierarchy of needs
(p.311)

McClelland's motive types
(p.313)

motivational appeal (p.315)

motive cluster (p.313)

oral briefing (p.331)

power motives (p.313)

social motives (p.311)

three needs theory (p.313)

visualization (p.323)

visualization process (p.315)

## ■ ASSESSMENT ACTIVITIES

1. In a short essay, indicate and defend the type of arrangement pattern (e.g., chronological, spatial, and so on) that you think would be most suitable for an informative speech on each of five of the following topics. For each topic, do a brief outline of first-level headings to show your reader what that speech might look like.

   a. The status of minority studies on your campus

   b. Recent developments in genetic engineering

   c. The search for the origins of human life in the Olduvai Gorge

   d. How the stock market works

   e. Five websites every college student should visit

   f. Working with a landlord

   g. Ways parents can control television viewing by their children

   h. How the U.S. presidential caucus and primary system works

2. Plan a 2- to 5-minute speech in which you give instructions. You might explain how to calculate one's life insurance needs, program a VCR so a person can watch one channel and record another, or do the Heimlich maneuver. Your instructor will grade you on the three essential criteria for all informative speeches: clarity, association of new information with old data, and use of relevant visualization.

3. What relevant motivational appeals might you use in addressing each of the following audiences? Be ready to discuss your choices in class.

   a. A group of students protesting federal reductions in financial aid programs

   b. A meeting of prebusiness majors concerned about jobs

   c. Women at a seminar on nontraditional employment opportunities

   d. A meeting of local elementary and secondary classroom teachers who are seeking smaller classes

   e. A group gathered for an old-fashioned Fourth of July picnic

## ■ REFERENCES

1. Consult any of the following: Roderick Wong, *Motivation: A Biobehavioural Approach* (New York: Cambridge University Press, 2000); David C. Edwards, *Motivation and Emotion: Evolutionary, Physiological, Cognitive, and Social Influences* (Thousand Oaks, CA: Sage, 1999); Denys DeCatanzaro, *Motivation and Emotion: Evolutionary, Physiological, Developmental and Social Perspectives* (Upper Saddle River, NJ: Prentice Hall, 1999); and Robert C. Beck, *Motivation: Theories and Principles* (Upper Saddle River, NJ: Prentice Hall, 2000). Psychologists are divided over several important issues. For example, some (e.g., Maslow) argue that all motives are innate, whereas others (e.g., McClelland) argue that at least some are learned. Likewise, psychologists differ on the issue of conscious awareness of motives: Are we aware of the drive, and if not, how do we control it? We won't get into such controversies in this text, but we take the

position that whether innate or learned, conscious or not, motives are the foundations for motivational appeals and, hence, are reasons for action. It is this characteristic that makes motives important to the student of public speaking.

2. Abraham Maslow, *Motivation and Personality*, 2nd ed. (New York: Harper and Row, 1970). In the 1970 revision, Maslow identified two additional desires—to know and understand and an aesthetic desire—as higher states. These frequently operate as part of the satisfaction of self-actualization; hence, we've included them in that category. For more recent work, see Abraham H. Maslow with Deborah C. Stephens and Gary Heil, *Maslow on Management* (New York: John Wiley, 1998).

3. For additional information on theories of motivation, see the following: Janice Cheung, "Theories of Motivation and Its Practical Application in Public Libraries," thesis, University of Alberta, 1999, available online: <http://www.slis.ualberta.ca/cap99/jcheung/emotive.htm>, accessed August 25, 2001; Roderick Wong, *Motivation: A Biobehavioural Approach* (New York: Cambridge University Press, 2000); David C. Edwards, *Motivation and Emotion: Evolutionary, Physiological, Cognitive, and Social Influences* (Thousand Oaks, CA: Sage, 1999); and Denys DeCatanzaro, *Motivation and Emotion: Evolutionary, Physiological, Developmental and Social Perspectives* (Upper Saddle River, NJ: Prentice Hall, 1999).

4. Harold W. Scheffler, *Filiation and Affiliation* (Boulder, CO: Westview Press, 2000).

5. To understand the power of verbal depiction, read Michael Osborn, "Rhetorical Depiction," in *Form, Genre, and the Study of Political Discourse*, edited by Herbert W. Simons and Aram A. Aghazarian (Charleston: University of South Carolina Press, 1986), 79–107.

6. Excerpted from a speech by Jesse Jackson, presented during Communications Week at Ohio University, Athens, OH, April 27, 1998.

7. See Osborn (note 5) and Paul Messaris, *Visual Persuasion: The Role of Images in Advertising* (Thousand Oaks, CA: Sage, 1997).

8. Information for this outline is from several sources: Phyllis Barrier, "Diabetes: It Never Lets Up," *Nation's Business*, November 1992, p. 77; David Bradley, "Is a Pill on the Way for Diabetes?" *New Scientist*, 27 June 1992, p. 406; Charles Kilo and Joseph R. Williamson, *Diabetes* (New York: Wiley, 1987); Mark Schapiro, "A Shock to the System," *Health*, July–August 1991, pp. 75–82; Carrie Smith, "Exercise Reduces Risk of Diabetes," *The Physician and Sports Medicine*, November 1992, p. 19; and John Travis, "Helping Diabetics Shed Pins and Needles," *Science News*, 6 July 1991, p. 4.

9. Adapted from a speech by Lam Sui Wah (Brenda), Ohio University, Athens, OH, 1996. Used with permission.

10. For information on this topic, see Sasha Khokha, "Paper Chase," *ColorLines*, 4 (Summer 2001): 26–29. Reprinted with permission from *ColorLines* magazine.

11. Outline adapted from Khokha (note 10). Reprinted with permission from *ColorLines* magazine.

12. "The Geisha" by Joyce Chapman, from *Communication Strategy: A Guide to Speech Preparation*, edited by Roselyn Schiff et al. Copyright © 1981 by Scott, Foresman/Addison-Wesley. Reprinted by permission of Addison-Wesley Educational Publishers, Inc.

Chapter **14**

# Speeches to Persuade and to Actuate

*In early 2001, Newsweek economist Robert Samuelson faced a dilemma: He had opposed large federal tax cuts on the grounds that any extra income the federal government has should be channeled into paying down the debt. Yet he saw many economic indicators—slumping industrial production, miserable Christmas retail sales, declines in auto sales, and the death of Montgomery Ward—that portended trouble for the United States. But how could he change his position on a tax cut without undermining his own credibility and without appearing inconsistent?*

*He decided on a three-part strategy: (1) Come up with a plan that would work faster than President Bush's plan would; (2) echo the Democrats' "Help the middle class" appeal; and (3) offer a quick fix that would seem much narrower than Bush's long-term plan. Thus, Samuelson proposed to (1) cut rates across the board immediately, not in 2002–2006; (2) distribute more of the rate cuts to the middle tax brackets; and (3) defer the phase-out of the estate tax, the so-called marriage penalty, and new deductions for charitable giving until there was evidence of how the economy was doing in a few years. Samuelson's persuasive strategies, therefore, were based on his hopes to protect his own credibility, maintain his psychological appeal to more liberal readers, yet respond to the economic problems the country was facing about the time President Bush was being inaugurated.*

Samuelson's persuasive goals were influenced by his knowledge of the public's skeptical attitudes toward both government giveaways and economic projections. He had to make the tax proposal seem both politically and economically reasonable. And he certainly wanted to maintain his own credibility as an understandable, commonsensical analyst. The strategies were useful, as he was asking people to change their ideas or actions in ways that ran contrary to what he had advocated in earlier articles. He managed to rationalize his change in policy and action.[1]

The speaker or writer who persuades makes a very different demand on an audience than the speaker who informs. Informative communicators are satisfied when listeners understand what's been said. Persuaders, however, attempt to influence listeners' thoughts or actions. Occasionally, persuaders seek to reinforce ideas or actions, urging listeners to defend the present system and reject proposed changes. Whatever their specific purposes, the general purpose of all persuaders is to convince audiences of something. Persuasive speaking is the process of producing an oral message that reorients an audience psychologically or induces them to act in new and different ways.

Broadly, persuasion encompasses a wide range of communication activities, including advertising, marketing, sales, political campaigns, and interpersonal relations. Given this book's focus on speechmaking, however, we narrow our thinking in this chapter to two types of speeches: speeches to persuade and speeches to actuate. Before we can talk about these types of speeches, however, we need to consider some general problems you will face as a persuader:

1. The need to adapt your work to listeners' psychological orientations

2. The selection of motivational appeals that reflect the lifestyles of different segments of the audience

3. The requirement to recognize the diversity of your audience and provide each group with reasons for accepting your claims

4. The absolute need to enhance your credibility when selling ideas to an audience

These topics were discussed earlier, but as we reintroduce them here, the focus will be on specific strategies that you, like Samuelson, have available when addressing particular audiences in particular situations. It's how-to-do-it time.

## Contemporary Approaches to Changing Minds and Behaviors

Persuading others is a challenging task. No matter what advertisers assume, people do not change their long-standing beliefs, values, or behaviors on a whim. They need to see change as consonant with how they see the world, with how they see themselves, and with what they want out of life for themselves and others. The natural question of *Why should I believe or act as you desire?* must be met by **good reasons** for asking listeners to alter their thoughts or actions.[2] Reasons are not *good* simply because they are perceived as rational or logically reasonable. Rather, their status is always determined by (1) listeners' psychological orientations, (2) the motives, needs, and desires that grow out of people's life experiences, (3) the sources of ideas (i.e., reference groups) acceptable to listeners, and (4) their assessment of the speaker's personal credibility.

*Persuasive speaking is the process of producing an oral message that increases personal commitment; modifies beliefs, attitudes, or values; or induces action.*

More specifically, at the dawn of the twenty-first century, it is very clear that the world of persuasive speaking has changed radically over the last 100 years. Marketers, especially, began to realize about 25 years ago that "throughout the nation, Americans live in distinctive community types, refusing to blend into the mythical melting pot."[3] As a country, the United States has become less and less organized by ideological tenets and ethnic blocs and more and more assembled out of a variegated web of what we will call *lifestyles*. Think of this term as generally vague and subject to many different category systems (three of which we'll look at in this chapter). It is used to suggest that you probably cannot use idealist value systems (thinking of people as having sociological, economical, or political motivations in general) or even old ethnic labels (the habits of Irish Americans, Asian Americans, African Americans) when conceptualizing how the country organizes itself routinely. Rather, you're better off seeing where people live, examining what they do and what products they buy, and asking them concrete preference questions ("Do you prefer to watch TV or go to a sports event in the evening?"). Then, what you'll find are pockets of people in different parts of the country who are more like people living in similar neighborhoods elsewhere than they are like their neighbors in another part of their own town.

We live in a fragmented society, in many ways, as books such as Robert Putnam's *Bowling Alone* and Joseph Turow's *Breaking Up America* tell us.[4] Some want to call this condition *postmodern*, and you certainly can, if you like—though only so long as you realize that modernist science and technology still are central to our lives. The point for you and this book is not what you call the condition but rather what it means to you as a persuader. It means that you have to think of audiences as *segmented*, with different segments—clusters, cultures—often demanding their own motivational appeals and prompts to act. That is why we'll begin this chapter by looking at various approaches to understanding and thinking about groups or clusters of people before talking about persuasive and actuative speechmaking.

## VALS: Adapting Messages to Listeners' Psychological Orientations

The phrase **psychological orientation** refers generally to the complex of beliefs, attitudes, and values that listeners bring to a speech occasion. There are hundreds of ways to talk about psychological states, but in this chapter, we limit ourselves to two.

**Psychological Orientation and the VALS Program**    A popular book from the early 1980s was Arnold Mitchell's *The Nine American Lifestyles.*[5] He and some teammates set up the Stanford Research Institute's **Values and Lifestyles (VALS) Program** to examine the motives, lifestyles, and governing values of groups of people. They set up the program for two reasons: First, they understood that people are governed by entire constellations of attitudes, beliefs, opinions, hopes, fears, needs, desires, and aspirations that are too complex to chart neatly on paper. Second, people nonetheless have relatively consistent ways of acting at any given time of their lives. There are patterns to people's development and actions that reflect both their psychological orientations and their behaviors. These can be defined as **lifestyles**—the relatively systematized ways of believing and acting in the world and the fairly consistent orientations people bring to their decision making.

The VALS program is an effort to capture those lifestyles in an analytically useful way. After considerable surveying and interviewing of Americans, Mitchell's team divided participants into four comprehensive groups that, in turn, were subdivided into nine lifestyles (see Table 14.1). The categories and the percentages

---

**TABLE 14.1**    **Mitchell's VALS Typology**

**Need-Driven Groups (11% of U.S. adults)**

Survivor lifestyle (4%)
Sustainer lifestyle (7%)

**Outer-Directed Groups (67% of U.S. adults)**

Belonger lifestyle (35%)
Emulator lifestyle (10%)
Achiever lifestyle (22%)

**Inner-Directed Groups (20% of U.S. adults)**

I-Am-Me lifestyle (5%)
Experiential lifestyle (7%)
Socially Conscious lifestyle (8%)

**Combined Outer- and Inner-Directed Groups (2% of U.S. adults)**

Integrated lifestyle (2%)

of U.S. adults in each came from 1980 research, so the specific numbers may have changed by now; in additon, VALS2 has altered this scheme. Even so, the original system is useful for the more informal uses to which persuaders can put it.

The VALS program defines groups of people who habitually respond to problems and their solutions in comparatively predictable ways:

- *Survivors* are poverty-driven people—ill, depressed, withdrawn, undereducated, and lacking self-confidence.

- *Sustainers* are closely related to Survivors but are more angry, distrustful, and anxious and have the motive to advance economically, if possible.

- *Belongers* are stereotypical middle-class Americans—traditional, conforming, family oriented, moral, mostly white, and often female.

- *Emulators* are the great strivers, those who work hard to become richer and more successful than they are; members of this group often are young, competitive, and ambitious.

- *Achievers* are more successful models of Emulators and often are professionals—comfortable, affable, and wealthy.

- *I-Am-Me's* lead off the inner-directed group; they are highly emotional and flighty, both aggressive and retiring, conforming and innovative, and always searching for their true selves.

- *Experientials* are adventure seekers, willing to experience life intensely; unlike I-Am-Me's, they are more involved with others.

- The *Socially Conscious* are driven by their concern for others, societal issues, trends, and events.

- *Integrated* people balance the strengths of the outer- and inner-directed people—these are the great leaders of most societies.

As these classifications attest, your audiences seldom are drawn purely from one group or another. Hence, the best approach is to segment the listeners and then target appeals to each segment. See the "How to" box on page 348, which takes you through an example using the VALS approach. Even a general analysis of psychological orientation, therefore, will help you choose from among the different ways you can urge change and even phrase the specific appeals that you use.

Why is VALS useful to speakers? As you observe members of your audience, you'll likely see behaviors and hear opinions that give you clues to their values and lifestyles. Indeed, the VALS questionnaire is a 40-question survey that integrates psychological information ("I am often interested in theories") with behavioral information ("I would rather make something than buy it").[6] By listening to audience members talk and by observing some of their behaviors, you should be able to assess them in ways suggested in the "How to" box. Casually gathered information about people, of course, is not as reliable as scientifically structured data, but it may be good enough to suggest some motivational appeals that will work.

**Psychological Orientation and Your Topic**   You should also try to assess most listeners' attitudes toward your specific topic. An audience can have any of five possible attitudes toward a speaker's topic and purpose: (1) favorable but not aroused to act; (2) apathetic toward the situation; (3) interested but undecided about what to do; (4) interested in the situation but hostile to the proposed

# How to
# Use VALS to Craft a Persuasive Message for a Diverse Audience

A cursory examination of your classmates should reveal something like the following:

- There will be few representatives of the need-driven groups (i.e., "Survivors" and "Sustainers").
- There will be several outer-directed students ("Emulators" and "Achievers").
- There also will be several inner-directed students (especially from the "Socially Conscious").

Based on this quick review, suppose you are suggesting that your classmates help a neighborhood association clean up some nearby vacant lots to create a park. For your classmates, you would want to feature appeals aimed at their particular psychological orientations:

I. We should help the neighborhood association clean the lots and build the park for several reasons:
   A. You would be demonstrating that even busy college students have the ambition to take on serious community projects. **[Achievers]**
   B. You would show the community that you have the leadership skills and technical abilities to carry it out. **[Achievers]**
   C. You would have done something of which you could be proud and that you could put on your résumé under "Community Service." **[Socially Conscious]**

If you were to shift your focus to the neighborhood association, a cursory examination might find these qualities:

- A larger percentage of need-driven people would be found among the community members than in your college class (i.e., "Survivors" and "Sustainers").
- A majority of outer-directed people would be found in the association (i.e., "Belongers").
- Some association members would be "Socially Conscious."

For this audience, a different set of reasons would be appropriate:

I. You should be involved in the neighborhood clean up and park construction for these reasons:
   A. The lots are now breeding grounds for rats and other vermin that make your life miserable. **[Socially Conscious]**
   B. Drug dealers might be driven out of the neighborhood if those lots are cleaned up. **[Inner-Directed Groups and Socially Conscious]**
   C. The presence of a park would increase your property value and even help those who are renters pressure your landlords to fix up your apartments. **[Need-Driven Groups]**
   D. A park would give you a free place to visit and enjoy on spring days and summer nights. **[Inner- and Outer-Directed Groups]**

attitude, belief, value, or action; or (5) hostile to any change from the present state of affairs. Given this sort of variability, consider the following suggestions as you design your speech:

**A message that incorporates both sides of an issue—and contains arguments refuting one side—will be more effective across diverse persuasive situations.** Thus, if your goal is to stimulate more favorable thoughts about your proposal, use a **two-sided message** with refutation. A **one-sided message**, which focuses on the arguments for your position only, also can be effective—and is more effective than simply outlining both sides of an issue without adding refutative arguments.[7] You might also consider how to make your listeners more resistant to ideas that run contrary to yours. The "Communication Research Dateline" box on the next page reviews research on counterpersuasion.

**A message that recognizes the logical interdependence between ideas will target those people for whom beliefs are highly integrative.** There will be people in the audience for whom beliefs are interlocked—altering or affecting one belief will have a dominolike impact on other beliefs. Thus, a speech that praises statin drugs—cholesterol-reducing drugs such as Zocor and Lipitor—for their primary effects on LDL (low-density lipids) and thus heart disease could also point out that they can stabilize plaque in blood vessels, work as an antiinflammatory generally, have anti–blood clotting effects, and even strengthen bones and hence reduce the risk of fractures.[8] But also remember that many audiences are sensitive to the advertising hype surrounding these drugs, and some will know that one of the statin drugs, Baycol, was recalled by its manufacturer in 2001 because of negative side effects—liver problems, muscular pain, and even deaths. Knowing enough about an audience's attitudes toward the topic to guess at what it already thinks will help you produce a balanced but effective speech.

**You must address not only the strengths of attitudes but also their saliency.** **Saliency** refers to the relevance and current interest level of a belief, attitude, or value for an individual. For example, topics currently on the front page often are highly salient, as are topics of regular conversation. The saliency of an issue should affect your persuasive strategies in significant ways: Issues will mean more or less to different members, so you need to decide how much detail to offer. The more often an issue is in the news, the more likely the audience will have opinions about it, affecting what arguments you should frame. Think again about a speech recommending statin drug therapies. The more the audience knows, the more careful you must be in framing arguments.[9]

**Recognize that audience members differ in their willingness to accept your ideas.** Audience members will have different ranges of acceptance or rejection, depending on how your proposal relates to their own views. Think in terms of not going too far in either direction from your proposal for a flat tax: A rate of 2 percent might be rejected by a moderate audience simply because it would seem to generate too little revenue; conversely, a rate of 35 percent might seem too high. A proponent of the flat tax will have a larger **latitude of acceptance;** conversely, an opponent would have a larger **latitude of rejection.**[10]

Attempting to gauge values and lifestyle choices from people's talk and behavior, of course, is not always easy. And as we've noted, unless you can do it with the precision of a market researcher, you cannot base all of your strategies on such effort. It's a start, however.

## COMMUNICATION RESEARCH DATELINE

### Resistance to Counterpersuasion

In this chapter, we've concentrated on the issue of persuading—increasing or otherwise changing people's acceptance of certain beliefs, attitudes, and values. We have not, however, focused on the ways in which you can increase your listeners' resistance to ideas that run counter to your own. Besides persuading them to accept your beliefs or attitudes, you also may need to protect them against *counterpersuasion*—attempts by others to influence your audience away from your position.

As in taking a vaccine to ward off a disease, you may inoculate your audience against your opponents' arguments. Studies by Pfau and others about political advertising have found that voters who received previous messages that an opponent would attack the candidate and voters who also received additional refutative arguments against the purported attack were far more resistant to the opponent's message. This offers practical support for the view that forewarning an audience may be helpful in increasing their resistance. As Benoit's analysis of the research on inoculation has suggested, it does not appear to matter whether the type of forewarning—letting audience members know in advance they'll be exposed to a counterpersuasive attempt—is general, as in "An attack on me is imminent from my opponent" or more precise with respect to the topic and position to be taken by the attacker. Nor does it appear to matter whether the attack really is imminent or comes later.

Another strategy that increases listeners' resistance involves the amount of knowledge that they bring to a situation. For example, Hirt and Sherman found that individuals with greater knowledge are more resistant to refutational arguments. Thus, you can increase potential resistance to messages that are contrary to your own by adding to the audience's knowledge about the issues involved.

#### For Further Reading

Benoit, William L. "Forewarning and Persuasion," in *Forewarning and Persuasion: Advances through Meta-Analysis*, edited by Mike Allen and Roy W. Preiss (Dubuque, IA: Brown and Benchmark, 1994), 159–184.

Hirt, E. R., and S. J. Sherman. "The Role of Prior Knowledge in Explaining Hypothetical Events." *Journal of Experimental Social Psychology* 21 (1985): 591–643.

Pfau, Michael. "The Potential of Inoculation in Promoting Resistance to the Effectiveness of Comparative Advertising Messages." *Communication Quarterly* 40 (1992): 26–44.

Pfau, Michael, and Michael Burgoon. "Inoculation in Political Communication." *Communication Monographs* 15 (1988): 91–111.

## PRIZM: Adapting Messages
## to Listeners' Behavioral Patterns

Another popular marketing technique that you can adapt to the process of selecting persuasive strategies is **PRIZM,** which, like VALS, is a so-called lifestyle segmentation system. Its special appeal is that it is geography sensitive. Constructed
out of data from the 1990 census (which will be updated soon), it defines every
neighborhood in the United States behaviorally and demographically, not psychologically, as did VALS. Once the census was tabulated by zip codes, it made
possible precise demographic descriptions, and when marketing (purchasing or
consumption) data were added to those descriptions, 62 types of areas or neighborhoods were defined. The distribution of those areas or neighborhoods could
be charted by zip code.[11]

Consider the usual habitat of one of this book's authors. The zip code
52240 is that for Iowa City, Iowa, a smallish town where the highest percentage of
residents come from PRIZM cluster 36, "Towns & Gowns: College Town Singles."
This cluster is described as a half-local ("Towns") and half-student ("Gowns")
population with "thousands of penniless 18–24 year-olds and highly educated
professionals, all with a penchant for prestige products that are beyond their evident means."[12] This cluster is dominated by lower-middle-income people, large
numbers of whom are under 24; they are largely white, but there is a strong Asian
population. The zip code of this author's residence, however, is 52361, the countryside around Williamsburg, Iowa. The dominant cluster here is 57, "Grain Belt:
Owners & Tenants," with strong ties to farming and the land, "mostly self-
sufficient, family- and home-centered." These likewise are lower-middle-income
people (who make somewhat more than the "Towns & Gowns" group) but much
older—55 to 64 and over 65—and white intermixed with a Hispanic rather than
an Asian population, largely because of Latino migrant workers. Given these differences between clusters 36 and 57, a persuasive speech delivered in Iowa City
will have a very, very different audience from one given in Williamsburg, even
though the towns are only a few miles apart.

For the persuader, PRIZM and other consumption-oriented methods for
identifying particular segments of audiences are corrective devices. As we discussed motivational appeals in Chapter 13, we identified motive clusters in a more
or less rational way. What PRIZM does is recognize that motives aren't always so
easy to chart in clear ways and that motivational appeals must be understood as
operating within environmentally defined situations. We could find Iowans representing almost all of the PRIZM categories, and of course the populations of cities
vary markedly as one moves from neighborhood to neighborhood. Trying to convince the citizens of even a 70,000-person city to vote for a bond issue to construct
a new sewer system would demand considerable adjustment of motivational appeals as you move from one part of town to another.

Let's return to Iowa City, Iowa, for a moment. There are five prominent
PRIZM clusters there, each of which would have to be approached on the question of a bond issue for a new sewer system in a somewhat different way:

*Seeking Votes through PRIZM for a New Sewer System in Iowa City, Iowa*

1. *"Towns & Gowns":* Have little money and no enduring place in the community. Will not be faced with the tax burden. Easy to persuade to vote for a sewer system, though hard to get them to actually get out and vote.

2. *"Starter Families":* The "townies" of Iowa City who opted for early marriage and children. Less prosperous neighborhoods, less expensive housing. Probably can be convinced to vote for increased taxes by emphasizing swimming pools and other recreational areas made possible by increasing water supply and control.

3. *"Boomtown Singles":* Somewhat older and more affluent than "Starter Families." More likely single and in technical/technology-centered jobs and living in newer rental units or condos. Harder to get them to understand a long-term commitment to community development. Must have the cost minimized for them.

4. *"Middleburg Managers:"* Doctors, lawyers, younger faculty, and local politicians and government service people. About half over 55, and about half are 35 and younger. These are likely voters; must be convinced to part with additional cash they're probably spending on clubs, sports, and exotic travel.

5. *"Upward Bound":* Top managers, professors, and company middle- and upper-level executives living in new, single-family homes. Smaller than some other groups but will bear the brunt of the cost of the sewer system. More liberal professoriate can be sold the system with humanitarian appeals to providing for others. More conservative business community will have to be convinced that better water supplies and control of waste water will help with future community investment, growth, and hence economic potential.

So, what should be done to pass the bond issue in Iowa City? In terms of motivational appeals, pleas to vote for civic improvement and environmental improvement (a social obligation in the affiliation cluster) should be aimed at the "Towns & Gowns" and the "Boomtown Singles." The "Starter Families" should be told about the improved recreational services to tap the achievement cluster of motivational appeals (especially adventure and personal enjoyment). Affiliation appeals to loyalty and tradition can form the bases for arguments aimed at the "Middleburg Managers," while appeals from the power cluster, especially dominance—the responsibilities of leadership—should be manufactured for the "Upward Bound" neighborhoods.

We leave the rest to you. Think about how to frame the specific appeals, all of which will require serious attention to the visualization step in the motivated sequence. Sewer and water systems take a long time to build, so benefits have to be projected in visionary terms. The point of all this, however, is to demonstrate that using a PRIZM-like analysis of audience segments can provide a rationale for particular approaches to motivational appeals and hence for reason giving in support of persuasive and actuative claims.

## Reference Groups: Adapting Messages to Listeners' Group Loyalties

A third approach to audience segmenting features the collectivities to which they belong. **Reference groups** are collections of people and organizations that affect individuals' beliefs, attitudes, and values. They are the groups "from which an individual derives attitudes and standards of acceptable and appropriate behavior and to which the individual refers for information, direction, and support for a given lifestyle."[13] You may or may not hold actual membership in such groups; you might belong to the Young Republicans Club and not to the Sierra Club (i.e., an environmental lobby) yet be influenced strongly by both. You voluntarily join some reference groups; you might believe in the legal rights of everyone and so join the American Civil Liberties Union. You are a part of other reference groups involuntarily—for example, you are born male or female and a member of an ethnic group. Thus, reference groups can be classified as *membership and nonmembership groups*, *voluntary and involuntary groups*, and *positive and negative groups*.

With this background, now consider some of the ways you can use reference groups in your persuasive and actuative speeches:

**Make reference groups you want to use salient to your listeners.** You need to bring some group to a conscious level and make sure it seems relevant to the topic at hand. For example, most students these days are heavy World Wide Web users, so appeal to their online experiences when talking about ways to build new circles of friends.

**Cite the opinions of voluntary, positively viewed groups whose values coincide with positions you're taking.** This is a kind of testimony—and useful, as we saw in Chapter 6, as orienting and probative supporting materials. Before

*Beliefs, attitudes, and values are based, in part, on the traditions and customs of reference groups, although people will differ in their degree of direct reliance on such groups.*

invoking the National Rifle Association in a speech opposing gun control legislation, you will need to sense whether that group is viewed positively or negatively by your audience

**Cite voluntary, negative groups that the audience does not belong to when they oppose the position you're advocating.** Such groups are *devil-groups,* or groups people vilify and actively act against. Such references play into an "Us versus them" orientation, and whether you like it or not, some listeners are as willing to act *against* something as *for* something else. Drawing on the position of a right-to-life group in a speech delivered to a prochoice gathering would be an example of this strategy.

**The more significant a person's role in any group, the more the group's norms and beliefs influence that person's thoughts and behaviors.** The more committed you are to a group's goals, the more likely the values of that group will influence your attitudes and behaviors. Groups have a normative influence with respect to setting standards—the more active you are in the group, the more impact it will have on you.[14]

**Talk about reference groups to create a sense of security and belongingness.** Aligning your views specifically with those of positive membership groups that are important to listeners not only helps you create acceptance but long-lasting acceptance. If you talk to students who are active members of student clubs and organizations, noting those reference groups and their positions on issues will be helpful in gaining support for your ideas.

Finally, as noted throughout this book, you're usually facing diverse audiences, which means you must work many reference groups into most speeches to reach various segments of your audience. You must aim for broad-based support of your position.

## Credibility: Adapting Messages to Your Own Strengths

The issue of authority brings us to the fourth essential dimension of the persuasive process: credibility, or *ethos*. This issue brings the analysis of segments home—to you and your relationship to the various targeted clusters of listeners. In Chapter 1, we outlined several factors that can determine listeners' perceptions of your credibility—their sense of your expertise, trustworthiness, competency, sincerity or honesty, friendliness and concern for others, and personal dynamism. You should work to maximize the potential impact of all these factors whenever speaking, regardless of purpose, but they are especially important when you seek to change someone's mind or behavior. The following guidelines can assist you in making decisions about the use of credibility as an effective tool in persuasion.

First, when speaking to people who are relatively unmotivated and do not have enough background information to critically assess what they hear, the higher your credibility, the better your chances of being a successful persuader.

Conversely, if your credibility is low, even strong arguments will not overcome your initial handicap.[15] Sure, this is obvious, but it's amazing how many speakers think that if they know what they're talking about or have power over a group of listeners, they don't need to worry about how those they're talking to will view them. That's not true. Furthermore, you must realize that your credibility will vary from audience cluster to cluster, and you'll have to think about that seriously when constructing speeches.

Second, you can increase the likelihood of being judged as credible when seeking to persuade an audience by taking steps to enhance your image of competence and sincerity. People are unlikely to change their beliefs and values if they think you've done a poor job of researching the issues or are insincere—they are less likely to judge you as trustworthy. So, do these three things:

1. Carefully set forth all of the competing positions, ideas, and proposals relevant to a topic before you come to your own judgment.
2. Review various criteria for judgment—criteria that different segments can apply—to show that your recommendations or positions flow from accepted measures.
3. Show that the recommendations you offer actually will solve the problems you identified in the need step of your speech.

You can increase the audience's sense of your sincerity by (1) opening yourself to correction and criticism (i.e., a calmly delivered, relevant response does more to defuse hecklers than responding in kind); (2) talking directly and warmly with various audience clusters; (3) maintaining direct eye contact; and (4) thanking modestly anyone who has helped you understand and work on the issue.

Third, heighten audience members' sense of your expertise, friendliness, and dynamism, especially when seeking to move them to action. People will more likely follow your lead if they feel you know what you're talking about, have their best interests in mind, and are excited about your own proposal. Expertise can be demonstrated by (1) documenting your sources of information; (2) using a variety of sources as cross-checks on each other, especially sources recognized as authoritative by various segments; (3) presenting your information and need analyses in well-organized ways; (4) using clear, simple visual aids when they are appropriate or necessary; (5) providing adequate background information on controversial issues; (6) competently separating causes from effects, short-term from long-term effects, hard facts from wishes or dreams, and one proposal from others; and (7) delivering your speeches in a calm and forthright manner.

A sense of friendliness and concern for others can be created by recognizing their human concerns and condition, handling disagreements without personal animosity, depersonalizing the issues, and offering solutions geared to the specific situations in which they live or work. An audience's sense of your dynamism can be enhanced by speaking vividly, drawing clear images of the events you describe; using sharp, fresh metaphors and active rather than passive verbs; and expressing your ideas with a short, hard-hitting oral style rather than a long, cumbersome written style and with varied conversational vocal patterns, an animated body, direct eye contact rather than reliance on your notes, and a firm, upright stance.[16]

A public speaker's principal communicative virtue is that she or he is a living, active human being—a person who embodies a message and whose own values are expressed in and through the message. People command more attention and interest than written words, and unlike films and videotapes, people can feel, react to audience members, and create a sense of urgency and directness. Hence, personal credibility is an extremely valuable asset for the persuader and actuator.

Another take on credibility is this: Human communication always operates at two levels—the **content level** and the **relational level**.[17] Listeners understandings of the world and their relationships to the speaker, to each other, and even to others not present are always being negotiated. In selling the citizens of Iowa City a new sewer system, you not only must convince them about the importance of more water and cleaner water but also about the kinds of relationships they have with the speaker and should be having with everyone else in their community—the need for social commitments to others now and in the future. Human credibility and common commitments always lie at the foundation of strong and successful persuasion.

# Basic Types of Persuasive and Actuative Speeches

There are many ways to classify persuasive and actuative speeches, but here, in an introductory textbook, we will examine them most simply as speeches that reorient people psychologically (persuasive speeches) and those that provide people with impetuses to action (actuative speeches).

## Persuasion as Psychological Reorientation

In discussing **psychological reorientation**, we are focusing on speeches that, in some way, remake how people look at or think about the world around them or even themselves. The center of psychological reorientation is a reworking of people's factual understanding of things as well as their beliefs, attitudes, and values. There are two principal species of reorienting speeches: speeches of reinforcement and speeches of modification.

**Speeches of Reinforcement**     Americans are joiners. To get our political, economic, social, and personal work done, we constantly organize ourselves into groups and associations. Action-oriented groups gather and package the latest information, keep on top of issues that are important to group members, and propose solutions to specific problems. Service groups organize charities, perform volunteer work, and provide support for other activities in communities. An inevitable fact of group life is that as time goes by, members' interest in activities declines, membership drops, and the cause for which the group was formed gets lost in the myriad other causes competing for the attention and support of people in the community. Periodically, people need to be reminded why they joined a group, what its services are, and how the group helps them meet their personal goals.

So, suppose you addressed a meeting of your county Democratic party. Most or all of these people probably worked to elect Bill Clinton, and most or all probably were disappointed at how his presidency ended. What could you say to fire them up again, to get them to actively support funding for the William J. Clinton Presidential Foundation, which would create a policy and research center and help fund the Clinton Presidential Library? Most likely, your best chances for success would be a **speech of reinforcement** that emphasized the highlights of his campaigns and political achievements:

- The United States's economic expansion during the 1990s
- His work on clean air and water
- His efforts to find new public policies for reducing crime
- His international negotiations in Ireland, the Middle East, Haiti, Bosnia, and Kosovo
- His efforts to expand the Internet's reach and operations

These topics—rather than, say, his lack of success in health care reform, the ambiguities surrounding the North American Free Trade Association, and, of course, the Lewinsky affair—would likely ring positively with his former supporters. The appeals to economic welfare, environmental responsibility, freedom from fear, diplomacy, and futuristic technology could have to power to reinforce the kind of thinking in which this audience was engaging back in 1992 and 1996, when it worked to elect him.

**Speeches of Modification**   Unlike a speech of reinforcement, a **speech of modification** seeks specific psychological changes in one's belief state, attitude toward an object, or basic values. Speeches of this type have been the central feature in the art of rhetoric since the time of the early Greeks. Whether your present or future role is that of a student, businessperson, lawyer, minister, salesclerk, doctor, or parent, the task of changing the views of others is a constant demand of your daily life. Using the categories of beliefs, attitudes, and values described in Chapter 5, we can examine three subtypes of speeches aimed at modifying the views of listeners.

**Changing beliefs.**   The psychological basis for most speeches aimed at changing someone's beliefs about the world is *differentiation*. Persuaders who want you to differentiate between your old way of looking at something and a newer way of seeing it may use one (or more) of three basic strategies:

1. *Descriptive accounts:* A focus on specific characteristics of a product, event, or issue is one means of providing good reasons for accepting a proposal. Someone might persuade you to consider tofu as an acceptable food by assuring you that its vitamin and mineral content is superior to that of foods in your normal diet.

2. *Narratives:* A persuader may use narrative forms, for example, by telling a story about the United States's preparedness going into the Korean Conflict and ending with the moral that the country can never let down its guard.

3. *Appeals to uniqueness:* Someone attempting to get you to change your beliefs about a politician may convince you that candidate is "not like all the others," pointing to unique aspects of that person's background, experience, public service, honesty, and commitment to action.

**Changing attitudes.** Attitude change probably is the most heavily researched type of psychological change of the last 100 years.[18] Given the previous discussion of attitude as predisposition, you're already aware that this form of change involves modifying one's evaluation of an object from "good" to "bad"—or at least to "neutral." Two tactics for changing attitudes are popular. First, because attitudes are attached to beliefs (e.g., "Opportunities for women are increasing in this country [belief] and that is good [attitude]"), sometimes persuaders attempt to change an attitude by attacking a belief. But attitudes also can be by *direct assault.* Parents attempt to instill any number of attitudes in their children by repeatedly offering short lectures (e.g., "Spinach is good for you," "Don't give in to peer pressure—be an individual"). Repetition often has the desired effect because children accept the attitude as their own and live by its creed.

**Changing values.** Perhaps the most difficult challenge for any persuader is to change people's value orientations. As noted in earlier chapters, *values* are fundamental anchors, basic ways of organizing our view of the world and our actions in it. They are difficult—but not impossible—to change. Three techniques often are used:

1. *Valuative shifts:* Like differentiation, this technique asks audience members to look at an issue or proposal from a different valuative vantage point. The person asking you to buy insurance, for example, tells you to look at it not simply as financial protection (a pragmatic value) but as family protection and a source of peace of mind (sociological and psychological values).

2. *Appeals to consistency:* When members of the Nature Conservancy hear appeals beginning with "We favor . . . ," they are being asked to approve a certain measure to remain consistent with others in their reference group. This will have an effect if approval of the reference group is a positive social value for them.

3. *Transcendence:* This sophisticated method for getting you to change your values approaches the issue from the perspective of a higher value. Notice the speeches by Representatives Richard Gephardt and J. C. Watts at the end of this chapter: Both asked listeners to view the impeachment of President Clinton in 1999 from higher values—social harmony built around "respect and fairness and decency" to Gephardt and basic issues of "right and wrong" to Watts.

Thus, speeches of modification may seek changes in beliefs, attitudes, or values. Speeches designed to bring about these kinds of changes in listeners demand a higher level of communicative competence than most other types of speeches. Again, preparation time spent thinking about the motivational springs within your listeners is key.

## Persuasion as Impetus to Action

Now, we move to the hardest kind of persuasion. Moving uncommitted or apathetic people to action is a chore many prefer to avoid. For example, you may have heard such expressions from friends and acquaintances as "I don't like to ask people to contribute money to a cause, even if it's worthy," "Don't ask me to solicit signatures for that petition—I feel like I'm intruding on others' privacy," and "I'm just not persuasive enough to get people to volunteer to work at the Big Brothers/Big Sisters auction—ask Maria." If all of us felt this way, little would be accomplished. In some cases, simply making a living requires that we move others to action. Even if you take one of these positions, you've undoubtedly asked others to act on your behalf in other ways ("I need a ride to Fargo this weekend; would you take me up there?"). Even though such a request is an interpersonal encounter, it shares the same features as a more elaborate speech of **actuation**—the listener may well respond with "What's in it for me?" Getting people to see and accept the benefits that will accrue from acting as you desire is the primary purpose: An actuative speech seeks, as its final outcome, a set of specifiable actions from its audience.

There are two types of audiences for whom actuative speeches generally are appropriate: those who believe in the idea or action but are lethargic about doing anything and those who doubt the value of the action and are uninformed or uninvolved. The first group needs a kind of reinforcement speech with a call for action. The second kind of audience will be our concern here.

As in the case of speeches of psychological reorientation, the key to effective actuation is motivation. No matter how wonderful the new product, how exciting the political candidate, or how worthy the cause, unless listeners are personally convinced that it will make a significant change in their lives, your speech will fail to have its intended effect. And as always, that call to act must be made in such a way that listeners apply it to themselves, in their own situations and within the array of lifestyle values they possess.

Is a motivational appeal based on *fear* a valid foundation for a persuasive actuative speech? Is fear an effective motivation? Think about these questions as you read the scenarios in the "Ethical Moments" box on page 360.

## Structuring Persuasive and Actuative Speeches

The overall structure of a persuasive or an actuative speech incorporates the features of the motivated sequence—attention, need, satisfaction, visualization, and action. Within each step, as appropriate to the topic and occasion (as we saw in

# ETHICAL MOMENTS

## Using Fear Appeals

Common sense tells you that fear appeals are among the most potent appeals to audiences. After all, if you can make your audience feel afraid for the future if a problem is not resolved, your proposal will be just the antidote. Unfortunately, a comprehensive review of decades of research on fear appeals suggests that this common-sense notion is not that well grounded, as "existing explanations of the effects of fear arousing persuasive messages are inadequate."* The inability to generate advice from the research on fear appeals raises ethical questions about the use—and potential misuse—of fear appeals. Consider the following scenarios:

**1**  You give a speech on the increased incidence of date rape on college campuses. To convince your audience that date rape is extremely common, you create scenarios that appeal to the fears of your listeners. Your scenarios are so vivid that several of your listeners—who are rape survivors—are visibly overcome with emotion. One of them is so upset that she leaves the classroom during your speech; everyone in the audience sees her leave.

**2**  You feel very strongly that the college president is wrong to continue investing college money in countries where torture and imprisonment without trial are legal. You present a very persuasive speech about your feelings. In your speech, you appeal to your audience's fears by suggesting that the college president actually is propagating torture and corrupting the values of U.S. citizens to the point that, someday, torture and imprisonment without trial might be legal in the United States. Your listeners become so incensed as a result of your speech that they march to the president's house and set his car on fire.

**3**  You're preparing to give a speech on hate crimes in the United States. You want to make sure you have your audience's attention before you begin, so you decide to present the details of a series of grisly murders committed in your town by a psychopath—even though these murders were not motivated by hate but by mental illness (and so are not examples of hate crimes).

*Frank J. Boster and Paul Mongeau, "Fear-Arousing Persuasive Messages," in *Communication Yearbook*, 8th ed., edited by Robert N. Bostrom (Beverly Hills, CA: Sage, 1984), 371.

Chapter 7), other patterns of organization can be used to bring a sense of coherence and cohesiveness. The idea of the overall structure, however, is our focus here, for it's a central challenge to any speaker: Given the diversity of audience interests, needs, background, and lifestyles, how can a variety of motivational appeals and supporting materials be packaged into a coherent, powerful oral message? That's the big question.

## Using the Motivated Sequence for Psychological Reorientation

The visualization and action steps are crucial elements in the first kind of reorientation speech, the reinforcement speech, because listeners already are convinced of the problem and are predisposed to accept particular solutions. Thus, the most important goal in a reinforcement speech is to get listeners to renew their previous commitment and charge once more into the public arena to accomplish a common objective.

### Using the Motivated Sequence in a Reinforcement Speech
#### You're Never Too Old to Learn—Virtually!

**The Situation:** As a project for a community education class, you decide to work with the recreation and education center at a local elderly housing project. The center is woefully short of educational materials, and the only teachers who show up are offering crafts classes. You figure out that here's a group of less-mobile people who are ripe for Internet educational experiences.

**Specific Purpose:** To reinforce the listeners' beliefs in serious education, telling them about Internet-based classes from around the United States[19]

#### ATTENTION

I. It's too easy to assume that older adults only want to play checkers and make Christmas presents out of plastic milk jugs.

II. In fact, retirees haven't given up living and learning—they're still curious and now have the time for a broad range of educational experiences.

#### NEED

I. Cognitive psychology has shown that exercising the brain keeps it alive and active longer.

II. Mental activity—especially structured activity, such as formal learning—helps prevent cognitive deterioration.

III. Yet the elderly often have trouble traveling to a three-times-a-week class at a local college to get that stimulation.

IV. Today's retirees are going to live longer than ever and so must keep learning to avoid falling significantly far behind the rest of society.

#### SATISFACTION

I. The Internet and the growing number of high-quality World Wide Web–based classes—more than 500,000 now available online—create great opportunities for people living at this housing project.

*(continued)*

   A.  You have plenty of computer terminals with browsers.

   B.  Because Internet courses often cost much less than bricks-and-mortar classes—most classes run $300 to $500—you can afford college-level schooling.

   C.  You're chatters—good conversationalists—which is just what turns a good web-based class into a rewarding experience.

II.  I will spend this semester as a resource person and tutor for you.

   A.  I'll provide technical help for any of you who are new to computer work.

   B.  I'll help you surf the net to find a course to your liking.

   C.  I'll be your tutor, as well, even setting up some study groups for people interested in similar kinds of things.

**VISUALIZATION**

I.  Think of what you have available on the Internet:

   A.  The California Virtual Campus has over 2,000 courses available online.

   B.  Indiana University will let you earn a bachelor's degree in general studies electronically.

   C.  The Rochester Institute of Technology has serious science and technology courses available to those of you who come out of technical backgrounds.

   D.  The University of California at Berkeley lets you start courses anytime.

   E.  Western Governors University will even give you credit for life experience.

II.  While virtual connections with faculty and fellow students are not as good as face-to-face contact in most people's opinions, they can be very rewarding.

   A.  Think of the pleasure you can have in chatting about Charles Dickens's *Oliver Twist* in an Introduction to Victorian Literature course offered by an urban eastern university.

   B.  Just consider what your life will be like when you can tune into a lecture by a professor working in Cairo while you stay home but are listening alongside a fellow classmate living in Tokyo.

   C.  Because you no longer have to worry about everything you learn being practical, you can take a course in world politics from the New School for Social Research in New York, a basic course in midwifery from the University of Pennsylvania, and a course in drawing and design from the University of Washington.

**ACTION**

I.  You all know the value of education—otherwise, you wouldn't have come to this meeting.

II.  You all know the value of thinking and understanding and evaluating for your own enjoyment and mental health.

III.  You all know that these computers would be doing a lot more good around here if they were being used more productively.

IV.  And you all know, I hope, that my commitment to your personal and collective development means that today's the day to sign up for the virtual ride down the Information Highway of your lifetime!

The motivated sequence works even better in speeches of modification. When asking an audience to accept your judgments about a person, practice, institution, or theory, you can seek to modify their beliefs by supplying new information, reorient their attitudes by changing negative stereotypes to positive ones (and vice versa), and seek transcendent values that will cause them to see their relationships with others through different lenses. These are the strategies that Henri Mann Morton employed some years ago.

## Using the Motivated Sequence in a Modification Speech
### *Strength through Cultural Diversity*

**The Situation:**  Henri Mann Morton presented a keynote speech at the Northwest's Colville and Okanogan National Forest Conference on Cultural Diversity on March 23, 1989. As a Native American woman, she was in an excellent position to comment on the issues related to gaining workforce parity for all peoples. During the speech, she differentiated the Native American experience from that of others in the hope of modifying her audience's beliefs about the values and interests of Native Americans.

**Specific Purpose:**  To modify audience beliefs about the values and interests of Native Americans[20]

### ATTENTION

I.  "Thanks for honoring me with your gracious invitation to speak."

II.  "We must never forget that American Indians were the first people to live in this beautiful country."

### NEED

I.  The beliefs of Native Americans are unique.
   A.  They believe in "the dualities of life: sky-earth; sun-moon; love-hate; wisdom-ignorance."
   B.  The most important duality is man-woman as together they are "part of the great sacred circle of life."

II.  Tribal views also are unique—with different tribes holding different beliefs about women being sacred.
   A.  The Hopi believe in the Spider Grandmother, who made the four races of people.
   B.  The Iroquois give status to the Clan Mother.
   C.  The Cherokee give status to the Beloved Woman.
   D.  Each tribe grants respect to Indian women.

III.  As a woman, I am part of that which has preceded me.
   A.  "My grandmothers have been here for all time."
   B.  "The land you strive to protect is my grandmother—my mother."

*(continued)*

IV. Once the majority, we are now the "minority of minorities."
  A. We number less than 1 percent of the population.
  B. Due to our small number, policymakers are generally uninformed about our culture.
  C. "I would characterize American society as 'culturally disrespectful.'"
V. Historically, American Indians have had three "agencies of oppression."
  A. Church: Christianize the pagans.
  B. Government: Assimilate them.
  C. Education: Civilize the "savages."

**SATISFACTION**

I. Policymakers should acknowledge five basic truths.
  A. "Indians have been here for thousands of years."
  B. This is their homeland.
  C. Their own distinct cultures have evolved.
  D. We were not forced into abandoning our cultures.
  E. "Assimilation and acculturation occur on individuals' terms."
II. The American Indian culture can contribute without changing.
  A. To the Iroquois, for example, "peace was the law."
    1. The same word is used for both *peace* and *law*.
    2. "Peace was a way of life."
  B. The allegory of the Great White Pine represents the unity of peace with law and land.
    1. For the Iroquois, the Tree symbolizes law.
    2. The Tree's branches symbolize shelter within the law.
    3. The Tree's roots symbolize the law's ability to stretch out and embrace all peoples.

**VISUALIZATION**

I. With recognition of the Indian's true nature and contribution can come change.
  A. Change is a cause for celebration.
  B. "With clarity of vision we can celebrate the natural diversity of our universe and our world."
II. The Indian values—patience, honesty, acceptance, respect—can serve as the foundation for good interpersonal relationships in a culturally diverse world.

**ACTION**

I. I applaud your commitment to a culturally diverse workforce.
II. My tribute to you is to share with you a Cheyenne philosophical belief: "A nation is not conquered until the hearts of its women are on the ground. Then it is done, no matter how brave its warriors nor how strong its weapons."
  A. This is the power of women as equals.
  B. This is why the most powerful pairing is men and women working together.

## Using the Motivated Sequence for Behavioral Actuation

Demands for action can be issued and defended very efficiently by using the motivated sequence. In fact, the desire to structure speeches that move people to action (e.g., to buy a product or engage in another specified behavior) was the impetus behind Alan Monroe's development of this organizational scheme. Read the outline that follows to get a clear sense of how the motivated sequence can be used in developing an actuative speech. Notice the adaptation of national statistics and information to the local situation in which students find themselves and the use of motivational appeals aimed particularly at a student population (service, yes, but also use of academic knowledge and ways of gaining academic credit while performing that service).

### Using the Motivated Sequence to Call for Action

#### The Chain Never Stops

**The Situation:** You are attending college at Buena Vista University, in Storm Lake, Iowa. It's home to a large meat-processing plant run by IBP (Iowa Beef Producers, Inc.). IBP has diversified the community by bringing in a significant Hispanic population to work at the plant. Yet you know that these workers' wages are low compared to those in other U.S. industrial plants and that meat-processing plants are notorious for accidents and lack of support for workers who have had accidents. You want your classmates to help do something about the problems you see.

**Specific Purpose:** To convince at least five classmates to join you in finding IBP workers who have suffered serious work-related injuries and in helping them get fair compensation for their injuries[21]

#### ATTENTION

I. "In the beginning he had been fresh and strong, and he had gotten a job the first day; but now he was second-hand, a damaged article, so to speak, and they did not want him.…They had worn him out, with their speeding-up and their carelessness, and now they had thrown him away!"
   A. These are words from Sinclair Lewis's 1906 novel *The Jungle.*
   B. Though written a hundred years ago, they still apply to the same place they were written about—slaughterhouses.

II. The meat-processing industry in the United States has grown into a wondrous mixture of industrial technology and human labor, yet Sinclair Lewis could have been writing about an Iowa Beef Processing, Inc., plant in South Dakota, Texas, or even Storm Lake, Iowa.
   A. I'm not singling out IBP or even the local plant.

*(continued)*

B.  But I am saying that the meat-processing industry does not have an enviable track record of care for labor.

C.  It's the kind of record, as a matter of fact, that some of you might be willing to help correct.

III.  Today, I want to review the safety and labor relations record of meat-packing plants and suggest some steps we can take toward bettering that record right here in Storm Lake, Iowa, as part of your education at Buena Vista University.

**NEED**

I.  First, you need to understand something about the history of meat processing in this country and the role of IBP in modernizing it.

A.  Begun as Iowa Beef Packers, Inc., in 1961, IBP revolutionized the meat-packing industry.

1.  It moved slaughterhouses out of the cities and into the countryside, nearer supplies, to save money.

2.  It automated the process through division of labor, meaning that it needed less-skilled workers who could be paid less than traditional, unionized butchers.

3.  It quit shipping carcasses to grocery outlets but instead packed them in smaller, more specialized boxes that were vacuum sealed and distributed directly to stores, which, in turn, did not need to hire such experienced meat cutters—saving still more money.

B.  The rest of the meat-processing industry could compete with IBP only by imitating its plant locations, meat-cutting processes, and distribution system, like IBP, economizing the production of consumable meat products that most of you enjoy at extraordinarily low cost.

II.  Along with these great innovations, however, came other changes.

A.  While the top four meat-packers in 1970 controlled just 21 percent of the beef market, today the top four—IBP, ConAgra, Excel, and National Beef—control about 85 percent of the market.

B.  Wages in the meat-packing industry fell by as much as 50 percent over the last three decades, making it one of the lowest-paying industrial jobs in the United States.

C.  Lower wages were possible because new workers were recruited heavily from Mexico.

1.  A wage of $9.50 an hour is a great boon to a Mexican who was making $7.00 a day at home.

2.  The power of unions in the meat-packing industry could be broken when labor was afraid that bosses would send them back to Mexico.

III.  All of these changes have adversely affected workers in the industry.

A.  In 1999, more than one-quarter of all meat packers—40,000 of the 150,000 workers—suffered a job-related industry or illness.

1. Because "The chain never stops"—the chain on which meat carcasses move down the assembly line—up to 400 animals an hour must be processed by workers cutting meat at lightning speed. (Twenty-five years ago, about 175 cattle went through per hour.)
2. Workers are regularly cut, hit, hooked, caught in meat tenderizers, burned by beef tallow and other hot solutions, and even decapitated or killed by stun guns. *[Be very careful on how graphic descriptions become]*

B. Those who are hurt are encouraged to sign a waiver when they're treated, meaning they give up their right to sue for damages in exchange for medical treatment.
   1. If workers want treatment by the company, they must sign the waiver.
   2. The waiver allows companies to get around workers' compensation laws in states like Texas, where one-quarter of the U.S. beef supply is processed.

C. Workers who are seriously injured are encouraged to quit or are forced to take menial jobs that they find humiliating.
   1. If you quit, you lose health benefits and have to go on welfare.
   2. If you stay, you might get a job like Michael Grover did—IBP had him picking up dropped dirty towels and toilet paper from the restroom floor all day, every day.

D. Further, some states are seeking to reduce workers' compensation levels, being lobbied by politicians with connections to the meat-processing industry.
   1. Texas Senator Phil Gramm's wife, Wendy Lee, sits on the board of IBP.
   2. Colorado state Senator Tom Norton, sponsor of a bill to limit compensation, has a wife, Kathy, who was vice president of ConAgra Red Meat the year he sponsored that bill.

**SATISFACTION**

I. What can a class of college students in northern Iowa do about any of this?
   A. We can volunteer at the local meat cutters' union hall and the recreation center downtown, where most of the workers' families come for daytime crafts and activities.
      1. We don't want to go off half-cocked: We need information on injuries, their seriousness, their treatment, and workers' compensation from the company.
      2. We need to establish a level of trust with those families before helping them with whatever work-related and injury- or health-related problems they have.
   B. Those of you who are prelaw majors can get a little practice by reading up on Iowa's workers' compensation laws and the conformity requirements for meat processors.
      1. You can't give advice until you know what you're talking about.
      2. Anyone who's taken Introduction to Business Law will be especially valuable as a resource.
   C. Someone can get hooked up with ICAN—the Iowa Citizens Action Network—to check on the status of workers' compensation law reform (proposed limitations) in Iowa.

*(continued)*

D. Then, once you know the situation of workers here in Storm Lake and what you need to know about Iowa law more generally, you can become a family counselor.
   1. Working a few hours per week in the counseling desk we're setting up at the recreation center will be easy to work into your schedule.
   2. You even can earn research practicum credit in the Department of Communication, thereby helping yourself move toward graduation.

**VISUALIZATION**

I. If the meat-processing industry, as a whole, does not become more worker conscious, horror stories will continue to pour out of gigantic plants across the country.
   A. Kenny Dobbins's story about his life with Monfort Beef Company [*Tell his story with good taste, including details about the falling 90-pound box of meat, his blown disc and back surgery, chlorine inhalation, damaged rotator cuff, broken leg, shattered ankle, and innumerable lacerations*]
   B. Albertina Rios's story about her life with IBP in Lexington, Nebraska
   C. Rual Lopez's story about being hung on a chain and crushed in Greeley, Colorado, while working for ConAgra

II. If the industry, however, even just lets workers get compensated under the usual state laws, a great stride forward will have been taken.
   A. Workers who have been injured will not be so easily fired.
   B. They'll be able to go to arbitration for compensation in cases of debilitating injury.
   C. And they'll be able to get proper financial help while recovering and state-mandated payments for nondebilitating yet bodily harm.

III. As well, if unions are reinstituted in all meat-packing plants, negotiations for health care, treatment, time off, and necessary retirement will be carried on by the people who count—the local managers and their own labor force.

**ACTION**

I. "The chain never stops"—that's the cry of workers who kill, skin, clean, cut up, box, and finally ship the meat that appears on American tables every morning, noon, and evening.
   A. If the chain doesn't stop, someone—many someones—will get hurt.
   B. Those of us who enjoy the products of their labor—bacon, burgers, a nice steak—have a moral obligation, it seems to me, to make their life in service to us as good as we can.

II. Come join me tonight at 7:30 in Room 123 down the hall to talk about the kinds of help you can provide, given your interests and schedules.
   A. I'll tell you how you can volunteer to meet with families.
   B. I'll show you some research projects we need to pursue, if you'd rather do that.
   C. I'll give you a list of Buena Vista University instructors who'll give you academic credit for your work of various kinds.

III. It's time for all of us—at least five of us, if they'll join me—to make sure that Sinclair Lewis's *The Jungle* no longer reflects factory life in Storm Lake, Iowa, and all of the other packer towns in the United States.

# Assessing Sample Speeches

The following two persuasive speeches were offered during the dramatic debate in the U.S. House of Representatives over Articles of Impeachment focused on President Bill Clinton, December 18–19, 1998.[22] On Saturday, December 19, both Democrats and Republicans gave time to their best speakers to offer short, persuasive statements to justify the votes for and against impeachment that occurred in the afternoon. Among the best speakers that day were Rep. Richard Gephardt (D–Missouri) and Rep. J. C. Watts (R–Oklahoma). Both chose transcendent strategies based on value appeals, arguing that valuative commitments should guide specific actions (votes for or against impeachment).

Rep. Watts spoke first. His strategy was dual: Appeal to our care and sympathy for children (*affiliation, companionship*) and to their clear, uncomplicated sense of honesty (*conformity, loyalty, tradition*). Especially in paragraphs 2–5, the theme of listening to our children and their clear sense of rightness was sketched expertly and in ways sensitive to audience segments with their own children or grandchildren. Rep. Watts contrasted their sense with adult attitudes, which he said we could see in public opinion polls (paragraphs 6–7). Having transcended the politics of impeachment with these appeals primarily to the affiliation cluster of motivational appeals, he then asked his listeners to apply those clear moral guidelines from children to the impeachment proceedings (paragraph 8), aiming at the "Belongers" and the "Social Conscious" groups from among the VALS typology. He concluded with a negative visualization: "In this moment, our children's future is more important than our future. If our country looks the other way, our country will lose its way" (paragraph 9).

Rep. Gephardt spoke later that morning. He, too, went to affiliative motivational appeals when talking about the Founding Fathers (*tradition*) and "the altar of an unattainable morality" (*reverence*). By paragraphs 7 and 8, he was contrasting "the death of representative democracy" (*fear*) from the power cluster with "healing" (*companionship*) from the affiliation cluster. Like Rep. Watts, therefore, Rep. Gephardt sought to transcend the political situation with social and communal appeals, going after the same "Belongers" that Watt did but major parts of the "Achievers" group, as well. He ended with negative and positive visualizations: The House now on "the brink of the abyss" (paragraph 10) contrasted with "a new politics of respect and fairness and decency" (paragraph 11). Such a new politics, he concluded, was possible only if Congress had "the wisdom and the courage and the goodness to save itself today" (paragraph 12). So, both Rep. Watts and Rep. Gephardt had warnings for their colleagues, though only Gephardt tried to turn the negative into a positive vision—and thereby, he hoped, to turn some votes *for* to votes *against* impeachment.

That there were Republican and Democratic votes both for and against impeachment—and that not all of the proposed Articles of Impeachment were passed—is testament to the power of persuasive speech.

### Speech for Impeachment
**Rep. J. C. Watts**

Mr. Speaker, there is no joy sometimes in upholding the law. It is so unpleasant sometimes that we hire other people to do it for us. Ask the police or judges. It is tiring and thankless. But we know it must be done, because if we do not point at lawlessness, our children cannot see it. If we do not label lawlessness, our children cannot recognize it. And if we do not punish lawlessness, our children will not believe it. 1

So if someone were to ask me, "J. C., why did you vote for the articles of impeachment?" I would say I did it for our children. How can we tell our children that honesty is the best policy if we do not demand honesty as a policy? How can we expect a Boy Scout to honor his oath if elected officials do not honor theirs? How can we expect a business executive to honor a promise when the chief executive abandons his or hers? 2

Whether it is a promise or a truth or a vow or an oath, a person's word is the firm footing our society stands upon, and the average kid understands that. They do not need a grand jury to enforce it. They say "cross your heart, hope to die"; "pinkie promise"; "king's X"; "blood brother." These are the childhood instincts that seek to draw a line between the honest and the dishonest, between the principled and the unprincipled. 3

Ask the children. The kid who lies does not last, and they do not bicker over what is and what is not a lie. They know. So do I. So do the American people. 4

Time and again, we wanted the essence of truth and we got the edges of the truth. We hear, "Let's get on with the business of our country." What business is more important than teaching our children right from wrong? Some say it is all about politics and party lines. If that were true, I would have given in to popular opinion. But what is popular is not always what is right. 5

Some say polls are against this. Polls measure changing feelings, not steadfast principle. Polls would have rejected the Ten Commandments. Polls would have embraced slavery and ridiculed women's rights. 6

Some say we must draw this to a close. I say we must draw a line between right and wrong—not with a tiny fine line of an executive fountain pen, but with the big, thick lead of a Number 2 pencil. We must do it so every kid in America can see it. 7

The point is not whether the president can prevail, but whether truth can prevail. We need to cease the cannibalizing of members of Congress. We need to cease the attacks on the president and his family because, friends, this is not about the President of the United States. He is not the injured party. Our country is. 8

In this moment, our children's future is more important than our future. If our country looks the other way, our country will lose its way. 9

## *Speech against Impeachment*
### Rep. Richard Gephardt

1 Mr. Speaker, I stood on this floor yesterday and implored all of us to say that the politics of slash and burn must end. I implored all of us that we must turn away from the politics of personal destruction and return to the politics of values.

2 It is with that same passion that I say to all of you today that the gentleman from Louisiana [Mr. Bob Livingston] is a worthy and good and honorable man.

3 I believe his decision to retire [after sexual indiscretions were revealed] is a terrible capitulation to the negative forces that are consuming our political system and our country, and I pray with all my heart that he will reconsider this decision.

4 Our Founding Fathers created a system of government of men, not of angels. No one standing in this House today can pass the puritanical test of purity that some are demanding that our elected leaders take. If we demand that mere mortals live up to this standard, we will see our seats of government lay empty and we will see the best, most able people unfairly cast out of public service.

5 We need to stop destroying imperfect people at the altar of an unobtainable morality. We need to start living up to the standards which the public in its infinite wisdom understands, that imperfect people must strive towards, but too often fall short.

6 We are now rapidly descending into a politics where life imitates farce, fratricide dominates our public debate, and America is held hostage to tactics of smear and fear.

7 Let all of us here today say no to resignation, no to impeachment, no to hatred, no to intolerance of each other, and no to vicious self-righteousness.

8 We need to start healing. We need to start binding up our wounds. We need to end this downward spiral which will culminate in the death of representative democracy.

9 I believe this healing can start today by changing the course we have begun. This is exactly why we need this today to be bipartisan. This is why we ask the opportunity to vote on a bipartisan censure resolution, to begin the process of healing our nation and healing our people.

10 We are on the brink of the abyss. The only way we stop this insanity is through the force of our own will. The only way we stop this spiral is for all of us to finally say "enough."

11 Let us step back from the abyss and let us begin a new politics of respect and fairness and decency, which realizes what has come before.

12 May God have mercy on this Congress, and may Congress have the wisdom and the courage and the goodness to save itself today.

# ■ CHAPTER SUMMARY

The rhetorical arts of persuasion and actuation are fundamental to any democratic society. Not only are they the heart and soul of capitalism, American mass media, and politics, but they are necessary to the operation of daily life. Effective persuasive and actuative speeches in an age of social-economic-political fragmentation are functions of the following:

- Adapting to an audience's psychological orientations (psychological orientation to lifestyles, as in VALS, and predispositions toward the topic)
- Selecting motivational appeals that will resonate with behaviors and community lifestyles (as in PRIZM clusters of audience members)

- Drawing upon a diverse mix of external reference groups
- Enhancing personal credibility

The strategies discussed under each of these topics are not exhaustive, but they suggest mental habits of audience analysis that speakers must employ each time they attempt persuasion. To increase your effectiveness, use them whenever you seek to reinforce an audience's commitment to shared values; to modify their beliefs, attitudes, and values; or to move them to action. Using the motivated sequence will assist you in adapting your content and style to the audience.

# ■ KEY TERMS

actuation   (p. 359)
content level   (p. 356)
good reasons   (p. 344)
latitude of acceptance   (p. 350)
latitude of rejection   (p. 350)
lifestyles   (p. 346)
one-sided message   (p. 349)

PRIZM   (p. 351)
psychological orientation   (p. 346)
psychological reorientation   (p. 356)
reference groups   (p. 353)
relational level   (p. 356)

saliency   (p. 349)
speech of modification   (p. 357)
speech of reinforcement   (p. 357)
two-sided message   (p. 349)
Values and Lifestyles (VALS) Program   (p. 346)

# ■ ASSESSMENT ACTIVITIES

1. Do a PRIZM-type analysis of your class. Download a copy of the PRIZM questionnaire available from Claritas (see the References, p. 373, note 12). Reproduce the questionnaire, distribute it, and appoint a small committee to tabulate it (or ask your instructor to do it, if your classmates don't want others seeing their individual questionnaires). Distribute the tabulation and discuss the results as a class: As you think about yourselves as an audience, can you find some specific clusters with three to five or

more people in each? What lifestyle characteristics or behavioral patterns most centrally define each cluster? What are some of the important differences between clusters—differences that will require speakers on certain kinds of topics to adjust their motivational appeals? Take notes, and use the PRIZM analysis in planning your future speeches.

2. Develop and present to the class a 5- to 7-minute speech. Follow the steps in the motivated sequence appropriate to the type of

speech chosen: reinforcement, modification, or actuation. As you construct your speech, remember the strategies discussed in this chapter, both in terms of the essential features of all persuasive speeches and those specific to your speech. Adapt to the audience as you deem appropriate from your analysis of the different segments or clusters of people in your class.

# REFERENCES

1. Information from Robert J. Samuelson, "It's Now Time for a Tax Cut," *Newsweek*, 15 January 2001, p. 25.

2. *Good reasons* must be understood as rational or reasonable, though not necessarily logical in a technical sense. They seem relevant and grounded in the world as audiences understand it. *Facts* are relevant when they are thought of or conceived of as relevant by people to their life experiences. Good reasons must be understood as a human (psychological, social) concept, not a logical (systemic) one. A full theory of good reasons is developed in Walter R. Fisher, *Human Communication as Narrative* (Columbia: University of South Carolina Press, 1987), esp. Chs. 2 and 3.

3. Michael J. Weiss, *The Clustering of America* (New York: Harper & Row, 1900), 2, as quoted in Joseph Turow, *Breaking Up America: Advertisers and the New Media World* (Chicago: University of Chicago Press, 1997), 45.

4. Robert D. Putnam, *Bowling Alone: The Collapse and Revival of American Community* (New York: Simon & Schuster, 2000), and Turow (note 3).

5. Arnold Mitchell, *The Nine American Lifestyles: Who We Are and Where We're Going* (New York: Macmillan, 1983). The VALS research program grew out of developmental psychology but soon was turned into a business-consulting operation, SRI (Stanford Research Institute) Consulting Business Intelligence. An article describing the original VALS system, "SRI's Values and Lifestyle Program," can be found in *In Context*, available online: <http://www.context.org/ICLIB/IC03/SRIVALS.htm>, 1983/1996. The business operation can be accessed at <http://future.sri.com/VALS/VALSindex.shtml>, 2001. They work from a late-1980s modification of the original categories, now called VALS2.

6. Details of the survey are available online: <http://future.sri.com/vals/surveynew.shtml>.

7. For a clear explanation, with illustrations of one- versus two-sided messages, see Herbert W. Simons with Joanne Morreale and Bruce Gronbeck, *Persuasion in Society* (Thousand Oaks, CA: Sage, 2001), 201–202.

8. "Benefits of the Statins: Beyond Cholesterol," *Harvard Men's Health Watch*, 6:1 (August 2001): 1–5.

9. An excellent source on saliency research is Richard E. Petty and John T. Cacioppo, *Communication and Persuasion: Central and Peripheral Routes to Attitude Change* (New York: Springer-Verlag, 1986).

10. Latitudes of acceptance and rejection are concepts developed within social judgment theory. See James B. Stiff, *Persuasive Communication* (New York: Guilford Press, 1994), 139–142; and Stephen W. Littlejohn, *Theories of Human Communication*, 6th ed. (Belmont, CA: Wadsworth, 1999).

11. The PRIZM *neighborhood lifestyle segmentation* system was developed by Claritas, Inc., a market research firm from San Diego, CA. It is built around five-digit zip codes, which typically means 2,500 to 7,500 households per *cluster*. Those wanting (and willing to pay for) more precise breakdowns—say, by nine-digit zip codes—can get demographic/consumption data on groups as small as 6 to 12 households at <http://www.velocity.claritas.com/YAYL/yawyfaq.wjsp#where>. A full discussion of the uses to which such segmenting systems can be put socially, economically, and politically is available in Turow (note 3).

12. The following information and quotations are available online: <http://www.qmsoft.com/solutions/prizm.htm>. The Claritas website (note 11) provides more concrete data by zip code.

13. Philip Zimbardo, *Psychology and Life*, 13th ed. (New York: Allyn and Bacon, 1992), 580–581.

14. See Stiff, 52–54 (note 10).

15. Petty and Cacioppo, 205 (note 9).

16. Still the most complete summary of credibility research is found in Stephen Littlejohn, "A Bibliogra-

phy of Studies Related to Variables of Source Credibility," in *Bibliographical Annual in Speech Communication: 1971*, edited by Ned Shearer (Washington, DC: National Communication Association, 1972), 1–40.

17. Simons, 49 (note 7), drawing upon the original research of Paul Watzlawick, J. H. Bevin, and D. D. Jackson, *Pragmatics of Human Communication* (New York: Norton, 1967).

18. Kay Deaux and Lawrence S. Wrightsman, *Social Psychology*, 5th ed. (Pacific Grove, CA: Brooks/Cole, 1988), 160–206. For a review of various theories of attitude change and its relationship to beliefs, values, and schemas, see Simons, Ch. 2 (note 7).

19. Information for this outline is from several sources: Eyal Press and Jennifer Washburn, "Digital Diplomas," *Mother Jones*, January–February 2001, pp. 34–39, 82–85; Jon Spayde, "College @ home," *Modern Maturity*, July–August 2001, pp. 60–62; and Don Steinberg, "The Lowdown on Online: Everything You Need to Get Plugged In," *Modern Maturity*, July–August 2001, p. 63.

20. This outline is based on a speech by Henri Mann Morton, "Strength through Cultural Diversity," in *Native American Reader: Stories, Speeches and Poems*, edited by Jerry D. Blanche (Juneau, AK: Denali Press, 1990), 400–474. Direct quotes from the speech are indicated as such. Used with permission of Denali Press.

21. Information for this outline is from several sources: Eric Schlosser, "The Chain Never Stops," *Mother Jones*, July–August 2001, pp. 38–47, 86–87; <http://www.ibpinc.com/index.htm>; <http://www.ibpinc.com/about/IBPNewHistory.stm>.

22. The texts for Rep. Watts's and Gephardt's speeches on December 19, 1998, are from the *Congressional Record*, Proceedings and Debates of the 105th Congress, 2nd sess. (Washington, DC: Government Printing Office, 1998), 144, no. 155:H11973-4, H2031-2.

Chapter **15**

# Argument and Critical Thinking

*Should the United States embark on a missile defense program?*

*Should our university institute a new technology fee?*

*Should we rent a movie tonight?*

These are very different questions, yet they are alike in one major respect: Each is debatable. None of the questions automatically suggests a right or true answer with which all would agree. Answering any of these questions with a simple yes or no will invite others to ask, "Why do you believe as you do?" You will be expected to provide reasons and evidence for your position, and in turn, your response may be challenged by your listeners.

In short, this exchange involves you and your listeners in **argumentation**—the give and take involved in advancing reasons for and against a particular claim (see Figure 15.1, p. 376). This process can be discussed in terms of **argument**—the actual *product* that results from the combination of a claim plus supporting reasons and evidence—as well as the *act* of **arguing** itself.[1] As you argue, you also engage in **critical thinking**—the process of examining the relationship between your own reasons and the claim you are advocating and the reasons or evidence offered by those challenging your argument.[2]

If the questions raised are capable of being answered truthfully, without any concern for being mistaken at some later point, there is no cause for challenge. Few such questions, however, have such answers available. Hence, argument is a constant companion of those issues and ideas for which there are no certain answers. In arguing, our search is for the *best answer* we can offer given the knowledge available. We do not know for certain if taking action against Iraq will end the threat of chemical weaponry, nor do we know if a technology fee is the right way to raise money for new computer equipment. Finally, we cannot be certain

**FIGURE 15.1**

**The Levels
of Argumentation**

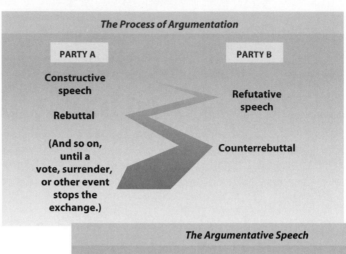

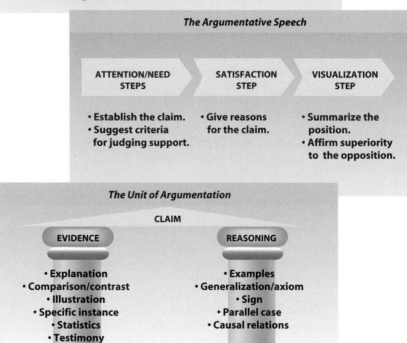

that renting a movie is the optimum choice (especially if we have an exam tomorrow). Given this uncertainty, the best solution is to think critically about our choices by testing the evidence offered in support of reasons—Is it reliable?—and examining the relationship between reasons and claims—Do the reasons really support the claim?

As we do, two features of argumentation are worthy of comment. First, argument is a social process. Second, argument is aimed at justifying our beliefs and actions. We begin with an examination of the social process involved in arguing with others, and we then consider what is involved in justifying claims, with a focus on improving your effectiveness as an arguer.

## Argument and Cultural Commitments

Argument and critical thinking are bound together in public communication. Exchanging views in the social world automatically includes the critical assessment of those ideas. Engaging in argument commits you to the social conventions governing deliberation, whether in private interchanges with close friends or in public settings among friends and strangers.[3]

### Commitment to Change Your Mind

You—and those who challenge you—must be open to the possibility that the position you each challenge is the weaker of the ones in dispute.[4] This does not mean that you approach an argument thinking you are wrong but simply that you need to acknowledge that others may well have good or even better justifications for their positions. They still have an obligation to illustrate that theirs is the better rationale, and they also have the reciprocal obligation to recognize you may in fact have the stronger argument. *Arguing,* as we define it, requires greater flexibility in positions taken. You've experienced the frustration of arguing with someone who does not accept this social convention: a stubborn friend or other opponent who believes only what he or she is saying and simply refuses to acknowledge the possibility that the position being advanced is wrong.

### Commitment to Knowledge

"Argument fails where ignorance prevails." In addition to accepting the possibility of being wrong, both parties to an argument also must accept a commitment to learn from each other, search for new information, and test evidence to ensure that the best possible information is being used to support alternative positions. Those who are certain of their own beliefs ("Don't confuse me with facts—my mind is made up") are closed to information that was counter to that which they already accept or which supports their position.

### Commitment to Worthy Subjects

Have you ever been in a silly argument? Unfortunately, many arguments can be summarized in the following statement: "Argumentation concerns talk between the uninformed and the misinformed about the inconsequential." The value of critical thinking and the need to test ideas in private or in public are wasted on people who are just plain disagreeable and nasty. Although some have a psychological need to be contentious, more important, there is a social need for argument about issues that matter, about causes that do, in fact, make a difference in how we treat and live with each other.

## Commitment to Rules

Argument is a rule-governed process of arriving at a conclusion that, to the best of one's knowledge, is justifiable as a basis for belief or action. The rules may focus on the overall procedures for engaging in argument, as in using parliamentary procedures to govern who talks, when, and for how long. The rules also focus on the product itself: Not any reason will support any claim. Some kind of logical, rational connection is needed between a given reason and the claim being offered.

The reliance on reasons given for a belief or action constitutes the major difference between argumentation and mere fighting. As such, argumentation is a form of *persuasion* in that it seeks to change the beliefs, attitudes, values, and behaviors of others. At the same time, it also is a form of mutual *truth-testing*, helping participants arrive at the best possible conclusions given the information available at the time. Thus, the process is more thoroughly rule governed than other forms of public presentation.

These four commitments define the social parameters of argument in the social community. Whether you are engaging in private discussion or public deliberation, the same conventions apply. The process of thinking critically about how argument proceeds depends, in addition, on understanding how to arrive at a justifiable defense—or attack—of another person's position.

 # Argument as Justifying Belief and Action

The analysis of how one justifies a position begins with the claim being advanced. Then, the nature of the evidence used in support of the claim and the major **reasoning patterns** (sometimes referred to as the *warrants* or *inferences*) used to connect evidence to claims are examined.

## Types of Claims

Most argumentative speeches assert that something is or is not the case, is desirable or undesirable, or should or should not be done. The first step in constructing a successful argument is to determine clearly the nature of your claim.

**Claims of Fact**   If you are trying to convince your listeners that "Raising tuition to the levels proposed will result in fewer applications to attend this university," you are presenting a **factual claim**—asserting that an audience is justified in believing this state of affairs will occur. When confronted with a factual claim, two questions are likely to arise among critical listeners:

*Knowing your audience is critical in arguing on behalf of a client.*

**By what criteria or standards of judgment should the accuracy of this claim be measured?** Some standards are rather obvious. If you were asked to judge a person's height, using a yardstick or other instrument would provide the answer. Listeners look for similar kinds of "yardsticks" when asked to evaluate more complex claims. Before agreeing that a tuition hike will result in fewer applications, critical thinkers want to know exactly what the proposed tuition hike is as well as what constitutes "fewer"—and when does this become a significant loss to worry about?

**Do the facts of the situation fit the criteria as set forth?** Has the speaker identified what is meant by "fewer" such that it will be clear this is a reasonable criteria? Will 5 to 10 fewer applications constitute the truth of the claim? (In a narrow, literal sense, yes, but then what is the point of the claim if it is satisfied with one less application?) The criteria must be seen as reasonable and making a significant difference regarding the risk associated with raising tuition. Realize that the audience may choose to disagree with your criteria as well as with your evidence. Hence, you need to be prepared to defend both.

**Claims of Value** A claim also may incorporate value judgments in asserting that your idea is worthy or that the idea of an opponent is undesirable or unjustified. In these cases, you are articulating a **value claim.** As with a factual claim, a value claim is supported by standards or criteria and by the illustration of how your value term meets those criteria. The claim that "Decriminalizing undocumented workers will destroy American jobs" implies a value—actions that are destructive of jobs are not worthy of consideration. You must, however, do more than simply suggest a preference ("I don't like the decriminalization proposal"). You need to know how decriminalization would function and what negative effects it may create. This knowledge leads you to the criteria for judging the worth of the proposal, which makes it easier to argue for its inadequacy because of the negative effects created.

**Claims of Policy**     A **policy claim** recommends a course of action you want the audience to approve. For example, you might claim that "The federal government *should* decriminalize undocumented workers." The policy claim incorporates fact and value claims as its primary *proofs:*

> **Policy:** The federal government should decriminalize undocumented workers because . . .
>
> **Value:** Decriminalization recognizes the humanity of migrant workers.
>
> **Fact:** Undocumented workers are working at rates far below minimum wage.
>
> **Fact:** Legalizing undocumented workers will not constitute a hardship for others. (Note that this is a far more difficult fact to support than the prior one!)

The key term in the policy claim is *should*—it identifies a proposed policy or defends a policy or action that currently is the case. For our purposes, those policy claims examined will challenge the present system, procedure, or way of doing things. When establishing or analyzing a policy claim, four questions are relevant:

**Is there a need for such a policy or course of action?**  If your listeners do not believe a change is called for, they aren't likely to approve your proposal. This does not mean you should avoid new ideas; rather, it suggests that the importance of establishing a need for change depends upon the audience's level of comfort with the present situation.

**Is the proposal practical or workable?**  Can we afford the expenses it would entail? Will it meet the need as identified? Is the proposal merely being advocated for symbolic reasons, or does it actually have a chance of being passed and effecting change? If the policy cannot meet these basic tests, what chance does it have?

**Will the benefits of your proposal be greater than the disadvantages?**  You may be familiar with the expression "The cure is worse than the disease." People are reluctant to approve a proposal that promises a cure but creates conditions worse than the ones it's designed to correct. Burning a building to the ground to get rid of rats may be efficient, but it is hardly desirable. The benefits and disadvantages must be carefully weighed in concluding that a proposal is, indeed, comparatively better than the present course.

**Is the offered proposal superior to any other plan or policy?**  Listeners are hesitant to approve a plan if they have reason to believe the current policy is more practical and beneficial. Requiring citizens to move their cars every two hours on downtown streets or be ticketed may seem a simple means of easing the parking crunch. Wrong! Any policy will affect some portion of the community more than others, and those whose lives are disrupted will make that known. Policy changes have consequences, and not all people will see the consequences as you do.

These claims—fact, value, policy—make different demands on you as an arguer (see Table 15.1). Your best strategy is to set forth a claim, the criteria on which it is based, and the evidence used to support the claim in a straightforward, honest manner. In that way, your audience can see what standard of judgment you are using and determine how you see the evidence functioning in relation to the criteria and claim. In some cultures, the context in which you place the claim and evidence and how you argue the point mean more than the actual content of your message.[5]

Previewing the underlying logic of your argument at the start (unless there are solid reasons for delaying this information) enables your audience to follow your line of reasoning. Forecast your argument by saying something like the following:

> I hope to convince you that there should be a salary cap on the income earned by professional athletes; if we take this action, it will result in fair and equitable treatment for all athletes and will restore faith in the sport for the paying fans.

## Evidence

As you discovered in Chapter 6, supporting materials clarify, amplify, and strengthen the ideas in your speech. They also provide evidence for the acceptance of a claim and its supporting points. **Evidence** is a crucial part of developing a clear, compelling argument, and it can be presented in any of the forms discussed in Chapter 6: explanation, comparison and contrast, illustration, specific instance,

**TABLE 15.1    Types of Claims**

| CLAIM | DESCRIPTION | ANALYSIS |
|-------|-------------|----------|
| Fact | Assertion that something exists | 1. By what criteria is the accuracy of the claim measured? <br> 2. Do the facts of the situation fit the criteria? |
| Value | Assertion that something is worthy or unworthy | 1. By what standards is something to be judged? <br> 2. How well does the thing measure up? |
| Policy | Recommendation of a course of action | 1. Is there a need? <br> 2. Is the proposal practical? <br> 3. Are the benefits greater than the disadvantages? <br> 4. Is the proposal better than other courses of action? |

## E T H I C A L   M O M E N T S

### The Use of Evidence

The use of evidence generates several potential ethical dilemmas:

**1**  Should you suppress evidence that contradicts a point you are making? If your opponent is not aware of the information, should you mention it?

**2**  What about the use of qualifiers? Should you leave in each "maybe" and "possibly" when you read or paraphrase a quotation? If you have to submit a written text or outline, you can use ellipses (i.e., the three dots that indicate something is missing from the original) where the qualifiers once were. Would that be acceptable?

**3**  Does it make any difference if you overqualify a source? If you've discovered an article by a staff researcher at the National Endowment for the Arts on the issue of funding controversial art, will it hurt to suggest the information is from an associate director of the agency, even if no specific person is cited? If it increases the credibility of the information, should the new (although false) title be used?

**4**  What difference does it make if a poll is conducted by the National Right-to-Life Committee or Planned Parenthood's Pro-Choice Committee? What if each organization asks polling questions in such a way as to encourage a response favorable to its position? Can you just say that "A recent national poll found that 75 percent of U.S. citizens favor abortion rights"? You haven't really lied in suppressing the polling agency or the actual questions asked, have you? Is this acceptable?

statistics, and testimony. As you conduct your search for information, the primary goal is to find supporting materials that are both rationally and motivationally relevant to the claim being advanced.

**Rationally Relevant Evidence**    The type of evidence you select should reflect the type of claim you advocate. For example, if you are defending the claim that censorship violates the First Amendment guarantee of freedom of speech, testimony from legal authorities will be useful in supporting your argument. On the other hand, examples, illustrations, and statistics work better if you are arguing that a problem exists or a change in practices is needed. If you argue that shark fishing should be more heavily regulated, you'll find that examples of poor fishing practices and statistical evidence related to overfishing and potential loss to the ecosystem will be relevant to your purpose. Always ask yourself: Given this claim, what evidence is naturally suggested by the subject matter? What type of evidence is logically relevant?

*Public advocates use argumentation to convince others, at times through active protest. What is the argument being promoted in this situation?*

**Motivationally Relevant Evidence**   Listeners often require more than logically relevant support. Your evidence also must create a compelling desire on their part to be involved, endorse the belief, or undertake a course of action. Why should an audience be concerned about regulating shark fishing? To motivate your listeners, you must answer the "So what?" question. To select motivationally relevant material, consider two issues:

**What type of evidence will this audience demand?** To orient your thinking, turn this question around and ask: As a member of the audience, what would I expect as support for this claim to accept it? What motivates you to accept the argument may well motivate the audience. As noted earlier, some evidence also seems naturally connected to certain subjects. A claim regarding relative costs of competing plans suggests things like statistical graphs or charts. If the audience is able to say "Yes, but . . ." after hearing your evidence, you have not motivated them to accept your claim.

**What evidence will generate the best response?** You should pose this question once you've determined the type of evidence required by your argument. For example, if you've decided to use expert testimony, whom should you quote? If you're using an illustration, should you use a factual example from the local group or develop your own? Will your listeners be moved more by a personal story than by a general illustration? Also, what ethical issues might be involved in decisions to use evidence? See the "Ethical Moments" box on the previous page for some possible scenarios.

## Forms of Reasoning (Inference)

You make connections among claims, criteria, and evidence using different forms of reasoning, or **inferences**. Forms of reasoning are the habitual ways in which a culture or society uses inferences to connect the material supporting a claim with the claim itself. In U.S. culture, there are five primary patterns: reasoning from example, generalization, sign, parallel case, and causal relations (see Table 15.2).

**Reasoning from Example**    The first pattern, **reasoning from example**, which also often is called **inductive reasoning**, is the process of examining a series of known occurrences and drawing a general conclusion or of using a single instance to reason to a future instance of the same kind. The conclusion is probable rather than certain:

> In every election in our community over the past few years, when a candidate leads in the polls by 10 or more points with a month to go, he or she has won. Thus, my candidate will surely win next month.

Maybe so—but maybe not. The inference in this case can be stated as "What is true of the particular cases is true of the whole class or, more precisely, future instances of the same class." Most reasoning from example uses multiple instances in inferring a conclusion; however, a single instance can be a powerful illustration on which to base a conclusion. You can argue, for example, that one death at an intersection supports the need for a traffic light. Using relevant examples will ensure a high degree of probability and provide strong justification for the adoption of a claim.

**Reasoning from Generalization or Axiom**    Applying a **generalization** or basic truism to a specific situation is a form of **deductive reasoning**. Whereas inductive reasoning is typified by an inferential leap on the basis of the evidence, deductive reasoning produces a conclusion that is true only if the premises are true. For example, you may know that generic drugs are cheaper than brand-name drugs. On the basis of this general truism, you ask your druggist for the generic prescription whenever possible because it will save you money. To the extent the generalization holds true, your experience will hold true, as well.

**Reasoning from Sign**    This pattern uses an observable mark, or symptom, as proof of the existence of a certain state of affairs. **Sign reasoning** occurs, for example, when you note the appearance of a rash or spots on your skin (evidence) and conclude you have the measles (claim). Signs are not causes: A rash does not cause measles, and an ambulance siren does not cause the accident or crisis it responds to. What the rash or the siren means remains open to further examination. While it may be the case that the rash is a sign of measles, it also may be a sign of an allergic

| TABLE 15.2 | Distinguishing and Testing Types of Reasoning | | |
|---|---|---|---|
| **FORM** | **DESCRIPTION** | **EXAMPLE** | **TESTS** |
| Example | Drawing a general conclusion from one or more examples | "I enjoy Bach, Beethoven and Ravel; I like classical music." | 1. Sufficient instances? 2. Fairly selected? 3. Important exceptions? |
| Generalization or axiom | Applying a general truism to a specific example | "Bichons are friendly dogs; I'll buy a Bichon." | 1. Generally accepted? 2. Applies to this instance? |
| Sign | Using a symptom or other observable event as proof of a state of affairs | "The petunias are dead. Someone forgot to water them." | 1. Fallible sign? 2. Accurate observation? |
| Parallel case | Asserting that because two items share similar characteristics, they will share results | "Tougher enforcement of existing laws reduced drunk driving in Indiana; hence, such laws will work in Iowa." | 1. More similarities than differences? 2. Similarities are relevant, important? |
| Causal relation | Concluding that one event influences the existence of a second, later event | "The engine won't start; the carburetor is flooded." | 1. Causes and effects are separable? 2. Cause sufficient to produce effect? 3. Presence of intervening events? 4. Any other cause possible, important? 5. Cause or correlation? |

reaction to medication. The meaning of the siren comes closest to an *infallible sign* relationship—that is, you would normally infer someone was hurt, but whether from an accident or a sudden illness, you could not say. Hence, the inference that evidence is a sign of the conclusion you want to draw is not always true.

**Reasoning from Parallel Case**    Another common reasoning pattern involves **parallel case**—comparing similar events or things and drawing conclusions based upon that comparison. The claim that your state should adopt a motorcycle helmet law might be supported by noting that a neighboring state with similar characteristics passed one and has experienced lower rates of death and head injury. In essence, you are claiming "What happened there can happen here." The political candidate's claim that what she or he has done for a community or state can be repeated in a larger arena, though not precisely parallel, draws strength from this type of argument. As the variables separating the cases grow in size and significance, however, this reasoning pattern will become less forceful.

**Reasoning from Causal Relation**   Causal reasoning assumes that one event influences or controls other events. You can reason from a specific cause to an effect or set of effects or vice versa. For instance, assume that alcohol abuse on a campus appears to be increasing. Is this increase the result of lax enforcement of existing rules? Do loopholes allow for more abusive situations to develop, despite the best intentions? Are students today more prone to abuse than in previous years? Pointing to one or more of these as the cause sets the stage for an analysis of potential solutions. The key is to point to connections between lax enforcement or loopholes and the resulting effect of increased alcohol abuse. The principle underlying this pattern is one of *constancy:* Every effect has a cause.

## Testing the Adequacy of Forms of Reasoning

Central to thinking critically is testing the reasoning pattern for weaknesses, both as a user and a consumer. Each pattern has its own unique set of criteria for establishing a valid, sound argument. For each pattern, apply the questions in the "How to" box on pages 388–389 to your own arguments and those of others.

These patterns of reasoning and their tests are not the only means of evaluating the effectiveness of arguments. Arguments can be flawed in other ways, as well. The following section describes common flaws, or fallacies, in reasoning.

## Detecting Fallacies in Reasoning

In general, **fallacies** interrupt the normal process of connecting claims, criteria, and evidence. Here, we discuss 10 of the most common, "garden variety" fallacies; these are argument errors that you already have committed or have experienced as you listen to others provide reasons for their claims:

- **Hasty generalization** (faulty inductive leap): This fallacy occurs when the conclusion is based on far too little evidence. If the answer to the question *Have enough instances been examined?* is no, a flaw in reasoning has occurred. Urging a ban on Boeing 747 airliners because one was involved in an accident or on aerosol sprays because one blew up in a fire is insufficient support for the claim being urged.
- **Genetic fallacy:** This argument rests on an origin, historical tradition, or sacred practice: "We've always done it this way; therefore, this is the best way." That an idea or institution or practice has been around a long time may have

little bearing on whether it still should be. Times change and new values replace old ones, suggesting that new practices may be more in tune with present values.

- **Appeal to ignorance:** The expression "You can't prove it won't work" illicitly a uses double-negative. Incomplete knowledge also does not mean a claim is or is not true: "We cannot use radio beams to signal extraterrestrials, because we don't know what languages they speak." In countering such claims, use arguments from parallel cases and from examples because they both transcend the unknown in providing support for a claim.

- **Appeal to popular opinion** (bandwagon fallacy): "Jump on the bandwagon" and "Everyone is going" are appeals to group support. If others support the position, then you're pressured into supporting it, as well: "There are a gazillion people who already think that Ricky Martin is one of the best." As an older advertisement put another appeal: "Eat chicken; 10,000 coyotes can't be wrong." While these may, in truth, have value, such claims have little probative (proof) value with respect to justifying an action. Nonetheless, this is precisely the kind of argument that has potency in changing people's minds. If audience members are receptive to popular opinion, then using that as a form of evidence will make a major difference in whether your idea is accepted. Politicians will use poll data to reflect the support that exists, even though such data, in and of itself, is not proof that the policy should be adopted. These claims may function as evidence of what people believe or value, but they are not, for that reason, true. The world has witnessed hundreds of widely believed but false ideas, from the idea that night air causes tuberculosis to panic over an invasion by Martians.

- **Appeal to authority:** Citing someone who is popular but nonexpert as the basis for accepting a claim is an inappropriate use of appeal to authority. The critical question in using authoritative testimony is: Is the source an expert on this topic? If not, why should you accept the claim?

- **Sequential fallacy:** This phrase literally translates from the Latin *Post hoc, ergo propter hoc* as "After this; therefore, because of this." This is a primitive kind of causal argument because it is based on the sequence of events in time: "I slept near a draft last night and woke up with a nasty head cold." (The draft did not cause the cold; a virus did.) Although the sequence may be appropriate ("The coach gave an inspirational half-time speech, and the players came out on fire"), there often are other circumstances (the players hate the coach but are motivated by each other) that help produce the effect. Timing alone is not sufficient to draw causal connections.

- **Begging the question:** This is circular or tautological reasoning: "Abortion is murder because it is taking the life of the unborn" rephrases the claim ("It is murder") to form the reason ("It is taking life"). Nothing new has been said. In other cases, begging the question occurs in the form of a complex question:

"Have you stopped cheating on tests yet?" assumes you have cheated in the past, when that may not be known. Saying yes admits past cheating; saying no admits to both past and present cheating. You cannot win either way. Evaluative claims are especially prone to this abuse of reasoning.

■ **Ambiguity:**  A word may have more than one meaning, or a phrase may be misleading. Using a term without clarifying its specific meaning can result in confusion and inaccurate claims: "Dog for sale: Eats anything and is fond of children." Does "eats anything" include the children? Sure sounds like it. Or "Wanted: Man to take care of cow that does not smoke or drink." When was the last time you saw a cow smoking? Former President Bill Clinton introduced a new phrase into the national lexicon with his explanation of sexual relations: "It depends on what 'it' is."

# How to
# Test Arguments

## Reasoning from Example

1. *Have you looked at enough instances to warrant generalizing?*  Just because you passed the last test without studying doesn't mean that not studying is the way to approach all future tests.

2. *Are the instances fairly chosen or representative?*  Deciding never again to shop in a store because a clerk was rude isn't exactly working on the basis of a representative, let alone sufficient, sample. You'll want to judge the store in a variety of situations. If you find that rudeness is the norm rather than the exception, your claim may be justified.

3. *Are there important exceptions to the generalization that must be accounted for?*  While it is generally true, from presidential election studies, that "As Maine goes, so goes the nation," there have been enough exceptions to this rule to keep candidates who lose in a Maine primary campaigning until the general election.

## Reasoning from Generalization or Axiom

1. *Is the generalization accepted?*  "Those who go on diets generally gain back the weight lost," and "People who marry young are more likely to divorce." Each of these is a generalization; you need to determine whether sufficient evidence

exists to justify the claim, if it is not already accepted as a general truism.

2. *Does the generalization apply to this particular case?*  Usually, discount stores offer the best deals, but on occasion, prices are better at sales at local neighborhood stores. While "Birds of a feather flock together" applies to birds, it may not apply to a group of humans.

## Reasoning from Sign

1. *Is the sign error proof?*  Many signs constitute circumstantial evidence rather than absolute, certain proof. Be especially careful not to confuse *sign reasoning* with *causal reasoning*. If sign reasoning were error proof or infallible, weather forecasters would never be wrong.

2. *Is the observation accurate?*  Witnesses sometimes testify to things that later prove to be wrong. People differ in their interpretations of events. Be certain that the observation is accurate—that the sign did exist as described or explained.

## Reasoning from Parallel Case

1. *Are there more similarities than differences between the two cases?*  Two items may have many features in common, but they also may

- **Persuasive definition:** Value terms and other abstract concepts are open to special or skewed definitions that are unique to the person or group offering them: "Liberty means the right to own military weapons"; "Real men don't wear cologne"; and "A true patriot doesn't protest against this country while on foreign soil." Each of these definitions sets up a particular point of view that is capricious and arbitrary. You could say that persuasive definitions are self-serving because they promote an argument at the expense of more inclusive definitions of the same terms. If you accept the definition, the argument is essentially over.[6] Substituting a definition from a respected, widely accepted source is a way of challenging this fallacy.

- **Name-calling:** There are several forms of this fallacy; all involve attacking the person, rather than the argument. You may attack special interests ("Of

have significant differences that will weaken your argument. Just because two states appear similar, they may also have many more differences that will weaken the effectiveness of the parallel being drawn.

2. **Are the similarities you've pointed out the relevant and important ones?** Suppose that two students down the hall dress in similar clothes, have the same major, and get similar grades. Does this mean that if one is nice, so is the other one? Probably not because the similarities you've noticed are relatively unconnected to niceness. The students' personal values and their relations with others would be more important criteria on which to base a parallel case.

### Reasoning from Causal Relations

1. **Can you separate causes and effects?** We often have trouble with "Which came first?" kinds of issues. Do higher wages cause higher prices or the reverse? Does a strained home life cause a child to misbehave, or is it the other way around?

2. **Are the causes sufficient to produce the effects?** Causes not only must be necessary to produce effects, but they also must be sufficient. While air is necessary for fire to exist, it isn't all that's required, or we would be in a state of constant fire.

3. **Did intervening events or persons prevent a cause from having its normal effect?** Causes do not always produce their expected effects; they may be interrupted by other factors. An empty gun does not shoot. A drought will drive up food prices only if there is insufficient food on hand, the ground was already dry, or cheap alternatives are unavailable.

4. **Could any other cause have produced the effect?** Some effects may be produced by different causes; thus, you need to search for the most likely cause in a given situation. Although crime often increases when communities deteriorate, increased crime rates also can be caused by many other changes. Perhaps crime only appears to have risen; in actuality, maybe people are just keeping better records.

5. **Is the cause really a correlation?** Correlations aren't necessarily causally related. Two phenomena may vary together without being related in any way. For example, since Abraham Lincoln's assassination, every president elected in a year divisible by 20 (until President Ronald Reagan) died in office. However, in each case, the year was inconsequential in causing the death.

course you're defending her; she's your cousin") or personal characteristics ("No wonder you're arguing that way; dweebs [or geeks] always think that way"). In these two cases, being related is not proof of defense, and dweebs may have ideas as good as anyone else's. Claims should be judged on their own terms, not on the basis of the people or ideas with which they may or may not be connected. On the other hand, note the powerful effect of name-calling as used by political candidates—and others. To label someone is also to reject other possible labels for that person. Name-calling, or what is sometimes called *ad hominem* ("to the person") argument, may well be persuasive.

These are some of the fallacies that find their way into casual and formal argumentation. A good, basic logic book can point out additional fallacies.[7] If you know about fallacies, you'll be better able to construct sound arguments and assess the weaknesses in your opponent's arguments. In addition, thinking critically can protect you from being taken in by unscrupulous politicians, sales personnel, and advertisers. The process of protecting yourself from irrelevant appeals can benefit from the model for organizing and evaluating arguments that is presented next.

## A Model for Organizing and Evaluating Arguments

As noted earlier, arguments are about contingent matters—events that could be other than they are or than what is proposed. The **Toulmin model** uses a visually clear pattern that isolates all the implicit and explicit elements in the argument (see Figure 15.2). This patterning of relationships will aid you in analyzing and critiquing your arguments and the arguments of others:

1. **Claim:** Put simply, what are you proposing for audience consideration— fact, value, or policy?

2. **Data:** What materials—illustrative parallels, expert opinion, statistical information, research studies, and the like—can you advance to support the claim?

3. **Warrant:** What is the relationship between the parallel case, statistical data, or expert opinion and the claim? On what kind of assumption or inferential pattern does its acceptance as support for the claim depend? Materials do not function as evidence or support for no reason; facts do *not* speak for themselves. What makes an audience believe in the strength of the reasons as support lies in the following kinds of assumptions that warrant acceptance of the link between data and claim:

    An expert knows what he or she is talking about.

    Past economic, social, and political practices are reliable predictors of future occurrences.

    Inferential patterns (e.g., a cause or sign) suggest that the linkage is rational.

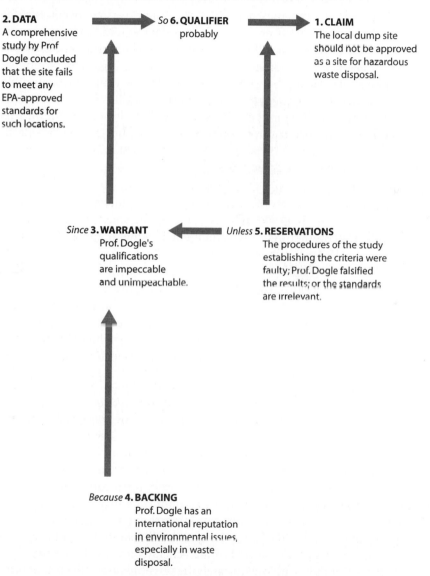

**FIGURE 15.2**    **The Toulmin Model of Argument**

*These six elements operate as a general framework for the construction and analysis of an argument. The interrelationships among the elements can best be displayed through a visual diagram. The numbers in the diagram correspond to the elements discussed.*

**2. DATA**
A comprehensive study by Prof. Dogle concluded that the site fails to meet any EPA-approved standards for such locations.

*So* **6. QUALIFIER**
probably

**1. CLAIM**
The local dump site should not be approved as a site for hazardous waste disposal.

*Since* **3. WARRANT**
Prof. Dogle's qualifications are impeccable and unimpeachable.

*Unless* **5. RESERVATIONS**
The procedures of the study establishing the criteria were faulty; Prof. Dogle falsified the results; or the standards are irrelevant.

*Because* **4. BACKING**
Prof. Dogle has an international reputation in environmental issues, especially in waste disposal.

We know, for instance, that an expert's credibility is a major determinant in gaining acceptance of the opinions being offered. In the development of the argument, this factor operates as an implicit warrant connecting the opinion to the claim. In matters involving economics, we know that the regularity of certain marketplace functions, such as supply and demand, exerts a powerful influence on events. Hence, when we claim the prices of finished products will rise because of an increase in the cost of raw materials, we are tacitly assuming the normal operation of the marketplace. Likewise, the value of using parallel cases as support for a position rests on the regularity of an inferential pattern: When two cases are parallel, similar results can be expected.

4. **Backing:** Does the audience accept the relationship between the data and the claim as given? If not, what further data would help support the warrant? When the warrant linking a reason and claim is accepted by the audience, explicit development of this facet of the argument is unnecessary. When a relationship between the reason and the claim is not automatically accepted, however, the speaker must provide additional support focused on the warrant rather than the original claim. Thus, in supporting an argument claiming that price controls would cause food shortages with authoritative testimony from a politician, you may need to establish her or his expertise to increase audience acceptance.

5. **Reservations:** Can significant counterarguments be raised? In most cases, arguments on the opposite side not only are readily available but even may be as strong as your own reasons. Anticipating reservations in advance will help you strengthen your own argument. In general, these can be thought of as "unless" clauses in your argument.

6. **Qualifiers:** How certain is the claim? Note that we do not ask how certain *you* are; you may be absolutely sure of something for which you cannot offer verifiable support. How much can your listeners bank on the claim you are putting forward as an acceptable basis for belief or action? Are you sure that price controls will have the claimed effect? Qualifiers such as *probably, presumably, virtually,* and *may* should be incorporated into the claim to reflect the strength of the argument.

This model has three principal uses in organizing your arguments. First, by setting forth the arguments' components in the manner indicated, you'll be able to capture visually the relationships among the components. How, for example, are the data you present linked to the claim? What sort of warrants (assumptions, precedents, rules of inference) are you using to ensure the audience sees the connection between the data and the claim? Second, once you've written a brief description of the data and identified the warrant on which its relationship to the claim rests, you can more clearly determine whether you wish to offer the claim as definite, only probable, likely, or possible. You'll also be reminded to reflect on the audience's grasp of the warrant. Is it a generally accepted relationship? Will it be in this case? Finally, thinking through the possible reservations that others will have to your argument puts you in a better position to shore up weaknesses in advance and, where necessary, build a stronger base from which to respond to issues that might undermine rather than directly refute your case.[8]

Applying the elements also sharpens your ability to question an argument. The data may be misleading or in error. The relationship between the data and claim may be highly questionable (lacking a strong warrant). There may be so many reservations that the claim must be highly qualified, and advocates may be pushing claims harder than the data warrant. Using the model as a means of thinking about arguments can help you determine whether a claim goes beyond what can reasonably be supported by the evidence and available warrants. In addition, use the guidelines provided in the "How to" box below to help in developing an argumentative speech.

## Assessing a Sample Speech

Policies are supported by particular factual assertions as well as values. The advisability of an action is based on the credibility of the facts offered in its support and on the audience's willingness to accept the value judgments being made. In many cases, a speaker must reorient listeners' thinking, especially if they take something for granted, such as their own listening skills.

## How to
## Develop Argumentative Speeches

Consider the following practical suggestions in developing an argumentative speech:

- ***Organize your arguments, using the strongest argument first or last.*** This takes advantage of a **primacy-recency effect.** That is, presenting strong arguments at the outset sets the agenda for how listeners will think about your claim. On the other hand, your last argument will be retained more easily; hence, you may wish to build toward it, carrying your audience with you as you provide stronger and stronger reasons for adopting the claim.

- ***Use a variety of evidence.*** You cannot bank on any one piece of material to move an audience toward your position; instead, use a broad variety of evidence appealing to relevance and motivation to strengthen your effectiveness. For example, if you wish to argue for restrictions on shark fishing, you can cite statistical evidence of overfishing depleting the population or present a graphic video clip showing definned sharks being dumped back into the ocean to die. (Shark

fin soup is an expensive delicacy in some countries.) The latter is a more moving illustration of the reasons for restrictions on fishing.

- ***Know the potential arguments of your opponent.*** "The best defense is a good offense," but it stands to reason that prior knowledge of the opponent's reasons will go a long way toward strengthening your own claims. Investigating your opponent's position as thoroughly as possible will give you a competitive advantage; you'll be less likely to be surprised or caught off guard by an argument.

- ***Finally, practice constructing logical arguments and detecting fallacious ones.*** Ultimately, arguing well depends upon your understanding of logical reasoning. The common denominator of all arguments, despite their different content, is the patterns of reasoning people use. If you have a clear grasp of the basic building blocks—including the materials presented in this chapter—your skill development will proceed at a much faster pace.

Professor Carol Koehler addressed this problem in arguing that one of the reasons for poor physician-patient relationships can be traced to an inadequate appreciation for—and skill in—listening.[9] As a professor of communication and medicine, she is in a unique position to develop an argument. The problem is set up in paragraphs 1 to 6, and the reasons that link poor listening to the problem then are evaluated (paragraph 7). She next raises a rhetorical question regarding what solution is available: providing "care over cure" (paragraph 8). In the remainder of her argument, she illustrates how her solution responds to the problem (paragraphs 9–14). In her conclusion, she uses an appropriate quotation to pull together the strands of her argument that *caring* is as essential as *curing* in the medical arena.

---

### Mending the Body by Lending an Ear: The Healing Power of Listening
### Carol Koehler

**Setup of the argument**

I would like to start this morning by telling you two different stories. Each story has the same two characters and happens in the same location. Both stories occur within a 24-hour period. **1**

Over the Christmas holidays my husband and I were invited to a formal black tie wedding. This was to be an elegant event so we put on our best evening clothes. Adding to that, I wore my mother's diamond jewelry and this fabulous mink coat that I inherited. Just before we left the house I telephoned my 86-year-old mother-in-law for her daily check up. When she answered, her voice sounded a little strange so my husband and I decided to stop at her apartment to make sure she was alright before we went to the wedding. **2**

When we arrived she seemed slightly disoriented (she was 86 years old but wonderfully healthy, sharp-witted and self-sufficient). We called her physician to ask his advice and he said to bring her to the local Emergency Room and have her checked out. We did that. This was a Saturday night so the Emergency Room was pretty active. When we arrived, I in my mink and my husband in his tux, we looked noticeably different from the general population in the waiting room. While my husband filled out forms, the doctors took my mother-in-law into a makeshift curtained room. When I noticed that the staff had removed both her glasses and her hearing aid, I realized she would experience some anxiety, so at that point I decided to stay with her to keep her from being frightened. As I went into the room, a young doctor said, "Ma'm, you can't go in there." Without missing a beat I said, "Don't be ridiculous." With that I went and found a chair in the waiting room, brought it into the examination room and sat down. I remember thinking the staff looked a little bewildered but no one challenged me at any time. When my mother-in-law's hands felt a little cool, I asked for a heated blanket and one was brought immediately. So it went for the entire evening. We missed the wedding but finally got my mother-in-law in a permanent room about 2 A.M. **3**

4    The next morning I went to the hospital about 10 o'clock in the morning, dressed in tennis shoes, a sweat suit and no make-up. As I arrived at my mother-in-law's room, an unfamiliar doctor was just entering. I introduced myself and asked him to speak up so my mother-in-law would be aware of why he was there and what he was doing. I told him that she tends to be frightened by the unexpected and without her glasses or hearing aid, she was already frightened enough. This 30-something male doctor proceeded to examine my mother-in-law without raising his voice so that she could hear, and without acknowledging me or my request in any way. Actually he never really looked at either one of us.

5    In both those scenarios, I was listened to, not by ears alone, but by eyes, by gender, by age judgments, and by social status assessments. That started me thinking....

6    Why did a recent article in the *Journal of the American Medical Association* indicate high dissatisfaction in traditional doctor-patient appointments? Why is it the *Wall Street Journal* claims that perception of physician concern and not physician expertise is the deciding factor in the rising number of malpractice suits? Why did the *New England Journal of Medicine* report that the care and attention quotient is causing "alternative" medical practices to grow by leaps and bounds? Given this litany of events, what does it really mean to listen? And why, in the name of science, don't we produce better listeners in the medical profession?

**Transition to the claim**

7    The reasons are so obvious that they are sometimes overlooked. First, listening is mistakenly equated with hearing and since most of us can hear, no academic priority is given to this subject in either college or med school (this by the way flies in the face of those who measure daily time usage). Time experts say we spend 9% of our day writing, 16% reading, 30% speaking and 45% listening—just the opposite of our academic pursuits. Second, we perceive power in speech. We put a value on those who have the gift of gab. How often have you heard the compliment, "He/she can talk to anyone?" Additionally, we equate speaking with controlling both the conversation and the situation. The third and last reason we don't listen is that we are in an era of information overload. We are bombarded with the relevant and the irrelevant and it is easy to confuse them. Often it's all just so much noise.

**Causes of the problem**

8    How can we address this depressing situation? Dan Callahan, a physician and teacher, argues that primacy in health care needs to be given to the notion of care over cure. Caring as well as curing humanizes our doctor patient relationships.

9    Let's talk about what that might mean for health care. What comes to mind when someone is caring? (The audience responded with the words warm "giving," "interested," "genuine" and "sincere.") Now, what comes to mind when you think of the opposite of care? (The audience volunteered "cold," "uninterested," "egotistical," "busy," "distracted" and "selfish.")

**Transition to the solution**

10    What might a caring doctor be like? If we take the word CARE and break it down, we find the qualities that are reflective of a therapeutic communicator, in other words, someone who listens not with ears alone.

*(continued)*

**Breakdown of the solution**

*C* stands for concentrate. Physicians should hear with their eyes and ears. They should avoid the verbal and visual barriers that prevent real listening. It may be as simple as eye contact (some young doctors have told me they have a difficult time with looking people in the eye, and my advice is, when you are uncomfortable, focus on the patient's mouth and as the comfort level increases, move to the eyes). In the placement of office furniture, try and keep the desk from being a barrier between you and the patient. Offer an alternative chair for consultations—one to the side of your desk and one in front of the desk. Let the patient have some control and power to decide their own comfort level.                **11**

*A* stands for acknowledge. Show them that you are listening by using facial expressions, giving vocal prompts and listening between the lines for intent as well as content. Listen for their vocal intonation when responding to things like prescribed medication. If you hear some hesitation in their voice, say to them, "I hear you agreeing but I'm getting the sound of some reservation in your voice. Can you tell me why?" And then acknowledge their response. Trust them and they will trust you.                **12**

*R* stands for response. Clarify issues by asking "I'm not sure what you mean." Encourage continuing statements by saying "and then what?" or "tell me more." The recurrent headache may mask other problems. Provide periodic recaps to focus information. Learn to take cryptic notes and then return your attention to the patient. (Note taking is sometimes used as an avoidance tactic and patients sense this.) Use body language by leaning toward the patient. Effective listening requires attention, patience and the ability to resist the urge to control the conversation.                **13**

*E* stands for exercise emotional control. This means if your "hot buttons" are pushed by people who whine, and in walks someone who does that very thing, you are likely to fake interest in that patient. With your mind elsewhere, you will never really "hear" that person. Emotional blocks are based on previous experiences. They are sometimes activated by words, by tone of voice, by style of clothes or hair, or by ethnicity. It is not possible for us to be free of those emotional reactions, but the first step in controlling them is to recognize when you are losing control. One of the most useful techniques to combat emotional responses is to take a long deep breath when confronted with the urge to interrupt. Deep breathing redirects your response and as a bonus, it is impossible to talk when you are deep breathing. Who of us would not choose the attentive caring physician?                **14**

**Conclusion**

As it nears time for me to take that deep breath, I would just like to reiterate that listening is a learned skill and learning to listen with CARE has valuable benefits for health care professionals and patients. As a wise man named J. Isham once said, "Listening is an attitude of the heart, a genuine desire to be with another which both attracts and heals."                **15**

Thank you very much.                **16**

# ■ CHAPTER SUMMARY

Argumentation is a persuasive activity in which a speaker offers reasons and support for claims in opposition to claims advanced by others. Arguing with others engages people in tasks central to critical thinking; that is, assessing the reasons offered in support of claims. Within single argumentative speeches, a particular argument consists of the claim to be defended, the evidence relevant to the claim, and the reasoning pattern, or inference, used to connect the evidence to the claim.

Claims of fact assert that something is or is not the case, claims of value propose that something is or is not desirable, and claims of policy attempt to establish that something should or should not be done. Evidence is chosen to support these claims because it is rationally or motivationally relevant.

There are five basic reasoning patterns: reasoning from example, reasoning from generalization or axiom, reasoning from sign, reasoning by parallel case, and reasoning from causal relation. Each of the inferential, or reasoning, patterns can be tested by applying specific questions to evaluate the strength or soundness of the argument. Critical thinkers also should be on the alert for fallacies committed during an argumentative speech. The "garden variety" fallacies or flaws in the construction of arguments discussed in this chapter are hasty generalization; genetic fallacy; appeals to ignorance, popular opinion, and authority; sequential fallacy; begging the question; ambiguity; persuasive definition; and name-calling. Through the use of the Toulmin model of argument and its elements (claim, data, warrant, backing, reservations, and qualifiers), you can better assess the quality of your arguments as well as the arguments addressed to you. If you are seeking to develop argumentative speeches, either to initiate support for a position or to refute an opponent's position, you should consider the general strategies presented in this chapter. As you become more adept at constructing your own presentations, you'll also increase your skill in critically appraising the arguments of your opponents.

# ■ KEY TERMS

ambiguity  (p. 388)

appeal to authority  (p. 387)

appeal to ignorance  (p. 387)

appeal to popular opinion
(p. 387)

arguing  (p. 375)

argument  (p. 375)

argumentation  (p. 375)

backing  (p. 392)

begging the question  (p. 387)

causal reasoning  (p. 386)

claim  (p. 390)

critical thinking  (p. 375)

data  (p. 390)

deductive reasoning  (p. 384)

evidence  (p. 381)

factual claim  (p. 378)

fallacies  (p. 386)

generalization  (p. 384)

genetic fallacy  (p. 386)

hasty generalization  (p. 386)

inductive reasoning  (p. 384)

inferences  (p. 384)

name-calling  (p. 389)

parallel case  (p. 385)

persuasive definition  (p. 389)

policy claim  (p. 380)

primacy-recency effect  (p. 393)

qualifiers  (p. 392)

reasoning from example
(p. 384)

reasoning patterns  (p. 378)

reservations  (p. 392)

sequential fallacy  (p. 387)

sign reasoning  (p. 384)

Toulmin model  (p. 390)

value claim  (p. 379)

warrant  (p. 390)

## ■ ASSESSMENT ACTIVITIES

1. How influential are political debates in campaign years? Locate studies of presidential debates, and present your critical summary in written form or as part of a general class or small-group discussion.

2. Assume you're going to give a speech in favor of paying student athletes to play to an audience of students hostile to your proposal. Outline your arguments using the Toulmin model of argument. What factors do you consider as you construct and frame your argument? Assume that several counterarguments are offered by your fellow students. What new factors must you consider in rebuilding your case for service?

3. Prepare a 10-minute argumentative exchange on a topic involving you and one other member of the class. Dividing the available time equally, one speaker will advocate a claim and the other will oppose it. Adopt any format you both feel comfortable with. You may choose from the following:

   a. *A Lincoln/Douglas format*—The first person speaks 4 minutes; the second, 5; and then the first person returns for a 1-minute rejoinder.

   b. *An issues format*—Both speakers agree on, say, two key issues, and then each speaks for 2½ minutes on each issue.

   c. *A debate format*—Each speaker talks twice alternately: 3 minutes in a constructive speech, 2 minutes in rebuttal.

   d. *A heckling format*—Each speaker has 5 minutes, but during the middle of each speech, the audience or opponent may ask questions.

## ■ REFERENCES

1. For the classic statement on the senses in which the term can be employed, see Joseph Wenzel, "Three Perspectives on Argument: Rhetoric, Dialectic, Logic," in *Perspectives on Argument*, edited by Janice Schuetz and Robert Trapp (Prospect Heights, IL: Waveland Press, 1990), 9–26.

2. For critical-thinking studies, see any of these sources: Andrew P. Johnson, *Up and Out: Using Creative and Critical Thinking Skills to Enhance Learning* (Boston, MA: Allyn and Bacon, 2000); M. Neil Browne and Stuart M. Keeley, *Asking the Right Questions: A Guide to Critical Thinking* (Upper Saddle River, NJ: Prentice Hall, 2001); and Sherry Diestler, *Becoming a Critical Thinker: A User Friendly Manual*, 3rd ed. (Upper Saddle River, NJ: Prentice Hall, 2001). For a recent analysis of critical thinking in relation to propaganda studies, see Michael Sproule, *Propaganda and Democracy: The American Experience of Media and Mass Persuasion* (New York: Cambridge University Press, 1997).

3. For a discussion of argument as justification, see Raymie E. McKerrow, "The Centrality of Justification: Principles of Warranted Assertability," in *Argumentation Theory and the Rhetoric of Assent*, edited by David Cratis Williams and Michael David Hazen (Tuscaloosa: University of Alabama Press, 1990), 17–32.

4. For a discussion of cultural constraints on arguing, see Iris Varner and Linda Beamer, *Intercultural Communication: The Global Workplace* (Boston: Irwin, 1995).

5. For a classic discussion of why one should acquiesce in the face of a stronger argument, see Douglas Ehninger, "Validity as Moral Obligation," *Southern Speech Communication Journal* 33 (1968): 215–222.

6. First referenced by Charles L. Stevenson in *Ethics and Language* (New Haven, CT: Yale University Press, 1944). A contemporary explanation is available online: <http://www.xrefer.com/entry.jsp?xrefid=551767>, accessed August 26, 2001. Also go to <www.xrefer.com>, a major resource for online encyclopedia and dictionary references.

7. For further study of informal logic, see Robert J. Fogelin and Walter Sinnott-Armstrong, *An Introduction to Informal Logic*, 6th ed. (New York: Harcourt, 2001).

8. Herbert W. Simons, with Joanne Morreale and Bruce Gronbeck, *Persuasion in Society* (Thousand Oaks, CA: Sage, 2001).

9. Carol F. Koehler, Ph.D., "Mending the Body by Lending an Ear: The Healing Power of Listening," *Vital Speeches of the Day* 64 (15 June 1998): 543–544. Used with permission of the author.

# Chapter 16

# Building Social Cohesion in a Diverse World

## Speeches on Ceremonial and Corporate Occasions

Informing, persuading, and arguing within the public domain carries an obligation to provide as full and complete a picture of the event or issue as you can. In these speeches, your ideas about what exists—and what should be created or altered—are of paramount importance. Nowhere is this process of adapting your message to the audience as critical as in speeches that are presented on ceremonial and corporate occasions. The task of creating, maintaining, or strengthening the community's sense of togetherness is critical to both kinds of occasions, whether one is speaking on a major holiday or keynoting a business conference. In these settings, such presentations aim to uplift the human spirit, acknowledge humility in the face of adversity, and praise the generosity of others.

On these and other **special occasions**, our consciousness of the role we should play as a representative of a select community—as in the case of entertainers, poets, and athletes—dictates the ground rules for speaking. Prior tradition—how speakers have handled their duties on previous occasions—at awards presentations, at Fourth of July commemorations, and other events specifies how we should perform. As presenters, we have a natural desire to do well, to earn the respect and admiration of the social or corporate community on our return from the podium.

In this chapter, we look at several kinds of speeches you may give in the presence of or as the representative of such a select community. Before we discuss those speech types, however, we return to an issue dealt with in Chapter 4: the challenge of communicating in an age of diversity. Ceremonial and corporate presentations are absolutely crucial types of public talk. Unless we're willing to think about what holds us together—what makes us a community—informative, argumentative, and persuasive speaking will produce no results. In this chapter, therefore, we return to our discussion on the nature of cultural diversity and then turn our attention to speeches of introduction and goodwill, after-dinner talks, and keynote presentations.

# Ceremony and Ritual in a Diverse Culture

The word *community* comes from the Latin *communis*, meaning "common" or, more literally (with the *-ity* ending), "commonality." A community is not simply the physical presence of people—say, those who live in the same town (i.e., a local community) or who worship together (i.e., a religious community). A **community** is a group of people who think of themselves as bonded together—by blood, locale, class, nationality, race, occupation, gender, or other shared experiences or attributes.

The phrase *who think of themselves* is key here. Of course, you share a blood type with members of your family, but why is that important to your concept of *family*? There are biological differences between males and females, but why should gender be a factor in determining who gets paid more, draws combat duty in time of war, or generally is expected to raise the kids? Yes, skin comes in many different colors, but why have we made so much of that fact? To understand why, we need to recognize one fundamental truism: While physiological, psychological, and social differences between people are real, the importance attached to those differences is socially constructed in arbitrary ways.

## Social Definitions of Diversity

A **social construction** is a mechanism used by group members to understand, interpret, and evaluate the world around them. There is no such thing, as Nelson Goodman notes, as "perception without conception."[1] Human beings cannot *see* their world without framing it, usually in language. Words store our experiences of the world. Just uttering *pit bull* brings to mind, for most people, frightening stories of their own or other people's experiences. Words encode our common attitudes. As noted in Chapter 10, we have multiple words for the same object (*officer of the law, cop*) because our feelings about such people vary. Words express our evaluations. The difference between a *student-athlete* and a *jock* is a difference in how we value what the person does while at school. Saying that "We socially construct our world" is not to say that we create it in some brute way; the physicality of the world is real, solid—and you'll literally hurt your toe when it bumps into a desk. Rather, human beings orient themselves to the world via language. We see, interpret, and evaluate the world via language.

It follows, then, that at one level or another, communication is always the attempt to get others to see, interpret, and evaluate the world as you do. The language you share within your social community builds a socially cohesive world; unfortunately, that language may not have the same impact outside your own community. Words vary from time to time, from place to place, from context to context, and even from person to person. *Democracy* means one thing in the United States and another in Thailand because of differing traditions, governmental institutions, and personal experiences. When U.S. and Thai citizens talk to each other about democratic institutions, they must be careful to indicate very concretely how each is seeing, interpreting, and evaluating the world when using that term. Within our own communities, such care is critical: Building consensus

> *On one level or another, communication is always the attempt to get others to see, interpret, and evaluate the world as you do.*

across diverse ethnic, racial, and class groupings in large cities is not an easy task. One thing we have learned: In an age of diversity, there is a tendency to fragment society rather than to share beliefs, attitudes, and values as a community.

The great challenge of special occasion speaking is to get a society to live together while valuing their individual differences. We can become *one*—we can live in harmony with others—without sacrificing our own identities through the language that we employ in building social cohesiveness, a sense of togetherness as we struggle to define our common purpose.

## Public Address as Community Building

Within your own community, the groups you belong to have special influences on your beliefs and actions. Whether you are part of a religious group, a member of the university swim team, a fraternity or sorority member, or an active member of a residence hall council, the group functions as a reference point in your life. You draw self-definition from the groups you belong to, and you use these same groups for reinforcement and for new information on problems. As noted in Chapter 4, culture is performed through language. The specific cultural frame that you choose to communicate from is heavily influenced by your **reference group.** The cultural frame serves as a guide in defining you and your role in the community.

When seen as relevant to a problem or event, a group helps direct the choices you have and even may dictate what should be done to remain in good standing within one or more of the groups. Just as your group memberships change over time, so does the power of any particular group to affect your thoughts and actions.[2] Yet traces of groups from your youth follow you through life. The question we face in this chapter goes beyond that social-psychological truth: Your sense of group identity, of community, is created largely through public talk. The language of reference groups is inscribed in your memory. If you were a Boy Scout or a Girl Scout, you can still, to this day, recite the oath expressing your commitment to the group. Your civic education begins with pledging allegiance to the flag; it broadens when you participate in Memorial Day, Fourth of July, and Labor Day ceremonies (which include public addresses); and it is reviewed every time the president appears on television or a candidate campaigns for local, state, or national office. Your sense of community undoubtedly is built out of bits and pieces of social constructions reinforced in you since childhood.

As Michael Walzer puts it, "The state is invisible; it must be personified before it can be seen, symbolized before it can be loved, imagined before it can be conceived."[3] The same is true with most reference groups in your life. You cannot see group standards, only the behaviors of individuals; you cannot feel the influence of groups outside the words and other symbols they use to define their claims upon you. You may not be consciously aware of the influence of a particular reference group, but its claim on your self-identity, beliefs, and actions is brought home to you on special occasions, in special rituals. David Kertzer has described **ritual** as follows:

> Ritual action has a formal quality to it. It follows highly structured, standardized sequences and is often enacted at certain places and times that are themselves endowed with special symbolic meaning. Ritual action is repetitive and, therefore, often redundant, but these very factors serve as important means of channeling emotion, guiding cognition, and organizing social groups. I have defined ritual as action wrapped in a web of symbolism.[4]

*Symbolization* is the key here. Some highly standardized sequences of behavior, such as brushing your teeth and getting dressed, have little or no symbolic significance; they are simply habits or routines. Rituals, however, are structured actions to which we attach particular collective significance—often about how the past relates to the present and how the present should affect the future. A political ritual, Kertzer notes,

> helps us cope with two human problems: building confidence in our sense of self by providing us with a sense of continuity—I am the same person today as I was twenty years ago and as I will be ten years from now—and giving us confidence that the world in which we live today is the same world we lived in before and the same world we will have to cope with in the future.[5]

As a community, we celebrate our pasts and construct our futures in the present; ritual is the mechanism of that celebration.

The notion of *power* comes into the picture when we consider politics as the process whereby vested interests in a society struggle for domination: Republicans fight Democrats for legislative or executive control. Parents in a local school neighborhood come together to protest the school's closing. The Hispanic voters of Texas ask presidential candidates to take stands against the English-language-only movement. Political struggle can be harsh—even fatal, in some societies. Citizens attempt to ritualize political fighting: They invent rules of parliamentary procedure to ritualize partisan debate, and the transfer of power from one executive to another is ritualized in inaugural ceremonies. The power in such rituals, according to Kertzer, lies in their ability to control the actual struggles for power and to help convince the populace that authority is being wielded benevolently, in their name. The rhetoric of ceremonial occasions, in particular, is a two-edged discourse of power and community maintenance. This can be seen in such activities as confirmation or bat mitzvah services, "hooding" a new Doctor of Philosophy during graduation, and reciting the Pledge of Allegiance in school—these are the kinds of ritual actions that Kertzer is talking about. All rituals are structured, standardized, and repetitive, with times and places set aside for their observances. Ritual is imbued with symbols and with public address to provide the means of channeling, guiding, and organizing that Kertzer mentions.

## Building Community on Corporate Occasions

Walk into any hotel with meeting space in the United States, check the "Activities Today" listing of events, and you'll find at least one meeting that has a featured speaker scheduled. Examine the various texts of speeches published in *Vital Speeches of the Day* and note the occasion—in most instances, the speech selected for publication was presented at a conference or celebratory event. Meetings and speeches seem to go together in U.S. society. Whether a speech of tribute or goodwill, a formal keynote, or a more entertaining after-dinner event, the speech is the glue that links the broader societal values with those of the corporate community.

Speakers do well if they use the larger community's values and reflect them in their more specific addresses dealing with economic or other business related issues. In each case, the ritualistic nature of the performance depends on the speaker adhering to the conventions associated with the kind of address being presented. As we have said, speeches on ceremonial and corporate occasions are ritualized—they follow a set pattern and, hence, may seem trite or even uninteresting. In these speeches, you meet expectations by following the ritualized tradition—you invite revolutionary change when you violate those traditions. In one form or another, the goal of such a speech is always to socially construct the world in ways consonant with group traditions: to get you to see, interpret, and evaluate the world through the eyes of the group in which the public address is occurring.

You are well advised to pay particular attention to the *culture* of the group to whom you are being asked to speak. It may be a weekly luncheon meeting of a service organization, such as the Rotary Club or the Kiwanis, or it may be a campus meeting of the student activities board seeking advice on programming for the coming year. In each case, a safe presumption is that the group has been meeting for a time and has its own, informal rules about what to expect from invited speakers. Rotary or Kiwanis members, for example, will be looking for a speech that connects to their reason for being at the meeting, so whatever information or policy argument you present must acknowledge their role as members of a service organization. In a campus group, the culture may be much less well developed, but the group still will have a serious concern about receiving information that fits within its purview as an organization. Speaking to a student activities board about the administration's antagonism toward "Greeks," for example, may find a sympathetic ear, but it also may cause members to wonder, "Why talk to us? Isn't this more appropriate for the student senate?" They may well be correct in their assessment of your topic choice. As with other special occasions, the freedom to talk about anything, in the manner you desire, is constrained by the tradition of the group that has invited you to speak.

Extending an invitation to speak does have an advantage: The audience has gathered for a distinct purpose and already has decided that you will be a credible, capable spokesperson for a particular topic. Knowing that purpose in advance—and adapting your comments so that they meet the expectations of the audience—is far easier when the audience comes with a shared sense of what they want to accomplish. In a classroom, the instructor may give you fairly free rein in choosing a subject—with the provision that its purpose be to inform or persuade. In a meeting or conference, on the other hand, the selection of the subject often is predetermined or highly restricted. Even in meetings such as those of Optimist or Civitan service organizations, the choice of what to speak about is not wide open. Members do not wish to waste their time with frivolous subjects, nor do they wish to be put on the spot regarding their commitment to particular causes without advance warning. If you are coming in as a director of a local American Cancer Society chapter or a representative of the Red Cross, the expectation is that a portion of your talk will be about ways in which the service organization can assist you in meeting your goals. Hence, in these instances, audiences will not feel accosted by a plea when it is presented. On the other hand, if you are invited not in that capacity but because you recently took a trip to the Middle East and have been asked to speak about your experiences, adding a special plea on behalf of your organization will not be as well received. The members may remain polite, but their willingness to assist—even at a later time—will have been lessened by your poor choice of timing. (Recall the discussion of *kairos* in Chapter 12.)

In many ways, the challenge that is set before us on such occasions is the most daunting of those faced by any speaker: In an age of diversity, when each of us has been socialized into any number of specific ethnic, social, political, and religious groups, each of which makes demands upon our beliefs, attitudes, and values, how can we create a sense of shared community?

We proposed five strategies for building cohesive communities in Chapter 4: recognizing diversity while calling for unity, negotiating among diverse values, accepting multiple paths to shared goals, working through the lifestyle choices of others, and maintaining self-identity in the face of cultural difference. Through use of these strategies, you'll find developing appropriate themes and the language to express them a much easier task than it may, at first, seem. With these strategies, it is possible to share community when people are divided into two genders, innumerable religions, age groups ranging from the young to the elderly, multiple ethnic groups, a growing number of political parties, and even Mac versus PC users.

We will first examine speeches of tribute and goodwill and then consider speeches to entertain, keynote speeches, and participating in panel discussions at conferences. Central to the discussion is this question: How do we create unity while retaining our diversity? That is the challenge as we review the special occasions you may encounter.

# Speeches of Tribute

As a speaker, you may be called upon to give a **speech of tribute** to praise a person's qualities or achievements. Such occasions range from awarding a trophy after a successful softball season to dedicating a new recreational facility to delivering a eulogy at a memorial service. Sometimes, tributes are paid to entire groups of people—teachers, soldiers, mothers—rather than to individuals. In all these circumstances, however, the focus is upon relationships between the community and the individual or group being paid tribute. This focus is reflected in the sample speech at the end of this chapter—Susan Au Allen, President of the Pan Asian American Chamber of Commerce (PAACC), speaking in honor of a 10-year Excellence 2000 Awards program initiated by PAACC, reminded her listeners of past award winners and the values they reflected. Honorees were held up for praise because they personified the community's values. Her speech is an excellent illustration of how community building takes place through ceremonial discourse. The following occasions—farewells, dedications, and memorial services—call for tributes of one kind or another.

### Farewells

In general, the **speech of farewell** falls into one of three subcategories: when people retire or leave one organization to join another or when persons who are admired leave the community where they've lived, the enterprise in which they've worked, or the office they've held. In each case, public appreciation of their fellowship and accomplishments may be expressed by associates or colleagues in speeches befitting the circumstances. Individuals who are departing may use the occasion to present a farewell address in which they voice their gratitude for the opportunities, consideration, and warmth given them by co-workers and, perhaps, call upon those who remain to carry on the traditions and long-range goals that characterize the office or enterprise. In both situations, verbal tributes are being paid. What distinguishes them is whether the departing person is speaking or is being spoken about.

More rarely, when individuals—because of disagreements, policy differences, or organizational stresses, for example—resign or sever important or long-standing associations with a business or governmental unit, they may elect to use their farewell message to present publicly the basis of the disagreement and the factors prompting the resignation and departure from the community. Using a special occasion to challenge an audience raises some ethical issues, as examined in the "Ethical Moments" box on the next page.

# ETHICAL MOMENTS

## A Counterexample: Challenging the Community's Values

A special occasion also is open to the possibility of challenging an audience. Even so, such an occasion may or may not represent what the community or nation needs at that moment. Over the years, several notable acceptance speeches have been given by celebrities—some notable because they violated the expectations of the audience. At a recent American Music Awards, for example, Garth Brooks was named Artist of the Year. His acceptance speech was decidedly nontraditional, however, because he refused to accept the award, leaving it on the lectern as he exited the stage.

Two decades earlier, three women were nominated for a National Book Award. As the following excerpt suggests, they, too, used the occasion to make a statement that violated audience expectations:

> We, Audre Lord, Adrienne Rich, and Alice Walker, together accept this award in the name of all the women whose voices have gone and still go unheard in a patriarchal world, and in the name of those who, like us, have been tolerated as token women in this culture, often at great cost and in great pain. We believe that we can enrich ourselves more in supporting and giving to each other than by competing against each other; and that poetry—if it is poetry—exists in a realm beyond ranking and comparison. We symbolically join together here in refusing the terms of patriarchal competition and declaring that we will share this prize among us, to be used as best we can for women.*

The three women had agreed in advance that should one of them win, this acceptance would be delivered by the award recipient on behalf of all three. What was going on here? This was, after all, a special occasion—a time to thank the award sponsors and those whose assistance made it possible for one person to win. It's as if instead of making a stirring call to national pride on the Fourth of July, a speaker were to soundly berate Americans for small-mindedness.

What was going on was that the speakers believed their approach was the only viable one if they were to remain true to their own values. Consider these questions:

1. Do you agree with this analysis? Why or why not?

2. What ethical commitments are placed in question in this kind of challenge to community practices?

3. When a speaker violates audience expectations, is it ever ethical?

4. When would it not be ethical to violate expectations, even if to remain consistent with the community would mean contravening your own values?

*From Adrienne Rich, Andre Lord, and Alice Walker, "A Statement for Voice Unheard," in *Inviting Transformations*, edited by Sonja K. Foss and Karen A. Foss (Prospect Heights, IL: Waveland Press, 1994), 148–149.

## Dedications

Buildings, monuments, and parks may be constructed or set aside to honor a worthy cause or commemorate a person, group, significant movement, historic event, or the like. At such a **dedication,** the speaker says something appropriate about the purpose to be served by whatever is being set aside and about the person or persons, event, or occasion thus commemorated.

## Memorial Services

Services to pay public honor to the dead usually include a speech of tribute, or **eulogy.** Ceremonies of this kind may honor a famous person or persons, perhaps on the anniversaries of their deaths. For example, many speeches have paid tribute to President John F. Kennedy and Dr. Martin Luther King, Jr. More often, however, a eulogy honors someone personally known to the audience and recently deceased. At other times, a memorial honors certain qualities for which that person stood. In such a situation, the speaker uses the memorial to renew and reinforce the audience's adherence to ideals possessed by the deceased and worthy of emulation by the community.

## Style and Content in Speeches of Tribute

When delivering a speech of tribute, suit your manner of speaking to the circumstances. A farewell banquet usually blends an atmosphere of merriment with a spirit of sincere regret. Dignity and formality are, on the whole, characteristic of memorial services, unveilings of monuments, and similar dedicatory ceremonies. Regardless of the general tone of the occasion, a simple, honest expression of admiration presented, in clear and unadorned language, is the most appropriate form.

Frequently, a speaker attempts to itemize all the accomplishments of the honored person or group. This weakens the impact, however, because in trying to cover everything, it emphasizes nothing. Instead, focus your remarks:

- *Stress dominant traits.* If you are paying tribute to a person, select a few aspects of her or his personality that are especially likable or praiseworthy and relate incidents from the person's life or work to illustrate these distinguishing qualities.
- *Mention only outstanding achievements.* Pick only a few of the person's or group's most notable accomplishments. Let your speech say "Here is what this person [or group] has done; see how such actions have contributed to the well-being of our business or community."
- *Give special emphasis to the influence of the person or group.* Show what effect the behavior of the person or group has had on others. Many times, the importance of people's lives can be demonstrated not so much by their particular material accomplishments as by the influence they had on associates.

See the "How to" box on the next page for useful strategies in organizing a speech of tribute.

## Speeches to Create Goodwill

A **speech to create goodwill** works from the values of the community in building a positive atmosphere for the acceptance of an idea, a product, or a service. In the process, the goal is to enhance the listeners' appreciation of a particular institution, practice, or profession. As a hybrid, or mixed type, of address, it combines the features of an informative speech with a strong, underlying persuasive purpose.

## How to
## Organize Speeches of Tribute

Consider these strategies in preparing your tribute:

1. *Direct the attention of the audience toward those characteristics or accomplishments that you consider most important.* There are two common ways of doing this: Make a straightforward, sincere statement of these commendable traits or achievements or of the influence they have had upon others, and relate one or more instances that vividly illustrate your point.

2. *Dramatize the impact of the person's accomplishments by noting obstacles that were overcome.* Thus, you might describe the extent of the loss to a family when their home burned before praising the Habitat for Humanity group that came to their aid, with special mention of the college students who participated in the rebuilding of the home.

3. *Develop the substance of the tribute itself.* Relate a few incidents to show how the personal or public problems you have outlined were met and surmounted. In doing this, be sure to demonstrate at least one of the following:

   ■ How certain admirable traits—vision, courage, and tenacity, for example—made it possible to deal successfully with these problems

   ■ How remarkable the achievements were in face of the obstacles encountered

   ■ How great the influence of the achievement was on others

3. *Synthesize the attributes of the person or group into a vivid composite picture of the accomplishment and its significance.* There are several ways to do this:

   ■ Introduce an apt quotation. Try to find a bit of poetry or a literary passage that fits the person or group to whom you're paying tribute, and introduce it here.

   ■ Draw a "word picture" of a world (e.g., community, business, profession) inhabited by such persons. Suggest how much better things would be if more people had similar qualities.

   ■ Mention the sense of loss that will occur after the individual or group leaves. Show vividly how much he, she, or they will be missed. Be specific: "It's going to seem mighty strange to walk into Barbara's office and not find her there ready to listen, advise, and help."

5. *In closing, connect the theme of the speech with the occasion on which it is presented.* Thus, in a eulogy, suggest the best tribute the audience can pay the person being honored is to live as that person did or to carry on what she or he has begun. In a dedication speech, suggest the appropriateness of dedicating this monument, building, or plaque to such a person or group, and express hope that it will inspire others to emulate its accomplishments. At the close of a farewell speech, extend to the departing person or persons the best wishes of those you represent and express a determination to carry on what they have begun. If you are saying farewell, call upon those who remain to carry on what you and your associates have started.

There are numerous situations in which goodwill speeches are appropriate. The most common include luncheon meetings of civic and service clubs, such as Rotary or Kiwanis; training programs, such as those sponsored by schools and companies; and special demonstrations at conventions and product shows. In all of these cases, the speakers have the opportunity to show their appreciation for being invited to speak and to increase appreciation for the company or product they represent.

## Style and Content in Goodwill Speeches

Three qualities—modesty, tolerance, and good humor—characterize the manner of speaking that is appropriate to goodwill speeches. On most occasions, you'll find the audience well disposed to hear you speak. The company you represent or the product you wish to introduce already is viewed positively by the audience— they simply want to know more about what is going on or how to use the product in their own work. In other cases, the audience may be downright hostile. A state official coming into a community to indicate why a proposed school cannot be built will likely have more difficulty creating goodwill. Speakers must be able to act not only as information sources but also as persuaders, working to change uninformed beliefs and hostile attitudes. You must know and present the facts clearly and show a tolerant, patient attitude toward others. You also can communicate your awareness of the depth of feelings you face and recognize that alternative opinions have merit.

On these occasions, you also face the challenge of diversity because audiences are likely to have stereotypical views that may make your task more difficult. If you are speaking to a local group about your fraternity's proposal to build a new house for its members, you'll face problems if they believe all college students are lazy no-accounts whose only goal is to party. Overcoming such views is never easy. The

*An educational program provides the public with critical information while creating goodwill in the process.*

challenge is to organize information and valuable appeals in such a way as to attack those stereotypes. On most occasions, you must speak as a modest, tolerant, good-humored individual—not as someone who is angered by the attitudes you hear.

In selecting materials for a goodwill speech, keep three suggestions in mind:

1. *Present novel and interesting facts about your subject.* Make your listeners feel that you're giving them an inside look into your company or organization. Avoid talking about what they already know; instead, concentrate on new developments and on facts and services that are not generally known.

2. *Show a relationship between your subject and the lives of your listeners.* Make them see the importance of your organization or profession to their personal safety, success, or happiness.

3. *Offer a definite service.* This offer may take the form of an invitation to the audience to visit your office or shop, to help them with their problems, or to answer questions or send brochures.

# How to
## Organize Goodwill Speeches

Use the following advice in organizing your speech:

1. *Attention step.* Establish a friendly feeling, and arouse the audience's curiosity about your profession or the institution you represent. You can gain the first of these objectives by giving a tactful compliment to the group or making a reference to the occasion that has brought you together. Follow this with one or two unusual facts or illustrations concerning the enterprise you represent.

2. *Need step.* Point out certain problems facing your audience—problems with which your institution, profession, or agency is vitally concerned. For example, if you represent a radio or television station, show the relationship of good communications to the social and economic health of the community. By so doing, you'll establish common ground with your audience. Ordinarily, the need step is brief and consists largely of suggestions developed with only an occasional illustration; however, if you intend to propose that your listeners join in acting to meet a common problem, the need step will require fuller development.

3. *Satisfaction step.* Tell your audience about your institution, profession, or business, and explain what it is or what it does. Relate interesting events in its history. Explain how your organization or profession operates. Describe the services your organization renders. Tell what your firm or profession has done for the community: people employed; purchases made locally; assistance with community projects; or improvements in health, education, or public safety. Do not boast, but make sure that your listeners realize the value of your work to them.

4. *Visualization step.* Crystallize the goodwill that your presentation of information in the satisfaction step initially created. Do this by looking to the future. Rapidly survey the points you have covered, or combine them into a single story or illustration. To approach this step from the opposite direction, picture for your listeners the loss that would result if the organization or profession you represent should leave the community or cease to exist. Be careful, however, not to leave the impression there is any real danger that this will occur.

5. *Action step.* Make your offer of service to the audience. For example, invite the group to visit your office or point out the willingness of your organization to assist in a common enterprise.

As with every type of speech, the style, content, and organization of the goodwill speech must be adapted to meet the demands of the subject or occasion. You should, however, never lose sight of the central purpose for which you speak: to show your audience that the work you do or the service you perform is of value to them, that it will somehow make their lives happier, more productive, interesting, or secure. For more advice on organizing a goodwill speech, see the "How to" box on the preceding page.

In general, even when audiences disagree with your position or argument, they may be more receptive in these settings because they will assume you are talking to them about issues they deem important. Indicating at the outset that you, likewise, value their position and their sense of the importance of the issues will increase the chance of the audience giving you a fair hearing. If they believe you to be sincere in your respect for their position while remaining committed to your own, they may continue to disagree but will more likely be cordial and hospitable in hearing your ideas.

The same will be true of speaking at conferences. On such an occasion, special pleading on behalf of a specific cause will depend largely on the purpose of your invitation to speak as well as on the goals of the conference itself. If it is meeting to determine the ways to best advance a city parks proposal, then placing before the group a special-interest plea that competes with that goal will not be in your best interest. If the conference is an academic one, the presenters generally will be expected to eschew political presentations and, instead, engage in discussions that may be critical of political events but in a manner designed to provide greater knowledge about how such events have occurred—or ways to prevent their reoccurrence. Your contribution to intellectual ideas also may well be what the audience seeks; students in various majors participate in such events through honors organizations as well as student chapters of various national organizations. Submitting a paper to an undergraduate research conference in your discipline may be a way to experience such an occasion firsthand. In fleshing out more precise advice with respect to meetings and conferences, we now deal with discrete meetings first and then consider conference speaking.

## After-Dinner Talks: Entertaining with a Purpose

Although it is by no means the only form of speaking at specific meetings, we focus here on the **speech to entertain** as a specific type of after-dinner presentation. To entertain an audience—especially one that meets late in the evening and is just finishing a banquet meal—presents special challenges to speakers. As you may recall, we identified *to entertain* as an independent type of speech in Chapter 2 because of the peculiar force of humor in speechmaking. Discounting slapstick (or the "slipping-on-a-banana-peel" genre), most humor depends primarily upon a listener's sensitivities to the routines and mores of society; this is obvious if you have ever listened to someone from a foreign country tell jokes. Much humor cannot be translated, in part because of language differences (e.g., puns do not translate well) and in even larger measure because of cultural differences. After-dinner occasions are not the only situations for entertaining speeches, but they are an apt use of this genre of speaking. Because the audience is at the end of what, for many, may be an already long day, to hit them hard with a serious, intellectually demanding talk is asking of them more than they may have to give in terms of attention and focus at that moment.

At the same time, humor does not work well if used only as an end in itself. Merely being funny is not enough in these occasions—the audience may well wonder why they didn't just invite a professional comedian. (At least then, the jokes would be better.) In place of humor for itself, the speech to entertain combines humor with a moral purpose. It seeks to ease the audience into more serious thought rather than beating them over the head with abstract theoretical musings. Hence, the title of this section: Entertaining with a Purpose. More often than not, that purpose is to make a point about some facet of society's values or some event of mutual concern to you and your audience.

## Style and Content in Speeches to Entertain

Like most humor, in general, a speech to entertain usually works within the cultural framework of a particular group or society. Such speeches may be merely funny, of course, as with a comic monologue, but most are serious in their force or demand on audiences. After-dinner speeches, for example, usually are more than dessert. Their topics normally are relevant to the group at hand, and their anecdotes usually are offered to make a point. That point may be as simple as deflecting an audience's blasé attitude toward the speaker, as group centered as making the people in the audience feel more like a group, or as serious as offering a critique of society.

To entertain does not always have to mean "Be funny all of the time." You want the audience to relax and enjoy the moment, but you also want to say something worth their listening. Simply stringing together unrelated anecdotes, as in a

 **How to**
**Organize Speeches to Entertain**

The following sequence works well for a speech to entertain:

1. Relate a story or anecdote, present an illustration, or quote an appropriate passage.
2. State the essential idea or point of view implied by your opening remarks.

3. Follow with a series of additional stories, anecdotes, quips, or illustrations that amplify or illuminate your central idea. Arrange these supporting materials so they are thematically or tonally coherent.
4. Close with a restatement of the central point you have developed. As in step 1, you can use another quotation or one final story that clinches and epitomizes your speech.

comic monologue, is not what we have in mind in discussing this type of speaking. The difference between *to entertain* and *to inform or persuade*, then, is in the emphasis placed on humor as a vehicle for obtaining audience attention and interest in your views. The "How to" box on the previous page presents a useful sequence to follow in organizing a speech to entertain.

Speakers seeking to deflect audience antipathy often use humor to ingratiate themselves. For example, Henry W. Grady, editor of the *Atlanta Constitution*, expected a good deal of distrust and hostility when, after the Civil War, he journeyed to New York City in 1886 to tell the New England Society about "The New South." He opened the speech not only by thanking the society for the invitation but also by telling stories about farmers, husbands and wives, and preachers. He praised former President Abraham Lincoln, a Northerner, as "the first typical American" of the new age; told another humorous story about shopkeepers and their advertising; poked fun at the great Union General Sherman ("who is considered an able man in our hearts, though some people think he is a kind of careless man about fire"); and assured his audience that a New South, one very much like the Old North, was arising from those ashes.[6] Through the use of humor, Grady had his audience cheering every point he made about the New South that evening.

Group cohesiveness also can be created through humor. Politicians, especially when campaigning, spend much of their time telling humorous stories about their opponents, hitting them with stinging remarks. In part, of course, biting political humor degrades the opposition candidate and party. However, such humor also can make one's own party feel more cohesive.

## Keynote Speeches

The **keynote speech** requires a clear sense of the mission or purpose of the conference being addressed. The audience will expect that you have asked the right questions in advance and that your presentation conveys an implicit—if not explicit—understanding of who they are and why they have gathered at this time and place. The keynotes you may well recall are those traditionally delivered during Republican and Democratic National Conventions. In each instance, the speaker serves as a symbolic representative of the party gathered to select a presidential candidate. Likewise, in each case, the speaker spends some time acknowledging the work of the party members attending—and also offers a critique of the other party as a means of solidifying support for the agenda of those listening.

On other occasions, the keynote speaker is brought in from outside, as in the case of John Hope Franklin's keynote address at a recent National Communication Association Convention. In this instance, Franklin acknowledged the connection between communication faculty concerns and his own concerns as Chair of the Advisory Board to President Clinton's Initiative on Race. Franklin's remarks were preceded by a speech of introduction, in which the association leader conveyed to the audience Franklin's qualifications and purpose. See the "How to" box that follows for more on how to organize a speech of introduction.

## Panel Discussions at Meetings

Inviting experts to appear as participants in a **panel discussion** is a common feature of most conferences or conventions. Generally, four to six individuals are asked to present a brief *position statement* and then discuss the issues raised, both among themselves and with members of the audience. These can be *pro/con sessions*, with experts invited to speak on either side of a controversial issue, or they can be *random sessions*, with experts asked to present their personal views and with mixed agreement/disagreement between and among the panelists.

# How to
## Organize Speeches of Introduction

The speech of introduction usually is given by the group's leader or the person responsible for bringing the speaker before the group. This type of speech is designed to prepare that group to accept the featured speaker and her or his message into the group's community and standards. In a sense, a speech of introduction paves the way; it gains permission to speak. In the case of a nonmember of the group or community, that permission is based upon what the person brings. What knowledge or skill, above and beyond what the group itself might already possess, does the speaker offer? If the speaker is a member of the group, the introduction should serve as a reminder of his or her role and accomplishments within the community.

Always, the introductory speech should motivate the audience to listen to the presentation. Everything else must be subordinated to this aim. In giving the introduction, you're only the speaker's advance agent; your job is to sell her or him to the audience. This task carries a twofold responsibility. First, you must arouse the listeners' curiosity about the speaker and subject, thus making it easier for the speaker to get the attention of the audience. Second, you must do all that you reasonably can to generate audience respect for the speaker, thereby increasing the likelihood that listeners will respond favorably to the message that's presented.

When giving a speech of introduction, your manner of speaking should be suited to the nature of the occasion, your familiarity with the speaker, and the speaker's prestige. Match your introduction to the seriousness of the occasion. Observe these principles:

1. *Talk about the speaker.* Who is the speaker? What's her position in business, education, sports, or government? What experiences qualify the speaker to talk on the announced subject? Build up the speaker's identity, and tell what she or he knows or has done. Don't praise her or his ability as a speaker, however. Let the speaker demonstrate her or his own skills.

2. *Emphasize the importance of the speaker's subject.* For example, in introducing a speaker who will talk about the budget cuts facing your university, you might say, "All of us pay tuition, and we know firsthand that budget cuts may mean a tuition hike for us. Knowing why the budget cuts are imperative, and what is likely to happen as a result, is in our self-interest."

3. *Stress the appropriateness of the subject or the speaker.* If your town is considering a program of renewal and revitalization, a speech by a city planner is likely to be timely and well received. If an organization is marking an anniversary, one of the speakers may be its founder. As in the previous example, you could go on to note the speaker is the university's vice-president for finance and administration and, hence, is in a position to know the reasons for the current crisis.

## Preparing for Panel Participation

As part of a group of presenters, you have an obligation to take the possible positions of others into account as well as to prepare remarks that permit others equal time to convey their thoughts. Speaking "off the cuff" seldom is a good idea in these settings because the audience will rather quickly conclude you have not given much thought to how your ideas will fit with those of others. Hence, it is incumbent on you to spend some time thinking about the situation and how your ideas will fit—and to prepare an outline from which you might speak extemporaneously. Adhering to the following guidelines will make it easier to make the best use of your time as part of the panel:

**Address the theme.** This constrains your choice a bit more than in other speaking situations, because you need to address the issues that others will also be considering. Your views of the issues may be different from those of others, and you may emphasize different facets of the problem or theme. Still, you will need to satisfy the other panel members and the audience that you have, indeed, paid attention to the reason for being a participant.

**Consider whether it would be wise to divide issues in advance of the presentation.** If you know the other participants, a conference call organizing the presentation may be in order. In this way, you will avoid duplication as well as the feeling that as the last speaker, everything you planned to say has already been noted by preceding speakers.

**Plan your own remarks in advance.** This may include reviewing the information you already have for significant gaps that need to be filled before you participate. Doing additional research on the issue, whether to fill gaps or bring your own knowledge up to date, may be essential if you are to come across as well versed in the issues. If the issue is controversial, you also may want to develop a more specific point of view to assemble your points in support. Rambling around, within, and under a topic does little to merit confidence that you have a commitment to the ideas. You also should anticipate the impact your thoughts will have on the panel as well as the audience. If your position will be controversial, think about the kinds of objections that will be raised and consider how you might answer queries and arguments counter to your position.

**When the moment arrives that you have the floor, speak in a direct, friendly, conversational style.** Even if your ideas are not well accepted, be willing to address others in a cordial and collegial manner. Doing so will assist in keeping the follow-up questions in a similarly civilized tone. Your specific contribution to the panel should be presented so that it appears straightforward, precise, and succinct. Being succinct will make it easier to keep your remarks within an allotted timeframe, so as not to monopolize the time set aside for the rest of the panel presentation. In most conferences, events are tightly structured, with only so much time allotted for each program. As the first or second speaker, in particular, you will want to make sure the remaining participants have ample time to present their own views.

**Speak in a conciliatory tone during the follow-up discussion.** By and large, the purpose of a panel session is not to come to specific decisions about what to do but to stimulate audience thought about the options available, with each speaker giving a specific slant to the possibilities. Thus, being perceived as open to alternatives—even though you may have a favorite solution in mind—is essential if the panel is to achieve its objective. You may marshal evidence and critique other alternatives as part of the follow-up discussion, but the overriding objective is to get as many ideas on the floor for discussion as possible. Hence, remaining calm and tolerant of dissenting views is as important as saying something meaningful.

With these guidelines in mind, you are well on your way to having a successful and productive panel session.

## Assessing a Sample Speech

As noted, Susan Au Allen presented the following remarks at the tenth anniversary of the Excellence 2000 Awards and in Celebration of Asian Pacific American Heritage at a meeting of the U.S. Pan Asian American Chamber of Commerce in Washington, DC.[7] In the first two paragraphs, she acknowledges her connection to the awards program, sets forth the objective of her presentation—to examine "where we are heading in the future"—and sets the rationale for a review of the preceding decade's awards—a task well suited to a tenth-anniversary celebration. In paragraphs 3–13, she reviews the principal themes and values underlying the celebration of Asian Pacific American Heritage months in the preceding years. She then extends the review of the current year, 1998, and its accomplishments before returning to her central question in paragraph 20. In the remainder of the presentation, she extols the values central to the organization, including the presentation of awards to people who are not of Asian descent; past recipients have been African American and Bosnian because they were deemed "the most qualified" applicants.

---

### *In Pursuit of the Tiger: Traditions and Transitions*
**Susan Au Allen**

I am honored that you are here to celebrate this occasion with us tonight. When I started    1
this program ten years ago, I could only dream that it would become what it is today.

The 10th anniversary Excellence 2000 Awards program of the U.S. Pan Asian Ameri-    2
can Chamber of Commerce brings forth a vital question—Where are we heading in the future, based on the traditions and transitions we have been through? But before we can answer that question, let us look together at where we have been in the last ten years.

In 1989, when we inaugurated the program, there was a serious need to celebrate    3
achievements by the many Asian Americans in the arts, science, sports, business, education and public service. We looked back and praised 15 Asian Americans for their

extraordinary achievements in these areas. They demonstrated vividly that America remains a land of opportunity for any and all who embraced its basic concept of freedom and personal accountability.

4      For each of the ensuing years, in May during Asian Pacific American Heritage month, we would celebrate our heritage and chose a theme to guide our lives and businesses in the coming year.

5      In 1990, our theme reflected what we all believed—that we were "Proud to be Americans."

6      In 1991, we embraced "Success through Merit"—not preferential treatment based on race, national origin or gender.

7      In 1992, our theme was the "Asian American Success Story," to underscore and perpetuate the profound belief shared by our members, that we are an integral part of America and its unique history wherein neither ethnic nor racial origin decides the main characters.

8      Then a year later in 1993, the debate over militant and government-mandated cultural diversity exploded across the land. In response to this dangerous trend toward division and group conflict, we embraced "A New Horizon" to remind the country that although injustices still remained, the doors of opportunity were opening wider to ever increasing numbers of Americans. We affirmed that for us, just as for others who previously had faced barriers, hardship, and prejudices in America, with opportunity when combined with hard work, skills and merit, comes success.

9      That tumultuous year was followed in 1994 with a surging rise in national crime rate. Our response was "A New Palladium," a metaphor we borrowed from Washington's farewell address and he borrowed from the ancient Greeks, signifying a strong unified foundation. In our case, it is a foundation of good citizens of all creeds, colors and races, unified to form a solid foundation built on the principles of equality, justice, freedom and the pursuit of happiness. We urged the country to use these vital forces to ward off the evil spirits of greed and crime.

10     In 1995, when the U.S. Congress threatened new restrictions on legal immigration, we responded with "We Immigrants. We Citizens," to remind the Congress, as President Franklin Roosevelt did, that we are all descended from immigrants and revolutionists.

11     Throughout these years, as we continued to do in 1996, we involved ourselves in "Reaching, Teaching and Inspiring," to lay the foundation for more promising futures. And over these years we awarded 38 college scholarships.

12     For 1997, we celebrated "An Auspicious Journey," to memorialize that Asian Americans are strangers no more to the American Dream. We have been and are in all walks of life. From building the Trans Continental Railroad, to fighting for America during World War II, to winning Olympic Gold medals and Nobel Prizes, Asian Americans had undeniably become an essential part of the American fabric. For example, in December 1996, *Time* Magazine named Dr. David Ho "Man of the Year" because of his groundbreaking AIDS research.

13     In 1998, he joined our Asian American Hall of Fame, with world class architect I. M. Pei, cellist Yo-Yo Ma, Nobel Laureate Subrahmanian Chandrasekhar, Olympians Sammy Lee and Kristi Yamaguchi and 63 others, all featured in tonight's program book.

14     This brings us up to date on the Excellence 2000 story.

*(continued)*

For 1998, we have the theme "In Pursuit of the Tiger: Traditions and Transitions."    **15**

1998 is the Year of the Tiger in Chinese culture. Coincidentally, one of our honorees    **16**
tonight is named Tiger. Also, my father will celebrate his 80th birthday this year and he
was born in the Year of the Tiger—and so was his much younger son-in-law Paul, my
husband. Both are in the audience with my mother and one of the jewels in the family
crown, our younger son Edward. Our older son, Mark, is at the University of Chicago,
studying, I hope. My sister May May is also here. They are my backbone.

I'd like my family to stand so that I can thank them publicly for their patience,    **17**
support and love.

The tiger in Chinese folklore is known for its valor, power and readiness to take    **18**
risks to preserve his or her values. And I propose the spirit of the Tiger be the guiding
philosophy for the Excellence 2000 program in the next ten years.

In pursuit of the tiger, we intend to preserve the time-honored traditions that have    **19**
been the Asian American legacy—family, personal responsibility, knowledge, industry,
self-restraint, respect for those who came before us, care for those who come after us,
compassion for those less fortunate than us, and the wisdom to pass the torch of
excellence from one generation to the next.

Importantly, these are the very same values honored by millions of people who    **20**
arrived on these shores over the last 220 years. Many of us have succeeded because we
have held onto these traditions, and have done well on account of our own efforts. As
one Excellence 2000 scholarship recipient said to me, "I am responsible for my life. I do
not ask for breaks. I make them, instead."

Now, the vital question is—Where are we heading in the next ten years? Now that    **21**
we have achieved success in so many areas, Asian Americans are moving into politics
and government. More than ever, we are participating in the political process. This is a
good thing. However, we must be careful not to fall prey to reliance on the government
to do the work for us.

As a minority group with little political power, we have come a long way without    **22**
government help. The formulae we used, the traditions I mentioned earlier, have
worked for us, as they have worked for other ethnic groups. They are the proven means
to success, and we should preserve them at all costs.

Here at the U.S. Pan Asian American Chamber of Commerce, we embrace voluntary    **23**
diversity and merit. As a result, many of our members are non-Asian.

Our Bruce Lee Scholarship was awarded to an African American student in 1996.    **24**
Why? Quite simply because she was the most qualified applicant. This year, the Bruce Lee
Scholarship will be awarded to an immigrant from Bosnia. He, too, is the most qualified.

Correctly, we support legislation that would open the doors for competition to small    **25**
businesses. For example, the proposed Small Business Lawsuit Abuse Protection Act would
prevent frivolous lawsuits and arbitrarily large punitive damage awards that have ruined
countless small businesses, destroyed jobs and reduced American competitiveness.

The free market economy is the ideal environment to practice and preserve the    **26**
traditions that we hold dear. All Americans involved in politics must honor this sacred
truth. Such an economy promotes a limited and responsive government, one that
would reduce taxes and reform regulations and act as the arbiter of right from wrong,
instead of an advocate for endless special interests.

27　　As we have looked back together tonight at the history of Excellence 2000 and look forward to our 1998 honorees, we see that all of the honorees—Tiger Woods, Andrea Jung, Scott Oki and Robert Nakasone—personify the traditions we value.

28　　Now as we stand at this important transition to the next century, it is my hope that these traditions will continue to be the guiding force for our lives, businesses and organization.

29　　Like the Chinese adage, "When we drink the water, we remember the source." So as we embark on new careers and new frontiers, such as politics and government, we ought to remember the source—our traditions.

30　　So, it is to the vital task of preserving this miracle of the free market that the U.S. Pan Asian American Chamber of Commerce must bring the valor, power and readiness to take risks embodied in the spirit of the Tiger.

31　　Welcome to the 10th Anniversary Excellence 2000 Awards program, and I ask you to join me in the noble challenge before us.

## ■ CHAPTER SUMMARY

Speeches on special occasions are grounded in the ceremonies or rituals that define and reinforce the fundamental tenets of a community. On such occasions, speakers face the special challenge of getting diversified audiences to see, interpret, and evaluate the world through the beliefs, attitudes, values, and rituals of the group observing the occasion. We define ourselves and live up to standards of behavior within reference groups, yet when those groups clash, unifying social constructions of the world must be built through language. Types of speeches on special occasions include speeches of tribute (farewells, dedications, memorial services) and speeches to create goodwill. Most of these forms are built to construct and reinforce community standards.

The guidelines for speaking at meetings and conferences are, in general, no different than those for other ceremonial and special occasion speeches. The key difference between such events and those involving classroom speeches is that there are more constraints on your freedom to select and develop a topic of your own choosing. After-dinner speaking—and particularly entertaining with a purpose—is one of the common types of speech occasions that you will encounter. You also may be asked to present a keynote address or participate in a panel discussion at a conference; in these cases, it will be important to adapt your presentation to fit the conference or the panel's theme and convey to the audience an appreciation for their reasons for coming to the meeting. Following the guidelines for participation in panel discussions, in particular, will be helpful in making the best use of your time—as well as the time of the audience.

## ■ KEY TERMS

community (p. 400)
dedication (p. 407)
eulogy (p. 407)
keynote speech (p. 413)
panel discussion (p. 414)

reference group (p. 401)
ritual (p. 402)
social construction (p. 400)
special occasions (p. 399)
speech of farewell (p. 405)

speech of tribute (p. 405)
speech to create goodwill (p. 408)
speech to entertain (p. 411)

## ■ ASSESSMENT ACTIVITIES

1. This chapter has argued that goodwill speeches usually are informative speeches with underlying persuasive purposes. Describe various circumstances under which you think the *informative* elements should predominate in this type of speech, and then describe other circumstances in which the *persuasive* elements should predominate. In the second case, at what point would you say the speech becomes openly persuasive in purpose? If you prefer to work with advertisements, scan magazines to find public service ads that emphasize what companies are doing to help society with its problems or to promote social-cultural-aesthetic values. Then, ask yourself similar questions about these ads.

2. Develop a speech that entertains as it promotes a specific point of view or moral. As you collect specific jokes or humorous stories, consider whether anyone in the intended audience might find them offensive. Can you adapt the joke or story so as not to give offense? What might be the consequence of going ahead with the story or joke as written? Is this a consequence you want to accept? Ask the audience, in particular, to evaluate your choices of entertaining stories and jokes—how accurate is your sense of what might be funny as well as nonoffensive?

3. Select a conference or convention that focuses on an issue, product, or theme that is important to you. You can use the *Chronicle for Higher Edu-* cation's list of conferences (though that will be limited primarily to academic conferences) or student organizations you belong to as one resource, or you can check trade publications in your university library to see when and where such conferences are held. Once you have a conference in mind, develop a keynote address that fits the theme. If you have the opportunity to present the speech in class, indicate in advance the nature of the conference and its theme and ask the audience to role-play conference attendees in evaluating your presentation.

4. Divide the class into small groups. Each group will consider one of the following topics and develop a panel presentation centered on it:
   a. *The ethics of lying:* When is it OK to tell a lie?
   b. *The ethics of plagiarism:* Is it ever OK to borrow from the works of others? (Note that some cultures do not have the same strictures placed on "borrowing" as does U.S. culture.)
   c. *The status of civil discourse in U.S. society:* Are we in an age of incivility, and if so, what should we do to increase the occurrence of civil discourse?
   d. *Select a topic that is of current concern on your campus or in your community:* What are the causes of the problem, and what solutions might be proposed?

## ■ REFERENCES

1. Nelson Goodman, *Ways of Worldmaking* (Indianapolis, IN: Hackett, 1978), 6.

2. For a discussion of the kinds of group activity that reinforce the power of groups over your life, see James E. Combs, "The Functions of Ritual," in *Dimensions of Political Drama* (Santa Monica, CA: Goodyear, 1980), 20–22. For comparison, see Philip G. Zimbardo, "Constructing Social Reality," in *Psychology and Life*, 13th ed. (New York: HarperCollins, 1992), 595–607.

3. Michael Walzer, "On the Role of Symbolism in Political Thought," *Political Science Quarterly* 82 (1967): 194.

4. David I. Kertzer, *Ritual, Politics, and Power* (New Haven, CT: Yale University Press, 1988), 9.

5. Kertzer, 10 (note 5).

6. Henry W. Grady. "The New South," in *American Public Addresses: 1740–1852*, edited by A. Craig Baird (New York: McGraw-Hill, 1956), 181–185.

7. Susan Au Allen, "In Pursuit of the Tiger: Traditions and Transitions," *Vital Speeches of the Day* 64 (15 July 1998): 605–607. Used with permission of the author.

# Index

*Note: Bold numbers indicate pages on which key terms are defined.*

**A**bbreviations, 72
Accuracy (of word choice), **234**
Achievement motives, **313**, 314
Action step (of motivated sequence), **177**, 186.
    *See also* Motivated sequence
Active listening, **67**, 69, 70. *See also* Listening
Activity (as audience attention strategy), **192**, 197
Actuation, **359**. *See also* Actuative speeches
Actuative speeches, 28, 359–360, 365–368. *See also*
    Persuasive speeches
  audiences of, 359
  definition of, **28, 359**
  motivated sequence and, 174–175, 180, 359–360,
    365–368
  organization of, 34, 174–175, 180, 359–360,
    365–368
  outlines/outlining for, 34, 180, 365–368
  purposes of, 27, 28–29, 31, 32, 34, 180
Ad hominem attacks, 243, **244**, 247, 390
Additive method (of audience unification), 125
Adulojo, Stephanie, 194, 240–241
Advertising, 249, 344,
Affect displays (and facial signals), **300**
Affiliation motives, **312**–314
After-dinner talks, 411–413. *See also* Entertainment
    speeches; Special occasion speeches
Aggregative quality (of speech), **288**
Agonistic quality (of speech), 80–81, **288**
Alda, Alan, 249
Allen, Susan Au, 405, 406–419
Amanpour, Christiane, 199
Ambiguity (as type of fallacy), **388**
American Management Association, 73
American Music Awards, 406
Americans with Disabilities Act, 83
Analogical definitions, **239**
Animate objects (as visual aids), **267**–268
Ansen, David, 155
Appeal to authority (as type of fallacy), **387**
Appeal to ignorance (as type of fallacy), **387**
Appeal to popular opinion (as type of fallacy), **387**
Appreciative listening, **66**
Appropriateness (of word choice), **238**

Archie (as search tool), 146
Arendt, Hannah, 13
Arguing (as act), 375, 377. *See also* Argumentative
    speeches
Argument (as process), **375**. *See also* Argumentative
    speeches
Argumentation (as exchange), **375**–377. *See also*
    Argumentative speeches
Argumentative speeches, 375–396
  assessment of, 393–396
  audience and, 377–378, 383
  claims in, 376, 378–381, 390–393
  counterarguments to, 392, 393
  critical thinking and, 375, 377–378, 392–393
  culture and, 377–378, 383
  definition of, 375–376
  elements of, 378–384, 390–393. *See also* Claims;
    Evidence
  ethical issues in, 382, 383
  language use in, 392
  levels of, 376
  model for, 390–393
  motivated sequence for, 376
  motivational appeals in, 383
  organization of, 376, 390–393
  persuasion and, 378
  purposes of, 376–377
  reasoning behind, 376, 378, 384–390
  sample of, 393–396
  supporting materials for, 382–383, 393
Aristotle, 13, 55, 197
Armstrong, Neil, 231
Articles of Impeachment, 369–371
Articulation, 293–294, 297
Assessment (of speeches), 43–45, 73–74
  of after-dinner talks, 416–419
  of argumentative speeches, 393–396
  of informative speeches, 337–340
  of use of motivated sequence, 181–185
  of persuasive speeches, 46–48, 369–371
  of special occasion speeches, 416–419
  of use of motivated sequence, 181–185
Atmosphere (of speaking occasion), 247–249, 283

Attention, **191**. *See also* Audience attention
Attention gaining/maintaining strategies, **192**–196,
    197, 289. *See also* Audience attention
Attention step (of motivated sequence), **171**, 185.
    *See also* Motivated sequence
Attitudes
    approaches to changing, 358
    of audiences, 36, 37, 56, 70–71, 108–109, 110–112,
        113, 123, 349, 358
    definition of, **108**
    research on, 358
    of speakers, 52, 53–54
Attribution process (as verbal association), **315**, 316
Audience analysis, 104–127. *See also* Audiences
    definition of, **36**–38, **56**
    demographic approaches to, 103, 104–106, 120,
        122, 129, 351–352
    ethical issues in, 126
    goal of, 103
    language use and, 106, 124
    outlines/outlining and, 217, 218
    psychological approaches to, 107–114, 120, 122,
        129, 217, 218, 309, 311–319, 320, 321, 344–356
    reference groups and, 353–354, 401–402
    sample of, 127–130
    targeting, 118–122
    use of, 105–106, 114, 117–127
Audience attention, 189–196, 197, 309, 311–319
    culture and, 190–196
    definition of, **189**
    handouts and, 278–279
    humor and, 192, 195, 197
    motivation appeals and, 309, 311–319, 359, 360,
        383
    strategies for gaining/maintaining, **192**–196, 197,
        289
Audience segmentation, 122–125 **(123)**, 345. *See also*
    Audience analysis
Audience targeting, **118**–122. *See also* Audience
    analysis
Audience-centered emphasis (of speech), **249**–250
Audiences (of speeches), 189–210
    actions by, 36, 121–122, 177, 206, 359
    of actuative speeches, 359
    analysis of. *See* Audience analysis
    of argumentative speeches, 377–378, 383
    attention of. *See* Audience attention
    attitudes of, 36, 37, 56, 70–71, 108–109, 110–112,
        113, 123, 349, 358
    behaviors of, 122, 344–356
    beliefs of, 107–108, 109, 110–112, 113, 123

body language and, 298, 301, 302–303
body of speech and, 196
claims/central ideas and, 31, 34, 68
commitments of, 377–378
as community, 11–12, 399, 400–405
conclusion and, 189–190, 196, 197, 198, 208
culture and, 190–196
demographic characteristics of, 103, 104–106, 120,
    122, 129, 351–352
desires/visions/fantasies of, 112–113, 123
ethics and, 126
expectations of, 116–117
feedback from, 43, 57
framing and, 114
generational differences in, 59
humor and, 192, 195, 197
introduction and, 189–190, 196, 197–198, 208
knowledge of, 36, 37, 56, 70–71, 208, 281, 377
language use and, 106, 124
listening skills/styles of. *See* Listening
motivated sequence and, 169–177
motivational appeals to, 309, 311–319, 359, 360,
    383
multicultural nature of, 37, 51–52, 56, 86–97,
    104–106, 255, 345. *See also* Multicultural society
nonverbal communication and, 298, 301, 302–303
of informative speeches, 309, 311–319
organization and, 161, 162, 169, 169–177,
    189–190, 217, 218
outlines/outlining and, 217, 218
perceptions of speakers, 54–55, 70–71
of persuasive speeches, 344–356
psychological characteristics of, 103, 107–114, 120,
    122, 129, 217, 218, 309, 311–319, 320, 321,
    344–359
purposes and, 27–31, 35, 36, 118–120
reference groups of, 353–354, 401–402
responses of, 169–177, 191
segmented nature of, 122–125 (123), 345
speakers' relationships with, 43, 290–291, 296,
    298, 301, 302–303
of special occasion speeches, 399, 400–405, 406,
    409–410
subject selection and, 24–25, 26–27, 37, 88, 208
supporting materials and, 71, 106, 114, 129
targeting of, 118–122
unifying members of, 86–97, 125–127
values of, 109–112, 113, 123, 358, 405, 406
visual aids and, 278–279, 281, 282
visualization and, 192, 195–196, 197, 315, 323
Auditory imagery, 240, **241**

Auditory listeners, 63, **64**
Aural channel, **58**
Austin, Gilbert, 229
Authority to act (by audience), **36,** 121–122
Authority, Appeal to (as type of fallacy), **387**
Axioms (reasoning from), **384, 385,** 388

**B**acking (in argumentation), 391, **392–393.** *See also*
    Evidence; Supporting materials
Baird, A. Craig, 5
Bandwagon (as type of fallacy), **387**
Bar graphs, **274,** 277
Begging the question (as type of fallacy), **387–388**
Beliefs (of audiences), **107**–108, 109, 110–112, 113, 123
Benoit, William L., 350
Bible, 8, 92–93
Bilingualism, 51–52, 294
Biographical dictionaries, 152
Biological needs, **311,** 312
Bird, Elizabeth, 90
Body (of speech), 161–169, 185, 196
Body language (and public speaking), 290–291,
    297–304
    audience and, 298, 301, 302–303
    culture and, 290–291, 298, 300, 301, 302
    emotional state and, 298, 300–301, 303
    facial expressions, 300–301
    gestures, 301–302, 303
    guidelines for, 297 298, 302–304
    movement and, 299–300, 301–304
    occasion and, 299, 300, 302–303
    posture and, 299–300
    proxemics and, 299, 302
    self-confidence and, 43, 53
    visual aids and, 267–268
Books (as supporting materials), 152
Boolean searching, **145.** *See also* Electronic source
    materials, searches of
Bossuet, Jacques-Bénigne, 6
Bowers, John Waite, 237
Breath control (during speaking), 297
Breznik, Evelyn, 198
Brin, Amy, 202, 206
Brooks, Garth, 406
Bryant, Donald C., 103
Buchanan, Pat, 288
Burke, Kenneth, 5, 112, 252
Bush, George W., 133, 248, 287, 343

**C**ampbell, Ben Nighthorse, 19
Campbell, George, 307

Captive audience, **117**
Card catalogs, 143–145
Carter, Stephen, 14
Causal patterns
    of organization, 162, **166**–167, 185
    of reasoning, **385, 386,** 389
Cause-effect pattern (of organization), 166, 167, **219**
CD-ROMs, **145,** 149
Central ideas (of speeches), **31,** 32, 34, 55, 68, 172
Ceremonial speaking occasions, 400–405. *See also*
    Special occasion speeches
Chalkboards (as visual aids), **273**
Challenge (issued in conclusion), 204–205
Channels (of public communication), 52, 58
Chapman, Joyce, 337–340
Charts (as visual aids), **276**–277, 283
Chronological patterns (of organization), **162**–164,
    185, **219**
Cicero, 1, 4, 13, 19, 138
CIOS, 143, 145
Civil language use, 252–261
Civil rights movement, 83, 84–85, 95, 96
Civility, 14. *See also* Ethics
Claims (of speeches), 378–381
    in argumentative speeches, 376, 378–381, 390–393
    audiences and, 31, 34, 68
    causal patterns of organization and, 166, 167
    central ideas vs., 31. *See also* Central ideas
    content and, 55
    culture and, 381
    definition of, **31,** 390
    listening and, 68
    motivated sequence and, 172
    organization and, 166, 167, 169
    outlines/outlining and, 33, 34, 214
    proofs of, 380
    purpose and, 31, 32–33, 34
    types of, 378–381
    word choice in, 32–33
Clichés, **243**
Clinton, Bill, 13–14, 69, 139, 246, 248, 357,
    369–371, 413
Clinton, Hillary, 246
Closure (as principle of verbal order), **160**
Coakley, Carolyn, 66
Co-cultures, **83.** *See also* Culture
Codes (as language channels), **232**
Coherence (of word choice), **235**–236
Color (use in visual aids), 277–278, 279
Color coding (in notetaking), 72
Common ground (among listeners), **78**

Communication competence, **61**

Communication rules, **60**

Community (and public speaking), 11–12, 399, **400–405**

Compact disks (CD-ROMs), **145,** 149

Comparisons (as supporting materials), **135–136,** 137, 144

Comparisons and contrasts (as supporting materials), 134, 135–137, 144

Competent language use, 234–243
   definition of, **234**
   definitions and, 238–239
   imagery and, 239–242
   metaphors and, 242–243
   word choice and, 234–238. *See also* Word choice

Complete enumeration (of subject), **168**

Comprehension (listening for), 66, **67,** 68–69

Computer-generated visual aids, **283–284**

Conclusion (of speech), 204–207
   audience and, 189–190, 196, 197, 198, 208
   definition of, **198**
   framing speech and, 209
   guidelines for, 207–209
   introduction and, 204
   motivated sequence and, 185–186, 190
   occasion and, 208
   outlines/outlining of, 209, 210
   purposes of, 162, 198, 204, 207
   rhetorical orientation and, 196, 198, 207
   types of, 204–207

Concrete reality (as audience attention strategy), **192–193,** 197

Concreteness (as quality of speech), **80**

Conferences (speeches for), 405, 411, **414–416**

Conflict (as audience attention strategy), 192, **195,** 197

Connectives (as transitions), **236**

Consumer imperative (as purpose of public speaking), **5**

Content (of speeches). *See also* Messages; Subjects; Supporting materials
   definition of, **55**
   elements of, 68
   of special occasion speeches, 407, 409, 412–413

Content level (of language/communication), **356**

Content-centered emphasis (of speech), 249–250

Contextual definitions, **239**

Contrast method of visualization, **176**

Contrasts (as supporting materials), 135, **136,** 137, 144

Conventional gestures, **301**

Conversationality (of speaker's voice), **291,** 296

Corporate culture, 110, 403–404

Corporate speaking occasions, 403–405. *See also* Special occasion speeches

Counterarguments, 392, 393. *See also* Argumentative speeches

Counterpersuasion, 349, 350. *See also* Persuasive speeches

Couric, Katie, 291

Craig, Dena, 46–48

Creating the title, **34–35**

Credibility (of speakers)
   definition of, **54–55**
   ethics and, 13–14, 55
   facial expressions and, 301
   persuasion and, 354–356
   ways to improve, 14

Critical listening, 66, **67**

Critical thinking, **73, 375,** 377–378, 392–393. *See also* Reasoning

Critiquing domination, 243, 245–**246**

Cross-cultural presentations, 60. *See also* Culture; Multicultural society

Cubbins, Elaine, 147

Cultural diversity, **79.** *See also* Multicultural society

Culture
   argumentation and, 377–378, 383
   audience attention and, 190–196
   body language and, 290–291, 298, 300, 301, 302
   characteristics of, 78–85
   claims and, 381
   co-cultures with, 83
   communication rules and, 60
   community within, 11–12, 399, 400–405
   as context for public speaking, 3–4, 8–9, 15–16, 19–20, 58–61, 73, 77–78, 85, 252, 255, 399, 400–405
   corporate level of, 110, 403–404
   definition of, **60, 78**
   dimensions of, 82–85
   diversity of. *See* Multicultural society
   entertainment and, 411–412
   feedback and, 57
   humor and, 409–411
   language use and, 252–255, 400–401
   as lived, 82–83
   motivational appeals and, 317
   orality and, 79–82, 287–288
   as performed, 82, 84–85
   persuasion and, 344–356
   rituals and, 402–403
   subcultures within, 83

as thought, 82, 83–84
values of, 84–85
visual aid use and, 265–266, 267
voice qualities and, 291, 298, 300, 301

**D**ata (in argumentation), **390–393**. *See also*
    Evidence; Supporting materials
Databases, 143–145
Deavenport, Earnest, 202–203
Decentering (of ideas), 68–69
Decoding (of words), **232**
Dedication speeches, **407**
Deductive reasoning, **384**, 385, 388. *See also* Reasoning
Definitional speeches, 323, **324–327**
Definitions, 238–239, 389
Delayed feedback, **57**
Delivery (of speeches), 41–43
    body language and. *See* Body language
    occasion and. *See* Occasion
    presentation methods, 41–42
    self-confidence and, 43
    timing of, 36–38, 117, 292
    voice and. *See* Voice
Delivery time (of speech), 36–38, 117, 292
Demographic analysis
    of audience, 103, **104**–106, 120, 122, 129, 351–352
    of culture, 82–83
Demonstration speeches, 268, 323, **328–331**
Demosthenes, 287
Descriptive gestures, **301**
Desires (of audiences), **112–**113, 123
Diagrams (as visual aids), 283. *See also* Charts;
    Drawings; Graphs
Dialects, **294**
Dictionary definitions, **238**
Differentiation
    as basis for persuasion, 357–358
    as principle of verbal order, **160**
Discriminative listening, 66, **67**
Document cameras (Elmos), 226, **271,** 273
Documents and reports (from government agencies),
    151
Dole, Robert, 287
Doublespeak, 247, **248**
Douglass, Frederick, 10
Drawings (as visual aids), 272–273, 283. *See also*
    Graphs

**E**ducational Resources Information Center (ERIC),
    145
Effect-cause pattern (of organization), 166, 167, **219**

Ekman, Paul, 300
Electronic Age, 7–8
Electronic source materials, 143–149
    availability of, 38–39, 133–134
    card catalogs, 143–145
    CD-ROMs, 145, 149
    databases, 143–145
    evaluation of, 38–39, 147, 148
    searches of, 143–145, 146–148, 149, 150
    World Wide Web. *See* World Wide Web
Ellsworth, Phoebe, 300
Elmos (document cameras), **226**, 271, 273
Embodiment (of ideas in communication), **84–85**
Emotional characterizers (and vocal quality), **296**
Emotions (of speakers), 298, 300–301, 303
Enactment (of cultural values), **84–85**
Encoding (of ideas), **232**
Encyclopedias, 151
End, The (and finality of speech), **198**. *See also*
    Conclusion
Entertainment speeches, 405, 411–413
    culture and, 411–412
    definition of, **29, 411**
    general purposes of, 27, 28, 29, 31, 32
    humor in, 29, 175, 409, 411–413
    language use in, 411–412
    motivated sequence and, 175, 180–181
    organization of, 175, 180–181, 412, 413
    outlines/outlining of, 181
    purposes of, 181
    for special occasions, 405, 411–413
    style of, 412–413
Enthymematic speech, **233**
Enunciation, **293**, 297
ERIC (Educational Resources Information Center),
    145
Ethical listeners/listening, 59, **69–71**. *See also* Listening
Ethically appropriate speech, **289**. *See also* Ethics
Ethics (in speaking), 13–16
    ad hominem attacks, 243, 244, 247, 390
    appropriateness and, 289
    argumentative speeches and, 382, 383
    audience analysis and, 126
    controversial issues and, 126
    credibility of speaker and, 13–14, 55
    critiquing domination, 243, 245–246
    definition of, 13
    doublespeak, 247, 248
    introduction and, 197
    language use and, 234, 243–247, 248
    linguistic erasure, 243, 244–245, 247

Ethics (in speaking) *(continued)*
  listening and, 59, 69–71
  moral bases of, 14–16
  motivational appeals and, 315, 318, 319, 359, 360
  use of statistics and, 141, 142
  use of supporting materials and, 39, 40, 141, 142–143, 154–157, 269, 270, 276, 382, 383
  use of visual aids and, 269, 270, 276
Ethos, 13–14, **55**, 197, 266, 354
Etymological definitions, **238**–239
Eulogies, **407**
Evaluation (of speeches), 43–45, 73–74
  of after-dinner talks, 416–419
  of argumentative speeches, 393–396
  of informative speeches, 337–340
  of persuasive speeches, 46–48, 369–371
  of special occasion speeches, 416–419
  of use of motivated sequence, 181–185
Evidence (in argumentation), **381**–383, 393.
    *See also* Supporting materials
Examples
  reasoning based on, **384**, 385, 388
  as supporting materials, 134, **137**–139, 144
Exemplar definitions, **239**
Exercises (for vocal control), 296, 297
Explanations (as supporting materials), 134, **135**, 144
Explanatory speeches, 323, **334**–337
Extemporaneous speeches, **42**
Eyes (and facial expression), 301

**F**acial expression, 300–301
Facts
  claims based on, **378**–379, 381
  knowledge and, 309, **310**–311
  as types of beliefs, **107**, 109
*Facts on File*, 149
Factual claims, **378**–379, 381
Fallacies (in reasoning), **386**–390, 393
Familiarity (as audience attention strategy), 192, **193**–194, 197
Family values, 88–89
Fantasies (of audiences), **112**–113
FAQs (Frequently Asked Questions), 146
Farewell speeches, **405**, 407
Farrakhan, Louis, 86–87, 125–127
Fear (as basis for motivational appeal), 359, 360
Feedback (from audience), 43, **57**
File Transfer Protocol (FTP), 147
Films, 272
Final summaries (and organization), **236**
First Amendment, 254

Fisher, Mary, 95
Fitch-Hauser, Margaret, 59
Fixed beliefs, **108**, 109
Flipcharts (as visual aids), 272, **277**
Flowcharts (as visual aids), **277**
Forecast (in introduction), **198**, 203
Formality (of speaking occasion), 233, 247–249, 291, 299, 300
Framing (of ideas/speeches)
  audience analysis and, 114
  conclusion and, 209
  definition of, **9**, **15**, **91**
  introduction and, 209
  moral bases for, 15
  motivated sequence and, 178–181, 190
  organization and, 178–181, 190
  rhetorical orientation and, 196–199
  types of speeches and, 178–181
Franklin, John Hope, 413
Frequently Asked Questions (FAQs), 146
Friesen, Wallace V., 300
FTP (File Transfer Protocol), 147

**G**allagher, Erin, 138–139, 191, 205
Gandhi, Mahatma, 6, 141
Gender-linked words, **252**–254
Gender-neutral words, **252**–254
General audience expectations, **116**–117
General purposes (of speeches), 27–29, 31, 32, 33, 34
Generalization (reasoning from), **384**, 385, 386, 388
Genetic fallacy, **386**–387
Geographical pattern (of organization), **165**
Gephardt, Richard, 368, 369, 371
Gestures, **301**–302, 303
Goldberg, Whoopi, 29
Good reasons (and persuasion), **344**
Goodman, Nelson, 400
Goodwill speeches, 405, **408**–411
Gopher (as search tool), 146
Gore, Al, 287
Government publications, 151
Grady, Henry W., 413
Graphic design (of visual aids), 277–278, 279, 284
Graphs (as visual aids), 274–276, 277
Grassian, Esther, 147, 148, 149
Greeting (as introduction), 200
Gustatory imagery, 240, **241**

**H**all, Edward, 8, 299, 303
Hammer, Kari, 201
Handouts (as visual aids), 278–279

Harris, Mary ("Mother Jones"), 200
Harris, Thomas, 241
Hart, Roderick P., 5
Hasty generalization (as type of fallacy), **386**
Hate speech, **254**–255
Hearing, **62**. *See also* Listening
Hebdige, Dick, 112
Hegemony (of culture), **84**
Hierarchy of needs, **311**–312, 313, 314
Hierarchy of prepotency, **312**, 317
Hirt, E. R., 350
HTML (HyperText Markup Language), 146
http (HyperText Transport Protocol), 146
*Humanities Index*, 143, 151
Humor
    atmosphere and, 247–249
    as audience attention strategy, 192, 195, 197
    culture and, 409–410
    definition of, **195**
    in entertainment speeches, 29, 175, 409, 411–413
    guidelines for use of, 195, 202, 207–208, 247–249
    in introduction of speech, 202–203, 207–208
    purposes of, 29
    in special occasion speeches, 409, 411–413
    style and, 247–249
Hypertext, 147
HyperText Markup Language (HTML), 146
HyperText Transport Protocol (http), 146

**I**deology (of culture), 83–84, 89, **110**–111
Ignorance, appeal to (as type of fallacy), **387**
Illustrations
    in conclusions, 206, 207
    in introductions, 203, 207
    personal experience and, 207–208
    as supporting materials, **137**
Imagery, **239**–242
Immediate feedback, **57**
Impeachment (of President Clinton), 369–371
Impromptu speeches, **41**
Inanimate objects (as visual aids), **267**, 268
Indentation (in outlines), 216–217
Indicators (as body movements), **301**–302
Inducement to belief/action (supplied in conclusion), 206
Inductive reasoning, **384**, 386. *See also* Reasoning
Inference, **383**. *See also* Reasoning
Information Superhighway, **145**, 310. *See also* World Wide Web
Information, 309–311 **(310)**. *See also* Supporting materials

Informational interviews, **152**–153
Informative speeches, 309–340
    audience and, 309, 311–319
    characteristics of, 319–323
    content of, 55
    definition of, **28**, 311
    framing of, 178
    general purposes of, 27, 28, 31, 32, 34
    motivated sequence and, 173–174, 178
    motivational appeals and, 309, 311–319
    organization of, 34, 173–174, 178, 320, 324–325, 326–327
    outlines/outlining for, 34, 219–227, 325–327
    purposes of, 178, 311
    supporting materials for, 309
    types of, 323–337. *See also* Definitional speeches; Demonstration speeches; Explanatory speeches; Instructional speeches; Oral briefings
    visual aids for, 268, 328
Instructional speeches, 323, **328**–331
Instrumental values, **109**–110
Integration (as quality of speech), **79**
Integrative method (of audience unification), 125–127
Integrity (of speakers), 16
Intellectual imperative (as purpose of public speaking), 5–6
Intelligibility (of speaking voice), 291–294 **(292)**
Intensity (of word choice), **237**
Intercultural contact, 60. *See also* Culture; Multicultural society
Internal transitions, **235**–236
Internet. *See* World Wide Web
Interviews/Interviewing, 152–153
Intrinsic motivation (of audience), **172**
Introduction (of speech), 199–203
    audience and, 189–190, 196, 197–198, 208
    conclusion and, 204
    definition of, **197**
    ethical issues in, 197
    framing speech and, 209
    guidelines for, 207–209
    humor in, 202–203, 207–208
    motivated sequence and, 185, 190
    occasion and, 199–200, 208
    outlines/outlining of, 209–210
    purposes of, 197–198, 207
    rhetorical orientation and, 196–197, 207
    subject and, 199–200
    types of, 199–203
Introduction speeches, 413, 414

Invitational rhetoric, **289**
Iowa City, Iowa, 351–352
Isocrates, 5

**J**ackson, Jesse, 15, 87, 92, 125, 323
Jacques, Elliott, 110
Johnson, Ben (student speaker), 239
Johnson, Jack, 68
Johnson, Lyndon, 95
Jordan, Barbara, 6, 11

**K**airos, **289**, 404. *See also* Ethics
Kennedy, John F., 112, 287, 288, 407
Kertzer, David, 402, 403
Keynote speeches, 405, **413**, 414
Kinesthetic imagery, 240, **242**
King, Larry, 294
King, Martin Luther, Jr., 6, 10, 112, 196, 243, 407
Kirchhefer, Travis, 203
Knowledge, 309, 310–311
    of audiences, 36, 37, 56, 70–71, 208, 281, 377
    definition of, **310**
    facts and, 309, 310–311
    of speakers, 16, 52, 53, 208
Koehler, Carol, 394–396

**L**aDuke, Winona, 136
Language use (in speeches/speaking), 231–261
    in argumentative speeches, 392
    audience analysis and, 106, 124
    bilingualism, 51–52, 294
    characteristics of, 232–234
    civility in, 252–261
    competence in, 234–243
    culture and, 252–255, 400–401
    definition of *language*, 231
    dialects, 294
    in entertainment speeches, 411–412
    enunciation, 293, 297
    ethical issues in, 234, 243–247, 248
    gender issues and, 252–254
    levels of language, 231–232, 356, 400–401
    literary types of. *See* Definitions; Imagery;
        Metaphors
    multicultural issues in, 51–52, 255, 400–401
    offensive use of, 252–255
    oral style and, 232–234. *See also* Style
    orality and, 232
    organization and, 160–161
    perception and, 400
    processes of language, 232

pronunciation, 293–294
qualifiers, 391, 392–393
transitions, 160–161, 235–236, 304
voice qualities and. *See* Voice
word choice. *See* Word choice
Latitude of acceptance, **350**
Latitude of rejection, **350**
Lauer, Matt, 291
Leary, Timothy, 202
LEXIS-NEXIS, 145, 151
Library of Congress photo archives, 280
Lifestyle rhetorical visions, 112
Lifestyles, 346–348
    definition of, 345, **346**
    in multicultural society, 86, 92–94, 345–356
    research on, 346–347
    types of, 346–347, 348, 351–352
Lincoln, Abraham, 6, 112, 234, 235, 287, 413
Line graphs, **274**, 275, 277
Linguistic erasure, 243, **244–245**, 247
Listeners. *See* Audiences
Listening
    behaviors involved in, 63–65
    central ideas/claims and, 68
    content and, 68
    definition of, **62**
    ethical issues in, 59, 69–71
    hearing vs., 62
    interviewing and, 153
    message and, 71
    in multicultural society, 65
    notetaking and, 72
    occasion and, 69–70
    purposes of, 66–68
    skills needed for, 5, 7, 63, 75, 72, 73–74
    to speakers, 70–71
    styles of, 63–65, 70
    supporting materials and, 68–69, 71, 73
    types of, 66, 67, 69, 70
Listening for comprehension, **67**
Lord, Audre, 406
Love, Courtney, 137–138, 139, 238

**M**acArthur, Douglas, 242
Macro-structure (for organizing speeches), **160**,
        169–177. *See also* Motivated sequence
    action step, **177**, 186
    attention step, **171**, 185
    meso-structures and, 185–186
    need step, **172–173**, 185
    overview of, 169–171

satisfaction step, **173**–175, 185

visualization step, **175**–177, 185

Magazines, 151

Main points (of speech), **161**, 205, 214, 215. *See also* Body; Outlines/Outlining

Mandela, Nelson, 10

Markers (in demographic audience analysis), 105

Marketing, 344, 345

Marx, Karl, 96

Maslow, Abraham, 311

Maslow's hierarchy of needs, **311**–312, 313, 314

Mass media, 7–8

Materials (for speeches). *See* Supporting materials

Mayo, Adrienne, 193

McCarthy, Joseph, 246

McClelland's motive types, 312–**313**, 317. *See also* Motivational appeals, types of

MEDLINE, 145

Meetings (speeches for), 405, 411, **414**–416

Mehrabian, Albert, 301

Memorial services (speeches for), **407**

Memorized speeches, **41**

Meso-structures (for organizing speeches), 160, **161**–169

causal patterns, 162, 166–167, 185

chronological patterns, 162, 164, 185, 219

definition of, **160**

macro-structures and, 185–186

motivated sequence and, 185–186

outlines/outlining of, 163–164, 165, 166, 167, 168

selection of, 169

spatial patterns, 162, 165, 185

topical patterns, 162, 167–169, 185, 219

Messages (of speakers/speeches), 52, **55**–56, 71, 349. *See also* Central ideas; Claims

Metaphorical frames, 91

Metaphors, **242**–243

Michigan Education Portal for Interactive Content, 110–111

Micro-structures (for organizing speeches), **160**–161, 186

Million Man March, 86–87, 125–127

Mitchell, Arnold, 346–347

Model of the speechmaking process, **52**. *See also* Speechmaking process

Models (as visual aids), **272**

Modification speeches, **357**–359, 363–364

Monroe, Alan, 169, 365

Monroe's motivated sequence, **169**. *See also* Motivated sequence

Moon, Donald, 15

Moral codes, 94

Moral frames, **15**. *See also* Framing

Mores, **14**. *See also* Ethics; Values

Morton, Henri Mann, 11–12, 90–91, 113, 363–364

"Mother Jones" (Harris, Mary), 200

Motivated sequence (as organizational pattern), 169–177

action step, 177, 186

for actuative speeches, 174–175, 180, 359–360, 365–368

for argumentative speeches, 376

attention step, 171, 185

audience and, 169–177

claims and, 172

conclusion and, 185–186, 190

content and, 172

definition of, **169**–170

for definitional speeches, 324–325, 326–327

for demonstration speeches, 328–331

for entertainment speeches, 175, 180–181

for explanatory speeches, 335–337

framing speeches using, 178–181, 190

for goodwill speeches, 410

for informative speeches, 173–174, 178

for instructional speeches, 328–331

introduction and, 185, 190

meso-structures and, 185–186

for modification speeches, 363–364

need step, 172–173, 185

for oral briefings, 332–334

overview of, 169–171

for persuasive speeches, 174–175, 179–180, 359–368

psychological reorientation and, 361–362

for reinforcement speeches, 361–362

sample speech using, 181–185

satisfaction step, 173–175, 185

types of speeches and, 178–181

visualization step, 175–177, 185

Motivational appeals (to audiences), 309, 311–319

in argumentative speeches, 383

clusters of, 313–316

culture and, 317

definition of, **315**

ethical issues in, 315, 318, 319, 359, 360

in informative speeches, 309, 311–319

supporting materials and, 383

types of, 311–316

use of, 316–319

Motive clusters, 313–316. *See also* Motivational appeals

Movements (and body language), **299**–300, 301–304
Multicultural society, 60–61, 85–97
  achieving goals in, 86, 90–92, 404
  audience in, 37, 51–52, 56, 86–97, 104–106, 255, 345
  communication competence and, 61
  communication rules and, 60
  community within, 11–12, 399, 400–405
  feedback and, 57
  humor and, 409–410
  language use in, 51–52, 255, 400–401
  lifestyle choices in, 86, 92–94, 345–356
  listening in, 65
  moral agreement in, 15–16
  persuasion in, 344–356
  public speaking in, 8–9, 15–16, 51–52, 85
  recognizing diversity of, 86–88, 106
  self-identity in, 86, 94–97
  subject selection in, 88
  values of, 86, 88–90, 94
Multicultural vision, **255**
Multiculturalism, **83**

**N**ame-calling (as type of fallacy), **389**–390
Narrative frames, 91
Narrative sequence (as chronological organization), **163**–164
Narrative style (of speaking), 250–252
Narratives (as supporting materials), **137**, 144
National Book Awards, 406
Neal, Justin D., 181
Need step (of motivated sequence), **172**–173, 185. *See also* Motivated sequence
Negative definitions, **238**
Negative method of visualization, **176**–177
Neuharth, Allen H., 249–250, 251–252
*New York Times*, 149
Newspapers, 149
Nixon, Richard, 6
Nonverbal communication, 297–304
  audience and, 298, 301, 302–303
  culture and, 290–291, 298, 300, 301, 302
  definition of, **297**–298
  emotional state and, 298, 300–301, 303
  facial expressions, 300–301
  gestures, 301–302, 303
  guidelines for, 297–298, 302–304
  movement and, 299–300, 301–304
  nature of, 398
  occasion and, 299, 300, 302–303
  posture and, 299–300

  proxemics and, 299, 302
  self-confidence and, 43, 53
  visual aids and, 267–268
Notecards, 72, 154, 156, 224, 225
Notetaking, 72, 154, 156
Novelty (as audience attention strategy), 192, **194**, 197

**O**'Donnell, Rosie, 141
Oasis system, 143
Occasion (of speaking), 52, 58–59
  analysis of, 37–38, 103, 114–117
  atmosphere of, 247–249, 283
  audiences of. *See* Audiences
  body language and, 299, 300, 302–303
  ceremonial types of, 400–405. *See also* Special occasion speeches
  community and, 11–12, 399, 400–405
  conclusion and, 208
  corporate types of, 403–405. *See also* Special occasion speeches
  definition of, **115**–116
  elements of, 115–117
  expectations of, 116–117, 117, 208, 233
  formality of, 233, 247–249, 291, 299, 300
  goals of, 115, 117
  introduction and, 199–200, 208
  listening and, 69–70
  nonverbal communication and, 299, 300, 302–303
  organization and, 161, 169
  physical setting and, 38, 54, 70, 115, 117, 299, 300, 302–303
  planning strategy and, 36
  scheduling of, 115, 117
  social context and, 58–60, 116. *See also* Culture
  subject selection and, 25, 299
  supporting materials and, 299
  time limits and, 26, 36–38, 117, 292
  visual aid use and, 282
  voice characteristics and, 292
Ocularcentric age (and use of visual aids), **265**–266, 267, 304
Olfactory imagery, 240, **241**
One-sided messages, **349**
Ong, Walter, 8, 79, 80, 288
Ono, Kent, 246–247
Opinions (as types of beliefs), **107**–108, 109
Optimum pitch level, **295**
Oral briefings, 323, **331**–334
Oral delivery, **288**. *See also* Speakers; Style
Oral language skills, 16, 17
Oral style, **232**–234. *See also* Style

Orality. *See also* Public speaking
   characteristics of, 79–82, 232–234, 288–289
   culture and, 79–82, 287–288
   definition of, 7–**8**, 79, **232**
   history of, 232, 287–288
   language use and, 232
Organic imagery, 240, **242**
Organization (of speeches), 159–187
   of actuative speeches, 34, 174–175, 180, 359–360, 365–368
   of argumentative speeches, 376, 390–393
   audience and, 161, 162, 169, 169–177, 189–190, 217, 218
   body, 161–169, 185, 196
   causal patterns of, 162, 166–167, 185
   central ideas and, **31**, 32, 34, 55, 68, 172
   chronological patterns of, 162–164, 185, 219
   circular nature of, 204
   claims and, 166, 167, 169. *See also* Claims
   conclusion. *See* Conclusion
   of definitional speeches, 324–325, 326–327
   of demonstration speeches, 328–331
   of entertainment speeches, 175, 180–181, 412, 413
   of explanatory speeches, 335–337
   framing and, 178–181, 190
   geographical patterns of, 165
   of goodwill speeches, 410, 411
   of informative speeches, 34, 173–174, 178, 320, 324–325, 326–327
   of instructional speeches, 328–331
   internal structure, 161–169
   introduction. *See* Introduction
   of keynote speeches, 413, 414
   language use and, 160–161
   macro-structure, 160, 169–177
   meso-structures, 160, 161–169
   message and, 55
   micro-structures, 160–161
   of modification speeches, 363–364
   motivated sequence and, 169–177, 185–186.
      *See also* Motivated sequence
   occasion and, 161, 169
   of oral briefings, 332–334
   outlines/outlining and. *See* Outlines/Outlining
   of panel discussions, 415
   of persuasive speeches, 174–175, 179–180, 359–368
   of reinforcement speeches, 361–362
   spatial patterns of, 162, 165, 185
   of special occasion speeches, 407, 408, 410, 411, 412, 413, 414, 415

   subject selection and, 169
   supporting materials and, 161, 172–173, 215, 216–217
   topical patterns of, 162, 167–169, 185, 219
   of tribute speeches, 407, 408
   types of speeches and, 173–175, 178–181.
      *See also specific types of speeches*
Outlines/Outlining, 213–227
   of actuative speeches, 34, 180, 365–368
   audience analysis and, 217, 218
   claims/central ideas and, 33, 34, 214
   of conclusion, 209, 210
   of definitional speeches, 325–327
   of demonstration speeches, 330–331
   of entertainment speeches, 181
   of explanatory speeches, 335–337
   guidelines for, 213, 214–217
   indentation in, 216–217
   of informative speeches, 34, 219–227, 325–327
   of instructional speeches, 330–331
   instructors' requirements for, 221
   of introduction, 209–210
   main ideas in, 214, 215
   meso-structures and, 163–164, 165, 166, 167, 168
   of modification speeches, 363–364
   of narrative sequence, 163–164
   notetaking and, 72
   of oral briefings, 333–334
   for panel discussions, 415
   of persuasive speeches, 179–180, 361–362, 363–364, 365–368
   preliminary drafts of, 39
   purpose of constructing, 213
   purpose of speech and, 33, 34
   of reinforcement speeches, 361–362
   rough outlines, 218, 219–220
   speaking outlines, 218, 222–226
   stages in, 218–227
   subpoints in, 215, 217, 218
   supporting materials and, 215, 216–217, 220
   symbols used in, 216
   technical plot outlines, 218, 220–222
   types of, 213, 218–227
   visual aid use and, 226

**P**acker, Billy, 291
Panel discussions, 405, **414–416**
Paralinguistic channel, **58**
Paralinguistics (between speaker/audience), **296**
Parallel case, **385–386**, 388–389
Paraphrasing (of supporting materials), 156

Partial enumeration (of subject), **168**

Participatoriness (as quality of speech), **81**

Pauses (during speeches), **295**–296

PC (political correctness), 113, **254**

Perceptual grouping, 217, 218

Performance (and nature of public speaking), 85, 289, 290–291

Pericles, 6

Personal intention (in conclusion), 207

Personal reference (in introduction), 200

Persuasive definition (as type of fallacy), **389**

Persuasive speeches, 343–371
   approaches to persuasion, 344–356
   argumentation and, 378. *See also* Argumentative speeches
   audience and, 344–356
   challenges of, 344
   content of, 55
   culture and, 344–356
   definition of, **28**
   general purposes of, 27, 28–29, 31, 32
   motivated sequence and, 174–175, 179–180, 359–368
   multicultural society and, 344–356
   organization of, 174–175, 179–180, 359–368
   outlines/outlining of, 179–180, 361–362, 363–364, 365–368
   purposes of, 179, 344
   resistance to, 349, 350
   subjects of, 348–350
   supporting materials for, 353–354
   types of, 356–359, 378. *See also* Actuative speeches; Argumentative speeches
   values and, 346–347, 369

Pfau, Michael, 350

Photographs, 268–269, 270, 280

Physical objects (as visual aids), **267**–268

Physical setting (of speaking occasion), 38, 54, 70, 115, 117, 299, 300, 302–303

Pictographs, **274**, 276, 277

Pictorial channel, **58**

Pie graphs, **274**, 275, 277

Pitch (of voice), **295**, 297

Pitch variation, **295**

Pitt, William (the Elder), 6

Plagiarism, 142–143, **154**–157

Policy claims, **380**–381

Political correctness (PC), 113, **254**

Political power, 402–403

Popular opinion, appeal to (as type of fallacy), **387**

Positive method of visualization, **175**, 176

Postman, Neil, 155–156

Posture (and body language), **299**–300

Power motives, **313**, 314–315

PowerPoint presentations, **226**, 227, 265, 270–271, *277*, 278–279

Practicing (for public speaking), 7, 39–40

Preexisting attitudes (of audiences), **36**

Preliminary summaries (and organization), **236**

Preview (in introduction), **198**

Primacy-recency effect, **393**

Print sources (of supporting materials), 149–152

Private aims (for public speaking), **36**

Private speech, **234**

PRIZM, **351**–352

Process-oriented listeners, **63**

Pronunciation, **293**–294

Proofs (of claims), 380

Propositional style (of speaking), **250**–252

Protected speech, 254

Proxemics, **299**, 302. *See also* Body language

Proximity (as audience attention strategy), 192, **193**, 197

*Psychological Abstracts*, 143

Psychological orientation (of audience), **346**–350, **356**–359, 361–362

Psychological profile (of audience), 103, **107**–114, 344–356. *See also* Audience, psychological characteristics of

Psychological reorientation (of audience), **356**–359, 361–362

Public distance, 299, 300, 303

Public speaking. *See also* Orality
   analysis of, 7
   audiences of. *See* Audiences
   characteristics of, 79–82, 232–234, 288–289
   community and, 11–12, 399, 400–405
   cultural context of, 3–4, 8–9, 15–16, 19–20, 58–61, 73, 77–78, 85, 252, 255, 399, 400–405. *See also* Culture
   definition of, 62, 82, **234**
   enduring examples of, 6
   ethical issues in. *See* Ethics
   freedom and, 19–20
   functions of, 4–5, 7–13, 36
   as liberal art, 18–20
   methods of, 41–42
   in multicultural society, 8–9, 15–16, 51–52, 85
   nature of, 3–4
   as performance, 85, 289, 290–291
   practicing for, 7, 39–40
   process of. *See* Speechmaking process

skills needed for, 7, 12, 16–17
steps in, 23–24. *See also specific steps*
study of, 4–7
subjects for. *See* Subjects
types of, 41–42. *See also* Speeches
Public speech, **234**. *See also* Public speaking
Purposes (of speakers/speeches), 27–37, 52, 53
   audiences and, 27–31, 35, 36, 118–120
   central ideas/claims and, 31, 32–33, 34
   content and, 31, 32, 34
   emphasis and, 249–250
   general, 27–29, 31, 32, 33, 34
   organization and, 169
   outlines/outlining and, 33, 34
   specific, 30–31, 33, 34
   supporting materials and, 133–134
   types of speeches and, 178, 179, 180, 181
Putnam, Robert, 345

**Q**ualifiers (in argumentation), 391, **392–393**
Question (as introduction), 201
Questionnaires, 153–154
Quintillian, 101, 103
Quotations
   in conclusions, 206
   in introductions, 200
   recording of, 225
   from supporting materials, 156, 224

**R**ate (of speaking), **292**, 294, 295, 304, 329
Rather, Dan, 296
Read speeches, **41–42**
*Readers' Guide to Periodical Literature*, 151
Reality (as audience attention strategy), **192–193**, 197
Reasoning, 376, 378, 384–390
   fallacies in, 386–390
   patterns of, 378
   testing adequacy of, 386, 388–389
   types of, 376, 384–386
Reasoning from example, **384**, 385, 388
Reasoning patterns, **378**
Reasons-oriented listeners, **63**
Redundancy (as quality of speech), **80**
Reference books, 151, 152
Reference groups, **353–354**, **401–402**
Referential level (of language), **231**
Reflecting complaining/compliments, 5
Reflective listening, **67–68**
Reinforcement speeches, 356–**357**, 361–362
Relational level (of language/communication), **231**, 356

Reports and documents (from government agencies), 151
Representations of objects/relationships (as visual aids), **267**, 268–277
Reservations (in argumentation), 391, **392–393**
Results-oriented listeners, **63**
Rhetoric of the body, 290. *See also* Body language
Rhetorical frame of mind, **23**
Rhetorical framing, 91. *See also* Framing
Rhetorical orientation, 189–190, **196–199**, 207
Rhetorical sensitivity, **16–17**
Rhetorical vision, **112**–113, 117
Rich, Adrienne, 406
Rituals (and special occasions), **402–403**
Rogers, Will, 29
Roosevelt, Eleanor, 287
Roosevelt, Franklin, 112
Rough outlines, 218, **219**–220. *See also* Outlines/ Outlining
RRA technique (for listening), **70**
RRP listening styles, **63**, 64, 65
Rules-driven listeners, 63, **64–65**

**S**aliency (and persuasion), **349**, 353
Sample speeches
   analysis of, 45
   argumentative types of, 393–396
   on Asian Pacific American heritage, 416–419
   on cell phone use, 127–128
   on cigar smoking, 46–48
   on civil language use, 255–261
   on drug testing, 181–185
   on geishas, 337–340
   on impeachment of president, 369–371
   informative types of, 337–340
   on listening, 394–396
   motivated sequence and, 181–185
   outlines/outlining of, 127–128. *See also* Outlines/ Outlining
   persuasive types of, 46–48, 369–371
   special occasion types of, 416–419
Samuelson, Robert, 343, 344
Satisfaction step (of motivated sequence), 173–175, 185. *See also* Motivated sequence
Schuller, Robert, 288
Scope (of situation described by statistics), **139**, 140
Search engines, **149**, 150
Segmentation (of audience), 122–125 **(123)**, 345. *See also* Audience analysis
Segments (of statistics), **140**
Self-absorbed listeners, 63, **64–65**

Self-confidence (of speakers)
  audience and, 43
  body language and, 43, 53
  communication of, 43
  development of, 8, 9, 12, 18, 43, 52, 53–54
  need for, 16, 17
  settings and, 54
  voice and, 43, 53
Self-identity (in multicultural society), 86, 94–97
Self-image (of speakers), **53–54**. *See also* Self-
    confidence
Sequential fallacy, **387**
Settings (of speaking occasions), 38, 54, 70, 115, 117,
    299, 300, 302–303
70–30 rule (for listening), 68
Sexist language, 252–254
Shakespeare, 8
Sherman, S. J., 350
Sherman, William, 413
Sign reasoning, 384–385, 388
Signposts (and coherence), **235**
Silence (during speeches), 295–296
Simplicity (of word choice), 234–**235**
Sinbad, 29
Situationalism (as quality of speech), **81**
Situations (for speeches). *See* Occasions
Size (of situation described by statistics), **139**, 140
Skyhook principle, **15**
Slides, 270–271
Social constructions, **400**
Social contexts (for speeches), **58–60**
Social imperative (as purpose of public speaking), 4–5
Social motives, **311**, 312. *See also* Motivational appeals
*Social Sciences Index*, 143, 151
Soros, George, 110
Sounded word, 79–82. *See also* Language use; Public
    speaking
Source materials (for speeches). *See* Supporting
    materials
Spatial patterns (of organization), 162, **165**, 185
Speaker-centered emphasis (of speech), **249–250**
Speakers, 52–55, 287–304
  attitudes of, 52, 53–54
  audiences' perceptions of, 54–55, 70–71
  audiences' relationships with, 43, 290–291, 296,
      298, 301, 302–303
  body language of, 43, 290–291, 297–304
  breath control of, 297
  characteristics of, 16–17, 354–356, 414
  credibility of, 13–14, 52, 54–55, 301, 354–356
  emotional state of, 298, 300–301, 303

eyes of, 301
  facial expressions of, 300–301
  gestures, 301–302, 303
  integrity of, 16
  introductions of, 413, 414
  knowledge of, 16, 52, 53, 208
  listening to, 70–71
  movements of, 299–300, 301–304
  oral skills of, 17
  posture of, 299–300
  purposes of, 52, 53. *See also* Purposes
  rate of, 292, 294, 295, 304, 329
  rhetorical sensitivity of, 16–17
  self-confidence of. *See* Self-confidence
  self-image of, 53–54
  voice of. *See* Voice
Speaking outlines, 218, 222–226 **(223)**. *See also*
    Outlines/Outlining
Special occasion speeches, 399–419
  after-dinner talks, 411–413
  assessment of, 416–419
  audiences of, 399, 400–405, 406, 409–410
  community and, 399, 400–405, 406
  for conferences, 405, 411, 414–416
  content of, 407, 409, 412–413
  dedications, 407
  definition of, **399**
  for entertainment, 405, 411–413. *See also*
      Entertainment speeches
  farewells, 405, 407
  for goodwill, 405, 408–411
  humor and, 409, 411–413
  introductions, 413, 414
  keynotes, 405, 413, 414
  for meetings, 405, 411, 414–416
  for memorial services, 407
  organization of, 407, 408, 410, 411, 412, 413, 414, 415
  panel discussions, 405, 414–416
  rituals and, 402–403
  sample of, 416–419
  style of, 407, 409, 412–413
  tributes, 405–407, 408
Specific audience expectations, **116**–117
Specific instances (as supporting materials), **137**
Specific purposes (of speeches), **30–31**
Speech. *See* Voice
Speeches (types of). *See also* Sample speeches
  to actuate, **28, 359**. *See also* Actuative speeches
  of argumentation, 375–376. *See also* Argumentative
      speeches
  for dedications, **407**

to define, 323, **324–327**
to demonstrate, 268, 323, **328–331**
to entertain, **29**, 405, **411–413**. *See also*
    Entertainment speeches
to explain, 323, **334–337**
extemporaneous, **42**
of farewell, **405**, 407
of goodwill, 405, **408–411**
impromptu, **41**
to inform, **28**. *See also* Informative speeches
to instruct, 323, **328–331**
of introduction, 413, 414
keynotes, 405, **413**, 414
for memorial services, 407
memorized, **41**
of modification, **357–359**, 363–364
oral briefings, 323, **331–334**
in panel discussions, 405, **414–416**
to persuade, **28**. *See also* Persuasive speeches
read, **41–42**
of reinforcement, 356–357. *See also* Reinforcement
    speeches
for special occasions, **399**. *See also* Special occasions
of tribute, **405–407**, 408
Speechmaking process (model of), 52–62
    channels in, 52, 58
    cultural context and, 60–61. *See also* Culture
    definition of, **52**
    elements of, 52, 53, 61–62
    feedback in, 52, 57
    listener in, 52, 56. *See also* Audiences
    message in, 52, 55–56. *See also* Messages
    situation in, 52, 58–59. *See also* Occasions
    speaker in, 52–55. *See also* Speakers
Stanton, Elizabeth Cady, 10
Startling statement (as introduction), 201
*Statistical Abstracts of the United States,* 151
Statistics (as supporting materials), 134, **139–141**,
    142, 144, 224
Stereotypes (as types of beliefs), **108**, 253
Stipulative definitions, **238**
Stress (of spoken words), **295**
Structure (of speeches). *See* Organization
Style (of speakers/speeches), 55–56, 112, 247–252
    atmosphere and, 247–249
    definition of, 55–56, **232**
    emphasis and, 249–250
    of entertainment speeches, 412–413
    of goodwill speeches, 409–411
    humor and, 247–249
    narrative type of, 250–252

propositional type of, 250–252
of special occasion speeches, 407, 409, 412–413
tone and, 247
of tribute speeches, 407
Subcultures, **83**. *See also* Culture
Subjects (for speeches)
    assigned vs. free choice, 25
    audience and, 24–25, 26–27, 37, 88, 208
    introduction and, 199–200
    multicultural issues with, 88
    narrowing of, 26–27
    occasion and, 25, 299
    organization and, 169
    of persuasive speeches, 348–350
    psychological orientation and, 348–350
    selecting of, 24–25
    time limits and, 26
    visual aids and, 276
Subpoints (and organization), **165**, 215, 217, 218.
    *See also* Outlines/Outlining
Summaries (and organization), **236**
Summarizing (in conclusion), 205
Sunday, Billy, 235
Supporting materials (for speeches), 133–157
    for argumentative speeches, 382–383, 393
    audience and, 71, 106, 114, 129
    citing sources of, 40, 142–143, 272
    content and, 55
    electronic sources of, 143–149. *See also* Electronic
        source materials
    ethical use of, 39, 40, 141, 142–143, 154–157, 269,
        270, 276, 382, 383
    evaluation of, 69, 73, 143, 144, 147, 148
    forms of, 134–143. *See also specific forms*
    gathering of, 38–39
    for goodwill speeches, 410
    for informative speeches, 309
    interviews as, 152–153
    listening and, 68–69, 71, 73
    motivated sequence and, 172–173
    motivational appeals and, 383
    occasion and, 299
    organization and, 161, 172–173, 215, 216–217
    outlines/outlining and, 215, 216–217, 220
    for persuasive speeches, 353–354
    print sources of, 149–152
    purpose and, 133–134
    recording of, 154
    relevance of, 382–383
    sources of, 38–39, 69, 129, 143–154, 279–281,
        376, 393. *See also specific sources*

Supporting materials (for speeches) *(continued)*
 surveys/questionnaires as, 153–154
 types of. *See* sources of *(above)*
 visual aids. *See* Visual aids
 from World Wide Web. *See* World Wide Web
SUR listening styles, 63, **64**–65
Surveys, 153–154
Suspense (as audience attention strategy), 192, **194**,
 197
Sweeney, Jennifer, 204–205
Symbolic level (of language), **231**–232
Synchronicity (of speaker and audience), **290**–291

**T**ables (as visual aids), **276**–277
Tactile imagery, 240, **241**–242
Tactile listeners, 63, **64**
Target populations, 123. *See also* Audience
 segmentation
Targeting (of audience), **118**–122
Technical plot outlines, 218, **220**–222. *See also*
 Outlines/Outlining
Temporal sequence (as chronological organization),
 **163**
Terminal values, **109**–110
Terministic screens, 112
Testimony (as support material), 134, **141**–143, 144,
 353–354
Textual materials (as visual aids), 277–279, 284
The End (and finality of speech), **198**. *See also*
 Conclusion
The Vital (as audience attention strategy), 192, **195**, 197
Therapeutic listening, 66, **67**
Third persona, 244–245
Thonssen, Lester, 5
Thorne, Gary, 291
Three needs theory, **313**
Time limits (for speeches), 26, **36**–38, 117, 292
Titles (of speeches), **34**–35
Tocqueville, Alexis de, 15
Tone (of speech/speaker), **247**. *See also* Style
Topical patterns (of organization), 162, **167**–169,
 185, **219**
Topics (of speeches). *See* Subjects
Toulmin model (of argumentation), **390**–393
Traditionalism (as quality of speech), **80**
Transactional experience, **58**
Transitions (and internal organization), 160–161,
 **235**–236, 304
Transparencies, 271
Trends (illustrated by statistics), **140**
Tribute speeches, **405**–407, 408

Truth, Sojourner, 6
Turow, Joseph, 345
Twitchell, Michael, 206
Two-sided messages, **349**
Type (use in visual aids), 277, 278, 284

**U**ltimate aims (for public speaking), **36**
Unfocused listeners, 63, **64**–65
Uniform Resource Locators (URLs), 145–146
URLs (Uniform Resource Locators), 145–146
U.S. Constitution, 254
Usenet, 147

**V**ALS Program, **346**–347, 348, 351, 369
Valuative frames, 91
Valuative vocabulary, **124**
Value claims, **379**–380, 381
Value orientations, **88**, **110**–111
Values, 109–112
 approaches to changing, 358
 of audiences, 109–112, 113, 123, 358, 405, 406
 challenges to, 405, 407
 claims based on, 379–380, 381
 of cultures, 84–85
 definition of, **109**, 358
 enactment of, 84–85
 of multicultural society, 86, 88–90, 94
 persuasion and, 346–347, 369
 types of, 88–89, 109–110
 word choice and, 124
Values and Lifestyles (VALS) Program, **346**–347, 348,
 351, 369
Variable beliefs, **108**, 109
Variety (in voice qualities), 291, **294**–296
VAT listening styles, 63, **64**, 75
Verbal channel, **58**
Vernacular language, 241
Veronica (as search tool), 146
*Vertical File Index*, 151
Videotapes, 39, 272
Vietnam War, 248
Visions (of audiences), **112**–113
Visual aids, 265–284
 audience and, 278–279, 281, 282
 body language and, 267–268
 citing sources of, 272
 color use in, 277–278, 279
 computer-generated types of, 283–284
 culture and use of, 265–266, 267
 definition of, **266**
 for demonstration speeches, 268, 328

equipment needed for, 226, 265, 268, 270–271, 272, 273, 281

ethical use of, 269, 270, 276

graphic design of, 277–278, 279, 284

handouts, 278–279

for informative speeches, 268, 328

occasion and, 282

for oral briefings, 332

outlines/outlining and, 226

physical objects as, 267–268

PowerPoint presentations, 226, 227, 265, 270–271, 277, 278–279

purposes of, 266–267

representations of objects/relationships as, 267, 268–277

size of, 329

skill in use of, 265, 282, 329–330

sources of, 279–281

statistics and, 141

subject selection and, 276

textual materials as, 277–279, 284

types of, 226, 227, 267–279. *See also specific types*

use of, 281–284

World Wide Web and, 271, 272, 280–281

Visual channel, **58**, 281, 297

Visual imagery, 240, 241

Visual listeners, 63, **64**

Visualization

  as audience attention strategy, 192, 195–196, 197

  definition of, **196, 323**

  motivational appeals and, 315, 323

Visualization process, **315**

Visualization step (of motivated sequence), **175**–177, 185. *See also* Motivated sequence

Vital, The (as audience attention strategy), 192, **195**, 197

*Vital Speeches of the Day*, 403

Vocal emphasis, **295**

Vocal quality, **296**

Vocal stereotypes, **294**

Voice (of speaker), 291–296

  culture and, 291, 298, 300, 301

  emotional state and, 296

  intelligibility of, 291–294

  occasion and, 292

  pronunciation, 293–294

  qualities of, 287–289, 291–296

  training of, 287, 296, 297

  variety in, 291, 294–296

Volume (of speaking), **292**, 293

**W**AIS (Wide Area Information Servers), 146

Waldock, Valerie, 239

Walker, Alice, 406

*Wall Street Journal*, 149

Walters, Barbara, 296

Walzer, Michael, 402

Wander, Philip, 245

Warrants (in argumentation), **390**–393

Washington, Booker T., 90

Watts, J. C., 368, 369, 370

Website visuals, **280**

Websites, 146–147, 280. *See also* World Wide Web

White space (and text design), 277

Whiteboards (as visual aids), **273**

Wide Area Information Servers (WAIS), 146

Wiesel, Elie, 135

William the Conqueror, 6

Wilson, Andrew B., 135–136

Winans, James Albert, 191

Winfrey, Oprah, 291

Wolfe, Stephanie, 201, 205

Wolvin, Andrew, 66

Women's movement, 83, 96

Word choice, 234–238. *See also* Language use

  in argumentative speeches, 392

  characteristics of effective, 234–230, 320–322

  in claims, 32–33

  definition of, **232**

  enunciation, 293, 297

  gender issues in, 252–254

  in informative speeches, 320–322

  organization and, 160–161

  pronunciation, 293–294

  qualifiers, 391, 392–393

  technical vocabulary and, 321, 322

  transitions, 160–161, 235–236, 304

  values and, 124

World Wide Web (WWW)

  access to, 38–39, 133–134

  definition of, **145**, 147

  searches on, 143–145, 146–148, 149, 150

  supporting materials from, 146–148, 149, 150, 271, 272, 280–281, 309, 310

  useful research sites, 147–146

  visual aids from, 271, 272, 280–281

  vocabulary of, 145–146

WWW (World Wide Web). *See* World Wide Web

**Y**earbooks, 151

*This constitutes a continuation of the copyright page.*

## Photo Credits

**Page 1:** Bob Daemmrich, Stock, Boston; **Page 3:** © David Brauchli, Corbis Sygma;
**Page 6:** Corbis-Bettmann; **Page 10:** © David Brauchli, Corbis Sygma; **Page 19:** AP/Wide World
Photos; **Pages 23 and 31:** © Bob Daemmrich, Stone/Getty Images; **Page 42:** © Bob Daemmrich,
The Image Works; **Page 51:** © James Marshall, The Image Works; **Page 54:** Reuters, Joe Traver,
Archive Photos/Getty Images; **Pages 66, 77, and 83:** © James Marshall, The Image Works;
**Page 87:** © AFP/Corbis; **Page 101:** PhotoDisc/Getty Images; **Page 103:** © Frank Siteman,
IndexStock Imagery; **Page 115:** © Elizabeth Crews, The Image Works; **Page 119:** © Frank
Siteman, IndexStock Imagery; **Pages 133 and 139:** © Jon Feingersh, Corbis Stock Market;
**Page 155:** © John Coletti, Stock Boston; **Page 159:** © Allen Russell, IndexStock Imagery;
**Page 162:** © Jeff Isaac Greenberg, Photo Researchers; **Page 174:** © Allen Russell, IndexStock
Imagery; **Page 189:** © UPI/ Corbis-Bettmann; **Page 190:** © Mark Richards, PhotoEdit;
**Page 196:** © UPI/Corbis-Bettmann; **Pages 213 and 223:** © Tony Freeman, PhotoEdit;
**Page 229:** PhotoDisc/Getty Images; **Page 231:** © Newsmakers/Getty Images; **Page 235:** Chicago
Historical Society; **Page 244:** © Newsmakers/Getty Images; **Page 265:** © Kaluzny/Thatcher/
Getty Images; **Page 269 (both):** Courtesy of Rollerblade; **Page 273:** © Kaluzny/Thatcher/
Getty Images; **Page 280:** Library of Congress; **Pages 287 and 294:** © Bob Daemmrich,
The Image Works; **Page 298:** © Rhoda Sidney, Stock Boston; **Page 307:** Tony Freeman,
PhotoEdit, Inc.; **Page 309:** © Eastcott/The Image Works; **Page 317:** © Michael Newman,
PhotoEdit; **Page 324:** © Eastcott/The Image Works; **Page 329:** © Matusow/Monkmeyer;
**Page 343:** © Lawrence Migdale, Stock Boston; **Page 345:** © Peter L. Chapman, Stock Boston;
**Page 353:** © Lawrence Migdale, Stock Boston; **Page 375:** © Herb Snitzer, Stock Boston;
**Page 379:** Bob Daemmrich, Stock Boston; **Page 383:** © Herb Snitzer, Stock Boston;
**Pages 399 and 401:** © Robert Ulmann, Monkmeyer; **Page 409:** © Ellis Herwig, Stock Boston.